BIOFEEDBACK AND BEHAVIOR

NATO CONFERENCE SERIES

- I Ecology
- II Systems Science
- III Human Factors
- IV Marine Sciences
- V Air–Sea Interactions

III HUMAN FACTORS

Volume 1 Monitoring Behavior and Supervisory Control
Edited by Thomas B. Sheridan and Gunnar Johannsen

Volume 2 Biofeedback and Behavior
Edited by Jackson Beatty and Heiner Legewie

Volume 3 Vigilance: Theory, Operational Performance, and Physiological Correlates
Edited by Robert R. Mackie

BIOFEEDBACK AND BEHAVIOR

Edited by

Jackson Beatty
University of California
Los Angeles, California

and

Heiner Legewie
Max Planck Institut für Psychiatrie
Munich, Federal Republic of Germany

Published in coordination with NATO Scientific Affairs Division by

PLENUM PRESS · NEW YORK AND LONDON

Library of Congress Cataloging in Publication Data

Conference on Biofeedback and Behavior, Munich, 1976.
Biofeedback and behavior.

(NATO conference series: III, Human factors; v. 2)
Proceedings of a conference held at the Max Planck Institut für Psychiatrie in Munich, Germany, July 27-30, 1976, sponsored by the NATO Special Program Panel on Human Factors.
1. Biofeedback training—Congresses. I. Beatty, Jackson. II. Legewie, Heiner. III. NATO Special Program Panel on Human Factors. IV. Title. V. Series.
BF319.5.B5C66 1976 152.1'88 77-830
ISBN 0-306-32882-8

Proceedings of a conference on Biofeedback and Behavior held at the Max Planck Institut für Psychiatrie in Munich, Federal Republic of Germany, July 27-30, 1976, sponsored by the NATO Special Program on Human Factors

ORGANIZING COMMITTEE:

ROLF ENGEL
POLA ENGEL-SITTENFELD
LAVERNE C. JOHNSON
GEORGE H. LAWRENCE
GARY E. SCHWARTZ
DAVID SHAPIRO

PROCEEDINGS PRODUCTION:

NANCY GAYNOR

A Division of Plenum Publishing Corporation
227 West 17th Street, New York, N.Y. 10011

Printed in the United States of America

Preface

Biofeedback and Behavior: A NATO Symposium, held on 27-30 July 1976 at the Max Planck Institut für Psychiatrie in München, was a multidisciplinary meeting that explored both theoretical and applied issues arising from the use of biofeedback procedures for the control of visceral, central nervous system and skeletal events. The symposium was multinational in its composition.

Financial support for the symposium was initially provided by the Scientific Affairs Division of the North Atlantic Treaty Organization as part of their continuing series of scientific symposia. Funds made available by a grant from the United States Office of Naval Research permitted wide-spread international participation in the symposium. The facilities for the meeting were graciously provided by the Max Planck Institut für Psychiatrie. We thank each of these organizations for their support in making this symposium possible. A special thanks is due to Dr. B.A. Bayraktar of the Scientific Affairs Division of NATO and Dr. Donald Woodward of the U.S. Office of Naval Research, whose counsel contributed substantially to the organization of this meeting.

The planning of this symposium was carried out in consultation with members of the organizing committee: Rolf Engel, Pola Engel-Sittenfeld, Laverne C. Johnson, George H. Lawrence, Gary E. Schwartz, and David Shapiro. The final form of this symposium reflects their contributions, for which we are grateful.

The rapid publication of these proceedings is due in large part to the support of our publisher, Plenum Press, and especially our editor, Paulette Cohen, whom we thank.

We would like to express our particular appreciation to Nancy Gaynor who prepared these proceedings for production and, as secretary to the symposium, was responsible for coordinating various aspects of this symposium from its inception. We would also like to thank Petra Bottger, who provided additional secretarial assistance in München.

Jackson Beatty and Heiner Legewie
Los Angeles
September 1976

Contents

BIOFEEDBACK AND BEHAVIOR: INTRODUCTION TO THE PROCEEDINGS

Jackson Beatty
Department of Psychology
University of California at Los Angeles

and

Heiner Legewie
Max Planck Institut für Psychiatrie
München

This volume is the record of a symposium, Biofeedback and Behavior, which was part of the NATO Human Factors Conference and Symposia Program for 1976. Seventy scientists from nine nations assembled at the Max Planck Institut für Psychiatrie in München in the last week of July, 1976, to present and discuss recent work on the learned modification of bodily processes using "biofeedback" procedures.

"Biofeedback" is an increasingly common term now used with reference to a wide variety of experimental procedures that present information obtained from biological signals to an organism in an attempt to modify underlying physiological processes. For this reason, the phrase "biofeedback research" describes a large and diverse body of experimental and clinical investigations that, in many instances, are unified only at the level of method, and not at the deeper levels of mechanism or theory. The München symposium reflects this diversity and the substantive issues discussed were wide-ranging.

The symposium was organized to fulfill two objectives. The first was to provide an overview of current experimental and clinical research in laboratories in both Europe and North America. In this respect the symposium was quite successful. Virtually every major laboratory was directly or indirectly represented. In reading these proceedings, one cannot help but note the diversity of substantive research interests represented and the varying degrees of success with which biofeedback methods have been employed in the study of behavioral problems.

The second objective of the symposium was to evaluate the usefulness of biofeedback methods as clinical and experimental research instruments. Opinions differed among the participants, but the general consensus of the symposium was critical: Biofeedback methods were seen to be useful in some experimental contexts and perhaps appropriate in some clinical settings, but the range of these applications was generally considered to be quite restricted. No participant expressed the once-common view that biofeedback procedures represent a unique and powerful technique for clinical treatment or method for scientific inquiry. Instead, the continuity between biofeedback procedures and other clinical and experimental methods was emphasized.

For the reader, these proceedings provide an opportunity to share with the participants of the symposium an international view of the current state of biofeedback research. From the many excellent presentations, the reader may learn why the mood of the symposium was critical and why some problems appear appropriate for biofeedback research or therapy and others do not. Most important, however, is for the reader to share in the developing understanding that these methods have many ties with other, more traditional methods of experimental research and clinical treatment. Biofeedback is no longer an unknown procedure with unknown promise. Instead it must be seen as a collection of experimental and clinical procedures, with particular strengths and weaknesses that may play some part in the study of man and in the treatment of human disorders. That part may not be large, but in selected areas it may be important.

Further it should be noted that, although this symposium was comprehensive, it was certainly not complete. The research contributions to the symposium primarily reflected new experimental and clinical work. It was not the purpose of the symposium to provide extended introductory material or to review previous research in depth. However several other sources may be consulted for an introduction to the area and a review of experimental work not presented by the symposium's participants. For a general treatment of both experimental and clinical issues, the reader is referred to a recent volume edited by Schwartz and Beatty (1977), Biofeedback: Theory and Research, which serves as a useful complement to these proceedings. Various aspects of learned regulation of central nervous system events are treated also by Chase (1974) in Operant Control of Brain Activity. The reader who is interested in clinical issues should consult Biofeedback-Therapie by Legewie and Nusselt (1975) and Biofeedback: Behavioral Medicine by Birk (1973). Biofeedback and Behavior reflects the present state of biofeedback research and provides a context for evaluating its scientific and clinical importance.

These proceedings of the symposium have been organized in five sections. The first provides an introduction to the general issues treated in the meetings. The present chapter explains the purposes of the symposium and sketches its contents. In the second chapter, Black and Cott provide an overview of the state of our knowledge and some major problems facing biofeedback research. The third chapter by Anliker gives a broad theoretical framework for a cybernetic approach to psychobiological research. The following chapter by R. Engel is concerned with some methodological questions that are more specific to research using biofeedback methods. In the final paper of the introductory section, Garcia and Rusiniak present some new facts and concepts from the behavioral study of learning that may come to be extremely important for understanding the plastic properties of visceral response.

The second section of the proceedings addresses the question of the modification of central nervous system events. Johnson begins this section with a comprehensive and critical overview of research on the operant modification of brain rhythms in man. In Chapter 7, Mulholland describes an application of biofeedback procedures for the analysis and quantification of the mechanisms regulating the alpha rhythms of the human electroencephalogram. The following two chapters are concerned with the control of alpha activity in the human brain, with Orne and Wilson (Chapter 8) raising the important question of individual differences and Plotkin (Chapter 9) providing a social psychological approach for the study of the so-called "alpha-experience." In Chapter 10, Birbaumer reviews some of the literature concerning the regulation of theta frequency activity in the EEG and suggests that these rhythms may reflect different processes in different brain regions. O'Hanlon, Royal and Beatty next (Chapter 11) show that theta activity in the posterior portions of the cerebral cortex is closely related to the state of behavioral alertness in vigilance-type tasks. This section is concluded by Sterman's comprehensive review of research on the regulation of the "sensorimotor rhythm" with an emphasis on therapeutic applications in epilepsy.

The third section contains a diverse collection of papers addressing issues related to the control of autonomic functions. The question of visceral learning is first treated in Chapter 13 by Harris, Goldstein and Brady, who present the results of a detailed and long-term investigation of blood pressure and heart rate conditioning in primates. In Chapter 14, Pickering, Brucker, Frankel, Mathias, Dworkin and Miller present data on the acquisition of control of blood pressure in patients with generalized bodily paralysis. Intimately related to the question of control of visceral functions is the problem of visceral perception, which is treated in the following two chapters. Brenner (Chapter 15) gives a comprehensive review of the western contribution to the study of visceral perception and describes a series of experiments performed in his laboratory. Roberts (Chapter 16) considers the problem of visceral perception from the perspective of discrimination theory. The patterning of learned responses in the autonomic nervous system is first treated by Kimmel and Burns from the perspective of learning theory (Chapter 17). In the following chapter, Schwartz proposes that different behavioral consequences arise from learning different patterns of autonomic activity.

The behavioral effects of visceral learning are also considered by Shapiro in Chapter 19, who describes a series of experiments investigating the effects of learned control of autonomic response under conditions of experimentally-induced stress.

Theoretical models of visceral learning are treated in the next three chapters. Lang, in Chapter 20, presents evidence that visceral learning may be analogous to the acquisition of motor skill, a proposition that Johnston questions in Chapter 21. Furedy (Chapter 22) discusses experimental results suggesting that neither the operant nor the Pavlovian models may be fully satisfactory in accounting for the learned control of heart rate.

The next three chapters present new methodological procedures for the study of plasticity of autonomic functions. Steptoe (Chapter 23) describes a non-invasive indirect method that may be clinically useful in measuring blood pressure. Ernst and Kordenat (Chapter 24) present some preliminary findings on the regulation of coronary blood flow in animal preparations. Welgan (Chapter 25) is concerned with the operant modification of gastrointestinal activity.

The remaining two chapters of this section address the clinical applicability of biofeedback procedures for the control of autonomic dysfunctions. In Chapter 26, B. Engel gives a critical review of the application of biofeedback methods in the treatment of cardiovascular disorders. In Chapter 27, Surwit and Shapiro present the results of a comparative therapeutic study with hypertensive patients.

The fourth section of this volume examines the use of operant techniques to modify responses of the skeletal muscle system. Fetz, in Chapter 28, shows how operant procedures may be used to study the functional relationships of different cell populations in the central motor system, an extremely fruitful approach that combines operant procedures with more standard methods of neurophysiological analysis. In Chapter 29, Engel-Sittenfeld presents a comprehensive overview of the application of operant procedures to the treatment of neuromuscular disorders. Next, DeBacher and Basmajian (Chapter 30) describe a large-scale project for the treatment of spasticity and other neuromuscular disorders. In the last paper of the section, Stoyva (Chapter 31) discusses one of the most popular applications of electromyographic feedback, the clinical use of relaxation training.

The final section presents two evaluative summaries of the issues posed by the symposium. In the first, Legewie (Chapter 32) reviews the evidence for the clinical utility of biofeedback procedures and concludes that a balanced approach to treatment is necessary. In the second, Beatty (Chapter 33) reviews the contributions made by biofeedback methods to the scientific understanding of the psychobiology of behavior and concludes that these procedures are helpful new tools that have been profitably employed in conjunction with other experimental methods in the study of selected research problems.

Thus, in evaluating the state of an area of scientific research that is barely a decade old, the München symposium revealed progress. Over the past ten years, increasingly specific and difficult scientific questions have received experimental treatment. The level of scientific rigor in the field has increased. Although the early hopes that biofeedback would produce major scientific and clinical breakthroughs have not been fulfilled, a more moderate and potentially more productive sense of biofeedback as a part of the scientific and therapeutic enterprises has emerged. These we believe are healthy trends. We hope that this perspective is communicated to the reader in the present volume.

REFERENCES

Birk, L. (Ed.). Biofeedback: Behavioral medicine. New York: Grune & Stratton, 1973.

Chase, M. H. (Ed.). Operant control of brain activity. Los Angeles: Brain Information Service/Brain Research Institute, UCLA, 1974.

Legewie, H., & Nusselt, L. (Eds.). Biofeedback-Therapie. München: Urban & Schwarzenberg, 1975.

Schwartz, G. E., & Beatty, J. (Eds.). Biofeedback: Theory and research. San Francisco: Academic Press, 1977.

A PERSPECTIVE ON BIOFEEDBACK

A.H. Black and A. Cott
McMaster University

INTRODUCTION

When beginning to prepare the opening address for a symposium such as this, one immediately feels the hand of tradition attempting to guide his own. There are certain topics that should be covered, and certain forms that should be followed. In such an address, the history of the field is reviewed, and attention is focused on interesting and impressive contributions. Above all, there is a compulsion to be positive--to praise what has been done, and to forecast an even more rosy future.

The thought of breaking with these traditions arouses anxiety. Our first reaction to this anxiety was to return to the folds of orthodoxy. But, we resisted the temptation to do so for the following reason. There is a real danger that the misrepresentations and overblown claims that have been made about biofeedback will lead to a rejection of the field by many scientists. We can no longer, therefore, be satisfied to stand by while unsubstantiated claims are made for biofeedback--not only in popular literature, but even in psychology textbooks. In short, unless we are honest about the failures, the inadequacies, and the problems of biofeedback research, we face a serious danger that biofeedback will be unable to make those contributions that it is capable of making. Therefore, this opening address will not be as positive as tradition would dictate. We shall not, however, break completely with tradition because we will begin with a few historical comments.

The beginning of modern biofeedback is usually identified with the research of five people in the 1960s--Basmajian, Kamiya, Kimmel, Miller and Olds. At first glance, the differences in their research seem so great that one wonders why they should be grouped together. For one thing, the response systems that they studied were very different. In addition, their goals varied. Kamiya was interested in developing voluntary control over complex psychological states (Kamiya, 1968). Kimmel and Miller were interested in testing certain theories of learning, which postulated that autonomic responses are not amenable to instrumental or operant control (Fowler & Kimmel, 1962; Kimmel, 1967; Miller, 1969; Miller & DiCara, 1967). Basmajian was interested in understanding the neural systems that control striate muscles (Basmajian, 1963, following up the work of Harrison & Mortensen, 1962). Olds thought that the operant conditioning of single unit activity would be a valuable analytic technique for studying the physiology of the brain, and in particular for understanding the neural basis of learning (Olds & Olds, 1961).

It is on the basis of two common features that the research of these men is grouped together. First, the responses which they studied could not be observed directly by the experimenter nor by the subject himself; some device had to be employed to record the response and display it. Second, the goal of the research was to train the subject to acquire control over the response by making some stimulus which the subject could observe contingent on the response. (Whether one could describe this contingent stimulus as an operant reinforcer or a biofeedback stimulus is an issue which we shall consider later.) In summary, it is the concern with responses that cannot be directly observed, and the goal of producing control over these responses by providing the subject with response contingent stimulation that are the common features of the work of these five men.

Following these beginnings, one would, we think, have expected the gradual accumulation of both basic and applied research on biofeedback. To some extent, this expectation was met--most noticeably by research which was concerned with the use of biofeedback as an analytic tool for studying brain function in animals. This development follows directly, in our opinion, from the work of Olds (Olds & Olds, 1961). We have employed biofeedback techniques to train various patterns of electrical activity in the hippocampus in an attempt to further our understanding of hippocampal function (Black, 1971, 1975). Fetz, who will describe his research later in the symposium, Fox, Rudell and Rosenfeld, and Sterman and his associates had also been carrying out successful research with the purpose of analyzing brain function. (See Fetz (1969), Fox & Rudell (1968), Sterman, Wyrwicka, & Roth (1969) for some early papers on this topic.)

There were, however, three additional developments during this period that we consider to be very disturbing. First, public interest in biofeedback grew rapidly and it became especially popular with people who wanted to help their fellowman but who were not particularly interested in a scientific approach. These people did not, and do not, seem to be concerned with a careful evaluation of the data nor with the systematic investigation of the limits of the technique. They believed in biofeedback, and believing, they set out to employ the technique and to convince others how wonderful the technique is. The sensationalism of the approach made many scientists skeptical about the value of biofeedback and turned them away from it. It also became difficult for those in the field to sort things out. With so many strong claims, often accompanied by inadequate research, it was difficult to decide what the technique could really do.

The second major problem concerns the failure of Miller and his colleagues to replicate their results with the curarized rat.[1] This has been discussed often enough, and we don't want to repeat the discussion (Obrist, Black, Brener, & DiCara, 1974; see, in particular, summary comments by Black and Brener). The main point is that Miller's research provided the most impressive and methodologically sound data on the biofeedback training of autonomic responses. It is these results which convinced many respectable scientists that there was "something to" autonomic biofeedback training. When the results could not be replicated, the basis for autonomic biofeedback training was called into question.[2]

The third development which is disturbing was the inability to substantiate the claim that the biofeedback training of certain types of brain electrical activity results in the control of psychological states in human subjects. In this area the major effort has been directed toward the conditioning of alpha waves recorded from electrodes attached to the scalps of human subjects primarily over the occipital cortex. A great many of the claims for the power of biofeedback were made for such alpha wave training. But as the data accumulated it became clear that the claims were not supported. As Mulholland pointed out in an address to the Massachusetts Psychological Association in 1971,

> The ALPHA cult is not scientific, prone to grandiose claims, attracts the naive, the desperate and the superstitious. It has also been a source of simple fraud, misrepresentations and quackery. The fact of the matter is this--to date there has been no evidence presented to the scientific or medical community that the occurrence of lots of alpha rhythms in the normal person is associated with any special mental powers. There is no evidence that lots of EEG alpha brings relief from physical or mental disease.

There is little reason, in our opinion, to change this evaluation today; this conclusion is supported by the contributions of L. Johnson and W. Plotkin to this symposium.

In summary, the mainstream of biofeedback research was not in a very healthy state in the early 1970s--with the major exception being animal research that was designed to analyze brain function. Overblown claims were being made for the power of the biofeedback technique. At the same time Miller's research, which had provided much of the support for claims about the power of biofeedback, could not be replicated, and the claims for therapeutic effects of alpha wave conditioning remain unsubstantiated.

In the past few years, the situation has improved somewhat. Well designed research has begun to appear more often in the literature. The evidence for the effectiveness of biofeedback is convincing in some cases. At the same time certain "old" problems are still with us, and new problems have arisen. We would like to discuss these problems next. These can be classified into two types. The first are empirical questions that arise from a lack of specific information; they can be dealt with by providing the required data. The second set of problems are those which arise from a concern with theoretical issues.

EMPIRICAL QUESTIONS

We would place the following issues in this class of empirical questions:

1) Which autonomic and central nervous system responses can be modified by biofeedback training?
2) What are the limits to which the modification of a given response can be carried?
3) What are the best procedures for modifying a given response?
4) Are the optimum procedures different for different response systems?
5) What, in fact, are the therapeutic effects of biofeedback training?

These questions could be answered in a straightforward way if the data were available. Unfortunately, the data are inadequate. We still do not know how many and which autonomic and central nervous system responses in a given species are amenable to operant or biofeedback control. We still do not know the degree to which we can change a given autonomic response, nor the best procedures for accomplishing such changes. As a consequence, when negative results are obtained with biofeedback training in a given experiment, we cannot decide whether this result occurred because the response cannot be trained or because the training procedure was inadequate.

We shall not deal with these questions further. Their importance is obvious and it will be easier to see how far we can go in answering them after some data have been discussed during the next few days.

THEORETICAL QUESTIONS

At this point we would like to turn to the second type of problem. Biofeedback seems to have been treated by some as a unique and very special process. We shall take a different position and assume that biofeedback can be analyzed best if we treat it as a form of learning. From this point of view, it may appear that the first logical step would be to attempt to assign biofeedback to one of the well-established categories of learning. For example, one might ask, "Is biofeedback most like simple instrumental or operant conditioning, or is it best described as a form of motor skills learning?" Once this has been accomplished, the second step would be to apply to biofeedback the theory relevant to the type of learning that biofeedback is supposed to resemble. If, for example, biofeedback is thought to resemble motor skills learning, it would be assumed that the available theories of motor skills learning will be appropriate for biofeedback. This is essentially theory formation by analogy. While this approach may be helpful in suggesting that certain variables are important, it may not be particularly fruitful in the long run as the papers by Johnston and Lang seem to indicate. Perhaps, it is more likely that a useful theory of biofeedback will be developed by simply asking the two questions that are central to most theories of learning.

1) What is learned as a consequence of the training procedure?
2) What variables are necessary and sufficient for producing learning, and by what mechanisms do they have their effect?

What is Learned?

Let us begin with the problem of what is learned during biofeedback training. One would expect that a great deal is learned--as in any training situation. For example, the subject may be learning about the temporal and spatial relationships among stimuli, about the associations between stimuli and responses, about the consequences of responses, and so on.

These possibilities--traditional areas of interest to learning theorists--appear, from a consideration of the literature, to be of no interest to most biofeedback researchers. Rather, their main concern is "the development of operant or voluntary control over a given response." This seems simple but the simplicity is more apparent than real.

In order to facilitate the discussion of this issue we shall distinguish between two aspects of the notion of "response control" and discuss them separately. The first is the event that leads to the occurrence of the response--that is, the stimulus which elicits the response or sets the occasion for its occurrence. The second is what the subject actually does. The former is usually referred to as stimulus control and the latter as the response strategy or response mechanism.

Stimulus control. The main point that we would like to make in this case is straightforward. There is a dearth of research on this topic in the biofeedback area. Consider the fact that there is a variety of types of stimulus control that we can establish. Which do we want in a given situation? Do we want stimulus control to be exerted by the life situation of the subject so that the response is performed continuously? Do we want stimulus control to be exerted by a specific stimulus that the experimenter presents to the subject so that the response is performed only when the experimenter wants it to be performed? Do we want stimulus to be exerted by some internal state so that the response is performed only when the subject is in this state? Do we want control to be voluntary? How much transfer or generalization to other stimuli do we want, and so on? These are very important questions--especially in therapeutic situations; they have not been dealt with adequately and, in fact, some are rarely even considered. We must specify what type of stimulus control is appropriate for particular situations, and determine whether and under what conditions we can establish it.

Probably the most notable lack of precision in this respect is found in discussions of the term "voluntary." This is one of the most common of the terms used in the biofeedback literature. Yet we still do not have an adequate description of what we mean by it. We shall discuss just one aspect of this problem. Most recent attempts to define "voluntary" have emphasized the ability to "comply with instructions" as the basic feature of voluntary control. But it may be that subjects can still have voluntary control without being able to follow instructions. A consideration of the conduction apraxias makes this clear. In such cases, subjects cannot perform a given response--say picking up a pencil--when instructed to do so because there seems to be a break in the pathways between the neural mechanism underlying language and those controlling motor functions. At the same time, the subject seems to be able to perform the response when he "wants to do so"--when, for example, the pencil falls to the floor (Geschwind, 1975). Is not the latter voluntary control? Another difficulty arising from the emphasis on "instructions" in the definition of voluntary can be mentioned. Since the definition of voluntary that we have been discussing requires that the response always follow a specific stimulus, that is, an instruction, does this mean that voluntary responses should be considered to be reflexively elicited? The concept of voluntary is complex and difficult, and the best strategy may be simply to stop using it. In any case, the problem of what is learned cannot be dealt with adequately until we come to grips with the problems of stimulus control.

Response strategy. Similar questions can be raised about response strategies. For example, is it necessary to train a precise response or will some gross response do? Do we want to establish a particular pattern of activity involving several responses? In contrast to the case for stimulus control, considerable attention has been focused on these and related questions (such as the problem of medication) by biofeedback researchers. This is illustrated by a number of papers in this symposium, see especially the papers by Pickering et al. and Schwartz.

At the same time, it is important to note that we need more information on what the subject is actually learning to do to obtain reinforcement. The importance of this question can be illustrated by considering the problem of the target response. What response should we reinforce when we are trying to alleviate a set of symptoms? Some researchers seem to assume that the most efficient procedure for producing a change in a response or symptom is to make the feedback stimulus directly contingent on that response or symptom. But this need not be the case. Consider, for example, a series of experiments that we carried out recently in collaboration with S. Smith and C. Vanderwel-Johnson (1975). One experiment was concerned with the development of an efficient procedure for reducing the blood pressure in patients suffering from labile hypertension. Four groups of subjects were employed. One group received biofeedback training only, a second group received relaxation training only, a third group both, and a fourth group was subject to blood pressure measurements without training. Relaxation training was successful in lowering baseline systolic blood pressure significantly; neither biofeedback training alone nor the no-treatment control condition were as effective in lowering the baseline blood pressure, even though subjects in the biofeedback groups could increase and decrease blood pressure. Data comparing the two groups receiving relaxation training with the other two groups are shown in Figure 1.

This result indicates that the training of general muscle relaxation

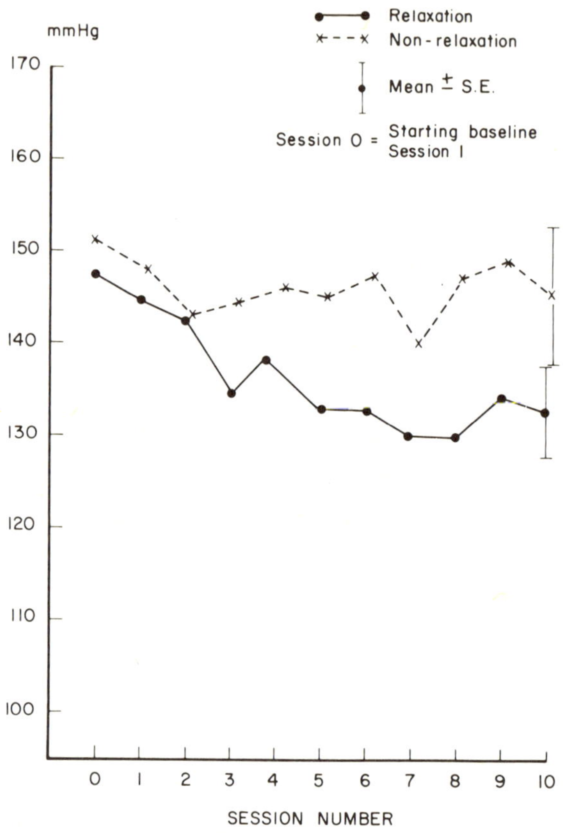

Figure 1. Baseline blood pressure (systolic) for two groups of hypertensive patients that were subject to relaxation training and two groups that were not. Measurements were taken over a series of ten weekly sessions.

had a much more profound effect on baseline blood pressure than attempts to develop direct biofeedback control over blood pressure--at least in our situation.[3] The papers in this symposium by B.T. Engel, R.S. Surwit and D. Shapiro, and J. Stoyva support this conclusion. In fact these papers--along with those on electromyographic activity by P. Engel-Sittenfeld, and G. DeBacher and J.V. Basmajian--tempt one to suggest that the most well-established therapeutic effect of biofeedback is related to the reinforcement of skeletal muscle changes. But at this point it is probably wise to resist this temptation.

One further point. In our experiments on blood pressure, it appeared that the most profound therapeutic effects occurred in subjects whose entire lifestyles were modified as a result of the treatment. This suggests that the therapeutic effects of biofeedback training may depend on a much more general modification of the behavior of the subject than we have been willing to consider so far, as is also suggested by Legewie in his comments. In short, the alleviation of a set of symptoms may be related to learning which is taking place in response systems not even being monitored, and of which the experimenter and subject are unaware.

This possibility raises another clearly related problem. One goal of research on the mechanisms of therapeutic techniques is to isolate the specific contributions of a given treatment from the effects of other unknown variables that operate simultaneously. The effect resulting from these unknown variables is usually called "the placebo effect." In the context of the medical model, it is often viewed as an annoyance--not a "real" therapeutic effect. But the placebo effect is a powerful one, worth analyzing on its own. If we could understand its mechanisms better we could use it to advantage--maximizing its contributions when it is desirable to do so and minimizing its contributions when undesirable. Ironically, biofeedback may be an excellent vehicle for studying placebo effects, particularly when the response on which the feedback stimulus is made contingent is not directly related to the symptoms of interest. An example is provided by alpha wave biofeedback where it is becoming clear that alpha activity per se is unrelated to subjective states. Melzack and Perry (1975), for example, found that alpha feedback alone had no effect in alleviating pain, although alpha activity increased as a result of training. However, when alpha feedback was employed in conjunction with a form of relaxation training, significant reductions in pain were reported. Substantial but statistically unreliable reductions in pain resulted from relaxation training alone. It was concluded that additional beneficial effects of alpha biofeedback training were attributable not to increases in alpha activity but rather to such things as "the distraction of attention, suggestion, relaxation, and a sense of control over pain." We think that such uses of biofeedback could provide some very interesting information about placebo effects.

Learning Mechanisms

Consider next the second question that we listed above. What are the variables and mechanisms that are thought to be involved in the acquisition of the response? Two major approaches to this question can be identified: One is the operant conditioning approach, and one we have called the awareness approach (Black, Cott, & Pavloski, in press). We think that the operant approach provides a more adequate framework for carrying out research. But, in our opinion, neither approach is particularly useful at present in dealing with the nature of the underlying mechanisms of learning. Attempts to deal with these mechanisms by the awareness approach are open to question and are practically non-existent in the operant approach.

We shall discuss the awareness approach briefly in order to justify this conclusion. We have defined awareness as the ability to distinguish between the occurrence and nonoccurrence of a response. That is, when the response itself (or internal stimuli and states that are a direct cause, correlate or consequence of the response) can act as discriminative stimuli, we have "awareness" of the response. If one accepts this definition, the "awareness" hypothesis can be stated as follows. When a subject learns to discriminate the occurrence and nonoccurrence of an internal response, he becomes aware of the response and, as a consequence, achieves voluntary control over that response.

The evidence does not support this hypothesis. We will not go into any detail at this time, but it is worth making two points. First, there are cases where subjects are "aware" of their responses but do not have voluntary control over them. Therefore, awareness is not sufficient for control. Second, consider the possibility that a subject can learn to perform a response as a result of biofeedback training and then lose control quickly when the contingent stimulus is removed (Alexander et al., 1975). It seems to us that such a result casts very serious doubts on the notion that the addition of an external feedback stimulus acts to make the subject aware of internal responses during training. For those who accept this position, the loss of control suggests that either 1) the subject was not aware of the internal response and control was achieved nevertheless, or 2) the subject was aware of the internal response but that awareness was not sufficient to maintain control. Both conclusions are damaging to the awareness view.

It seems to us that the results of research employing this transfer design are very important to the awareness view and that additional data on this transfer data would be useful. In any case, our main point is, we hope, clear. Neither of the two approaches that have been taken in attempting to develop a theoretical account of biofeedback is adequate. Again, we need more research on the relevant issues in order to develop an acceptable theory.

CONCLUSION

These are some of the empirical and theoretical problems with which we are currently faced. We hope that the papers that will be presented during the course of the week will help to solve them. In addition, we anticipate vigorous discussion of some specific issues that we have not mentioned--for example, the significance of the theta rhythm and the control of seizure activity in epilepsy. As new information comes in, biofeedback may be able to take its place as one more tool in the armamentarium of behavior modification procedures that can be employed in conjunction with each other. In this way, it may be useful therapeutically in the same way that it has been demonstrated to be useful as another analytic tool for studying brain function. But, as we stated at the outset, we are not particularly sanguine about the future of biofeedback unless its checkered history is faced honestly and an attempt is made to deal with its only too obvious failures and deficiencies. We hope that this symposium will provide a step in the right direction.

REFERENCES

Alexander, A. B., Holland, P. W., & Wallace, H. M. Training and transfer of training effects in EMG biofeedback assisted muscular relaxation. Proceedings of the Society for Psychophysiological Research, Fifteenth Annual Meeting, Toronto, Canada, 1975. (Abstract)

Basmajian, J. V. Control and training of individual motor units. Science, 1963, 141, 440-441.

Black, A. H. Autonomic aversive conditioning in infrahuman subjects. In F. R. Brush (Ed.), Aversive conditioning and learning. New York: Academic Press, 1971. (a)

Black, A. H. The direct control of neural processes by reward and punishment. American Scientist, 1971, 59, 236-245. (b)

Black, A. H. Hippocampal electrical activity and behavior. In R. L. Isaacson & K. H. Pribram (Eds.), The hippocampus (Volume 2). New York: Plenum, 1975.

Black, A. H., Cott, A., & Pavloski, R. The operant learning theory approach to biofeedback training. In G. E. Schwartz & J. Beatty (Eds.), Biofeedback: Theory and research. San Francisco: Academic Press, in press.

Blanchard, E. B., & Young, L. B. Self-control of cardiac functioning: A promise as yet unfulfilled. Psychological Bulletin, 1973, 79, 145-163.

Fetz, E. E. Operant conditioning of cortical unit activity. Science, 1969, 163, 955-957.

Fowler, R. L., & Kimmel, H. D. Operant conditioning of the GSR. Journal of Experimental Psychology, 1962, 63, 563-567.

Fox, S. S., & Rudell, A. P. Operant controlled neural event: Formal and systematic approach to electrical coding of behavior in brain. Science, 1968, 162, 1299-1302.

Geschwind, N. The apraxias: Neural mechanisms of disorders of learned movement. American Scientist, 1975, 63, 188-195.

Harrison, V. F., & Mortensen, O. A. Identification and voluntary control of single motor activity in the tibialis anterior muscle. Anatomical Record, 1962, 144, 109-116.

Kamiya, J. Conscious control of brain waves. Psychology Today, 1968, 1, 57-60.

Kimmel, H. D. Instrumental conditioning of autonomically mediated behavior. Psychological Bulletin, 1967, 67, 337-345.

Melzack, R., & Perry, C. Self-regulation of pain: The use of alpha-feedback and hypnotic training for the control of chronic pain. Experimental Neurology, 1975, 46, 452-469.

Miller, N. E. Learning of visceral and glandular responses. Science, 1969, 163, 434-445.

Miller, N. E., & DiCara, L. V. Instrumental learning of heart-rate changes in curarized rats: Shaping and specificity to discriminative stimulus. Journal of Comparative and Physiological Psychology, 1967, 63, 12-19.

Obrist, P. A., Black, A. H., Brener, J., & DiCara, L. V. (Eds.). Cardiovascular psychophysiology: Current issues in response mechanisms, biofeedback, and methodology. Chicago: Aldine, 1974.

Olds, J., & Olds, M. E. Interference and learning in paleocortical systems. In J. F. Delafresnaye (Ed.), Brain mechanisms and learning. Oxford: Blackwell, 1961.

Smith, S. L., Black, A. H., Vanderwel-Johnson, C., & Cott, A. Successful behavioural treatment for hypertension: A study of methods and predictors. Paper presented at the Canadian Psychiatric Association Meetings, Calgary, Alberta, September 1975.

Sterman, M. B., Wyrwicka, W., & Roth, S. Electrophysiological correlates and neural substrates of alimentary behavior in the cat. Annals of the New York Academy of Sciences, 1969, 157, 723-739.

NOTES

1. It is ironic to note that replication of these experiments on curarized rats is no longer important as far as one of their major original purposes is concerned. This purpose was to demonstrate operant autonomic conditioning with somatic mediation. But as we and others have pointed out previously, the curarized preparation is inadequate for this purpose. Curare blocks the peripheral neuromuscular junction. If the relationship between autonomic and somatic responses involves central rather than peripheral circuits, as often seems to be the case, curare will not block that relationship.

2. One could argue that the results obtained by Miller and his associates were not historically important for applied biofeedback research because Miller's work was with animals and because these data were not relevant to human subjects. But in the early 1970s when Miller's results were not being replicated, there weren't many data on human subjects that one could fall back on. The lack of data on the human biofeedback training of autonomic responses during this period has been amply documented in the review paper by Blanchard and Young (1973).

3. An analogous example is provided by Sterman's work. He has implied that it is more efficient to control the sensorimotor rhythm than to control abnormal EEG activity directly in attempting to reduce epileptic seizures. Unfortunately, this conclusion must be questioned since data from appropriate control groups are unavailable.

The preparation of this paper and the research described in it were supported by Ontario Mental Health Foundation Grant #258-69D, Medical Research Council of Canada Grant #MA-5854, and Ontario Ministry of Health Grant #PR-335. Dr. Cott is an Ontario Mental Health Foundation Research Scholar.

BIOFEEDBACK FROM THE PERSPECTIVES OF CYBERNETICS AND SYSTEMS SCIENCE

James Anliker
Biotechnology Division
NASA Ames Research Center

The great French mathematician Laplace, whose monumental *Mécanique celeste* summarized the work of several generations of mathematicians on the behavior of celestial bodies under the influence of gravitational forces, captured the imagination of scientists and philosophers with his famous pronouncement that

> "An intelligence knowing all of the forces acting in nature at a given instant, as well as the momentary positions of all things in the universe, would be able to comprehend in one single formula the motions of the largest bodies as well as the lightest atoms, provided that its intellect were sufficiently powerful to subject all data to analysis; to it (i.e., to such an intelligence) nothing would be uncertain, the future as well as the past would be present to its eyes."

However, he went on to say that "All the mind's efforts in the search for truth tend to approximate to the intelligence we have just imagined, although it (the mind) will forever remain infinitely remote from such an intelligence." It should be noted that Laplace's analysis of celestial mechanics was based on three assumptions: 1) the solar system is isolated in space; 2) the solar system is devoid of diffuse matter (i.e., there is no friction to retard the movement of heavenly bodies); 3) the observer does not disturb the system observed. In addition, of course, there had to be the tacit assumption that the sun could exist indefinitely without an appreciable change in state. Thus, with respect to gravitational forces, the solar system is what the physicist would call a closed system, i.e., a system which is isolated from external influences. As you probably know, conventional physics is concerned only with closed systems. The laws of thermodynamics, for example, apply only to closed systems.

In dealing with the more mundane behavior of living organisms, we are clearly confronted by systems which are not isolated from their environments, which are subject to many "frictions," and which are both self-observing and self-controlling. Obviously, they must be classified as open systems. This raises the question of whether there are any practical ways to achieve some substantial reduction in our uncertainties concerning the behavior of organisms. More specifically, can human intelligence discover predictable local order, as contrasted with global or universal order, in human behavior? Can human intelligence utilize this knowledge to control human behavior in particular individuals? And, can the individual use such information to control his own behavior? Although the answer must be "yes" to all three questions, they must be qualified affirmatives because there are serious limitations to both prediction and control of human affairs.

There is a tradition that attributes to Archimedes the boast: "give me a place to stand and I will move the earth." One might say that it is the search for this vantage point that motivates human science. The particular vantage point sought depends upon the aims or purposes of the seeker. As students of biofeedback mechanisms, our aim is not to move the earth but rather to "move" living organisms. To be more exact, our purpose is to discover the vantage points from which a man may "move" his own behavior.

At this conference held at the Max-Planck-Institut fur Psychiatrie it seems of particular interest to report the view of this matter expressed by Max Planck himself. In a remarkable book entitled Where is Science Going? (1932), the great physicist wrote:

> "The fact is that there is a point in the immeasurable world of mind and matter, where science and every causal method of research is inapplicable, not only on practical grounds but also on logical grounds, and will always remain inapplicable. This point is the individual ego. It is a small point in the universal realm of being; but in itself it is a whole world, embracing our emotional life, our will and our thought. This realm of the ego is at once the source of our deepest suffering and at the same time of our highest happiness. Over this realm no outer power of fate can ever have sway, and we lay aside our own control and responsibility over ourselves only with the laying aside of life itself.

"And yet there is a way which the causal method can be applied within the limits of this inner realm. In principle there is no reason whatsoever why the individual should not make himself the observer of what has happened within himself. In other words, he can look back over the experiences through which he has passed and endeavor to link them up in their causal relations. There is no reason indeed, at least in principle, why he should not scrutinize each experience--by which I mean each decision and line of conduct which he has taken--and study it from the viewpoint of finding out the cause from which it has resulted. Of course that is an extremely difficult task; but it is the only soundly scientific way of dealing with our own lives. In order to carry out this plan of action the facts of our own lives which we now place under observation would have to be distanced in the past, so that our present complex of living emotions and inclinations would not enter as factors in the observation. If we could carry out the plan in this detached way, then each experience through which we have passed would make us immeasurably more intelligent than we were before, so intelligent indeed that in relation to our earlier condition we should rise to the level of the super-intelligence postulated by Laplace." (pp. 161-162)

"...I am not preaching a moral sermon here or suggesting what ought to be aimed at for the sake of the moral uplift of one's own being. I am only treating the case of individual freedom from the viewpoint of its logical coherence with the principle of causation, and I am saying that in principle there is no reason why we should not discover the causal connections in our own personal conduct, but that in practice we never can do so because this would mean that the observing subject would also be the object of research. And that is impossible; for no eye can see itself. But in so far as any man is not entirely to-day (i.e., at this moment) what he was years ago (i.e., at a previous moment) there is a relative degree to which he might subject his own experiences to causal scrutiny..."

One might expect that the great physicist, having made this much of a concession to causal relativism might have generalized the principle. Unfortunately, he did not. To Planck the physicist, science meant objectivity; therefore, "private science" would not really be science because it would lack the essential objectivity. On the other hand, he recognized the usefulness to the individual of employing scientific procedures in the analysis of private events. This attitude is similar to that of the "pure" mathematician toward the activities of the "applied" mathematician. The former has no objection to the latter's "applications" as long as no mathematical rules are violated; but the application is of no mathematical relevance. In other words, these provincial or private games and their outcomes are not of interest to the theoretician qua theoretician, however important they may be to the individual.

It seems reasonable to assume that higher organisms, with or without authoritative approval, are perpetually engaging in some form of subjective causal analysis, however crude or sophisticated. If so, each organism's covert models of its "world" (including models of its self or selves) would constitute one of the two principal classes of controllers of its overt and covert actions. The other principal class of controllers is composed of the environmental influences. In the case of a civilized person's environment, we should recognize that educational process arranges for attentional priorities to be assigned to similarly educated social partners and to the cultural institutions.

The individual has limited information concerning his covert behavior. Of this private store of information the individual can only communicate a small amount of his subjective experiences of which he can only communicate to other individuals, and then only to individuals sharing the same language and similar experiences. Thus, behavior which to the behaving individual is orderly and consistent with his plans may appear random to another individual. The limits of behavioral control are, in large measure, determined by the ability of science (public or private) to reduce the unpredictable disturbances to a minimum by discovering methods of extracting predictable order from apparent disorder.

In undertaking the task of looking at biofeedback from the perspectives of cybernetics and systems science, I hope to narrow somewhat the wide gap that seems to separate the intensely empirical biofeedback research from the theoretical developments embodied in cybernetics and systems science. I realize, of course, that empiricists are inclined to be skeptical about the usefulness of theoretical formulations. This attitude is often justified because the theorist is seldom competent to cope with practical affairs. In this regard, you may be amused to learn of the ill-fated attempt by Napoleon to harness the intelligence of Laplace to the problems of state. Napoleon, when he became first consul in 1799, optimistically appointed Laplace to the important position of minister of the interior. But he was forced to remove Laplace after only six weeks (the great scientist was discreetly "promoted" to the senate) because he brought "the spirit of infinitesimals into administration." Thus, while I hope to interest (or re-interest) some of you in technological control concepts, I realize that I may only succeed in causing others to reaffirm their opposition to what they consider to be "misguided" attempts to apply technological concepts and procedures to the analysis of the exceedingly complex behavior of living organisms of a high order. Nevertheless, it seems to me that the biofeedback area is one in which the lack of a clear theoretical formulation is a serious obstacle to progress. Behavioral scientists can and should help to close the fact-theory gap in this area by making a great er effort to formulate their techniques and observations in terms that are more accessible to engineers and control theorists. In order to achieve this they will have to learn something about engineering language and procedures. I firmly believe that systems analysis and control theory are destined to play a dominant role in the future of the psychology of learning and conditioning.

WHAT IS CYBERNETICS?

The term cybernetics was selected by Norbert Wiener (1948), a professor of mathematics at the Massachusetts Institute of Technology, to represent the complex of scientific disciplines that deal with various aspects of communication and control processes in machines and in living organisms. This name, derived from the Greek word for "governor" or "steersman," was selected to focus attention upon the unifying property which justifies the drawing together of a wide-ranging collection of phenomena, concepts, and methods of analysis. Cybernetics includes such diverse fields of inquiry as computer science, probability theory, information theory, control theory, neurophysiology, perceptual theory, and so forth. Presumably, membership in the cybernetics family is open to any discipline that can make a substantial contribution to the prediction and control of machine and/or man. The function of the cybernetic theorist, according to Wiener (1948) is to provide the unifying theory that describes the transformational relations between the member disciplines. It would seem that very little progress has been made in achieving the unifying theory envisioned by Wiener although there has been a noticeable weakening of the boundaries separating the various disciplines. Although there is some tendency to identify systems theory with control theory and cybernetics, von Bertalanffy (1968) believes that cybernetics "is but a part of a general theory of systems." In his view, cybernetic systems are merely a subset of a larger family of systems, the cybernetic systems being those characterized by self-regulation. For this reason it seems worthwhile to begin at a rather general level and then try to "focus in" on self-regulating or self-controlling systems.

WHAT ARE SYSTEMS?

A collection of elements or entities may be characterized, according to von Bertalanffy (1968), 1) by the species to which the various elements belong (i.e., by the intrinsic properties of the elements that permit their assignment to classes as in nominal scaling), 2) by their numbers (i.e., the sums according to classes), and 3) by their relations (i.e., the constraints or interactions between elements). The properties of elements which are the same whether the elements are located inside the complex or outside may be described as summative; "they may therefore be obtained by means of summation of characteristics and behavior of elements as known in isolation." By contrast, properties which are dependent on specific relations within the complex may be described as constitutive; such properties are lost when elements are isolated from each other. Von Bertalanffy illustrates the usefulness of this distinction as follows:

> "The meaning of the somewhat mystical expression, "the whole is more than the sum of parts" is simply that the constitutive characteristics are not explainable from the characteristics of the isolated parts. The characteristics of the complex, therefore, compared to those of the elements, appear as "new" or "emergent." If, however, we know the total of parts contained in a system and the relations between them, the behavior of the system may be derived from the behavior of the parts. We can also say: While we can conceive of a sum as being composed gradually, a system as total of parts with its interrelations has to be conceived of as being composed instantly."

A constitutive (or interactive) arrangement of parts (i.e., elements, components, entities, sub-systems) is said to constitute a system. This definition is sufficiently general to encompass systems which vary widely along the dimensions of complexity and abstraction. A system has inputs and outputs, but is isolated otherwise. Naturally, the systems of greatest interest to us here are the ones that exhibit dynamic properties, i.e., systems that are "behavioral" in character. A dynamic system is simply one whose state is varying with time. Mathematically, the variables of a dynamic system are expressed as vector quanitites. From a functional viewpoint, a behavioral system is composed of a network of interactive components. The "flow" of causal influences within the system must be suitably represented in the abstract models. However, one must constantly be reminded that the term "system" can be defined and used at a number of different levels on the continuum from concrete to abstract. That is, the system in question might range from functional machinery through scaled replicas and computerized analogies to mathematical models. Thus, when one speaks of the "behavior" of a "system" it is important to distinguish clearly among these various levels of abstraction and to observe carefully the rules and conventions that constrain proper usage at each level of discourse. With the proliferation of maps and models, one has to watch labels carefully in order to avoid semantic confusion.

It is necessary, of course, to have some methods for defining which entities are to be included in a particular system and which entities are to be excluded from the system under consideration. Logically, this can be broken down into three distinct operations: 1) the recruitment of entities as candidates for inclusion in the system; 2) the classification of the candidates into "members" and "non-members"; 3) the selective elimination of the unwanted candidates or "non-members"; and 4) the selective retention of the "members."

A systems analyst usually begins by developing a greatly simplified description or model of his problem. To obtain a useful model, he must start with an insightful selection of system variables, a selection presumably based on a careful review of the relevant facts and principles. He then usually generates what is often termed a "black-box" description of the properties (or behavior) of the components of his system when they are connected according to his scheme. To keep his description manageable, he will usually contrive to linearize the nonlinear relationships (or merely choose to disregard them in the model). Finally, he must settle upon effective criteria for defining an optimal performance (by an ideal system) and for evaluating actual performance. Each of the above-mentioned operations can be either simple or extremely complex depending upon the nature of the system that is modelled.

Typically, the scientist is concerned with the systematic exclusion of all non-essential parts, i.e., the isolation of the mechanisms essential to the function. As mentioned earlier, a completely isolated system is called a closed system (not to be confused with a "closed loop"). Obviously, a closed system is simpler to account for than an open system because the former contains fewer variables than the latter. Once the properties of a closed system have been analyzed into manageable order, it is then of interest to open the system to external influences on a limited basis. The external influences should be selected preferrably from the output of another system whose properties are predictable. And so the systems scientist is supposed to progress "from meaner things to higher" without overloading his understanding of the processes in question.

FEEDBACK CONTROL SYSTEMS

In the engineer's description of a piece of machinery, a distinction is made between the power variables and the control variables. In general, the power variables are concerned with one or another form of energy required for the operation of the system, and with transformations of this energy within the system. The control variables, on the other hand, are concerned with information and planning. This distinction can be clarified by considering an important class of control systems called servomechanisms. These devices are automatic control systems in which the output of a (usually high-power) sybsystem (or effector) is made to comply with the commands or instructions given to it by a (usually low-power) subsystem called a controller. The controller and the effector (or "plant") can be, and frequently are, placed in locations which are remote from one another. We may note in passing that the existence of "remote control" mechanisms greatly complicates the analysis of living systems. The use of a low-power controller to guide the behavior of a high-power plant provides many advantages. For instance, since the high-power element is only brought in at the final stage prior to the output, the rest of the control system need not be burdened with the problems associated with high power operations. Another advantage is that the ratio of the power of the plant output and the control signal input can be very large indeed. For instance, in an observatory with suitable servomechanisms, the light emitted by a star can control the movements of a massive telescope so that it "tracks" the star's location with a very high degree of accuracy.

The high-power output device in a servosystem is sometimes called the controlled member. Suppose that the controlled member is a motor: we might elect to control the speed of rotation of its output shaft or its angle of rotation. The low-power mechanism that issues instructions to the plant is often called the controller or the command sybsystem; in the example of a motor, its commands to the controlled member might be in terms of rotational speed or rotational angle.

There is an important characteristic that distinguishes servosystems as a class from other automatic control systems: namely, its use of negative feedback. In a negative feedback control system the operation of the high-power subsystem is controlled or regulated by the difference or error between 1) the desired state or input reference of the controller and 2) the existing state or output of the high-power system. The output is monitored by an appropriate sensor and the sensor's output signals are relayed to the controller. The controller performs two functions: First, it compares the input reference signal with the sensor signal and computes the magnitude and sign of the error; second, it computes the compensation that should null (in accordance with its control law) the difference between the reference signal and the output signal, i.e., between the desired output and the actual output. This type of feedback is termed negative because the error quantity is subtracted from the (subsequent) output.

If the error were added to the (subsequent) output, the system would be called a positive feedback system. It is understandable that positive feedback would cause an increase or growth of error; therefore positive feedback is of limited interest from the standpoint of autocontrol although it is of considerable interest in the matter of reducing another system's self-control since, by increasing the confusion (or error) of the controllee, it can reduce the controllee's capacity to resist external forces.

The dynamic compensatory capability of the negative feedback control system or servomechanism allows it to maintain the commanded output under a wide range of unpredicted or unpredictable operating loads, i.e., process disturbances. "The purpose of feedback control," according to Bryson (1972), "is to reduce to acceptable levels the effects of unpredictable disturbances and uncertain parameters, using acceptable levels of control action." However, since to predict is not to foresee (i.e., forecasts are subject to error), an error-compensating system assists in "taking up the slack" between the predicted and the observed output quantities. It should not be too surprising, therefore, to find this highly useful error-compensating mechanism incorporated into many systems, both natural and man-made.

The external influences acting upon a negative feedback control system may be classified as "control variables" or disturbance variables" depending upon whether their effects are "accepted" or "resisted" by the system. That is, the recipient system is usually designed so as to respond preferentially (i.e., without reluctance) to one class of input variables (i.e., the control variables) and to act to resist or to minimize the influence of another class of variables (i.e., disturbance variables) on the system's output. A machine that is designed to be thoroughly controlled by another machine is often called a "slave." In the design of machines, a slave system has no options other than to carry out the commands issued to it by the controlling system; the slave may contain many feedback control subsystems but the full resources of the slave are expendable in executing the commands received from the superordinate system. Human behavior is enormously complex, having the capacity to be "controllable" by some external forces and to be "uncontrollable" by others. It seems that the education of the individual serves the purpose of making the cultured individual both unnaturally sensitive and unnaturally resistant to environmental controllers and, what is of great interest here, to potential controllers in the internal environment including the control of one subsystem of the nervous system by another subsystem of the nervous system.

Those variables which are not a part of the system (i.e., external variables) but which can influence the behavior of the system are referred to as parts of the system's environment. These environmental variables are, by definition, outside the system (i.e., not a system component) but their physical location may be either "inside" or "outside" the physical locus of the physical system in question. Not all environmental variables are equally influential upon the behavior of a system. Of special interest are the higher order environmental variables that are capable of communicating higher order control messages to the system. The hierarchical ordering of control systems into subordinate and superordinate subsystems is based on an analysis of the flow patterns within the system.

FEEDBACK VERSUS FEEDFORWARD

With increasing frequency we encounter the term "feedforward" in the literature and this raises the question as to what is meant by "forward" and "backward." The term "feedback" means that there is a connection between the output from a chain of components and the input to the chain. This recurrent pathway must not be construed as running backwards against time inasmuch as "time's arrow" travels relentlessly forward. With respect to time, we must understand that the so-called loop is merely a conceptual convenience for dealing with repetitious sequences of events. If a boy tosses a ball into the air, catches it, tosses it up again, catches it, etc., it must be understood that with respect to time the boy who catches the descending ball is not the same boy who previously tossed it aloft. Since, however, the catcher has a lot in common with the tosser, we may ignore for certain conceptual purposes the difference between Tosser (time one) and Tosser (time two) and deal with a cycle of phases with the sequence Toss-Catch, Toss-Catch, etc. In phase-time we re-set the clock at the beginning of each cycle. This permits us to "coil" the chain of temporal events into a recurrent phase-time concept or model. It is merely a convenient way of abstracting the time-order of sequences of events. For example, the structural changes as a function of time, say, from conception to parturition are sequentially more orderly, in general, than the events transpiring between parturition and the next conception in the history of the "same" female; therefore, the embryologist is justified in re-setting his clock, so to speak, between pregnancies so that he can match the initial phase (i.e., conception) of the history of one embryo with the equivalent initial phase in the history of another embryo. By this means he is able to compare the histories of two or more embryos as a function of phase-time in which phase-time (zero) is understood to be the moment of conception in the history of each embryo.

In describing a feedback system as a closed loop, we are exploiting the fact that the components of the loop are sufficiently invariant in time that we can dissociate their activities from their stationary properties and concentrate our attention upon detecting the order in the time-varying properties. Thus, to return to our example, the ball-tossing boy is divisible conceptually into 1) some stationary components (i.e., constants) which do not change appreciably from one ball-toss to the next and 2) some nonstationary components (i.e., variables) whose states may change with time. We then focus our attention upon the nonstationary components and undertake to conceptualize this behavior in such a manner that we can extract some further invariance such as the phase cycle of tossing and catching. And so forth.

Now, after our small philosophical digression (a conceptual loop, if you will) we can continue our explanation of the "back" in the term "feedback." If a component persists long enough for the feedback loop to be traversed, the state of the component can be affected by the arrival of the feedback message. In short, it is as if the component were carried forward in time (i.e., persists) until an environmental consequence of its prior output arrives to influence the component. This arrival causes a revised output, and so forth. Strictly speaking, of course, a component cannot directly influence itself, but its output to the environment can set in motion an activity which, in turn, may affect the initiator if the initiator can be said to persist long enough to receive the feedback. Thus, by feedback we refer to a connection between a prior and a subsequent component in a phase cycle.

Now what is meant by feedforward? Here we do not mean merely the forward connection between two components in a phase cycle, although this is an acceptable trivial meaning. The term "feedforward" is used at times to describe a condition in which the input to the system in question is also sampled by a superordinate system which intervenes in the affairs of the subordinate system; without waiting for the feedback response of the subordinate system, the superordinate system orders a change in the output of the subordinate system. Usually this type of mechanism acts to suppress or over-ride the feedback effects generated in the subordinate system. Feedforward can also mean that a parallel system (superordinate) receiving different input can seize control of the output of the subordinate system by bypassing certain sequences in the subordinate system. For example, in the game of Monopoly a player may receive the order "go directly to jail" which over-rides the normal sequence of steps around the board. Or, the superordinate system by observing factors outside the scope of the subordinate system, may intervene to advance the output of the system rapidly to some state of interest before relinquishing further control to the subordinate system.

The basic strategy of hierarchical systems is to minimize the use of the higher level (i.e., more decisive and widely influential) computational facilities and to maximize the use of more peripheral (more unconditional or automatic, hence less generally useful) control mechanisms. When the upper centers are being overloaded with work (or if they anticipate being overworked), they can intervene in the affairs of the lower levels in ways calculated to reduce the workload of the upper levels of the system. Generally, feedforward operations, i.e., superordinate intervention in subordinate affairs) serve to rapidly and directly advance the system into the most probable range of operation (or "ball park") before the superordinate system relinquishes control to the subordinate feedback control system which then takes over and reduces the remaining error. This combination of coarse and fine tuning, where applicable, serves to expedite error-reduction. "When feedforward is applied to a complex system, the complexity of control is reduced because the system is kept within a ball-park region of the operation. As a result, feedback is applied to a resultant, much simpler system" (Szentagothai & Arbib, 1975). Many feedback systems can function as intended only if they are initially directed to the "ball park" and/or are prevented from wandering outside the "ball park" limits. This is particularly true of an automatic tracking system which must be returned to its "ball park" after losing track of its target. In orher words, the nervous system must employ a strategy which allows the major error factors to be anticipated so that the initial state as seen by the feedback mechanism is within the compensatory range (or "ballpark") of the feedback mechanism. The intelligent system, therefore, is not a bottom-up organizer but is, instead, a top-down organizer. Instead of blindly groping for the optimal filter design on each occasion, the intelligent computer preserves its most successful filters for subsequent "best guess" deployment. What we have here is essentially a parameter vs. variable distinction. That is, the rate of change allowable for the parameter is necessarily slower than that of its associated variables. Thus, the parameter settings of the most probably optimum filter are altered less frequently (because they are more predictable) than the associated variables. More attention (high level participation) is required in getting a complex operation "going" than in simply sustaining the operation after it is functioning successfully. The higher level parameters (slowest changing variables) in the system are, so to speak, more "eternal" than the lower level parameters. Once properly launched on the right track, the simpler feedback mechanisms may have sufficient tracking power to sustain the target-tracking behavior. Then, only when the lower level feedback circuits begin to allow the target to get away (i.e., when maximal compensation fails to reduce error) is it necessary to invoke higher level intervention, the higher level being presumed to have additional compensatory powers. Thus, it is useful to distinguish between the initialization operations or start-up adjustments and the continuation operations. Finding the ball-park requires more brain power than merely remaining within the ball-park once you are there. For this reason, we must suppose that the efficient nervous system calls into play its higher level intelligence during the start-up operations (or after losing track which is equivalent to starting from scratch). The activity of a superordinate system will normally inhibit automatically or over-ride the lower level, less intelligent feedback mechanism.

FEEDFORWARD AND INTELLIGENCE

From the foregoing remarks, it will be immediately apparent to most students of learning and conditioning that the successful application of the feedforward principle is the very essence of "intelligent" behavior. That is to say, rather than blindly pursuing a chain of simple feedback reactions, the intelligent organism is able to utilize stored information (memory) concerning previous problem-solving responses to bypass activities which have a low probability of pay-off and skip ahead (i.e., advance directly) to the responses which have a higher probability of pay-off. Of course, relevant stored information must be available for otherwise, as Emerson phrased it, he who cannot remember the past is condemned to repeat it. We may note once again that it is the invariance of certain sequences of environmental events that makes possible the use of experiential maps (abstractions of past experiences which are preserved by some form of memory into the present) to anticipate or predict the future. This is the strategy of the advanced form of adaptive control mechanism exhibited by higher organisms. The cultured man utilizes sophisticated mnemonic media in his external environment to extend his functional mnemonic capacity far beyond his natural limits. By devising methods for encoding (e.g., writing) and decoding (e.g., reading) messages stored in entropy-resistant form, he is able to utilize the external environment as a repository for some of his experiential maps. By conforming to social agreements (rules and regulations) concerning allowable encoding and decoding procedures, men are (to some extent) able to utilize the environmentally recorded experiential records of men who lived thousands of years ago by deciphering their surviving records.

We have already described a feedback control system as one that compares the system's output with the system's reference input and acts to reduce any error or discrepancy between the desired output and the observed output. Such a system must wait for a discrepancy to appear before it can begin its compensatory action.

However, it is possible to use input information to begin to prepare responses and corrections without waiting for the feedback effects to arrive. This arrangement allows the system to start corrective action moving in the right direction without waiting for the input to work its influence on the output. Another feedforward approach to control is to use a model to predict the input. It should be recognized that prediction is prerequisite to control. The farther into the future a system can successfully predict, the greater the time available to prepare the responses to these anticipated events. As we shall see, the nervous system is able to utilize its hierarchical control structure to launch its "reactions" prior to the arrival of the environmental stimuli. In this manner, the nervous system gives the impression of "going out to meet" the arriving stimuli. I believe that this type of feedforward control allows the nervous system to make its most powerful controlling responses. Our anticipatory activities (inferences about future inputs and future output needs) allow us to prepare our responses in advance (as a kind of control ammunition) and hold the final stage of implementation until the actual need arrives. I would argue that the elaborate standby services, or options, provided by higher order nervous systems account for the remarkably smooth transitions from one form of behavior (overt or covert) to another. At the higher levels of the nervous system fewer activities are "reactive" in the sense that the response begins only after the stimulus arrives, and more behaviors are pro-active or anticipative in the sense that the response begins before the disturbance or load occurs. It seems clear that the higher levels of the nervous system prepare not only the ultimately utilized response but also a host of alternative responses corresponding to a variety of future probabilities. Most of these standby responses are not completed because the environment "selects" one of them and the rest are discarded covertly (i.e., they are not allowed to influence the output.)

Queen Victoria had the services of a Scottish chamberlain who was so skillful in anticipating her needs that the queen would simply sit down without asking for a chair or looking to see whether there was one waiting to receive her. Her servant anticipated her action and would shove a chair under her as she descended. In many respects your brain is like the anticipative chamberlain inasmuch as it tends to prepare all of the responses which you are likely to need. In fact, it is so anticipative that it is usually difficult for you to conceive of unanticipated responses. It is this wealth of anticipation that creates the great sense of ease which is associated with elaborately prepared responses. You have the impression that your organism does most if not all of the work while your conscious attention appears to be free to engage in other activities. In the perceptual sphere, your brain anticipates what you will probably see when you move your eyes or turn your head, etc. Again, the result is that there are relatively few surprises.

In negative feedback control systems, the work of the system is often largely covert in that it acts to prevent environmental disturbances from affecting the output of the system. This compensation has the effect of producing extremely nonlinear input-output relationships. Naturally, such mechanisms greatly complicate the business of making relevant measurements. For example, in a classical study by Gasnier and Mayer (1939) it was found that the poor relationship between food consumption (energy intake) and metabolic expenditures exhibited by rabbits in the normal laboratory environment could be greatly improved by depriving the rabbits of their compensatory reserves; this was accomplished by shaving the rabbits and placing them in a cold environment so that the cold stress was so great the animals had to "burn" everything they ate in order to maintain a viable body temperature. In other words, if you knock out the compensatory mechanism by keeping its energy reserves completely depleted, you may restore a linear input vs. output relation. This is such a powerful compensatory mechanism that if you wish, for example, to lower the core temperature of a rat, it is necessary to inactivate the neuromuscular response of shivering in the presence of a cold environment; this can be achieved by CO_2 narcosis. Neal Miller (1969) reported that in the conditioning of visceral responses he found that "paralyzing the animal with curare not only greatly simplifies the problem of recording visceral responses without artifacts introduced by movement but also apparently makes it easier for the animal to learn, perhaps because paralysis of the skeletal muscles removes sources of variability and distraction." It is also possible that just as a barrier or detour serves to hold the organism until it emits a less probable behavior which allows it to escape further learning (Guthrie & Horton, 1946), the blockage of overt responses and their normal feedback effects might cause the less probable visceral response to be differentially exposed to reinforcement. That is, if the stronger competitors are prevented from entering the feedback race, the weaker competitors have a better chance to win. In any case, much experimental ingenuity must be expended in the business of controlling (or disabling) compensatory mechanisms that drastically interfere with the linearity of output measurements of interest.

MODEL-BUILDING AND CORRESPONDENCE

One more point needs to be considered before we turn our attention to a cybernetic view of brain functions. That is, the aim of model-building is to achieve a useful correspondence between the process and the model. Systems analysis ordinarily proceeds by a series of progressive approximations between the abstract systems model and the available set of measurements or observations. If the initial modelling effort succeeds in making qualitative predictions, the next step is to generate a mathematical model which makes quantitative predictions. This may lead to a series of revisions in both the model and in the set of measurements (especially if the initial data were not sufficiently extensive or if they were subject to excessive measurement error). At each revision or iteration of the model and/or the data-set, the guiding criterion is to reduce the discrepancies between the model and the data. From a pragmatic engineering point of view, the model is said to be an "adequate" characterization of the real system if it generates a satisfactory (for some defined purpose) level of prediction and/or control. In other words, a model can be evaluated in terms of its usefulness. A model does not have to be "correct" or "true" in order to be useful, but it will have to correspond (i.e., be equivalent rather than identical) in certain respects to the correct or true model of the process. To borrow a line from the poet T.S. Eliot, it is possible "to do the right thing for the wrong reason."

THE LIVING BRAIN: A PROTOPLASMIC COMPUTER

From the viewpoint of a cyberneticist, the human nervous system is regarded as an extremely large and complex protoplasmic computer that functions as an adaptive control system. In other words, it is just another control system, albeit an extraordinarily interesting one. The concept of the brain-as-computer was first advanced in a systematic fashion by Kenneth Craik (1943). Considering the fledgling state of electronic computers at that time, his insight was remarkable. The critics of the man-as-machine hypothesis are usually quick to point out what they regard as crucial differences between the functional capacities of man and the most advanced machines; and they are especially difficult when it comes to conceding that man's crowning organ is merely a biological computer. It is easy to become so distracted by the more emotional claims and counter-claims that one fails to realize that the inventors of machinery, i.e., engineers and scientists, are relentlessly designing and building progressively more sophisticated machines that have fewer and fewer functional limitations. These advanced machines provide useful models and they also perform the logical work required for examining the implications of complex models. A functional approach is to use a model you understand as a stand-in for the process you would like to predict and control. From this point of view, electronic computers provide the most attractive models of complex brain functions.

The most penetrating study of the man-machine similarities and contrasts must come, of course, from those who have a sustained motivation for systematic research in this area. Who are they? It seems to me that they can be divided roughly into two groups: On the one hand, there are those individuals and groups who are primarily interested in man but who believe that a better understanding of machines is the royal road to reducing human limitations; on the other hand, there are those individuals and groups who are primarily interested in building better machines but who believe that a better understanding of living control mechanisms may reveal design principles which can be used to reduce the limitations of machines. Obviously, there is no sharp boundary between these two groups since the roles of advocate and judge are assumable by the same individual at different times; that is, intellectual progress usually requires that something be taken for granted (at least temporarily) while a "minor premise" is explored.

At any rate, the idea of the brain as a control system was adopted and expanded by McCulloch and Pitts (1943), Wiener (1948) and others. Needless to say, advocates of the brain-as-computer hypothesis are under considerable pressure to formulate a common ground between man and machine in the performance of perceptual functions. In my opinion, one of the most remarkable advances in this area came from a rather surprising source, namely from a distinguished economist, Friedrich Hayek, in his treatise on The Sensory Order (1952). The essential task accomplished by Hayek was to show how the perceptual problems might be handled by a nervous system having certain very basic properties which neuroscientists have agreed upon. What this theory provides is an intellectual framework for reconciling a very large number of seemingly incompatible facts and principles. Since Hayek's writing is unusually lucid, I shall attempt as much as possible to present his views in his own words.

The task of perceptual theory, according to Hayek, "is to show in what sense it is possible that within parts of the macrocosm a microcosm may be formed which reproduces certain aspects of the macrocosm and through this will enable the substructure of which it forms a part to behave in a manner which will assist its continued existence" (p. 127). He goes on to say that "the human mind itself may in a certain sense be conceived as a model of the macrocosm within which it exists" (p. 127). Hayek recognized that there would have to be "definite limits to the extent to which such a microcosm (i.e., the nervous system) can contain an adequate reproduction of the significant factors in the macrocosm." "If it were not possible for practical purposes to isolate quasi-self-contained substructures, containing no more parts which significantly affect the relevant result than can be reproduced, or matched point by point, by 'representative' elements within our organism, prediction and purposive adaptation would be impossible" (p. 131). In contrast to "the old idea that individual stimuli and individual nervous impulses are invariably and uniquely related with particular individual sensory qualities," Hayek proposed that "the essential characteristic of the order of sensory qualities is that, within that order, each stimulus or group of stimuli does not possess a unique significance represented by the particular response, but that they are given different significance if they occur in combination with, or are evaluated in the light of, an infinite variety of other stimuli which may originate from the external world or from the organism itself" (p. 84). There is a centripetal ascent of nerve impulses derived both from exteroceptive and proprioceptive sources. "(T)he sensory order with which we are concerned is both a result and a cause of the motor activities of the body. Behavior has to be seen in a double role: it is both input and output of the activities of the higher nervous centres."

"Just as at the higher centres it will not be only one particular sensory impulse, but any one of a class of many different combinations of impulses, which will give rise to a particular response, so the motor signal sent out from the higher centres will be for the execution not of one particular pattern of co-ordinated movements but for any one of a class of such patterns" (p. 94).

"At the higher centres the connexions will thus increasingly exist, not between particular stimuli and particular responses, but between classes of stimuli and classes of responses and between classes of classes of stimuli and classes of classes of responses, etc. The order given at the highest centre in response to a particular situation may thus be of the kind which we have called a general 'directive' for an action of a certain class, and it may be only at the lower levels that the appropriate response is selected from the class of behaviour patterns which in different situations may produce the required result."

"The selection of the particular behaviour pattern from the class of such patterns appropriate to the results aimed at, must not be conceived of as taking place in one act. The choice of a kind of behaviour pattern and its continued control, modification, and adjustment while it takes place, will be a process in which the various factors act successively to produce the final outcome. It is not as if the whole behaviour pattern were determined upon before any movement takes place, but rather that during the process of execution further adjustments are constantly made to secure the result."

It is "in connexion with these continuous adjustments, made while the movement proceeds, (that) the interaction between the exteroceptive and the proprioceptive impulses and the operation of the 'feed-back' principle become of special significance....the sensory representation of the environment, and of the possible goal to be achieved in that environment, will evoke a movement pattern generally aimed at the achievement of the goal. But at first the pattern of movement initiated will not be fully successful. The current sensory reports about what is happening will be checked against expectations, and the difference between the two will act as a further stimulus indicating the required corrections."

Of great concern to us here is Hayek's observation that "guidance by a model which reproduces, and experimentally tries out, the possibilities offered by a given situation, can produce action which is purposive to any desired degree..." (p.126).

"The representation or model of the environment will...constantly tend to run ahead of the actual situation. This presentation of the possible results following from the existing position will, of course, be constantly checked and corrected by the newly arriving sensory signals which record the actual developments in the environment. The newly arriving impulses, on the other hand, in turn will always be evalued against the background of the expectations set up by the previously existing pattern of impulses (par. 5.58).

"The representations of the external environment which will guide behavior will thus be not only representations of the actually existing environment, but also representations of the changes to be expected in that environment" (p. 121). The result of every step in the course of the actions will, as it were, be evaluated against the expected results, and any difference will serve as an indicator of the corrections required.

From these excerpts of Hayek's work, it may be seen that his views provide a useful interface between the psychology of perception and the cybernetic view of the brain as a protoplasmic computer that manages information and communication processes.

COMMENTS ON BIOFEEDBACK RESEARCH

I should like to preface these comments by saying that I shall consider behavior from a general point of view that is commensurate in generality with the overview I have given of cybernetics and systems science. Obviously, I shall have to be quite selective. Therefore I shall confine my remarks to four questions concerning the application of the concepts of cybernetics and systems science to behavioral self-control and biofeedback research.

1. HOW MUCH OF THE ORGANISM'S HISTORY IS REQUIRED FOR EXERCISING USEFUL CONTROL OVER BEHAVIOR?

One might easily obtain the impression from reading Skinner (1953) that it is necessary to trace all controlling variables to their historical roots in the external environment. While this is a laudable goal from the standpoint of generating a comprehensive scientific explanation of behavioral control, one normally takes a more pragmatic approach to the control of behavior. We assume, for instance, that more recent samples of an organism's behavior in specified environment have more predictive value than samples taken from the more remote past. This is based on the general principle that physical systems change as a function of time; thus the greater the time distance between two observations, the greater the opportunity for change. In other words, uncertainty propagates as a function of the time elapsing between two measurements of the same process. The error propagation characteristics set time limits on the usefulness of one sample as a predictor of another sample at some specified time distance (forward or backward) in the time series.

2. DOES FILTER THEORY PROVIDE MODELS THAT ARE USEFUL FOR CHARACTERIZING CONTROL PROCESSES IN THE BEHAVIOR OF ORGANISMS?

An arrangement of environmental variables that produces learning effects in an organism can be usefully conceptualized as a filter. This environmental filter is interposed between the organism and the generator of reinforcing stimuli. This filter rejects some responses and passes other responses. For instance, the confining structure of the Skinner box is response-rejecting while the manipulandum is designed to be response-accepting. There is an instrumental loop that begins in the organism's accessible environment with the manipulandum, makes an excursion (or circuit) through an environment that is inaccessible to the organism, and returns to, say, the food-cup which is also in the organism's accessible environment. A schedule of reinforcement may be viewed as an additional filter imposed on this circuit. With exposure to such a conditional feedback mechanism, the organism exhibits a modification of its response probabilities which we call learning. It is clear that the instrumental portion of the process is (or should be) deterministic in the sense that the law governing its input/output characteristics is unchanging.

And what of the learned modification of the organism? The organism would be modelled as an adaptive filter that adjusts its responses in accordance with the differential feedback it receives from its environment. In other words, the organismic adaptive filter is "tuned" by the environmental filter. Subsequently, the organismic filter can operate independently of the environmental filter. For example, the organism which has been conditioned on a fixed interval schedule of reinforcement will not detect an arbitrary change to a variable interval schedule of reinforcement until it happens to make an "early" post-reinforced response and interacts with a shorter interval of reinforcement (see Anliker, 1955). However, the behavioral adjustment which is optimal for the fixed interval schedule is maladaptive if the environment shifts to variable interval reinforcement, and vice versa. In order to account for adaptive behavior, therefore, we must discover sources of behavioral variation because if the organism's response never varied, learning would be impossible; but we must also account for certain invariances in the organism's behavior because without these the acquired organization would be quickly dissipated. To do justice to the multiple input/multiple output characteristics of organisms, it will usually be necessary to make use of an advanced form of filter such as the Kalman-Bucy filter instead of the single input, single output models of classical filter theory (i.e., Wiener-Kolmogorov filter). Although there are many problems to be overcome in adapting such a filter concept to behavioral measurements, it seems likely that the behavioral scientist will be forced to avail himself of the services of such potent abstract models and computerized analysis of their implications in order to escape being overloaded by the complexity of behavioral control systems.

3. ARE THE CONCEPTS OF FEEDBACK AND FEEDFORWARD APPLICABLE TO THE BEHAVIOR OF ORGANISMS?

We have seen in Hayek's model of the nervous system that the higher levels of the nervous system are concerned with more abstract models which are, relatively speaking, timeless whereas the lower levels of the nervous system are concerned with more specific or concrete matters which require a higher rate of compensation for error. The upper eschelons are buffered from the necessity for dealing with specifics by the labor of the lower eschelons. The upper levels "earn their keep," so to speak, by guiding the lower eschelons to their compensatory ball parks. In a block diagram of the organismic system we would have to provide for at least 1) a basic controller, 2) an adaptive controller (which can modify the parameters of the basic controller, and 3) an anticipative controller which initiates output changes prior to the reception of current feedback information. The anticipative controller, in other words, stores information about successful adaptive parameters used in the past. On the assumption of a correspondence between past and future, the system then employs feedforward control to quickly approximate the previously successful "ball park" output settings. It is apparent that the decisiveness or tentativeness of the feedforward activity depends upon some calculus of the probable relevance of the higher order model. It seems to me that the association of feedback control with the lower levels of nervous organization and the association of feedforward control with the higher levels of the nervous system is a useful way of resolving many apparent paradoxes in organismic behavior which are not resolvable by less complex models. The hierarchical structure of nervous organization doubtless would be evident in a suitably-conceived probability analysis of behavioral processes.

4. HOW MIGHT A SYSTEMS ANALYST APPROACH THE PROBLEM OF COVERT BEHAVIOR AND ITS CONTROL?

A wise engineer is always searching for the best possible set of observations on which to base his modelling. He generally avoids getting caught up in the illusion that there is one best measurement. Instead he is quite accustomed to the idea that every measurement is truth-telling in some respects and biased in other respects. Therefore, he would prefer to build a composite filter that utilizes multiple information sources and cancels out biases. Skinner (1953) admits that the individual enjoys a unique perspective on his private events. The systems analyst would treat the subject's information about his subjective processes as an information source which may well contain useful information albeit vulnerable to certain biases. On the other hand, an external observer of the individual's behavior is also biased by what he can observe and what he cannot observe. By integrating the information from various perspectives it is possible to approximate a synthesis which is relatively independent of the biases associated with the various perspectives.

In this context it is enlightening to consider the concepts of observability and controllability which were first introduced by Kalman (1960). In general terms, a system is said to be controllable if any initial state can be transformed to any final state within a finite time by some control operation. A system is said to be observable if every state of the system can be determined exactly from measurements of the output over a finite interval of time. If there are states which are decoupled from the output, they are obviously unobservable. And if there are states which are decoupled from the input, they are obviously uncontrollable. Gilbert (1963) has used these concepts to divide systems into classes of subsystems having different properties of controllability and observability. There are, in his view, four possible classes of subsystems. They are the following: 1) a class of subsystem which is both controllable and observable (Sco); 2) a class which is controllable but unobservable (Scu); 3) a class which is uncontrollable but observable (Suo); and 4) a class which is uncontrollable and unobservable (Suu). It will be seen that this set is logically exhaustive of the possibilities. Therefore, we can immediately enter these four subsystems into our analysis of any system. It will be obvious that a variable which is uncontrollable by one input might be controllable by another input. However, the two inputs belong to two different subsystems although they might share the same component. Since systems are defined at the output, these two subsystems would be conceived as having independent inputs and a common output. By locating a subsystem which has one of the missing properties and adding the subsystem to a larger system, the larger system gains the attributes of its various components and is not subject to their individual limitations. I should like to suggest that there is within the individual a no-man's land, or deadspace, between the external observer-controller and the internal observer-controller. The limits of behavioral control are dependent upon the ability of science (public and private) to conquer this territory, by making it completely observable and controllable--and therefore devoid of uncertainty. This is, of course, an ideal which can only be approximated. A coordinated two-pronged assault on this autonomous realm by an internal observer-controller and an external observers-controllers is probably the best way, if not the only way, to minimize or eliminate this no-man's land. Skinner (1953) states "The line between public and private is not fixed. The boundary shifts with every discovery of a technique for making private events public....The problem of privacy may, therefore, eventually be solved by technical advances." However, pursuing Skinner's suggestion that "Behavior which is of such small amplitude that it is not ordinarily observed may be amplified" is fraught with difficulties because as the output signal is attenuated the signal-to-noise ratio becomes increasingly unfavorable to signal analysis. Even if we had a complete account of the activity of each and every motor unit influencing audible speech, we would still be faced with the enormously difficult task of developing a workable translating scheme which would accurately predict the audible sounds. As the speech became increasingly inaudible, this task would become increasingly difficult. It is all too easy to forget that a shift to another level of observation carries with it the need for reorientation. For example, early microscopists naively expected to be able to "see" the microscopic world through their microscopes. They did not anticipate that they would not know how to look at what was to be seen through the microscope and that observational and interpretative disciplines would have to be laboriously developed in order to "see" and to "understand" the exceedingly strange and exotic microscopic world. Neither did they anticipate the fact that magnification also increases the effective size of the domain which must be surveyed. The problem is similar to that of using micro-electrodes versus macro-electrodes. In avoiding the complexities of covert behavior, behaviorists have had to accept rather severe limitations in the amount of behavioral control they can achieve. Homme's suggestion (1965) that behaviorists study "coverants" or "covert operants" is probably a step in the right direction. Still it seems doubtful that anything less than a large-scale investigation into the subjective phenomena accompanying overt behavior will produce the desired results.

REFERENCES

Anliker, J. E. Reversal of discriminations of temporal schedules of reinforcement. Unpublished thesis, Harvard University, 1955.

Bertalanffy, L. von. General system theory. New York: George Braziller, 1968.

Bryson, A. E. Control theory for random systems. Stanford: Stanford University Department of Aeronautics and Astronautics Report Number 447, 1972.

Craik, K. J. W. The nature of explanation. Cambridge: University Press, 1943.

Gasnier, A., & Mayer, A. Recherches sur la regulation de la nutrition. III. Mecanismes regulateurs de la nutrition et intensite du metabolisme. Annales de Physiologie, 1939, 15, 186-194.

Gilbert, E. G. Controllability and observability in multi-variable control systems. Journal Soc. Ind. Appl. Math., series A, Control, 1963, 1, 138-151.

Guthrie, E. R., & Horton, G. P. Cats in a puzzle box. New York: Holt, Rinehart, and Winston, 1946.

Hayek, F. A. The sensory order. Chicago: University Press, 1952.

Homme, L. E. Perspectives in psychology, XXIV: Control of coverants, the operants of the mind. Psychological Record, 1965, 15, 501-511.

Kalman, R. E. On the general theory of control systems. Proceedings IFAC Moscow Congress (Vol. 1). Washington, D.C.: Butterworth, 1960.

McCulloch, W. S., & Pitts, W. A logical calculus of the ideas immanent in nervous activity. Bulletin of Mathematical Biophysics, 1943, 5, 115-133.

Miller, N. Learning of visceral and glandular responses. Science, 1969, 163, 434-445.

Planck, M. Where is science going? New York: W. W. Norton, 1932.
Skinner, B. F. The behavior of organisms. New York: Appleton-Century-Crofts, 1938.
Skinner, B. F. Science and human behavior. New York: Macmillan, 1953.
Szentagothal, J., & Arbib, M. A. Conceptual models of neural organization. Cambridge: MIT Press, 1975.
Wiener, N. Cybernetics. Cambridge: Technology Press, 1948.

METHODOLOGICAL AND TECHNOLOGICAL ISSUES IN BIOFEEDBACK RESEARCH

Rolf R. Engel
Psychiatric Hospital
University of Munich

Stemming from two rather different psychological disciplines, psychophysiology and learning, biofeedback research combines the methodological problems of both fields in a very distinct fashion. It is questionable whether biofeedback is an independent scientific discipline today. A scientific discipline is determined by its methods. Current biofeedback methodology is lacking a comprehensive theoretical framework that could classify the various procedures that are used. Discussions of methodological issues in biofeedback research have been either very conceptual (e.g. Katkin & Murray, 1968; Crider, Schwartz, & Shnidman, 1969; Katkin, Murray, & Lachman, 1969) or have been addressed to specific problems that are found in biofeedback research but are not unique for this discipline. Recent examples regarding heart rate feedback are the papers by McCanne and Sandman (1975), Gatchel (1974), Lang and Twentyman (1974) and Borchard and Corson (1976), to mention just a few.

Instead of trying to overview all those methodological issues that have some relevance in biofeedback research, the present paper will focus on those methodological and theoretical problems that are unique for the biofeedback approach. It will be shown, how some of the problems might be conceptualized within a comprehensive system, though it is beyond the purpose of this paper to present such a system.

PARTIAL NONREPEATABILITY OF EXPERIMENTAL CONDITIONS

The main point of the problems I would like to discuss relates to the fact that in biofeedback research the dependent variable, e.g. heart rate, is fed back to the subject and, thus, becomes part of the independent variables. This means that the defining property of biofeedback research--the mere existence of the feedback loop--poses serious questions, when it is seen in the light of the usual experimental strategies. Besides the possibility to manipulate and vary the independent variables, the repeatability of an experiment is one of the three principles of scientific experimentation. In feedback experiments, however, one integral part of the independent variables, the feedback signal itself, varies with the dependent variable and is not completely under the control of the experimenter. This means that the independent conditions are not fixed but vary at every moment within a single experiment. Biofeedback studies are thus partly non-repeatable and--if one looks at it from the other side --this non-repeatability forms a constituent factor in all biofeedback experimentation.

The difficulties encountered with yoked control procedures (Church, 1964) may be seen as a necessary consequence of this basic fact.

OPERANT CONDITIONING AND BIOFEEDBACK COMPARED

Biofeedback is not the only and not the first discipline that has to live with what I would like to call the partial non-repeatability of experimental conditions. In particular the field of operant conditioning is well acquainted with this dilemma: The response of an organism, i.e. the behavior under study, determines partly the experimental manipulations, i.e. the reinforcement stimulus. Operant conditioning is a healthy and growing field that obviously is not at all hindered in its development--basic as well as applied--by the partial non-repeatability of its experimental conditions. Why should this fact then constitute a problem for biofeedback research? The reason is probably to be found in two important differences between operant conditioning and biofeedback research, one more conceptual and one primarily technical in nature.

Concepts

The conceptual dissimilarity results from the fact that operant conditioning in the sense of Skinner has its very own theoretical framework which differs in many regards from the other fields of experimental psychology. To mention just a few points: the strong emphasis on an individual-centered approach, the use of single-case designs instead of group studies, the deliberate omission of statistical inference, the preponderance of inductive search rather than deductive hypothesis testing. In its short history biofeedback has not adopted this theoretical approach. In most of the published experimental literature in biofeedback authors have formulated explicit hypotheses, have used group designs and statistical inference and have placed their work within the traditional scientific approach. Partial nonrepeatability of experimental conditions is therefore more consequential in this area of research than in operant conditioning.

Measurement Scales

The second point concerns the different measurement concepts in operant conditioning and biofeedback and is a rather technical problem, though it might also be seen as a consequence of the theoretical difference. In classical operant conditioning there is only one kind of datum: response rate, i.e. frequency of a response per time interval, often conceptualized as probability of occurrence of a response. The response itself is coded in binary form: Either there is a response or there is no response. The measurement scale is a two-step nominal scale--quite simple in comparison to physiological measures. This schematic measurement facilitates a schematic scheduling of reinforcement. There is abundant information on the different effects of fixed-interval, variable-interval, fixed-ratio and various other reinforcement schedules. Since the publication of Ferster and Skinner's (1957) "schedules of reinforcement" this information is constantly being broadened and refined, a process which probably is caused by the inductive "analytical" nature of operant research. This very narrow type of experimental design favors the replicability and communicability of scientific research and tends to diminish the partial nonrepeatability of experimental conditions.

To summarize: In operant research the partial nonrepeatability is reduced 1) by only one well standardized and simple response measure (response rate) and 2) explicit schedules of reinforcement based on this measure.

This does not apply to biofeedback research. Physiological processes are usually measured--and are certainly best represented--in form of quantitative scales and so far there exist virtually no "schedules of feedback" that are comparable in standardization to the contingency schedules in operant research. Thus, the partial nonrepeatability of experimental conditions is likely to have a stronger influence on the communicability and replicability of biofeedback experiments.

CONCEPTUALIZATION OF THE FEEDBACK PROCESS

So far, there is no theory and no uniform methodological concept in biofeedback research that tries to account for those difficulties. If one checks the method sections of biofeedback articles the conflict between the use of operant concepts and the quantitative nature of physiological measurements is obvious. One large group of researchers holds the classical Skinnerian position and defines binary classes of responses by dichotomizing a quantitative variable and uses reinforcement stimuli in accordance with a definite schedule, in most cases a simple nonintermittent reinforcement schedule. This procedure has the advantage of being imbedded in a definite theoretical framework, but it also has serious drawbacks. Usually it is necessary to change the cut-off point for dichotomizing "response" and "no response" several times within one single session, a procedure that is similar to the shaping of complex chains of operant responses. Again, this procedure reduces the repeatability of a study, since the shaping process depends on the performance of the individual subject. In order to be both effective and repeatable a very complex chain of schedules would probably be necessary. Obviously, within the methodological framework of operant conditioning the three criteria of effectivity, repeatability and simple structure are never met together, as long as quantitative variables are involved.

Another large group of researchers does not follow the operant approach. They use different terms like control for conditioning, feedback for reinforcement, and usually provide a continuous quantitative feedback signal. It is difficult to conceptualize this as operant conditioning; however, there is no other theoretical framework to take its place. Both methodological concepts struggle with difficulties that arise through the very nature of physiological processes as quantitative variables.

FEEDBACK STIMULI AS VARIABLE TRANSFORMATIONS

Let us consider what usually happens when someone is using a continuous feedback signal. Everyone of us is used to interpret continuous feedback as linear feedback: We implicitly assume that there is a linear correspondence between changes of the feedback signal and changes of the physiological variable. This simply means that large changes in the feedback signal correspond to large physiological changes and small feedback changes correspond to small physiological changes--independent of the tonic level of the physiological variable.

From a statistical point of view, deriving a feedback signal from a physiological signal represents a transformation. One signal is transformed into another one and this transformation can be described as a function that very often will be a short and simple equation. From a technological point of view in biofeedback experiments this transformation is performed in real time either by means of analog data processing as in commercial and special-purpose equipment or by digital techniques in computer controlled experiments.

The formalization of the feedback signal as a transformation of a certain source signal has several advantages. One obvious advantage is that this concept allows a thorough analysis of the functional relation between the basic biological process and a certain kind of feedback signal. Since there is so much technology involved in biofeedback research, it might sometimes be quite difficult to realize the various non-linear transformations that take place during the feedback-generating process. Such hidden transformations occur 1) at the raw-score level, 2) in combination with the feedback generation itself and 3) as a function of the sensory modality of the feedback signal.

Effects of Raw-Score

Nonlinear transformations are often involved in heart-rate feedback. Heart period as the primary raw-score will yield different results than instantaneous heart rate, since either one of the two measures is a nonlinear hyperbolic transformation of the other. Parametric statistics (and this includes the calculation of the arithmetic mean of just two scores) are not invariant against nonlinear transformations. This fact was only recently recognized by psychophysiologists, at an empirical level (Khachaturian, Kerr, Kruger, & Schachter, 1972; Jennings, Stringfellow, & Graham, 1974) as well as mathematically (Thorne, Engel, & Holmblad, 1976). Feedback signals generated by rate or period data differ most at both extreme ends of the heart activity range, i.e. at high or low heart rates.

Usually--but not necessarily--technology plays the major role in deciding on the measurement scale: The output of a cardiotachometer is linear regarding rate while digital computers usually are programmed to be linear regarding heart periods.

Effects of Data Processing

The possibilities for nonlinear transformations at the level of feedback generation are manyfold. In EMG-feedback, e.g., a favorite feedback modality is auditory feedback in form of either clicks changing in rate or a tone changing in pitch. Most published systems for EMG or continuous EEG-feedback (e.g. Budzynski & Stoyva, 1969; Emde & Shipton, 1974; Fetz & Barenstein, 1975; Hertz, Legewie, & Nusselt, 1973; Krausman & Lenox, 1974; Weiss, Sobolewski, & Drury, 1972) use a linear voltage-to-frequency converter.

There are, however, nonlinear systems as well. Leaf and Gaarder (1971) recommend explicitly a logarithmic transformation (realized by means of a logarithmic operational amplifier), because this transformation tends to stretch the scale at the low end and to compress it in the high EMG ranges. Thus recognition of small differences is facilitated when EMG level is low.

Radl (1972) gives circuit descriptions that allow different transformations, some being continuous and some discrete. Among the continuous transformations he recommends a circuit that gives the first derivation of the original signal, thus emphasizing only changes in level without considering the tension level itself.

Commercial manufacturers of EMG-feedback devices have started to incorporate these features in their devices. There exist some machines that offer a choice of several transformations resulting in continuous or discrete feedback signals, visual as well as auditory. What is still missing is a theoretical or empirically derived system that tells us what to use, when, and why.

Effects of Modality

The last point, where transformations could take place is in the choice of the feedback modality. Let us assume a continuously changing voltage level as source of the feedback signal. This could be e.g. a cardiotachometer output. Two modalities are commonly encountered: a visual signal, e.g. a large voltmeter, whose needle varies with the cardiotachometer output, or an auditory signal, usually produced by a linear voltage-to-frequency converter that transforms the signal into a tone changing in pitch. There exist, however, differences regarding the linearity of the signal between both modalities. While the visual perception is directed by the scaling of the meter, that usually is linear and thus represents a linear transformation of the source signal, the auditory feedback involves a specific though hidden transformation. With a linear voltage-to-frequency converter the tone frequency itself is a linear function of the source voltage, of course. The perception of tone frequencies, however, is not at all linear but follows roughly a logarithmic function as all psychologists know since the days of Fechner. Consequently, even those modalities that have been studied and compared most frequently differ not only in modality but also regarding the linearity of the psychophysical relation involved. There is a systematic difference: Compared with visual feedback auditory feedback facilitates the perception of small changes at the low end of the scale.

BIOLOGICAL MEANING OF MEASUREMENT SCALES

So far the discussion has been conducted mainly in technical and mathematical terms. It is, however, even more important to consider the biological meaning of a linear scale. Imagine for example a clinician who is interested in giving relaxation training to a patient using an EMG-feedback device. Imagine further that the device is quite simple, with only a linear feedback meter and a gain control. Most probably the experimenter will start with a low gain and increase it as the patient learns to relax. Most clinicians would probably think that this is the most effective procedure, since it allows an individualized shaping. Hard-core experimentalists could argue that this kind of treatment is not standardized, irrepeatable, and therefore open to criticism.

What this clinician actually does is to apply a transformation to the signal, before he feeds it back. The transformation could easily be formalized as a series of stepwise transformations, whose graph resembles that of a negatively accelerated function. The whole procedure could easily be standardized using a square-root or generally speaking an inverse-power transformation. In this formalized structure, the clinical approach would be standardized and repeatable.

If we now conclude, that each single kind of feedback procedure may be formulated as a distinct function--stepwise or continuous--between source and feedback signal, we have to turn to the basic question, which kind of transformation is appropriate for a certain problem or variable. The question is if there is a rationale to decide whether one scale of measurement is more meaningful regarding the biological process in question than another one.

EXAMPLE: A LINEAR SCALE FOR EMG-BIOFEEDBACK

In answer to this question I would like to report some data from an experiment that was designed to study the effects of EMG-feedback on subjects with high and subjects with low initial muscle tension (Engel, 1973). A pretest was conducted with 160 subjects to obtain two groups with extreme high or low muscle tension. Figure 1 shows--in the lower part--the initial EMG level at the forehead for the 160 unselected subjects. The measurement scale is microvolt. These raw-scores have a skewed distribution, a fact that may be expected with all variables having an absolute limit on only one (in this case on the left) side of their distri-

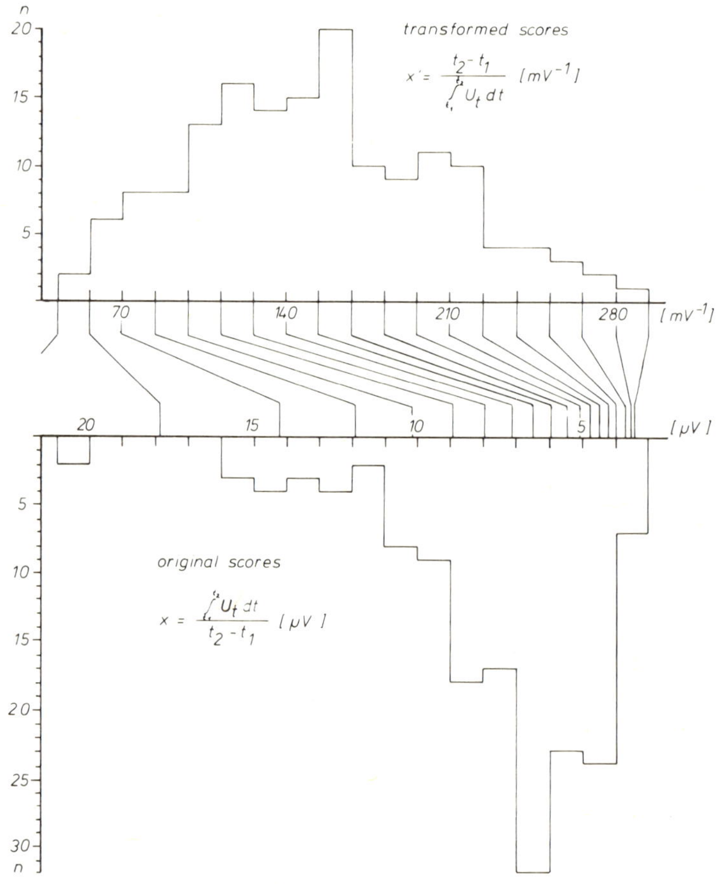

Figure 1. Resting forehead EMG level in 160 unselected subjects (see text).

bution. The same kind of skewness is likely to be found with reaction time scores for instance, and it makes no difference whether those distributions are collected between or within subjects.

The upper part of the figure shows the distribution that results from a hyperbolic transformation of the raw-scores. Regarding skewness as well as curtosis the distribution of the transformed scores is normal, while the raw scores are significantly different from a normal distribution ($p \leq .001$). A normal distribution, however, is not a fetish of some statisticians. The most important point about a normal distribution is that it implies a linear scale. In interpreting a linear scale we know that there are equal differences between every two adjacent points on the scale. This does not hold for nonlinear scales. With regard to the lower scale (the original one) every clinician would argue that a drop from 20 μV to 15 μV is much easier to achieve than one from 10 uV to 5 μV, and, thus, the numbers seem to be of little value for him. The skewed distribution shows that he is completely right. Only the upper scale is linear and it is only on this scale that the scores correspond to their biological meaning. The use of the original scales would imply that subjects with high EMG can relax better through muscle feedback than subjects with low EMG. This, however, is just a by-product of the nonlinearity of the μV-scale and it is apparently more economical to use linear scales without any level-by-change interactions.

These data show that in EMG-relaxation-feedback a good measurement scale (and hence a good feedback scale) would be one that removes the right-skewed distributions of the μV-scores by means of an appropriate transformation. Having the relevant data for this variable, we can give the respective recommendations. It is clear, however, that for most physiological variables we do not have data that tell us the details of a certain scale of measurement. This issue goes beyond the immediate concern of biofeedback research and is actually a central methodological issue in psychophysiology. One of the long-standing questions in psychophysiology, Wilder's "Law of initial value," is based on a level-by-change interaction that is characteristic for non-linear scales.

CONCLUSIONS

The present paper has tried to highlight several methodological problems that are specific for biofeedback research. Based on the fact that in biofeedback experiments the existence of a feedback loop induces a partial nonrepeatability of experimental conditions, strong emphasis was laid on the necessity to standardize feedback procedures. As one way to categorize the various feedback procedures according to the functional relations between the physiological variable and the feedback signal the formulation of mathematical functions between source and feedback was advocated. In analyzing existing feedback paradigms according to the transformations involved some widely unrecognized differences between apparently similar procedures were found. Regarding the selection of appropriate transformations those scales were shown to be of central importance that have a linear relationship to the biological process under study.

REFERENCES

Bouchard, C., & Corson, J. A. Heart rate regulation with success and failure signals. Psychophysiology, 1976, 13, 69-74.

Budzynski, T. H., & Stoyva, J. M. An instrument for producing deep muscle relaxation by means of analog information feedback. Journal of Applied Behavior Analysis, 1969, 2, 231-237.

Church, R. M. Systematic effect of random error in the yoked control design. Psychological Bulletin, 1964, 62, 122-131.

Crider, A., Schwartz, G. E., & Shnidman, S. On the criteria for instrumental autonomic conditioning: A reply to Katkin and Murray. Psychological Bulletin, 1969, 71, 455-461.

Emde, J. W., & Shipton, H. W. A dual digital integrator for EEG studies. Electroencephalography and Clinical Neurophysiology, 1974, 37, 185-187.

Engel, R. R. Measurement and quantification of surface EMG signals in states of relaxation. In D. Shapiro, T. X. Barber, L. DiCara, J. Kamiya, N. E. Miller, & J. Stoyva (Eds.), Biofeedback and self-control, 1972. Chicago: Aldine, 1973.

Ferster, B. B., & Skinner, B. F. Schedules of reinforcement. New York: Appleton-Century-Crofts, 1957.

Fetz, E. E., & Barenstein, R. I. An electronic activity integrator for operant conditioning of patterns of neural and muscular activity. Electroencephalography and Clinical Neurophysiology, 1975, 38, 87-89.

Gatchel, R. J. Frequency of feedback and learned heart rate control. Journal of Experimental Psychology, 1974, 103, 274-283.

Herz, H., Legewie, H., & Nusselt, L. Ein linearer Integrator zur Digitalisierung und Rückmeldung der elektrischen Muskelaktivität. Biomedizinische Technik, 1973, 18, 195-197.

Jennings, R. J., Stringfellow, J. C., & Graham, M. A comparison of the statistical distributions of beat-by-beat heart rate and heart period. Psychophysiology, 1974, 11, 207-210.

Katkin, E. S., & Murray, E. N. Instrumental conditioning of autonomically mediated behavior: Theoretical and methodological issues. Psychological Bulletin, 1968, 70, 52-68.

Katkin, E. S., Murray, E. N., & Lachman, R. Concerning instrumental autonomic conditioning: A rejoinder. Psychological Bulletin, 1969, 71, 462-466.

Khachaturian, Z. S., Kerr, J., Kruger, R., & Schachter, J. A methodological note: Comparison between period and rate data in studies of cardiac function. Psychophysiology, 1972, 9, 539-545.

Krausman, D. T., & Lenox, J. R. An on-line integrator for alpha quantification. Behavior Research Methods & Instrumentation, 1974, 6, 317-320.

Lang, P. J., & Twentyman, C. T. Learning to control heart rate: Binary vs. analogue feedback. Psychophysiology, 1974, 11, 616-629.

Leaf, W. B., & Gaarder, K. R. A simplified electromyograph feedback apparatus for relaxation training. Journal of Behavior Therapy and Experimental Psychiatry, 1971, 2, 39-43.

McCanne, T. R., & Sandman, C. A. Determinants of human operant heart rate conditioning: A systematic investigation of several methodological issues. Journal of Comparative and Physiological Psychology, 1975, 88, 609-618.

Radl, G. W. Einsatz eines hybrid-analogen Laborrechners mit kleiner Rechenkapazität zur Ansteuerung von Rückmelde-Signal-gebern durch die Elektromyogramm-Amplitude. Biomedizinische Technik, 1972, 17, 96-102.

Thorne, P. R., Engel, B. T., & Holmblad, J. B. An analysis of the error inherent in estimating heart rate from cardiotachometer records. Psychophysiology, 1976, 13, 269-272.

Weiss, M. S., Sobolewski, J. S., & Drury, R. A multipurpose electronic filter and integrating level detector. IEEE Transactions on Biomedical Engineering. 1972, BME-19, 395-397.

VISCERAL FEEDBACK AND THE TASTE SIGNAL

John Garcia and Kenneth W. Rusiniak
Departments of Psychology and Psychiatry
University of California at Los Angeles

BIOFEEDBACK AND GUSTATORY-VISCERAL CONDITIONING

Visceral feedback after eating a meal modifies the taste of the food and drink by psychological processes which are of special interest to students of biofeedback. For simplicity, consider an unlimited amount of a tasty fluid placed before a hungry subject. The taste of the fluid is the perceptual signal, ingestion is the process to be controlled and homeostatic well-being is the state to be achieved. If the fluid is a creamy substance, rich in calories, it tastes delicious at the beginning of the meal and the subject drinks heartily. As the caloric mass accumulates in the gut, satiety is achieved before tissue needs are redressed, as if the viscera has sensing devices which accurately estimate the amount of food needed to achieve the ultimate homeostatic balance (Novin, 1976; Schachter, 1971; McHugh, Moran, & Barton, 1975).

Satiety is a complex multidimensional perceptual process, and again for simplicity, we will only consider what happens to the taste signal. Taste resembles the external signal coupled to the physiological transducer which informs the biofeedback subject he has achieved the desired functional state, such as the production of alpha electroencephalographic rhythm or the reduction of cardiovascular tension. In a typical biofeedback arrangement, the subject is acutely aware of this external signal but only dimly, if at all, aware of the internal homeostatic process he attempts to control. Often he gives up direct attempts to cope with the internal process; instead, he attends to the signal and utilizes thought and fantasy as mediators to achieve the desired state. So it is with ingestive control where taste quality changes perceptibly and is reportable before the diffuse internal consequences of ingestion terminating the meal become acute. There may be one important difference. As satiety approaches, it is the hedonic value of taste that is progressively altered. The rich fluid is no longer palatable or pleasant to the taste so that ingestion tends to cease under ideal conditions (Cabanac, 1971; Cabanac & Ducleaux, 1970; Garcia, Hankins, & Rusiniak, 1974). Parenthetically, it would be interesting to know if the hedonic value of the external signals changes approximately as the subject achieves beneficial biofeedback states. However, the main point is that the subject can more effectively regulate his food through this hedonic modulation of taste signal than he can by directly heeding his internal changes. Indeed, he may be completely unconscious of the ultimate internal effects, as when sleep follows a full meal, and still adapt appropriately through perception of taste quality in subsequent meals.

These changes in palatability of food during the course of a meal, as the subject moves from hunger to surfeit, are superimposed upon an initial baseline hedonic value. Even the neonate comes into the world with a preference for sweet and an aversion to bitter, preferences that are clearly related to the natural food stores and the natural toxins found in the world in which his species has evolved (Garcia & Hankins, 1975). This baseline hedonic value changes dramatically with experience. If the food proves homeostatically useful, its baseline hedonic value in subsequent meals is more or less permanently raised through what appears to be a classical conditioning process. If internal distress follows ingestion, the baseline hedonic value is reduced in subsequent meals. In extreme cases, the food becomes aversive and disgusting (Green & Garcia, 1970; Garcia, Rusiniak, & Brett, 1976).

VARYING THE TASTE SIGNAL DURING VISCERAL FEEDBACK

We will now present some empirical evidence on the hedonic changes which occur in rats when ingestion of flavored fluid is followed by visceral feedback from lithium illness. Licking records will allow us to look at the palatability changes which occur during a drinking bout as well as the changes in baseline values between bouts. Perhaps what is more important for biofeedback purposes, these data allow us to assess the usefulness of two sets of controlling stimuli in the adaptive process: perception of the peripheral taste signal against perception of the internal malaise.

Our experimental situation is extremely simple. The animal is accustomed for several weeks to receiving his daily allotment of water in a 15 minute confinement to a special box where a drinkometer records each lick. In most cases, the rat is drinking salty water (0.12M NaCl) which he prefers to distilled water when given a choice; hereafter we will call this sodium water. On test days, he is given a mildly toxic salty solution (0.12M LiCl) which we will call lithium water. The two solutions taste very much alike. Graduate students cannot reliably distinguish between the two solutions, nor can rats tell sodium water from lithium water in a shock avoidance discrimination task. Our previous studies indicate that rats show first signs of lassitude about 10 to 15 minutes after an intragastric load of a 0.12M LiCl.

Figure 1 illustrates the cumulative drinking records of a group of rats encountering lithium water for the first time after weeks on sodium water. In all seven cases, lithium consumption is less than the previous day's sodium consumption. However, only four rats show a convincing discrimination of the two fluids.

Two questions immediately arise from these data. First, have the four rats detected a subtle difference in the taste signal provided by lithium water or have they utilized the visceral feedback from toxicosis to distinguish the effects of the two fluids? Second, can rats improve their discrimination of the two fluids with repeated trials? To answer these

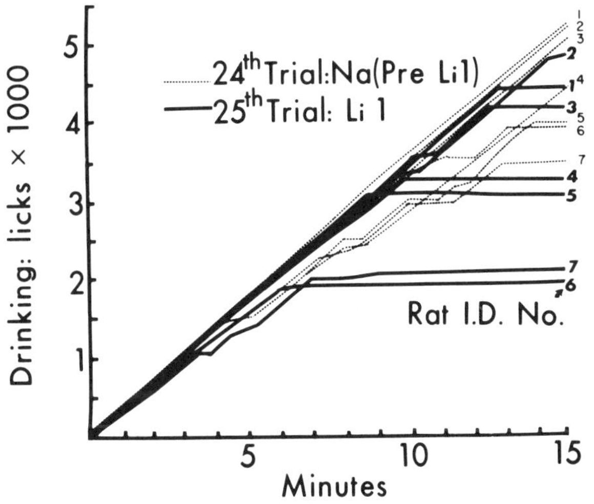

Figure 1. Detection of lithium illness by rats drinking 0.12M LiCl for the first time. Note that all seven rats drink less lithium than sodium on the preceding day.

questions, lithium water was presented every third day for a total of five lithium trials. In addition, taste signals were varied for different groups of rats by adding a mild saccharin flavor (0.5 g/L) to the toxic lithium water and/or to the safe sodium water which they received during habituation and continued to receive on two days between lithium trials. We present cumulative lithium drinking records of rats typical of their group since individual curves suit our biofeedback purposes more effectively. However, group data is provided elsewhere so that "typicalness" can be objectively assessed (Rusiniak, Garcia, & Hankins, 1976). For comparison, the sodium drinking scores on the day prior to the first lithium trial (Pre), the sodium score following the last lithium trial (Post) and the lowest sodium score (Low) portray both the temporal and quantitative excursions of sodium water records for the individual animals.

The upper left quadrant of Figure 2 illustrates the effect of merely repeating the lithium trials. The first lithium record of this rat (No. 12) was within the range of his sodium records. The first clear sign of a lithium discrimination appeared after four minutes of the second trial as a change in lick rate (slope), indicating that the initial baseline value had not changed very much after one trial. It is possible that Rat 12 recognized the early feedback signs from the previous lithium toxicosis and slowed his ingestion rate to avoid further toxication. However, in the last three trials, he showed rate changes in less than one minute, suggesting that he was detecting lithium through a change in its hedonic baseline taste, rather than through direct toxicosis feedback. In one minute, he could have hardly consumed enough to produce symptoms of illness. All seven rats in this condition learned the discrimination well within five trials.

When the flavor of the toxic lithium water was enhanced by the addition of saccharin, Rat 25 (Figure 2, upper right) made a reasonable discrimination on the first lithium trial; his rate for the last six minutes and his total consumption was generally below his sodium range and specifically well below his Post sodium curve. On trials 4 and 5, he drank virtually no sweet lithium beyond a few sampling licks, indicating a clear hedonic baseline shift. All five rats in the sweet lithium vs. sodium condition displayed the same rapid acquisition of a profound aversion for the taste of lithium water.

In contrast, when the flavor of safe sodium water was enhanced by saccharin, Rat 32 (Figure 2, lower left) did not perform as well as Rat 25. This seems curious for two reasons: First, both rats were making the same discrimination between sweet salty and plain salty solutions; second, the addition of preferred saccharin to the safe sodium might be

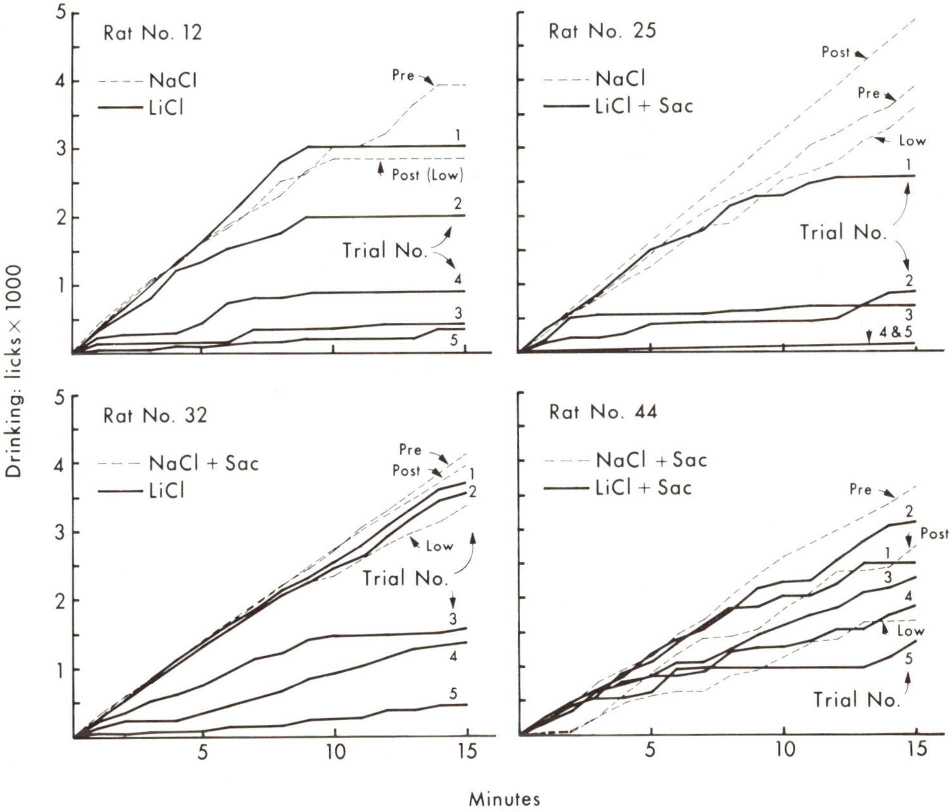

Figure 2. Effects of varying the taste signal during lithium illness feedback. Enhancing the taste of toxic lithium water facilitates acquisition (Rat 25) enhancing the safe sodium water does not (Rats 32 and 12) and masking with saccharin disrupts learning (Rat 44).

expected to increase its consumption over that for plain lithium thus augmenting the difference between the scores. Nevertheless, the performance of Rat 32 and the other four rats in the sweet sodium group was no better than that of the animals in Rat 12's group who had the toxic salty vs. safe salty discimination task. This asymmetry is reminiscent of effects obtained by Jenkins and Sainsbury (1970), who demonstrated that pigeons performed more effectively when the distinctive feature was placed on the positive rather than the negative stimulus panel in a discrimination problem. In our case, the asymmetry may have been facilitated because the salt signal and the sweet signal operate via relatively independent channels. The rationale is as follows. Rat 25 was habituated only to salty safe sodium water, so his sweet detectors were stimulated for the first time when he became ill. Sweet, therefore, was a clear taste signal for poison. On the other hand, Rat 32 was habituated to both sweet and salty safe sodium water, so no new stimulus was added on the lithium day. The deletion of a safe signal on the lithium trial was of no particular help.

The notion that sweet and salty are handled by relatively independent systems is not completely substantiated by the data from Rat 44 (Figure 2, lower right), who had saccharin added to both solutions from beginning to end. Sweet sodium vs. sweet lithium proved to be a difficult discrimination. A clear rate difference was not manifested until the last nine minutes of the fifth trial. While most of the six rats in this group showed a discrimination during the fourth trial, they were definitely inferior to the sodium vs. lithium group, indicating that the saccharin was masking some subtle difference between the two salty solutions. Analysis of the lick records in the very beginning of the fifth trial indicated the sodium vs. lithium discrimination (e.g. Rat 12) required only a five second sample; adding saccharin to both solutions (e.g. Rat 44) extended the sampling interval to 90 seconds.

In summary the data from these experiments indicate that the taste signal is of paramount importance in controlling the ingestion process. However these data do not completely eliminate the possibility that rats can use visceral feedback from lithium toxicosis to discriminate the toxic salt from a safe salt.

DEGRADING THE TASTE SIGNAL DURING VISCERAL FEEDBACK

In the next series of studies we attempted to reduce the effectiveness of the taste signal to zero, thus forcing the rats to rely solely on visceral feedback. We used two approaches. First we attempted to mask the taste differences between the safe sodium and toxic lithium solutions by adding a sour flavor and a bitter flavor as well as a sweet flavor to both solutions. This was an effort to mask the taste differences via all four "primary" taste qualities. Our "cocktail" recipe was 1.0 ml concentrated acetic acid, 15 mg quinine monohydrochloride and 0.5 g saccharin added to a liter of the 0.12M lithium or the 0.12M sodium solution. Second, we attempted to eliminate the taste differences by requiring the animals to lick tapwater and using the lick to drive an intragastric pump which delivered an equivalent amount of 0.24M salt solution directly into the stomach, thus bypassing the oral taste receptors. The amount of water consumed orally by licking was calculated to reduce the double (0.24M) concentration delivered intragastrically to the 0.12M standard used in our other studies. For the same reason, the increments on the ordinate in Figure 3 have been doubled for the pump rats.

Rat 58 was typical of most of the rats drinking the toxic and safe cocktails. He drank progressively less lithium water with each trial, but he also drank progressively less sodium water. Recall that animals were given two sodium water days following each lithium trial. In general, on the first day after a lithium trial, the cocktail animals drank less sodium water than lithium water the previous day; but on the second day they drank more sodium. In other words, the hedonic baseline value of

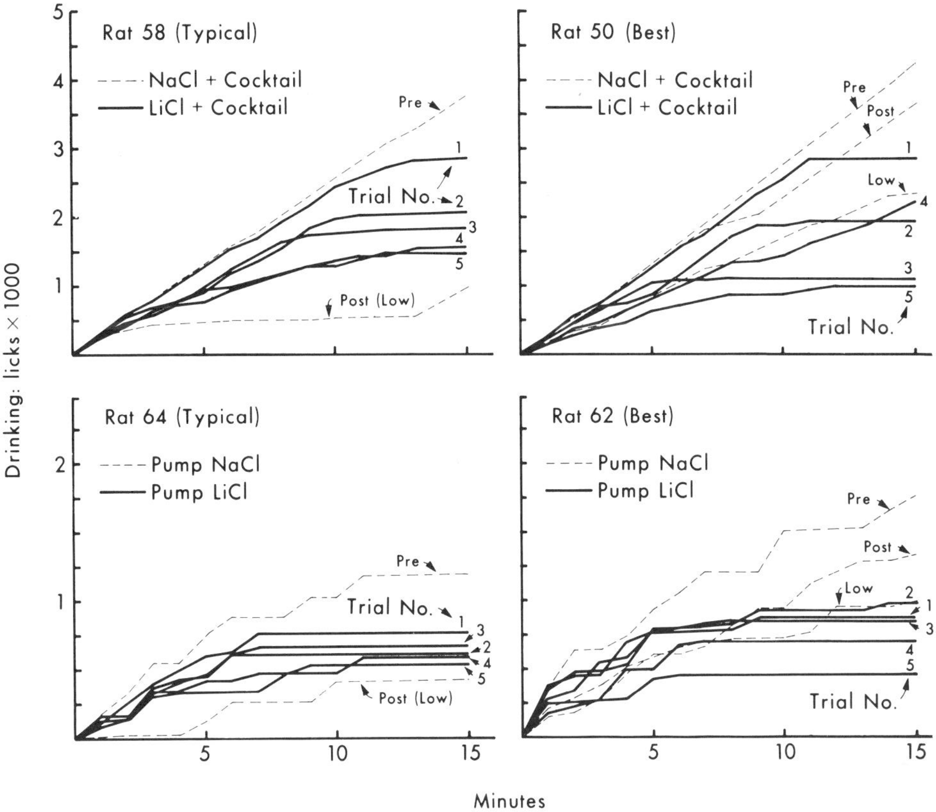

Figure 3. Effects of masking the taste signal during visceral feedback. Both a complex flavor stimulating all four flavors and intragastric delivery typically abolished learning (Rats 58 and 64, respectively). When a discrimination did develop, it was never as distinct as when taste cues were present (Rats 50 and 62; cf. Figure 2).

the cocktail depended upon the previous day's visceral feedback effect. However, despite these fluctuations, there was a general decline in consumption over the experiment and the animals were unable to maintain their body weights or their general appearance of health. Only two of the eight cocktail animals gave any evidence of discrimination and we have presented data from Rat 50, the best of the group. Rat 50 displayed the most rapid discrimination on trials 3 and 5 where slope differences appear between three to five minutes. It is possible for lithium symptoms from larger doses to appear this rapidly, so this animal may have been detecting visceral feedback but we cannot discount the possibility that he was making a taste discrimination.

The data of the intragastric pumping group was characterized by wider variation between rats and between trials for individual rats. In general, the results were the same as for the cocktail group. As typified by Rat 64, most of the rats tended to drink progressively less of both fluids. Only two of seven rats gave any evidence of discrimination and we have presented the data for Rat 62, the best of the pump group. Rat 62 appears to make his earliest discrimination at about five minutes on Trial 5. Hence he too, may have been detecting early feedback. However, we cannot exclude the possibility of a taste discrimination since substances in the bloodstream can be detected by the taste receptors (Fishberg, Hitzig, & King, 1933; Greenfield, 1950; Bradley & Mistretta, 1971; Bradley, 1973).

In summary, these experiments demonstrate that when the taste signal is masked or eliminated, most rats cannot learn to discriminate a toxic solution from a safe solution, at least within the bounds of our experiments. While some rats appear to form a discrimination, perhaps on the basis of visceral feedback, the learning seems too ineffective to insure their survival under prolonged exposure.

PRESENTING THE VISCERAL FEEDBACK UNDER DEGRADED AWARENESS

These data on the development of a taste-illness aversion seem paradoxical. While the rat can utilize the taste signal efficiently to avoid delayed toxicosis, it cannot use early internal signs very effectively to escape the distress of more intense illness. Such early internal signs are temporally more proximal and functionally more closely related to the ultimate aversive distress. According to traditional conditioning principles, they should serve as better signals than the more distal taste stimuli. Nevertheless, there is another source of evidence that visceral feedback mechanisms are functionally independent of the cerebral cortex, of cognitive coping mechanisms, and of phenomena such as attention, awareness, and consciousness.

Cortical spreading depression (CSD) has been used to examine the neural and behavioral mechanisms underlying associative learning (Bures, Buresova, & Krivanek, 1974). This disruption of cortical electroencephalographic activity (EEG) is produced by bilateral application of potassium chloride (KCl) directly on the surface of the brain through trephine holes in the skull. Slow high amplitude EEG waves radiate from the point of KCL application and in about fifteen minutes the normal electrical activity is virtually abolished. Motor coordination, placing responses and righting responses are impaired. Spontaneous eating and drinking is abolished, though the rat will swallow reflexively if food is placed in the back of the mouth. Under CSD, the rat will jump and squeal at footshock and acquire simple conditioned responses when stimulus parameters are favorable and task requirements are simple. However there is a progressive impairment as tasks become complex and the rat is required to anticipate consequences of signals. Behaviorally, the rat under CSD acts as if he is functionally decorticate.

In one study, rats were given saccharin water followed by bilateral KCl. A single dose of lithium injected fifteen minutes after CSD onset produced an aversion comparable to that observed in control animals. Similarly, when CSD was given five minutes after the lithium injection, the rats acquired an aversion as great or greater than control animals. Since illness onset is estimated to occur 5 to 15 minutes after injection, visceral feedback while the animal is in the CSD state seems to be as effective as when its brain surface is electrically functional (Buresova & Bures, 1973a).

In another study, rats were allowed to drink saccharin water and 15 minutes later CSD was induced and maintained during the taste-illness interval. If lithium was administered within 60 minutes, the aversion of the experimental animals was comparable to controls. If lithium was delayed for 120 minutes the aversion was disrupted, so CSD may have an effect upon the delay gradient (Buresova & Bures, 1973b, 1974).

In contrast, CSD has a profound effect upon an aversion if it is administered before the taste signal. Since rats under CSD will not spontaneously drink, a number of force feeding techniques were used on both CSD animals and their controls. Saccharin was either rinsed through the oral cavity, reflexively swallowed or intubed into the stomach. Force feeding tended to attenuate the aversions in control animals, but the results were clear. Presenting the saccharin signal under CSD disrupted the acquisition of a flavor-illness aversion (Buresova & Bures, 1973a, 1973b).

Rats can acquire a taste aversion even when the illness agent is presented under general anesthesia (Roll & Smith, 1972). Rats were given saccharin water, then injected with chloroproxithene, to facilitate CNS depression and enhance respiration, and anesthetized with Nembutal. When they failed to display the corneal reflex or respond to a tail pinch, the rats were exposed to 100 r of ionizing radiation. Both experimental and control groups were anesthetized for eight hours, a period calculated to cover the aversive feedback from radiation. The animals were then tested in their home cages with a saccharin bottle and a water bottle continuously available for one week. Control animals initially displayed a mild distaste for saccharin as they drank only forty percent of their fluid from that bottle on the first day. This effect, presumably due to the general anesthesia, rapidly extinguished as the rats were drinking ninety percent of their fluid from the saccharin bottle by the fourth day. In contrast, the rats irradiated during anesthesia displayed a profound aversion, never taking more than ten percent of their daily fluid from the saccharin bottle during the entire week.

In summary, it appears that agents which degrade awareness drastically disrupt the perception of the taste signal as we would expect; but these same agents have surprisingly little effect upon the capacity of visceral feedback to alter the hedonic baseline value of the taste signal. Though we need more evidence on this point, it appears that the animal can acquire an aversion even though the visceral feedback occurs while it is completely unconscious.

SOME IMPLICATIONS FOR BIOFEEDBACK TRAINING

In a traditional conditioning experiment, the subject must be able to clearly discriminate the unconditioned stimulus following the signal and the reinforcement following his response for rapid acquisition. The unconditioned or reinforcing stimulus is usually a stimulus which contacts his peripheral surface. For avoidance conditioning, electrocutaneous shock is often employed, and for approach, the taste of food in the mouth is most often used. The animal must be able to discriminate these reinforcing stimuli as clearly as he discriminates the distant visual or auditory signal which warns him away from pain or beckons him toward food. But in taste-illness conditioning he need only discriminate the peripheral taste signal, for he can be cortically impaired, anesthetized or asleep when the reinforcing internal feedback is applied. Furthermore, after delayed illness, there is powerful conditioning specifically to taste. Conditioning to visual aspects of food, the place where food is eaten, and even to the smell of food is too weak to be of survival value in most mammals tested. It is the hedonic quality of the taste that is changed; after illness, appetizing food becomes disgusting (Garcia, Hankins, & Rusiniak, 1974; Garcia, Rusiniak, & Brett, 1976).

Obviously, taste-illness conditioning does not conform to the usual notions of behavior modification through associative conditioning or cognitive learning. Taste-illness conditioning is representative of another class of conditioning, incentive modification through homeostatic utilization. A stimulus which is useful in the homeostatic economy is pleasant on contact to the peripheral receptors. For example, when the body core temperature is too cool, warm rays impinging on the skin give immediate pleasure. As his core temperature rises, the warmth becomes unpleasant, but the subject is unaware, in any clear sense, of the vegetative process which dictates the hedonic changes (Cabanac, 1971). So it is with flavor-illness conditioning; a flavor contacting the peripheral gustatory receptors becomes aversive after it has disrupted the internal vegetative economy.

Biofeedback training is also concerned with control of internal vegetative processes. These states are difficult to describe in meaningful behavioral terms. Hence, operant conditioning methods are often employed. The subject is attached to electronic devices monitoring the internal process and when he approaches the desired state, he is signalled through the telereceptors, i.e., through the visual or auditory channels. The timing of the signal is usually delivered at the first sign of the desired state because of the immediate reinforcement assumption borrowed from traditional operant principles. However, immediate feedback signaling may be counterproductive because early signs of the state may be functionally useless to the subject. It may be more effective to let him obtain a deep state and then signal him after the fact, as Kamiya did in his early studies (see Stoyva & Kamiya, 1968; Nowlis & Kamiya, 1970). In this way, the signal informs the subject that he has achieved the required feeling state, serving an instructional function rather than reinforcement function (see Beatty, 1972).

The choice of a telereceptive signal to cognitively inform the subject of his vegetative state may be counterproductive also. Informative signals may disrupt the desired state, particularly forms of relaxation, by arousing the subject into a coping and achievement mode. It might be more fruitful to couple a radiant head source rather than an auditory speaker to the biofeedback device. Then the subject attempting to relax in a cool room could receive a pleasant feedback sensation conducive to further relaxation. In any case, it is clear that behavioral models derived from animals actively coping with external problems, informative distal signals and discrete distal goals are inappropriate for biofeedback training. The hedonic changes sensed by peripheral receptors are more intimately related to the control of the diffuse sluggish vegetative processes, as sought in biofeedback training.

REFERENCES

Beatty, J. Similar effects of feedback signals and instructional information on EEG activity. Physiology and Behavior, 1972, 9, 151-154.

Bradley, R. Electrophysiological investigations of intravascular taste using perfused rat tongue. American Journal of Physiology, 1973, 224, 300-304.

Bradley, R., & Mistretta, C. Intravascular taste in rats as demonstrated by conditioned aversion to sodium saccharin. Journal of Comparative and Physiological Psychology, 1971, 75, 186-189.

Bures, J., Buresova, O., & Krivanck, J. The mechanism and applications of Leão's spreading depression of electroencephalographic activity. New York: Academic Press, 1974.

Buresova, O., & Bures, J. Cortical and subcortical components of the conditioned saccharin aversion. Physiology and Behavior, 1973, 11, 435-439. (a)

Buresova, O., & Bures, J. Cortical and subcortical components of conditioned saccharin aversion in rats. Acta Neurobiologia Experimentalis, 1973, 33, 689-698. (b)

Buresova, O., & Bures, J. Functional decortication in the CS-US interval decrease efficiency of taste aversion learning. Behavioral Biology, 1974, 12, 357-364.

Cabanac, M. Physiological role of pleasure. Science, 1971, 173, 1103-1107.

Cabanac, M., & Duclaux, R. Specificity of internal signals in producing satiety for taste stimuli. Nature, 1970, 227, 966-967.

Fishberg, A. M., Hitzig, W. M., & King, R. H. Measurement of the circulation time with saccharin. Proceedings of the Society for Experimental Biology and Medicine, 1933, 30, 651-652.

Garcia, J., & Hankins, W. G. The evolution of bitter and the acquisition of toxiphobia. In D. A. Denton & J. R. Coghlan (Eds.), Olfaction and taste V. New York: Academic Press, 1975.

Garcia, J., Hankins, W., & Rusiniak, K. Behavioral regulation of the milieu interne in man and rat. Science, 1974, 185, 824-831.

Garcia, J., Rusiniak, K. W., & Brett, L. P. Conditioning food-illness aversions in wild animals: Caveant canonici. In H. Davis & H. M. B. Hurwitz (Eds.), Operant-Pavlovian interactions. New Jersey: Lawrence Erlbaum Associates, 1976, in press.

Green, K., & Garcia, J. Recuperation from illness: Flavor enhancement for rats. Science, 1970, 173, 749-751.

Greenfield, I. Sodium succinate as a test of circulatory efficiency. Annals of Internal Medicine, 1950, 32, 524-527.

Jenkins, H. M., & Sainsbury, R. S. Discrimination learning with the distinctive feature on positive or negative trials. In D. Mostofsky (Ed.), Attention: Contemporary theory and analysis. New York: Appleton-Century-Crofts, 1970.

McHugh, P. R., Moran, T. H., & Barton, G. N. Satiety: A graded behavioral phenomenon regulating caloric intake. Science, 1975, 190, 167-169.

Novin, D. Visceral mechanisms in the control of food intake. In D. Novin, W. Wyrwicka, & G. A. Bray (Eds.), Hunger: Basic mechanisms and clinical applications. New York: Ravin, 1976.

Nowlis, D. P., & Kamiya, J. The control of electroencephalographic alpha rhythms through auditory feedback and the associated mental activity. Psychophysiology, 1970, 6, 476-484.

Roll, D., & Smith, J. Conditioned taste aversion in anesthetized rats. In M. E. P. Seligman & J. Hager (Eds.), Biological boundaries of learning. New York: Appleton-Century-Crofts, 1972.

Rusiniak, K. W., Garcia, J., & Hankins, W. G. Baitshyness: Avoidance of the taste without escape from the illness. Journal of Comparative and Physiological Psychology, 1976, 90, 460-467.

Schachter, S. Some extraordinary facts about obese humans and rats. American Psychologist, 1971, 26, 129-144.

Stoyva, J., & Kamiya, J. Electrophysiological studies of dreaming as the prototype of a new strategy in the study of consciousness. Psychological Review, 1968, 75, 192-205.

NOTE

This research was supported by USPHS-NIH Research Grant 1-R01-NS-11618 and USPHS Program Project Grant HD 05958.

LEARNED CONTROL OF BRAIN WAVE ACTIVITY

Laverne C. Johnson
Naval Health Research Center
San Diego, California

I understand the purpose of my presentation is to present a tutorial and to set the stage for those presenting research papers this afternoon. My function thus is to review the work of others rather than present our own research, but I will not be able to strictly adhere to this guideline as I will present some of the work from our Naval Health Research Center laboratory.

In keeping with the tutorial format, I would like to restate the title of my talk in the form of a question: Has Learned Control of Brain Wave Activity Been Demonstrated; i.e., has operant conditioning occurred. For this presentation, I will restrict the discussion to feedback studies with humans.

Dr. Black (1973, 1974), our opening speaker, asked the same question in a 1972 paper. For Black, as for many others, if it is assumed that the observed changes in the electrical activity of the brain are produced by operant conditioning, the crucial question then is: "Were the changes produced directly by the operant conditioning of CNS electrical activity, or indirectly by the operant conditioning of some other response which mediated the observed changes in CNS electrical activity?" (Black, 1973, p. 96).

With respect to the types of possible mediators, Black states "It would seem that most of the CNS patterns of electrical activity over which we have obtained control by means of operant conditioning are related to motor processes" (Black, 1973, p. 132). This observation is appropriate for both the control of alpha activity and for the sensory motor rhythm (SMR) which I will discuss later. The role of the visuomotor system in the control of alpha activity has been stressed by Mulholland and his associates (Mulholland & Runnals, 1962; Mulholland & Evans, 1966; Mulholland & Peper, 1971; Mulholland, 1972, 1974). Their studies indicated that to increase or decrease alpha, one learned to inhibit or to increase looking behavior which involves control of his oculomotor activity.

Dr. Plotkin (1976) has recently presented a series of studies which led him to conclude that "in the feedback augmentation of occipital alpha, enhancement and suppression of this rhythm is always mediated by learned control of oculomotor processes" (p. 92).

Others have also raised questions as to the mediating mechanisms involved in the feedback control of alpha rhythms. Lynch and Paskewitz (1971) identified three general sources of influence on alpha density: constitutional, physiological, and cognitive-attentional factors. Paskewitz and Orne (1973) and Lynch, Paskewitz, and Orne (1974) concluded that the alpha densities observed in the feedback situation have very little to do with feedback or direct learning processes. From their results, they concluded that increases in human alpha activity occur in feedback situations when the individual learns to disinhibit various stimuli, attentional and arousal factors that normally block this rhythm.

Paskewitz and Orne (1973) also found that it was impossible to enhance alpha beyond that found during eyes-closed baseline or above the baseline alpha recorded in a darkened room. Significant enhancement was obtained with eyes open in a dimly lighted room. Paskewitz and Orne's data did not support the popular view (at that time) that alpha-feedback training permits individuals to increase alpha densities significantly above those obtained during a comfortable baseline session with eyes closed in a relaxed, nondrowsy state.

With respect to Paskewitz and Orne's finding that alpha activity cannot be raised above the eyes-closed resting level, some years earlier in studies of photic driving of EEG activity, George Ulett and I (Ulett & Johnson, 1958) came to a similar conclusion. We found that when there was a large amount of resting alpha activity, we produced little increase in alpha during photic stimulation at alpha frequencies, but, conversely, when there was little resting alpha activity, as when eyes were open, there was a significant increase.

In discussing alpha feedback, Travis, Kondo, and Knott (1974) observed that, with respect to operant conditioning, one of the critical points that emerged was that the performance curves did not resemble typical acquisition curves found in the development of conditioned responses.

In addition to possible mediating responses, in operant conditioning the relation between the reinforcer and the response is a critical factor. The relation between the reinforcing feedback stimulus and the alpha response was soon found to be highly variable. Hord and Barber (1971) found that it made no difference whether a tone-on or tone-off signal was used to indicate the presence of alpha. The level of alpha was similar when the subjects were told to keep the tone off as it was when they were told to keep the tone on.

For those researchers who believed that some feedback was necessary, a tone-off was as informative as a tone-on, Beatty's (1972) report that a feedback stimulus was not necessary to control brain activity must have been disturbing. Subjects who were verbally given appropriate strategies for producing alpha and beta frequencies could control these two brain activities as well as those subjects given second-by-second feedback. Beatty's subjects were able to develop cognitive strategies in the absence of feedback that resulted in the desired brain activity (see Plotkin, 1976). Data suggesting that biofeedback effects may not even be limited to the target response are provided in a study examining the direct and cross modality effects of EEG alpha, EMG frontalis feedback (DeGood, Chisholm, & Valle, 1976). While both groups increased their alpha activity, the increase was larger for the 10 subjects receiving EMG relaxation training. Only EMG subjects demonstrated any reduction of frontalis activity during training.

Other studies have also found no significant correlation between changes in alpha activity and other physiological measures. Both Hord and Barber (1971) and Beatty and Kornfeld (1972) found that EEG changes during biofeedback were relatively independent of cardiac activity. Beatty and Kornfeld also reported no significant correlation of EEG changes with respiratory activity.

The above is not an exhaustive review of the various concerns and problems that have been raised relative to the question of learned control of alpha activity in humans, but I believe the results are sufficient to justify the conclusion that unmediated learned control of alpha activity per se has not been achieved. This statement is in agreement with Lynch and Paskewitz (1971) who stated, "One conclusion does seem apparent, however, alpha activity is mediated by a whole host of factors, and the likelihood of ever controlling or eliminating all these factors to observe only simple alpha conditioning is extremely small. Thus, in the more restricted sense, any discussion of the 'operant control of alpha activity' seems to us, operationally indefensible" (pp. 208-209).

BEHAVIORAL CORRELATES OF ALPHA

Laboratory studies exploring the mechanism of alpha control were far exceeded by papers attesting to its virtues. In addition to the subjective reports of well being, serenity, relaxation, Nowlis and Kamiya (1970) implied that alpha enhancement aided task performance, and Green, Green and Walters (1970) asserted that alpha enhancement improved delayed recall. Enhanced alpha appeared to raise the pain threshold (Gannon & Sternbach, 1971), facilitate extrasensory perception (ESP) (Honorton, Davidson, & Bindler, 1971), and decrease the need for sleep (Regestein, Buckland, & Pegram, 1973). Nideffer (1973) listed three ways in which subjects may benefit from alpha training. First, it could be useful in the treatment of hypersensitive conditions and it may increase the subject's ability to withstand stress; second, it may increase self-acceptance, tolerance, and understanding, as well as empathy for others; and third, the alpha state may be used to train individuals to recognize and experience a non-critical, ego-free environment. For some scientists, as for many laymen, further research was unnecessary; it was a proven scientific fact that high alpha universally enhanced both work and play.

Results from carefully controlled studies have not supported this view of alpha as a panacea. It soon became apparent that the glowing subjective reports of the alpha state were influenced by subject and experimenter expectations. In our laboratory, when our alpha-naive subjects were not instructed as to what or how they should feel or act to keep the feedback tone on, they generally described the alpha state as "boring," "no different," "not unusual," and in some instances "relaxing." Regestein, Pegram, Cook, and Bradley (1973) reinforced seven subjects for high and then low amounts of alpha rhythm during two separate 12-hour periods. It was easier for their subjects to maintain high alpha for this long period than no alpha. It also made no difference to the subjects whether they were paid or whether they had a tone associated with alpha. With respect to the subjective feelings during the 12-hour regimen, Regestein et al. stated, "Given the subjective boredom of our prolonged alpha subjects, we disagree with the numerous advertisements for alpha-rhythm feedback machines now appearing in the popular press and elsewhere, which suggest that much time spent in alpha rhythm will psychologically benefit the purchaser of these devices" (p. 222). Walsh (1974), in a study of the interactive effects of alpha feedback and instructional set on subjective state, concluded that "for an 'alpha experience' to occur, both alpha activity and alpha set are necessary; neither alone is sufficient" (p. 428). Plotkin (1976), in his extensive study, provides further data on the role of instructions in determining the subjective response during alpha feedback.

With respect to alpha as a substitute for sleep, research at the Naval Health Research Center clearly demonstrated that self-enhancement or inhibition of alpha activity is not a substitute for sleep. The deleterious effects of acute sleep loss on performance and mood were not ameliorated by alpha-contingent feedback (Hord, Tracy, Lubin, & Johnson, 1975; Hord, Lubin, Tracy, Jensma, & Johnson, 1976).

In the cognitive domain, Beatty (1973) found no relationship between occipital alpha feedback and two measures of information-processing capacity: short-term memory for digits and choice-reaction times. As a part of the same research program concerned with self-regulation as an aid to human effectiveness (Lawrence & Johnson, 1976), Kamiya (1972), like Beatty, found EEG activity unrelated to both memory for words and a simple reaction-time test. Kamiya also attempted to determine whether subjects trained to control alpha amplitude would show improvement in performance tasks if break periods from the tasks were used to maintain high alpha amplitude. The reasoning underlying this hypothesis was that alpha is often regarded as indicative of a resting or idling condition which may be characteristic of rest periods from performance tasks. Five young male adults were given a battery of performance tasks with 4-minute break periods between each task. The control group was told merely to wait for 4 minutes between tasks while the experimental group was trained to produce alpha and received 4 minutes of alpha feedback between tasks. The tasks were verbal auditory vigilance, rod and frame, Guilford creative intelligence, visual memory, mental arithmetic, digit memory span, and tone tracking. The results were negative. Kamiya concluded that the self-regulated high alpha break period did not facilitate task performance.

Martin Orne and his associates (1975) explored the ability of subjects to maintain a high alpha state while performing cognitive tasks. Nine well-trained subjects were able to maintain the alpha activity while counting backwards by one, but counting backwards by seven significantly blocked alpha when compared to non-task trials. Complexity of the task, subject's ability to perform the task, and level of effort by subject were all related to the degree of alpha blocking during the tasks. In a series of related studies, Orne et al. (1975) were unable to find a relationship between alpha training and performance on various other cognitive tasks.

Thus, enhanced alpha activity does not prevent sleep-loss effects or substitute for sleep (Hord et al., 1975, 1976), is not related to memory or choice-reaction performance (Beatty, 1973), does not provide a recuperative break period (Kamiya, 1972), and is incompatible with cognitive tasks requiring effort (Orne et al., 1975).

THERAPEUTIC EFFECTS OF ALPHA

With respect to self-regulated alpha and pain, Melzack and Perry (1975) used alpha feedback and hypnotic training for the control of chronic pain. They report that the combined procedures produce a substantial decrease in pain (by 33% or greater) in 58% of the patients during the training sessions. They conclude, however, that since alpha alone had no significant effect on pain reduction, the contribution of the alpha-training procedure to pain relief when combined with hypnosis was "not due to increased EEG alpha as such but, rather, to the distraction of attention, suggestion, relaxation, and sense of control over pain which are an integral part of the procedure" (Melzack & Perry, 1975, p. 452).

Our session chairman, Dr. Lehmann, and his associates have also failed to reduce headaches by use of alpha feedback (Lehmann, Lang, & Debruyne, 1976). In their study, alpha-EEG feedback training was administered in 12 sessions to tension-headache patients and healthy controls. One patient group (N=9) and the control group (N=6) received auditory alpha EEG feedback, another patient group (N=10) received auditory pseudofeedback from a random generator. Headache pain was assessed by self-rating, and decreased systematically within the limits of a placebo effect during training; there was no difference in headache decrease between feedback and pseudofeedback patients.

Increase of alpha EEG over sessions was observed under feedback and pseudofeedback. However, there was always more alpha during resting periods than during training. The results suggested, for Dr. Lehmann, that alpha increase over time in training is a habituation effect (as per Martin Orne). The results did not support the notion that one can learn to produce more EEG alpha.

Therefore, alpha feedback has no unique recuperative or therapeutic powers. In those instances where a positive psychological experience occurred, these were influenced by subject and experimenter expectations aided by instructions. Where "therapeutic" gain has been noted, it probably was due in large part to the general relaxation that often is associated with maximum alpha activity.

If alpha feedback has little to do with learned control of brain activity and controlled studies contradicted the early positive claims, why did alpha feedback research go off like a rocket? Certainly the knowledge that one could control his own alpha activity by opening or closing his eyes or by controlling his thoughts was not new. It was not until Kamiya began to report his findings on the operant control of EEG alpha rhythm and its effects on consciousness that the alpha turn-on began (Kamiya, 1969). Brown (1970) soon supported Kamiya's findings in her laboratory. For both Kamiya and Brown, the point of departure of their work was that the "learned" physiological activity seemed to have behavioral effects. As noted above, the initial reports on the behavioral properties of the "alpha state" were predominantly positive. Science had not only found a way to control brain activity, but perhaps a way to expand consciousness. Maslow (1969) viewed alpha training as a way to produce serenity, meditativeness, even happiness. "That is to say that it is already possible to teach people how to feel happy" (p. 728). Gardner Murphy (1969) viewed this new technique as a way of identifying the many kinds of phenomenological states that are anchored upon particular types of EEG.

In their zeal to discover and to identify new behavioral states by EEG wave forms, most feedback researchers paid little attention to the argument that EEG and autonomic activity per se cannot be used to define states of consciousness. When we suggested that one must first infer the subject's state from his verbal reports and overt behavior before determining the significance of the EEG and autonomic activity (Johnson, 1970), the response was Alpha is the state.

We should also remember that alpha feedback was introduced when the Zeitgeist was to seek new experiences, new highs, and drug use was prevalent. A technique to achieve a "high" without drugs was too important to keep buried in a laboratory. Perhaps others felt that alpha biofeedback would help subjects rapidly achieve the meditational state reported by yoga and Zen masters.

Grossberg (1972), also noting the disproportionate excitement generated by such modest evidence, suggested "that metaphysical assumptions about psychic powers of the brain are still obstacles to scientific progress in psychology" (p. 248). Whatever the reason for its ready acceptance, the alpha balloon was pricked by the overwhelming data from carefully controlled laboratory studies. I hasten to add, however, that it still appears through the pages of some of our most popular publications.

THETA ACTIVITY

While most of the focus has been on control of alpha activity, there have been attempts to self-regulate other brain activity. These efforts have focused on the 3-7 Hz theta rhythm, the 12-16 Hz sensory motor rhythm (SMR), and, most recently, 40 Hz activity. Since there has been limited work in feedback training for 40 Hz activity, I will not discuss it in this paper and refer the reader to Sheer (1975). Let's look first at theta. Theta waves are most prevalent during the drowsy period, stage 1 in the APSS Sleep Scoring Manual (Rechtschaffen & Kales, 1968). Relative to alpha, theta waves are rare in the awake, relaxed state. Thus, there is little opportunity for feedback information to the subject. It is not surprising, then, that the results from the few attempts to enhance theta by feedback training have been inconsistent. Brown (1971), Klug and Brown (1974), and Beatty, Greenberg, Deibler, and O'Hanlon (1974) reported positive results. Lutzenberger, Birbaumer, and Wildgruber (1975) noted, however, that the work from Brown's laboratory did not include controls, and they were uncertain as to the learning procedure and data in the Beatty et al. paper. It should be noted that Beatty et al. were more interested in training subjects to suppress theta than to augment theta, and their theta measure used to trigger the feedback tone stimulus was a ratio of 3-7 Hz waves over the total number of waves in the 3-30 Hz range. Also, the significance level reported by Beatty et al. for theta augmentation during a vigilance task was 0.10, while the significance level for decrease in theta from baseline was 0.05. Thus, Beatty et al.'s subjects were better at suppressing than augmenting theta activity.

Lutzenberger et al., in a controlled cross-over design study with contingent feedback and noncontingent feedback, found no significant difference in theta enhancement in any of their subjects when contingent and noncontingent feedback conditions were compared.

Noting that learning to produce theta waves was a subtle and demanding task for most subjects, Sittenfeld, Budzynski, and Stoyva (1976) hypothesized that sequential or graduated training might be more effective than one which provided only theta feedback for the entire training period. Also noting that subjects who produce theta waves often report strong feelings of drowsiness, Sittenfeld et al. chose muscle relaxation for the first phase of their sequential training. Budzynski and Stoyva (1969) had earlier noted that with low EMG levels, theta activity frequently appeared.

Subjects with high and low EMG levels were chosen. A comparable number of subjects in each level were given either one-phase or two-phase sequential training. In the latter, the subjects were given EMG relaxation training before theta feedback.

The subjects with high frontal EMG levels increased theta only if they were initially given EMG training followed by theta training. High EMG subjects did not increase their theta when given only theta feedback training. Subjects with low frontal EMG levels did best at increasing theta output if they were given theta feedback from the outset. Low EMG subjects did not profit from sequential training.

Correlations of theta with other activity showed an inverse relation with EMG levels. A heart rate decrease was found with theta increase in the high EMG group but not in the low EMG subjects. There was no consistent relation between alpha and theta, and alpha activity did not vary systematically between baseline and post-baseline sessions.

Sittenfeld et al. concluded that by individualizing the feedback procedure, most subjects could produce theta waves and this finding was of potential value as a technique to help induce sleep.

THETA AND PERFORMANCE

In their initial paper, Beatty et al. (1974) reported that suppression of theta by operant methods enhanced monitoring efficiency whereas theta augmentation led to performance degradation over a 2-hour watch period. After many negative alpha studies, Beatty et al. were encouraged by their theta-suppression results and stated, "This is the first demonstration, to our knowledge, of a lawful relationship between operantly regulated cortical phenomena and performance in man" (p. 873).

The nature of this relation, however, turned out to be influenced by both task and subjects. In a 1-hour vigilance task, subjects trained to suppress theta performed no better than a nonfeedback group, though the theta-suppression subjects did detect signals more rapidly than subjects trained to augment theta. Beatty and O'Hanlon then shifted from college students to trained radar observers in their UCLA laboratory. The level of self-regulated theta suppression was less with the 11 radar observers than with college students though, like the college students, the naval subjects required significantly fewer sweeps for target detection when theta-suppression feedback was provided (Beatty & O'Hanlon, 1975). But more troublesome was the finding that in an operational test at a nearby Naval Air Station involving 14 naval petty officers trained as air controllers or radarmen, self-regulation of theta had no significant effect on the detection time during a 3-hour vigilance task, but I will leave the detailed presentation of this work to Dr. O'Hanlon.

As a further test of theta suppression, Wilson, Hord, Townsend, and Johnson (1976) studied 19 naval subjects in a 3-hour sonar task. One group of 7 subjects used biofeedback to suppress theta activity, 7 subjects were yoked controls (each yoked control received the same feedback tones as those of a feedback subject but had no control over the tone), and 5 subjects received no theta feedback or tones. There were no significant differences among the three groups in time to detect sonar signals or in number correctly detected. While the theta-feedback group learned to suppress theta during training, during the vigilance task there was no difference in theta between the two groups.

Beatty and O'Hanlon felt that the theta-feedback procedures provided the subject with new information concerning his state of nervous system arousal, permitting him to maintain alertness in a manner not otherwise possible. It is likely that this effect--if it turns out to exhibit reliability and robustness--reflects state changes comfortably subsumed under most conceptualizations of arousal; perhaps Beatty and O'Hanlon have discovered a way to teach people to stay awake without drugs or peripheral stimulation. There are, however, no consistent data indicating that background theta activity per se (i.e., theta activity generally present and not associated with drowsiness) is related to performance levels in rested subjects (Williams, Granda, Jones, Lubin, & Armington, 1962). Recent findings at the Naval Health Research Center support the conclusions of Williams et al. No significant relation was found between reaction time or errors of omission and the amount of theta activity in either the 8 seconds (average correlation .01, N = 18) or 1-second period (average correlation .01, N = 13) before the signal presentation in rested subjects. If theta feedback has any value, it may allow the subject to become aware of changes in state which are reflected by changes in theta levels, rather than in theta activity per se. In the sleep-deprived subject, there is a significant relation between appearance of theta and lapses in performance (Williams et al., 1962).

Has learned control of theta activity been demonstrated? Beatty et al. referred to their technique as "operant control of occipital theta," and Sittenfeld et al. felt that changes in EEG frequencies were feedback contingent, i.e., "the changes were selective to theta, the response being trained" (p. 43). While Sittenfeld et al. acknowledged that the theta results could have been due to general "slowing down," the thrust of their arguments indicated they wanted to believe their subjects had learned to control theta. The fact that in the title of their article they refer to "shaping" of theta activity may reflect their concern over whether operant control of theta actually occurred. I believe that EEG theta activity is an epiphenomenon of a general lowering of arousal level. Until it can be clearly shown that theta activity is uniquely feedback contingent in a subject who shows no other physiological changes of lowered arousal, it would appear most parsimonious to view changes in arousal level as the response being controlled.

SENSORY MOTOR RHYTHM

Earlier, I quoted Black's observation that the CNS patterns of activity over which control had been obtained by means of operant conditioning are related to motor responses. The SMR clearly supports Black's observation. In the cat, the SMR has been related to processes involved in the inhibition of movement; i.e., as the animals were producing SMR, they remained rigid or posturally motionless (Chase & Harper, 1971; Roth, Sterman, & Clemente, 1967; Sterman, Wyrwicka, & Roth, 1969). Based upon the finding that cats given SMR training when awake had more spindling when asleep, Sterman, Howe, and MacDonald (1970) stated, "the neural mechanism common to the SMR and the sleep spindle burst is concerned with the suppression of movement, as indicated by the absence of phasic motor behavior when these rhythms are present in wakefulness and in sleep" (p. 1148). A functional similarity was thus inferred between the awake SMR and the 12-14 Hz spindles during sleep.

Johnson, Hanson, and Bickford (1976) found no significant relation between sleep spindle bursts and the onset of or the rate of body movements during sleep. Sleep spindles often occurred just before a movement. They therefore questioned whether sleep spindles functioned to inhibit motor activity and doubted there was a functional similarity between the awake SMR and sleep spindles in humans.

It is, however, as a technique to reduce seizures that the SMR has stimulated most interest. The possible usefulness of the SMR for controlling seizures in humans was suggested by the work in cats by Sterman, LoPresti, and Fairchild (1969). They found that in cats trained to produce SMR, the onset of convulsions was delayed following injection of a convulsion-producing drug. In cats with no SMR training, there was no delay.

The effectiveness of SMR training and whether the therapeutic effect is specific to the SMR is at present unresolved. The absence of well-controlled studies using an adequate number of patients has been a severe shortcoming of work in this area. Sterman's original observations were on 4 patients of various ages and types of seizures.

Rundell (personal communication) used SMR feedback in the absence of theta; i.e., if theta were present, the feedback tone would not come on to successfully reduce psychomotor attacks in a 13-year-old and a 28-

year-old female. A 19-year-old male with mixed petit mal and grand mal seizures showed no EEG learning or seizure control.

Finley, Smith, and Etherton (1975) reported SMR training reduced the seizure frequency of a 13-year-old epileptic, and Seifert and Lubar (1975) reported a reduction of seizure frequency in 6 patients following SMR feedback. Lubar and Bahler (1976) used SMR feedback to treat a heterogeneous group of 8 chronic seizure patients. The group included 4 males, age range 12 to 19, and the age range for the 4 females was 14 to 26. Seizure history ranged from 4 to 18 years. Four patients had temporal lobe discharges (one with focal slowing, one general slowing, one temporal lobe seizure discharges as a result of suspected structural lesion, and one characteristic of temporal lobe seizure disorder). The other 4 patients had generalized dysrhythmias. The types of seizures were psychomotor, myoclonic, and akinetic. One patient was mentally retarded.

Lubar and Bahler report that most of the patients showed a reduction in seizures during SMR training. They also reported the seizures were of shorter duration and of less intensity than they were initially. "Overall, our data indicate that the use of sensorimotor rhythm training for the management of epileptic seizures seems to be effective for several different types of epilepsy" (p. 100). Inspection of their seizure curves indicates that 5 of the 8 patients had a seizure rate at the end of treatment lower than that during pretreatment, two were nearly identical, and one's seizure rate was higher. During one or more periods of training, all patients had lower rates, but the seizure rate per 10-day period varied widely. The statistics were all computed from within-subject data and consisted of the correlation of seizure frequency with days. To compute significance levels using within-subject data, one must assume all the scores are independent--an assumption that could hardly be met in this study. It also is extremely risky to generalize to a larger population from an N of 1 regardless of the obtained within-subject significance level. No statistical tests were made over subjects on any measure. Also, there was no correlation of level of SMR activity, or level of success in training with seizure frequency. The closest they come to such an analysis is the statement, "Accompanying the decreased seizures in many patients is an increase of 12-14 Hz activity in the raw EEG over the recording sites from which training is instituted (specifically C3-T3 and C4-T4)" (p. 101). This statement does not provide the quantitative data necessary to support a specific relationship between SMR activity and seizure rate. But the major difficulty is that no control group of patients was run.

Though Kuhlman (1974) was unable to locate the 12-14 Hz rhythm in 6 human subjects and Kaplan (1975) was unable to find positive results with SMR training, interest in this technique as an adjunct treatment for epileptics appears to be growing. Neither the patient's age, duration of seizures, type of seizures, type of EEG abnormality, nor whether the abnormality is focal or generalized appear to be related to the efficacy of the SMR. No one can or would dare to claim such universal applicability for any pharmacological agent.

This universality of the effect of SMR suggests that the results are probably not due to a specific learned CNS rhythm. It is hard to imagine how the SMR could have equal inhibitory effects on all types of seizures regardless of etiology, locus of seizure activity, and behavioral manifestations. A mediator which could serve to block various types of seizure activity must be present. That mediator might be focused attention or arousal. In our early studies on cognitive functioning during seizure activity (Johnson & Davidoff, 1964; Davidoff & Johnson, 1964), I was impressed by how frequently we could abort the EEG seizure activity and thus the clinical seizure by asking the subject to solve a simple arithmetic problem or repeat digits. Rhythmic photic stimulation, in contrast, would synchronize the EEG activity and stimulation at the critical frequencies for a particular patient, usually between 7-20 Hz, would elicit EEG seizure activity.

Kuhlman (1976) also questioned the specificity of the SMR rhythm when he found a reduction of seizure activity in 3 of his 5 patients with no enhancement of SMR. Kuhlman did report significant increases in the amount and frequency of the alpha rhythm and felt that feedback training served to facilitate normal resting synchrony. Kaplan (1975) suggested that perhaps seizure reduction, when it occurred, was due to the lowered "arousal level of the patient." Johnson and Meyer (1974) reported a 46% decrease in monthly seizure rate in an 18-year-old female with a combination of EMG relaxation training and EEG biofeedback training of alpha and theta activity.

Pertinent to this question of SMR specificity is the work by Wyler, Fetz, and Ward (1974) on the effects of operantly conditioning epileptic unit activity on seizure frequencies, and that by Wyler, Fetz, and Ward (1975) on the firing patterns of the epileptic and normal neurons. Based upon these findings, Wyler, Lockard, Ward, and Finch (in press), questioned whether production of synchrony is the mechanism behind seizure reduction. They argue just the converse; i.e., "that the most obvious factor correlative with the diminution of ictal occurrences with operant conditioning was not the production of any specific EEG frequency, but simply the production of desynchronized single unit activity within the epileptogenic cortex." The decreased neuronal synchrony presented was thought to prevent recruitment of surrounding neurons into a critical mass necessary for the propagation of an ictal event.

To test their desynchronization hypotheses, Wyler et al. studied 5 seizure patients, 4 of whom were reinforced for production of EEG frequencies about 14 Hz. Reinforcement was withheld for the occurrence of activity below 10 Hz. The fifth patient was given only EMG feedback though led to believe the feedback was related to her brain activity. Blood samples were taken to monitor drug level, and seizures were observed during preconditioning, conditioning, and pseudo-conditioning periods. Reduced seizure frequency was observed in two patients. The two other patients receiving feedback had more seizures but they were of a milder form. The patient receiving EMG feedback showed no change in seizure frequency. Though recognizing the possibility of more faithful drug use and the ever present placebo problem, Wyler et al. felt their success with use of only faster frequencies supported their desynchronization hypothesis. Though the authors used within-subject statistical analysis to determine significance of change in seizure frequency, these four improved patients join the list of those benefiting from EEG feedback.

While rejecting the idea that the SMR has specific and unique functions for reduction of seizure activity, or that the SMR represents the electrophysiological correlates of cortical inhibition, the authors speculate that similar results may have been obtained by SMR feedback training. "The obvious conclusion to this is that there is not a particular rhythm exclusive to rolandic cortex which if reinforced will provide adjunctive therapy in all types of epileptics" (Wyler et al., in press).

In my review, I did not cover the animal studies concerned with operant conditioning of CNS activity or the intriguing reports of learned control of specific components of the cortical evoked response. These two topics deserve a tutorial of their own. I refer the reader to the studies of Black and his colleagues, to the review papers by Black (1973, 1974), as well as the papers by Fetz (1974), Rosenfeld (1974), Fox (1970), and Fox and Rudell (1970). In animals, the response-reinforcer relationship is easier to establish. Thompson (1976) has recently demonstrated a relationship between unit activity in the hippocampus and the conditioned nictating membrane response in the rabbit.

At the outset, I asked the question "Has learned control of brain wave activity been demonstrated?" Based upon my review and evaluation of the literature, I would say "No" with respect to alpha and theta EEG activity as indices of CNS activity. I did not include the SMR with alpha and theta because I am still uncertain whether there is an SMR, as delineated in the cat, present in humans. There is certainly 12-14 or 12-16 Hz activity in the EEG. But there are also 18-20, 21-24 Hz waves and, as Wyler et al. demonstrated, the occurrence of these faster waves can also be enhanced by feedback. Until there are more data indicating that the SMR is a unique rhythm with a specific relation to sensory motor activity in man, caution should be exercised in extrapolating to man the functional significance of the SMR inferred from the cat. Regardless of the label for the 12-16 Hz, or faster frequencies in the awake human, it appears that control over these frequencies is mediated by arousal level or focused attention.

In sleep research, my major area of interest, it is quite easy for us to speak of the EEG indices of sleep and, on one level, even believe the electrical activity inked on our yards and yards of paper is sleep. During these lapses, probably induced in part by sleep loss, we forget that the cortical brain activity we score into sleep stages is only an epiphenomenon of the complex biological state of sleep. Those who would study cortical brain activity as a correlate of altered states of consciousness and behavior should be careful to avoid the lapses of some sleep researchers.

I would like to end this paper with a quote from Black in his 1972 paper dealing with operant conditioning of CNS activity: "A second set of questions concerns the significance of the research. Does it provide useful information? If so, does it add to the information provided by more familiar procedures for analyzing and controlling the electrical activity of the brain?" (p. 96). There are, of course, other reasons for doing biofeedback of brain activity than to contribute new information on CNS activity, but I will leave the formulation of these reasons as an exercise for the individual researchers. Whether there is operant conditioning of brain electrical activity may, in the long run, be the least interesting question.

REFERENCES

Beatty, J. Similar effects of feedback signals and instructional information on EEG activity. Physiology and Behavior, 1972, 9, 151-154.

Beatty, J. Self regulation as an aid to human effectiveness. Annual Progress Report under Contract N00014-70-C-0350 submitted to San Diego State University Foundation. Los Angeles: University of California, 1973.

Beatty, J., Greenberg, A., Deibler, W. P., & O'Hanlon, J. F. Operant control of occipital theta rhythm affects performance in a radar monitoring task. Science, 1974, 183, 871-873.

Beatty, J., & Kornfeld, C. Relative independence of conditioned EEG changes from cardiac and respiratory activity. Physiology and Behavior, 1972, 9, 733-736.

Beatty, J., & O'Hanlon, J. F. EEG theta regulation and radar monitoring performance of experienced radar operators and air traffic controllers. UCLA Technical Report. Los Angeles: University of California, March 1975.

Black, A. H. The operant conditioning of central nervous system electrical activity. In D. Shapiro, T. X. Barber, L. V. DiCara, J. Kamiya, N. E. Miller, & J. Stoyva (Eds.), Biofeedback & self-control, 1972. Chicago: Aldine, 1973. (Reprinted from G. H. Bower (Ed.), The psychology of learning and motivation: Advances in research and theory. New York: Academic Press, 1972.)

Black, A. H. Operant conditioning of CNS electrical activity and the neural basis of learning. In M. H. Chase (Ed.), Operant control of brain activity. Perspectives in the brain sciences. Volume 2. Los Angeles: Brain Information Service/Brain Research Institute, University of California, 1974.

Brown, B. B. Recognition of aspects of consciousness through association with EEG alpha activity represented by a light signal. Psychophysiology, 1970, 6, 442-452.

Brown, B. B. Awareness of EEG-subjective activity relationships detected within a closed feedback system. Psychophysiology, 1971, 7, 451-464.

Budzynski, T. H., & Stoyva, J. M. An instrument for producing deep muscle relaxation by means of analog information feedback. Journal of Applied Behavior Analysis, 1969, 2, 231-237.

Chase, M. H., & Harper, R. M. Somatomotor and visceromotor correlates of operantly conditioned 12-14 c/sec sensorimotor cortical activity. Electroencephalography & Clinical Neurophysiology, 1971, 31, 85-92.

Davidoff, R. A., & Johnson, L. C. Paroxysmal EEG activity and cognitive-motor performance. Electroencephalography & Clinical Neurophysiology, 1964, 16, 343-354.

DeGood, D. E., Chisholm, R. C., & Valle, R. S. The interrelationships of parietal alpha and frontalis muscle activity during biofeedback training. Psychophysiology, 1976, 13, 164. (Abstract)

Fetz, E. E. Operant control of single unit activity and correlated motor responses. In M. H. Chase (Ed.), Operant control of brain activity. Perspectives in the brain sciences. Volume 2. Los Angeles, Brain Information Service/Brain Research Institute, University of California, 1974

Finley, W. W., Smith, H. A., & Etherton, M. D. Reduction of seizures and normalization of the EEG in a severe epileptic following sensorimotor biofeedback training: Preliminary study. Biological Psychology, 1975, 2, 195-209.

Fox, S. S. Evoked potential, coding, and behavior. In F. O. Schmitt, G. C. Quarton, T. Melnechuk, & G. Adelman (Eds.), The neurosciences: Second study program. New York: Rockefeller University Press, 1970.

Fox, S. S., & Rudell, A. P. Operant controlled neural event: Functional independence in behavioral coding by early and late components of the visual cortical evoked response in cats. Journal of Neurophysiology, 1970, 33, 548-561.

Gannon, L., & Sternbach, R. A. Alpha enhancement as a treatment for pain: A case study. Journal of Behavior Therapy & Experimental Psychiatry, 1971, 2, 209-213.

Green, E. E., Green, A. M., & Walters, E. D. Self-regulation of internal states. In J. Rose (Ed.), Progress of cybernetics: Proceedings of the International Congress of Cybernetics, London, 1969. London: Gordon & Breach, 1970.

Grossberg, J. M. Brain wave feedback experiments and the concept of mental mechanisms. Journal of Behavior Therapy & Experimental Psychiatry, 1972, 3, 245-251.

Honorton, C., Davidson, R., & Bindler, P. Feedback-augmented EEG alpha, shifts in subjective state, and ESP card-guessing performance. Journal of the American Society for Psychical Research, 1971, 65, 308-323.

Hord, D., & Barber, J. Alpha control: Effectiveness of two kinds of feedback. Psychonomic Science, 1971, 25, 151-154.

Hord, D., Lubin, A., Tracy, M. L., Jensma, B. W., & Johnson, L. C. Feedback for high EEG alpha does not maintain performance or mood during sleep loss. Psychophysiology, 1976, 13, 58-61.

Hord, D., Tracy, M. L., Lubin, A., & Johnson, L. C. Effect of self-enhanced EEG alpha on performance and mood after two nights of sleep loss. Psychophysiology, 1975, 12, 585-590.

Johnson, L. C. A psychophysiology for all states. Psychophysiology, 1970, 6, 501-516.

Johnson, L. C., & Davidoff, R. A. Autonomic changes during paroxysmal EEG activity. Electroencephalography & Clinical Neurophysiology, 1964, 17, 25-35.

Johnson, L. C., Hanson, K., & Bickford, R. G. Effect of flurazepam on sleep spindles and K-complexes. Electroencephalography & Clinical Neurophysiology, 1976, 40, 67-77.

Johnson, R. K., & Meyer, R. G. Phased biofeedback approach for epileptic seizure control. Journal of Behavior Therapy & Experimental Psychiatry, 1974, 5, 185-187.

Kamiya, J. Operant control of the EEG alpha rhythm and some of its reported effects on consciousness. In C. T. Tart (Ed.), Altered states of consciousness: A book of readings. New York: Wiley, 1969.

Kamiya, J. Self-regulation as an aid to human effectiveness. Annual Progress Report under Contract N00014-70-C-0350 submitted to San Diego State University Foundation. San Francisco: Langley Porter Neuropsychiatric Institute, June 1972.

Kaplan, B. J. Biofeedback in epileptics: Equivocal relationship of reinforced EEG frequencies to seizure reduction. Epilepsia, 1975, 16, 447-485.

Klug, J. W., & Brown, B. B. Learned control of EEG theta activity. Paper presented at the meeting of the Biofeedback Research Society, Denver, February 1974.

Kuhlman, W. N. Topography and long term feedback training of sensorimotor area EEG activity in normal human subjects. Paper presented at the meeting of the Biofeedback Research Society, Denver, February 1974.

Kuhlman, W. N. EEG feedback training in epileptic patients: Clinical and neurophysiological analysis. Paper presented at the meeting of the Biofeedback Research Society, Colorado Springs, February 27 - March 2, 1976.

Lawrence, G. H., & Johnson, L. C. Biofeedback and performance. In G. E. Schwartz & J. Beatty (Eds.), Biofeedback: Theory and research. New York: Academic Press, 1976, in press.

Lehmann, D., Lang, W., & Debruyne, P. Kontrolliertes EEG-alpha-feedback-training bei gesunden und kopfschmerzpatientinnen. Archiv für Psychiatrie und Nervenkrankheiten, 1976, 221, 331-343.

Lubar, J. F., & Bahler, W. W. Behavioral management of epileptic seizures following EEG biofeedback training of the sensorimotor rhythm. Biofeedback and Self-Regulation, 1976, 1, 77-104.

Lutzenberger, W., Birbaumer, N., & Wildgruber, Ch. An experiment on the feedback of the theta activity of the human EEG. European Journal of Behavioural Analysis & Modification, 1975, 1, 119-126.

Lynch, J. J., & Paskewitz, D. A. On the mechanisms of the feedback control of human brain wave activity. Journal of Nervous & Mental Disease, 1971, 153, 205-217.

Lynch, J. J., Paskewitz, D. A., & Orne, M. T. Some factors in the feedback control of human alpha rhythm. Psychosomatic Medicine, 1974, 36, 399-410.

Maslow, A. Toward a humanistic biology. American Psychologist, 1969, 24, 724-735.

Melzack, R., & Perry, C. Self-regulation of pain: The use of alpha-feedback and hypnotic training for the control of chronic pain. Experimental Neurology, 1975, 46, 452-469.

Mulholland, T. Occipital alpha revisited. Psychological Bulletin, 1972, 3, 176-182.

Mulholland, T. Objective EEG methods for studying covert shifts of visual attention. In N. E. Miller, T. X. Barber, L. V. DiCara, J. Kamiya, D. Shapiro, & J. Stoyva (Eds.), Biofeedback and self-control, 1973. Chicago: Aldine-Atherton, 1974.

Mulholland, T., & Evans, C. R. Oculomotor functions and the alpha activation cycle. Nature, 1966, 211, 1278-1279.

Mulholland, T., & Peper, E. Occipital alpha and accommodative vergence, pursuit tracking, and fast eye movements. Psychophysiology, 1971, 8, 556-575.

Mulholland, T., & Runnals, S. Increased occurrence of EEG alpha during increased attention. Journal of Psychology, 1962, 54, 317-330.

Murphy, G. Psychology in the year 2000. American Psychologist, 1969, 24, 523-530.

Nideffer, R. M. Alpha and the development of human potential. In D. Shapiro, T. X. Barber, L. V. DiCara, J. Kamiya, N. E. Miller, & J. Stoyva (Eds.), Biofeedback and self-control, 1972. Chicago: Aldine, 1973.

Nowlis, D. P., & Kamiya, J. The control of electroencephalographic alpha rhythms through auditory feedback and the associated mental activity. Psychophysiology, 1970, 6, 476-484.

Orne, M., Evans, F., Wilson, S., & Paskewitz, D. The potential effectiveness of autoregulation as a technique to increase performance under stress. Final Summary Report under Contract N00014-70-C-0350 submitted to San Diego State University Foundation. Philadelphia: University of Pennsylvania, 1975.

Paskewitz, D. A., & Orne, M. Visual effects on alpha feedback training. Science, 1973, 181, 360-363.

Plotkin, W. B. On the self-regulation of the occipital alpha rhythm: Control strategies, states of consciousness, and the role of physiological feedback. Journal of Experimental Psychology: General, 1976, 105, 66-99.

Rechtschaffen, A., & Kales, A. (Eds.) A manual of standardized terminology, techniques and scoring system for sleep stages of human subjects. Washington, D.C.: U.S. Government Printing Office, 1968.

Regestein, Q. R., Buckland, G. H., & Pegram, G. V. Effect of daytime alpha rhythm maintenance on subsequent sleep. Psychosomatic Medicine, 1973, 35, 415-418.

Regestein, Q. R., Pegram, G. V., Cook, B., & Bradley, D. Alpha rhythm percentage maintained during 4- and 12-hour feedback periods. Psychosomatic Medicine, 1973, 35, 215-222.

Rosenfeld, J. P. Evoked potential conditioning in neuroscience research. In M. H. Chase (Ed.), Operant control of brain activity. Perspectives in the brain sciences. Volume 2. Los Angeles: Brain Information Service/Brain Research Institute, University of California, 1974.

Roth, S. R., Sterman, M. B., & Clemente, C. D. Comparison of EEG correlates of reinforcement, internal inhibition and sleep. Electroencephalography & Clinical Neurophysiology, 1967, 23, 509-520.

Seifert, A. R., & Lubar, J. F. Reduction of epileptic seizures through EEG biofeedback training. Biological Psychology, 1975, 3, 157-184.

Sheer, D. E. Biofeedback training of the 40-Hz EEG and behavior. In N. Burch & H. L. Altshuler (Eds.), Behavior and brain electrical activity. New York: Plenum, 1975.

Sittenfeld, P., Budzynski, T., & Stoyva, J. Differential shaping of EEG theta rhythms. Biofeedback and Self-Regulation, 1976, 1, 31-46.

Sterman, M. B., Howe, R. C., & MacDonald, L. R. Facilitation of spindle-burst sleep by conditioning of electroencephalographic activity while awake. Science, 1970, 167, 1146-1148.

Sterman, M. B., LoPresti, R. W., & Fairchild, M. D. Electroencephalographic and behavioral studies of monomethylhydrazine toxicity in the cat. Technical Report AMRL-TR-69-3. Wright-Patterson Air Force Base, Ohio: Aerospace Medical Research Laboratories, 1969.

Sterman, M. B., Wyrwicka, W., & Roth, S. Electrophysiological correlates and neural substrates of alimentary behavior in the cat. Annals of the New York Academy of Sciences, 1969, 157, 723-739.

Thompson, R. F. The search for the engram. American Psychologist, 1976, 31, 209-227.

Travis, T. A., Kondo, C. Y., & Knott, J. R. Alpha conditioning: A controlled study. Journal of Nervous & Mental Disease, 1974, 158, 163-173.

Ulett, G. A., & Johnson, L. C. Pattern, stability and correlates of photic-electroencephalographic activation. Journal of Nervous & Mental Disease, 1958, 126, 153-168.

Walsh, D. H. Interactive effects of alpha feedback and instructional set on subjective state. Psychophysiology, 1974, 11, 428-435.

Williams, H. L., Granda, A. M., Jones, R. C., Lubin, A., & Armington, J. C. EEG frequency and finger pulse volume as predictors of reaction time during sleep loss. Electroencephalography & Clinical Neurophysiology, 1962, 14, 64-70.

Wilson, C., Hord, D., Townsend, R., & Johnson, L. Lack of a theta suppression effect on performance during a complex visual sonar vigilance task. Paper presented at the meeting of the Biofeedback Research Society, Colorado Springs, February 27 - March 2, 1976.

Wyler, A. R., Fetz, E. E., & Ward, A. A., Jr. Effects of operantly conditioning epileptic unit activity on seizure frequencies and electrophysiology of neocortical experimental foci. Experimental Neurology, 1974, 44, 113-125.

Wyler, A. R., Fetz, E. E., & Ward, A. A., Jr. Firing patterns of epileptic and normal neurons in the chronic alumina focus in undrugged monkeys during different behavioral states. Brain Research, 1975, 98, 1-20.

Wyler, A. R., Lockard, J. S., Ward, A. A., Jr., & Finch, C. A. Conditioned EEG desynchronization and seizure occurrence in patients. Electroencephalography & Clinical Neurophysiology, in press.

BIOFEEDBACK METHOD FOR LOCATING THE MOST CONTROLLED RESPONSES OF EEG ALPHA TO VISUAL STIMULATION

Thomas B. Mulholland
Psychophysiology Laboratory
Veterans Administration Hospital
Bedford, Massachusetts

This paper demonstrates a new scientific method for testing hypotheses that "links" or a causal chain exists between a stimulus (independent variable) and an EEG response (dependent variable). The uniqueness of the method lies in the way feedback is used to reduce the "noisy" variation of the response compared to its average value.

There are analogies between models of non-living control systems and paradigms of scientific method. The following are analogous open-loop systems:

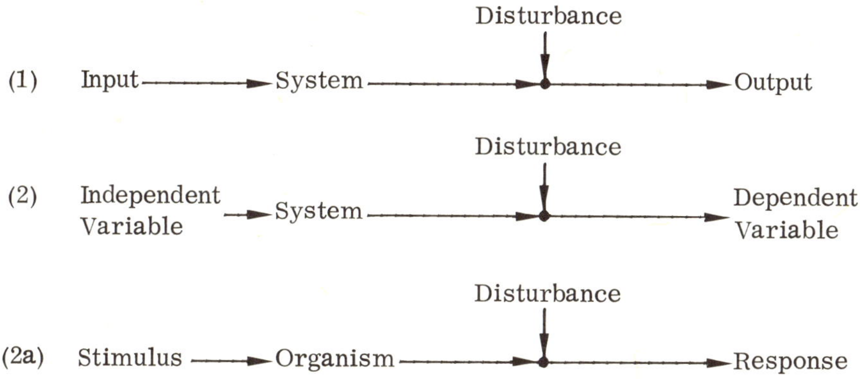

All systems include random, unpredictable variations which are lumped under the term "Disturbance" in the previous diagrams. If there is too much disturbance which is uncorrected, the output or response will be excessively variable relative to its central tendency, e.g., the "signal-to-noise" ratio would be low. If there is too much variance of the dependent variable, then a central tendency relative to unsystematic variance may not be reliably observed because the "signal/noise" ratio of the dependent variable would be too low.

When the signal/noise ratio is too low for a relation between stimulus (independent variable) and EEG response (dependent variable) to be demonstrated with "open loop" methods then feedback could prove the existence of a real correlation between an independent and a dependent variable, a "link" in the feedforward path, by increasing the correlation (Mulholland, 1976).

The control engineer uses feedback from the output to the controller at the input to reduce unsystematic variation, to correct "errors," to increase the signal/noise ratio of the output, i.e., to improve control of the output. Analogously, the scientist can also use feedback to achieve improvement of the signal/noise ratio of the output response so that the response is better controlled.

The following are closed-loop analogies:

(4)

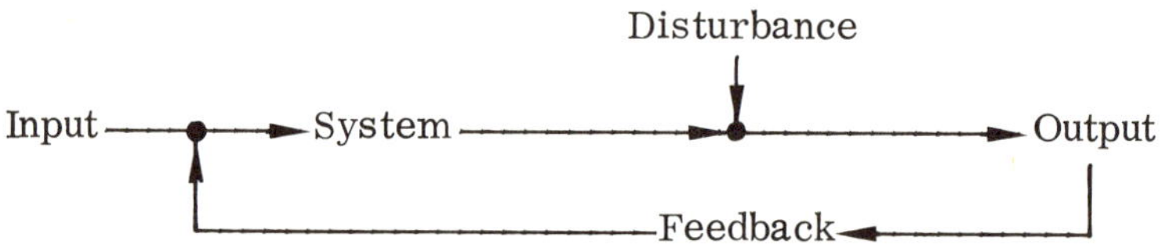

(5)

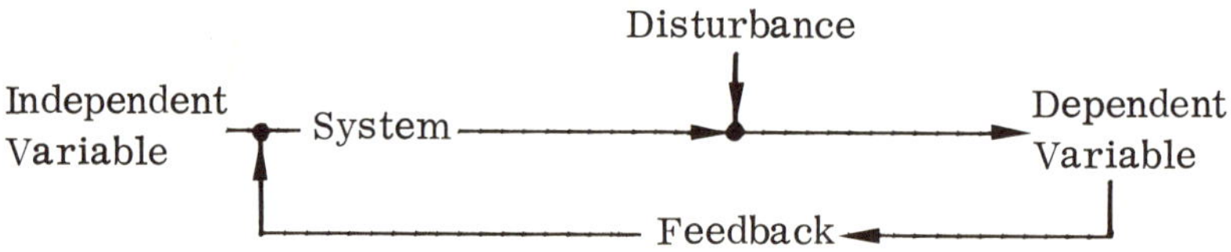

(5a)

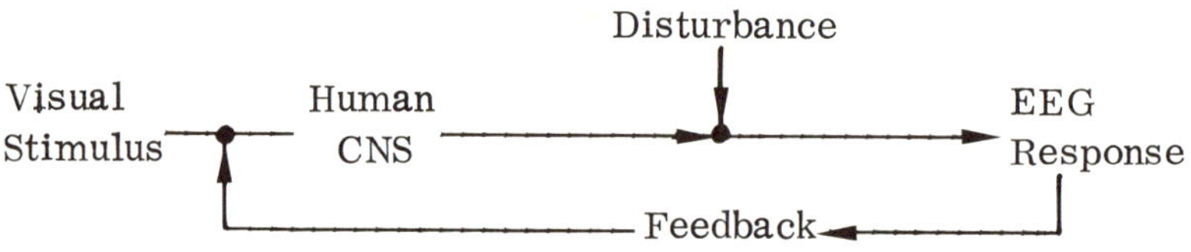

In previous research it has been shown that a feedback between EEG alpha occurrence and non/occurrence and a visual stimulus increases the control of the EEG, as indexed by Mean/Standard Error ($\overline{X}$/SE), compared to conditions of steady stimulation (Mulholland, 1973; McLaughlin & Lewis, 1976) and non/contingent stimulation (Eberlin & Mulholland, 1976). For instance, control, measured by $\overline{X}$/SE, increased bilaterally with a unilateral connection between EEG and a visual stimulus. However, control increased significantly more in that EEG which was externally connected to the stimulus compared to the contralateral EEG which was recorded simultaneously but not externally connected to the stimulus.

By extension of those results, which were obtained by changing the external feedback contingency between EEG and stimulus, it was hypothesized that the control of the EEG could also be modified by changing the internal contingency in the "feedforward" path from stimulus through receptor processes and CNS to the EEG.

METHOD

Subjects

Twelve right-handed subjects from a local community college (ages 18-37) volunteered as subjects for the experiment. All were right-eye dominant and had 20-20 vision or an acuity corrective to at least 20-20. Glasses were worn during the experiment if needed.

None of the students was acquainted with experimental details, especially that one's EEG actually controlled the stimulus presentations. Although no monetary compensation was offered, all subjects were extremely cooperative and highly motivated. Each person exhibited alpha rhythms with eyes closed in the dark and showed the classical alpha "block" when looking at a visual stimulus.

Apparatus

EEGs were recorded using standard polygraphic techniques. Feedback was produced by connecting an EEG to a visual stimulus so that when alpha occurred in that EEG the stimulus was presented; when no-alpha occured, the stimulus was not presented. Details of the EEG apparatus and the feedback system have been described elsewhere (Boudrot, 1973).

Procedure

The procedure was the same for each subject except for the sequence of conditions during the session. Five EEG electrodes were attached to the scalp spaced equidistantly along a line from O_1-P_3 - C_3 and from O_2-P_4 - C_4. For some subjects it was possible to use the "10-20" system to place electrodes at standard locations O, P and C and an electrode between O and P and between P and C. For other subjects, the close spacing of electrodes was associated with insufficient amplitude. For these subjects, O_1 and O_2 were located and the rest of the electrodes placed 4 cm apart along a line connecting O, P, and C. Consequently, the electrodes were placed at O, and near P, near C and near a location between O and P and between P and C. From these, four bipolar recordings were made from adjacent locations. Whatever EEG was connected into the feedback system, the contralateral EEG was recorded too, though it was not connected to feedback (non-contingent). Thus, in each trial a contingent EEG and a contralateral non-contingent EEG were recorded. The location of the contingent and non-contingent bipolar EEGs was designated by letters I, II, III, and IV from posterior to central on each side. The temporal sequence of the location of the contingent EEGs in the experimental session was given by a Latin Square design of the four bipolar bilateral recordings.

Each experimental session was in three parts: 1) an initial calibration, 2) recording under eyes-closed and eyes-open baseline conditions, and 3) recording during visual stimulation. The baselines were recorded from whichever EEG location (I, II, III, or IV) which was to be the first stimulation condition for that subject. Every location was tested for each baseline, eyes closed and eyes open.

For each trial, the alpha detectors were calibrated so that maximum alpha with eyes closed was full scale value on the alpha metering circuits. Alpha threshold was set at 25% of full scale. The aim of these calibrations was to "normalize" alpha detection to reduce bilateral differences and differences among the EEG locations due to alpha amplitude.

The stimulus conditions were each in two parts: 1) prehabituation and bilateral alpha amplitude matching and 2) a test condition. The purpose of prehabituation was to reduce the initial response to the stimulus so that the test measurements would be a sample of habituated responses to feedback stimulation. Final amplitude matching was also done during the prehabituation run in some trials. Sometimes a prehabituation condition was repeated until alpha amplitude matching was completed. Also, test conditions were repeated if artifacts or errors of procedure occurred which obviated a proper test condition.

The stimulus was a circular spot of light projected onto a screen 10 feet in front of the viewer. The stimulus was presented about 60 times in each trial. The last 30 responses from each trial were analyzed. This was done to exclude the contribution of the initial response (prehabituation part of trial) to the stimulus from the estimate of EEG control during feedback.

The data analyzed were the time durations (Δt) of the alpha detector ON (alpha) and OFF (no alpha) measured to the nearest 0.1 sec. The series of 30 alpha and 30 no alpha durations during each feedback trial were fitted with a line which described a trend in the case that a trend existed. This was done to enhance the estimate of random variability of alpha and no alpha durations. The procedure has been described before (Goodman, 1973). The following best-fit functions were fitted to alpha and no alpha durations in each trial.

1. $\Delta ta = (AN + B) \pm SE$

2. $\Delta tna = (C/N + D) \pm SE$

The Mean of the functions ($\overline{X}$), the Standard Error (SE) and the ratio of the Mean of the function to the Standard Error ($\overline{X}$/SE) were computed for each trial. These statistics were analyzed with analysis of variance (ANOVA) for the feedback trials and for the baseline conditions. Variance was partitioned among subjects, sequences of conditions, EEG locations, feedback contingency, ordinal place in the sequence, Latin Square "cells," and their interactions. The residual variance was a single estimate obtained by subtracting partioned variance from the total.

RESULTS

Baseline Conditions

Bilateral differences. The EEG was recorded bilaterally during Eyes Closed and Eyes Open conditions. No significant bilateral differences were found between the $\overline{X}$ durations, SE of the durations and the ratio $\overline{X}$/SE for alpha and no-alpha. This result also shows that alpha amplitude matching to reduce the differences between right and left sides was successful. See Table 1.

Differences among EEG Locations. No significant differences among EEG locations during the baseline conditions were obtained for $\overline{X}$, SE, or

Table 1

Average Mean, Standard Error (SE) and $\overline{X}$/SE (Computed in Each Trial) for Alpha (a) and No-Alpha (na)

		Feedback EEG Locations								Baselines				
		I		II		III		IV			E.O.		E.C.	
Statistic	Contingency	a	na	a	na	a	na	a	na		a	na	a	na
MEAN	LC	.36	2.35	.36	2.85	.36	3.29	.32	2.88	L	.80	4.98	.63	2.31
	RNC	.37	2.84	.36	2.77	.35	2.88	.34	2.90	R	.44	3.68	.45	1.78
SE	LC	.19	1.95	.19	2.25	.20	3.11	.21	2.84	L	1.04	4.73	.54	2.66
	RNC	.22	2.69	.20	2.60	.20	2.48	.22	2.79	R	.39	4.21	.37	2.40
$\overline{X}$/SE	LC	2.13	1.58	2.25	1.55	2.09	1.25	1.59	1.18	L	1.33	0.94	1.43	0.97
	RNC	1.93	1.26	1.88	1.32	1.80	1.23	1.67	1.11	R	1.23	1.01	1.43	0.98

$\overline{X}/SE$. This shows that the normalization of alpha amplitude reduced differences among locations.

Eyes Closed vs. Eyes Open. No-alpha durations were significantly longer in the Eyes Open condition ($\overline{X} = 4.33$ sec) compared to Eyes Closed ($\overline{X} = 2.04$ sec).

Feedback Conditions

Control of the EEG by Feedback ($\overline{X}/SE$). The control of alpha and no alpha durations, as measured by $\overline{X}/SE$, was greater in all feedback conditions compared to baseline conditions. Control of alpha durations was greater than control of no-alpha durations. These results confirmed those reported previously (Mulholland, 1973; McLaughlin & Lewis, 1976; Eberlin & Mulholland, 1976).

Contingency. Control. The average ratio $\overline{X}/SE$ was greater for contingent EEGs compared to the non-contingent EEG. Alpha $F_{1,53} = 8.2$; $MS_e = 0.159$. No Alpha $F_{1,53} = 4.2$; $MS_e = 0.140$. See Table 1 and Figure 1.

Location of EEG. Control. The ratio $\overline{X}/SE$ was least in the parieto-central location. The largest ratio was anterior to O_1 and O_2 at II. Alpha duration $F_{3,53} = 5.6$; $MS_e = 0.159$. For no-alpha $F_{3,53} = 3.31$; $MS_e = 0.140$. See Table 1 and Figure 1.

To estimate the consistency of the differences among EEG locations in the sample of 12 subjects, non-parametric tests were applied. For each subject the values of $\overline{X}/SE$ in the test conditions were ranked over the EEG locations, the lowest receiving a rank of 4, the highest a rank of 1. The ranks at each location were summed and the statistic χ^2_r of ranks was calculated (Friedman, 1937). The results are presented in Table 2. Differences among EEG locations are significant for the contingent EEGs but not for the non-contingent EEGs.

Mean duration. No significant differences among EEG locations were found.

Standard error. No significant differences among EEG locations were found.

Interaction of contingency and location for $\overline{X}/SE$. The interaction of contingency by location was not statistically significant for any of the

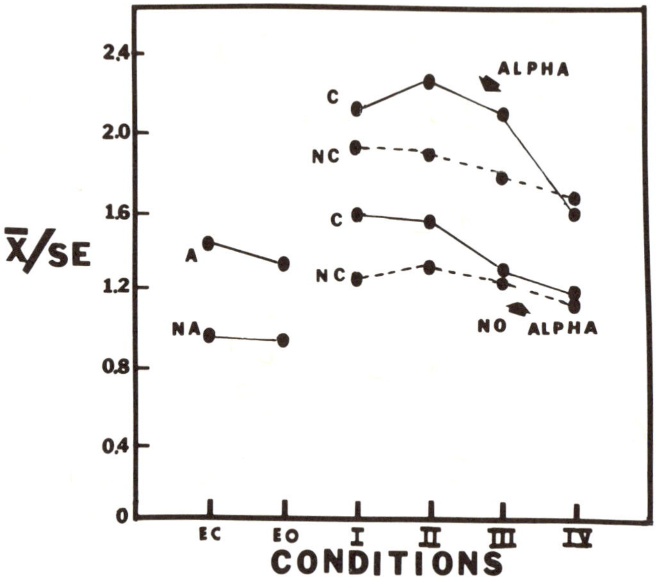

Figure 1. Control ($\bar{X}$/SE) of alpha and no-alpha durations in baseline conditions (eyes closed and eyes open) and during feedback conditions at each of four EEG locations (I, II, III, IV) and for the contingent (C) and non-contingent (NC) EEG.

Table 2

Non-Parametric Analysis of Ranks to Test for Differences among EEG Locations (χ_r^2 of Ranks)

	Contingent EEG	Non-Contingent EEG
Alpha	15.4; $p < .001$	4.9; $p < 0.10$
No-Alpha	8.9; $p < .05$	2.4; $p < 0.50$

ANOVA. The differences between contingent and non-contingent EEG were numerically smaller at location IV than the other locations. See Figure 1. The non-parametric analysis showed significant differences among locations for the contingent EEG only. See Table 2.

Habituation across experimental trials. In each trial a pre-test habituation condition was run to eliminate the initial response to the stimulus from the test trial. The measures analyzed are from habituated responses. Consequently there was relatively little change from trial-to-trial during the experiment. Mean durations showed significant changes over trials. For alpha, $F_{3,53} = 5.5$, $MS_e = 0.006$. No-alpha $F_{3,53} = 3.40$, $MS_e = 1.52$. Standard error also showed significant changes over trials. No-alpha $F_{3,53} = 3.71$, $MS_e = 1.62$. The mean no-alpha durations decreased from the beginning to the end of the experimental session and SE for no-alpha decreased also.

Individual differences. The ANOVA showed that differences among subjects were statistically significant for all measures.

DISCUSSION

The main results were: 1) visual feedback from the EEG improved control of the EEG at all locations compared to baselines; 2) control was improved most in posterior EEGs and least in the parieto-central EEG; 3) control was improved most for an EEG somewhat anterior to the posterior occipital location, an occipito-parietal EEG; 4) control was improved most for EEGs most reliably contingent with the visual stimulus; EEGs externally connected to the stimulus (contingent) were more controlled than were contralateral EEGs which were simultaneously recorded but not externally connected to the stimulus (non-contingent); 5) the difference between contingent and non-contingent EEGs was greatest in posterior EEGs and practically nil in the parieto-central EEG; 6) there were small differences among EEG locations which were non-contingent; differences among locations were larger and significant for contingent EEGs; 7) control was greater for alpha durations compared to no alpha durations; 8) measures of central tendency were not different for different locations or different contingencies.

Control

The measure of feedback control is the ratio of the mean duration to the standard error of a best-fit function computed for a series of 30 alpha and of 30 no-alpha durations. The "signal" can be defined as the mean duration: The aim of control is to hold all durations as near to the mean as possible. Deviations from the mean are "errors" and feedback is used to correct errors. Though not producing signal/noise ratios comparable to non-living feedback control, there is an improvement of control with feedback stimulation at all locations compared to baseline conditions. These general results confirm those reported previously (Mulholland, 1973; McLaughlin, 1976; Eberlin & Mulholland, 1976). Yet, even with feedback the durations of alpha and no-alpha are not perfectly controlled.

Location of the EEG

Control of the EEG by feedback is greatest in posterior occipital-parietal recordings, less in parieto-central recordings. The EEGs from cortical regions which are less controlled by feedback are less reliably responsive to the stimulus. Such an inference requires an explanation of why one cortical region would be less reliably responsive to a visual stimulus than another cortical region.

The cortical regions sampled at the eight EEG locations differ in terms of the inputs they receive from receptor-afferent processes, subcortical "arousal" processes (which are facilitory and inhibitory) and in terms of their role in cortical and subcortical processes which eventuate in the adjustment of the visual receptor to optimize vision. In terms of the hypothesis tested here, all of the cortical regions sampled are responsive to feedback because the ratio $\overline{X}/SE$ increases at each location relative to baseline. The cortical regions differ in the reliability of their response to visual stimulation and the degree of control is different.

The signal/noise ratio of the EEG output is determined by the average duration of the signal and the unpredictable variability of durations. ANOVA revealed no evidence for a difference among locations for the Mean durations. Differences were found for SE and for $\overline{X}/SE$. It follows that the level of unpredictable variation of the EEG response to the visual stimulus is greatest at the parieto-central location. The transfer of information around the loop from eye - CNS - cortical processes - EEG - visual stimulus - eye is less reliable for the parieto-central EEG compared to the others. Since the EEGs are associated with different cortical processes and these with different subcortical influences, the EEG differences reflect the greater relevance of the cortical processes underlying the posterior EEG especially at location II, to the visual stimulus and the lesser relevance of cortical processes underlying the EEG at location IV.

Summarizing, the response of the parieto-central EEG to a simple spot of light is least salient because it is part of an internal path which includes cortical processes which are less relevant to this stimulus than the other, more posterior, locations. This is tantamount to locating the EEG response to stimulation in terms of a salient cortical response which was sampled by the EEG at location II.

Contingency

The detection of the salient EEG response is facilitated by feedback. A comparison of contingent and non-contingent EEGs at each location shows that the $\overline{X}$/SE is less at all locations for the non-contingent EEGs confirming previous results (Eberlin & Mulholland, 1976). The differences among EEG locations is less for the non-contingent EEGs, and even less for baseline EEGs.

This means that intermittent stimulation which is not feedback would not be as efficient in the detection of differences among EEG locations as is feedback contingent stimulation. On the practical level this translates into a larger sample of responses to achieve comparable levels of confidence. With non-contingent stimulation the signal/noise ratio is so low that it is not a sensitive detector of differences.

Analogously, when the EEG is not reliably responsive because of its less-than-optimum location, its signal/noise ratio may be so low that even contingent feedback does not increase the $\overline{X}$/SE anymore than non-contingent stimulation does. This is perhaps the reason why contingent and non-contingent EEGs at location IV have the same $\overline{X}$/SE.

The precision of this method for localizing EEG responses to visual stimulation is not known. The evidence from this experiment indicates that a difference in location of less than 6 cm is associated with different $\overline{X}$/SEs. The gross relation between EEG and cortical process limits the precision of the method. Such a limitation does not hold for macro-electrodes on the cortex (ECoG) and even less so for micro-electrodes inserted into brain cells. These latter applications of feedback method may be much more fruitful because of the improved reliability of response to a stimulus and inherently better discrimination among different locations. In short, where the feedforward path is more reliable, feedback can improve the signal/noise ratio more than for a much less reliable feedforward path. Feedback method could be a useful tool in cortical electrophysiology and a method for testing hypotheses about the existence of a feedforward path (Mulholland, 1976).

REFERENCES

Boudrot, R. An alpha detection and feedback control system. Psychophysiology, 1972, 9, 461-466.

Eberlin, P., & Mulholland, T. Bilateral differences in parietal-occipital EEG induced by contingent visual feedback. Psychophysiology, 1976, 13, 212-218.

Friedman, M. The use of ranks to avoid the assumption of normality implicit in the analysis of variance. Journal of the American Statistical Association, 1937, 32, 675-701.

McLaughlin, T., & Lewis, C. Baseline and EEG correlates of interview behavior. Psychophysiology, 1976, 13, 302-306.

Mulholland, T. Objective EEG methods for studying covert shifts of visual attention. In F. J. McGuigan & R. A. Schoonover (Eds.), Psychophysiology of thinking. New York: Academic Press, 1973.

Mulholland, T. Biofeedback as scientific method. In G. E. Schwartz & J. Beatty (Eds.), Biofeedback: Theory and research. San Francisco: Academic Press, 1976, in press.

NOTES

The experiment reported here has been repeated with the right EEG contingent with the feedback stimulus. The results confirm the reported experiment: the posterior location II was most controlled; contingent (right) EEGs were more controlled than non-contingent (left) EEGs; differences of control among locations were statistically significant for contingent EEGs but not for non-contingent EEGs.

The assistance of Peter Eberlin, David Goodman, Robert Boudrot and Anne Davidson was very much appreciated.

ALPHA, BIOFEEDBACK AND AROUSAL/ACTIVATION

Martin Orne and Stuart Wilson
Institute of Pennsylvania Hospital
and
University of Pennsylvania

Dr. Johnson has reviewed several issues in the operant control of EEG alpha rhythm as well as the interactions among cortical electrical activity, general physiological reactivity and subjective experience. Our presentation seeks to expand and clarify somewhat the nature of the interaction between alpha and high levels of arousal/activation associated with fear.

As many others, we were encouraged by the early reports that positive subjective experience was linked to alpha production. Therefore, Orne & Paskewitz began a collaboration to explore the apparent potential of alpha feedback as a means for the individual to gain direct control over neurophysiological arousal and therefore subjective tension-anxiety. Initially we replicated the early findings both to confirm them and to gain experience with the general phenomenon of brain wave feedback.

As Dr. Johnson reported earlier we found that, although subjects did show increasing alpha density with training, the effects seemed to be a function of the presence of ambient light or the use of lights to signal the presence and absence of alpha. Subjects in total darkness began with a spontaneously high level of alpha density which was immediately depressed by visual stimuli such as the feedback signals. Subjects then increased their alpha production, typically by learning to observe the feedback light's change in color in a passive manner by not focusing their eyes on the light.

Further, experimentation carried out by using tones as the feedback signals and varying the presence or absence of ambient light, as reported by Paskewitz and Orne in 1973, clearly documented that visuomotor activity was of primary importance in the results of the usual alpha feedback training experiment. It seemed that the apparent augmentation of alpha density occurred only when alpha had previously been depressed, primarily by visuomotor activity, from the individual's optimum nondrowsy resting baseline obtained in total darkness. Thus, learning to increase alpha from these depressed levels seemed to involve the individual's gradually learning to ignore the stimulus that had been responsible for alpha suppression in the first place. What is more, subjects trained in the dark did not significantly increase their alpha density over that found in an optimal baseline in total darkness, even after six days of alpha increment training.

Thus, we had begun to recognize that the original assumptions about the control of alpha density by a subject's conscious intent, effort or learning were valid only in conditions which somehow had depressed an individual's moderate to high baseline alpha density. Therefore, we reconceptualized the effects of alpha feedback training as an experience which taught the subject to augment alpha under circumstances which would ordinarily reduce the amount of alpha in the EEG (Paskewitz, Lynch, Orne, & Costello, 1970). The visuomotor system seemed to be the overriding factor determining alpha levels in those circumstances in which the person could see visual patterns (or even in a totally dark room attempt to see them) a point which among those interested in feedback training, only Mulholland (1968, 1972) and Peper (Peper & Mulholland, 1970) had emphasized.

With the assumption that different mechanisms might be involved in blocking alpha it seemed to follow that different skills might be necessary to learn to augment alpha activity. We assumed that what was learned during alpha feedback training would depend on the nature of the primary stimulus which was depressing alpha density. Because of the disproportionate significance of visual effects for alpha density, if the individual were trained in the presence of light, he would first need to learn to disregard visual stimuli before the alpha blocking effect due to other factors would be affected. In order to focus on other potential blockers, in particular arousal/activation, we chose to avoid the presence of ambient light in subsequent studies of the function.

In a complex experiment on alpha and activation (Orne & Paskewitz, 1974) subjects came initially to the laboratory to participate in a simple alpha feedback study. Every effort was made to produce a comfortable and relaxing environment so that the initial baselines and feedback alpha densities were obtained from a minimally aroused subject little affected by fear, anxiety or an active visual system. At the conclusion of this initial session subjects with greater than 25% resting eyes closed alpha density in the dark were invited to return for a second session that would involve electric shock which would "not cause tissue damage but would range from mildly uncomfortable to quite painful."

Of the 22 eligible subjects ten were persuaded to continue. During the second session the same sensory electrodes for EEG, electrooculogram, electrodermal activity and heart rate were attached; finally, the experimenter ostentatiously attached two large silver electrodes and a ground over the right calf and explained that these were for the shock stimuli. Subjects were purposefully not informed when the shocks would be given since it was felt that this ambiguity would maximize anxiety. The lights were turned off and the second day's baselines obtained.

Four five-minute feedback trials preceded any further instructions regarding shock. Only after these were over were the shock instructions given. These explained that during the next part of the experiment he would from time to time be in jeopardy of receiving electric shocks ranging from barely perceptible to extremely painful. These jeopardy periods would be signaled by a third tone different from the feedback tones. This tone would be on only when he wasn't producing alpha. Since these jeopardy periods would be the only time that he would be shocked, he could, simply by turning on alpha, turn off the jeopardy tone and prevent himself from being shocked. Thus, it was explained that the more alpha he could produce, the less the likelihood of being shocked.

Subsequent to these shock instructions five five-minute feedback trials, each divided into ten half-minute segments, were given. Five of these segments were in fact jeopardy segments during which the third tone was always present simultaneously with the no-alpha tone. During the other five segments only the usual alpha, no-alpha tones were present. This same procedure was repeated on a third visit to the laboratory.

The findings were as puzzling as they were complex. First, one would expect that a subject anticipating an experiment which includes painful shock would be anxious and have lower alpha density than that on the first day. However, the anticipated drop in initial alpha baselines did not appear; instead, there was a non-significant rise from the first day mean of 35.2 seconds per minute. We expected that the initial feedback trials would permit the subject to augment reduced baseline levels; however, since alpha densities were not lower it was hardly surprising, therefore, that we also failed to observe a significant increment in alpha

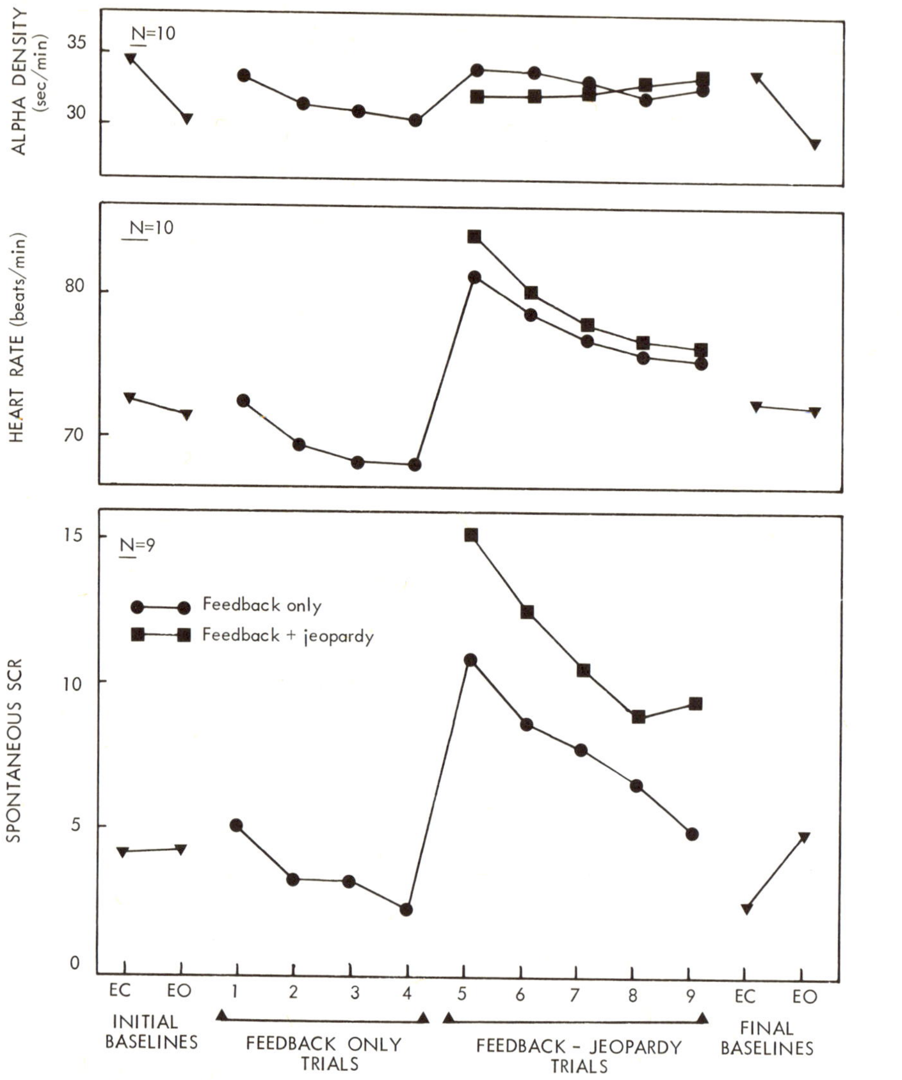

Figure 1. Alpha density, heart rate and skin conductance responses as a function of experimental conditions in Experiment 1. Shock instructions were given between Trials 4 and 5.

density during the first four feedback trials. Finally, we had expected that following the shock instructions the increased apprehension would again decrease alpha. Most striking, however, was the total absence of alpha blocking following the shock instructions. Further, even during the jeopardy periods themselves, there was only a very small and transient drop in alpha density, which disappeared by the third feedback trial.

In interpreting these data, the first possibility we considered was whether the shock manipulations were unsuccessful in making the subjects anxious and/or aroused. However, post-experimental inquiries as well as physiological data, notably heart rate and electrodermal response, clearly substantiated that subjects were indeed aroused and anxious as shown in Figure 1.

For example, the heart rate baseline during the first shock session was clearly and significantly higher than that during the first day. Further, it dropped during the first four feedback periods in the precise manner we had anticipated alpha density would rise. Again when shock instructions were given an instantaneous and dramatic increase in heart rate took place, well over ten beats per minute. On both days heart rate was significantly higher during jeopardy periods than during nonjeopardy periods. The electrodermal activity showed a closely analogous pattern of change.

Thus it appeared that neither the apprehension about the shock session, which might have been reflected in the second session baseline, nor the more intense concern following the shock instructions, nor even the acute fear of being shocked, resulted in the anticipated sharp drop in alpha density. The expected relationship between high levels of activation and reduced alpha density did not materialize.

Although this study appears to have a number of ramifications, care must be taken in generalizing from it in view of the lack of additional relevant controls that in retrospect would have been helpful in understanding the results and the special nature of the volunteer sample. In particular, more data are needed comparing the effect of specific stimuli and tasks on subjects' alpha density in the presence as well as the absence of feedback. However, the present data do clearly indicate the lack of a necessary relationship between alpha density and the subject's level of arousal, fear, anxiety or apprehension. Clearly, this finding challenges the widely accepted view concerning the inverted U-shaped relationship between level of arousal and alpha density. It is this view which in large part suggested that high alpha density would index a particular state of the organism characterized by relaxation without drowsiness. It is perhaps now worth examining more carefully the data upon which this theory is based.

The empirical observations which led to the inverted U hypothesis on the relationship between alpha density and arousal included: First, as an individual becomes drowsy and approaches stage one sleep alpha density is dramatically reduced and tends to approach zero; second, that if an individual is confronted with a stimulus evoking sudden arousal such as a loud noise, a period of alpha blocking is observed; third, some studies have demonstrated a moderate relationship between anxiety levels and alpha baselines. What is different about the conditions in the experiment just reported that failed to demonstrate a drop in alpha density associated with a highly arousing stimulus--the threat of shock--when compared with circumstances in which previous observations were made?

One major difference between our studies and others reported in the literature is that we used dark adapted individuals in a situation totally devoid of light. We emphasize the importance of dark adaptation since it is not the presence of light but rather the attempt to see which is responsible for alpha blocking.[1] Second, as one considers the nature of the stimuli which have been used to block alpha, it can be seen that they are all of a nature to also cause an orienting response which has a strong visual component. Certainly in dim light and, with subjects not dark adapted, even in total darkness this visual component of the orienting response might well serve to mediate the alpha blocking which has in the past been ascribed to the effect of arousal/activation. However, early studies did not systematically and purposefully vary the level of arousal without using stimuli that are prone to produce a concurrent visual orienting response.

Third, one must consider the relationship of alpha density to low arousal. These data appear considerably more satisfactory. Thus, all subjects show a dramatic drop in alpha density with approaching sleep. For example, Paskewitz and Orne (1973) have demonstrated a remarkably high association between periods of unusually low alpha density within a subject's record and the presence of independently assessed slow rolling eye movements--well known precursors of sleep.

It is tempting, therefore, to accept these data as documenting the relationship between low arousal and the absence of alpha. Here too, however, caution is needed. The drop in alpha density may not be a function of low arousal at all but rather it may be an incidental manifestation of the active processes associated with sleep.

For example, if one examines night time sleep records, there are periods when individuals show a great deal of arousal. Notably, REM is associated not only with the rapid eye movements which give the sleep state its name but also with penile erection and marked variation in heart rate, suggesting a heightened level of arousal. Nonetheless, during these periods there is usually no alpha or only a very small increase in alpha.

This absence of any change is especially striking when one considers the amount of mentation associated with dreaming and the level of autonomic arousal as indexed by penile erection and cardiovascular changes.

A similar paradox is associated with the periods of GSR storms during stage four sleep first described by Johnson's group. While this fascinating phenomenon does not seem to be accompanied by changes in other physiological parameters such as heart rate and respiration the presence of spontaneous GSR tends to be one of the better indices of arousal and has been closely linked to the level of activation of the reticular formation. Again, we are unaware of any evidence suggesting that alpha density normally increases during such periods.

Thus, during what may be considered the extremes of activation within sleep, both resembling, as it were, major fragments of waking physiological arousal, no considerable emergence of increased alpha density has been documented. Rather, we see an apparent clear separation of processes signaling increased neurophysiological arousal from cortical alpha production. It seems to follow that, were the progressive drop in alpha density seen as an individual falls asleep primarily the result of the associated low level of activation, one ought to find differences in alpha density during sleep itself as the widely variable levels of activation manifest themselves. The absence of such changes strongly suggests that the decrease in alpha density seen as an individual approaches sleep reflects an active inhibition of alpha by the mechanisms associated with sleep rather than a low level of arousal per se.

In considering the basic logic underlying the use of alpha feedback for the control of arousal one final point which has been important in justifying alpha feedback is Kamiya's casual observation that subjects could learn to identify the presence or absence of alpha in their EEG. This clearly suggested that, potentially at least, some form of cortical representation of alpha existed. While perhaps not directly related to arousal, this point was a crucial link in previous arguments justifying the use of alpha feedback training to bring about a special state of consciousness.

In attempting to replicate this study it became clear to us that temporal cues could easily serve to mediate the apparent ability of the individual to recognize the presence or absence of alpha. Thus, if an individual has high alpha density and the experimenter intends to have the next trial be during a nonalpha event, the inter-trial interval will tend to be considerably longer than if he were looking for an alpha event. It follows that subtle temporal cues, which in casual experimentation might well escape the notice of both experimenter and subject, could have accounted for

Kamiya's findings.

Controlling for temporal cues by using a modified signal detection procedure, we were unable to observe any increase in the subject's skill in identifying the presence or absence of alpha.[2] Pavloski, Cott, and Black (1975) and Legewie (1975) have reported similar difficulties. While it is of course possible that it is necessary to train individuals with longer windows than those which were used in these studies, it would seem essential that more carefully controlled positive observations be obtained before it is justified to assume that the simple presence of alpha has cortical representation.

To summarize our observations thus far: One, subjects do not appear to learn to increase their alpha density above their optimal resting baseline through feedback; two, visuomotor activity is of prime importance in depressing optimal alpha density and in subsequently learning to enhance alpha; three, high levels of alpha density can be present even during the very high arousal and subjective fear; further, the absence of alpha during sleep seems equally unrelated to arousal levels; and four, subjects may not be able to discriminate directly between alpha and non-alpha waking states. In sum, the views that alpha production is closely related to subjective experience, has specific cortical representation and alone reflects the level of arousal cannot be justified with presently available data.

Given these observations it would seem that the entire basis justifying the potential benefits of alpha feedback training is lacking and accordingly one might well choose to dismiss this entire line of inquiry. However, throughout our efforts to understand alpha feedback we have become increasingly aware of the need to also understand the underlying processes and have been forced to reevaluate issues that had been assumed to be resolved by previous work in order to reconcile the conflicting reports in the literature. Of the several issues that arise, the single most important factor, which has been essentially ignored in the reported work to date, relates to systematic individual differences in the dynamics of the alpha response. Such differences will be discussed more extensively in a paper in progress by Wilson, Orne, and Paskewitz, but it is possible to explore a few of them here.

As you will recall in regard to the shock study I discussed earlier, no group mean alpha density changes were found either in the baselines or during the anticipation of being shocked nor even when electric shock was imminent. However, striking individual differences are masked when the data are grouped in means. For example, consider the Day 2 baselines. Of the ten subjects there are two who during the initial baseline on Day 2 decreased alpha by 16 seconds per minute below Day 1 levels while two others increased alpha by 16 seconds per minute. Again after shock instructions, one subject shows an alpha density decrease of 70% while two subjects show increases of 40% over that day's baseline levels.

These findings that some subjects increase, others decrease, while still others show no change in response to the identical stimulus are consistent across Day 2 and 3 and appear to represent different patterns typical of the individual. In this study the alpha response to arousal was investigated in the context of experimentally induced fear and arousal. Analogous observations have been reported by Lemere (1936), Simonova (1968) and Birbaumer (1970) in nonfeedback settings. In each of these instances different kinds of alpha density responses to intense arousal were noted. It seemed important to establish whether these differences in alpha dynamics require intense arousal or represent a more general pattern of response to some other stimuli which alter alpha density.

An earlier study by Paskewitz and Orne had explored the differences between counting backward by one and counting backward by seven across days in a feedback setting. The interpretation of the seemingly consistent drop in alpha density associated with counting backward by seven--but not with counting backward by one--was confounded by the combination of the two tasks, counting backward by seven and attempting to augment alpha. In order to explore the nature of potential differences in basic alpha density dynamics, an experiment was performed without feedback on changes in alpha density during cognitive task performance.[3] Eleven subjects, while in total darkness, on three different days performed serial subtractions by several different numbers as well as a descending subtraction task. For the latter the person began by subtracting nine from a three digit number, then eight from the remainder, then seven from that remainder and so on until reaching two, when he began again with nine, eight, seven, etc., until told to stop. We have found performance of this task to be extremely demanding for our subjects, as opposed to counting backwards by one, which presents no difficulty.

Two different major patterns of alpha response to such a task emerge when one examines the data for individual differences in subjects well adapted to the laboratory and performing the task on the second day. For example, during subtraction by one, one group increases alpha and another group decreases alpha relative to their own baseline. In order to evaluate the consistency of such response styles we examined the individual's response during a much more difficult descending subtraction task. Thus subjects were divided on the basis of whether they increased or decreased alpha density while counting backward by one in order to see if this split also differentiated them when they performed the very difficult descending subtraction task. Remarkable similarities are seen. Subjects who block alpha while counting backward by one also do so during descending subtraction. What is more, those who increase their alpha density while performing the simple task increase it during the difficult one as well. This phenomenon can be seen clearly in Figure 2.

This figure shows the mean percent left hemisphere alpha density in two groups, four alpha blockers (dotted lines) and seven alpha augmenters (solid lines), defined by alpha changes, either decrease or increase relative to baseline, during subtraction by one on Day 2. As you can see these two groups have comparable resting alpha density both during the initial baseline and the rests preceding the tasks. Since the two groups were defined by the direction of their alpha response during subtraction by one it is hardly surprising that the difference in alpha density between them is significant during this task.

These individual differences in reaction are not related to the individual's success or speed in counting backward but one perhaps could attribute the result to the general ease with which everyone can perform the task. One might then expect that everyone would block alpha during the difficult descending subtraction task. However, on the second day this task evokes mean alpha changes during trial one very similar to those during subtraction by ones ($t = 1.82$, $p = .05$). Indeed, the split becomes even more significant on the second trial ($t = 3.09$, $p < .01$).

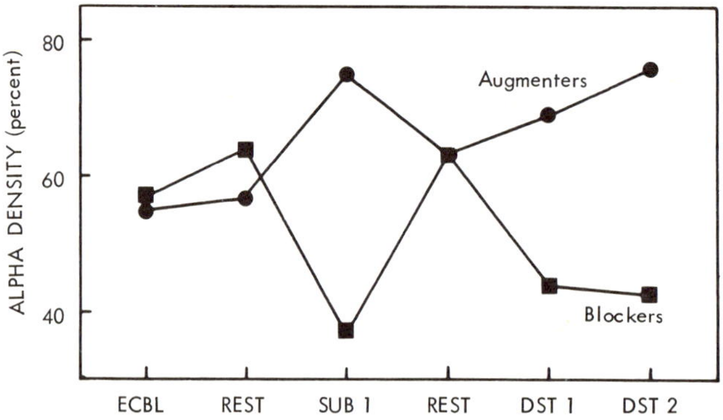

Figure 2. Mean percent left hemisphere alpha density for four alpha blockers (■) and seven alpha augmenters (●) in Experiment 2.

The stability of the direction of change depends partially on the individual's characteristic amount of phasic blocking. Those showing little change in alpha during performance of a task tend to oscillate between increasing and decreasing alpha during tasks in an apparently random fashion. However, the consistency of an individual's alpha augmenting or blocking response is further demonstrated by the continued significant differences between these two groups, separated by alpha changes with subtraction by one on Day 2, during Day 3 descending subtraction. The t for the differences between the two groups on Day 3 descending subtraction trial one is 3.02 and on trial two is 3.58, thus demonstrating the stability of the differences first seen on Day 2. Thus, perhaps contrary to expectations that there might be little blocking to the rote task and a uniform strong blocking effect from the descending subtraction task, there is a remarkable within individuals consistency in the direction of alpha change during various tasks across days. These kinds of differences, although observed by others in the past, have tended to be ignored because they are masked either by the presence of light or by novelty on the first day of testing and were therefore considered to be random variation. However, our data suggest that the individual's style of alpha density response to task situations is consistent across tasks and across days. Further, if one splits subjects on the basis of performance on Day 2 significant differences in alpha blocking in the Day 1 data become apparent.

Clearly, these kinds of data are not reflected in current theories regarding alpha, activation, behavior and subjective experience outside of the feedback context. It is equally clear that we cannot expect to apply alpha feedback to obtain predictable results unless these powerful systematic individual differences are understood and integrated into our general set of assumptions about alpha phenomena during feedback.

What may we then consider to be established conclusions regarding the relationship between activation/arousal and alpha density? Perhaps first we must recognize that, contrary to our initial naive hopes, we cannot assume that high alpha density is uniformly accompanied by moderate physiological arousal or subjective calm. It is now clear that a number of different mechanisms influence alpha density and interact to determine an individual's tonic levels and phasic changes in alpha. Second, visuomotor activity is of primary importance in determining alpha density and in learning to augment alpha, in the presence of light. It would appear that feedback training carried out in light requires the development of different skills and may have very different subjective and objective results than that carried out in total darkness. Third, while in early work we could not get people to exceed baseline alpha levels, it is now clear that some subjects do exceed their baseline level--but in response to activation! Fourth, clearly the widely accepted inverted U-shaped function hypothesized to relate alpha density to activation needs to be reevaluated. Fifth, very important systematic individual differences in alpha dynamics must be accounted for in further explorations of the relationships between cortical electrical activity, subjective experience and behavior as well as in alpha feedback training research. The individual differences reported here may help to direct further efforts at understanding results such as those of Travis, Kondo, and Knott (1975) who found that only about 60% of subjects feel the attempt to enhance alpha in the dark is relaxing or pleasant.

In sum, our findings suggest that the proposal to use alpha feedback training as a means of helping individuals to self-regulate arousal in the face of stimuli eliciting activation/arousal cannot be expected to be uniformly useful. However, we have begun to recognize that totally opposite alpha dynamics in the face of high arousal may exist in the population and that some individuals do respond to activation with drops in alpha density, even in total darkness. If we apply alpha feedback specifically to these subjects results in line with early optimistic reports by others may yet be obtained.

REFERENCES

Birbaumer, N. Praeventive alpha-inhibition und angst. Studia Psychologica, 1970, 12, 179-187.

Broughton, R. J. Sleep disorders: Disorders of arousal? Science, 1968, 159, 1070-1078.

Jasper, H. H. Cortical excitatory state and variability in human brain. Science, 1936, 83, 259-260.

Legewie, H. Subjective correlates of EEG feedback: Discrimination, learning or superstition? Paper presented in the symposium "EEG Alpha Learning: State of the Art" at 1975 meeting of the Biofeedback Research Society.

Lemere, F. The significance of individual differences in the Berger rhythm. Brain, 1936, 59, 366-375.

Mulholland, T. The concept of attention and the electroencephalographic alpha rhythm. In C. R. Evans & T. B. Mulholland (Eds.), Attention in neurophysiology. New York: Appleton-Century-Crofts, 1969.

Mulholland, T. Occipital alpha revisited. Psychological Bulletin, 1972, 78, 176-182.

Orne, M. T., & Paskewitz, D. Aversive situational effects on alpha feedback training. Science, 1974, 186, 458-460.

Paskewitz, D. A. A hybrid circuit to indicate the presence of alpha activity. Psychophysiology, 1970, 8, 107-112.

Paskewitz, D. A., Lynch, J. J., Orne, M. T., & Costello, J. G. The feedback control of alpha activity: Conditioning or disinhibition? Psychophysiology, 1970, 6, 637-638.

Paskewitz, D. A., & Orne, M. T. Visual effects of alpha feedback training. Science, 1973, 181, 360-363.

Pavloski, R., Cott, A., & Black, A. H. Paper presented at the Annual Meeting of the Eastern Psychological Association, April 1975.

Peper, E., & Mulholland, T. B. Methodological and theoretical problems in the voluntary control of electroencephalographic occipital alpha by the subject. Kybernetic, 1970, 7, 10-13.

Simonova, P. V. Basic (alpha) EEG rhythm as electrographic manifestation of preventive inhibition of brain structures. Progress in Brain Research, 1968, 22, 138-147.

Stennett, R. G. The relationship of alpha amplitude to the level of palmar conductance. Electroencephalography and Clinical Neurophysiology, 1957, 9, 131-138.

Travis, T. A., Kondo, C. Y., & Knott, J. R. Subjective aspects of alpha enhancement. British Journal of Psychiatry, 1975, 127, 122-126.

NOTES

1. In an unpublished study subjects were told to signal by pushing a button when they had found a faint pinpoint of light which would be turned on sometime after a signal was given. The light was not actually turned on until some thirty seconds after subjects were told to begin looking for it. However, alpha blocking took place as soon as subjects were signaled to begin looking for the light source. Incidentally, this effect is quite specific to visual attention and is not seen in an analogous situation using auditory stimuli.

2. We wish to thank Anthony L. Van Campen who served as Biomedical Engineer for this attempted replication.

3. Different aspects of this study were conducted by Frederick J. Evans, Betsy E. Lawrence and Anthony L. Van Campen.

The line of research reported here would not have been possible without the close collaboration of David A. Paskewitz who designed the equipment, ran the subjects, and supervised the analysis of all but the most recent studies. This later work was carried out in collaboration with Frederick J. Evans, Betsy E. Lawrence, Emily Carota Orne, and Anthony L. Van Campen. We would also like to express our appreciation to them and to William M. Waid for helpful comments and suggestions in the preparation of this manuscript.

The substantive work upon which this paper is based was supported in part by grant #MH 19156-04 from the National Institute of Mental Health, the Advanced Research Projects Agency of the Department of Defense and was monitored by the Office of Naval Research under contract N00014-70-C-0350 to the San Diego State College Foundation, and by a grant from the Institute for Experimental Psychiatry.

ON THE SOCIAL PSYCHOLOGY OF EXPERIENTIAL STATES ASSOCIATED WITH EEG ALPHA BIOFEEEDBACK TRAINING

William B. Plotkin
University of Colorado

Alpha feedback training involves presenting immediate moment-to-moment information feedback of the strength or density of the EEG alpha rhythm, providing the opportunity, in principle, to learn to increase, maintain, or decrease the strength of this brain rhythm. Of special significance is the observation by some researchers (Brown, 1970; Kamiya, 1968, 1969; Nowlis & Kamiya, 1970) that many persons report entering a quasi-meditational state of consciousness during alpha-enhancement feedback. This state of consciousness, often called the "alpha experience," is said to be a pleasant, relaxed, and serene state, characterized by a loss of body and time awareness, an absence or dimunition of thought, and "egolessness." Initially, researchers claimed that the alpha experience was intrinsically and directly associated with enhanced alpha levels, and that the alpha experience was achieved by virtue of enhanced alpha (hence, the name, alpha experience). However, more recently, several researchers have argued that the alpha experience is at least in part a result of certain social psychological variables such as suggestion, the demand characteristics of the experimental setting, expectation, and the degree of experienced success (Beatty, 1972; Lynch & Paskewitz, 1971; Lynch, Paskewitz, & Orne, 1974; Peper, 1971; Plotkin, 1976a, 1976b; Plotkin & Cohen, 1976; Plotkin, Mazer, & Loewy, 1976; Walsh, 1974). In addition, several studies have failed to find a significant occurrence of alpha experiences during alpha-enhancement feedback, especially when demand characteristics have been minimized (Beatty, 1972; Lynch, Paskewitz, & Orne, 1974; Orne & Paskewitz, 1974; Peper, 1971; Plotkin, 1976a; Plotkin & Cohen, 1976; Plotkin, Mazer, & Loewy, 1976; Regestein, Pegram, Cook, & Bradley, 1974). Hardt and Kamiya (1976) have argued that the failure of these latter studies to find a reliable connection between alpha-enhancement feedback and the alpha experience is due to the use of "deficient methodologies," such as too short training time. However, Plotkin (1976b) has criticized this observation of Hardt and Kamiya's on the grounds that most of the above studies used methodologies that were similar or nearly identical to the original studies of alpha feedback--those by Brown (1970), Kamiya (1968, 1969), and Nowlis and Kamiya (1970)--including the length of training. In addition, a recent study (Plotkin, 1976, in preparation) that employed Hardt and Kamiya's recommended methodology, including almost 9 hours of training time, found (a) no support for a reliable or direct connection between maintained or enhanced alpha and the alpha experience, and (b) little support for the claim that even long-term alpha training can lead to alpha strength levels that are much higher than those seen during pre-feedback eyes-closed baselines.

There have been two published studies which have specifically investigated the effects of suggestion or expectation on the occurrence of the alpha experience during alpha feedback (Plotkin, Mazer, & Loewy, 1976; Walsh, 1974). In Walsh's (1974) study, alpha-enhancement and alpha-suppression feedback were each paired with "alpha experience" and neutral instructional sets. He found the typical alpha experience to be reported only when persons were given both the alpha experience set and alpha-enhancement feedback. Either alone was not sufficient. Walsh interpreted these results as showing that the alpha experience is directly associated with the alpha rhythm, but that this association may be blocked by "situational factors" unless the person is provided with "appropriate preparation for the experience, including some concepts to use in describing it." (p. 433). However, Plotkin (1976a) argued that this interpretation is not clearly supported by Walsh's data, since there is the following equally plausible interpretation. Rather than showing that the alpha experience is directly associated with alpha activity, Walsh's study may have only shown that the absence of alpha activity (during alpha-suppression feedback) is incompatible with the alpha experience (as well as with numerous other kinds of experiences--see Plotkin, 1976a). The absence of alpha experiences in the groups that received alpha-suppression feedback (regardless of whether or not they also received the alpha experience set) could be explained by this incompatability rather than by a special, direct, or one-to-one relationship between the alpha rhythm and the alpha experience. The finding of significantly more alpha experiences in the alpha-enhancement group that also received the alpha experience set can straightforwardly be interpreted as demonstrating the effects of expectation. Studies reported in Plotkin (1976a), Plotkin and Cohen (1976), and the present article present data that support the above interpretation of Walsh's study.

It seems that a more adequate way of investigating the extent of the effects of suggestion or expectation on experiences reported during alpha feedback training would be to have two groups, both of which receive alpha-enhancement training, but which have been given expectations for different experiences. One group would expect the typical alpha experience, while the other would expect an experience as different from the alpha experience as possible within the constraints of the overall biofeedback situation. The reported experiences of these two groups can then be compared 1) with each other, 2) with the experiences reported by a group that has previously been tested (Plotkin, in preparation, 1976) which received a neutral set, and 3) with the degree of alpha enhancement achieved. This is the procedure that was used in the present research.

In the study by Plotkin, Mazer, and Loewy (1976), one group was given an alpha experience set while another received no set. Both groups received alpha-enhancement feedback. However, the results showed that the likelihood of an alpha experience was not significantly different for the two groups. Plotkin et al. interpreted the failure of this variable as being due to the fact that many persons felt very frustrated in their attempts to enhance alpha. Thus, the alpha experience set may have been ineffective due to an incompatability between frustration and the alpha experience. This interpretation suggests that the degree of experienced success at the feedback task may interact strongly with expectation (set). Therefore, the present research also investigated the effects on reported experience of the degree of experienced success by arranging for half of the trainees to feel successful at the feedback task and half to feel unsuccessful, while it was insured that both groups achieved the same degree of actual success at the task. By including this success variable in a 2 x 2 factorial design with the above discussed expectation variable, it was possible to assess the presence of the hypothesized interaction between these two social psychological variables.

METHOD

Research Participants

The research participants were 48 undergraduates from the Department of Psychology's "subject pool," who came to the lab in response to a request for "persons who are interested in learning how to voluntarily control aspects of their brainwave activity that are associated with altered states of awareness." The following restrictions were used in selection: 1) age range of 18 to 25, 2) no prior biofeedback experience,

3) no significant amount of meditation experience, and 4) neither too little nor too much eyes-closed alpha strength to produce any noticeable changes in the feedback signal. Six persons who began the experiment turned out to have too little alpha, and none had too much. In order to insure a high level of motivation for engaging in feedback training, these students were informed before they signed up that they would receive only three hours of "participation credit" for six hours of experimental time.

Apparatus

The EEG was recorded by electrodes attached to the middle of the occipital lobe (O_Z) and to the right mastoid, with the forehead as ground. This O_Z-ear placement is the most popular one in alpha studies, although Plotkin (in preparation, 1976) has shown that neither reported experiences nor success at alpha enhancement are different when using the O_2-F_4 placement, which was employed in the studies by Nowlis and Kamiya (1970), Plotkin (1976a), Plotkin and Cohen (1976), and Plotkin, Mazer, and Loewy (1976).

The feedback apparatus, manufactured by Biofeedback Systems, Inc., records the integrated alpha amplitude, presents an intensity-modulated feedback tone to the trainee via a headphone set, and has been described in greater detail in Plotkin, Mazer, and Loewy (1976).

Procedure

The basic design was a 2 x 2 factorial with two levels of expectation (Kappa or Lambda) and two levels of experienced success (Success or Failure). Each research participant was assigned randomly to one of the four conditions produced by these two variables, with the stipulation that there were equal numbers of each sex in each condition.

Although each participant engaged in a total of 2 hours of alpha-enhancement training (with lights out and eyes closed), it was insured that no participant thought that he or she was participating in research that was at all concerned with alpha waves. Instead, half of the persons were told that they were training to enhance their "lambda" waves, while the other half were told that they were going to learn "kappa" enhancement.

While the electrodes were being attached, the research participants were given the appropriate set of experimental instructions to read. They were told that they would find themselves in an altered state of consciousness (the "lambda" or "kappa" state, depending on the group) if they were very successful at lambda- (or kappa-) enhancement. The lambda state was described in the same way as the typical alpha experience. The kappa state was described in a way that is opposite to the lambda (i.e., alpha) state except that both states share the following four attributes: 1) pleasant, 2) relaxing, 3) unusual, and 4) characterized by a loss of body awareness. The two suggested states were defined at opposite poles as concerns 1) the deliberateness and speed of thought, 2) the degree of "ego" awareness, 3) emotionality, 4) awareness of time, and 5) the degree of concentration. The lambda state is at the low end of each of these five dimensions, while the kappa state is at the high end. Both experiences were described in such a way that they each would appear to be very valuable and worthwhile experiences. By various manipulations (described below), the Success groups were made to feel highly successful at the feedback task, while the Failure groups were made to feel totally unsuccessful. Efforts were made to motivate the Failure groups to maintain their efforts at alpha-enhancement, in order to insure that they achieve the same degree of actual success as the Success groups.

Each research participant trained on two different days. Each day included two half-hour feedback sessions, and each session was divided into three 10-min feedback periods, separated by 30-sec rest periods. During the rest periods, the lights were turned on and the participants were asked to open their eyes and to stretch. Each feedback period was subdivided into five 2-min trials. Each day began with a baseline recording with lights out and eyes closed. The baseline was taken for 10 min on the first day and for 6 min on the second day. (Previous work in our lab established that it takes less time for subjects to habituate to the lab on the second and subsequent days.) Then, after a 30 sec rest period, the tone was turned on and adjusted, and then the 30 min session began. During feedback, integrated alpha amplitude was averaged over 2-min periods. After each 2-min trial, the participant was read (via an intercom) a 3-digit number that was proportional to average alpha strength during the last trial, to provide information about trial-by-trial progress. However, persons in the Success groups heard their actual scores only after the first 2-min trial of the first of the four sessions. After that, each actual score was inflated by an additional (and accumulating) 2% of that day's baseline score. Thus, while these "success scores" were still responsive to the person's actual success, and while the actual feedback tones were still being used, these trainees were nevertheless led to believe that they were improving at a somewhat remarkable, yet convincing, rate. In addition, the Success persons were given frequent verbal reinforcement, such as "you're making remarkable progress." Persons in the Failure groups were given their actual feedback tones and their actual scores at all times (every 2 min). However, their instructions included a paragraph that informed them that the kappa (or lambda) experience does not even begin to occur until kappa (or lambda) strength is increased by at least 100% over the initial baseline levels. In this way, persons in this group were guaranteed to experience failure since 100% increases over eyes-closed baselines were never even approached in earlier research, even with almost 9 hours of training (Plotkin, in preparation, 1976). In addition, the experimenter did not reinforce the Failure persons for any improvements, but instead made such comments as "not much progress this session, but maybe you'll do better next time."

At the end of each of the four sessions, each research participant filled out a questionnaire (the same one for all groups), which included 26 1-to-9 scales, with which the trainee appraised his/her experience during the times when the tone was loudest and/or the scores the highest.

After day 2, each participant was scheduled for a third session, during which the Stanford Hypnotic Susceptibility Scale: Form C (SHSS:C) was individually administered. Following this, the participant was interviewed about experiences during the entire experiment and then was completely debriefed on the actual nature and purposes of the research.

RESULTS

In general, and with few exceptions, the analyses of the questionnaires showed, as hypothesized, that persons in the Kappa-Success group reported very powerful and genuine kappa experiences, while persons in the Lambda-Success group reported authentic lambda experiences. Most persons in both Failure groups reported "nothing unusual." Moreover, there were no differences even approaching significance between any of these groups in the degree of alpha-enhancement actually achieved (see Plotkin, 1976c, for a detailed report of the results of the present experiment).

Experiential Reports

For each of the 26 items on the questionnaire, a separate 2 x 2 x 2 x 2 x 2 ANOVA was performed, corresponding to two levels of expectation (Kappa or Lambda), two of experienced success (Success or Failure), two of sex, and two within-subject variables: days (1 & 2) and sessions (1 & 2). Without exception, the main effect of Success reached significance on the ANOVAs of those items which the kappa and lambda experiences had in common, such as the degree of relaxation, pleasantness, awareness of surroundings, value, and state of consciousness (from "normal" to "extremely altered"). On these ANOVAs, persons in the Success groups reported significantly more valuable or intense experiences, and there were only few and small differences between the Kappa and Lambda groups. Again, in nearly every case, the main effect of expectation and the interaction between expectation and experienced success reached significance on those items which differentiated the kappa and lambda experiences, such as the amount of thought (from "blank mind" to "extremely powerful and abundant thought"), awareness of time, emotionality, and awareness of self (from "totally unaware of oneself as a separate entity" to "very highly aware of oneself as a person in the world"). The combination of this main effect and interaction showed that the Kappa-Success and Lambda-Success groups scored significantly different on these items, while the two Failure groups scored nearly the same and midway between the two Success groups.

To illustrate the first group of effects discussed above, two special scales were constructed, one made up of the sum of 4 Sensory Deprivation (SD) items (degree of body awareness, experienced body weight, relaxation, and awareness of surroundings), and the other consisting of the sum of 8 General Intensity (GI) items (such as unusualness, pleasantness, and value). The ANOVAs for the SD and GI scales indicated significant main effects of Success ($F(1,40) = 23.59$, $p < .0001$; and $F(1,40) = 37.66$, $p < .00001$, respectively). In both cases, Success persons scored considerably higher than Failure persons.

To illustrate the second group of effects discussed above, a special scale (the K-L scale) was constructed which consisted of the ten items from the questionnaire that pre-experimentally differentiated the kappa and lambda experiences. This ANOVA indicated a significant main effect of expectation ($F(1,40) = 42.12$, $p < .00001$) and a significant interaction between expectation and experienced success ($F(1,40) = 24.59$, $p < .0001$). This interaction is drawn in Figure 1, and is self-explanatory. In addition, a significant interaction between days and expectation ($F(1,40) = 11.24$, $p < .005$) showed that the experiences of persons in the Lambda groups became more lambda-like across days, while the experiences of persons in the Kappa groups became more kappa-like.

Enhancement Scores

An Enhancement Score (ES) for each trial was calculated as X/B, where X = the integrated alpha amplitude for that 2-min trial and B = that

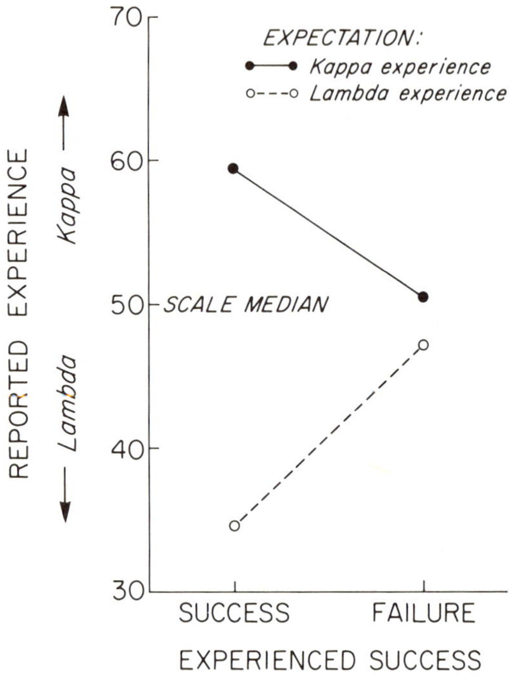

Figure 1. Interaction between Expectation and Experienced Success on the Kappa-Lambda Differentiation Scale.

day's baseline score. The baseline score was calculated with the following method: During the baseline period, integrated alpha amplitude was recorded in 1-min trials. The baseline score was then taken to be twice the score of the highest 1-min trial from this period. (This doubling was necessary in order for the baseline score to be comparable to the 2-min feedback trials.)

With the trial-by-trial ESs, three ANOVAs were performed: one with every trial-by-trial ES, one with just the highest ES from each period (Periods' Highests), and one with just the highest ES from each session (Sessions' Highests). These three Enhancement Measures (EM) were very highly intercorrelated, with an average $r = .92$. On all three ANOVAs, all of the expectation and experienced success main effects and their interactions indicated F ratios of less than unity, demonstrating no differences approaching significance between the EMs of these four groups.

How well persons actually did at alpha enhancement can be seen by the following data. Although none of the trial-by-trial group averages were greater than 1.00 ($\bar{X} = .91$), the Sessions' Highests ANOVA showed that each of the four groups enhanced their alpha strength significantly above baseline ($p < .05$) for at least 2 of the 4 sessions. Although the group means associated with this ANOVA were only about 8% above baselines, there were 16 individuals (33%) whose single highest ESs were between 25% and 74% above baseline. All in all, the analyses demonstrated that persons in this study showed the typical lack of progress and atypical learning curves of eyes-closed alpha training, but were nevertheless at least as successful at eyes closed alpha production as persons in any other research reported to date (see Plotkin, 1976b, and 1976, in preparation).

Correlations

Pearson product moment correlation coefficients were computed for the correlations between SHSS:C scores; averaged SD, GI, and K-L scores; averaged baseline scores; and the three averaged EMs. These analyses were performed for 1) all persons, 2) the Success and Failure groups separately, and 3) separately for the four groups of the expectation by experienced success interaction. These correlations showed that, for all groups considered alone or in combination, there were no significant relationships between any aspect of experiential reports and the degree of actual success at the feedback task, with one exception: For the Lambda-Success group, there was a significant negative correlation between the Sessions' Highests EM and the K-L scale, $r(10) = -.65$, $p < .05$. If we note that the lambda end of the K-L scale is the low end, then this looks like a positive correlation between this EM and the intensity of a lambda experience for this group. However, since 1) the correlation between the same EM and the K-L scale nearly reached significance in the opposite direction for the Kappa-Success group, $r(10) = .46$ (note that the kappa end of the K-L scale is the high end), and since 2) one cannot completely separate the degree of actual success from the degree of experienced success, we must conclude that this result is more likely to be reflecting a correlation between the degree of experienced success (within the Lambda-Success group) and reported experiences, rather than demonstrating a direct or one-to-one relationship between alpha enhancement and the lambda (alpha) experience. This interpretation has the virtue of being consistent with the rest of the data and is supported by three moderately high negative correlations within the Lambda-Success group between the three EMs and the degree of experienced frustration (reported on the questionnaire): $r(10) = -.50$, $p < .10$; $r(10) = -.49$, $p < .11$; and $r(10) = -.57$, $p < .06$.

Elsewhere, the correlation analyses showed that, across all participants, there was no relation between hypnotic susceptibility and baseline alpha strength, $r(46) = -.08$; that the lower a person's baseline, the higher he would score on the Sessions' Highests EM, $r(46) = -.32$, $p < .05$; and that, for the Failure group, hypnotic susceptibility was negatively correlated with actual enhancement success on the Sessions' Highests and Periods' Highests EMs, $r(22) = -.53$, $p < .05$, and $r(22) = -.47$, $p < .05$, respectively.

DISCUSSION

The present results dramatically demonstrate that 1) the general intensity, pleasantness, value, and the relaxation and sensory deprivation qualities of experiences that are reported to occur during alpha biofeedback training are very strongly influenced by the degree of experienced success at the feedback task, 2) for persons who do experience success at the feedback task, the specific qualities of the reported experiences are closely related to his/her expectations (or set); the "alpha experience" has no special relationship to EEG alpha, and 3) the quality and intensity of the experiences that occur during alpha training are independent of the actual degree of success at alpha enhancement.

The relative absence of unusual experiences in the Failure groups supports the interpretation that Plotkin, Mazer, and Loewy (1976) offered for their results: An instructional set to expect an alpha experience will not be influential unless the trainee sees himself as having been successful at the very task which, he believes, leads to the alpha experience.

Although the overall means demonstrate that the reported experiences were closely related to the participants' expectations, there were one or two atypical responses in each group. This finding points to the importance of considering individual differences. Persons may have greater or lesser ability and/or disposition to self-induce unusual experiences or to self-induce one kind of experience over another. In addition, persons differ as to their proneness to sensory deprivation effects, their susceptibility or openness to suggestion, their tolerance for self-altering experiences, their ability to be comfortable in an experimental situation, their disposition to follow instructions and cooperate with the experimenter, and to other relevant attributes. Additional research is needed to study the role of individual differences in the likelihood of having an alpha experience during alpha training.

The combined effects of the feedback situation, the explicit suggestion, and the experience of success seem to be sufficient to generate authentically powerful and profound experiences of high personal significance. On their questionnaires and during their post-experimental interviews, several persons in both of the Success groups spoke very colorfully and dramatically about their experiences, some claiming to have had one of the most valuable self-altering experiences of their lives. Thus, this research most certainly did not demonstrate that the lambda (alpha) or kappa experiences are inauthentic or trivial, but rather that the occurrences of these very meaningful and profound experiences are unrelated to either spontaneous or voluntary changes in EEG alpha, and that they are within the "reach" of "normal" persons who are exercising their normal skills and capacities. After the full nature of the experiment was explained to them, many of my research participants left the lab with a renewed sense of their natural powers of self-control--latent powers that they now realize were always there waiting to be tapped. Thus, although the present research serves as an additional demonstration that alpha training per se is neither necessary for, nor especially facilitative of, the achievement of the alpha experience, this finding adds up to a very exciting positive conclusion in the area of self-regulation: The research demonstrates that we have greater natural abilities of self-control than we have hitherto been willing to grant ourselves.

In this connection, we can now see a fascinating resemblance between the alpha feedback phenomenon and the hypnotic situation: Both are ways in which latent behavior potential can be effectively evoked, and in a similar manner. One way in which hypnotic inductions work (see Plotkin & Schwartz, 1976) is through the hypnotist's carefully timed redescriptions of behavior--he redescribes the hypnotic subject's behavior in such a way that the subject sees his own behavior differently; for example, the rising arm is redescribed in such a way that it is seen as autonomously rising, when the subject is actually raising it himself. Similarly, the biofeedback researcher unintentionally gives an inaccurate description of the alpha feedback situation such that the trainee believes that the promised experiential state is a causal result of biofeedback-produced alpha-enhancement, rather than a direct achievement of the trainee himself (the latter being, in fact, the case). By doing this, the researcher has managed to circumvent the typical trainee's self-doubts about his eligibility to simply put himself in this state, which leaves the trainee in the position where he can simply go ahead and do just that (as long as he does not see it that way at the time). In sum, although biofeedback researchers have not been fully aware of it, alpha feedback training has been a case in which biofeedback equipment has been used as an element in a social influence process which can lead to the evocation of latent (but natural) powers of self-control (of states of consciousness, in this case).

A recent finding closely related to the present experiment is reported in a study by Plotkin (1976, in preparation), which demonstrated that the sensory deprivation qualities of the biofeedback setting can account for much of the unusual content of experiences reported to occur during alpha training. Persons who engaged in ten one-hour sessions of eyes-closed alpha-enhancement feedback without rest periods reported experiences that were significantly more unusual and intense than those of persons who engaged in the same training with 20-second eyes-open rest periods interspersed every 4 minutes. There were no differences between the two groups in the actual degree of alpha-enhancement achieved, except that, on the first session, persons who had the rest periods performed better.

Finally, I would like to point out that it is not the case that the alpha rhythm has absolutely no relevant psychological significance. However, the significance seems to be in maintained (or simply not-suppressed) alpha, rather than in enhanced or "maximized" alpha. Alpha feedback appears to be one method among many that allows a person to essentially maintain his naturally occurring optimal alpha levels under circumstances in which they would normally decrease (Paskewitz & Orne, 1973). More specifically, to maintain one's alpha level at or around one's pre-feedback optimal level, and to do this in the alpha feedback situation (dark and quiet room, comfortable chair, restrictions on bodily movement, headphones, monotonous tone) requires one to habituate to the presence of the initially alpha-suppressing feedback tone and to stay alert in a sensory deprivation situation; if one begins to fall asleep, alpha will decrease or disappear (one of the oldest EEG findings). In addition, abundant alpha is known to accompany (or to be a sign of) sensory and/or motor inhibition at the cortical level (Peper, 1971). Thus, maintained alpha may also have some similarities to a self-imposed sensory deprivation state. However, we now have an empirical demonstration (similar to that of studies of sensory deprivation states; see Zubek, 1969) that the intensity, value, pleasantness, and other experiential qualities of states that may occur in the alpha feedback situation are unrelated to any special changes in alpha strength, and are instead closely related to the sensory deprivation qualities of the feedback situation and to the interactive effects of at least two social psychological variables: expectation (set) and the degree of experienced success at the feedback task.

REFERENCES

Beatty, J. Similar effects of feedback signals and instructional information on EEG activity. Physiology and Behavior, 1972, 9, 151-154.

Brown, B. Recognition of aspects of consciousness through association with EEG alpha activity represented by a light signal. Psychophysiology, 1970, 6, 442-452.

Hardt, J. V., & Kamiya, J. Some comments on Plotkin's self-regulation of EEG alpha. Journal of Experimental Psychology: General, 1976, 105, 100-108.

Kamiya, J. Conscious control of brain waves. Psychology Today, 1968, 1, 57-60.

Kamiya, J. Operant control of the EEG alpha rhythm and some of its reported effects on consciousness. In C. T. Tart (Ed.), Altered states of consciousness. New York: Wiley, 1969.

Lynch, J. J., & Paskewitz, D. A. On the mechanisms of the feedback control of human brain wave activity. The Journal of Nervous and Mental Disease, 1971, 153, 205-217.

Lynch, J. J., Paskewitz, D. A., & Orne, M. T. Some factors in the feedback control of human alpha rhythm. Psychosomatic Medicine, 1974, 36, 399-410.

Nowlis, D. P., & Kamiya, J. The control of electroencephalographic alpha rhythms through auditory feedback and the associated mental activity. Psychophysiology, 1970, 6, 476-484.

Orne, M. T., & Paskewitz, D. A. Aversive situational effects on alpha feedback training. Science, 1974, 186, 458-460.

Paskewitz, D. A., & Orne, M. T. Visual effects on alpha feedback training. Science, 1973, 181, 361-363.

Peper, E. Reduction of efferent motor commands during alpha feedback as a facilitator of EEG alpha and a precondition for changes in consciousness. Kybernetic, 1971, 9, 226-231.

Plotkin, W. B. On the self-regulation of the occipital alpha rhythm: Control strategies, states of consciousness, and the role of physiological feedback. Journal of Experimental Psychology: General, 1976, 105, 66-99. (a)

Plotkin, W. B. Appraising the ephemeral "alpha phenomenon": A reply to Hardt and Kamiya. Journal of Experimental Psychology: General, 1976, 105, 109-121. (b)

Plotkin, W. B. Social psychological variables in EEG alpha biofeedback training. Unpublished doctoral dissertation, University of Colorado, 1976. (c)

Plotkin, W. B. Longterm eyes-closed alpha-enhancement training: Effects on experiential state and on alpha amplitudes. In preparation, 1976.

Plotkin, W. B., & Cohen, R. Occipital alpha and the attributes of the "alpha experience". Psychophysiology, 1976, 13, 16-21.

Plotkin, W. B., Mazer, C., & Loewy, D. Alpha enhancement and the likelihood of an alpha experience. Psychophysiology, 1976, in press.

Plotkin, W. B., & Schwartz, W. R. An explication of altered states of consciousness and hypnosis. Submitted for publication, 1976.

Regestein, Q. R., Pegram, V., Cook, B., & Bradley, D. Alpha rhythm percentage maintained during 4- and 12-hour feedback periods. In N. E. Miller, T. X. Barber, L. V. DiCara, J. Kamiya, D. Shapiro, & J. Stoyva (Eds.), Biofeedback and self-control, 1973. Chicago: Aldine-Atherton, 1974.

Walsh, D. H. Interactive effects of alpha feedback and instructional set on subjective state. Psychophysiology, 1974, 11, 428-435.

Zubeck, J. P. (Ed.) Sensory deprivation: Fifteen years of research. New York: Appleton-Century-Crofts, 1969.

NOTES

This article is based on a dissertation submitted by the author to the University of Colorado in partial fulfillment of the requirements of the Ph.D. degree.

The author wishes to express special appreciation to Drs. Ekstrand, Ossorio, Budzynski, Bourne, and Kimble for their help with design and procedures; to John Davis, Wynn Schwartz, Bob Chereck, Barbara Cooper, Donna Culver, Rob Kauffman, Dedee Knapp, Ken Slenkovich, and Jerry Simms for their invaluable and expert help in data collection; to Biofeedback Systems, Inc., for their generous loan of equipment; to the staff of the Institute for the Study of Intellectual Behavior for their clerical and technical assistance; and to the staff of the Institute of Behavioral Science's computer center.

OPERANT ENHANCEMENT OF EEG-THETA ACTIVITY

N. Birbaumer
Institute of Psychology
University of Tübingen

SPECULATIONS ON THE BEHAVIORAL SIGNIFICANCE OF POSTERIOR THETA RHYTHM

During the last several years the interest in "operant" control of theta activity in the electroencephalogram (EEG) has rapidly increased. Apart from concern for actual scientific support, a wide range of clinical methods for "theta-control" are advertised by the biofeedback industry. This interest was partly stimulated by speculations on the involvement of theta activity in specific psychological and behavioral responses.

Pelletier (1974), for example, hypothesized that the presence of theta activity is a prerequisite for pain control. Studying an individual with abnormally high insensitivity to pain, he found an increase of posterior theta during painful stimulation.

A great deal of work is concerned with the significance of theta for meditative states. Most often cited in this respect is the paper by Banquet (1973). This investigation claims to have found in stage 1 of meditation a "dramatic increase in alpha abundance," high amplitude alpha waves in frontal areas, and no alpha blocking to external stimulation. Stage 2 was characterized by an increase of trains of occipital theta with a constant frequency that is different from the mixed frequencies found in drowsiness. Theta also persists when the eyes are opened and during the post meditation period. On the background of theta waves high frequencies in the beta range were observed. The work of Banquet (1973) failed to use an appropriate control condition, a flaw which characterizes most of the work on meditation. A group of beginners in transcendental meditation (TM) served as controls. It is therefore possible that the observed effects are due to the increased ability of trained TM practitioners to achieve a drowsy state, a criticism already confirmed by Fenwick (1974) who found no difference between TM patterns and drowsiness. Furthermore, in Banquet's study, no statistical analysis of the data was applied.

Williams and West (1975) confirmed the tendency of trained TM meditators to exhibit a significantly smaller alpha blocking effect during meditation; subjects instructed to relax served as the control group. The authors concluded that the meditation state is a state of prolonged drowsiness, but they also discussed the possibility of a state of sustained attention. Similar results are reported by Wallace et al. (1971) and Fenwick (1974). Generally, in spite of many interesting studies and speculations, there is little evidence for the existence of a special kind of theta state distinct from drowsiness in meditation.

Together with the increasing interest in meditation, theta was thought to be an indicator of hallucinatory and hypnagogic events as they occur during sleep stages 1 and 2 and other "twilight" states (Stoyva, 1973). Stoyva mentioned a special kind of "theta imagery." But as far as I know, no sufficiently controlled study exists which supports any of these speculations. The work of Green et al. (1971) claiming "vivid imagery" during theta stimulated a certain amount of practical applications of theta-training, but is based only on unsystematic observation and lacks an experimental design. From sleep research (Foulkes & Vogel, 1965) we know that with descending stages 1 and 2, reports of dreamlike experiences increase. Along with these speculations Budzynski and Peffer (1974) advanced the idea that "theta state" may be a prerequisite of very powerful memory consolidation as it occurs during posthypnotic suggestion; and in fact a machine for "twilight learning" has been built and is already being sold. However there is no solid evidence supporting this interesting hypothesis.

In the context of stress research the occurrence of theta activity is often considered as an indicator of a state of consciousness incompatible with anxiety (Stoyva, 1973). There are two controlled studies on the effect of alpha activity on anxiety relief during systematic desensitization (Birbaumer & Tunner, 1970; Benjamins, 1976). Both experiments support the notion that during and between imagination of anxiety provoking scenes, aversive arousal disappears with increasing alpha. Whether alpha presence or EEG synchronization is a necessary condition for anxiety reduction, as Birbaumer (1973) assumed, remains to be demonstrated empirically.

Better controlled studies exist on the relationship between theta activity and performance in vigilance tasks. Nevertheless the findings of the two main research groups (Lawrence & Johnson, 1976; Beatty, 1976) are contradictory. Since an excellent review by Lawrence and Johnson (1976) is available, only the main problems will be evaluated here. Beatty and his collaborators (Beatty et al., 1974; O'Hanlon & Beatty, 1975; O'Hanlon, Royal, & Beatty, see this volume) have reported an increased performance of student subjects in a radar monitoring task during posterior theta suppression and a decreased performance during theta augmentation in comparison to the same group of subjects without theta feedback. This effect was replicated using professional radar operators in a laboratory environment, but not in a natural radar monitoring situation, where no group decrement was observed under any condition (O'Hanlon, Royal, & Beatty, this volume).

As with biofeedback of other variables (e.g., heart rate), the effect of the training is either confined to the laboratory or there is no effect of training in those groups of subjects who need self-regulation. Lawrence and Johnson (1976) reviewed their own work in the light of Beatty's and O'Hanlon's research. Hord et al. (1975) used a yoked and one no-feedback group--a better controlled but less powerful design in comparison to the Beatty et al. (1974) within-subject bidirectional design (theta augmentation versus theta suppression). Hord et al. again used a 3-hour sonar task and applied theta suppression to their subjects, but used a different algorithm of EEG analysis. Beatty and his colleagues compute a theta ratio index for each second (number of theta waves divided by the total number of waves in the theta, alpha and beta frequencies) while Hord et al. worked with an analog filter system. It is not clear whether differences in the EEG analysis or in design are responsible for this discordance. Lawrence and Johnson (1976), after reviewing the relevant studies, state: "A performance decrement may be a necessary condition for the observance of any theta effect, and there are no data to suggest that theta suppression can lead to performance enhancement above initial levels."

Thus on the whole, the behavioral and psychological "meaning" of cortical theta activity is not clear. We believe one of the reasons for most of the problems in present research on theta is the fact that theta is not a unitary phenomenon. The characteristics of frontal theta and posterior or temporal theta may be entirely different. We observed unsystematically 10-20% high voltage theta trains during an alert awake state in frontal areas in comparison to a very weak posterior theta activity (Lutzenberger et al., in press). Low voltage theta with mixed frequencies in sleep stages 1 and 2 may be a very different physiological phenomenon than high amplitude regular theta during awake states and meditation. Different methods of analysis and feedback between the laboratories add a considerable amount of confusion; exact replications are virtually impossible because of different laboratory conditions. Most of the speculations on the psychological covariations of theta still await experimental support.

EFFECTS OF BIOFEEDBACK ON INCREASING THETA

It is generally assumed that high amplitude theta activity as an indicator of central synchronization is incompatible with the presence of central arousal patterns; low voltage theta is an integral part of the operational definition of sleep stages 1 and 2, and occurs also in REM sleep. Increased theta activity over large cortical areas should lead to a drowsy state or a state which is not characteristic of attentive wakefulness ("twilight state"). It may be a useful clinical goal to voluntarily increase the amount of theta in anxiety states, insomnia and other stress related disorders.

Unfortunately, the experimental setup of a biofeedback situation is incompatible with a drowsy state. It may be impossible to attend to the feedback during theta "state." On the other hand we know that operant learning is possible during a drowsy state and also in REM sleep (Salamy, 1970).

There are few controlled studies on the possibility of increasing theta activity through biofeedback. With the exception of our own work (Lutzenberger et al., in press) all investigators tried to control posterior theta. Brown (1971) and Klug and Brown (1974) reported a substantial increase in theta through biofeedback. Since they did not use a control group the effect may be due to increased drowsiness over the experimental session. The same effect could be responsible for the data reported by Green et al. (1971). Sittenfeld et al. (1976) similarly used a design which is inappropriate for the control of the drowsiness effect. Four groups of five subjects each with two different baseline frontal electromyogram (EMG) levels received theta feedback training (8 sessions), or combined EMG training (4 sessions) initially and theta training (4 sessions) afterwards.

They found that all groups with the exception of the group with high resting baseline EMG, which had only theta training for 8 sessions, increased theta activity over sessions. The second group with high EMG, which had the two stage training, increased theta activity as well. The authors interpret their results as supporting the "concept of shaping of low arousal" and as support of a "response patterning approach." In our opinion both explanations are inappropriate. The results could also mean that all groups adapt over sessions and became more and more drowsy, but the groups with a tonic higher tension level are unable to adapt as easily. This design again demonstrates the usefulness of EMG relaxation training for tensed subjects and it shows that muscular relaxed subjects have fewer difficulties in shifting to a drowsy state.

In summary, the possibility of increasing theta activity with feedback is still open to experimental testing. The clinical usefulness of theta biofeedback has not yet been demonstrated in controlled studies.

RESEARCH ON THETA BIOFEEDBACK FROM OUR LABORATORY

Two controlled studies were performed in our laboratory to test: 1) the effect of acoustic feedback on theta activity during increase task only; 2) the effect of the training session on a post training stress situation with and without feedback; and 3) the influence of simultaneous biofeedback of heart rate and frontalis EMG as pretraining on the biofeedback of EEG theta activity.

In the first study (Lutzenberger, Birbaumer, & Wildgruber, 1975) 10 subjects participated in eleven one-hour sessions (1 habituation session and 10 training sessions). A cross-over design was applied: Five subjects began with five sessions contingent feedback after a baseline session (CF, a soft pink noise on the right ear simultaneously with EEG activity of 3 to 7.8 Hz with a minimal amplitude of 10 μM) and continued with 5 sessions of non-contingent feedback (NCF, pink noise on the left ear in the sequence of the tape recorded feedback signals produced by the same subject in the previous session); the remaining five subjects received the same treatment in reversed order. After the 6th and 11th sessions both groups were shown an aversive movie and were simultaneously presented with either the "non-contingent" feedback signal or the "contingent" signal, depending on group assignment. The entire experiment was run by an on-line program on a PDP lab 8/e computer. Posterior EEG, EOG, heart rate (HR) and subjective changes were recorded. (For a more detailed description see Lutzenberger et al., 1975).

The EEG was analyzed by a method similar in some respects to the method used by Beatty et al. (1974), but instead of zero crossing a maximum-minimum algorithm was used. Further, subjects received immediate feedback if more than one theta wave was detected in the EEG. A moving baseline was used in computation of the results; the mean amount of theta during the baseline of the same session was calculated and subtracted from the mean amount of theta during training. The statistical analysis was made within and across the 10 subjects. There was no significant difference between the CF and NCF condition or the test conditions (aversive movie) in any of the subjects. In contrast to Beatty's work, all subjects were informed of the nature of the feedback. Furthermore, falling asleep was carefully controlled: EEG and EOG data which indicated sleep stages 1 and 2 were eliminated.

Due to a high correlation between heart rate slowing and the amount of theta activity, and the positive effect of EMG training on theta biofeedback reported by Sittenfeld et al. (1976), a second study was designed to test the influence of the pretraining in simultaneous heart rate slowing and reduction of frontalis EMG on theta biofeedback (Lutzenberger, Birbaumer, & Steinmetz, 1977; Birbaumer, Lutzenberger, & Steinmetz, 1976).

Twenty normal subjects were exposed to four half-hour sessions with simultaneous feedback of heart rate and frontalis muscle (pretraining) following one baseline session. Ten subjects received contingent (CF), the other ten noncontingent feedback (NCF). Subjects were asked to lower heart rate and muscle tension (EMG). The feedback display of the heart rate was very similar to that developed by Lang (1974). The subject is seated before a large oscilloscope screen. Each heart cycle initiates a line starting on the left, which then extends across the screen. The length of the line is proportional to the length of each successive R-R interval. There is also a vertical target line for the heart rate (see Figure 1).

In the slowing task the horizontal line must extend past the vertical target. The target line is set initially at the median R-R interval of the subject. If the subject succeeds in extending the horizontal "heart rate line" for more than 10 heart beats, a new target line is set which is midway between the subject's previous and current medians ("rule of halves" after Lang's procedure). At the same time the horizontal line is moved up and down the screen proportionally to the integrated EMG amplitude of the subject. There is a horizontal target line for the EMG amplitude which is again initially set at the median of the subject's amplitude. The subject is asked to reduce his muscle tension as much as he can and to keep the horizontal line as long as possible below the horizontal target line. Subjects in the noncontingent feedback group (NCF) faced the same display as the contingent feedback group (CF) (see Figure 1) except that the horizontal line and the two target lines were not computed from the actual HR and EMG of the subject, but instead represented a random combination of HR and EMG of the past 2 minutes of the same subject.

Heart rate decreased up to 19 bpm with a mean of 4 bpm for the CF

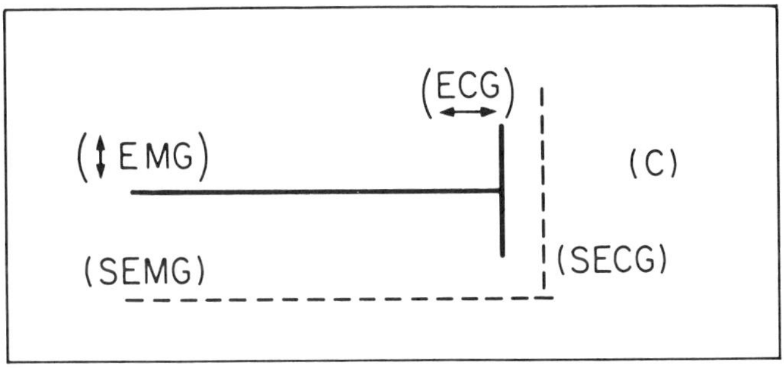

Figure 1. The solid line is moving up and down (EMG) and from right to left (HR). Dotted lines are target lines for EMG (horizontal line) and HR (vertical line). The counter (C) is placed in the right corner of the screen.

group within a session. There was only a weak decrease over sessions because of the strong adaptation effect.

EMG decreased substantially only in the first session and remained stable over the next three sessions. Differences between CF and NCF were significant for both measures. After pretraining subjects received eight sessions of acoustic feedback of their frontal EEG theta activity (Fz to mastoid), four sessions with CF and four sessions with NCF in balanced order. Again subjects were fully informed about the meaning of the feedback signal. In this study the feedback consisted of pink noise increasing in pitch against a steady soft background noise. Only theta periods longer than 1.5 sec produced feedback.

To correct for artificial signals from eye movement, the feedback was immediately terminated if an EOG signal larger than 50 uV was detected. The noncontingent feedback (NCF) consisted of the tape recorded sequence of feedback signals produced by the same subject during the previous session.

After the fourth and eighth sessions a 4 min video film was presented showing aversive scenes from surgical operations and electroshock therapy. Five min before the film was shown subjects were told to produce the feedback as frequently as possible while waiting for the film. During film presentation and after the film they were again asked to regulate theta without any feedback for 4 min with eyes opened.

There was a weak significant increase of theta (15 to 20%) for the

CF condition over sessions but a decrease within the sessions. Pretraining had no influence on the performance during theta training.

A certain amount of control over theta in the presence of the stress inducing film was demonstrated: The CF group did not reduce theta in comparison to the NCF group which did. Whether this result could have any effect on subjective or behavioral responses remains to be investigated.

In contrast to our previous study (Lutzenberger et al., 1975) which indicated no effect of feedback on the EEG theta activity, there is a weak effect of contingent feedback in this experiment.

DISCUSSION

This discrepancy between the first (Lutzenberger et al., 1975) and the second study (Lutzenberger et al., 1977) could be due to a variety of effects which are not easy to evaluate, since the second study was not an exact replication of the first.

As Stoyva has suggested (see below), the negative results of the study may be the result of the fact that we excluded stage 1 sleep. In the study by Sittenfeld et al. (1976) stage 2 sleep was deliberately included. The reason for excluding stage 1 was a theoretical one: "Self-regulation" of central nervous functions in humans in our opinion should be the result of "cognitive processing" of an awake subject and should not be compared with a sleeping subject. Stoyva's argument is therefore correct for the first study. In the second study we included sleep stage 1, but contrary to Sittenfeld et al. (1976), who recorded theta from C_4 - O_2, we recorded theta from frontal areas. Since we found a small but significant increase over sessions, Stoyva's argument is strongly supported. The question remains, why there was no influence of the pretraining on the theta production as Sittenfeld et al. (1976) have reported.

In our opinion there still exists the possibility--which I mentioned above--that the high EMG group which didn't show theta increase was the only group that did not fall asleep within the sessions nor was there an effect across sessions because they were more tense than the other three relaxed groups. In this case they are not an appropriate control for a specific feedback effect. To put it ironically, insomniacs were compared with normals and a difference in sleep onset was found. But again, our second study is not an exact replication of Sittenfeld et al. (1976); all our critical arguments rest on the unproved--and the certainly wrong--assumption that both studies are comparable. Both results await an exact replication before even tentative conclusions are possible.

We conclude in agreement with Johnson (in these proceedings), that a positive effect of biofeedback posterior theta rhythm with the instruction to the subjects to increase theta still awaits experimental support.

Stoyva (personal communication) noted that the "discrepancy between the two sorts of results is puzzling," and that "the task remains of defining precisely the conditions which improve the ability to increase (sleep onset) theta rhythms. One important possibility may be the nature of the training employed in the Sittenfeld et al. (1976) experiment. This training was conceptualized as the 'shaping of low arousal' in which subjects would begin with an easy task and then shift to a more difficult one. The subject's first task was relaxation of the forearm extensor (1 session), next relaxation of frontal EMG (3 sessions) and finally, production of theta EEG (4 sessions). With such techniques, both forearm and forehead EMG values fall to very low levels (see Sittenfeld et al., 1976 for precise details on the training technique--since the latter are frequently critical in biofeedback learning). It seems quite possible that muscle relaxation may have to be very extensive before the CNS is affected in the direction of sleep. Consistent with such an interpretation is the experiment of Hodos (1962) who recorded EEG changes in 24 cats injected with Floxedil, a drug which blocks conduction at the motor end-plate and causes complete relaxation of the entire striate muscle system. As hypothesized, the cats regularly showed EEG changes in the direction of synchrony and sleep. Hodos' result suggests that muscle relaxation, as produced by biofeedback or other techniques, should be extensive before a shift to elevated theta activity is likely to occur."

REFERENCES

Banquet, J. P. Spectral analysis of the EEG in meditation. Electroencephalography and Clinical Neurophysiology, 1973, 35, 143-151.

Beatty, J. Learned regulation of alpha and theta frequency in the human electroencephalogram. In G. E. Schwartz & J. Beatty (Eds.), Biofeedback: Theory and research. San Francisco: Academic Press, in press.

Beatty, J. Power spectrum shifts induced by reinforcement of theta frequency EEG activity using a period-analytic algorithm. UCLA Technical Report, June 1975.

Beatty, J., & Kornfeld, C. Relative independence of conditioned EEG changes from cardiac and respiratory activity. Physiology & Behavior, 1972, 9, 733-736.

Beatty, J., Greenberg, A., Deibler, W. P., & O'Hanlon, J. F. Operant control of occipital theta rhythm affects performance in a radar monitoring task. Science, 1974, 183, 871-873.

Benjamins, J. K. The effectiveness of alpha feedback training and muscle relaxation procedures in systematic desensitization. Proceedings of the Biofeedback Research Society, 7th Annual Meeting, Colorado Springs, 1976.

Birbaumer, N. Überlegungen zu einer psychophysiologischen Theorie der Desensibilisierung. In J. C. Brengelmann & W. Tunner (Eds.), Behaviour Therapy. Verhaltenstherapie. München: Urban & Schwarzenberg, 1973.

Birbaumer, N., Lutzenberger, W., & Steinmetz, P. The influence of simultaneous biofeedback of heart rate and frontalis EMG on the control of EEG theta activity: A controlled study. Proceedings of the Biofeedback Research Society, 7th Annual Meeting, Colorado Springs, 1976.

Birbaumer, N., & Tunner, W. EEG, evozierte Potentiale und Desensibilisierung. Archiv für Psychologie, 1971, 123, 225-234.

Brown, B. B. Awareness of EEG subjective activity relationships detected within a closed feedback system. Psychophysiology, 1971, 7, 451-467.

Budzynski, T. H., & Peffer, K. E. Twilight state learning: The presentation of learning material during a biofeedback-produced altered state. Proceedings of the Biofeedback Research Society, 5th Annual Meeting, Colorado Springs, 1974.

Fenwick, P. B. C. Metabolic and EEG changes during transcendental meditation. Paper presented at the conference on Transcendental meditation-research and application. University of Wales, Institute of Science and Technology, Cardiff, 1974.

Foulkes, D., & Vogel, G. Mental activity at sleep onset. Journal of Abnormal Psychology, 1965, 70, 231-243.

Green, E. E., Green, A. M., & Walters, E. D. Voluntary control of internal states: Psychological and physiological. In T. X. Barber et al. (Eds.), Biofeedback and self-control, 1970. Chicago: Aldine, 1971.

Hord, D., Wilson, C. E., Townsend, R., & Johnson, L. C. Theta suppression effects on complex visual sonar operation. Paper presented at the 5th Annual ARPA Self-regulation Symposium, Grand Teton, Wyoming, June 1975.

Klug, J. W., & Brown, B. B. Learned control of EEG theta activity. Paper presented at the 5th Annual Meeting of the Biofeedback Research Society (BRS), Colorado Springs, 1974.

Lang, P. J. Learned control of human heart rate in a computer directed environment. In P. Obrist et al. (Eds.), Contemporary trends in cardiovascular psychophysiology. Chicago: Aldine, 1974.

Lawrence, G. H., & Johnson, L. C. Biofeedback and performance. In G. E. Schwartz & J. Beatty (Eds.), Biofeedback: Theory and research. San Francisco: Academic Press, in press.

Lutzenberger, W., Birbaumer, N., & Wildgruber, C. An experiment on the feedback of the theta activity of the human EEG. European Journal of Behav. Anal. Modif., 1975, 1, 119-126.

Lutzenberger, W., Birbaumer, N., & Steinmetz, P. Simultaneous biofeedback of heart rate and frontalis EMG as a pretraining for the biofeedback of EEG theta activity. In press, 1977.

O'Hanlon, J., & Beatty, J. EEG and neuropharmacological predictors of detection efficiency in a monotonous monitoring task. In preparation.

O'Hanlon, J., Royal, J. W., & Beatty, J. EEG theta regulation and radar monitoring performance in a controlled field experiment. UCLA Technical Report 1738-F, September 1975.

Pelletier, K. R. Neurological, psychophysiological and clinical parameters of alpha, theta and the voluntary control of bleeding and pain. Proceedings of the Biofeedback Research Society, 5th Annual Meeting, Colorado Springs, 1974.

Salamy, J. Instrumental responding to internal cues associated with REM sleep. Psychonomic Science, 1970, 18, 342-343.

Sittenfeld, P., Budzynski, T., & Stoyva, J. Differential shaping of EEG theta rhythms. Biofeedback and Self-Regulation, 1976, 1, 31-46.

Stoyva, J. Biofeedback technique and the conditions for hallucinatory activity. In F. J. McGuigan & R. A. Schoonover (Eds.), The psychophysiology of thinking. New York: Academic Press, 1973.

Wallace, R. K., Benson, H., & Wilson, A. F. A wakeful hypometabolic physiologic state. American Journal of Physiology, 1971, 221, 795-799.

Williams, P. Self-control of occipital theta activity and task performance. Science, 1975, 188, 478-479.

Williams, P., & West, M. EEG responses to photic stimulation in meditation. Electroencephalography and Clinical Neurophysiology, 1975, 39, 519-522.

NOTES

This research was supported by the Deutsche Forschungsgemeinschaft and the Stiftung Volkswagenwerk.

The author is very grateful for comments and criticism made by P. J. Lang, R. Hölzl and B. Rockstroh.

The work reported here was done together with W. Lutzenberger, C. Wildgruber and P. Steinmetz.

THETA REGULATION AND RADAR VIGILANCE PERFORMANCE

James F. O'Hanlon and Jackson W. Royal
Human Factors Research Incorporated

Jackson Beatty
University of California at Los Angeles

INTRODUCTION

The "vigilance decrement" is the gradual, unconscious loss of the ability to react effectively to infrequent, unpredictable but critical events in passive, monotonous work. It was first identified from records of hostile submarine contacts reported by surface and airborne British radar operators during World War II (see Baker, 1962). That finding was rapidly confirmed by American and Canadian investigators in studies of military personnel operating simulated radar and sonar systems (Anderson & Lindsley, 1944; Solandt & Partridge, 1946). Mackworth's (1950) classic work followed, and established the methodological precedence which was later followed in literally hundreds of laboratory studies of vigilance phenomena (Davies & Tune, 1970). Mackworth's famous "clock test" was the first laboratory abstraction of the radarman's task, and although he was careful to validate the results it produced through comparison with data obtained in a simulated radar task, later workers generally lost sight of the raison d'être for vigilance research. Most workers chose to study vigilance using college student subjects who performed simplistic monitoring tasks in impoverished laboratory environments. To be sure, much valuable information was acquired over the years. In particular, basic psychophysiological concepts of arousal and habituation were studied in the context of prolonged monitoring tasks and a useful, though limited, picture of the relationship between vigilance and brain functions emerged. Nonetheless, the artificial nature of the usual experimental approach has recently caused some to question the practical relevance of the behavioral results and, by implication, the generality of laboratory-established psychophysiological relationships (Kibler, 1965; Teichner, 1972). Our work followed from earlier demonstrations of a basic relationship between the EEG theta rhythm and vigilance, and our own initial success in applying biofeedback for controlling theta. It was also intended to provide results that might be generalized to occupational settings with a minimum risk of exaggeration.

The 3 to 7 Hz theta rhythm is usually visible in EEG recordings taken over the posterior cortex of normal adults experiencing drowsiness or the first stage of sleep. Yet, an occasional wave in the theta frequency range intrudes on predominantly alpha (7 to 13 Hz) and beta (13 to 30 Hz) activity of the normal wakening EEG. The abundance of theta activity has been related to the efficiency of detection performance for subjects performing prolonged and monotonous monitoring tasks. Oswald (1962) described studies in which strip chart recordings revealed that most failures to respond to signals in an auditory monitoring task occurred as subjects were showing transient periods of continuous occipital theta activity, which he defined as "microsleeps." However, Oswald's subjects performed the task with eyes closed in a recumbent posture, conditions which are conducive to drowsiness and poor performance. Williams et al. (1962) noted a strong coincidence of occipital theta activity and failures to detect auditory signals by sleep-deprived subjects. That relationship did not exist before the two-day period of sleep deprivation, but apparently persisted for more than half of the subjects after one night of recovery sleep. Groll (1966) employed rested subjects in a visual monitoring task to extend the relationship between occipital theta and detection performance. Her subjects' average EEG frequency was 8.9 Hz during a one-second interval preceding the occurrence of signals which were detected, but only 5.6 Hz before signals which were missed. Recently, O'Hanlon and Beatty (1976) studied the relationship between average levels of performance and percentages of occipital EEG waves in the beta, alpha, and theta frequency ranges in subjects performing a simulated radar task. Their results revealed a significant intra-subject correlation of .44 between average theta percentage and target detection latency. The only conflicting evidence was provided in a study by Daniel (1967). He found that occipital theta incidence declined during a 30-second interval, centered on the occurrence of auditory signals which were missed, relative to the mean rate of theta production on all stimulus trials.

Still, we were encouraged to believe that vigilance might be improved if a method were developed that would allow persons to suppress theta activity during monotonous tasks that tend to put them to sleep. At the time we began this research we were aware of only one group who had attempted to employ biofeedback procedures for theta auto-regulation.

Their results (summarized by Stoyva & Budzynski, 1974) were not particularly encouraging. They had found it exceedingly difficult to condition theta augmentation in clinical subjects, suffering from various symptoms of chronic stress. Indeed, some subjects were only able to increase their theta levels after first learning to reduce frontalis EMG activity through the use of biofeedback. Considerable training was usually required for the subjects to achieve control of theta in this two-stage process, and even then the procedure was not always effective (Budzynski, 1973). We were further disturbed by the lack of any evidence showing that individuals actively engaged in visual search would be able to achieve and sustain theta control over periods of hours. Fortunately, both fears proved groundless. In our studies to date, nearly 80 subjects have been rapidly conditioned to either suppress or augment occipital theta activity and sustain theta control with biofeedback while performing a simulated radar task for prolonged and repeated test sessions.

With an effective operant method for conditioning theta auto-regulation we proceeded to demonstrate that theta suppression led to proficient target detection performance, and augmentation to unusually degraded performance for university students in a simulated sea-surveillance radar task (Beatty, Greenberg, Deibler, & O'Hanlon, 1974). This result could be of practical consequence if the performance sustaining effects of operant theta suppression were to occur for professional radar operators.

The professional radar operator is, however, the product of a long process of occupational selection. Individuals who cannot maintain adequate vigilance when others' lives depend upon it are usually discovered and replaced. Those who find the task unbearably boring either do not choose the profession or shortly leave it. Moreover, judging from McBain's (1970) observations of line-haul truck drivers, it seems likely that people who routinely perform monotonous work learn effective behavioral strategies for maintaining vigilance. In short, the factors of selection, experience, and high motivation might be expected to enhance the performance of real radar operators in any test situation, and thereby reduce the effectiveness of any procedure designed to further improve that performance. It was conceivable that the theta suppression technique, which had worked so well with task-naive college students, would prove totally ineffective when applied to skilled radar operators.

To evaluate the effectiveness of the theta suppression procedure when applied to skilled radar operators, a two-stage research program was designed. In the first experiment, we attempted to partially replicate our earlier results in a laboratory simulation of the radar monitoring task. In the second experiment, we moved the site of the research to an operational environment wherein the procedure was tested in an even more realistic version of the task. In both cases, the experimental task was modeled after the perceptually difficult sea-surveillance radar watch where faint contacts from small targets occur on a short-range scale in video "noise," simulating the radar returns from waves (i.e., "sea clutter").

GENERAL METHOD

Subjects

The subjects were volunteer enlisted personnel on active duty at the USN Pacific Missile Range at Point Mugu, California. All were Petty Officers currently rated as either Operations Specialists (radarmen) or Air Traffic Controllers. They ranged in grade from E-4 (Third Class) to E-9 (Master Chief). Their radar monitoring experience ranged from 2 years to 25 years. Their normal duties involved daily air-surveillance radar monitoring for the purpose of range control, and operating a sophisticated computer-assisted aircraft tracking system. While their duties normally required continuous radar monitoring for periods of one hour or less, all reported occasionally serving as the sole radar operator, essentially unrelieved for periods of 8 to 12 hours. They were drawn from the range's population of 21 to 24 elite radar operators, viewed by their command as among the best in the U.S. Navy.

EEG Conditioning

On a day preceding radar testing, each subject was conditioned to regulate his EEG theta activity in two successive sessions. The duration of the sessions varied between experiments, depending upon the availability of the subjects. In the first experiment sessions were one hour long, whereas in the second these were 30 minutes in duration.

The EEG was recorded from a bipolar occipital-parietal lead configuration (active electrodes over the 01 and P3 locations in the International 10-20 System (Jasper, 1958) and reference electrode over the ipsilateral mastoid bone). The EEG signal was amplified and filtered in a special-purpose, miniaturized, integrated circuit amplifier (Human Factors Research, Inc.). The system's spectral response was essentially flat between 2 and 30 Hz, down 3 db at 1 and 40 Hz, and dropping by 12 db per octave beyond. The signal was processed directly through an analog-to-digital converter (1000 Hz sampling rate) and into a Hewlett Packard 2114B digital computer for analysis. Beatty and Figueroa's (1974) version of the method of period analysis (Saltzberg, 1973) was used, where for each second the periods between positive-going zero crossings were measured, and the theta ratio (number of waves in the 3 to 7 Hz theta frequency band relative to the total number 3 to 30 Hz waves) was determined.

The EEG conditioning sessions were composed of 10 periods (210 seconds each in Experiment No. 1; 180 seconds in Experiment No. 2), of which periods 1, 4, 7, and 10 were baselines in which the subject received no reinforcement. In the remaining conditioning trials, the intensity of a quiet 400-Hz tone was elevated for one second if the value of the theta ratio in the preceding second was equal to, or different than, the criterion value in the desired direction (less for theta suppression, greater for theta augmentation). The measurement and decision process was repeated in each second of the period. The initial training criterion was based on the subject's baseline theta activity. During the trial, the criterion was reevaluated at the end of each 30-second period; the mean theta ratio for that period replaced the criterion if the new value differed from criterion in the desired direction. Thus, the program produced a shaping function, forcing the EEG to more extreme values if a constant level of reinforcement was to be maintained. In these conditioning sessions, subjects were asked to sit quietly with their eyes open and refrain from moving.

Task Training

On the same day as EEG conditioning, each subject was also trained to perform the experimental task. The task, and therefore the training, varied somewhat between the experiments. Complete details are provided elsewhere (Beatty & O'Hanlon, 1975; O'Hanlon, Royal, & Beatty, 1975). In general, both protocols involved 1) a brief introduction to the task, with examples of targets; 2) a short task trial with knowledge of results provided after every response by the subject; 3) further short trials with that information withheld until each trial's end; and 4) a prolonged period of performing under essentially the same conditions as would be encountered in the critical test on a later day. No EEG feedback was provided during task training. Performance records were inspected to determine that the subjects had all learned to perform in a stable and efficient manner but were not further analyzed.

EXPERIMENT 1

Specific Methods

Subjects. Ten male radarmen (seven Operations Specialists, E4 to E6, and three Air Controllers, E5 to E9) traveled individually to the UCLA laboratory for two consecutive days of training and testing (Part 1); six returned for one additional day of training and testing (Part 2).

Schedule

Part 1. On his first day, each subject was trained to perform the experimental radar monitoring task (0830-1200 hours). Then electrodes were attached and he was trained to suppress occipital theta activity in the manner described above (1300-1600 hours). On the second day, the subject returned to the laboratory at 0800 hours, electrodes were attached, and he was given a short period of practice with the simulator. Then he began the critical testing procedure which consisted of two standard sequences of Pretest, Long Watch, and Posttest. One sequence was with, and the other without, concurrent theta suppression feedback during the Long Watch. The order of conditions was counterbalanced between halves of the group. EEG was recorded in all test conditions and analyzed to yield the percentages of theta, alpha, and beta, and the theta ratio. One test sequence began at 0900 hours; the other, at 1300 hours.

Part 2. A subgroup of six subjects was obtained for one additional day. These subjects performed on the same experimental schedule as they had on the earlier test day. They were however, first instructed that another feedback procedure was being applied. Then, beginning at 0900 hours, they received a 55-minute period of EEG conditioning with reinforcement contingent upon augmented theta activity. After a short break, they undertook the standard test sequence (1000-1330 hours). The sequence was later repeated, beginning at 1400 hours. One session was with, the other without, concurrent theta augmentation feedback during the Long Watch. Counterbalancing and EEG recording were accomplished as before.

Radar Task and Standard Test Sequence

The subject's task was performed using a complex and realistic radar simulator. The simulator was comprised of the subject's display console and the experimenter's control console located in adjacent laboratory rooms. The former contained a 23 cm cathode ray tube presenting imagery on P-7 phosphor in the format of a conventional Planned Position Indicator (PPI). The radar sweep line rotated at 10 rpm, painting continuous video noise, and occasional single targets. Targets (3 mm x 2^0 at 4.5 db signal/rms noise ratio) were initiated by the computer at programmed times and random combinations of range and bearing. Targets were repainted on successive sweeps until detected by the subject.

The subject's immediate detection response was made by depressing a microswitch in a response console. He was further required to use other switches in the console for indicating the target's approximate range and bearing. This information was transmitted to the computer which evaluated the accuracy of each response sequence, scoring those correct by the number of successive target presentations before detection occurred (i.e., sweeps-to-detect). Responses in the absence of targets, or responses made when a target was displayed but which were incorrect with respect to range or bearing identification were scored as false. Targets were terminated when correctly detected or after 20 successive repaintings, whichever came first.

The Pretest was five minutes in duration and contained eight targets. The Long Watch followed after a one-minute break. It was 180 minutes in duration and contained six targets in each successive 20-minute period. It was followed by the Posttest after another one-minute break. The Posttest was similar in every respect to the Pretest. The occurrence of each test in this sequence was evident to the subject by the illumination of a corresponding panel on his response console.

The subjects were monitored visually and aurally by a low-light-level, closed-circuit TV system and a microphone/loudspeaker system. Illumination in the subject's room was provided by the radar display and a 25-watt darkroom (red) light. The ambient noise level was below 65 db (A).

Results and Discussion

The mean ($\pm$SE) target detection performance of the full group of radar operators (Part 1) is shown in Figure 1 for conditions where they performed without feedback, and when they attempted to use feedback for suppressing theta activity during the Long Watch. Also shown is their concurrent mean ($\pm$SE) theta ratio.

Without feedback, the operators' target detection proficiency dropped

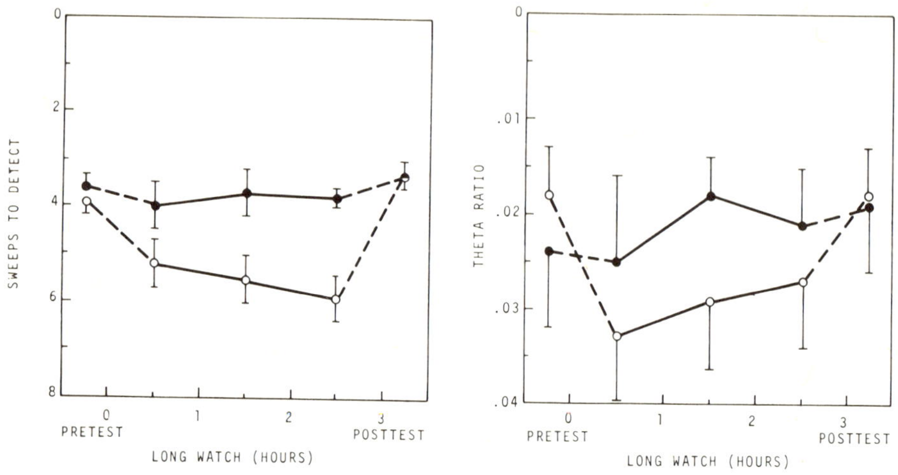

Figure 1. Mean (±SE) target detection performance (left) and theta ratio (right) for 10 radar operators in Pre- and Posttests and as functions of time during Long Watches accomplished with (solid circles) and without (open circles) theta suppression feedback.

from the alerted Pretest to the Long Watch. Therein, it continued to decline as a function of time. Performance returned to its initial level of proficiency during the Posttest. With theta suppression feedback, subjects' performance proficiency never dropped substantially below its Pretest level. The overall difference between the subjects' Long Watch performance in the two conditions was highly significant ($t = 2.84$; $df = 9$, $p < .02$).[1]

Several points deserve mention. First, the present experiment partially replicated our earlier results (Beatty et al., 1974). In that study we were able to demonstrate, using a bidirectional control procedure, that the contingency of feedback reinforcement alone determines whether EEG theta will increase or decrease as a function of feedback. Further, suppression of theta was associated with an absence of the vigilance decrement whereas the augmentation of theta increased the amount of behavioral decrement observed as compared with performance without simultaneous EEG regulation. We concluded that these data demonstrated a lawful relationship between operantly regulated cortical phenomena and human performance. The results of the present experiment confirm a portion of the data upon which that conclusion rests and extends the applicability of that finding to highly trained subjects.

Second, the demonstration of a facilitatory effect of EEG theta suppression feedback upon performance in experienced radar operators and air traffic controllers suggests that such feedback does not act to simply aid the naive subject in learning to monitor a complex display for prolonged periods under monotonous conditions. The subjects in the present experiment have had a wide variety of opportunities to learn many techniques of maintaining vigilance under monotonous conditions. Their overall performance levels and the relatively small decline in performance efficiency over time on watch shows them to be far more proficient at the task then were the naive college students employed in the earlier study. Nonetheless, even the performance of the present group was aided by theta suppression feedback. This suggests that such feedback provides the experienced operator with new information concerning his state of central nervous system arousal, permitting him to maintain alertness in a manner not otherwise possible.

One disturbing possibility remained--that the performance enhancing effects of theta suppression feedback observed in the present experiment might be attributed to nonspecific aspects of the experimental treatment, and not to the specific effects of the EEG-contingent reinforcement. Such an explanation is not likely in view of our previous experience, but it is logically possible. In our earlier experiment, we were able to discard any nonspecific interpretation of the experimental results through the use of a bidirectional control design. The present experiment did not embody the full bidirectional procedure, in which one group is trained to increase, and the other decrease EEG theta activity, but replicates only the theta suppression and EEG-unregulated conditions. Since the other procedures employed in the two experiments were identical, it was reasonable to assume that the facilitatory effects of learned theta suppression observed in the present experiment were due to the specific effects of the training procedure. Nonetheless, to provide further evidence of the specific nature of the feedback effect, the experiment was expanded to include the second part.

Using the theta augmentation reinforcement contingency, EEG-regulation acted to increase theta frequency activity as compared with the associated spontaneous EEG condition. These results are shown in Figure 2. That these effects of reinforcement are specific is shown in a comparison of EEG-regulation and spontaneous EEG conditions during the Long Watch for subjects in the main experiment (Part 1) and the theta-augmentation control procedure (Part 2). The difference in the mean theta ratio between spontaneous and EEG-regulation conditions on each of the two days of testing differed significantly in the predicted direction ($t = 2.27$, $df = 4$, $p < .05$, one-tailed. One subject's data omitted from analysis due to loss of

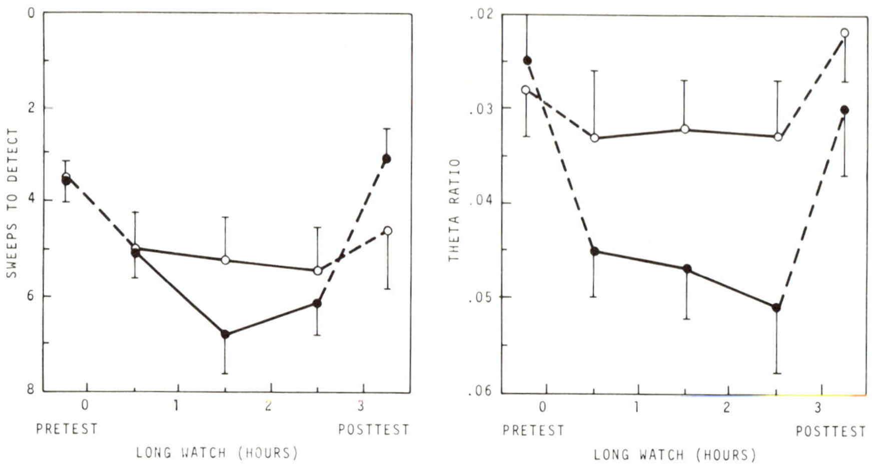

Figure 2. Mean (±SE) target detection performance (left) and theta ratio (right) for 6 radar operators in Pre- and Posttests and as functions of time during Long Watches accomplished with (solid circles) and without (open circles) theta augmentation feedback.

spontaneous EEG record in Part 1).

The mean (±SE) target detection performance in the theta augmentation condition of the six subjects who participated in both experiments is shown in Figure 2. Under this reinforcement contingency, the EEG-regulation acts to degrade performance. These effects are of the same magnitude as those previously reported and are significant by t-test on the difference between regulated and unregulated performance on each of the two days of testing ($t = 2.66$, $df = 5$, $p < .05$). Thus we may safely conclude that effects of theta-contingent reinforcement on both EEG and performance are specific to the reinforcement contingency employed, and not due to any non-specific factors in the training or testing situation.

EXPERIMENT 2

Specific Methods

Subjects. Thirteen male and one female Operations Specialists and Air Controllers, ranging in grade from E4 to E9, and in radar monitoring experience from 2 to 25 years, served as subjects. At the time, they represented 67% of the total compliment of actual radar operators at the USN Pacific Missile Range (PMR), Operations Headquarters at Point Mugu, California. Two of these subjects had previously participated in Experiment 1.

Schedule

Each subject participated in a training session, and two testing sessions, on separate days. Theta suppression conditioning and task training were administered during the first session as described above. One testing session involved the subject's use of theta suppression feedback; in the other, the subject performed without feedback. The order of conditions was counterbalanced between halves of the group. Both testing sessions were performed at the same time of day for a given subject, either in the morning beginning at 0900 hours, or in the afternoon beginning at 1300 hours. Sessions were scheduled at the convenience of the PMR command with no more than 2 days separating the first and second sessions, and no more than 1 week separating the second and third sessions.

Radar Task and Standard Test Sequence

Two subjects performed the task in a large room at the PMR Operations Building which was specially set aside for this purpose. The room contained two standard Navy SPA-8 radar consoles. Two subjects were tested in parallel at respective consoles. Plywood partitions were constructed around each console to isolate the subjects from each other, and from the experimenter's control station, located in the same room. Apparatus at the control station included a repeater display, a special-purpose target injection system, an EEG tape recording system, the digital computer for monitoring the subject's EEG and providing him with feedback, and special response recording equipment.

Naturally occurring radar imagery was presented in the conventional PPI display format on all consoles simultaneously from an ASR-7 radar system. The system was operated in a "Moving Target Indicator" (MTI) mode, so that returns from fixed objects did not appear on the console displays. The imagery did include signals from normal air traffic, atmospheric turbulance, additional clutter from a variety of unidentified sources, occasional interference from other radar transmissions, and system noise. Aircraft contacts, clutter, and noise varied widely during the day and over days in a normal manner.

The ASR-7 system was selected to provide background radar imagery from several alternative systems in continual use at PMR. The ASR-7 is a long-range, two-dimensional radar, transmitting in the S-band frequency range (i.e., 2,862 MHz) from an antenna atop the PMS Operations building. It is an airport-type, air-surveillance radar but similar to shipboard radar with respect to its scan-rate of 15 rpm. This means that targets were successively repainted on display consoles every 4 seconds by the rotating sweep line. Full display range was set at about 37 Km (20 nautical miles) to simulate the shipboard sea-surveillance display. Within that radius, the number of real aircraft contacts varied between 5 and 30, depending mainly upon time of day.

The target injection system permitted the display of a single artificial contact which first appeared at the farthest range and approached the center of the display, on a constant bearing, simulating a speed of 2,224 Km per hour (1,200 NM/hr). The contact was repainted on 15 consecutive revolutions of the sweep line as it moved from the periphery to the center of the display. Target size was approximately 3 mm by 3^0. Its brightness was set at a supra-threshold level approximating that of normal aircraft contacts.

The subject's task was modeled after one of the most difficult expected to be encountered by shipboard radar monitors in times of war; viz., that of detecting a surface-to-surface missile approaching at high speed and low altitude. The subject was required to monitor his display at all times and respond upon target detection by immediately depressing a response switch, then adjusting a potentiometer to indicate the "missile's" bearing. Missiles were initiated by the experimenter at prescribed times, from random bearings, and from a range slightly beyond that visible to the subjects. As each missile entered the subjects' displayed range, two separate elapsed time counters were activated. Each of these was stopped by the respective subjects' detection response. Detection latency was recorded as the performance measure. The subjects' potentiometer settings were read from respective dials on the experimenter's console for confirming the detection responses. No false detection responses were ever recorded during a testing session.

Pairs of subjects performed the task at corresponding consoles in three parts: a Pretest, Long Watch, and Posttest. The Pretest and Posttest were similar, being 10 minutes in duration and containing six missile attacks. The Long Watch was 180 minutes in duration and six missile attacks were generated in each consecutive 20-minute period. The timing of attacks was the same as the target presentation schedule used in Experiment 1; the shortest interval between attacks was 90 seconds; the longest, 300 seconds.

One subject in each pair performed the Long Watch with feedback. That is, his EEG was analyzed on-line by the computer, and the tone was presented from a loudspeaker located between the two working stations whenever he achieved his theta ratio criterion. He was instructed to keep the tone on as much as possible during his performance of the task. The other subject's EEG was recorded on electromagnetic tape for later computer analysis. He heard the feedback signal as it was presented to the other subject, but he was told that it was not contingent upon his EEG and should be ignored. In this manner, any nonspecific effect of the tone should have been equal for both subjects. Both knew the significance of the tone but only one had any control over its occurrence. The other served as a yoked, albeit knowledgeable, control. Later, of course, their roles were reversed in their second testing session.

Results and Discussion

The mean (±SE) missile detection for all subjects, with and without feedback, during the Long Watch is shown in Figure 3. It may be seen that the subjects performed in a highly proficient manner during the Pretest in both conditions. Performance efficiency dropped during the Long Watch in both conditions, the drop being greatest without feedback. The

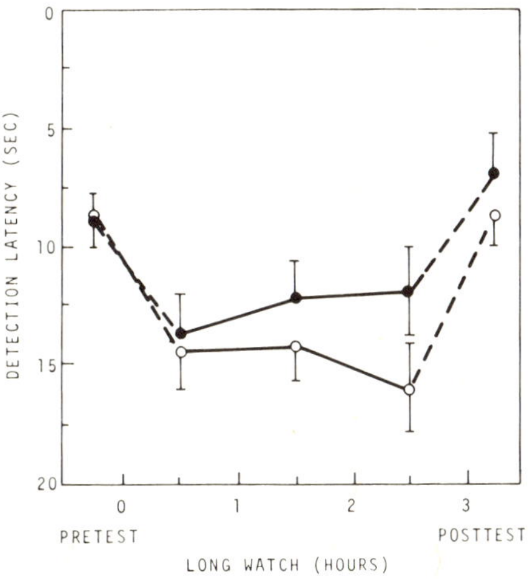

Figure 3. Mean (±SE) target detection latency for 14 radar operators in Pre- and Posttests and as functions of time during Long Watches accomplished with (solid circles) and without (open circles) theta suppression feedback.

apparent feedback effect was not statistically significant, although during the third hour on watch the mean difference between conditions was approaching significance ($t = 1.93$, $df = 13$, $p < .10$).

A defect in the EEG tape recording system resulted in the loss of data from eight subjects in the Long Watch performed without feedback. Complete data were collected from six subjects in both conditions. These were analyzed and this subgroup's average theta ratio during the Long Watch was determined to be .04 and .09, with and without feedback, respectively. All six showed lower values with feedback and the result was significant ($p < .05$ by sign test).

In recapitulating the results obtained from the group as a whole, it may be said that feedback allowed the subjects to suppress theta activity but that this treatment had little effect upon their detection performance. The latter finding was disconcerting in view of our previous success in applying the same procedures to improve performance in the laboratory simulator environment. Yet even there we had found it difficult to show any beneficial theta suppression effect upon the performance of individuals whose performance was stable and efficient in the absence of theta contingent feedback. Consequently, we wondered whether the marginal results of the current study could be interpreted to mean that the subjects, being highly motivated professional operators and using familiar equipment in their normal working environment, were performing near the maximum of human capability in the control condition, and whether their detection performance could be improved in the feedback condition by any means no matter how effective when applied to other populations in different working environments. After all, in the control condition, the group as a whole showed only about a 1-second drop in detection latency from the first to the third hours of the Long Watch, hardly enough to qualify as a vigilance decrement. There were, however, two subjects who showed striking changes in performance over time at the task. These individuals' average detection latencies fell by 12 and 18 seconds, respectively, from the first to the third hours at the task, showing not only the greatest decrements but also the overall poorest levels of performance during the Long Watch. Because these individuals may represent a small but important proportion of the professional radar operator population who are unable to sustain vigilance, their data were analyzed in detail. Figure 4 shows how their individual performance levels varied during all tests and how their respective theta ratios changed with theta-contingent feedback during the Long Watch.

It is clear from the data presented in Figure 4 that the performance of both subjects was markedly better while performing with feedback than

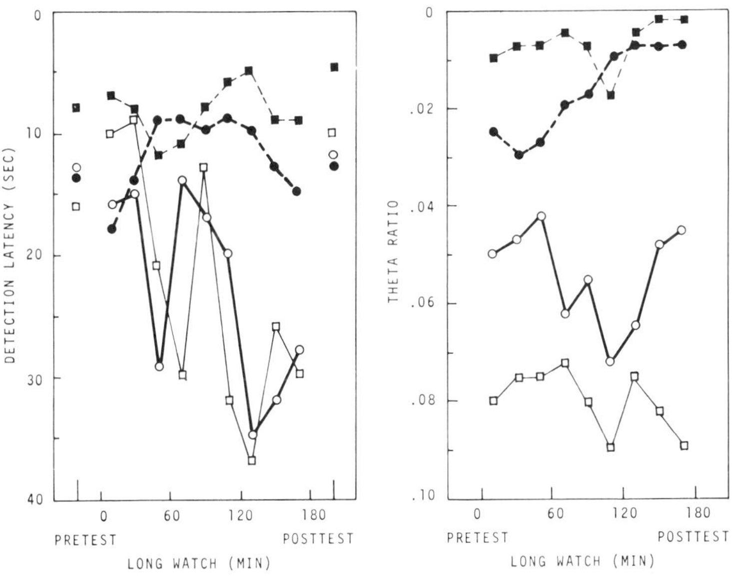

Figure 4. Average target detection latencies (left) and theta ratios (right) for the two worst radar operators (circles and squares, respectively). (Solid symbols indicate that feedback was given during the Long Watches; open symbols, that feedback was withheld.)

without. At the same time, each subject's theta ratio was much lower with feedback than without. These data are suggestive of a beneficial effect of theta suppression upon the radar detection performance of the least proficient radar operators.

GENERAL DISCUSSION

These results, and those collected in other phases of this program, have rather conclusively demonstrated the feasibility of operant conditioning of occipital theta through the use of EEG biofeedback. Very few subjects have failed to achieve control of their theta activity within the short time span allowed by our training procedure. Although we have concentrated on theta suppression conditioning in the hope of using it as an aid to performance, conditioning for theta augmentation has worked equally well.[2]

The effectiveness of theta suppression as an aid to enhancing performance in realistic monitoring tasks, such as radar watchstanding, is still open to question. Our earliest results, based upon data collected from a sample of naive college students, were highly encouraging. Nonetheless, the magnitude of the theta suppression effect diminished as we moved closer to the desired application. In Experiment 1, the professional radar operators' target detection efficiency showed statistically significant improvement with feedback, but the changes in performance were not as great as had been the case for the students. In Experiment 2, the professional operators, now using familiar equipment in their normal working environment, showed only a marginally significant improvement with feedback during the final hour of an arduous 3-hour watch. Still, the fact that the worst operators seemed aided by the feedback cannot be ignored. Without feedback, those individuals experienced a vigilance decrement which might have been dangerous if the task were real. With feedback, they maintained a level of vigilance close to their alerted maxima. Further research is indicated to determine whether the beneficial effect of theta suppression feedback will be reliable for professional operators whose vigilance normally declines over time on watch. Though their number may be relatively small, their tasks are often critical and every means for enhancing their performance should be thoroughly explored.

Hord et al. (1975) attempted to replicate parts of our work but failed to show any beneficial effect of theta suppression on the sonar watchstanding performance of inexperienced Naval personnel. Several procedural differences existed between our respective studies. Notably, their feedback signal was continuously provided by analog circuitry; ours was delivered after digital processing at discrete intervals only when subjects had achieved the criterion theta ratio level. It is not clearly stated in their report whether the subjects' initial task training involved a prolonged unaided exposure to the monitoring task. Because we have found that a 40- to 60-minute exposure is essential for overcoming peculiar first-day arousal effects of performing a novel task in an obvious testing situation, we remain in doubt as to whether those investigators fully replicated our procedure to obtain contradictory results.

However, we are in full agreement with the conclusions drawn by Lawrence and Johnson (1976, p. 9):

> ...theta suppression may be effectual in preventing performance decrement in vigilance tasks of long duration. In fact, it appears that a performance decrement is a necessary condition for the observance of any theta effect; certainly there is no suggestion in the data so far that theta suppression leads to performance enhancement above initial levels.

Our results have demonstrated the beneficial effect of theta suppression on the performance of college students and professional radar operators, who spontaneously showed a vigilance decrement in a simulated radar task, and on the performance of individual professional operators who atypically showed the decrement in a still more realistic task.

REFERENCES

Anderson, J. H., & Lindsley, D. B. (Eds.) Radar operator "fatigue": The effects of length and repetition of operating periods on efficiency of performance. Office of Scientific Research and Development Report No. O.S.R.D. 33334, 1944.

Baker, C. H. Man and radar displays. New York: Macmillan, 1962.

Beatty, J., & Figueroa, C. Period analytic algorithms for the estimation of selected spectral properties of short segments of EEG data. Behavior Research Methods & Instrumentation, 1974, 6, 293-295.

Beatty, J., Greenberg, A., Deibler, W. P., & O'Hanlon, J. F. Operant control of occipital theta rhythm affects performance in a radar monitoring task. Science, 1974, 183, 871-873.

Beatty, J., & O'Hanlon, J. F. EEG theta regulation and radar monitoring performance of experienced radar operators and air traffic controllers. UCLA Technical Report, March 1975.

Budzynski, T. Biofeedback procedures in the clinic. Seminars in Psychiatry, 1973, 5, 537-547.

Daniel, R. S. Alpha and theta EEG in vigilance. Perceptual and Motor Skills, 1967, 25, 697-703.

Davies, D. R., & Tune, G. S. Human vigilance performance. London: Staples Press, 1970.

Groll, E. Zentralnervose und periphere Aktivierungs variable gei Vigilanzleistungen. Z. Exp. Ang. Psychol., 1966, 13, 248-264.

Hord, D., Wilson, C. E., Townsend, R., & Johnson, L. C. Theta suppression effects on complex visual sonar operation. Paper presented at the Fifth Annual ARPA Self-Regulation Symposium, Grand Teton, Wyoming, June 1975.

Jasper, H. H. The ten-twenty electrode system of the International Federation. Electroencephalography and Clinical Neurophysiology, 1958, 10, 371-375.

Kibler, A. W. The relevance of vigilance research to aerospace monitoring tasks. Human Factors, 1965, 7, 93-99.

Lawrence, G. H., & Johnson, L. C. Biofeedback and performance. San Diego State University Foundation (San Diego, California) Technical Report, 1976.

Mackworth, N. H. Researches on the measurement of human performance. Medical Research Council Special Report No. 268, London, H.M.S.O., 1950.

McBain, W. N. Arousal, monotony, and accidents in line driving. Journal of Applied Psychology, 1970, 54, 509-519.

O'Hanlon, J. F., & Beatty, J. Concurrence of electroencephalographic and performance changes during a simulated radar watch and some implications for the arousal theory of vigilance. In R. R. Mackie (Ed.), Vigilance II: Relationships among theory, physiological correlates, and operational performance. New York: Plenum, in press.

O'Hanlon, J. F., Royal, J. W., & Beatty, J. EEG theta regulation and radar monitoring performance in a controlled field experiment. Human Factors Research, Inc. (Goleta, California), Technical Report 1738-F, September 1975.

Oswald, I. Sleeping and waking. New York: Elsevier, 1962.

Saltzberg, B. Period analysis. In M. Matousek (Ed.), Evaluation of bioelectrical data from brain, nerve and muscle, II. Part A. Frequency and correlation analysis. In A. Reymond (Ed.), Handbook of electroencephalography and clinical neurophysiology 5A. Amsterdam: Elsevier, 1973.

Solandt, D. Y., & Partridge, D. M. Research on auditory problems presented by Naval operations. Journal of Canadian Medical Services, 1946, 3, 323-329.

Stoyva, J., & Budzynski, T. Cultivated low arousal--an antistress response? In L. V. DiCara (Ed.), Limbic and autonomic nervous system research. New York: Plenum, 1974.

Teichner, W. H. Predicting human performance III: The detection of a simple visual signal as a function of time of watch. New Mexico State University (Las Cruces) Technical Report 72-1, June 1972.

Williams, H. L., Granda, A. L., Jones, R. C., Lubin, A., & Armington, J. C. EEG frequency and finger pulse volume as predictors of reaction time during sleep loss. Electroencephalography and Clinical Neurophysiology, 1962, 14, 64-70.

NOTES

1. One subject's EEG data were lost during his control session, due to electrode detachment. The subject's availability was not such to allow a replication of this session and for that reason all of his EEG data were omitted in the analysis.

Our previously reported (Beatty & O'Hanlon, 1975) analysis of the same theta ratio data included measurements taken only during periods when targets were present on the display. The analysis reported here includes all EEG data collected during periods when targets were present and absent. Consequently, these results differ slightly from those previously reported, with respect to absolute values and significance of effects.

2. In an as-yet unpublished study, college student subjects performed the simulated radar monitoring task in repeated 1-hour sessions over the course of a single day. Three groups of 16 subjects performed without feedback, with theta suppression feedback, and with theta augmentation feedback, respectively. Theta ratio in the group performing with theta augmentation feedback was always significantly higher than in the control group, and the difference increased across repeated sessions.

This research was supported by the Advanced Research Projects Agency of the Department of Defense, and monitored by the Psychophysiology Programs Office, Physiology Branch of the Office of Naval Research under Contract N00014-70-C-0350. We gratefully acknowledge the unhesitating cooperation of the officers and men of the USN Pacific Missile Range, NAS Point Mugu, California.

EFFECTS OF SENSORIMOTOR EEG FEEDBACK TRAINING ON SLEEP AND CLINICAL MANIFESTATIONS OF EPILEPSY

M.B. Sterman
Sepulveda Veterans Administration Hospital
Departments of Anatomy and Psychiatry,
University of California at Los Angeles

The formal application of behavioral conditioning techniques for therapeutic purposes in epilepsy is of relatively recent origin. A comprehensive review of this area of investigation is currently being prepared for publication by Mostofsky and Balaschak at Boston University. One of the first definitive papers on this subject, however, appeared in the mid-50s when Efron reported the interruption and eventual elimination of generalized tonic-clonic seizures in one female patient with a 26-year history of the disorder. This patient experienced a well-developed aura which was inevitably followed by a grand mal seizure. When a specific sensory stimulus (strong, unpleasant odor) was applied early in the aura, Efron (1956) reported that further seizure development was consistently prevented. Application of the stimulus late in the aura resulted either in a partial seizure or a failure to abort. In further studies on this patient, Efron (1957) successfully paired the olfactory stimulus to a nonspecific visual stimulus consisting of a silver bracelet. Staring at this bracelet for several moments soon became effective in preventing seizure development, and eventually simply thinking about it was sufficient. This patient remained free of clinical seizures for 14 months. During the later months of this follow-up period the incidence of warning auras had sharply decreased, also, in spite of complete withdrawal of anticonvulsant medication.

Stevens (1960, 1962, 1967) attempted to employ paroxysmal activity in the EEG of epileptic patients as conditional stimuli either to associate a sensory specific paroxysm to another sensory modality or to serve as a warning for an impending noxious stimulus (electric shock). These studies sought to affect an extinction of the epileptic process through generalization or aversive conditioning. This approach proved largely unsuccessful and, although some patients became more aware of their paroxysmal EEG discharges through aversive conditioning, the incidence of seizure was not reduced. It was concluded that "spontaneous epileptiform EEG transients have little influence on ongoing behavior or subjective state and can be conditioned to act as internal signals only with great difficulty" (Stevens, 1967).

A somewhat more fruitful line of research has been explored by Forster (1965, 1966, 1969) with epileptics whose seizures are triggered by specific sensory stimuli. He has employed various desensitization techniques in patients who were exposed to stimuli which gradually encroached upon the sensitive region for their seizure precipitation. Once the seizure was elicited, the stimuli were rapidly reduced and the process was repeated in a systematic fashion. This type of conditioned seizure inhibition proved successful in stroboscope-induced, startle, pattern and musicogenic epilepsies, but extinction occurred within several days unless reinforcement of the inhibition was supplied. It was discovered that the inhibitory process could be conditioned to a second conditional stimulus, and in the case of stroboscope-induced epilepsy, an auditory stimulus consisting of a "click" coupled to a flickering light proved successful in maintaining seizure suppression. Special eyeglasses equipped with a photocell and electronic circuits for generating audible clicks in response to flashing light in the environment were supplied to these patients. The eyeglasses provided the necessary reinforcement on an out-patient basis, and essentially complete protection against stroboscope-induced epilepsy was achieved in six individuals (Forster, 1969).

While a great many reports exist in the literature on various methods to produce epileptic seizures in experimental models, there is a surprising lack of information regarding the use of behavioral techniques in attempts to modify or interrupt the induced epileptogenic processes. Although a learning paradigm was not utilized per se, Guerrero-Figueroa et al. (1963) demonstrated that certain visual, auditory, olfactory and somatic stimuli were highly effective in inhibiting paroxysmal spike discharge induced in kittens and adult cats by alumina cream lesions. Direct electrical stimulation of the reticular activating system was equally effective. Suppression of seizure discharge was attributed to general attentive factors. Rouse (1971) reported that conditioned inhibition, generated by long interstimulus intervals and overlearning in aversive classical conditioning, generalized to protect a strain of mice susceptible to audiogenic seizures from a challenge auditory stimulus which would normally precipitate seizure activity.

Our research in this area was initiated with the observation in the EEG of a discrete 12-15 cps rhythm over sensorimotor cortex in the cat during learned suppression of movement (Sterman & Wyrwicka, 1967; Roth et al., 1967; Sterman et al., 1969). Since this activity was localized to sensorimotor cortex it was termed the "sensorimotor rhythm" or SMR, in deference to anatomy rather than Greek. Recordings from the same area during sleep indicated that the familiar sleep spindle was focused also in this region (Sterman et al., 1970). While the waking SMR appeared as sustained, rhythmic trains at moderate voltage in a background of low voltage fast (LVF) activity, sleep spindles developed at the same 12-15 cps frequency as envolopes of high voltage rhythmic activity in a context of diffuse slow waves (Figure 1). Rhythmic 12-15 cps activity also appeared occasionally during the REM stage of sleep, when phasic events characteristic of this state were absent, thus confirming an earlier report of this EEG pattern during REM in the cat (Sterman et al., 1965). These EEG-behavioral observations suggested that the appearance of rhythmic 12-15 cps sensorimotor EEG activity was closely correlated with the absence of movement, regardless of whether the animal was awake or sleeping. The correlation during wakefulness was supported subsequently by Rougeul and associates (1972). The relative suppression of motor activity during sleep is well documented in the sleep research literature (Chase et al., 1968).

To explore this relationship further cats were prepared with indwelling pairs of sensorimotor cortex electrodes and provided with food reinforcement for the production of 0.5 sec trains of SMR activity at a voltage 100% above background LVF activity. Most animals learned this operant conditioning task rapidly, and did so by assuming stereotypical motionless postures (Wyrwicka & Sterman, 1968). EMG activity from the neck was suppressed also during the conditioned production of this rhythm (Figure 2).

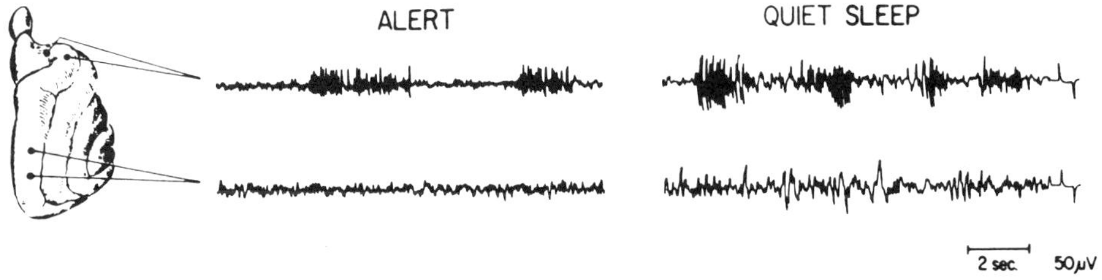

Figure 1. Examples of sensorimotor rhythm (SMR) during alert wakefulness and sleep spindles recorded from the same cat. (From Sterman et al., 1970).

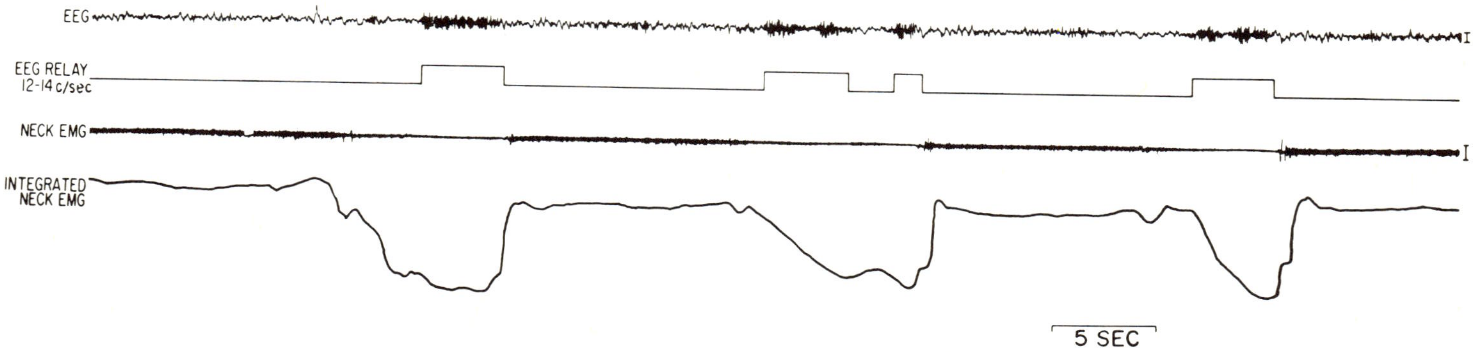

Figure 2. Neck EMG discharge during learned EEG feedback performance in the cat. Both direct and computer integrated neck EMG traces show suppression of tonic motor discharge during production of SMR activity. (From Chase & Harper, 1971)

The relationship between waking SMR and sleep spindles suggested by earlier observations was examined further by training two groups of cats to alternately produce and suppress this pattern in counterbalanced order (Sterman et al., 1970). Sleep spindle density and duration were measured systematically prior to training and before and after the reversal of training. Sleep spindle activity was enhanced significantly after SMR reinforcement, but not after SMR suppression, regardless of the training order. Moreover, phasic movements during sleep were significantly reduced after the period of SMR reward. Subsequently, it was observed that somatic afferent reflex responses in the cat (the monosynaptic masseteric, or jaw closing reflex) were suppressed during conditioned SMR activity (Babb & Chase, 1974), suggesting a depression of gamma motor system excitability similar to that observed during sleep and barbiturate spindles (Buchwald & Eldred, 1961; Honge et al., 1963). Moreover, extra-cellular unit discharge patterns in ventrobasal thalamic cells were found to be identical during conditioned SMR production and spindle burst sleep (Figure 3). Finally, somatosensory evoked responses were altered similarly during both waking SMR responses and sleep spindles, relative to adjacent EEG patterns in the cat (Howe & Sterman, 1973).

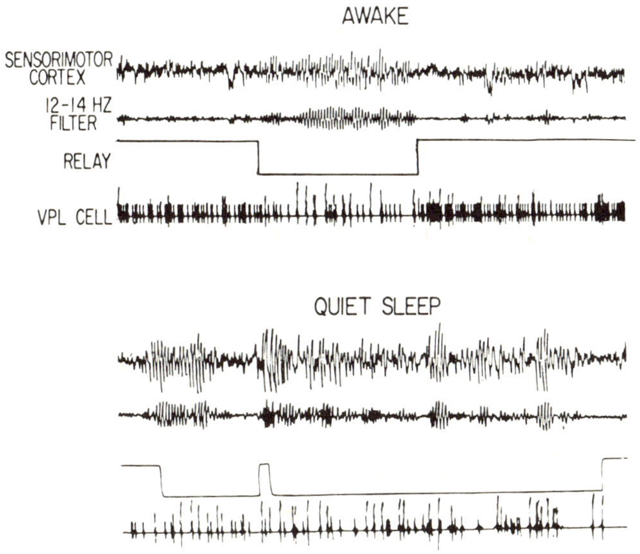

Figure 3. Examples of sensorimotor cortex EEG and corresponding unit activity from nucleus ventralis posterolateralis of thalamus during trained SMR response and sleep with spindles. Note similarity in pattern of neuronal discharge during SMR and sleep spindles.

These various findings indicated a functional relationship between the waking SMR and sleep spindles, and that these EEG patterns were both associated with a suppression of motor excitability.

As part of a separate ongoing study in our laboratory, all experimental cats were eventually injected with convulsant doses of a toxic hydrazine derivative, monomethylhydrazine (MMH). This compound induces generalized tonic-clonic seizures of subcortical origin after a characteristic sequence of preictal events, including emesis, salivation, hyperventilation and hyperkinesis (Figure 4). A profound activation of the EEG precedes these seizures, usually by 10-20 minutes, and even subconvulsive doses produce a significant EEG activation and reduction in sleep lasting up to six hours (Figure 5). When the animals from our EEG operant conditioning study were added to this series, it was noted that several did not show seizures at this dose, and the rest showed seizures only after an abnormally prolonged delay, despite the fact that the typical prodrome was apparent. It was determined that these animals were all from the group which had received SMR training as the last condition in the previous sleep study. Moreover, a number of these animals showed unusual trains of SMR activity in the EEG during the period in the preictal sequence associated typically with marked EEG activation (Figure 6). This accidental finding suggested that the EEG conditioning experience had increased seizure thresholds in these animals (Sterman et al., 1969), a suggestion which was supported later by studies in a larger group of animals (Sterman, 1976).

Because of the relationship established between the SMR, behavioral motionlessness, EMG depression and reflex attenuation, it was hypothesized that the increased seizure thresholds observed in SMR conditioned animals resulted either from an active, learned suppression of movement, or some sustained change in thalamocortical neural circuitry which increased motor control and, thereby, counteracted the seizure process. The implications of these findings for the treatment of epilepsy led to an extension of this work to man.

In a preliminary investigation, a 23-year-old, female epileptic, with a stable eight year history of uncontrolled generalized tonic-clonic seizures, was provided with three 30-min sessions per week of light and tone feedback for production of 0.5 sec trains of low voltage 11-13 Hz activity from central cortex. Anticonvulsant medications were maintained constant, a fact confirmed by clinical monitoring. During the initial three months of this training the patient demonstrated an abrupt reduction in seizures (Sterman & Friar, 1972). She was followed subsequently over a five year period, both within the context of expanded studies (see below)

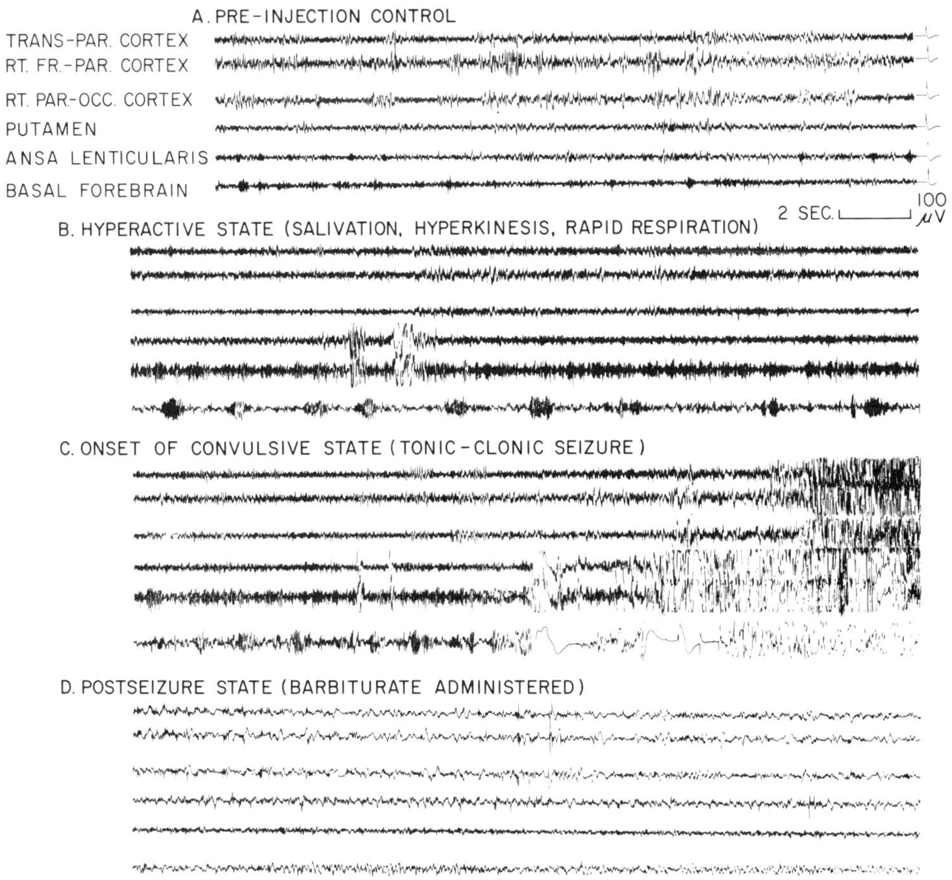

Figure 4. Cortical and subcortical EEG patterns in a cat before and at various stages after the administration of a convulsive dose of MMH (IP). These data indicate that seizures began subcortically and were propagated to cortex. Basal forebrain lead reflects burst discharge in adjacent olfactory cortex related to respiration in the waking animal. Note suppression of rhythmic EEG activity in cortex following exposure and preceeding seizure.

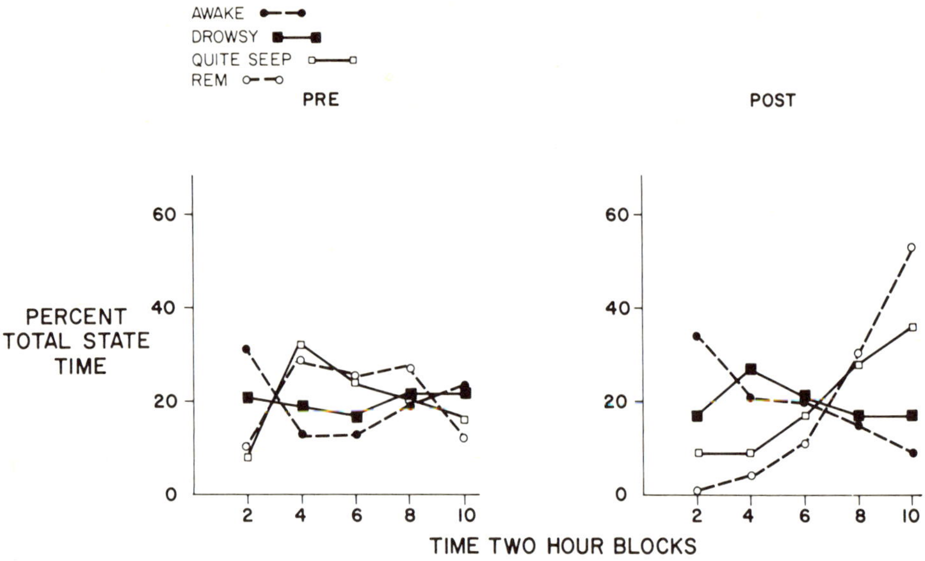

Figure 5. Comparison of the distribution of waking and sleep state patterns in a group of six cats during the same 10 hr period following administration of saline (pre) and administration of 5 mg/kg MMH (post). Mean percentages of total state time are plotted for this group in successive two hour blocks. Despite the fact that this dose is subconvulsive, and produced no overt symptoms of toxicity, there was a statistically significant suppression of both quiet and REM sleep up to six hours after IP injection when compared with saline. Waking patterns, and particularly arousal, were enhanced during this same period. Sleep rebound followed this effect. (From Sterman et al., 1974)

and as a pilot for improvements in methodology. First, a voltage inhibit circuit (amplitude detector) was added to the signal recognition and reward system (Neuro Feedback Instruments) which prevented large slow waves or high voltage transients, such as movement artifact and paroxysmal discharge, from activating the reward mechanism. During the subsequent seven month period of the first training year (February - August, 1972) the patient demonstrated a 60% reduction in reported seizures, as compared with the same period in the preceding year (Figure 7). A prototype portable training instrument, incorporating most of the features of the laboratory system, was developed by Neuro Feedback Instruments and tested with this patient during the next 12 month period. Practice consisted of six daily 30-min training sessions per week at a fixed time and location within the patient's home. Reported seizures during this period

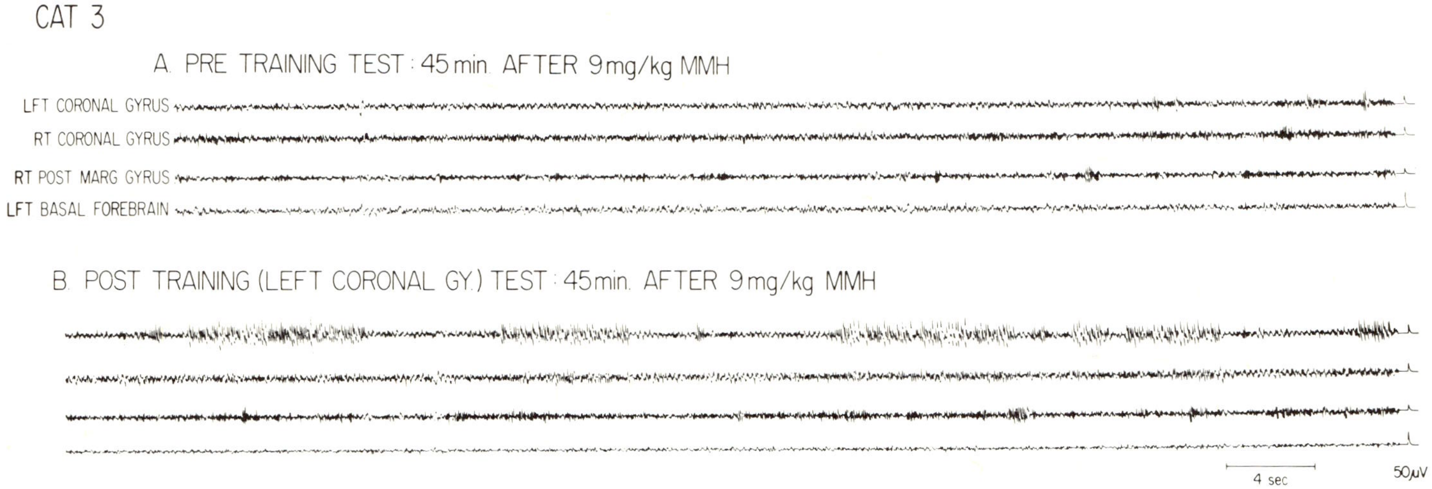

Figure 6. Sample EEG patterns recorded from the same cat 45 min after MMH administration, prior to and following SMR operant conditioning. Note intense EEG activation in both samples, but presence of recurrent SMR trains in sensorimotor cortex after conditioning. EEG training effect was primarily unilateral in this animal. (From Sterman et al., 1969)

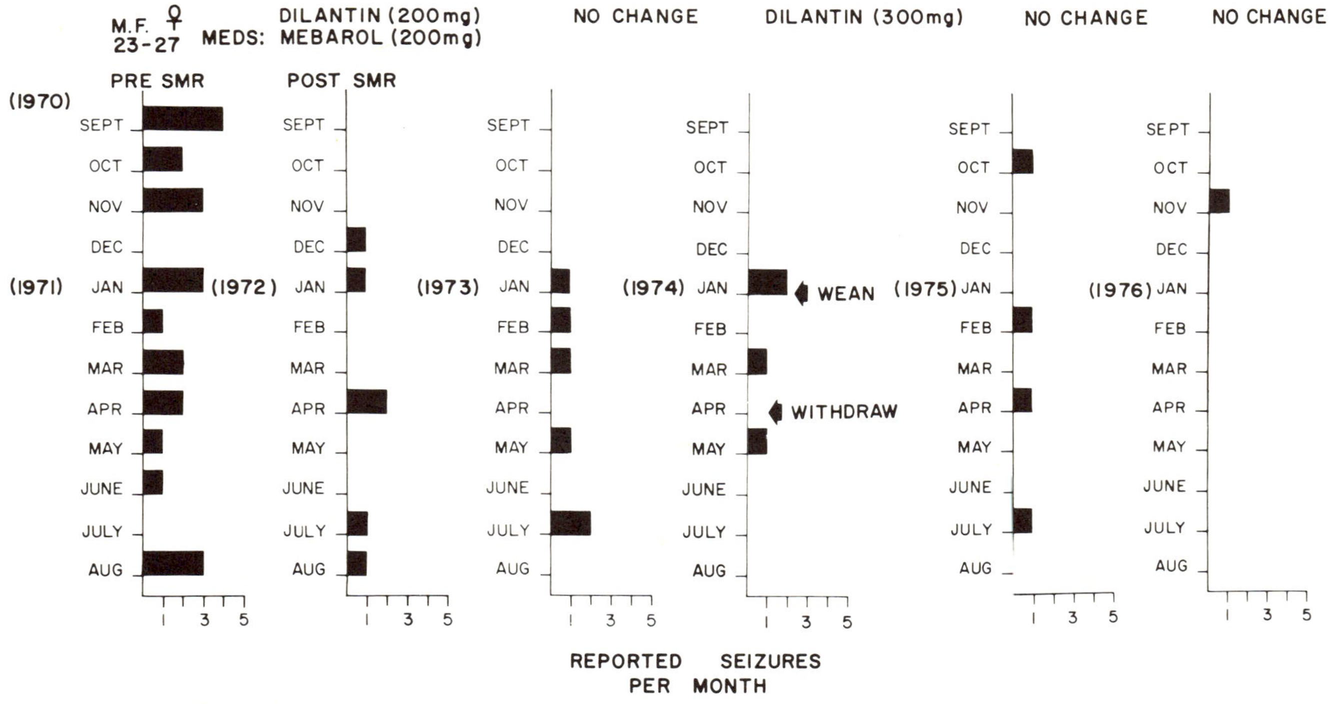

Figure 7. Six year seizure log showing generalized tonic-clonic seizures recorded by an epileptic subject before and after study in our laboratory. See text for details.

were reduced 74% when compared with the rate reported for the year preceding SMR training. In the third year of study, diphehylhydantoin medication was increased as indicated, and the patient was withdrawn gradually from home training (January - April, 1974). During this period seizure rate was further reduced (30%). The patient was followed for the subsequent 16-mo period without training (May, 1974 - August, 1975) and reported a total of five seizures (a reduction of 84% over the pre-training average rate. From September, 1975 through January, 1976 she was provided again with six months of training on advanced portable equipment (to be described below). The patient reported one seizure during this span. She was gradually withdrawn from training at the end of this period, and has reported no seizures during the subsequent six months.

At the same time that prolonged training and associated methodological refinements were being explored with this patient, three other epileptics were provided with systematic SMR feedback training in extended pilot studies. The epileptic subjects were evaluated over a two year period with three-per-week, 30-min laboratory training sessions only, and focusing exclusively on reward for production of 12-15 Hz central cortical rhythmic activity (0.5 sec trains at 5 µv or above), all subjects demonstrated improvement in both clinical and EEG manifestations of their seizure conditions (Sterman et al., 1974). At one point in the study these three patients were acutely withdrawn from training for a nine week period. Within four weeks all subjects reported an exacerbation of symptoms to pre-training levels, a fact which was confirmed through both clinical and laboratory EEG evaluations. Re-training led to rapid improvement, approximating previously reduced or altered seizure manifestations. An overall mean seizure reduction of approximately 65% was obtained with training. The best results were realized with major motor symptoms as compared with seizures involving disturbances of consciousness. Acute withdrawal was found to result in a delayed clinical regression, somewhat similar to that obtained with withdrawal from anticonvulsant medications.

As a result of these studies several other laboratories began investigating the effects of central cortical EEG feedback training on epilepsy. A summary of published findings to date is presented in Table 1. These findings are reviewed also in this text by Johnson ("Learned control of brain wave activity"). Data from six laboratories, involving 30 epileptics, have now been presented for scientific scrutiny. Of these, 25 (83%) have demonstrated reductions in seizure manifestations with central cortical EEG feedback training, utilizing frequencies ranging from 6-30 Hz. It is important to note that all of these patients had failed to respond adequately to previous anticonvulsant drug therapies. Moreover, the research represented by these studies involved a major investment in time and energy

Table 1

Summary of Central Cortical EEG Feedback Training Studies in Epileptics Indicating Selected Parameters for Comparison (Complete to May, 1976)

Investigator(s)	Frequency Rewarded	No. of Patients	No. Showing Seizure Reduction	Design & Approx. Duration of Training	
Sterman & Friar (1972)	11-13 Hz (+)	1	1	Single Case	3 mo.
Sterman et al. (1974)	12-14 Hz (+) < 10 (-)	4*	4	Group Pre-Post	6-18 mo.
Finley et al. (1975) and Finley (1976)	11-13 Hz (+) < 10 (-)	2	2	Two Single Case	10-22 mo.
Seifert & Lubar (1975) and Lubar & Bahler (1976)	12-14 Hz (+) 4-7 Hz (-)	8	7	Group Pre-Post	6-9 mo.
Kaplan (1975)	12-14 Hz (+) 6-12 Hz (+)	2 3**	0 2	Group Pre-Post	3-4 mo. 5-6 mo.
Kuhlman & Allison (1976)	9-14 Hz (+)	5	3	A-B	1-2 mo.
Wyler et al. (1976)	14-30 Hz (+) (Variable) < 14 Hz (-)	5	4	A-B-A (Variable)	1.5-6 mo.
Sterman (this paper***)	12-15 Hz (+) 18-23 Hz (+) 6-9 Hz (-)	3	3	A-B-A-B (Counter balanced)	12 mo.
Totals (Independent)		30	25 (83%)		

* Includes patient from earlier study

** Includes patient from other group (total N = 3)

*** Preliminary report of ongoing study (total N = 40)

in attempting to evaluate a complex procedure with a very elusive yet profound clinical problem. These facts should not be overlooked by critics who are quick to point out the small number of patients studied and the lack of textbook designs in this early work. Considering the alternatives presently available to uncontrolled seizure patients (or for that matter, to those who are controlled), these results must be viewed as most promising.

We have been acutely aware of the limitations of our initial studies in this area. In an effort to approach these problems systematically, it was necessary to first look carefully at central cortical EEG patterns in non-epileptic subjects provided with EEG feedback training.

Analysis of trained EEG responses in non-epileptic subjects indicated both pure and mixed frequency patterns that were bilaterally symmetrical or independently manifest in either hemisphere. The distribution and interactions among various sensorimotor cortex frequencies in the trained non-epileptic subject could sometimes be clarified by power spectral analysis. This was particularly true in control neurological patients with spinal cord injuries, who often showed enhanced SMR activity. An example is shown in Figure 8, which displays isometric power spectral plots from various bilateral pairs of recording leads obtained during 10 min of performance. In this example, various nonphysiologic artifacts such as eye or gross body movements are apparent in low frequency peaks localized to frontal recording leads. In other non-epileptic subjects there were often several partially independent frequencies apparent over central and frontal cortex, a 9-11 Hz rhythm associated with a similar but dominant frequency from parietal cortex (alpha), and multiple peaks between 12-15 Hz.

It was established that approximately 70% of normal non-epileptic subjects studied eventually developed trains of visible 12-15 Hz activity over central cortex with feedback training (Sterman et al., 1976). In contrast, it had been noted that epileptics, even after extensive training, showed visible bursts of SMR activity in the EEG only rarely if at all (Sterman et al., 1974). Moreover, in sleep recordings obtained from these patients a peculiar deficiency in sleep spindle activity was often observed. This correlation was reminiscent of the previously established relationship between waking SMR and sleep spindle activity in animal experiments. It had been suggested that these EEG patterns share a common neural substrate (Sterman et al., 1970). Additionally, there was substantial evidence relating this substrate to the suppression of motor excitability. It was possible, therefore, that this mechanism was deficient in some epileptics, and that this deficiency was related to the abnormality expressed

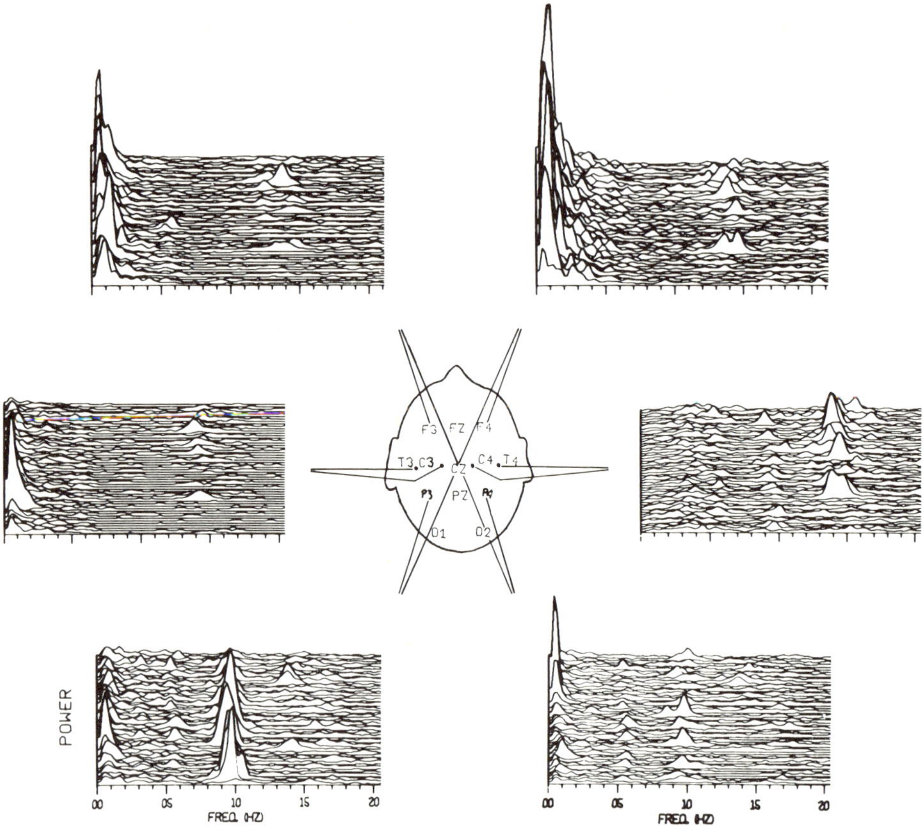

Figure 8. Power spectral analysis of cortical EEG activity during SMR training in a quadriparetic patient. Each trace represents analysis of a 17 sec epoch of EEG activity from electrode placements shown. Successive traces, plotted isometrically, represent a total of 10 min of EEG data (time in vertical dimension). The subject was rewarded for right central 12-15 Hz activity. Note central and frontal cortical peaks at these frequencies. Lower frequency (8-11 Hz) activity appeared to be attenuated in right parietal leads.

by their seizures. To further evaluate this hypothesis a comparative study of sleep EEG characteristics in epileptics and non-epileptics was initiated. The dependent variable in this study was the quality and quantity of central cortical EEG spindle activity during Stage 2 sleep.

To date, 13 neurologically normal subjects, ranging in age from 23-54 years, have been studied through all-night polygraphic sleep recordings. Data from these subjects are here compared to similar data from 17 epileptics. These patients ranged in age from 15-34 years. Each subject reported to the laboratory one hour before his usual bedtime. Recordings were obtained by standard methods with electrodes placed over left sensorimotor cortex at positions 10 and 30 percent lateral to vertex, with reference to the total interaural distance, or slightly medial to the C3 and T3 positions of the International 10-20 System. Electrodes were applied also to the skin at the outer canthus of each eye and over the chin and anterior digastric muscle, for recording eye movements and submental EMG, respectively. All data were recorded on a Grass Model 78 polygraph, with sensitivities set at 7.5 and low and high filters at 1 and 35 Hz, respectively, and on magnetic tape (Crown-Vetter, Model A). A time-code signal was recorded also on the polygraph record and on one channel of the magnetic tape recording.

Subjects slept in isolated, sound attenuated rooms with good ventilation and comfortable temperatures. Contact with the experimenter was maintained through an intercom system. After electrode impedances were checked and established at 10K or less, the recording was begun and continued until 8 A.M. the following morning.

Polygraph records were scored for stages of sleep according to the standardized criteria of Rechtshaffen and Kales (1968). The point of initial onset of Stage 2 sleep was determined and the subsequent 10 minutes of left sensorimotor EEG data were subjected to computer analysis. The signal was electronically pre-filtered between 0.5 - 40 Hz and digitized at a rate of 102.4 samples per second. Individual signals were equated for amplitude differences between subjects and recordings by reference to a standard 10 Hz, 50 μv calibration at the beginning of each record. A Fast Fourier Transform (Mason, 1970) was then used to calculate power spectral estimates for each 17.5 sec epoch of data. A three-point moving average filter was applied to the resulting spectra, and each spectrum was plotted isometrically (Bickford et al., 1972).

Examples of Stage 2 sleep power spectral profiles provided by isometric plots of consecutive 17.5 sec epochs over a 10 min period are shown in Figure 9 for five different non-epileptic subjects. Epileptics showed two significant deviations from this, one being irregular, abnormal peaks between 4-7 Hz (abnormal discharge), and the second reflected by irregular or deficient activity between 11-15 Hz (sleep spindles). These manifestations varied among patients, but the deficiency in 11-15 Hz spindle activity was most profound in patients with primarily generalized seizure disorders (Table 2). This deficiency is illustrated in Figure 10, which compares continuous isometric plots over an entire

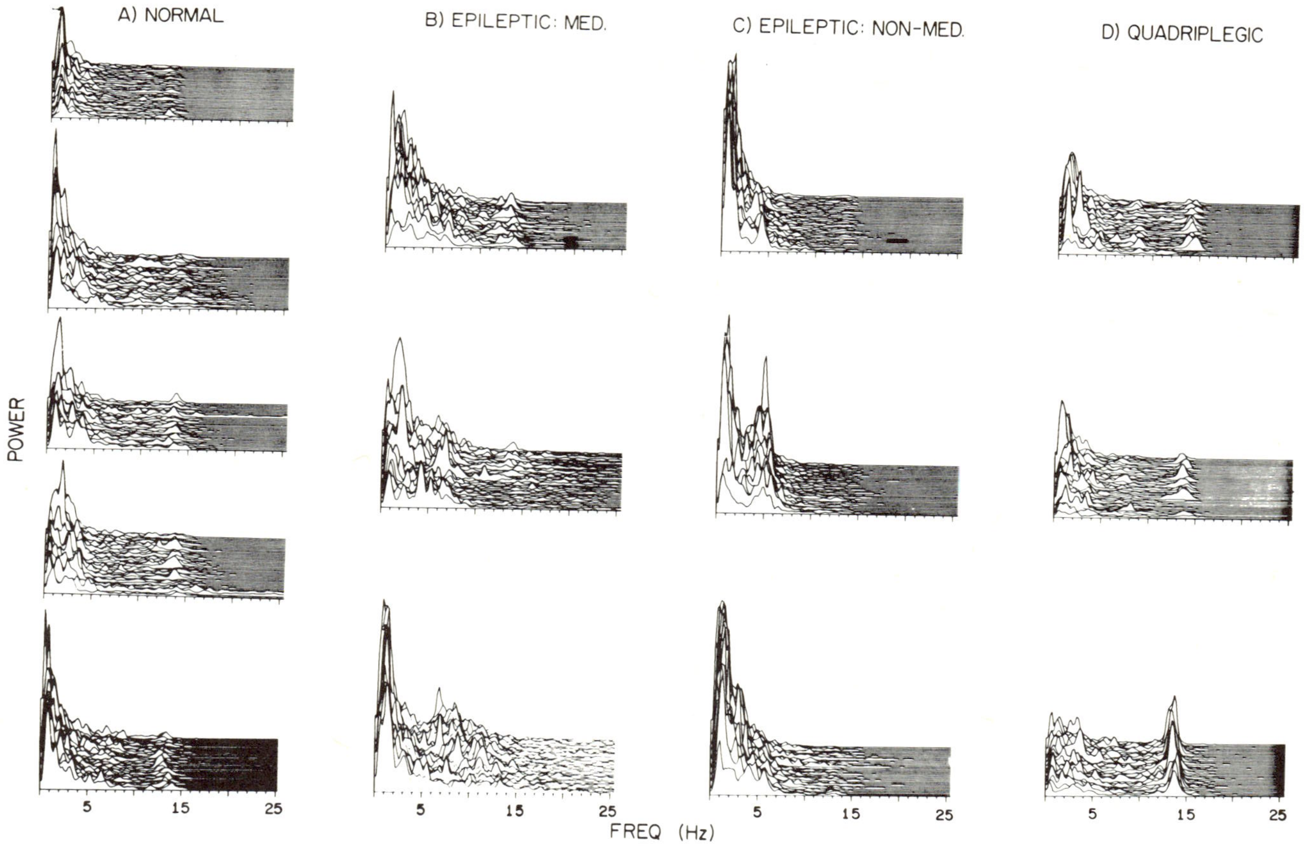

Figure 9. Comparison of isometric power spectral plots depicting central cortical EEG frequency distributions during the first 10 min of stage 2 sleep in five normal subjects (A), three medicated epileptics (B), three epileptics voluntarily withdrawn from medications (C), and three quadriplegic subjects. Note varia-

Table 2

Quantification of the Central Cortical EEG Power of two Frequency Bands in 17 Epileptics and 13 Neurologically Normal Subjects During the Initial 10 min of Stage 2 Sleep. Power is Expressed as the Percent Area Under the Curve between 0-9 Hz for the 4-7 Hz Band, and between 9-20 Hz for the 11-15 Hz Band. Data are Ordered on the Basis of Age

Non-epileptics				Epileptics					
Subject	Age	% 4-7 Hz	% 11-15 Hz	Subject	Age	% 4-7 Hz	% 11-15 Hz	Epilepsy Classification	Medications
1	23	23	64	1	15	36	41	Partial	Celontin & Phenobarb.
2	24	22	68	2	15	20	49	General	None
3	25	20	70	3	18	20	15	General	None
4	28	20	61	4	18	44	49	General	Celontin & Dilantin
5	30	28	61	5	18	30	64	General	Dilantin & Phenobarb.
6	32	21	64	6	22	16	66	Partial	Dilantin, Phenobarb., Valium
7	33	21	61	7	23	26	50	General	Dilantin & Mebarol
8	37	15	60	8	23	19	53	General	Dilantin & Tegretol
9	37	24	64	9	23	29	55	General	Dilantin
10	39	29	64	10	24	21	48	General	Dilantin & Tegretol
11	40	22	60	11	26	19	46	General	Mysoline, Tridione, Eskabarb.
12	48	15	68	12	28	34	37	General	Celontin & Dilantin
13	54	22	61	13	28	52	44	General	None
				14	28	34	73	Unclassified	Dilantin & Tranxine
				15	30	39	62	Partial	Dilantin & Phenobarb.
				16	30	29	64	Partial	Dilantin
				17	34	31	45	General	Tridione, Mysoline, Dilantin
Mean	34.6	21.7	63.5	Mean	23.7	29.3	50.6		
S.D.	9.3	4.0	3.3	S.D.	5.6	9.9	13.5		

three-hour sleep cycle in a non-epileptic and an unmedicated seizure patient. Statistical comparisons established a significant difference between the epileptic and non-epileptic subjects, with the former group showing more abnormal 4-7 Hz activity ($p = < 0.05$) and less normal 11-15 Hz activity ($p = < 0.01$). Individual differences were apparent in this regard, however, and suggested that these parameters may vary as a function of the particular epileptic condition and/or medications utilized by the patient.

We concluded from these findings that the Stage 2 EEG of many epileptics can provide several indices of abnormality, including increased low frequency activity (4-7 Hz) and deficient or irregular sleep spindle activity (11-15 Hz). Since these are physiological events which occur during the unconscious state of sleep, they provide an objective sign of epileptic pathology, which can be utilized in the assessment of potential therapies, including EEG feedback training.

A new study was initiated incorporating this measure and utilizing a sophisticated new portable training unit (Neuro Feedback Instruments, Neuroanalyzer 4000). This unit provided for positive reinforcement of one frequency-band contingent upon the suppression of activity in a second frequency band. Additionally, the reward system was aborted whenever a high frequency transient (> 50 μv + or -) occurred in the signal. The study in normals had indicated that central cortical 13 Hz activity and 15 Hz activity co-varied, while 10 Hz activity often changed in the opposite direction. One test band was established, therefore, as 12-15 Hz.[1] The 10 Hz frequency really represented a band noted frequently in normal subjects between 8-11 Hz, which is slowed somewhat in epileptics. Thus, a second test band was established at 6-9 Hz. Finally, to provide for assessment of higher frequency activity a third test band was set at 18-23 Hz. Thus, in a typical training situation the portable could provide a positive reward for the desired frequency (bright, continuous amber lamp as this frequency is held, flashing discrete green lamp when criterion amplitude and duration are reached, digital count on electronic counter and brief tone) and negative rewards (red lamps) for the presence of activity in the undesired frequency and the occurrence of a high voltage transient (movement, large slow wave or spike). The unit also contained a 4-channel strip chart recorder which registered home training time and counted each of the events described above on very slowly moving paper.

Recent studies have clearly established the fact that merely placing epileptics in an extended operant conditioning experiment and providing EMG feedback or random, non-contingent EEG feedback did not reduce their seizures (Kuhlman & Allison, 1976; Wyler et al., 1976). It was de-

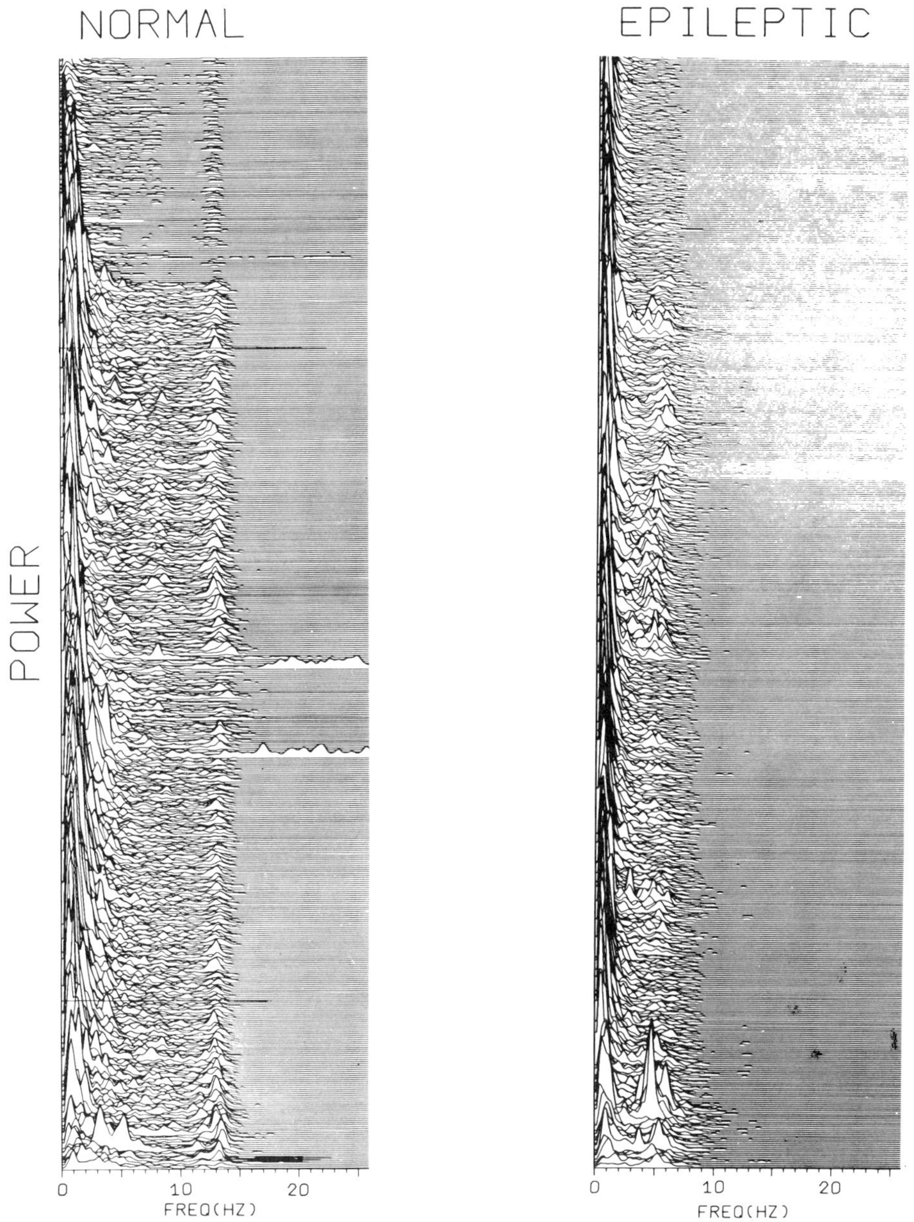

Figure 10. Comparison of isometric power spectral plots depicting central cortical EEG frequency characteristics during the first three hours of sleep in a neurologically normal subject (left) and a 15 year old, non-medicated epileptic with uncontrolled, generalized seizures (right). Epileptic showed abnormal 4-7 Hz discharge and marked attenuation of 12-15 Hz spindles during sleep. Both subjects are seen to enter REM sleep at top of continuous record. (From Sterman, 1976)

cided, therefore, to eliminate a non-contingent control group from our new design in favor of testing various frequency patterns in sensorimotor cortex. The design which has been initiated involves the evaluation of 40 epileptic patients over a four year period. Ten patients have been entered into this design to date, and three have completed the requisite year of participation. An attempt was made to select patients on the basis of 1) primary motor symptomatology, 2) previously uncontrolled and relatively frequent seizures, and 3) a history of reliable seizure logging.

Each patient is provided with a complete and independent neurological workup, including examination, clinical EEG and clinical anticonvulsant blood level determination. In addition, two all-night sleep polygraphic records with an extended EEG montage are obtained. Initial training is carried out in the laboratory, and preceded by three 30-min laboratory baseline recording sessions over a 10 day period. Patients are assigned, as accepted, to one of four training groups. The procedure for each involves an A-B-A design, in which the rewarded and suppressed frequency combinations are reversed at approximately three month intervals without the patient's knowledge (Table 3). The patient begins training in the laboratory with a portable unit and continuous EEG monitoring. Direct EEG recordings are compared to the EEG channel of the portable unit during this period. All recordings are obtained from left sensorimotor cortex with leads placed 10 and 30% lateral to vertex, as in sleep recordings. The subject is rewarded for criterion production of one frequency band only if a second frequency band is suppressed and no high voltage transients are present in the EEG.

Training continues daily during 30-min sessions for 1-3 weeks, depending upon the time required for the patient to demonstrate adequate use of the system. Initially, evidence of response acquisition was sought as a criterion for completion of the laboratory phase; however, this approach was dropped due to time restraints and the complex patterns of EEG response observed in this early phase. It was decided to let all patients proceed with the design as soon as they were comfortable with the training requirements and competent in the use of the equipment. The portable unit is then set up for use in a standard location and at a standard time in the patient's home. The patient is instructed to practice for a fixed 30-min period at least six days per week. At the end of two weeks the patient returns to the laboratory with the unit, is recorded during a standard training session and returns home without the unit. During this time the paper-tape record is removed from the unit for assessment of compliance, and the instrument sent home for a two week period with another patient in the same design group. In this way, two patients share a unit during alternate periods of two weeks on and two weeks off practice,

Table 3

Summary of A-B-A Design with Five Groups of Eight Subjects each, for Evaluation of EEG Operant Conditioning Effects

Condition	Group 1	Group 2	Group 3	Group 4	Group 5
Baseline	Lab EEG, Sleep EEG, Clin. EEG, Anticonv. Lev.	Lab EEG, Sleep EEG, Clin. EEG, Anticonv. Lev.	Lab EEG, Sleep EEG, Clin. EEG, Anticonv. Lev.	Lab EEG, Sleep EEG, Clin. EEG, Anticonv. Lev.	Lab EEG, Sleep EEG, Clin. EEG, Anticonv. Lev.
LABORATORY TRAINING PERIOD					
A_1	6-9 Hz + 12-15 Hz -	12-15 Hz + 6-9 Hz -	6-9 Hz + 18-23 Hz -	18-23 Hz + 6-9 Hz -	2-7 Hz -
REPEAT OF SLEEP AND CLINICAL MEASUREMENTS					
B	12-15 Hz + 6-9 Hz -	6-9 Hz + 12-15 Hz -	18-23 Hz + 6-9 Hz -	6-9 Hz + 18-23 Hz -	12-18 Hz +
REPEAT OF SLEEP AND CLINICAL MEASUREMENTS					
A_2	6-9 Hz + 12-15 Hz -	12-15 Hz + 6-9 Hz -	6-9 Hz + 18-23 Hz -	18-23 Hz + 6-9 Hz -	12-18 Hz + 2-7 Hz -
B TRAINING REPEATED WHERE APPROPRIATE					

with laboratory recordings obtained at each two week interval. After three months of this phase (condition A_1), the patient is again recorded during all-night sleep, clinical tests are again obtained and the patient started on a second three-month phase with reward contingencies reversed (condition B). The same schedule is maintained during this phase, after which complete sleep and clinical testing are repeated, and the third phase initiated with reward contingencies returned to their original configuration (condition A_2). Three patients have now completed this design.

The following is a summary of our findings with these initial cases.

Patient 1 was a healthy, 19-year-old Caucasian female of normal intelligence, with a six-year history of generalized tonic-clonic seizures of idiopathic onset. A variety of medicational regimes failed to adequately control these seizures. At the time of admission to our program the patient reported an average of one major motor seizure per month, despite a daily medication program of Dilantin, 300 mg, and phenobarbital, 90 mg, during the previous year. Medications were kept constant throughout participation in the study. Condition A_1 for this patient involved enhancement (+) of central 6-9 Hz activity concurrent with suppression (-) of central 12-15 Hz activity. Reward was contingent upon 0.5 sec trains of the former band, at 10 μv or above, in the absence of the latter band, or of paroxysmal discharge.

Comparisons of standard waking laboratory EEG records between baseline conditions and the three training phases are presented in Figure 11. Abnormal high voltage epileptiform activity is apparent prior to training and during the last laboratory record after three months of condition A_1. However, after three months of reversal training (condition B), with 12-15 Hz central activity as the rewarded frequency, overall EEG voltage was reduced significantly and abnormal discharge seen only rarely. A return to the original contingencies in condition A_2 was followed by a gradual deterioration of the EEG toward its earlier characteristics. This patient was provided with a three-month B_2 condition, so that the final training period would consist of the most therapeutic reward combination. The laboratory EEG data during training confirmed these observed results in that low frequency bands (0-3 Hz and 4-7 Hz) increased during conditions A_1 and A_2 (6-9 +), while high frequencies (16-19 Hz, 20-23 Hz and 24-27 Hz) decreased. The opposite was true during the B_1 and B_2 conditions (12-15 +), with low frequencies decreased and high frequencies increased. Surprisingly, neither 8-11 Hz or 12-15 Hz showed any significant changes throughout the design. However, the sleep EEG power spectra showed a specific increase in 12-15 Hz activity following condition B_1 (Figure 12). This analysis is presently being completed.

Reported clinical seizures throughout the experimental period were compared with seizures during identical periods in the preceding year. While this patient's seizure rate was relatively low, the pattern of seizures had been stable for several years. The condition prior to training represented the best control achieved with medications at a monthly average rate of 1.1 seizures evenly distributed over the calendar year. During conditions A_1 and A_2 the rate was 1.0 and 0.9 respectively, while the

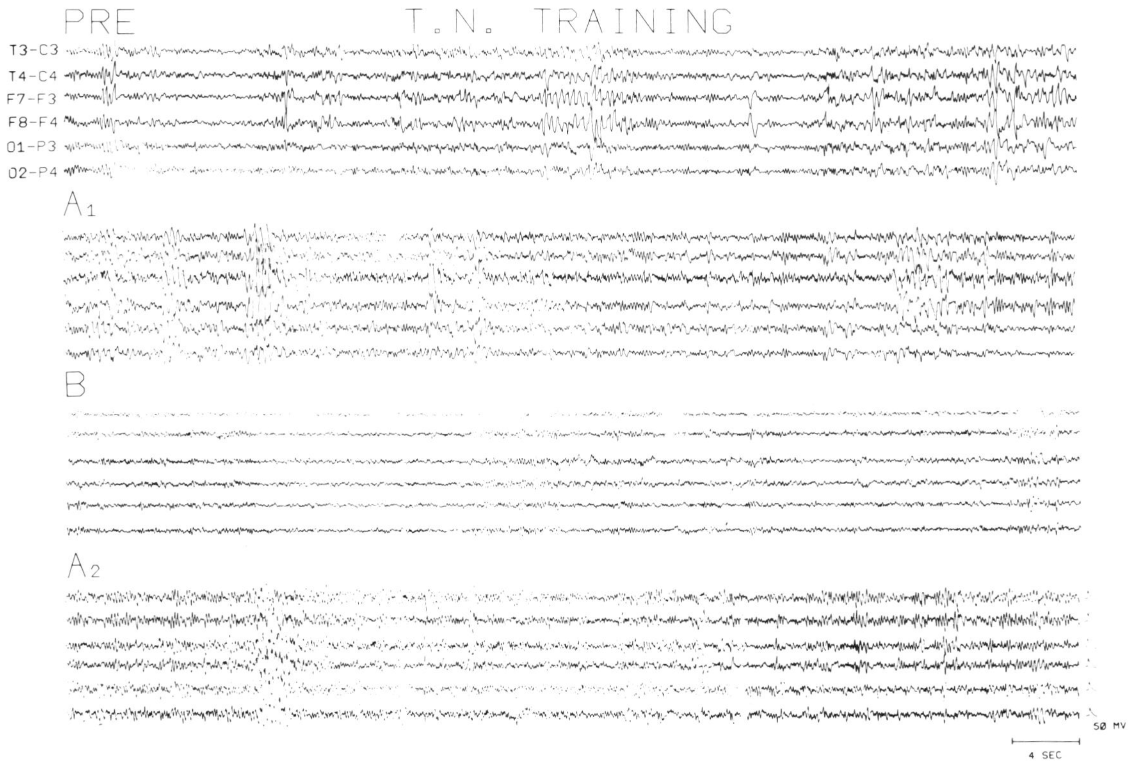

Figure 11. Sample EEG traces from laboratory recordings obtained during baseline and at end of each condition in the A-B-A design utilized for assessment of feedback training with this epileptic subject. Condition A_1 and A_2 consisted of feedback reward for 6-9 Hz central cortical activity in the absence of concurrent 12-15 Hz activity. Condition B provided reward for 12-15 Hz central cortical activity in the absence of concurrent 6-9 Hz. (From Sterman, 1976).

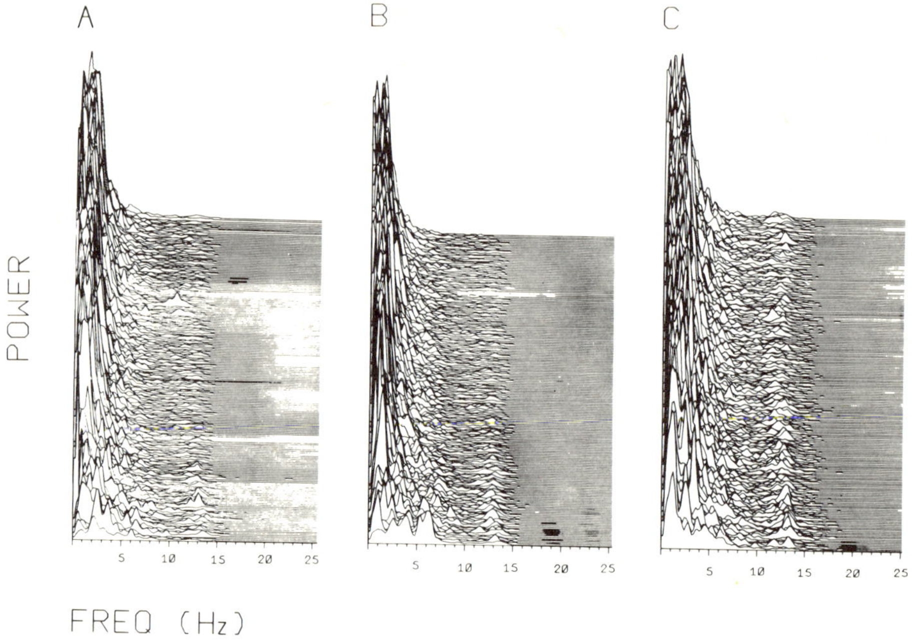

Figure 12. Comparison of isometric power spectral plots during the first 60 min of sleep in the epileptic subject whose training EEG samples are shown in Figure 11. Each trace represents 17 sec epoch of central EEG activity, with successive traces plotted vertically. Pre-training baseline sleep data are shown at A, while plot B shows sleep after three months of condition A_1 training (6-9 Hz +, 12-15 Hz -) and plot C shows sleep after reversal of these contingencies during three months of subsequent training (condition B, 12-15 Hz +). Note increase in 12-15 Hz sleep spindle activity in plot C.

rates reported during conditions B_1 and B_2 were 0.4 and 0.0.

In this patient, waking EEG data, sleep EEG data and reported seizure data all showed the same pattern during 12 months of experimental study. No sleep EEG or clinical changes were observed during or after three months of reward for 6-9 Hz central cortical activity. However, when reward parameters were changed such that 12-15 Hz activity was reinforced, the incidence of this frequency increased in the sleep EEG and seizure rate was reduced. Upon return to the previous reward contingencies, EEG and seizure rate data indicated a partial deterioration of this improved condition. A final training period, with reward for 12-15

Hz activity, again normalized the EEG and was accompanied by no reported seizures. During the three months of post-training follow-up to date, the patient continues to report no seizures.

Patient 2 was a 28-year-old, Caucasian male with a college education, who is married and has two children. Six years ago he was severely injured in an automobile accident and began a progressive seizure pattern during hospitalization from this accident. He was discharged from hospital on Dilantin therapy and subsequently began experiencing generalized tonic-clonic seizures with focal onset from the right parietal posterior temporal region. During the past five years these seizures were not controlled by anticonvulsants. As a result of undesired side effects from medication and unsatisfactory therapeutic effects, the patient voluntarily withdrew from anticonvulsants late in 1974. He entered our program in late spring of 1975 with an average reported seizure rate of 3-6 per month.

Condition A_1 for this patient was 18-23 hz (+) and 6-9 Hz (-). Spectral analysis of sleep EEG data indicated a high level of abnormal discharge in the 4-7 Hz range during Stage 2 sleep and an abnormally low level of 12-15 Hz activity. After three months of training in condition A_1 this pattern was changed significantly, with a 75% reduction in abnormal slow activity and an increase in spindle activity of approximately 15% (Figure 13-right). Reversal of training contingencies in condition B was followed by a partial restoration of the abnormal discharge during sleep and a reduction in 12-15 Hz activity. Analysis of sleep data following condition A_2 is incomplete at this time.

Concurrent seizure log data indicated that, within a month after the onset of condition A_1 training, seizures had essentially ceased. Reversal of training contingencies in condition B did not alter this picture, and throughout the remainder of the design this patient reported no further generalized seizures.

The third patient who has completed training was a 26-year-old male Caucasian suffering from frequent (40-50/mo) partial seizures with complex symptomatology (psychomotor). An atonic component to these seizures led to frequent falling episodes with associated head injuries, thereby requiring the use of a protective helmet during the day. Onset was idiopathic at age 12. This patient was assigned to Group 2 (Table 3) and received reward in condition A_1 for 12-15 Hz activity, in the absence of concurrent 6-9 Hz activity. Computer analysis of Stage 2 sleep activity indicated a very low level of 12-15 Hz spindles prior to training and a dramatic increase in this activity after three months of condition A_1 (Figure 13-left). A slight decrease in corresponding 4-7 Hz activity was docu-

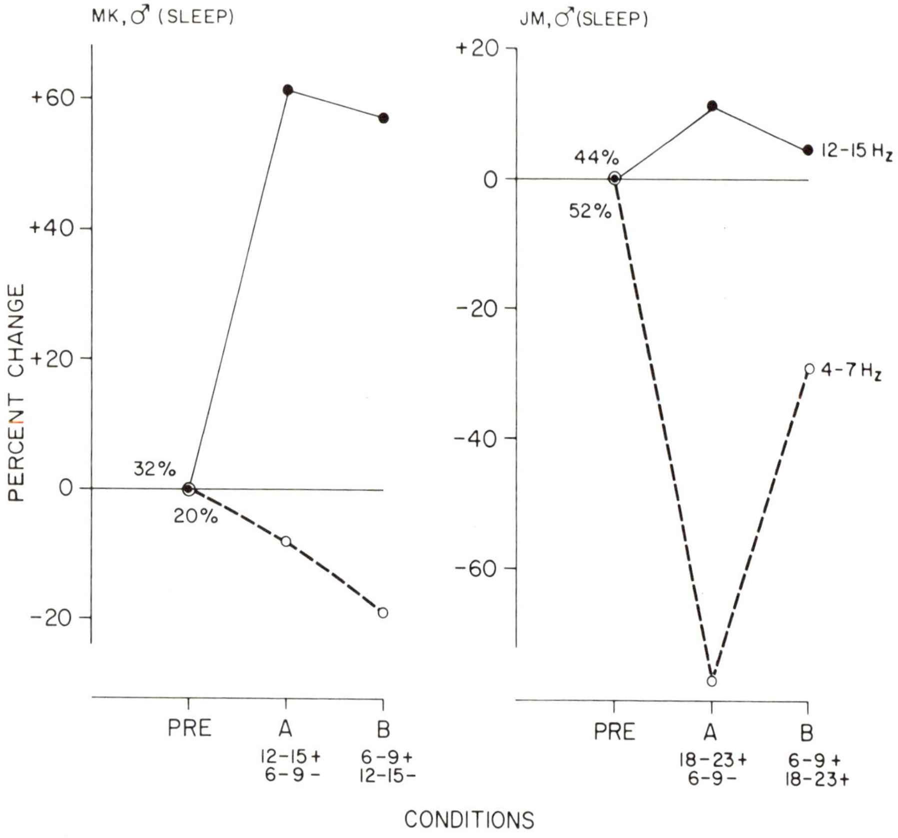

Figure 13. Quantitative analysis of power spectral data from central cortical EEG recordings during the first 10 min of stage 2 sleep in two epileptic subjects. Changes from pre-training baseline values are shown for sleep samples after successive three-month training conditions, A and B. Data points represent the percentage of 12-15 Hz activity (solid dots) within the 9-20 Hz band, and the percentage of 4-7 Hz activity (open dots) within the 0-9 Hz band during baseline sleep recordings (pre) and the percent change from these values following conditions A and B of the experimental design.

mented also. No significant change in spindle activity followed condition B, while a further decrease in low frequencies was observed. Sleep data from condition A_2 are presently being analyzed. Reported seizure rate dropped 20% in this patient during condition A_1, and stabilized at this level during condition B. There was a further fall in reported seizures of 30% during condition A_2, for a total reduction of 50% at the end of the nine month period of study.

While the data from these patients are definitive and most promising, any general conclusions derived must be considered as preliminary until adequate numbers of epileptics are tested in this manner. Nevertheless, it appears that meaningful changes in the EEG can be obtained through feedback training. Response to reward for the 6-9 Hz band with this method was less encouraging. Five patients have now completed an initial training period (A_1) during which 6-9 Hz activity was rewarded. In all of these subjects EEG patterns and reported seizure rates were clearly unaltered, and in several appeared to be exacerbated. Thus, reinforcement for this frequency band was not therapeutic, and may even be contraindicated, despite the fact that identical methods were used for all training conditions. Training at both higher frequencies (12-15 Hz and 18-23 Hz) reduced abnormal low frequency paroxysms, when present, and increased 12-15 Hz sleep spindles. It appears, however, that once therapeutic benefit is obtained in an effective training condition it becomes difficult to reverse this effect, regardless of the training paradigm. Thus, control training conditions (i.e., noncontingent or low frequency) can be documented most clearly only if they precede therapeutic training conditions, a fact noted also by Kuhlman and Allison (1976).

An additional training group was recently incorporated into our experimental design (Group 5, Table 3) in order to evaluate other potentially therapeutic parameters with this method. This group provides for the study of effects produced first by rewarding suppression of 2-7 Hz central cortical activity (condition A), followed by reward for a broad 12-18 Hz frequency band (condition B), and then a combination of the two (condition C). Three patients have now completed condition A in this group, without attendant EEG or clinical improvement.

Despite the clinical and theoretical debate which this area of investigation has provoked in some circles, there is now convincing evidence that EEG feedback training, involving central cortical frequencies ranging between 9-20 Hz, can produce quantitative reductions in both EEG and clinical manifestations of epilepsy. It is important to note that the studies leading to this conclusion have utilized the most difficult seizure conditions to be found, and have essentially ruled out explanations invoking altered compliance in the use of anticonvulsant medications, clinical peculiarities associated with increased attention on or by the patient, and the ubiquitous placebo effect.

This conclusion does not dispute the need for years of further investigation in this area. The effective parameters of the method remain to be determined, and its clinical utility for the vast majority of epileptics is as yet uncertain. Nevertheless, EEG feedback training has produced effects which justify serious consideration by those truly interested in the problem of epilepsy.

The potential therapeutic mechanism underlying this effectiveness has been the subject of increasing debate among investigators. While Kaplan (1975) suggested that relaxation associated with enhancement of central 6-12 Hz activity may account for the effect, Wyler et al. (1976) took the opposite view, invoking the well-established seizure disrupting influence of beta activity (EEG activation) which he felt may result from non-specific enhancement of higher frequencies. Wyler stated, also, that his findings implicate EEG spindles as a pathological sign, since abnormal cellular bursting discharge in monkey sensorimotor cortex was increased during locally recorded spindles (Wyler et al., 1974), and paroxysmal activity from epileptic foci in man was associated also with spindles recorded from these areas (Wyler et al., 1976).

The suggestion by Kaplan that reward for lower frequencies from central cortex might be therapeutic due to attendant relaxation is in direct contradiction of our recent findings, which show consistently that reward for these frequencies has either no effect on seizure manifestations or may, indeed, result in their intensification. It should be pointed out, however, that the electrode placements, signal detection method and data analysis procedures utilized in Kaplan's study were all different from ours. We are in basic agreement with Wyler and associates concerning the possible importance of cortical activation in the suppression of seizures. Using both band-pass and power spectral methods of analysis, we have observed several patterns of response in the waking EEG as a result of feedback training. As mentioned earlier, during training some patients showed a generalized increase in high frequency activity (16-27 Hz) combined with a decrease in lower frequencies (0-7 Hz). Despite these changes and the fact that reward was provided for 12-15 Hz activity, the incidence of the SMR often did not change with training, as reported also by Kaplan (1975) and Kuhlman and Allison (1976). However, other patients have shown training-specific increases in SMR activity.

Certainly, Wyler and co-workers do not suggest that sleep spindles are abnormal. They fail to stress the fact, however, that the spindles they describe were recorded from pathological cortical tissues. Whether or not they bear a functional relationship to normal sleep spindles is unclear. Since normal sensorimotor cortical neurons also showed bursting discharge in relation to sleep spindles, it is possible that abnormal neurons, which frequently display non-specific bursting, might show even more or faster bursting activity under this additional drive, without necessarily indicating increased abnormality.

Our interest in sleep spindles originally derived from an observed relationship between this pattern and SMR activity during both sleep (Sterman et al., 1965) and wakefulness (Sterman et al., 1970) in the cat. In this animal both SMR and spindle activity have been associated with decreased primary motor neuron excitability (Babb & Chase, 1974; Buchwald & Eldred, 1961; Hongo et al., 1964). Within this context, it is noteworthy that our analysis of Stage 2 sleep in epileptics, utilizing power spectral methods, indicated a significant deficiency in central 12-15 Hz activity for this group as compared with normal non-epileptics. Moreover, in the few patients who have completed the complex design of our current study, feedback reward for 12-15 Hz and 18-23 Hz, but not 6-9 Hz, produced consistent increases in this frequency band during sleep.

Several possibilities emerge from these considerations. Rhythmic 12-15 Hz activity represents a natural oscillatory discharge between undisturbed elements in sensorimotor thalamus and cortex (Anderson & Anderson, 1968). The resulting functional state of this system appears to be intermediate between a "highly engaged" condition during activation and a dissociated condition during slow waves. Empirically, the activated condition is usually associated with a suppression of seizure discharge, whereas the high voltage, slow patterns are associated with an increase in this activity. The intermediate condition of thalamocortical interaction during 12-15 Hz rhythmic activity would then represent an intermediate level of neuronal excitability. If some epileptics are deficient in this mechanism for intermediate control due to anatomical or neurochemical abnormalities, reduction in lemniscal or reticular drive could result in the synchronous activation of many neurons. This might explain the characteristic high voltage, slow EEG patterns seen in many epileptics during resting wakefulness and the typical enhancement and exacerbation of slow frequencies during non-REM sleep. Polyspike discharge may represent a different or extreme manifestation of this condition. The "exercise" of alternate pathways with feedback training, either of adjacent frequencies or of 12-15 Hz activity directly, could compensate for this deficiency, as indicated by increased higher frequencies and decreased lower frequencies during waking, and increased spindle activity during sleep. The inability of some epileptics to increase 12-15 Hz activity during training, therefore, may reflect underlying pathology rather than a failure in training.

One of the major factors responsible for the precipitation of seizures in epileptics is sleep loss (Berti Ceroni et al., 1967; Mattson et al.,

1965). In an ongoing study of a large series of severe, adult epileptics with mixed seizure types and etiologies, it was reported that 54% of these patients could associate seizures with sleep deprivation (Mattson et al., 1974; Pratt et al., 1968). While precipitating factors are often complex, a patient can be considered as significantly more vulnerable to seizures after a night with less than three hours of sleep. Thus, any influence which improves sleep might conceivably be therapeutic for the epileptic. It is interesting to note in this regard that many sedatives, and particularly the benzodiazepines, have anticonvulsant properties and produce increased sleep spindle activity (Johnson et al., 1976). We have observed, in both cats (Sterman et al., 1970; Lucas & Sterman, 1974) and man (Feinstein et al., 1974), that SMR feedback training can result in an improvement in the quality of sleep, as indicated by multiple sleep parameters, and an increase in the density and voltage of sleep spindle activity. Therefore, it is also possible that the observed reduction in seizure manifestations is a secondary consequence of improved sleep. It could be argued that a non-specific stress reducing influence, resulting indirectly from central cortical feedback training, or from increased alpha activity associated with such training (Kuhlman, 1976), might have the same effect; however, EMG and alpha rhythm feedback training, which are more direct methods for achieving relaxation, have not proven to be effective methods for improving sleep (Hauri et al., 1976). Additionally, in at least one patient, Wyler et al. (1976) found no decrease in seizures following feedback reward for EMG reduction.

There are many reasons to believe that the sleep spindle mechanism contributes significantly to the physiological organization of sleep. The notion that sleep spindle enhancement can be related to seizure reduction in patients who were previously deficient in this EEG parameter, therefore, raises the interesting possibility that some epilepsies may be associated with a specific, neurologically based disorder of sleep. We hope to explore this possibility in future studies.

Finally, we share the concern expressed by Kaplan (1975) and echoed by Gastaut (1975) over the present lack of a documented cause-effect relationship between EEG feedback effects and epilepsy. However, it seems inappropriate to be critical on such grounds in a field where pathological mechanisms remain unclear and the preferred method of treatment is empirical drug therapy. At this early stage in the development of a new area there is a greater need for research than for rhetoric.

REFERENCES

Andersen, P., & Andersson, S. A. Physiological basis of the alpha rhythm. New York: Appleton-Century-Crofts, 1968.

Babb, M. I., & Chase, M. H. Masseteric and digastric reflex activity during conditioned sensorimotor rhythm. Electroencephalography and Clinical Neurophysiology, 1974, 36, 357-365.

Berti Ceroni, G., Sabattini, L., Gambi, D., & Lugaresi, E. Effetti della "sleep deprivation" in epilettici. Riv. Neurol., 1967, 37, 56-57.

Bickford, R., Billinger, T. W., Fleming, N., & Steward, L. The compressed spectral array (CSA): A pictorial EEG. Proceedings of the Biomedical Symposium, San Diego, 1972, 3, 365-370.

Buchwald, J. S., & Eldred, E. Relations between gamma-efferent discharge and cortical activity. Electroencephalography and Clinical Neurophysiology, 1961, 13, 234.

Chase, M. H., & Harper, R. M. Somatomotor and visceromotor correlates of operantly conditioned 12-14 c/sec sensorimotor cortical activity. Electroencephalography and Clinical Neurophysiology, 1971, 31, 85-92.

Chase, M. H., McGinty, D. J., & Sterman, M. B. Cyclic variation in the amplitude of a brainstem reflex during sleep and wakefulness. Experentia, 1968, 24, 47-48.

Efron, R. The effect of olfactory stimuli in arresting unicate fits. Brain, 1956, 79, 267-281.

Efron, R. The conditioned inhibition of unicate fits. Brain, 1957, 80, 251-262.

Feinstein, B., Sterman, M. B., & Macdonald, L. R. Effects on sleep of EEG biofeedback training of sensorimotor cortical rhythms. Biofeedback and Self-Regulation, 1976, in press.

Finley, W. W. Operant conditioning of the EEG in two patients with epilepsy: Methodologic and clinical considerations. Pavolvian Journal of Biological Science, 1976, in press.

Finley, W. W., Smith, H. A., & Etherton, M. D. Reduction of seizures and normalization of the EEG in a severe epileptic following sensorimotor biofeedback training: Preliminary study. Biological Psychology, 1975, 2, 189-203.

Forster, F. M. Conditioning in sensory evoked seizures. Conditioned Reflex, 1966, 1, 224-234.

Forster, F. M. Conditional reflexes and sensory evoked epilepsy: The nature of the therapeutic process. Conditioned Reflex, 1969, 4, 103-114.

Forster, F. M., Ptacek, L. J., & Peterson, W. G. Auditory clicks in extinction of stroboscope induced seizures. Epilepsia, 1965, 6, 217-255.

Gastaut, H. Comments on "Biofeedback in epileptics: Equivocal relationship of reinforced EEG frequency to seizure reduction" by Bonnie Kaplan, Epilepsia, 16: 477-485, 1975. Epilepsia, 1975, 16, 487-490.

Guerrero-Figueroa, R., Barros, A., & DeBalbian Verster, F. Some inhibitory effects of attentive factors on experimental epilepsy. Epilepsia, 1963, 4, 225-240.

Hauri, P., Phelps, P. J., & Jordan, J. B. Biofeedback as a treatment for insomnia. Proceedings of the Biofeedback Research Society, Seventh Annual Meeting, Colorado Springs, 1976, p. 34. (Abstract)

Hongo, T. K. Kubota, K., & Shimazu, H. EEG spindle and depression of gamma motor activity. Journal of Neurophysiology, 1963, 26, 568.

Howe, R. C., & Sterman, M. B. Somatosensory system evoked potentials during waking behavior and sleep in the cat. Electroencephalography and Clinical Neurophysiology, 1973, 34, 605-618.

Johnson, L. C., Hanson, K., & Bickford, R. G. Effect of flurazepam on sleep spindles and k-complexes, Electroencephalography and Clinical Neurophysiology, 1976, 40, 67-77.

Kaplan, B. J. Biofeedback in epileptics: Equivocal relationship of reinforced EEG frequency to seizure reduction. Epilepsia, 1975, 16, 477-485.

Kuhlman, W. N., & Allison, T. EEG feedback training in the treatment of epilepsy: Some questions and some answers. Pavlovian Journal of Biological Science, 1976, in press.

Lubar, J. F., & Bahler, W. W. Behavioral management of epileptic seizures following EEG biofeedback training of the sensorimotor rhythm. Journal of Biofeedback and Self-Regulation, 1976, 1, 77-104.

Lucas, E. A., & Sterman, M. B. The polycyclic sleep-wake cycle in the cat: Effects produced by sensorimotor rhythm conditioning. Experimental Neurology, 1974, 42, 347-368.

Jason, J. R. Continuous Fast Fourier transform. DECUS #12-23, Digital Equipment Users Society, 1970.

Mattson, R. H., Lerner, E., & Dix, G. Precipitating and inhibiting factors in epilepsy: A statistical study. Epilepsia, 1974, 15, 271-272.

Mattson, R. H., Pratt, K. L., & Calverley, J. R. Electroencephalograms of epileptics following sleep deprivation. Archives of Neurology, 1965, 13, 310-315.

Pratt, K. L., Mattson, R. H., Weikers, N. J., & Williams, R. EEG activation of epileptics following sleep deprivation: A prospective analysis of 114 cases. Electroencephalography and Clinical Neurophysiology, 1968, 24, 11-15.

Rechtschaffen, A., & Kales, A. Manual of standardized terminology, techniques and scoring system for sleep stages of human subjects. Washington, D.C.: U.S. Government Printing Office, 1968.

Roth, S. R., Sterman, M. B., & Clemente, C. D. Comparison of EEG correlates of reinforcement, internal inhibition, and sleep. Electroencephalography and Clinical Neurophysiology, 1967, 23, 509-520.

Rougeul, A., Letalle, A., & Corvisier, J. Activite rhythmique du cortex somesthesizue primaire en relation avec l'immobilite chez le chat libre eveille. Electroencephalography and Clinical Neurophysiology, 1972, 33, 23-39.

Rouse, L. O. Conditioned inhibition of audiogenic seizures in DBA/2 mice. In S. Franklin (Ed.), Varieties of psychology. Fresno, California: Fresno State College, 1971.

Seifert, A. R., & Lubar, J. F. Reduction of epileptic seizures through EEG biofeedback training. Biological Psychology, 1975, 3, 157-184.

Sterman, M. B. Effects of brain surgery and EEG operant conditioning on seizure latency following monomethylhydrazine in the cat. Experimental Neurology, 1976, 50, 757-765.

Sterman, M. B., & Friar, L. Suppression of seizures in an epileptic following sensorimotor EEG feedback training. Electroencephalography and Clinical Neurophysiology, 1972, 33, 89-95.

Sterman, M. B., Howe, R. C., & Macdonald, L. R. Facilitation of spindle-burst sleep by conditioning of electroencephalographic activity while awake. Science, 1970, 167, 1146-1148.

Sterman, M. B., Knauss, B. A., Lehmann, D., & Clemente, C. D. Circadian sleep and waking patterns in the laboratory cat. Electroencephalography and Clinical Neurophysiology, 1965, 19, 509-517.

Sterman, M. B., LoPresti, R. W., & Fairchild, M. D. Electroencephalographic and behavioral studies of monomethylhydrazine toxicity in the cat. Technical Report AMRL-TR-69-3, Wright-Patterson Air Force Base, Ohio, Air Systems Command, 1969.

Sterman, M. B. Macdonald, L. R., Feinstein, B., & Bernsten, I. Analysis of extended narrow-band central cortical EEG biofeedback training. Biofeedback and Self-Regulation, 1976, in press.

Sterman, M. B., Macdonald, L. R., & Stone, R. K. Biofeedback training of the sensorimotor EEG rhythm in man: Effects on epilepsy. Epilepsia, 1974, 15, 395-416.

Sterman, M. B., & Wyrwicka, W. EEG correlates of sleep: Evidence for separate forebrain substrates. Brain Research, 1967, 6, 143-163.

Sterman, M. B., Wyrwicka, W., & Roth, S. R. Electrophysiological correlates and neural substrates of alimentary behavior in the cat. In J. P. Morgane & M. Wayner (Eds.), Neural regulation of food and water intake. New York: Annals N.Y. Acad. Sci., 1969.

Stevens, J. R. Electroencephalographic studies of conditional cerebral responses in epileptic subjects. Electroencephalography and Clinical Neurophysiology, 1960, 12, 431-444.

Stevens, J. R. Endogenous conditioning to abnormal cerebral electrical transients in man. Science, 1962, 137, 974-976.

Stevens, J. R., Milstein, V. M., & Dodds, S. A. Endogenous spike discharges as conditioned stimuli in man. Electroencephalography and Clinical Neurophysiology, 1967, 23, 57-66.

Wyler, A. R., Fetz, E. E., & Ward, A. A., Jr. Effects of operantly conditioning epileptic unit activity on seizure frequencies and electrophysiology of neocortical experimental foci. Experimental Neurology, 1974, 44, 113-125.

Wyler, A. R., Lockard, J. S., Ward, A. A., Jr., & Finch, C. A. Conditioned EEG desynchronization and seizure occurrence in patients. Electroencephalography and Clinical Neurophysiology, in press.

Wyrwicka, W., & Sterman, M. B. Instrumental conditioning of sensorimotor cortex EEG spindles in the waking cat. Physiology & Behavior, 1968, 3, 703-707.

NOTES

1. We recognize that the designation of frequency for both SMR and sleep spindles has varied in our work up to this point. This variation resulted from several valid considerations, but has not significantly altered the conclusions drawn from these studies. Current studies will focus upon the 12-15 Hz band.

The research reported here from our laboratory represents the collective efforts of many people over the past 10 years. Among these the author would like to give special credit to L. Macdonald and I. Bernsten and to Drs. W. Wyrwicka, M. D. Fairchild, R. H. Harper, R. K. Stone, M. Lucia, G. O. Walsh, L. Friar and R. LoPresti. This work was supported by the Veterans Administration, by U.S. Air Force Contract F33615-72-C-1885 and by NIH-NINDS Grant 5 R01 NS 10726.

VISCERAL LEARNING: CARDIOVASCULAR CONDITIONING IN PRIMATES

Alan H. Harris, David S. Goldstein, and Joseph V. Brady
Division of Behavioral Biology
Department of Psychiatry and Behavioral Sciences
The Johns Hopkins University School of Medicine

> "The importance of feed-back is clear. The organism must be stimulated by the consequences of its behavior if conditioning is to take place. In learning to wiggle one's ears, for example, it is necessary to know when the ears move if responses which produce movement are to be strengthened in comparison with responses which do not. In re-educating the patient in the use of a partially paralyzed limb, it may be of help to amplify the feed-back from slight movements, either with instruments or through the report of an instructor." (Skinner, 1953).

Behavior science developments over the past decade (Honig & Staddon, 1976), coupled with rapid advances in techniques for monitoring the circulation (Obrist, Black, Brener, & DiCara, 1974) have contributed substantially to the systematic experimental analysis of interacting cardiovascular-behavioral processes which define psychophysiological aspects of stress, anxiety, and emotional arousal. The results of rapidly expanding laboratory investigative efforts in this complex domain appear to reflect the emergence of two general models for the experimental analysis of such psychophysiological relationships (Brady & Harris, 1976). The first and more traditional concurrent model emphasizes the effects of antecedent or concurrent behavioral interactions upon the elicitation of physiological responses and has provided a productive framework for laboratory studies since at least the time of Pavlov (1879) and Cannon (1929). The second and more contemporary contingent model, in contrast, focuses upon the controlling effects of environmental-behavioral consequences which follow such physiological changes and bear a close temporal relationship to their occurrence.

The work of Forsyth and his colleagues (Forsyth, 1968, 1969, 1971, 1972; Forsyth, Hoffbrand, & Melmon, 1971; Forsyth & Harris, 1970) perhaps typifies more recent investigative programs within the context of concurrent psychophysiological models. In these experiments, rhesus monkeys were trained to perform on Sidman avoidance schedules (Sidman, 1953) which required the animals to maintain a continuous stream of responding in order to avoid receiving painful electric shock. During both acquisition and prolonged exposure to steady-state phases of this avoidance performance, several cardiovascular functions were monitored concurrently, including heart rate, systolic and diastolic blood pressure, regional blood flows, cardiac output, and total peripheral resistance. The results of these studies have contributed importantly to an understanding of cardiovascular-behavioral interactions at several critical levels. Most significantly, it was demonstrated that behavioral control of such avoidance schedules was accompanied by significant elevations of blood pressure and that these blood pressure elevations tended to persist throughout the day even after the termination of the avoidance conditioning session. Additionally, long-term exposure to the daily routine of a 12-hour "on", 12-hour "off" avoidance schedule often resulted in chronically elevated blood pressure levels that developed after four to five months of normal or hypotensive "off" period control pressures. Indeed, similar effects of recurrent acute sympathetic activation have been reported by Folkow and Rubinstein (1966) demonstrating that repeated stimulation of the anterolateral hypothalamus (i.e., "defense alarm area") for twelve hours per day resulted in a moderately sustained pressure elevation developing after several months exposure to such conditions. And McCubbin et al. (1965) have shown that subpressor doses of angiotensin, a powerful pressor agent, administered repeatedly over several days will eventually produce elevated pressure levels in rats, especially under conditions of environmental stress. These findings, along with the research of several other investigators including Charvat, Dell, and Folkow (1964), Pickering (1961), Henry and Cassel (1969) and Saslow and Blackly (1964), generally support a model of hypertension based upon the observation that repeated applications of environmental stressors which initially produce only transient cardiovascular pressor episodes, can eventually result in chronically elevated blood pressure. Descriptions of essential hypertension as a progressive disease which begins with a labile phase where blood pressure elevations are associated with an increased cardiac output, followed by a phase of chronically elevated blood pressure associated with increased peripheral resistance, are consistent with this model (Eich et al., 1962, 1966; Finkielman et al., 1965; Julius & Conway, 1968; Frohlich et al., 1970).

In later extensions of his work, Forsyth has also shown that avoidance schedules and other environmental stresses produce more marked pressor episodes in angiotensin-infused animals as compared with control (saline-infused) subjects (Forsyth et al., 1971). This finding supports the thesis that angiotensin can potentiate sympathetically mediated vasomotor activity, and is consistent with the reported interaction between environmental conditions, angiotensin, and the sympathetic nervous system (McCubbin et al., 1965). In addition, later studies have shown that continuous 72-hour exposure to the Sidman avoidance produces systematic changes in the cardiovascular pattern observed in the course of this 3-day stress interval. During the first several hours, heart rate and cardiac output are elevated, and a significant decrease in blood flow to the kidneys was observed to accompany the pressor response. Toward the end of the 72-hour period, the elevated blood pressure response was maintained by increased peripheral resistance with cardiac output and heart rate approximating control levels. Blood flow was redistributed to the heart, spleen, pancreas, and liver at the expense of the kidney, gastrointestinal organs, and skeletal muscle (Forsyth, 1972).

Additional psychophysiological studies within the framework of a concurrent model have also been reported by Brod and his colleagues (1959) showing that marked cardiovascular changes occur when humans are performing mental arithmetic problems under stringent time pressure. These cardiovascular changes included an elevation of arterial pressure, increased heart rate, increased blood flow to the muscles and markedly reduced blood flow to the kidneys and gastrointestinal tract. More recently, animals trained to respond to various reinforcement schedules of food reward and shock avoidance show concurrent schedule-specific cardiovascular patterns which include initially transient and sometimes chronic blood pressure elevations (Nathan & Smith, 1968; Forsyth, 1968; Herd et al., 1969; Brady et al., 1969; Forsyth & Harris, 1970; Anderson & Brady, 1971, 1972). And the results of several studies involving specific behavioral interaction patterns have demonstrated concurrent increases in the level of circulating catecholamines (Frankenhaeuser, 1971) and in the enzymes involved in the biosynthesis and metabolism of epinephrine and norepinephrine (Axelrod et al., 1970; Henry et al., 1971). Indeed, the involvement of the sympathetic-adrenal medullary system during emotional reactions to environmental stress was demonstrated many years ago by Cannon and De La Paz (1911) and has more recently been extensively studied within the context of a systematic concurrent analysis by Mason et al. (1968) and Brady (1970).

Relatively recent development of the more contemporary contingent model has been characterized by procedural arrangements which provide for physiological events (e.g., heart rate increases or blood pressure decreases) to exert a direct effect upon the occurrence of specific environmental events (e.g., food reward or shock punishment). The results of several recent experimental studies under such conditions, for example, have established that both heart rate (Engel & Gottlieb, 1970; Fields, 1970; Stephens et al., 1972; Harris et al., 1976) and blood pressure (Benson et al., 1969; Plumlee, 1969; Shapiro et al., 1969, 1970, 1971; Harris et al., 1971, 1973), among a wide range of other visceral and glandular responses (Miller, 1969; DiCara, 1970), can be modified by instrumental conditioning procedures involving contingent environmental consequences. During the past decade, several studies of both human and animal subjects have demonstrated the basic properties of such instrumental autonomic conditioning including response specificity (DiCara & Miller, 1968a; Fields, 1970), discriminative stimulus control (Miller & DiCara, 1976), reversibility (i.e., extinction) (Miller & Banuazizi, 1968; Fields, 1970), and the effectiveness of several modes of reinforcement (DiCara & Miller, 1968b). Although there continue to be a host of unanswered theoretical and methodological questions (Katkin & Murray, 1968), several clinical applications of such biofeedback conditioning procedures have been reported (Birk, 1974), including the treatment approaches to hypertension and cardiac arrhythmias (Engel & Melmon, 1968; Benson et al., 1971; Weiss & Engel, 1971). Indeed, changes in blood pressure produced by biofeedback conditioning procedures have been demonstrated in several different species of primates including squirrel monkeys (Benson et al., 1969), rhesus monkeys (Plumlee, 1968, 1969), baboons (Harris et al., 1971, 1973), and man (Shapiro et al., 1969, 1970, 1971; Benson et al., 1971; Schwartz et al., 1971).

Work in our own laboratories over the past several years with baboons as experimental subjects has focused upon the contingent psychophysiological model in analyzing the interaction between cardiovascular changes and environmental influences (Harris & Brady, 1974, 1976; Harris et al., 1971, 1973, 1976). Fifteen to twenty kg baboons (Papio sp.) have been used in this research because of the animal's size, hardiness, adaptability to surgery and long-term experimental conditions, and the similarity of their circulatory parameters (i.e., blood pressure, heart rate, clinical biochemistry) to man (McGraw & Sim, 1972; Weber, Brede, Retief, & Melby, 1971). Each animal was maintained in a primate restraining chair as shown in Figure 1 (Findley, Robinson, & Gilliam, 1971b), and housed in a sound-reducing experimental chamber provided with stimulus lights, an automatic food dispenser, a food tray, water spout, and a closed circuit TV monitoring system. Each baboon was surgically prepared, using a modification of previously described techniques (Werdegar, Johnson, & Mason, 1964) with two silicone-coated polyvinyl catheters, the arterial catheter implanted either in-

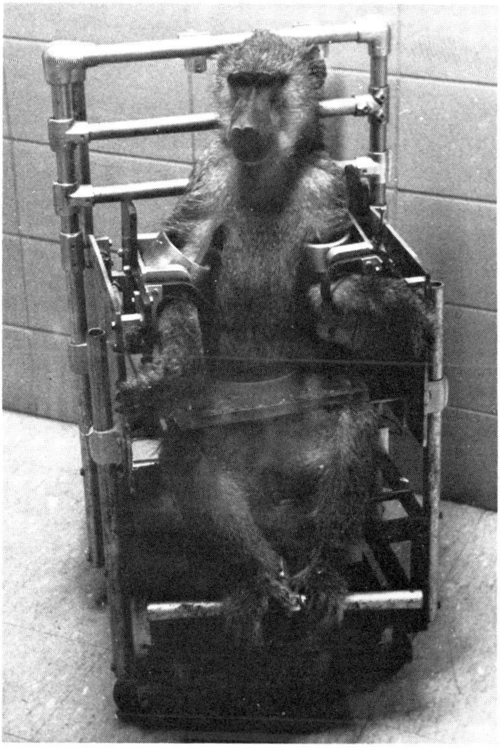

Figure 1. Baboon in restraint chair.

to a femoral or carotid artery and the venous catheter into the corresponding vein. The distal end of each catheter was tunneled under the skin and exited in the inter-scapular area, fitted with an 18-gauge Leur stud adapter, and the arterial catheters connected to a Statham transducer (P23De) mounted on the outside-top of the experimental chamber. The proximal end of each femoral catheter was advanced to just above the iliac bifurcation, while that of each neck catheter was advanced until intrathoracic. Patency of the arterial catheter was maintained by continuous infusion of lightly heparinized saline (5000 USP units per liter) at a constant rate of about 4 ml/hr and by a more rapid "flush" once each day. Daily calibration of the system was accomplished without dismantling the components by integration of a mercury manometer through a series of three-way valves (Findley, Brady, & Robinson, 1971a). Pressure signals from the transducer were amplified and displayed on an Offner polygraph (Type R) which provided continuous heart rate and beat-by-beat blood pressure recordings. In addition, the pressure and rate signals were analyzed by an electronic averager (Swinnen, 1968) which provided on-line printout of heart rate and systolic and diastolic blood pressure over consecutive prespecified intervals. Throughout the extended course of the experiments, blood pressure and heart rate were monitored continuously, 24 hours each day, and adjustable meter relays integrated with the physiological recording system provided for the selection of criterion diastolic blood pressure and/or heart rate levels. All programming of the experimental procedures and recordings of both physiological and behavioral responses were accomplished automatically and remotely using a system of relays, timers, switches, cumulative event markers, polygraphs, electronic averagers, and printout counters.

For the most part, the operantly controlled blood pressure increases and decreases described in the literature have been of limited magnitude and relatively short duration, and our initial studies with chair-restrained laboratory baboons focused upon the application of operant "shaping" techniques to generate and maintain large magnitude, enduring pressure changes (Harris et al., 1971). During the course of these experiments, both the amplitude and duration requirements for the blood pressure elevation response were systematically increased in small progressive steps to diastolic blood pressure levels above 125 mmHg maintained for intervals up to 5 minutes duration. The results of this study clearly demonstrated that large magnitude elevations in diastolic blood pressure, 50 to 60 mmHg above resting levels, could be generated under conditions which made shock-avoidance and food-acquisition contingent upon the required pressure elevations. Furthermore, these experiments confirmed that such instrumentally-conditioned circulatory changes could be brought under explicit exteroceptive environmental stimulus control and that they could be produced on a relatively acute basis (i.e., intervals up to 5 minutes in duration) seventy or more times each day over the extended course of these initial studies.

Ongoing studies of more chronic adaptations of the systemic circulation to operant control procedures involving food and shock-avoidance as contingent consequences of prespecified cardiovascular changes have focused upon the effects of daily 12-hour conditioning sessions ("conditioning on") alternating with a 12-hour rest period ("conditioning off"). As part of these operant conditioning procedures, the experimental subjects are provided with two "feedback" lights; a white light which is associated with cardiovascular levels above a prespecified criterion, and in the presence of which food pellet rewards are delivered; and a red light which is associated with cardiovascular levels below that of a prespecified criterion and in the presence of which aversive electric shocks are programmed. Under these conditions, a shock-free, food-abundant environment is made

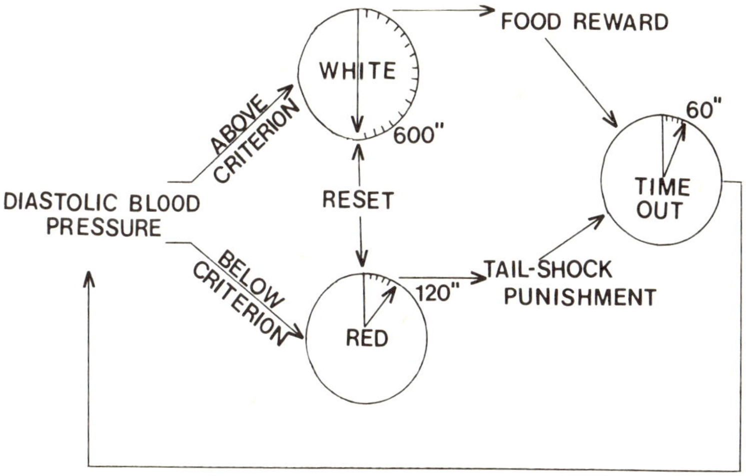

Figure 2. Blood pressure conditioning procedures. See text for procedural description.

contingent upon the maintenance of effective control over selected circulatory functions.

The conditioning procedures, diagrammed in Figure 2, required the animals to maintain prespecified diastolic blood pressure levels in order to obtain food and avoid shock. Five one-gram pellets were delivered to the animal for every 10 minutes of accumulated time that the diastolic pressure exceeded criterion, as indicated by the white light. Conversely, the animal received a single, 8 ma, 0.25 second electrical shock through stainless-steel electrodes applied to a shaved portion of the animal's tail for every 120 seconds of accumulated time that the diastolic pressure was below criterion, as indicated by the red light. Additionally, each food delivery reset the shock timer postponing the delivery of shocks for an additional 120 seconds, and each occurrence of an electric shock reset the food timer, postponing the delivery of food for at least an additional ten minutes. A one minute "time out" from stimuli and contingencies followed each food or shock delivery.

At the beginning of the training period, the criterion pressure levels were determined by the animal's pre-conditioning, resting, baseline diastolic pressure (approximately 75 mmHg). Increases in the criterion occurred at a gradual, progressive rate of about 1 to 2 mmHg per week over a period of two to three months. Conditioning sessions occurred daily dur-

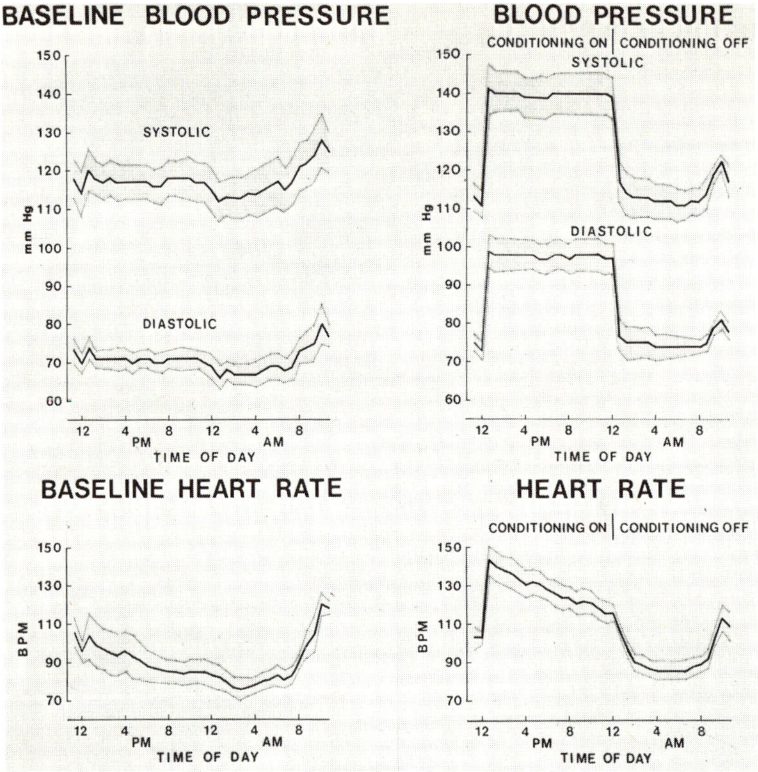

Figure 3. Average blood pressure and heart rate values (+ S.E.) for seven baboons over consecutive 40-minute intervals during 28 pre-experimental baseline determinations (left panels), compared with 28 12-hour conditioning-on, 12-hour conditioning-off sessions (right panels).

ing a 12-hour period from noon to midnight ("conditioning on") alternating with a 12-hour period from midnight to noon during which no programmed contingencies were in effect ("conditioning off"). In the course of a 2 to 3 month training interval, seven baboons attained diastolic blood pressure levels during the conditioning sessions which were elevated by at least 25 mmHg (approximately 33%) over baseline values, and they maintained these elevated pressures for more than 90% of each 12-hour session, as illustrated in Figure 3. This figure shows consecutive 40-minute interval averages, and summarizes, in the right hand panel, the stable response pattern which developed after the baboons had been exposed to at least 40 daily 12-hour conditioning sessions. During these daily conditioning sessions, the animals received on the average about 2 shocks (currently < 1)

and 25 pellets per hour. Characteristically, sustained elevations of 30 mmHg or more in both systolic and diastolic blood pressure were maintained throughout the 12-hour "conditioning on" period accompanied by elevated but progressively decreasing heart rate over the course of the 12-hour interval. During the ensuing 12-hour "conditioning off" recovery period, heart rate continued to fall somewhat precipitously, and blood pressure returned to approximately basal levels (or slightly above) within 6 to 8 hours.

That these large magnitude, sustained elevations in blood pressure are related directly and specifically to the programmed contingency requirements of the instrumental conditioning procedure is further confirmed by the results obtained with two additional baboons exposed to virtually identical experimental conditions with the exception that concurrent food-reward and shock-avoidance were made contingent upon decreasing diastolic blood pressure. Over extended intervals (6 months or more) of daily exposure to this instrumental procedure for lowering blood pressure (involving electric shocks, food deprivation and reward, surgery and chronic catheterization, confinement and chair restraint) neither animal showed any change from baseline cardiovascular levels under the same general laboratory condition prevailing for the seven baboons which showed contingent blood pressure elevations.

Two additional baboons have been similarly conditioned but with the contingency directed at heart rate increases. Specifically, the conditioning procedure required the animals to maintain prespecified heart rate levels in order to obtain food and avoid shock. Initially, the criterion heart rate was set 10 - 15 bpm above the animal's pre-experimental resting baseline levels, with progressive increases programmed to occur at a rate approximating 7 bpm per week over a period of 8 - 10 weeks. Within this 2 - 3 month interval, heart rate doubled, reaching levels maintained above 165 bpm for more than 95% of each daily 12-hour conditioning session. During these conditioning sessions, the animal received, on the average, less than 1 electric shock and more than 20 food pellets per hour.

Figure 4 compares the concurrent changes in blood pressure and heart rate during the 12-hour conditioning-on, 12-hour conditioning-off periods with the changes in blood pressure and heart rate during the pre-conditioning baseline period. The data plot in Figure 4 is in the form of averages for four consecutive 24-hour experimental conditioning sessions (right panel) for each of the two baboons and four consecutive 24-hour pre-experimental baseline sessions (left panel) for the same two animals before conditioning. This figure shows consecutive 40-minute interval aver-

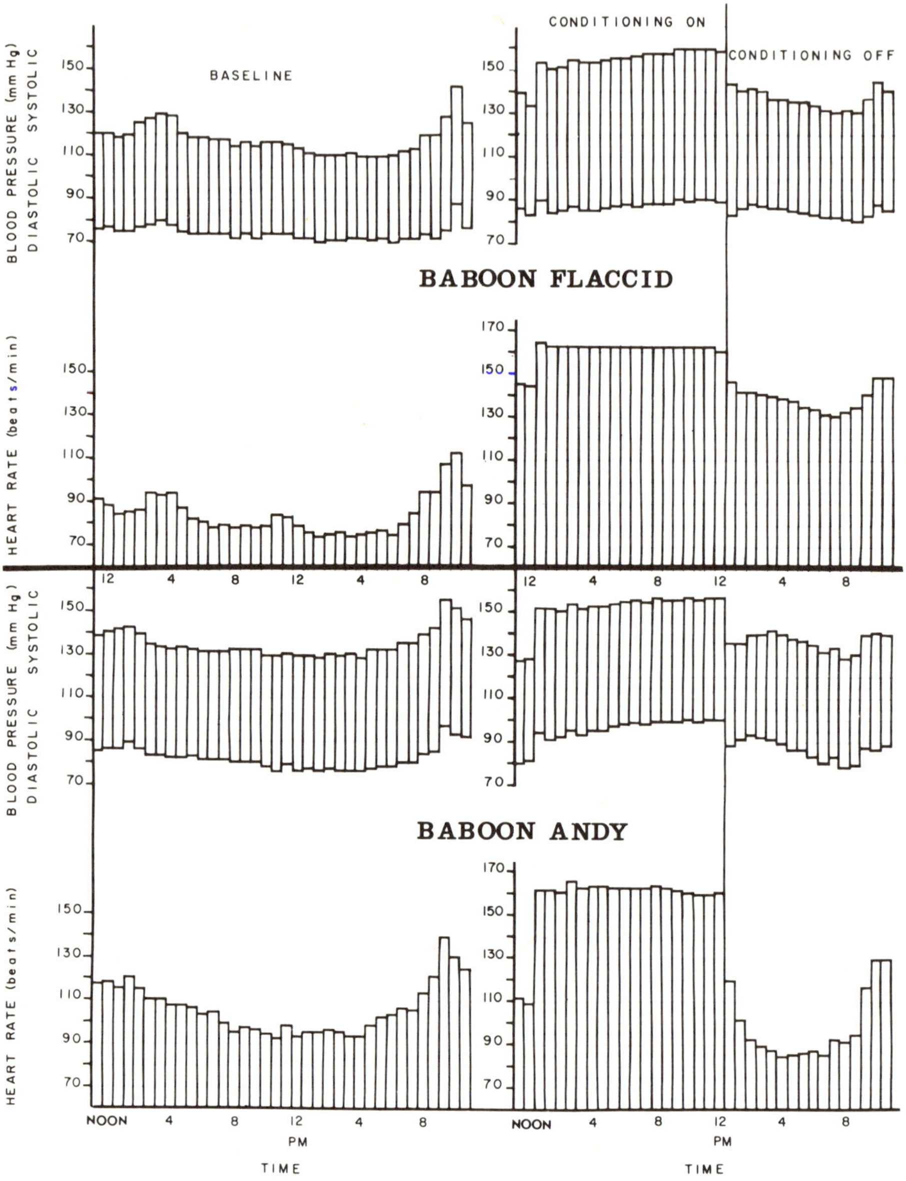

Figure 4. Heart rate and blood pressure values for baboons "Flaccid" (top) and "Andy" (bottom) averaged over 40-minute intervals during four consecutive pre-experimental baseline days (left panels) compared with four consecutive days during the 12-hr ON-12-hr OFF heart rate conditioning program (right panels).

ages, and summarizes in the right-hand panel the response pattern which developed after the baboons had been exposed to at least 40 daily 12-hour conditioning sessions.

Characteristically, the onset of the 12-hour conditioning sessions occasioned a rapid rise in heart rate which was sustained at levels approximating 165 bpm throughout the 12-hour conditioning-on periods for both animals. For baboon Andy, heart rate rose from a forenoon level of about 110 bpm to a sustained level (afternoon) of approximately 162 bpm. At midnight, when the 12-hour conditioning sessions terminated, heart rate rapidly returned to baseline levels below 100 bpm. Conditioning-on heart rate levels of similar magnitude were observed with baboon Flaccid though it is noteworthy that the cardiac rate did not return to pre-experimental baseline levels for this animal. As shown in Figure 4, Flaccid's conditioning-off heart rate remained elevated above 130 bpm (compared to a pre-experimental baseline approximating 80 bpm) and the conditioning-on levels approximating 165 bpm represented an increase of 20 to 30 bpm. For both subjects, blood pressure (both systolic and diastolic) showed a progressive rise of about 12 mmHg during the course of the 12-hour conditioning-on period and returned to baseline levels during the 12-hour conditioning-off interval.

These results show that marked and durable increases in heart rate can be produced in the baboon through the application of concurrent food reward and shock avoidance conditioning procedures. These heart rate elevations were sustained during daily 12-hour conditioning sessions and were accompanied by modest but progressive increases in blood pressure. Significantly, the heart rate increases generated in the animals under the heart rate contingency were at least 200% greater than the heart rate increases in the animals trained under the blood pressure contingency, while the blood pressure increase in the former was less than half as large as the pressure increase in the latter.

Adequate understanding of the physiological processes underlying these conditioned changes requires consideration of the complex system of interacting mechanisms controlling the circulation (Korner, 1971). The sympathetic adrenergic nervous system, by its influences on cardiac rate and contractility, arterial resistance, and venous capacitance, plays a major role in the modulation of blood pressure (Engleman & Braunwald, 1974; Leutscher, Boyers, Cuthbertson, & McMahon, 1973). Accordingly, we investigated the possible involvement of sympathetic adrenergic nervous activity in operantly conditioned hypertension. Because increased sympathetic nervous activity contributes to the transient hypertension observed in response to stressful environmental-behavioral interactions such as classical aversive conditioning (Bergasmaschi & Longoni, 1973; Klose, Augenstein, Schneiderman, Manas, Abrams, & Bloom, 1975; Randall & Smith, 1974) and operant avoidance conditioning (Anderson & Brady, 1973; Anderson, Yingling, & Brady, 1974; Kelleher, Morse, & Herd, 1972), we hypothesized that increased sympathetic adrenergic activity would also occur in association with operantly conditioned increases in blood pressure.

A technique for assessing sympathetic adrenergic nervous activity which is particularly useful in the behaving, conscious animal subject involves administration of specific adrenergic receptor blockers. On the basis of a systematic study of the effects of catecholamines, Ahlquist (1948) proposed the modern classification of adrenergic receptors as either alpha or beta. The heart is predominantly under beta-adrenergic control and the vasculature is under alpha-adrenergic control (Nickerson, 1973). Alpha-adrenergic agonists such as phenylephrine have no direct cardiac effect (Varma, Johnson, Sherman, & Youmans, 1960), but increase blood pressure by contracting peripheral vascular beds (Goodman & Gilman, 1970). Beta-adrenergic agonists such as isoproterenol increase heart rate and contractility and dilate skeletal muscular beds (Goodman & Gilman, 1970). The contribution of alpha- and beta-adrenergic receptor activity may be inferred from the effects of specific alpha receptor blockers such as phentolamine and phenoxybenzamine and specific beta receptor blockers such as propranolol.

We used this pharmacologic approach to assess the effects of specific alpha-, beta- and combined alpha- and beta-adrenergic blockers on the acute increases in blood pressure observed at the beginning of the daily 12-hour training sessions in baboons reinforced for increasing their diastolic blood pressures. Four baboons were tested under control (no blockade), beta-blockade, and alpha-blockade conditions. These four plus one additional baboon were also tested under combined alpha- and beta-blockade. Adequate alpha-blockade was inferred if phenylephrine, at a dose producing at least a 45 mmHg increase in systolic pressure prior to phenoxybenzamine, produced no detectable increase in systolic pressure after phenoxybenzamine. Adequate beta-blockade was inferred if isoproterenol, at a dose producing at least an 80 bpm increase in heart rate prior to propranolol, produced no detectable increase in heart rate after propranolol. These effects are illustrated in Figure 5.

By using a combination of food-reward, shock-avoidance, and visual biofeedback, all contingent upon diastolic blood pressure, the baboons were conditioned, in 3 - 4 months, to raise their blood pressure 30% above pre-conditioning baseline levels, and to maintain the increased pressure

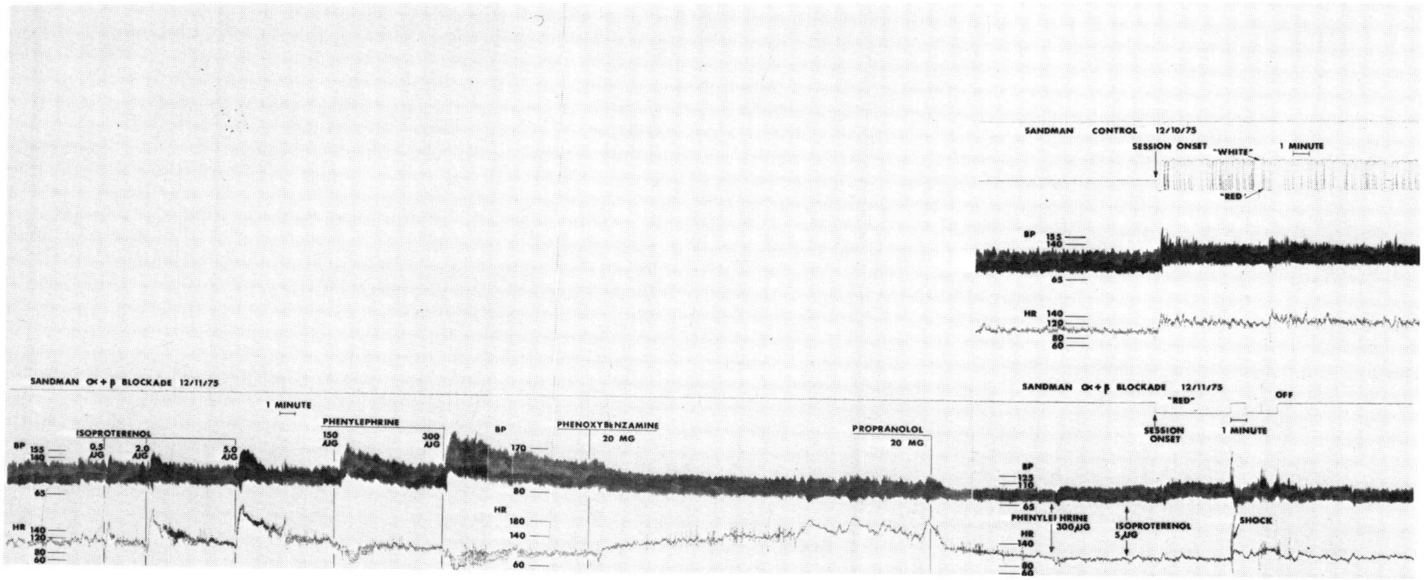

Figure 5. Polygraph records for baboon "Sandman" showing the sequence of events during an experimental session involving both alpha- and beta- adrenergic blockade. The blood pressure and heart rate effects of alpha (phenylephrine) and beta (isoproterenol) adrenergic agonists are shown before and after combined alpha and beta blockade with phenoxybenzamine and propranolol, respectively (lower record). Lower record (right side) also shows the blood pressure and heart rate response to the onset of the conditioning session following combined alpha and beta-adrenergic blockade. For comparison, the upper record on the right shows the characteristic conditioned cardiovascular effects one day prior to any drug administration.

during daily 12-hour training sessions. The typical conditioned cardiovascular response each day included a sharp rise in both blood pressure and heart rate at the beginning of each conditioning session, as shown for baboons "Sandman," "Kingfish," and "Charlie," in the control records of Figures 5, 6, and 8 respectively. Administration of the specific beta-adrenergic blocker, propranolol, virtually eliminated the tachycardia usually accompanying the conditioned hypertension, thereby demonstrating that augmented beta-adrenergic activity accounts almost entirely for the tachycardia. Propranolol did not, however, significantly attenuate the increase in diastolic pressure, as shown for baboon "Kingfish" in Figure 6. Similarly, alpha blockade did not significantly attenuate the conditioned blood pressure elevation, but increased tachycardia accompanied the pressor episodes after alpha blockade as shown for baboons "Flip," and "Kingfish" in Figure 7. Combined alpha and beta-adrenergic blockade did significantly attenuate the increase in blood pressure, however, indicating that sympathetic adrenergic activity does participate to some extent in the conditioned hypertension. Surprisingly though, even under conditions of extensive adrenergic blockade--as indicated by abolition of the tachycardic effect of doses of isoproterenol normally producing more than 80 bpm increases in heart rate and by abolition of the hypertensive effect of doses of phenylephrine normally producing more than 45 mmHg increases in blood pressure--clearcut, consistent, and statistically significant increases in systolic and diastolic pressure continued to occur, as shown in Figure 8 and Figure 5. It is possible that the blockade wore off quickly due to a massive sympathetic nervous or adrenal discharge at the beginning of the sessions; however, administration of adrenergic agonists after the session onset at 12:10 PM repeatedly showed continued effective blockade. The results suggest the participation of some non-adrenergic factor or factors in operantly conditioned hypertension. Possible factors include a direct effect of skeletal muscular contraction on circulatory variables (Dews & Herd, 1974), participation of renin-angiotensin system (Forsyth, Hoffbrand, & Melmon, 1971), and parasympathetically-mediated alterations in myocardial contractility (Higgins, Vatner, & Braunwald, 1973).

Other investigators have measured the effects of alpha- and beta-adrenergic blockade on the circulatory response to stressful environmental-behavioral interactions. Our results are similar to those of Kelleher, Morse and Herd (1972), who found that in squirrel monkeys undergoing avoidance conditioning, neither propranolol nor phentolamine attenuated episodic increases in blood pressure during the conditioning periods, although propranolol eliminated the associated episodic tachycardia. Anderson and Brady (1973) similarly found that beta-blockade attenuated the tachycardia usually associated with avoidance behavior in dogs, but did

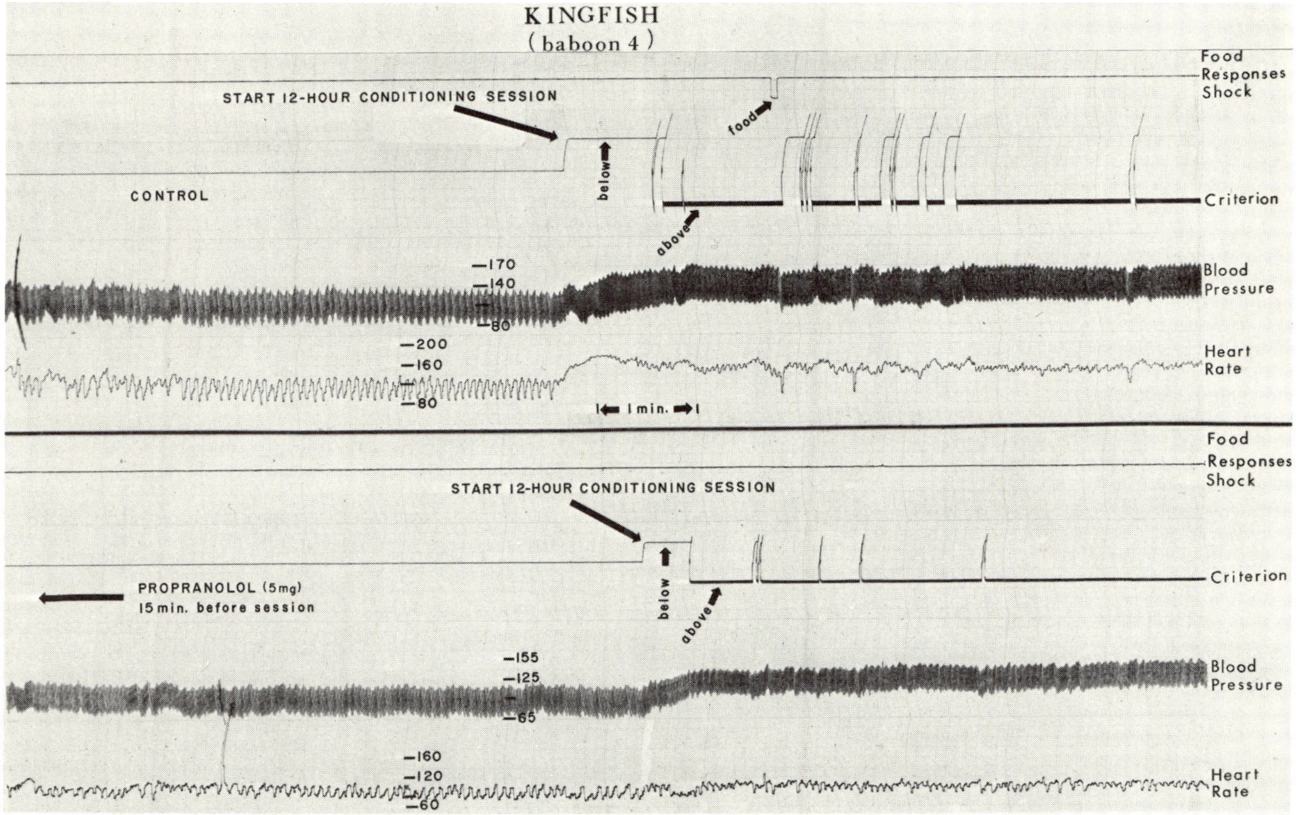

Figure 6. Polygraph records for baboon "Kingfish," showing the heart rate and blood pressure response to the conditioning session onset at noon, before (top record) and after (bottom record) beta-adrenergic blockade. Note the elimination of the heart rate increase that usually accompanies the blood pressure increase.

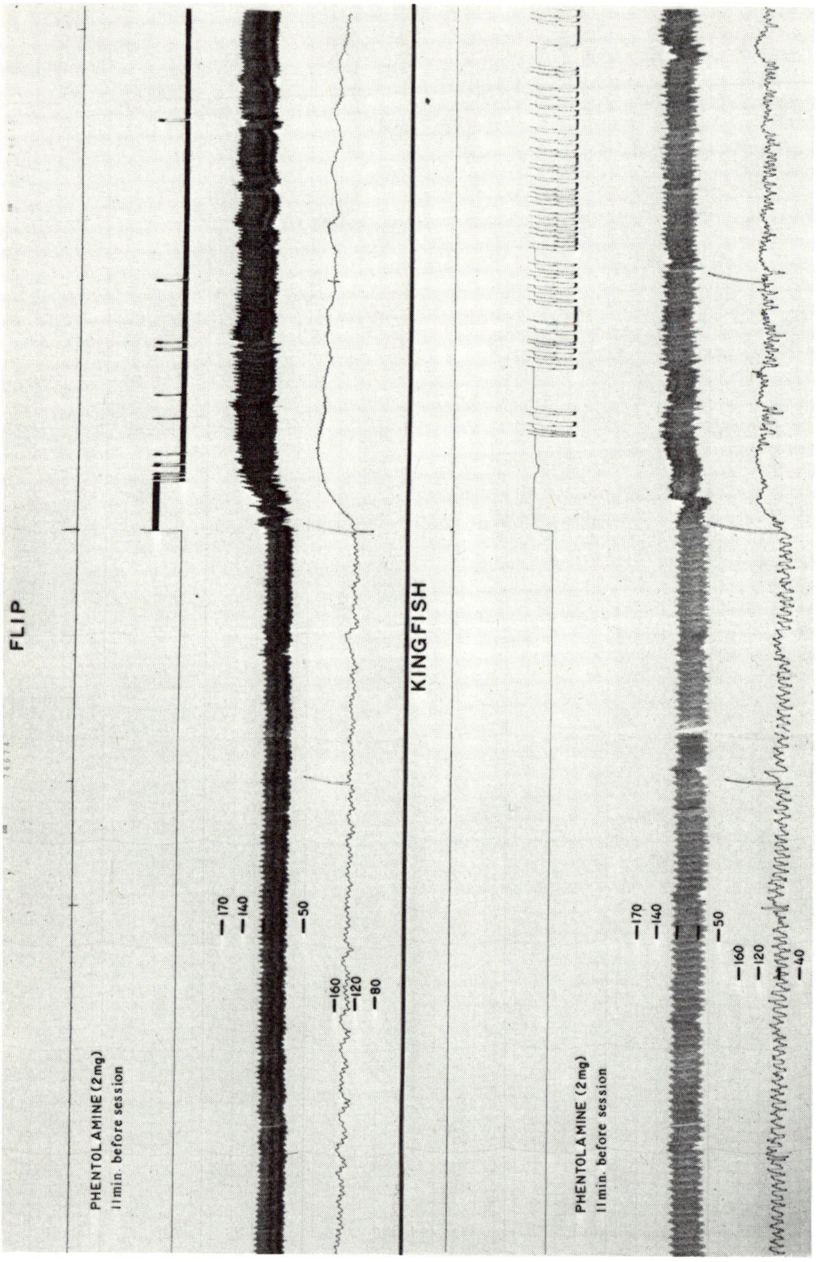

Figure 7. Polygraph records for baboons "Flip" (top record) and "Kingfish" (bottom record) showing the blood pressure and heart rate response to the conditioning session onset at noon following alpha-adrenergic blockade.

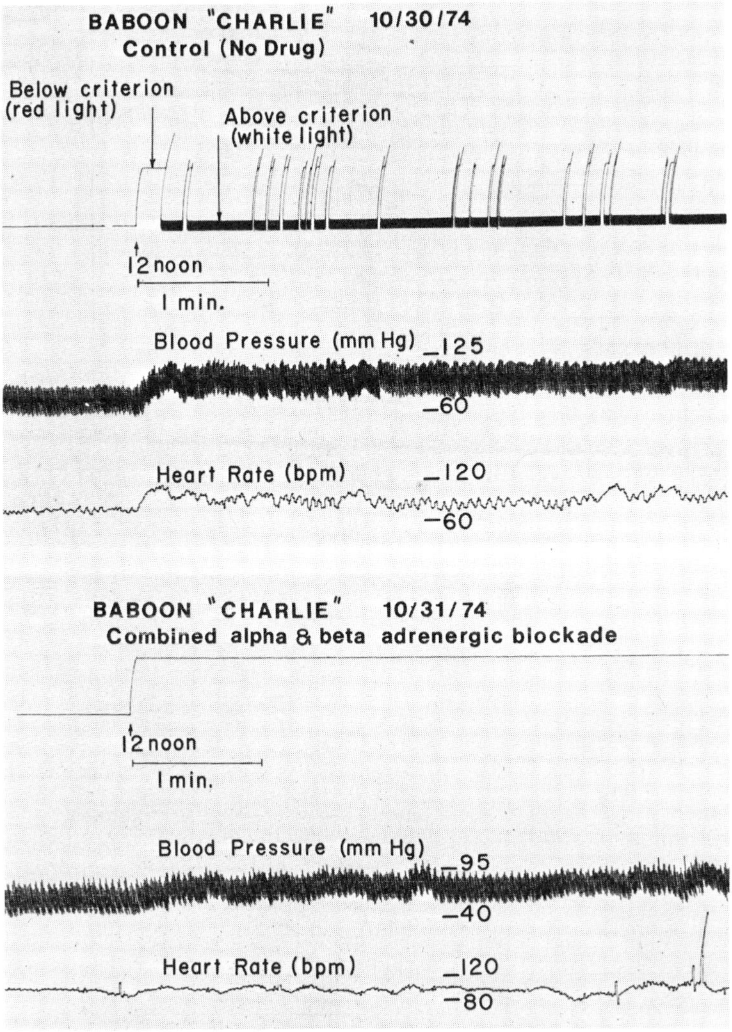

Figure 8. Polygraph records for baboon "Charlie," showing the heart rate and blood pressure response to the conditioning session onset at noon, before (top record) and after (bottom record) combined alpha- and beta-adrenergic blockade.

not attenuate the blood pressure elevations.

During the daily 12-hour conditioning sessions, a consistent change in the blood pressure - heart rate relationship occurs: The pressure elevation is maintained while heart rate decreases (see Figure 3). Our conclusions derived from an analysis of the first 10 minutes of the conditioning sessions may not apply to the potential contribution of sympathetic adrenergic activity later during the sessions, since alterations in temporal patterns of alpha- and beta-adrenergic activity may account for the observed blood pressure and heart rate trends. Further study is needed of adrenergic receptors both at various times within sessions and during the acquisition of operant control of blood pressure over the initial weeks of training.

In summary, our results support the participation of sympathetic adrenergic nervous activity in producing acute operantly conditioned blood pressure changes, but they are also consistent with the additional participation of non-adrenergic factors in operantly conditioned hypertension. Controversies regarding such mechanisms notwithstanding however, the evidence that operant conditioning procedures, whether centrally or peripherally mediated, exert orderly and specific effects upon the functional properties of physiological systems seems incontrovertible. Clearly, systematic analysis of such noninvasive, nonpharmacologic influences upon somatic processes holds considerable promise for enriching both clinical and experimental approaches to the physiopathology of health disorders. It is at least equally important that this work clearly confirms the importance of the contributions made by basic behavioral science to a comprehensive physiology of the intact, unanesthetized, conscious organism. Indeed, increasing emphasis upon the application of bio-telemetric techniques (McCutcheon, 1973) in psychophysiological investigations provides tangible recognition of this developing frontier. Certainly, the identification and operational definition of such "internal state" variables and their functional interactions is of central importance in delineating a research domain which emphasizes the critical role of environmental-behavioral influences in the production of physiological alterations.

REFERENCES

Ahlquist, R. P. A study of the adrenotropic receptors. American Journal of Physiology, 1948, 153, 585-600.

Anderson, D. E., & Brady, J. V. Preavoidance blood pressure elevations accompanied by heart rate decreases in the dog. Science, 1971, 172, 595-597.

Anderson, D. E., & Brady, J. V. Differential preparatory cardiovascular responses to aversive and appetitive behavioral conditioning. Conditional Reflex, 1972, 7, 82-96.

Anderson, D. E., & Brady, J. V. Effects of beta blockade on cardiovascular responses to avoidance performance in dogs. Psychosomatic Medicine, 1973, 35, 457.

Anderson, D. E., Yingling, J., & Brady, J. V. Effects of alpha adrenergic blockade upon cardiovascular responses of the dog to avoidance contingencies. Pavlovian Journal of Biological Science, 1975, 9, 173.

Axelrod, J., Mueller, R. A., Henry, J. P., et al. Changes in enzymes involved in the biosynthesis and metabolism of noradrenaline and adrenaline after psychosocial stimulation. Nature (London), 1970, 225, 1059-1060.

Benson, H., Herd, J. A., Morse, W. H., & Kelleher, R. T. Behavioral inductions of arterial hypertension and its reversal. American Journal of Physiology, 1969, 217, 30-34.

Benson, H., Shapiro, D., Tursky, B., & Schwartz, G. E. Decreased systolic blood pressure through operant conditioning techniques in patients with essential hypertension. Science, 1971, 173, 740.

Bergamaschi, M., & Longoni, A. M. Cardiovascular events in anxiety: Experimental studies in the conscious dog. American Heart Journal, 1973, 86, 385-394.

Birk, L. (Ed.) Biofeedback: Behavioral medicine. New York: Grune & Stratton, 1973.

Brady, J. V. Endocrine and autonomic correlates of emotional behavior. In P. Black (Ed.), Physiological correlates of emotion. New York: Academic Press, 1970.

Brady, J. V., & Harris, A. H. The experimental production of altered physiological states: Concurrent and contingent behavioral models. In W. Honig & J. E. R. Staddon (Eds.), Handbook of operant behavior. New York: Prentice-Hall, in press.

Brady, J. V., Kelly, D., & Plumlee, L. Autonomic and behavioral responses of the rhesus monkey to emotional conditioning. Annals of the New York Academy of Science, 1969, 159, 959-975.

Brod, J., Fenel, V., Hejl, Z., & Jirka, J. Circulatory changes underlying blood pressure elevation during acute emotional stress (mental arithmetic) in normotensive and hypertensive subjects. Clinical Science, 1959, 18, 269.

Cannon, W. B. Bodily changes in pain, fear, hunger and rage (2nd ed.). New York: Appleton-Century-Crofts, 1929.

Cannon, W. B., & De La Paz, D. Emotional stimulation of adrenal secretion. American Journal of Physiology, 1911, 27, 64.

Charvat, J., Dell, P., & Folkow, B. Mental factors in cardiovascular disease. Cardiologia, 1964, 44, 121.

Dews, P. B., & Herd, J. A. Behavioral activities and cardiovascular functions: Effects of hexamethonium on cardiovascular changes during strong sustained static work in rhesus monkeys. Journal of Pharmacology and Experimental Therapeutics, 1974, 189, 12-23.

DiCara, L. V. Learning in the autonomic nervous system. Scientific American, 1970, 222(1), 30-39.

DiCara, L., & Miller, N. E. Instrumental learning of vasomotor responses by rats: Learning to respond differentially in the two ears. Science, 1968, 159, 1485-1486. (a)

DiCara, L., & Miller, N. E. Changes in heart rate instrumentally learned by curarized rats as avoidance responses. Journal of Comparative and Physiological Psychology, 1968, 65, 1-7. (b)

Eich, R. H., Cuddy, R. P., Smulyan, H., & Lyons, R. H. Hemodynamics in labile hypertension: A follow-up study. Circulation, 1966, 34, 299.

Eich, R. H., Peters, R. J., Cuddy, R. P., Smulyan, H. I., & Lyons, R. H. Hemodynamics in labile hypertension. American Heart Journal, 1962, 63, 188.

Engelman, K., & Braunwald, E. Hypotension and the shock syndrome. In M. M. Wintrobe, G. W. Thorn, R. D. Adams, E. Braunwald, K. J. Isselbacher, & R. G. Petersdorf (Eds.), Harrison's principles of internal medicine. New York: McGraw-Hill, 1974.

Engel, B. T., & Gottlieb, S. H. Differential operant conditioning of heart rate in the restrained monkey. Journal of Comparative and Physiological Psychology, 1970, 73(2), 217-225.

Engel, B. T., & Melmon, K. L. Operant conditioning of heart rate in patients with cardiac arrhythmias. Conditioned Reflex, 1968, 3, 130.

Fields, C. Instrumental conditioning of the rat cardiac control systems. Proceedings of the National Academy of Sciences, 1970, 65(2), 293-299.

Findley, J. D., Brady, J. V., Robinson, W. W., & Gilliam, W. J. Continuous cardiovascular monitoring in the baboon during long-term behavioral performances. Communications in Behavioral Biology, 1971, 6, 49-58.

Findley, J. D., Robinson, W. W., & Gilliam, W. J. A restraint system for chronic study of the baboon. Journal of the Experimental Analysis of Behavior, 1971, 15, 69-71.

Finkielman, S., Worcel, M., & Agrest, A. Hemodynamic patterns in essential hypertension. Circulation, 1965, 31, 356-368.

Folkow, B., & Rubinstein, E. H. Cardiovascular effects of acute and chronic stimulations of the hypothalamic defense area in the rat. Acta Physiologica Scandinavia, 1966, 68, 48.

Forsyth, R. P. Blood pressure and avoidance conditioning. Psychosomatic Medicine, 1968, 39(1), 125-138.

Forsyth, R. P. Blood pressure responses to long-term avoidance schedules in the restrained rhesus monkey. Psychosomatic Medicine, 1969, 31, 300-309.

Forsyth, R. P. Regional blood-flow changes during 72-hour avoidance schedules in the monkey. Science, 1971, 173, 546-548.

Forsyth, R. P. Sympathetic nervous system control of distribution of cardiac output in unanesthetized monkeys. Federation Proceedings, 1972, 31(4), 1240-1244.

Forsyth, R. P., & Harris, R. E. Circulatory changes during stressful stimuli in rhesus monkeys. Circulation Research, 1970, 27 (Suppl.), 1-13.

Forsyth, R. P., Hoffbrand, B. I., & Melmon, K. L. Hemodynamic effects of angiotensin in normal and environmentally stressed monkeys. Circulation, 1971, 44, 119-129.

Forsyth, R. P., & Rosenblum, M. A. A restraining device and procedure for continuous blood pressure recordings in monkeys. Journal of the Experimental Analysis of Behavior, 1964, 7(5), 367-368.

Frankenhaeuser, M. Behavior and circulating catecholamines. Brain Research, 1971, 31, 241-262.

Frohlich, E. D., Kozul, V. J., Tarazi, R. C., & Dunstan, H. P. Physiological comparison of labile and essential hypertension. Circulation Research, 1970 (Suppl. 1), 26 & 27, 1-55.

Goodman, L. S., & Gilman, A. The pharmacological basis of therapeutics. New York: Macmillan, 1970.

Harris, A. H., & Brady, J. V. Animal learning: Visceral and autonomic conditioning. Annual Review of Psychology, 1974, 25, 107-133.

Harris, A. H., & Brady, J. V. Long-term studies of cardiovascular control in primates. In G. E. Schwartz & J. Beatty (Eds.), Biofeedback: Theory and research. San Francisco: Academic Press, 1976, in press.

Harris, A. H., Findley, J. D., & Brady, J. V. Instrumental conditioning of blood pressure elevations in the baboon. Conditioned Reflex, 1971, 6, 215-226.

Harris, A. H., Gilliam, W. J., & Brady, J. V. Operant conditioning of heart rate in the baboon. Pavlovian Journal of Biological Science, 1976, in press.

Harris, A. H., Gilliam, W. J., Findley, J. D., & Brady, J. V. Instrumental conditioning of large magnitude daily 12-hour blood pressure elevations in the baboon. Science, 1973, 183, 175.

Henry, J. P., & Cassel, J. C. Psychosocial factors in essential hypertension. American Journal of Epidemiology, 1969, 90, 171.

Henry, J. P., Stephens, P. M., Axelrod, J., & Mueller, R. A. Effect of psychosocial stimulation on the enzymes involved in the biosynthesis and metabolism of noradrenaline and adrenaline. Psychosomatic Medicine, 1971, 33, 227-237.

Herd, J. A., Morse, W. H., Kelleher, R. T., & Jones, L. G. Arterial hypertension in the squirrel monkey during behavioral experiments. American Journal of Physiology, 1969, 217, 24-29.

Higgins, C. B., Vatner, S. F., & Braunwald, E. Parasympathetic control of the heart. Pharmacological Reviews, 1973, 25, 119-155.

Honig, W., & Staddon, J. E. R. (Eds.) Handbook of operant behavior. New York: Prentice-Hall, 1976, in press.

Julius, S., & Conway, J. Hemodynamic studies in patients with borderline blood pressure elevation. Circulation, 1968, 38, 282-288.

Katkin, E. S., & Murray, E. N. Instrumental conditioning of autonomically mediated behavior: Theoretical and methodological issues. Psychological Bulletin, 1968, 70, 52-68.

Kelleher, R. T., Morse, W. H., & Herd, J. A. Effects of propranolol, phentolamine, and methyl atropine on cardiovascular functions in the squirrel monkey during behavioral experiments. The Journal of Pharmacology and Experimental Therapeutics, 1972, 183, 204-217.

Klose, K. J., Augenstein, J. S., Schneiderman, N., Manas, K., Abrams, B., & Bloom, L. J. Selective autonomic blockade of conditioned and unconditioned cardiovascular changes in rhesus monkeys (Macaca mulatta). Journal of Comparative and Physiological Psychology, 1975, 89, 810-818.

Korner, P. I. Integrative neural cardiovascular control. Physiological Reviews, 1971, 51, 312-367.

Luetscher, J. A., Boyers, D. G., Cuthbertson, J. C., & McMahon, D. F. A model of the human circulation. Circulation Research, 1973, Suppl. I to Vols. 32-33, I-84 - I-97.

Mason, J. W., et al. Organization of psychoendocrine mechanisms. Psychosomatic Medicine, 1968, 30, 565-808.

McCubbin, J. W., DeMoura, R. S., Page, I. H., & Olmsted, F. Arterial hypertension elicited by subpressor amounts of angiotensin. Science, 1966, 149, 1394.

McCutcheon, E. P. (Ed.) Chronically implanted cardiovascular instrumentation. New York: Academic Press, 1973.

McGraw, A. P., & Sim, A. K. Clinical biochemistry of the baboon. Journal of Comparative Pathology, 1973, 82, 193.

Miller, N. E. Learning of visceral and glandular responses. Science, 1969, 163, 434-445.

Miller, N. E., & Banuazizi, A. Instrumental learning by curarized rats of a specific visceral response, intestinal or cardiac. Journal of Comparative and Physiological Psychology, 1968, 65, 1-7.

Miller, N. E., & DiCara, L. Instrumental learning of heart rate changes in curarized rats: Shaping and specificity to discriminative stimulus. Journal of Comparative and Physiological Psychology, 1967, 63, 12-19.

Nathan, M. S., & Smith, O. A., Jr. Differential conditional emotional and cardiovascular responses - A training technique for monkeys. Journal of the Experimental Analysis of Behavior, 1968, 11, 77-82.

Nickerson, M. Adrenergic receptors. Circulation Research, 1973, Suppl. I to Vols. 32-33, I-53 - I-59.

Obrist, P. A., Black, A. H., Brener, J., & DiCara, L. V. (Eds.) Cardiovascular psychophysiology. Chicago: Aldine, 1974.

Page, I. H., & McCubbin, J. W. Renal hypertension. Chicago: Yearbook Medical Publishers, 1968.

Pavlov, I. P. Uber die normalen blutdruckshwanjungen beim hunde. Archiv Fur die Gesampte Physiologie des Menschen und der Tiere, 1879, 20, 215.

Pickering, G. W. The nature of essential hypertension. London: J & A Churchill, 1961.

Plumlee, L. A. Operant conditioning of blood pressure increases and decreases in the monkey. Psychophysiology, 1968, 4, 507.

Plumlee, L. A. Operant conditioning of increases in blood pressure. Psychophysiology, 1969, 6, 283-290.

Randall, D. C., & Smith, O. A., Jr. Ventricular contractility during controlled exercise and emotion in the primate. American Journal of Physiology, 1974, 226, 1951-1959.

Saslow, G., & Blackly, P. H. Introduction. In Timberline Conference on Psychophysiologic Aspects of Cardiovascular Disease. Psychosomatic Medicine, 1964, 26, 409.

Schwartz, G. E., Shapiro, D., & Tursky, B. Learned control of cardiovascular integration in man through operant conditioning. Psychosomatic Medicine, 1971, 33, 57-62.

Shapiro, D., Schwartz, G. E., & Tursky, B. Control of diastolic blood pressure in man by feedback and reinforcement. Psychophysiology, 1971, 8, 262.

Shapiro, D., Tursky, B., & Gerson, E. Effects of feedback and reinforcement on the control of human systolic blood pressure. Science, 1969, 163, 588.

Shapiro, D., Tursky, B., & Schwartz, G. Control of blood pressure in man by operant conditioning. Circulation Research, 1970 (Suppl. 1), 26 & 27, 1.

Sidman, M. Avoidance conditioning with brief shock and no exteroceptive warning signal. Science, 1953, 118, 157-158.

Skinner, B. F. Science and human behavior. New York: Macmillan, 1953.

Stephens, J., Harris, A. H., & Brady, J. V. Large magnitude heart rate changes in subjects instructed to change their heart rates and given exteroceptive feedback. Psychophysiology, 1972, 9, 283-285.

Swinnen, M. E. T. Blood pressure digitizer. Proceedings Annual Conference Engineering in Medicine and Biology, 1968, 10, 18.4.

Varma, S., Johnson, S. D., Sherman, D. E., & Youmans, M. D. Mechanisms of inhibition of heart rate by phenylephrine. Circulation Research, 1960, 8, 1182-1186.

Weber, H. W., Brede, H. D., Retief, F. P., & Melby, E. C., Jr. The baboon in medical research: Baseline studies in fourteen hundred baboons and pathological observations. Defining the laboratory animal, National Academy of Science, Washington, D. C., 1971.

Weiss, T., & Engel, B. T. Operant conditioning of heart rate in patients with premature ventricular contractions. Psychosomatic Medicine, 1971, 33, 301-321.

Werdegar, D., Johnson, D. G., & Mason, J. W. A technique for continuous measurement of arterial blood pressure in unanesthetized monkeys. Journal of Applied Physiology, 1964, 19, 519.

NOTE

Portions of the data reported here are from research supported by Grants HL17958 and HL06945 from the National Heart and Lung Institute, and by the Advanced Research Projects Agency of the Department of Defense and monitored by the Office of Naval Research under subcontract No. 225013 to the San Diego State College Foundation.

MECHANISMS OF LEARNED VOLUNTARY CONTROL OF BLOOD PRESSURE IN PATIENTS WITH GENERALISED BODILY PARALYSIS

T.G. Pickering
Radcliffe Infirmary, Oxford

B. Brucker
Goldwater Memorial Hospital, New York

H.L. Frankel and C.J. Mathias
Spinal Injuries Centre, Stoke Mandeville Hospital, England

B.R. Dworkin and N.E. Miller
Rockefeller University

Although there have been several reports of learned voluntary control of blood pressure in man (reviewed by Blanchard and Young, 1972), there is little information concerning the mechanism of such changes. In the experiments reported here, we have been particularly concerned to eliminate mediation of blood pressure changes occurring secondarily to alterations of breathing or muscle tension by working with paralysed patients in whom voluntary control of skeletal muscles was minimal, so that any learned blood pressure changes are likely to be produced by direct autonomic control.

VOLUNTARY CONTROL BY PATIENTS PARALYSED BY POLIOMYELITIS AND MUSCULAR DYSTROPHY

Methods

Eight subjects (four with polio, four with muscular dystrophy) were paired in two matched groups; one group was trained to raise diastolic pressure, the other to lower it. All subjects had virtually complete paralysis, requiring permanent hospital care and mechanically assisted ventilation.

Diastolic pressure was measured continually over 2 minute periods by a servo-controlled sphygmomanometer. This maintained the Korotkoff sound (recorded from a crystal microphone) at a constant intensity by automatically adjusting the cuff pressure. The device had previously been calibrated against directly recorded arterial pressures. The output of the diastolic pressure channel was fed into a Schmitt trigger which turned a tone on or off to indicate to the subject how his pressure was changing. Recordings of chin EMG, respiration, and ECG were also made.

Subjects were told that they were going to be trained to change their blood pressure, but not in which direction. They were instructed to try to keep the tone sounding, but not to tense their muscles or change their breathing. Each session consisted of ten 2-minute recordings, the first and last being baseline periods.

Results

The average changes of diastolic pressure and heart rate produced by training are shown in Figure 1 for the six subjects who completed seven sessions (two subjects dropped out after five sessions). Learned differences of diastolic pressure were significant between the increase and decrease groups for sessions 6 ($t = 3.37$, $p < .02$) and 7 ($t = 3.04$, $p < .05$), the actual changes during these sessions being +3.5 and +2.6 mmHg for the increase group, and -5.0 and -2.0 for the decrease.

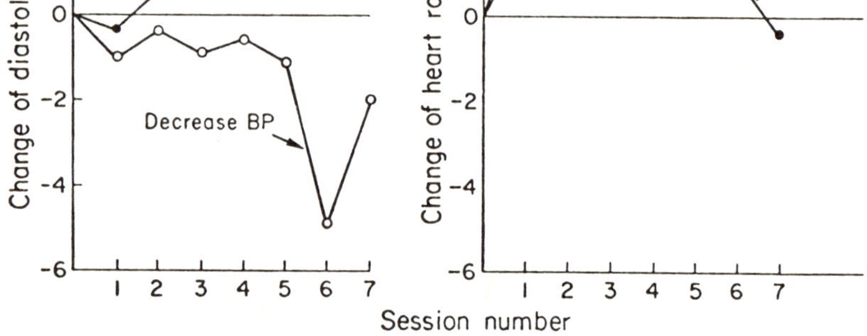

Figure 1. Average changes of diastolic pressure (left) and heart rate (right) for the increase and decrease groups.

Both groups showed a significant tendency for heart rate to increase during the earlier training sessions, but no significant change occurred in either group during the last two. No significant change of rate or pressure occurred during the baseline periods.

Changes of diastolic pressure, heart rate, and respiration were also examined for each subject individually, by comparing the changes occurring during the first two and last two sessions. During the first two sessions only one subject showed significant changes in the desired direction. By the last two, however, five out of six did (three in the increase group, and two in the decrease group). Two subjects (one in each group) showed small but significant increases in respiration rate.

Four of the subjects who learned to change their pressure (two from each group) attempted to do so while on constant ventilation from their respirators with monitoring of end-tidal P_ACO_2 in two further training sessions. Three did this successfully without any change of P_ACO_2; an example is shown in Figure 2 for one of the subjects in the decrease group.

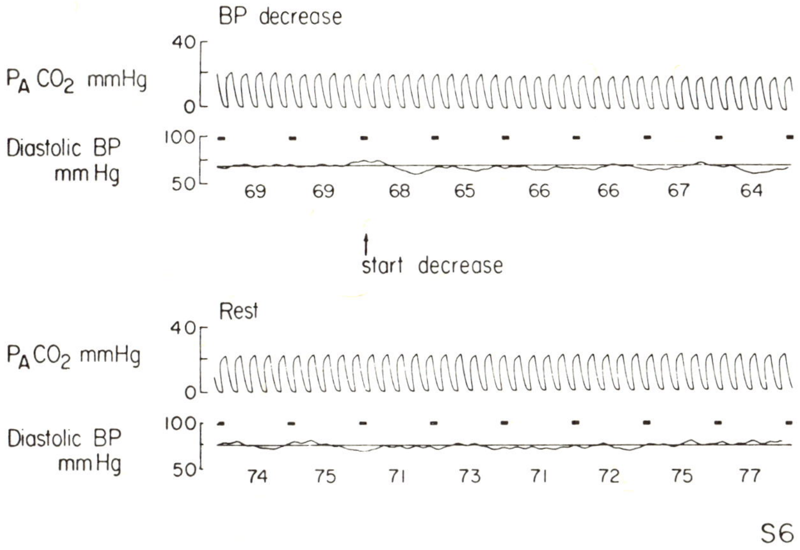

Figure 2. Upper half: records of P_ACO_2 and diastolic pressure during one 2 minute trial. Between the traces are 15 second time markers. Horizontal line on pressure record indicates average pressure for first 30 seconds. Subject began to attempt to change pressure at 30 seconds. Lower half: control record, with no attempt to change pressure. Numbers below pressure brace indicate average pressure for each 15 second period.

The three subjects who learned to raise their pressure also attempted a sustained hand grip for one minute. Changes of diastolic pressure and heart rate were compared with those occurring during training periods. In one subject the effects of the two procedures were very similar, but in the other two they were not: In one the attempted handgrip raised both rate and pressure, whereas the learned rise of pressure was not associated with a rate change; the other could not raise her pressure by attempted handgrip.

Discussion

These results show that small but reliable changes of diastolic pressure can be produced by instrumental learning in patients with virtually complete neuromuscular paralysis. Similar changes have been reported in non-paralysed man (Shapiro, Schwartz, & Tursky, 1972), but little attempt has been made to exclude skeletal mediation of the autonomic changes. Since contraction of very small muscles can significantly raise blood pressure, it is virtually impossible to exclude this in a non-paralysed subject. In these subjects with nearly complete paralysis, it is most unlikely that the blood pressure changes were secondary to changes in breathing or muscle tension. These results do not support the idea that paralysis per se enhances visceral learning.

It was a surprise to find that attempted contraction of atrophic muscles could result in a sizeable rise of blood pressure and heart rate, but in two of the three successful subjects in the increase group this response appeared to be different from the learned change. In a larger series of 13 untrained but severely paralysed subjects we found an average diastolic pressure rise of 8.5 mmHg over one minute, without any detectable muscle contraction. It is generally thought that the rise of blood pressure during an isometric contraction is produced reflexly (Lind & McNicol, 1976), but our findings are more consistent with the view that the mental activity producing such contraction may itself be partly responsible for the cardiovascular changes (Freyschuss, 1970; Goodwin, McCloskey, & Mitchell, 1972).

VOLUNTARY CONTROL BY PATIENTS PARALYSED BY COMPLETE CERVICAL CORD TRANSECTION

Cervical cord transection interrupts central sympathetic outflow and produces tetraplegic paralysis below the level of the lesion. Such patients are thought to show no blood pressure response to stimuli originating in the nervous system above the lesion, whereas they show exaggerated pressor responses ("Autonomic Hyperreflexia") to stimuli entering the cord below the lesion. Since central sympathetic outflow is cut they would not be expected to be able to learn voluntary blood pressure control.

Methods

Four subjects were studied. In addition to complete muscular paralysis and anesthesia below the lesion, all showed evidence of interruption of central sympathetic outflow, i.e., postural hypotension and autonomic hyperreflexia.

Systolic pressure was recorded from a cuff with a Korotkoff sound microphone, whose output was made audible to the subject. The cuff pressure was held at 2 mmHg above systolic for 30 second periods, during which time any increase of systolic pressure would produce Korotkoff sounds which would be audible as clicks. At the end of 30 seconds the cuff was deflated and a new reading of systolic pressure taken, and then reflated to 2 mmHg above systolic. Five such periods constituted one trial; there were four trials interspersed by rest periods in each training session. During three of the trials the subjects were instructed to raise their pressure by keeping the clicks going ("Raise" trials), and during the other to hold their pressure constant ("Hold" trials). Heart rate and respiration were also recorded. Subjects 1 and 2 were trained for 25 sessions or more, and subjects 3 and 4 for ten.

Results

Subject 1. S.S., a 25 year old woman, had a cord transection at C4-5. The learned changes of systolic pressure, heart rate, and respiration rate are plotted session by session in Figure 3. It is clear that from session 3 onwards she was able to raise her pressure by 10-15 mmHg during the "Raise" trials, without any consistent changes during the "Holds." Heart rate also increased. Comparisons of pressure at the beginning and end of each trial by t-tests showed highly significant changes for the "Raise" but not the "Hold" trials.

End-tidal P_ACO_2 fell slightly during the voluntary pressure increases, but neither hyperventilation nor hypoventilation could reproduce the learned changes, and neither could any attempted muscle contraction.

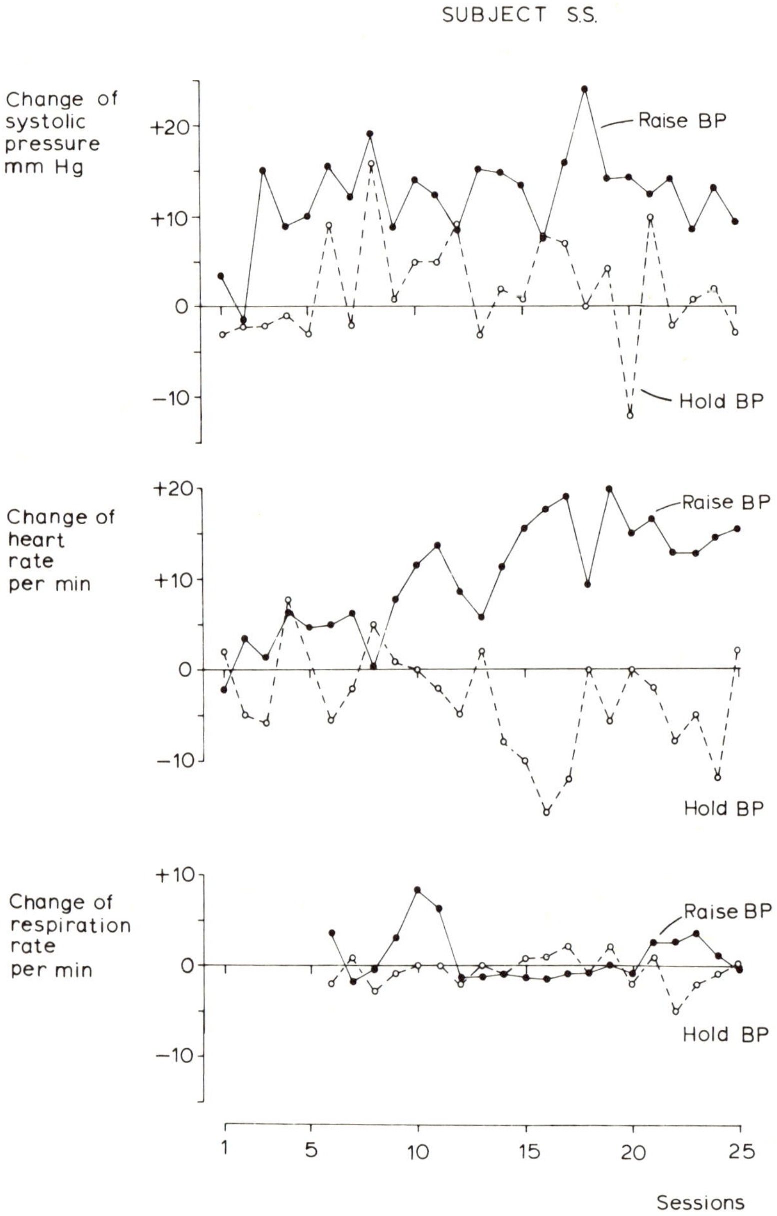

Figure 3. Subject S.S. Learning curve for changes of systolic pressure, heart rate, and respiration rate for each session. Closed circles: Raise BP; open circles: Control (Hold BP).

Subject 2. J. L. was a 20 year old man with a C7 transection. Significant increases of pressure were achieved after session 5 (average +7.1 mmHg), and heart rate also tended to increase (+5.1/minute), but respiration rate tended to slow.

Subject 3. G.S., a 41 year old man, had a C5 transection. After 10 sessions he could raise his pressure by 20 mmHg. Since the voluntarily produced rise of pressure was always accompanied by a tachycardia, it seemed possible that a withdrawal of vagal tone might be responsible for the changes. It was decided to test this possibility by testing the subject's ability to raise his pressure with intra-arterial pressure recording, and then to inject a blocking dose of atropine. If vagal withdrawal were the cause of the pressure rise, atropine should 1) raise the pressure itself, and 2) block his voluntary control.

During this last session the findings of the earlier ones were confirmed: During seven attempts to raise his pressure for two minute periods, he was successful every time, the average increase being +18.3 mmHg for systolic, and +16.0 mmHg for diastolic pressure. Heart rate rose by 13.1/minute. All these changes were significant at the .001 level. A typical example is shown in Figure 4.

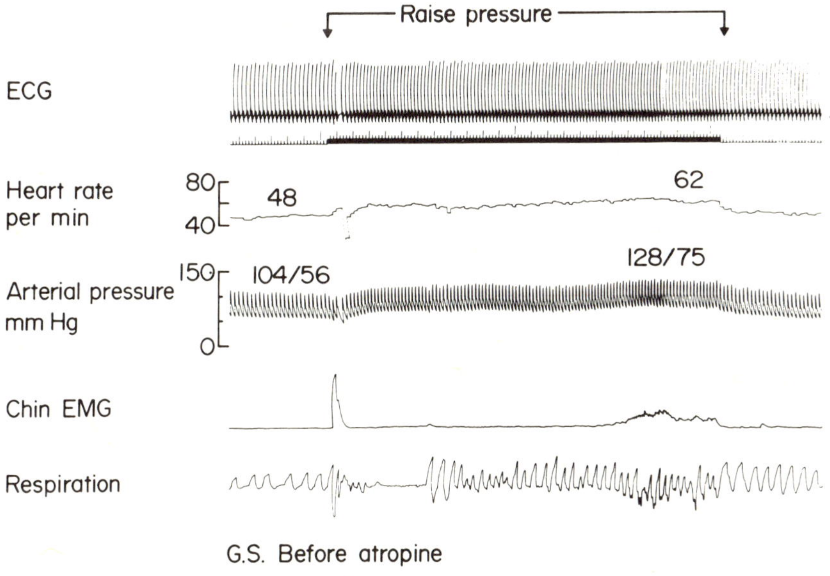

Figure 4. Subject G.S. Voluntary increase of blood pressure for 2 minutes. Onset is indicated by movement of chin (on EMG trace) and on atrial ectopic beat. Numbers above records show initial and final values of rate and pressure.

During the voluntary pressure increases the respiratory pattern became more irregular; arterial blood gases did not change, and neither hypo- nor hyper-ventilation could reproduce the learned changes. Attempted muscle contraction resulted in a smaller rise of pressure (+6/5 mmHg) but a much bigger rise of tension in the chin EMG.

Atropine was then given intravenously, in a dose (3 mg) sufficient to produce complete vagal blockade. This increased his heart rate from 47 to 80/minute, and his blood pressure from 108/50 to 146/90 mmHg. He was now unable to produce any voluntary change of rate or pressure (Figure 5). These findings were thus in agreement with the hypothesis that the voluntary increase of pressure was mediated vagally.

Subject 4. I. E., a 27 year old man, had a C5 transection. After ten sessions he could consistently raise his heart rate, but the changes of pressure were variable.

He was studied during one final session with intra-arterial pressure recording. He could raise his heart rate significantly (+8.4/minute, $p < .05$), but not his pressure. After atropine his rate rose for 84 to 129/minute, but there was no effect on his pressure.

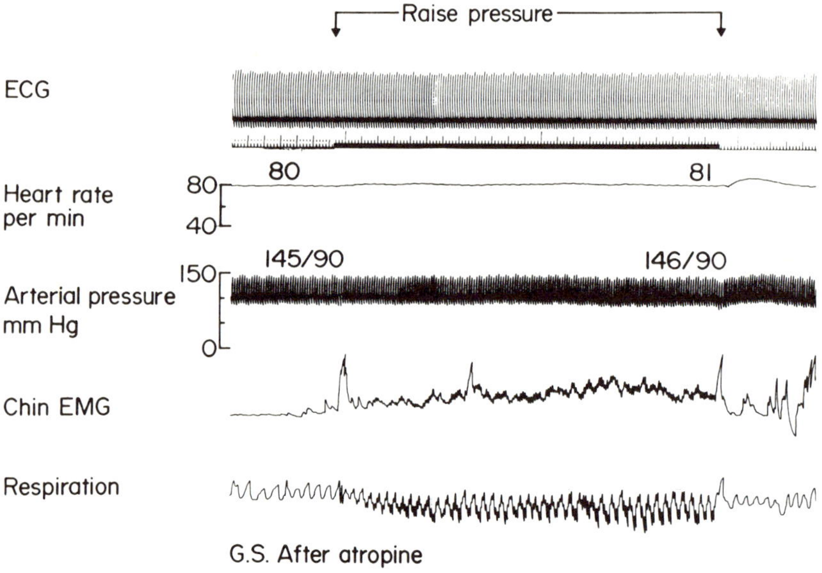

Figure 5. Subject G.S. Unsuccessful attempt to raise pressure for 2 minutes after atropine. EMG changes are bigger than in Figure 4.

Discussion

All these subjects had clinical evidence of complete cord transection at the cervical level, and contrary to our original expectation, three out of four were able to learn to produce large increases of arterial pressure. All four could raise their heart rates. The abruptness of the pressure rises (see Figure 4) rules out any humoral mechanism, such as changes of blood gases.

The preganglionic sympathetic outflow from the cord is from T1 to L4 (Bard, 1960), so that complete cord transection above T1 will result in a severance of cerebral control of the sympathetic. This loss of central control is manifest in ways such as postural hypotension and the absence of any vascular response to noxious stimuli applied above the lesion (Corbett, Frankel, & Harris, 1971). The vagus is of course unaffected in these subjects. Normally, vagal blockade by atropine increases heart rate to 120/minute, but blood pressure is unchanged (Fielder, Nelson, Andersen, & Gravenstein, 1969). In tetraplegic patients Frankel and Mathias (unpublished) have found blood pressure to be increased by atropine, as it was in our subject G.S. The effects of atropine were thus compatible with the hypothesis that he was controlling his blood pressure through his vagus. As in the first series of subjects, mediation of the blood pressure changes by skeletal muscle seems most unlikely.

These tetraplegic subjects demonstrated two different mechanisms by which blood pressure might increase. Spontaneous pressure increases are usually initiated by stimuli entering the cord below the level of the transection, which activate sympathetic centres in the isolated cord to produce a vasoconstriction. The rise of pressure stimulates the baroreceptors, resulting in a reflex vagal bradycardia. The heart rate response is thus quite different from the tachycardia which accompanies the learned voluntary pressure increase: In this instance the vagus is initiating the increase of pressure, whereas in the former it is opposing it.

REFERENCES

Bard, P. Anatomical organisation of the central nervous system in relation to control of the heart and blood vessels. Physiological Review, 1960, 40, 3-26.

Blanchard, E. B., & Young, L. B. Self-control of cardiac functioning: A promise as yet unfulfilled. Psychological Bulletin, 1973, 79, 145-163.

Corbett, J. L., Frankel, H. L., & Harris, P. J. Cardiovascular changes associated with skeletal muscle spasm in tetraplegic man. Journal of Physiology, 1971, 215, 381-431.

Goodwin, G. M., McCloskey, D. I., & Mitchell, J. H. Cardiovascular and respiratory responses to changes in central command during isometric exercise at constant muscle tension. Journal of Physiology, 1972, 226, 173-190.

Fielder, D. L., Nelson, D. C., Andersen, T. W., & Gravenstein, J. S. Cardiovascular effects of atropine and neostigmine in man. Anesthesiology, 1969, 30, 637-641.

Freyschuss, U. Cardiovascular adjustments to somatomotor activation. Acta Physiologica Scand. Suppl., 1970, 342.

Lind, A. R., & McNicol, G. W. Muscular factors which determine the cardiovascular response to sustained and rhythmic exercise. Canadian Medical Association Journal, 1967, 96, 706-714.

Shapiro, D., Schwartz, G. E., & Tursky, B. Control of diastolic blood pressure in man by feedback and reinforcement. Psychophysiology, 1972, 8, 296-304.

NOTE

We should like to acknowledge the help of Dr. L. Ince. This research was supported by the National Institute of Mental Health, the Wellcome Trust, and the British Heart Foundation.

VISCERAL PERCEPTION

Jasper Brener
University of Hull

INTRODUCTION

Perception is generally acknowledged to involve the processing of sensory input. Although many forms of perception appear to be genetically preprogrammed, it is also well established that perceptual processes may be reliably influenced by experience (Bower, 1974). Thus it is proposed that although not all perceptual processes are experientially determined, whenever a stimulus acquires response-controlling properties by virtue of experience, evidence of perception is thereby constituted. In terms of this requirement, visceral perception, a process long denied, emerges as a conspicuous and reliable aspect of our everyday behaviour. As it is employed here, the term "visceral perception" refers to processes related to the detecting and labelling of visceral states.

To a greater or lesser extent, visceral perception is based upon the processing of information from the interoceptors that sense the state of the milieu interieur. Chernigovskiy (1967) distinguishes the interoceptive classes: mechanoreceptors, chemoreceptors, osmoreceptors and thermoreceptors according to the type of internal stimuli to which they are sensitive. The prevalent assumption that afference from these receptors does not impinge upon consciousness is closely related to the rejection of a visceral perceptual capacity. However, the intimate relationship between perception and consciousness which most philosophers of mind assume, is not a necessary or indeed, a justifiable assumption for the experimental psychologist. Nevertheless the existence of visceral perception has been questioned precisely because the phenomenology of interoception differs qualitatively from that of exteroception and proprioception. One plausible reason for this relates to differences in the reference frameworks employed in organizing and processing afference arising from these different sources. Perceptions which are based upon exteroceptive input are generally referred to the instigating stimuli. Thus when I perceive an object through the visual modality the description of my perception is identical with my description of the object. However, in the case of very intense or painful stimulation, the perception is generally referred to the receptive site of the stimulus rather than to the stimulus itself. Finally perceptions may be referred to the bodily state produced by particular stimuli. James's theory of emotion exemplifies processes of this sort. This analysis is consistent with the hypothesis that there is a general tendency to ascribe the phenomenal properties of a percept to the earliest discriminable components of the perceptual process. Since individuals have not learned to label internal stimuli or localize interoceptors, visceral perceptions when they are expressed verbally tend to refer to states of the organism. Like other perceptual processes however, they may be manifested in many nonverbal ways.

The phenomenological differences between visceral perception on the one hand and environmental and proprioceptive perception on the other, are not, as has been commonly supposed, due to fundamental structural or functional differences between the afferent systems involved. Langley (1900), for example proposed that the autonomic nervous system was a purely efferent system. Although Sherrington (1906) acknowledged the interceptive or visceroceptive sensory system he emphatically denied that this system had access to consciousness. The viscera which were deprived of sensation were by the same token relegated to the subservient role of a vegetative, involuntary and reflexive effector system. That the viscera should be deprived not only of conscious sensation but also of voluntary control was acknowledgment of the relationship between the discriminability and the controllability of a response. Clearly there is no need for visceral activities to make themselves known to the CNS (or consciousness) if their vital purpose is reflexively to obey the peripheral commands of the striate muscles, which are the true instruments of consciousness. It is widely believed that an organism must be sensible of its actions in order to control them. As a demonstration of this principle Mott and Sherrington (1895) severed the afferent nerves serving the right forelimb of a monkey and observed that the monkey ceased to use this limb voluntarily.

In a view of this history, it is not surprising that a resurgence of interest in visceral perception has been precipitated by the research on voluntary control of the viscera. Biofeedback is reported to aid the development of voluntary control over responses that have hitherto been considered the reflexive consequences of somatomotor adjustments. This observation is in accordance with the notion that the viscera are not subject to voluntary control because of their impoverished afferent system. Although the argument is plausible the validity of its major premise, that the visceral afferent system is substantially different from the exteroceptive or proprioceptive systems, is severely compromised by an overwhelming body of evidence.

THE VISCERAL AFFERENT SYSTEM

Certainly there are differences between the afferent systems in terms of the degree of organization in their peripheral receptor systems and in the cortical representations of the different sensory domains but these differences are not as compelling as are the structural and functional similarities amongst the systems. Adam (1967), Chernigovskiy (1967) and Newman (1974) are agreed that the organization of the visceral afferent system follows the same principles as the proprioceptive and exteroceptive systems. "Like somatic afferents, their (visceral afferents) projections are found at every level of the central nervous system." (Newman, 1974, p. 11). Several points of similarity are noteworthy.

1) Impulses originating from exteroceptors and interoceptors alike reach the higher nervous centres through specific afferent pathways where they can influence the activity of single cells or groups of cells.

2) Visceral afferents may elicit visceral and somatic effects.

3) Interoceptive like exteroceptive impulses cause reticular activation resulting in nonspecific cortical arousal.

4) Pavlovian principles apply in the conditioning of somatic or visceral responses to interoceptive stimuli. This implies that interoceptive afferents are fully involved in the intersensory processes of associative learning (Bykov, 1957; Razran, 1961).

5) Interoceptive stimuli may also acquire discriminative control over operant responses indicating that their functions may be altered via

the Law of Effect (Cook et al., 1960; Schechter & Rosincrans, 1972; Schuster & Brady, 1964; Slucki et al., 1965; Slucki et al., 1969).

In view of the foregoing it must be conceded that there is no easy answer to the question of why visceral sensations appear to be absent from our conscious experience. As was suggested earlier this may have to do with our implicit criteria for attributing perceptions with the property of consciousness. Few people would deny consciousness of a stomach ache or of being thirsty or of intense fear but because these perceptions are not referred to the visceroceptors from which they arise or to the stimuli that act upon the visceroceptors, the concept of visceral awareness remains foreign.

COMMON EVIDENCE OF VISCERAL PERCEPTION

Not only are the anatomical means for the detection of visceral activities available to the central nervous system but as the experimental literature indicates, they are strenuously exercised in the ordering of our daily lives. Some of the more familiar manifestations of visceral perception are summarized below.

Visceral Pain

Visceral pain is an ubiquitous phenomenon that provides the skilled clinician with the basis of preliminary and, in some cases, accurate diagnosis. Many visceral pains are reported to arise from loci other than their point of origin. Sometimes they are referred to the body surface. Since cutaneous and visceral afferents enter the spinal cord through the same dorsal roots and excite the same thalamic relay cells, this referral of sensation is not surprising (Newman, 1974). In cases such as dysmenorrhea, childbirth, overdistended bladder, or coronary occlusion, the pain although diffuse and also referred to other structures is reported to arise within the organ itself. Pain in a normal viscus may also result from disease in a distant organ through a viscero-motor reflex. Thus painful contractions of the small intestine sometimes accompany appendicitis (Brobeck, 1973).

Biological Drives

The ability of individuals to exhibit adaptive learned behavior in response to variations in the milieu interieur provides evidence of the processing of visceral afference. The term hunger as it is employed in the subjective reports of individuals has been thought to label sensations arising from gastric contractions (Cannon & Washburn, 1912; Griggs & Stunkard, 1964), variations in blood glucose (Mayer, 1955), lipostatic effects and thermal variations in the hypothalamus (Brobeck, 1955). Thirst is a term used to label either dryness in the mouth (Cannon, 1918) or the outputs of interoceptive osmoreceptors (Verney, 1947).

Diet selection by animals in which nutritional deficiencies have been established by experimental means provides an example of the precision with which the interoceptive afferent system may govern behavior (Epstein & Stellar, 1955). The association of the taste of a substance with its nutritional consequences would appear to require the participation of the interoceptive signaling system. Hormonal influences must also be recognized to influence the organization of exteroceptive sensory input in the regulation of sexual behavior in a variety of species (e.g., Lehrman, 1964). Variations in reported mood associated with the menstrual cycle have been ascribed to associated changes in body chemistry (Little & Zahn, 1974) providing further support for a chemoreceptive perceptual capacity in humans. The homeostatic concept of motivation acknowledges that interoceptive stimuli are at the source of all activity. Interoceptive stimuli not only have strong reflex-eliciting properties, as the evidence indicates they also acquire conditional response-controlling properties when submitted to the appropriate classical or operant conditioning procedure.

Emotions

The concept of emotion is intimately linked with the viscera. The visceral metaphor has always been a favorite means of communicating emotional ideas. These metaphors assume that the pounding of the heart, the sweating and the trembling that accompany fear are universal experiences. Fear is the term we employ to label them (James, 1890). Experiments such as those of Schachter and Singer (1962) tend to discredit the idea that emotional terms are employed simply to label certain constellations of interoceptive sensations. They tend to suggest instead that the constellation of sensation labelled by an emotional term contains exteroceptive and proprioceptive elements as well. Nevertheless, individuals are sufficiently convinced of the association between visceral activities and emotions that when they are led to believe that a metronome beat is their heart beat, their moods can be manipulated by changing the rate of the metronome (Valins, 1970). The limbic system which is intimately involved in the control of emotional expression also contains a major receptive region for visceral afferent impulses (Newman, 1974).

Taken together these familiar phenomena establish that stimuli arising in the visceral field may give rise to behavioral adjustments that are characteristic of perceptual responses. The way in which a visceral percept differs from one that is based upon exteroceptive afference appears to be that the phenomenological properties of such responses as fear or thirst are remote from their sensory sources.

THE EXPERIMENTAL STUDY OF VISCERAL PERCEPTION

Although Pavlovian and operant conditioning techniques have proven to be effective in answering a number of basic questions regarding the functional attributes of the interoceptive system, these procedures are not necessarily appropriate to the investigation of visceral perception in the intact organism. Because these methods generally employ direct stimulation of interoceptors they have served to establish the anatomical feasibility of visceral perception. But by the same token direct stimulation of the visceral receptors is essentially abiological and bears little relation to the sensory processes associated with normal variations in visceral activity. Furthermore perception is by its nature an intersensory process involving the integration of multimodal sensory inputs. Thus although the traditional approaches to the study of interoception have established the sensory basis for visceral perception, other methods are required for examining the detection and labelling of variations in visceral activity.

In this context it is important to note that interoception is not an essential prerequisite to the detection of visceral responses. For example, an individual could conceivably sense the action of the heart through the afferent consequences of pulsatile changes on intracardiac mechanoreceptors, on baroceptors in the aortic arch or carotid body, on mechanoreceptors in the muscles of the thorax, a limb, or a digit, on the auditory receptors via pulsatile actions on the Eustachian Tubes, or on the eyes by watching some part of the body move. The detection of signals delivered through any of these modalities would enable the individual to discriminate the activity of the heart. By and large, procedures for examining visceral perception do not provide data that would permit firm conclusions regarding the sensory sources of perceptions of visceral activity. The data generated by these procedures can tell us whether individuals are capable of detecting particular variations in visceral activity and whether or not they are able to label these variations accurately. The data may also, in certain cases, enable the experimenter to broadly delimit the possible sensory sources upon which the visceral perception is based.

Tests Involving Verbal Identification of Visceral Responses

In the study of exteroceptively-based perception, one may ask a subject to report verbally on, for example, the relative size of two objects or the pitch of a tone. The most prevalent test of visceral perception employs the same methodology. Since visceral stimulus sources are not intersubjectively verifiable, the validity of a method which relies upon the consistent and accurate use of a verbal labelling system in describing the sensations that result from these stimuli is open to question.

Mandler et al. (1958) developed the Autonomic Perception Questionnaire (APQ) in an effort to measure the extent to which individuals are aware of the visceral changes that normally accompany emotional states such as anxiety and pleasure. They observed that persons who scored high on the APQ tended also to display significantly more visceral reactivity to psychological stressors in the heart rate, sudomotor and respiratory effector modalities than did those who scored low on the APQ. As the authors point out in the introduction to their study, the experiences that lead to the verbal labelling of visceral sensations are far more amorphous than those which lead to the labelling of exteroceptive stimulus complexes. In the latter case the stimulus source of the perception is intersubjective whereas in the case of visceral perception it is largely intrasubjective. Thus the APQ must be considered to be a very circumscribed test of visceral perception -- it measures the tendency of individuals to employ a standard verbal reference system in reporting their internal states. It does not provide information on the actual or potential acuity of visceral perception. The verbal calibration of internal sensations, like the visual calibration of kinesthetic sensations (Held, 1965) is a plastic process that is readily modifiable by experience. In the same way that we may teach an individual that a visual target is 7° to the right of its initially perceived position, so too may we teach an individual to categorize sensations using verbal categories other than those he might employ initially. For example, Hefferline and Perera (1963) were able to teach subjects to label the sensory correlates of muscle twitches as audible tones.

The suggestion that the APQ measures the tendency of individuals to employ certain lexical items in describing their experiences rather than their abilities to perceive visceral change is supported by experiments by Donelson (1966), McFarland (1975) and Whitehead et al. (1975a). All of these studies failed to find a significant relationship between APQ scores and objective indices of heart rate perception. Furthermore, Whitehead et al. (1975a) failed to obtain a significant correlation between APQ scores and performance on the rod-and-frame test (Oltman, 1968), a measure of vestibular sensitivity. These results are not surprising since Mandler et al.'s APQ questionnaire did not purport to measure the accuracy of visceral perception. In fact these investigators found that High Perceivers tended to overestimate, and Low Perceivers tended to underestimate their visceral reactions.

Despite this, experimenters in the area of biofeedback have consistently expected to find a positive relationship between performance of the APQ and the acquisition of voluntary visceral control. With equal consistency this expectation has been experimentally disconfirmed. Bergman and Johnson (1971) did find that subjects who scored in the middle range of the APQ were better at controlling their heart rates than high and low scorers. Although it is tempting to entertain the hypothesis that high and low scorers did badly because of their respective tendencies to over- and underestimate their visceral responses, four further studies have reported conflicting relationships between APQ scores and visceral control. Donelson (1966) and Whitehead et al. (1975b) both reported nonsignificant correlations between APQ scores and heart rate control under conditions of biofeedback whereas Greene and Nielson (1966) and Blanchard et al. (1972) both found negative correlations between APQ scores on the one hand and GSR and heart rate control respectively on the other.

A paper-and-pencil test that has yielded scores which correlate reliably with heart rate control is Rotter's (1966) locus of control (LOC) scale. It is interesting that this test which was developed in the context of social learning theory to measure the relative tendencies of individuals to respond to internal or external sources of stimulation is a better predictor of visceral control than tests which purport to measure visceral perception. Ray & Lamb (1974) and Ray (1974) found that internal LOC subjects were better at increasing their heart rates and that external locus of control subjects were better at decreasing. Fotopolous (1970) has also reported that internal LOC subjects were better at increasing their heart rates. From the data presented by Ray and Lamb it appears that external LOC subjects profited proportionately more from the provision of external heart rate feedback than did internal LOC subjects. Although these data fit well with assumptions regarding the relationship between the perception and control of visceral activities, this extrapolation of the data should be undertaken cautiously. Rotter's scale was not intended as a measure of visceral perception and the relationship between LOC scores and objective measures of visceral perception have not yet been investigated.

Furthermore the interpretation of data presented by Ray, Lamb and Fotopolous may be accommodated by the observation that when subjects are instructed to attend to internal stimuli, their heart rates increase and when they are required to attend to external stimuli their heart rates decrease (Porges & Raskin, 1969). In this connection it should be noted that only external LOC subjects in Ray's study reported "looking at objects in the room" significantly more often when they were trying to decrease their heart rates than when they were trying to increase. Lacey et al. (1963) has provided data which suggest that the heart rate decreases during the reception of environmental information and increases when environmental input is rejected.

However in order to assess these data in relation to the hypothesis concerning the perception and control of visceral activity, it is necessary to determine whether Rotter's scale does provide a valid index of visceral perception. Several techniques which purport to provide objective measurements of the acuity of visceral perception have been devised and these may be employed to verify indirect tests such as the Rotter Scale.

Objective Tests of the Detection and Labelling of Visceral States

One experimental approach to the investigation of interoceptive detection and labelling is to manipulate the state of the milieu interieur experimentally and then to train the individual to label the objectively-measurable consequences of these manipulations. Silverstein et al. (1974) subjected a group of four chronic alcoholics to a regimen of controlled drinking which resulted in their blood alcohol levels (BALs) increasing and then decreasing systematically over successive 48 hour periods. Variations in BAL were measured using a Breathalizer test. Subjects were intermittently required to rate their BALs on a 40-point scale. Following training in which they were provided with error feedback, rewards and punishments contingent upon the accuracy of their BAL estimates, the subjects learned to label their BALs accurately. This ability deteriorated significantly by the second day following training. In the second phase of the experiment, subjects were required to control their alcohol intake so as to achieve specified target BALs. When provided with knowledge of results and reinforcement subjects again acquired accurate control and maintained it throughout training. Although this method provides good evidence that individuals may learn how to label the sensory consequences of alcohol ingestion in terms of a standard scale, like most of the methods to be described, it does not identify the sensory source of these perceptions. The subjects in this experiment may, for example, have been rating their perceived levels of sensory-motor impairment.

Nevertheless, the evidence does indicate that the viscera are endowed with a sensory system capable of supporting perceptual processes. Since visceral activities are amenable to objective measurement, particular variations in such activities may be employed as stimuli in signal detection and discrimination paradigms in order to test whether their sensory correlates are amenable to identification and labelling. The prototype for this sort of experiment was described in 1912 by Cannon and Washburn. Stomach contractions were recorded during a procedure in which the subject was required to report the occurrence of hunger pangs. The substantial correlation between stomach contractions and reports of hunger observed by these investigators have been substantiated in a number of later studies employing similar procedures. A very thorough-going investigation of gastric perception has been reported by Stunkard and Koch (1964) and by Griggs and Stunkard (1964). These investigators observed that whereas people of normal weight tend to report hunger in the presence of gastric motility and not in its absence, obese people report hunger independently of stomach contractions. Obese men tend to report being hungry most of the time whereas obese women report never being hungry. In other words, unlike people of normal weight, obese people do not apply the term "hunger" to the labelling of gastric sensations. In a study of one obese and one non-obese individual, Griggs and Stunkard (1964) observed that in contrast to the normal subject, the obese subject reported hunger sensations independently of stomach contractions and was unable to detect stomach contractions. However under appropriate reinforcement conditions in which the subject was rewarded for correct identification of stomach contractions and punished for incorrect identification, his performance improved to the level of the non-obese subject. The authors of this study make the interesting observation that the pre-training discriminative performance of the obese subject was similar to that produced in the nonobese subject by reinforcement contingencies which punished false positive responses more severely than false negatives and provided greater rewards for true negatives than for true positives.

In the Griggs and Stunkard procedure, subjects were intermittently asked to indicate the presence or absence of a stomach contraction by saying "yes" or "no." On half the trials and in a random order stomach contractions were present when the discriminative response was called for and on the other half, they were absent. Variants of this procedure have been employed in studying the detection of sudomotor and heart rate responses.

In a study of heart rate discrimination, Mandler and Kahn (1960) instructed a subject to say "Fast" whenever he thought his heart rate was increasing and "Slow" when it was decreasing. When the subject was provided with feedback for correct discriminative responses, his performance improved from chance level to 100% correct performance. Although performance deteriorated somewhat when feedback was withdrawn, the subject did retain a substantial ability to correctly identify heart rate increases and decreases. Using a similar procedure Epstein and Stein (1974) instructed subjects to press a key either whenever their heart rates were high or low. Heart rate discrimination was assessed prior to, during, and following a training procedure in which subjects received feedback on correct responses. Although the subjects were able to discriminate high and low heart rates when feedback for correct discriminations was available, discriminative performance declined to a level not significantly different from pre-training levels when reinforcement was withdrawn. Whereas Mandler and Kahn conclude that heart rate discrimination in their experiment was based upon respiratory cues, Epstein and Stein discount this possibility in accounting for their results. The latter investigators do not however report examining respiratory amplitude, the most likely correlate of heart rate variation.

Although both of these studies provide evidence of learned heart rate discrimination, in a second study reported by Mandler and Kahn in which the subject was not informed of the actual task requirements, no evidence of heart rate discrimination was obtained. In this experiment, upon the occurrence of a signal, the subject was required to guess which of two lights ("right" or "left") would next be illuminated. Unbeknown to the subject, the right and left lights were illuminated in a random sequence but with the right light always contingent on a heart rate increase and the left, always contingent on a heart rate decrease. Although feedback was provided for correct performance, the subject's discriminative performance did not deviate from chance over 4675 training trials. These results suggest the instructional factors which have been shown to have an important influence on visceral control (Brener, 1974b) and exteroceptive perception (Houssiadas, 1964), also influence the development of visceral perception. It is quite possible that in Mandler and Kahn's second experiment, the instructions which led the subject to try and guess an imaginary sequence produced a set that was antagonistic to the development of a discriminative response.

Kleinman (1970) and McFarland (1975) employed similar procedures in the examination of heart beat discrimination. In both of these experiments, subjects were first of all presented with a brief exteroceptive stimulus on each heart beat, and then subsequently in the absence of the exteroceptive stimulus, they were required to press a button on each heart beat. During the first phase of the procedure, Kleinman instructed his

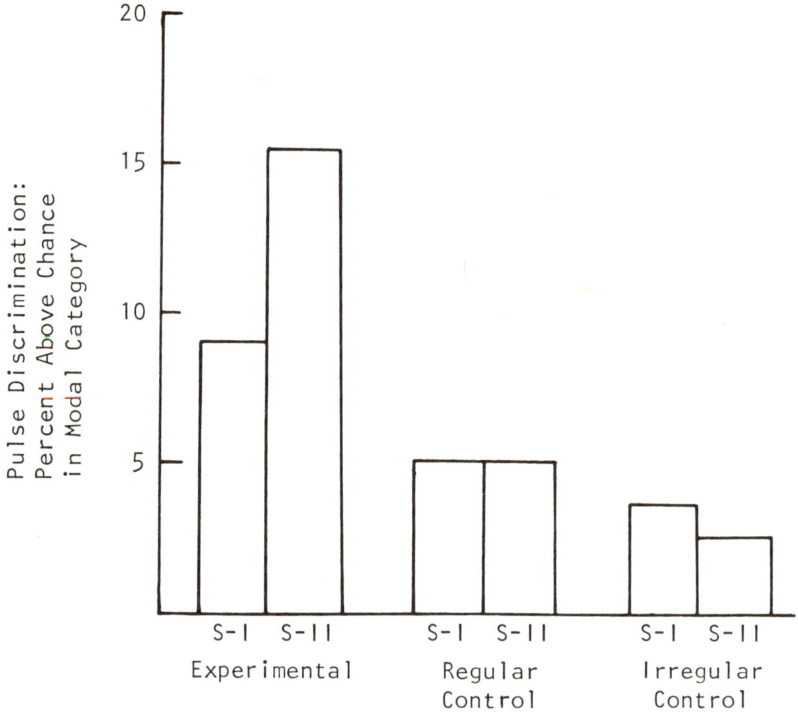

Figure 1. Pulse discrimination in one Experimental and two (Regular and Irregular) Control Groups. During training Experimental subjects were exposed to a light flash on each heart beat and instructed to attend to internal sensations that accompanied the external stimuli. During the discrimination assessment procedure from which these data were derived, they were instructed to press a button whenever and as soon as they sensed a heart beat Subjects in the control groups were exposed to either regular or irregular external light flash sequences during training trials and were instructed to replicate the periodicities of these sequences by pressing the button on assessment trials. It was assumed that if subjects were pressing the buttons independently of their heart beats, these latencies would be more-or-less rectangularly distributed but that clear evidence of a mode in the latency distribution would indicate that they were employing the sensory correlates of the heart beat as signals for pressing the button. The data presented her indicate the percentage of latencies falling into the modal cagegory of the distribution do not deviate significantly from chance estimates based upon the assumption of a rectangular distribution for the Control groups but do for the Experimental group. Furthermore the Experimental group displaye significantly more latencies in their modal categories than did the Control groups whose performance provides an empirical estimate of chance devia-

subjects to attend to internal sensations that may be associated with the external stimulus whereas McFarland instructed his subjects to press a button on each external stimulus. Kleinman examined the heartbeat-button press latencies for evidence of discrimination and on the basis of these data (Figure 1) concluded that subjects learned to use the sensory correlates of heart beats as signals for pressing the button. This conclusion is interesting in the light of an observation by Jammes and Rosenberger (1971) of cardiac-motor coupling amongst mentally-retarded individuals. In a study involving 101 patients, they found an almost perfect correlation between the frequency of rocking behavior, which is characteristic of mentally-retarded persons, and heart rate. Furthermore they found that drugs which produced substantial increases and decreases in heart rate produced precisely parallel changes in the frequency of rocking and did not disturb the correlations. They entertain the hypothesis that the stimulus for rocking is the ballistic effect of the cardiac pulse. McFarland assessed heart beat discrimination on the basis of the discrepancy between the number of heart beats and button presses on each discrimination trial. These discrepancies expressed as a percentage of the number of heart beats on discrimination trials varied from 52% to 2% with a mean of 15%. It will be appreciated that this index may reflect nothing more than the subject's ability to remember and reproduce the frequency of the heart beat contingent exteroceptive stimuli presented prior to the discrimination assessment procedure.

An attempt to deal with this source of artifact was contained in a study by Donelson (1966) on heart rate discrimination. On test trials, subjects were required to adjust the frequency of signals on an oscilloscope to match their heart rates. Interspersed between these test trials subjects received training trials during which they were permitted to observe heartbeat-contingent signals on the oscilloscope. In order to reduce the possibility of subjects relying upon their memories of these heartbeat-contingent signals in adjusting the signal frequency on test trials, Donelson required half her subjects to hyperventilate for 15 seconds prior to training trials and the other half to hyperventilate prior to test trials. This operation ensured that subjects' heart rates were different on test and training trials. Interestingly, she observed that subjects who were required to hy-

---

tions from rectangularity in the distribution. Finally, it will be seen that in contrast to the Control subjects, the Experimental subjects show an increase in the percentage of latencies falling into the modal category from Session 1 (S-I) to Session 2 (S-II). (From Kleinman, 1970).

perventilate prior to training trials acquired superior heart rate discrimination as measured by the discrepancy between their actual and estimated heart rates. She suggests that this finding may have been due to increased cardiovascular feedback consequent upon hyperventilation on training trials.

In most of the procedures so far described in this section, visceral perception is assessed in terms of the subject's ability to perform some discriminative responses in the presence of a particular visceral state and not in its absence. This method has also been employed to examine the detection and labelling of sudomotor responses. Stern (1966) required subjects, on the presentation of a signal, to press one of four buttons to indicate how certain they were that they had, or had not, just made a galvanic skin response (GSR). Prior to this assessment procedure all subjects were informed of maneuvers, mainly of a cognitive sort, that were associated with GSR production. Half of the subjects were permitted to practice producing GSRs with visual feedback of their skin resistance available whilst the other half had to practice without exteroceptive feedback. The group who were given practice with biofeedback did somewhat better discriminating GSRs than the group who were not provided with feedback during the practice phase of the experiment although neither group displayed strong evidence of discrimination. In this experiment, the instructional setting operations which identified GSRs with cognitive processes may have deflected subjects from employing more direct sources of discrimination. More recently Diekhoff (1976) has investigated the detection and labelling of GSR responses under a variety of training conditions. As in the Stern study, subjects were required, on the presentation of a signal, to indicate their certainty that a GSR had or had not just occurred by pressing one of four buttons. Four groups of subjects were run over three one-hour training sessions. The groups were differentiated according to the type of feedback they received contingent upon their discriminative responses. Following each discriminative response, one group received information on the presence or absence and relative magnitude of the GSR activity prior to the discriminative response, another group received information on whether a GSR had occurred or not, a third group received no feedback and a final group received incorrect feedback in which they were informed that GSRs had occurred on all the trials when they had not and on half the trials when they had. Subjects were not informed of any of the maneuvers that influence GSRs although presumably they were informed as to what a GSR is. The surprising outcome of this experiment is that the only group which displayed an improvement in their ability to detect GSRs was the one which was provided with no feedback. Subjects who received magnitude feedback displayed an improvement in the labelling of GSRs. Diekhoff concludes that the improvement in GSR detection displayed by the No Feedback Group is consonant with the predictions of Schema Theory (Evans, 1968). Although this theory may apply to understanding the formation of concepts based upon familiar stimulus dimensions, it is difficult to understand how it would apply in enabling subjects to distinguish GSR from nonGSR states.

Procedures in Which Subjects are Required to Distinguish Between Exteroceptive Stimulus Variations that Bear Different Relationships to Visceral Activity

In the procedures described thus far, subjects are required to indicate whether a simple stimulus did or did not follow a particular variation in visceral activity. In these cases the stimulus functions as an instruction to respond appropriately to the perceived visceral state. Variations in this response signal do not reflect variations in the visceral state under study. An alternative means of measuring the ability to detect variations in visceral activity is to determine whether the individual can distinguish between exteroceptive stimulus variations that bear different relationships to the visceral activity under study. In one variant of this procedure, the subject is presented with similar sequences of exteroceptive stimuli on successive trials. On half the trials and in a random order the exteroceptive stimuli are contingent on a particular variation in visceral activity; on the remaining trials the stimuli vary independently of the visceral activity. Following each trial, the subject is presented with a respond signal and is required to make one response if he believes that the exteroceptive stimulus train to which he has just been exposed was contingent upon his visceral activity and another response if he believes that the stimuli were independent of his visceral activity. This procedure is therefore a test of whether individuals are able to discriminate biofeedback stimuli (contingent exteroceptive stimuli) from stimuli that have similar physical characteristics but are independent of variations in visceral activity (noncontingent exteroceptive stimuli). This procedure was employed by Brener and Jones (1974) in an investigation of heartbeat discrimination. Experimental subjects were tested before and after training on their ability to discriminate between 10 second trains of vibratory stimuli that were or were not provided with feedback following their discriminative responses whereas on training trials they received a brief feedback stimulus contingent on each correct discriminative response. During noncontingent stimulus trials, the vibratory stimuli were presented at a rate equal to the subject's mean heart rate but with a fixed interstimulus interval. Since it was possible that subjects might learn to discriminate between contingent and noncontingent vibratory stimuli on the basis of the differences in their periodicities, a group of control subjects were given training with feedback for correct responses in discriminating stimuli that were contingent or noncontingent upon another subject's heart beats. A second control group was run under the same conditions as the experimental group except that they did not receive feedback for correct responses during the training phase. The results of the experiment (Figure 2) indicated quite clearly that only subjects who received feedback for correct discriminations learned to discriminate vibratory stimuli that were contingent on their heart beats from vibratory stimuli that were noncontingent. Since the periodicity control group failed to learn the discrimination between stimuli that were and were not contingent on another subject's heart beats, it may be concluded that variation in periodicity was not the basis of the discrimination. The observation that subjects who were not provided with feedback of correct responses did not learn to discriminate the two sorts of pulse trains is clearly opposed to the findings reported by Diekhoff (1976).

A similar procedure has been reported by Whitehead et al. (1975a, 1975b). These investigators required subjects to discriminate between ten second sequences of light flashes in which on half the trials each light

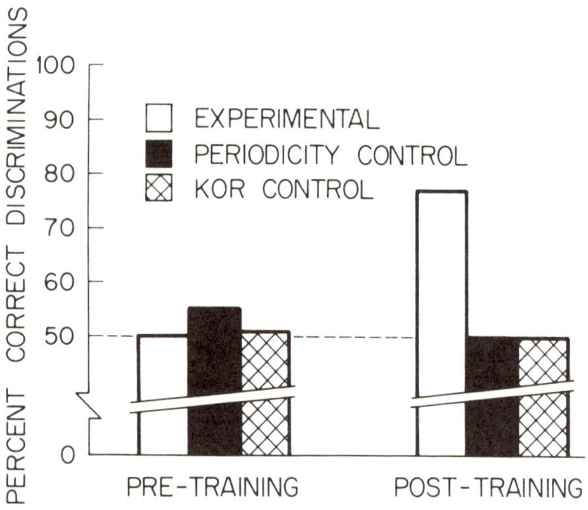

Figure 2. Median percentage of correct discriminations between heartbeat-dependent and heartbeat-independent vibratory stimuli during pre- and post-training tests for Experimental subjects (Exp); subjects who were not given feedback for correct discriminations during training (KOR C); and subjects who were trained to discriminate between sequences of vibratory stimuli that were and were not contingent on another subject's heart beats (PC). See text for full description of procedure. (From Brener & Jones, 1974).

flash followed a heart beat at an interval of 128 msecs, and on the other half, at an interval of 384 msecs. These investigators report d' values ranging from .053 (no discrimination) to 1.901 (good discrimination). They did not however investigate the influence of training on this ability. This is a particularly attractive procedure since it is difficult to imagine how a subject could solve this discrimination problem without actually detecting the sensory correlates of the heartbeat. In all of the other procedures described, the discrimination problem may be solved by discriminating any process that is systematically related to the visceral activity under study. For example, in the Brener and Jones study, subjects could learn to discriminate the contingent from the noncontingent stimuli by discovering that if they took a deep breath or tensed their muscles, the periodicity of the contingent but not the noncontingent stimuli would change. In the Whitehead et al. procedure, these maneuvers would have the same effect on the short- and long-delay stimuli.

Despite this difference between the Whitehead et al. and Brener and Jones procedures, Clemens and MacDonald (1975) and Clemens (1976) using the Brener and Jones procedure to assess heart beat discrimination obtained a range of d' scores very similar to that reported by Whitehead. Clemens (1976) also attempted to train discrimination between light flashes that were contingent upon or independent of heart beats but failed to obtain good evidence of discrimination. Two procedural differences could explain this discrepancy with the Brener and Jones study: 1) The vibratory stimuli employed by Brener and Jones to present the contingent and noncontingent stimulus trains may have been more easily associated with the internal sensory correlates of the heart beat than the visual stimuli employed by Clemens. It has been well established that a given stimulus will more readily form associations with stimuli of a one class than with stimuli of another class (see Mackintosh, 1975). 2) Although the number of training trials was approximately equal in the two experiments (150 vs. 180), those in the Clemens study were spaced over three sessions whereas those of Brener and Jones were massed in one session. Furthermore the criterion for solution of the discrimination problems was less stringent in the Clemens experiment than in the Brener and Jones experiment.

More recently Giacinto in my laboratory has applied this method to the study of heart rate rather than heart beat discrimination. During the contingent trials, each 26 heart beats long in this case, a tone came on whenever and as soon as the subject's heart rate exceeded (or fell below) a criterion based upon his heart rate distribution. On noncontingent trials, tones were controlled by a purpose-built simulator which reproduced a pattern of tones comprising the same number and distribution of durations as had occurred in the preceding contingent trials. Separate groups of

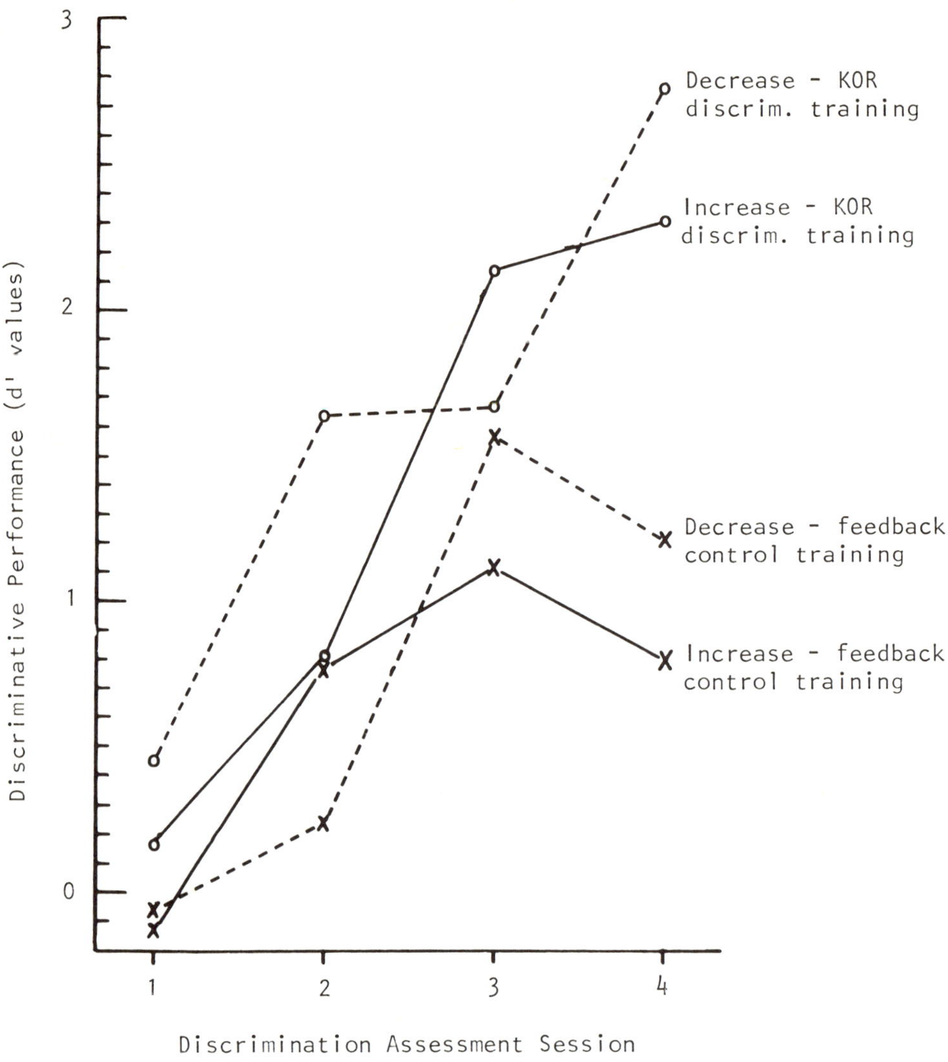

Figure 3. Discrimination of Heart rate Increases and Decreases in groups of subjects who either received discrimination training (KOR discrim. training) or heart rate control training under conditions of biofeedback (feedback control training). The d' measures presented are session means derived from discrimination tests in which subjects were required to press one button if they thought that the sequence of tones presented during a trial were associated with heart rate increases (or decreases) and another button if they thought that the tones were not associated with their heart rates. During training trials which occurred on each session, subjects in the discrimination training groups received feedback contingent upon cor-

subjects were assessed for discrimination of heart rate increases and decreases prior to and following each training session. Within each increase and decrease group, half the subjects were provided with discrimination response. The other half received heart rate control training under biofeedback conditions. Each subject in this condition was trained to produce changes in the direction he was required to discriminate. The d' data describing the discrimination test performances of the four groups of subjects is illustrated in Figure 3. Two aspects of these data are noteworthy: 1) There is no difference between the rates at which the discrimination of high heart rates and low heart rates is acquired. 2) Although the discrimination training procedure appears to result in better discrimination, it is not significantly different from the improvement in discriminative performance produced by the control training procedure.

THE PERCEPTION AND CONTROL OF VISCERAL ACTIVITY

The last observation brings us back to consider again the relationship between visceral perception and visceral control (Brener, 1976). A number of studies already described contained data relevant to the assessment of this relationship. It has already been mentioned that the relationship between APQ scores and the learning of visceral control is rather unclear. The only two studies that report a statistically significant correlation find a negative relationship. Blanchard et al. (1972) found that Low Perceivers were better at controlling their heart rates than High Perceivers and Greene and Nielsen (1966) found that only Low Perceivers showed any conditioning of increases in skin resistance. Perhaps High Perceivers have a strong but erroneous idea of what the correct responses feel like.

However, Whitehead et al. (1975b) found that their objective measure of heart beat detection also correlated negatively with ability to control the heart. Although this appears to support the findings mentioned above, it will be remembered that Whitehead et al. (1975a) found no correlation between this objective measure of cardiac sensitivity and APQ scores. McFarland who also found no correlation between an objective

---

rect button presses whereas subjects in the control training groups were provided with feedback contingent on heart rate changes (increases for one group and decreases for another). The biofeedback stimuli presented to subjects in the heart rate control groups were identical to those they were required to identify as contingent stimuli on discrimination assessment trials.

measure of heart rate perception and APQ scores did find that his objective index of heart rate perception was correlated with the ability to increase heart rate but not to decrease it. In support of McFarland we find that Clemens and MacDonald (1975) and Clemens (1976) both found a significant correlation between their objective test of heartbeat discrimination and ability to increase but not decrease the heart rate. It will be remembered that Ray (1974) and Ray and Lamb (1974) also found that internal LOC subjects as classified on Rotter's Scale were better able to increase heart rate whereas external LOC subjects were better able to decrease. Two further examples of a significant positive relationship between visceral perception and control may be mentioned. Kleinman observed that subjects who had been trained to discriminate their heart beats were better at controlling their heart rates with and without biofeedback, than subjects who had not received discrimination training. In their study of the perception of blood alcohol levels and control of alcoholic consumption, Silverstein et al. (1974) found that when subjects had been adequately trained, they were able to control consumption so as to produce target BALs. However the capacity to discriminate and recognize particular visceral states is no guarantee that the individual will moderate its behavior to achieve these states. This was certainly true of Silverstein's subjects and also of the obese subject described by Griggs and Stunkard (1964). Although this individual reported retaining the acute awareness of gastric motility he had acquired during discrimination training a year earlier, his weight gain continued unabated.

CONCLUSIONS

Western psychophysiology has long neglected the study of visceral perception and has concentrated its efforts in the investigation of perceptual processes that arise from stimulation of the more amenable exteroceptive system. However as the data presented here indicates, the problems of visceral perception are now being attacked with renewed vigor. The methodological problems associated with investigating the capacity of intact individuals to detect and label variations in visceral activity are, however, far from resolved. A great deal of work is still required before reliable and valid methods for investigating visceral perception are established. The intercorrelations that have been reported between different tests of visceral perception are uniformly low although as yet no comparisons of different objective tests have been undertaken.

One epistomological issue related to the validity of such tests requires special mention. This concerns the identification of the sensory sources upon which the discrimination of variations in visceral activity depends. Within the frame of analysis adopted here, an organism is said to discriminate an event if it reliably responds differently in the presence and absence of that event. Learned discriminations that conform to this operational criterion are accepted as evidence of perception. Thus if an individual learns to respond differently in the presence and absence of, for example, heart rate increases he thereby provides evidence of visceral perception. This is true regardless of the sensory modality through which he receives the signal for his discriminative responses. Clearly the sensory basis of the perception is of great theoretical and practical interest. It is not however germane to the question of whether or not the individual can detect or label variations of his heart rate.

I have previously argued that biofeedback training augments the development of visceral control by teaching individuals to label the sensory correlates of variations in visceral activity (Brener, 1974a; 1974b; 1976). Although neither conclusively confirmed nor falsified, this hypothesis has been wholly or partially supported by a majority of studies in which objective measures of visceral perception were employed. Disconfirmatory evidence has been derived by other studies most of which have employed paper-and-pencil tests of visceral perceptions such as the APQ. However the validity of such tests has not been adequately established. Clearly a final resolution of this issue will have to await the development of generally acceptable means of assessing not only visceral perception but also visceral control. Refinement of the methods described in this paper may well provide the basis for such developments.

REFERENCES

Adám, G. Interoception and behavior. Budapest: Adademiad Kiado, 1967.

Bergman, J. S., & Johnson, H. J. The effects of instructional set and autonomic perception on cardiac control. Psychophysiology, 1971, 8, 180-190.

Blanchard, E. B., Young, L. D., & McLeod, P. Awareness of heart activity and self-control of heart rate. Psychophysiology, 1972, 9, 63-68.

Bower, T. G. R. Development in infancy. San Francisco: Freeman, 1974.

Brener, J. A general model of voluntary control applied to the phenomena of learned cardiovascular change. In P. A. Obrist, A. H. Black, J. Brener, & L. V. DiCara (Eds.), Cardiovascular psychophysiology. Chicago: Aldine-Atherton, 1974. (a)

Brener, J. Factors influencing the specificity of voluntary cardiovascular control. In L. V. DiCara (Ed.), The limbic and autonomic nervous systems: Advances in research. New York: Plenum, 1974. (b)

Brener, J. Sensory and perceptual determinants of voluntary visceral control. In G. E. Schwartz & J. Beatty (Eds.), Biofeedback: Theory and research. San Francisco: Academic Press, 1976, in press.

Brener, J., & Jones, J. M. Interoceptive discrimination in intact humans: Detection of cardiac activity. Physiology and Behavior, 1974, 13, 763-767.

Brobeck, J. R. Neural regulation of food intake. Annals of the New York Academy of Science, 1955, 63, Art. 1, 44-55.

Brobeck, J. R. Best and Taylor's physiological basis of medical practice (9th ed.). Baltimore: The Williams and Wilkins Company, 1973.

Bykov, K. M. The cerebral cortex and the internal organs. New York: Chemical Publishing Company, 1957.

Cannon, W. B. The physiological basis of thirst. Proceedings of the Royal Society, London, 1918, B. 90, 283-301.

Cannon, W. B., & Washburn, A. L. An explanation of hunger. American Journal of Physiology, 1912, 29, 441-454.

Cook, L. A., Davidson, D. J., Davis, D. J., & Kelleher, R. T. Epinephrine, norepinephrine and acetylcholine as conditioned stimuli for avoidence behavior. Science, 1960, 131, 990-991.

Chernigovskiy, V. N. Interoceptors. Washington, D.C.: American Psychological Association, 1967.

Clemens, W. J., & MacDonald, D. F. The relationships between heart beat discrimination and heart rate control. Paper presented at the annual meeting of the Society for Psychophysiological Research, Toronto, 1975.

Clemens, W. J. Heart beat discrimination and the learning and transfer of voluntary heart rate control. Paper presented at the annual meeting of the Southeastern Psychological Association, New Orleans, 1976.

Diekhoff, G. M. Effects of feedback in a forced-choice GSR detection task. Psychophysiology, 1976, 13, 22-26.

Donelson, F. E. Discrimination and control of human heart rate. Unpublished doctoral dissertation, Cornell University, 1966.

Epstein, L. H., & Stein, D. B. Feedback-influenced heart rate discrimination. Journal of Abnormal Psychology, 1974, 83, 585-588.

Epstein, A. N. & Stellar, E. The control of salt preference in the adrenalectomized rat. Journal of Comparative and Physiological Psychology, 1955, 48, 167-172.

Evans, S. H. A brief statement of schema theory. Psychonomic Science, 1968, 8, 87-88.

Fotopolous, S. Locus of control and the voluntary control of heart rate. Paper presented at the meeting of the Biofeedback Research Society, New Orleans, 1970.

Greene, W. E., & Nielsen, T. C. Operant GSR conditioning of high and low autonomic perceivers. Psychonomic Science, 1966, 6, 359-360.

Griggs, R. C., & Stunkard, A. The interpretation of gastric motility: II. Sensitivity and bias in the perception of gastric motility. Archives of General Psychiatry, 1964, 11, 82-89.

Hefferline, R. F., & Perera, T. B. Proprioceptive discrimination of a covert operant without its observation by the subject. Science, 1963, 139, 834-835.

Held, R. Plasticity in sensory-motor systems. Scientific American, 1965, 213, 84-94.

Houssiadas, L. Effects of "set" and intellectual level on the perception of causality. Acta Psychologica, 1964, 22, 155-161.

James, W. The principles of psychology. New York: Henry Holt, 1890.

Jammes, J. L., & Rosenberger, P. B. Rocking behavior and heart rate in the mentally retarded. Journal of Nervous and Mental Disease, 1971, 153, 57-59.

Kleinman, R. A. The development of voluntary cardiovascular control. Unpublished doctoral dissertation, University of Tennessee, 1970.

Lacey, J. I., Kagan, J., Lacey, B. C., & Moss, H. A. The visceral level: Situational determinants and behavioral correlates of autonomic response patterns. In P. H. Knapp (Ed.), Expression of the emotions in man. New York: International Universities Press, 1963.

Langley, J. N. The sympathetic and other related systems of nerves. In E. A. Schafer (Ed.), Textbook of physiology (Vol. 2). London: Young & Pentland, 1900.

Lehrman, D. S. Control of behavior cycles in reproduction. In W. Etkin (Ed.), Social behavior and organization among vertebrates. Chicago: University Press, 1964.

Little, B. C., & Zahn, T. P. Changes in mood and autonomic functioning during the menstrual cycle. Psychophysiology, 1974, 11, 579-590.

Mandler, G., & Kahn, M. Discrimination of changes in heart rate: Two unsuccessful attempts. Journal of the Experimental Analysis of Behavior, 1960, 3, 21-25.

Mayer, J. Regulation of energy intake and the body weight: The glucostatic theory and the lipostatic hypothesis. Annals of the New York Academy of Science, 1955, 63, Art. 1, 15-43.

McFarland, R. A. Heart rate perception and heart rate control. Psychophysiology, 1975, 12, 402-405.

Mckintosh, N. J. The psychology of animal learning. London: Academic Press, 1974.

Mott, F. W., & Sherrington, C. S. Experiments upon the influences of sensory nerves upon movement and nutrition of the limbs. Proceedings of the Royal Society, London, 1895, 57, 481-488.

Newman, P. P. Visceral afferent functions of the nervous system. London: Edward Arnold, 1974.

Oltman, P. K. A portable rod-and-frame apparatus. Perceptual and Motor Skills, 1968, 26, 503-506.

Porges, S., & Raskin, D. Respiration and heart rate components of attentive observation to external and internal stimuli. Journal of Experimental Psychology, 1969, 81, 497-503.

Ray, W. J. The relationship of locus of control, self-report measures, and feedback to the voluntary control of heart rate. Psychophysiology, 1974, 11, 527-534.

Ray, W. J., & Lamb, S. B. Locus of control and the voluntary control of heart rate. Psychosomatic Medicine, 1974, 36, 180-182.

Razran, G. The observable unconscious and the inferable conscious in current Soviet psychophysiology: Interoceptive conditioning, semantic conditioning and the orienting reflex. Psychological Review, 1961, 68, 81-147.

Rotter, J. B. Generalized expectancies for internal versus external control of reinforcement. Psychological Monographs, 1966, 80 (Whole No. 609), 1-28.

Schachter, S., & Singer, J. E. Cognitive, social and physiological determinants of emotional state. Psychological Review, 1962, 69, 379-399.

Schachter, M. D., & Rosencrans, J. A. Atropine antagonism of acetylcholine-cued behavior in the rat. Life Science, 1972, 11, 517-532.

Sherrington, C. S. The integrative action of the nervous system. Cambridge: University Press, 1906.

Silverstein, S. J., Nathan, D. E., & Taylor, H. A. Blood alcohol estimation and controlled drinking by chronic alcoholics. Behavior Therapy.

Slucki, H., Adam, G., & Porter, R. W. Operant discrimination of an interoceptive stimulus in Rhesus monkeys. Journal of the Experimental Analysis of Behavior, 1965, 8, 405-414.

Slucki, H., McCoy, F. B., & Porter, R. W. Interoceptive S^D of the large intestine established by mechanical stimulation. Psychological Reports, 1969, 24, 35-42.

Stern, R. M. Detection of one's own spontaneous GSRs. Psychonomic Science, 1972, 29, 354-356.

Stunkard, A., & Koch, C. The interpretation of gastric motility: I. Apparent bias in the reports of hunger by obese persons. Archives of General Psychiatry, 1964, 11, 74-82.

Valins, S. The perception and labelling of bodily changes as determinants of emotional behavior. In P. B. Black (Ed.), Physiological correlates of emotional behavior. New York: Academic Press, 1970.

Verney, E. B. The antidiuretic hormone and the factors which determine its release. Proceedings of the Royal Society, London, B. 135, 25-106.

Whitehead, W. E., Drescher, V. M., & Blackwell, B. Lack of relationship between autonomic perception questionnaire scores and actual sensitivity for perceiving one's heart beat. Paper presented at the annual meeting of the Society for Psychophysiological Research, Toronto, 1975. (a)

Whitehead, W. E., Drescher, V. M., & Blackwell, B. Rate of learning to differentially control heart rate is negatively correlated with subjective awareness of heart beat. Paper presented at the annual meeting of the Society for Psychophysiological Research, Toronto, 1975. (b)

NOTE

The preparation of this paper was supported by MRC Grant No. G974/440/B.

THE ROLE OF EXTEROCEPTIVE FEEDBACK IN LEARNED ELECTRODERMAL AND CARDIAC CONTROL: SOME ATTRACTIONS OF AND PROBLEMS WITH DISCRIMINATION THEORY

Larry E. Roberts
McMaster University

The purposes of this paper are threefold. The first is to outline a class of theories that attempts to explain how subjects learn to comply with an instruction to change an autonomic or central nervous system response during biofeedback training. These accounts are described herein as "discrimination" theories of biofeedback training, for the prominence they assign to perceptual processes in the acquisition of learned control (Black, Cott & Pavloski, in press; Brener, 1974; Staudenmayer & Kinsman, 1976). The second purpose is to illustrate the organizing power of discrimination theory by applying it to data which suggest that experience with an exteroceptive feedback contingency is required for the performance of instructed changes in palmar sweating, but not for the performance of instructed changes in heart rate. The last purpose is to discuss some of the difficulties that arise when one attempts to assess discrimination theory, and to comment upon the utility of the theory in relation to some other approaches to the study of biofeedback training.

DISCRIMINATION THEORIES OF LEARNED CONTROL

The discrimination theories described below are characterized by two assumptions that warrant their inclusion in a common class. First, these theories assume that feedback presentations act to render discriminable interoceptive stimulus events which are related to the occurrence of target responding. Production of the target response in the absence of exteroceptive feedback can be taken to indicate that at least one source of afferentation related to performance of the response has been discriminated. Second, discrimination theories of learned control assume that the development of response strategies during training depends, at least in part, upon this perceptual process. A general statement of discrimination theory need not specify the source of afferentation the subject is assumed to have identified as a result of biofeedback training, nor need it imply that subjects are able to describe with precision either the sensory effects of such training or the response strategies which they have developed to produce target behavior. The minimum empirical requirement of theories of this class appears to be that interoception deriving from some process related to the occurrence of target responding can serve as a discriminative stimulus for choice behavior during a subsequent discrimination test, if subjects have successfully produced the response on transfer trials during prior biofeedback training.

One disadvantage in using a single term like "discrimination theory" to designate a class of theories which share these assumptions in common is that this practice tends to obscure important differences within the class that ought to be kept distinct. I would like to comment briefly upon three distinctions that define versions of discrimination theory which appear to differ in plausibility as well as in empirical support.

The first distinction has to do with the effect that feedback presentations are assumed to have upon interoceptive events related to target responding. Perhaps the most conservative position with respect to this issue is the notion that feedback presentations act merely to identify which aspects of current sensory experience are related to production of the response. Once identified, these sensations provide a basis for the development of response strategies during biofeedback training and act to protect these strategies from fragmentation when they are performed subsequently with exteroceptive feedback removed. Other accounts of discrimination theory go further than this and maintain that feedback presentations alter sensory experience in some way. For example, one might suggest that exteroceptive feedback renders detectable certain interoceptive stimulus events that were previously indiscriminable and did not intrude upon awareness in normal daily functioning. This notion seems implicit in the idea that biofeedback training leads to "awareness" of sensations produced by the response, as some researchers (Brener, 1974; Brown, 1971; Staudenmayer & Kinsman, 1976) appear to have suggested. Detectability may be enhanced by the acquisition of receptor-orienting acts which augment the interoceptive stimulus source, as is illustrated by the case in which subjects learn to adopt certain postures in order to discriminate their pulses. More complex processes might conceivably be involved in the enhancement of detection as well. Another possibility is that biofeedback training may act to differentiate the interoceptive stimulus source. In this instance the interoceptive j.n.d. is reduced, presumably by a process similar to that which accounts for improved discriminability of weights as described by Gibson (1953). Discrimination theories which propose enhanced detectability or differentiation appear to carry with them the implication that biofeedback training produces novel alterations in sensory experience, in the sense that such training allows subjects to attend to sensations that were previously inaccessible to consciousness, or to experience them more intensely (Staudenmayer & Kinsman, 1976). Discrimination theories which stress interoceptive identification as a product of biofeedback training, on the other hand, do not claim such effects.

A second distinction I would like to make between varieties of discrimination theory has to do with the source of afferentation the subject is assumed to have identified, detected, or differentiated when control of a visceral response is established. One possibility is that the afferentation that is discriminated may be directly or indirectly consequent upon visceral effector activity (or, in the case of a central nervous system response, of some unspecified mental process). Other possibilities are that the interoceptive events which are discriminated may be produced by somatomotor or respiratory activities which are related to target responding, or they may be simply motor or other central efferent commands. The discrimination models of visceral control described by Brener (1974) and Black et al. (in press) appear to have placed considerable emphasis upon the perception of effector afferentation. However, this emphasis is not a defining property of discrimination theory as the theory is developed here. In general, the source of afferentation which is discriminated during biofeedback training seems likely to depend upon the intrinsic discriminability of potential sources of response-related interoception, as well as upon the extent to which these sources are related to target responding and the frequency with which they are identified by exteroceptive feedback presentation. The act of attaching verbal labels to these sources is probably best depicted as a separate process. Choice of labels is likely affected by previous experiences subjects have had with the events they have discriminated and by details of the experimental situation which suggest how these events might be appropriately described.

The last distinction has to do with the role that stimulus identification, detection, or differentiation is assumed to play in the development and execution of response strategies during biofeedback training. One could take the position that the interoceptive events which are identified by perceptual processes serve as referents for response differentiation during biofeedback training, and that identification of these events is necessary if target behavior is to be produced on transfer trials where exteroceptive feedback is removed. The idea here is that preferential accessing of efferent processes that produce target behavior takes place only after afferentation deriving from these processes has been rendered discriminable by perceptual mechanisms. This is a conservative proposal in the sense that interoceptive discrimination is seen as an important and necessary component in the process of response differentiation, but other mechanisms are assumed to participate in differentiation and in performance as well. Thus it is possible that feedback presentation may establish the ability to discriminate sensations related to target responding, but that control of the response may not eventuate as a result of impediments to response differentiation and performance arising from other sources. An alternative view which appears to have been suggested by Brener (1974) and Kamiya (1969) is that response differentiation and the ability to produce target behavior follow automatically when an interoceptive stimulus source has been discriminated. Dissociation of discrimination and control does not appear to be compatible with this account of the acquisition process.

I have characterized theories suggested by these distinctions as "discrimination" theories because each proposes the existence of a perceptual process that renders discriminable some aspect of response state during biofeedback training. Each account further makes reference to a response differentiation process in which afferentation identified by the feedback contingency serves as a basis for the development of response strategies which are utilized subsequently to produce target behavior when exteroceptive feedback is removed. Black et al. (in press) have recently employed the term "awareness view" to denote models of the acquisition process which are similar in some respects to those discussed here. This term was proposed initially by Black (1974) to highlight the novel effect that biofeedback training was assumed to have by some researchers (for example, Brown, 1971) on sensory experience, and to call attention to the further and frequently made assumption that such experience is sufficient for control of target behavior. The present characterization appears to be broader than Black et al.'s (in press) in the sense that it includes models which maintain that feedback presentations render discriminable some aspect of response state without proposing that novel experiences in consciousness are produced, or that such experiences are sufficient for control of the response in a transfer test. As will be noted later, models which propose that biofeedback training alters stimulus detectability or differentiation appear to be particularly refractory to empirical test. The assumption that awareness of sensations produced by a response is sufficient for control of that response has been criticized by Black et al. (in press).[1]

THE ROLE OF EXTEROCEPTIVE FEEDBACK IN ELECTRODERMAL AND CARDIAC CONTROL

I was attracted initially to discrimination theory by its ability to account for the results of a recent study which found that prior experience with an explicit exteroceptive feedback contingency was necessary for successful performance when subjects were instructed to control palmar sweating, but not when they were instructed to control heart rate (Lacroix & Roberts, 1976). Operant conditioning and motor-skills approaches to the analysis of biofeedback training, on the other hand, appeared to offer little in the way of a retrospective explanation of differences between these two response systems.

The principal findings of this experiment are depicted in Figure 1. Subjects in Group I/SC were instructed to increase or decrease their palmar sweating on discrete 30-second trials, in the absence of exteroceptive feedback. No mention was made of possible response strategies, nor were explicit constraints placed on the subject's behavior. Changes in palmar hydration were assessed by measuring skin conductance. Inspection of Figure 1 shows that after three days of testing, subjects remained unable to comply with this request. Subjects in Group IF/SC received identical instructions but were in addition given auditory feedback when they performed successfully. Comparison of these groups shows that feedback training established control of skin conductance ($p < .025$), as evidenced by performance on test trials where exteroceptive feedback was removed. The remaining two panels of the figure depict the performance of subjects instructed to control heart rate. As before, no mention was made of response strategies or behavioral constraints in the instructions the subjects received. Provision of instructions alone (Group I/HR) was sufficient to produce a substantial change in this response. Inspection of acquisition in Figure 2 shows that performance improved over days under these conditions ($p < .05$), even though no exteroceptive feedback was given for successful responding. Subjects given exteroceptive feedback for heart rate (Group IF/HR) performed somewhat better than did subjects given instructions alone, but these groups did not differ significantly from one another. Experience with an explicit feedback contingency was not required for control of heart rate, since subjects evidenced substantial control when merely instructed to change this response.

Discrimination theory explains these findings by appealing to differences in the discriminability of afferentation deriving from electrodermal and cardiac responding. According to this view, untrained subjects tested under the conditions of the present experiment were able to distinguish between high and low heart rates on the basis of afferentation deriving from

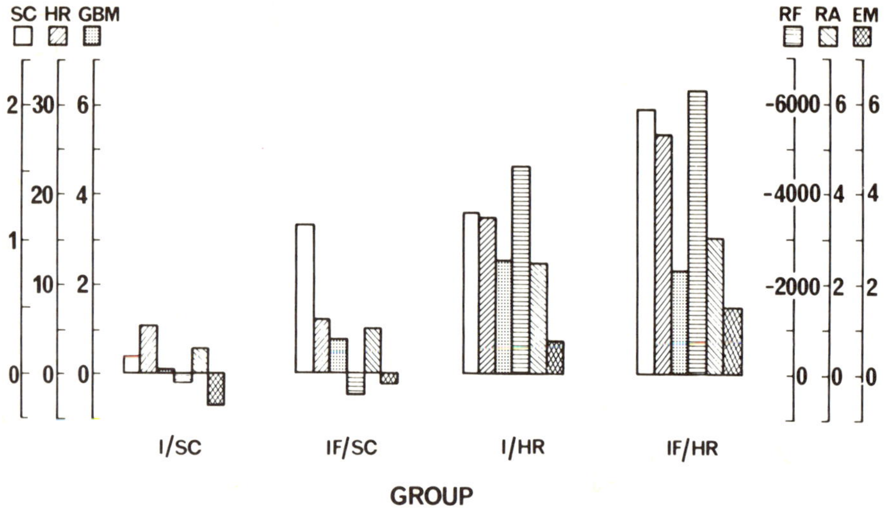

Figure 1. Control of skin conductance and heart rate in four groups of subjects (N=8 each). Experimental conditions are as described in the text. Subjects received 20 increase and 20 decrease trials daily for three consecutive days; trials lasted 30 seconds and were separated by an intertrial interval that averaged 40 seconds. The bars represent the difference in performance between increase and decrease trials on the last day of testing. Data for the feedback groups (IF/SC and IF/HR) were taken from test trials on which subjects were instructed to change the response with feedback removed. SC = skin conductance in micromhos; HR = heart rate in beats per minute; GBM = gross body movement in arbitrary units; RF = respiration frequency measured as respiratory period in milliseconds (negative-up); RA = respiration amplitude in arbitrary units; EM = eye movements in arbitrary units. The only reliable bidirectional difference under the skin conductance condition was SC responding in the IF/SC group. All variables differed reliably between increase and decrease trials when heart rate was the target response. From Lacroix & Roberts (1976).

cardiac effector action. Subjects instructed to change their heart rate without the aid of exteroceptive feedback (Group I/HR) utilized this skill to identify response strategies that produced cardiac change, and to refine them over the course of training. Adding exteroceptive feedback contributed relatively little to performance, because the cardiac changes identified by feedback presentation were discriminated and labeled appropriately in the absence of the feedback contingency. Changes in palmar sweating, on the other hand, were not intrinsically discriminable, owing to a lack of detect-

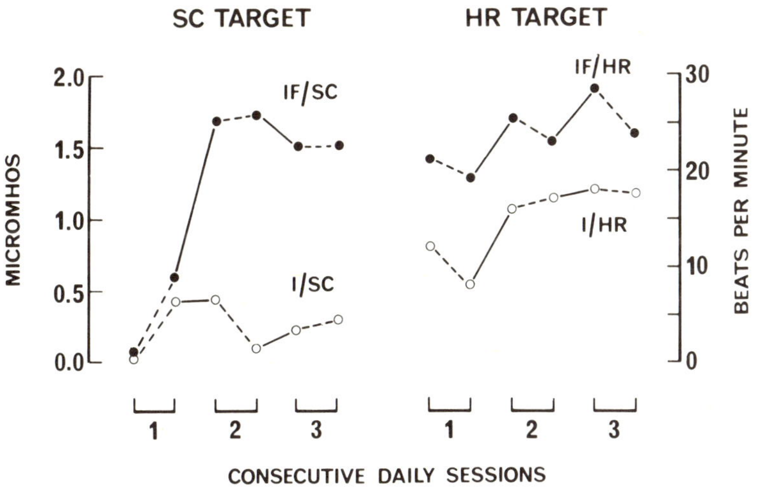

Figure 2. Compliance with instructions to increase and decrease palmar sweating (skin conductance target) or heart rate (heart rate target) over three days of training. Groups are as described in the text. Bidirectional performance is shown. Data for each day are depicted separately for the first and last half of the session and are taken from test trials on which feedback was removed for subjects in the feedback condition (IF Groups). From Lacroix & Roberts (1976).

able afferentation arising from this effector process under conditions of the present test. Consequently, experience with an explicit exteroceptive feedback contingency was necessary to identify other sources of afferentation which were related to performance of this response. Control was achieved when one such source was identified and used as a basis for developing response strategies that produced changes in this autonomic system.

This discrimination analysis made no reference to the subject's knowledge of effective response strategies or to his ability to change target behavior, prior to feedback training. However, inspection of Figure 2 shows that subjects instructed to change their heart rate evidenced changes exceeding 10 beats per minute on the first block of test trials, under both feedback conditions. This suggests that performance in the experiments of Figure 1 may have been affected by transfer to the experimental task of information about the response, that was mediated by the verbal labels used to designate the response systems in the instruction. If subjects adopted a particular strategy from prior knowledge that it works, discrimination theory assumes that subjects have discriminated variations in visceral responding and have identified activities that produce them, in their natural environments. If, on the other hand, subjects acted upon misinformation communicated by the verbal labels, as might have happened when instructed to change palmar sweating[2], discrimination theory explains why this information persisted as a basis for performance until corrected by an explicit feedback contingency. Both the presence and absence of prior knowledge about a response are explained as a consequence of whether interoceptive referents were available to serve as a basis for learning about the response prior to explicit feedback training. Thus it is possible that the effects of Figure 1 derived from differences in the discriminability of response-related afferentation, even though a portion of the effect was attributable to transfer from previous learning that was mediated by the verbal labels used to reference the response systems in the instructions the subjects received.

This explanation of how subjects learned to control heart-rate and electrodermal responding appears consistent with neurophysiological knowledge pertaining to potential sources of discriminable afferentation deriving from cardiac and sudomotor effector action. Subjects instructed to change their heart rate may have identified variations in this response on the basis of afferentation arising from several sources, including 1) pressure receptors in the heart, carotid sinus, and aortic arch, 2) auditory or visual sensations produced by the beating heart, or 3) mechanoreceptor stimulation arising from muscle and skin following arterial distention with each ventricular contraction. Potential sources of afferentation deriving from sudomotor activation, on the other hand, appear to be fewer in number. There is no interoception known to arise directly as a consequence of sudomotor effector action (Kuno, 1956). There is reason to believe that tactile and thermal sensations are altered when the palm is hydrated by sweat secretion (Edelberg, 1961), but it is doubtful whether the secretory effects that occur in typical biofeedback applications are of sufficient magnitude to yield measureable sensory experiences of this nature in the absence of sensitive psychophysical tests. Differences between the electrodermal and cardiovascular systems with respect to potential sources of afferentation may be amplified further by differences in the periodicity and consequently the sampling rate of sudomotor and cardiac effector activity. These considerations appear to provide adequate grounds for suggesting that changes in heart rate may be intrinsically more discriminable than changes in palmar sweating.

A discrimination analysis of the role of exteroceptive feedback in electrodermal and cardiac control is also attractive for its ability to integrate seemingly disparate observations with respect to the issue of whether provision of exteroceptive feedback facilitates learned control of heart rate (Levenson, 1976). A discrimination analysis suggests that exteroceptive feedback will facilitate control of heart rate only in those experimental situations in which the response strategies available to the subject are insufficient to generate changes in cardiac activity that are large enough to be discriminated. Under these circumstances, subjects both require and utilize exteroceptive feedback to identify sensations related to changes in heart rate, and to subsequently develop effective control strategies. The contribution of feedback under these circumstances is evidenced by improved performance when feedback is provided, as well as by the occurrence of somatomotor and respiratory correlates which appear to be necessary for the performance of heart-rate change even though these activities may have been discouraged by the instructions given to the subjects prior to training (Brener, Kleinman, & Goesling, 1969). If, however, somatomotor and respiratory constraints are rigorously enforced, as was done by Levenson (1976) who provided his subjects with respiration feedback and in one study required them to breathe through a respirometer, feedback may fail to facilitate performance because subjects are not permitted to utilize response strategies which are effective in producing cardiovascular change. The reluctance of subjects to capitalize on these strategies may persist when their performance is closely monitored, even though afferentation deriving from these strategies is identified by feedback presentation.[3]

The organizing power of discrimination theory does not appear to be limited to these applications. For example, the theory provides a basis for understanding the informal report by Upton and Longmire (1975) that epileptic subjects given exteroceptive feedback of paroxysmal activity in their EEGs subsequently report auras which previously had escaped their attention. The therapeutic benefits of such training presumably depend upon whether sensations identified by the feedback contingency serve successfully as referents for the development of seizure-inhibiting response strategies and are available to act as discriminative stimuli for the performance of these strategies after biofeedback training has been completed. Discrimination theory also suggests an explanation for the superiority of single-beat as opposed to multiple-beat feedback contingencies reported recently by Gatchel (1974) for the production of heart rate increases. Contingencies that provide feedback upon the completion of every heart beat may be expected to result in better control insofar as they provide additional opportunities to sample and identify afferentation related to changes in heart rate. The additional opportunity provided by the single-beat contingency in Gatchel's study derived from the fact that feedback was presented more frequently and was more likely to have been temporally contiguous with afferentation produced by the performance of heart rate change. The superiority of analog over binary feedback displays (Lang & Twentyman, 1974) may also derive in part from these effects, since in addition to information about the magnitude and direction of performance errors, analog displays typically present feedback more frequently than do binary procedures.

It is the ability of discrimination theory to suggest explanations for observations as diverse as these which makes it an attractive approach to the analysis of biofeedback training. At first glance the theory also seems open to a relatively straightforward experimental test. With respect to the results of Figure 1, one merely has to assess the ability of subjects to discriminate afferentation associated with heart rate and electrodermal responding, prior to and following exteroceptive feedback training. The expected results of such study are that subjects should be able to discriminate activities related to effector action only under those circumstances where control of target behavior is also evidenced. Unfortunately, however, this test is not as straightforward as it at first seems. Some of the difficulties associated with testing a discrimination account of the results of Figure 1 are considered next.

SOME PROBLEMS IN ASSESSING THE RELATIONSHIP BETWEEN DISCRIMINATION AND CONTROL

The difficulties in assessing the relationship of discrimination to control to be considered here arise from the inability of the experimenter to directly manipulate the stimulus (response state) whose discriminability is to be assessed. In practice the only method available for most response systems is to identify the stimulus to be discriminated by means of an exteroceptive feedback contingency. One arrangement that has been used for discrimination testing may be referred to as a contingency discrimination procedure (Brener & Jones, 1974). In this procedure, exteroceptive feedback is presented contingently upon the activity that is to be discriminated on some trials, and independently of such activity on other trials. The subject's task is to identify which type of trial he has received. Another method, referred to herein as a response-state discrimination procedure, asks whether subjects can tell when the same exteroceptive stimulus event is contingent upon high or low levels of activity in the visceral response that is to be discriminated (Baron, 1966). If multiple feedback presentations are given on trials in either procedure, control tests are required to establish that subjects cannot discriminate trial types on the basis of feedback presentations alone. Successful performance can occur on properly-conducted contingency and response-state discrimination tasks only if subjects are able to identify a source of interoception that is related to target behavior.[4]

There are, however, complications inherent in these procedures which give reason to suspect that subjects who fail to perform successfully on discrimination tasks may nevertheless be able to discriminate activities which are the target of the discrimination test. One potential source of difficulty is that the feedback contingency utilized in discrimination testing may not have identified just-noticeable-differences in the interoceptive stimulus that was to be discriminated. Feedback contingencies which identify variations that are more deviant in duration or magnitude may yield evidence of discrimination where other contingencies do not. Another problem is that subjects exposed previously to biofeedback training may have learned to discriminate, not peripheral interoceptive events arising directly or indirectly from effector action, but peripheral or central afferentation deriving from correlated processes that produce target behavior. Any feature of subsequent discrimination testing that restricts access to these processes (such as somatomotor constraints or brief trial durations) may be expected to affect the outcome of a discrimination task. Such restrictions might also affect performance insofar as subjects are not permitted to engage in activities which generate changes in effector action of sufficient magnitude to be discriminated. The thrust of these objections is that subjects may fail to perform successfully on a discrimination test, not because they are unable to identify some aspect of response state, but because the test procedure has failed to identify those aspects which they have discriminated.

One way to circumvent these objections is to examine discrimination performance as a function of the conditions of the discrimination task, and as a function of variations in the response unit upon which feedback is made conditional in a discrimination test. This information is useful and should be collected when the discriminability of response states is assessed. There appears, however, to be a difference between interoceptive and more traditional exteroceptive discrimination tasks that may pose still further obstacles to successful performance during discrimination testing, even when an internal stimulus source is present and detectable. Response-state and contingency discrimination procedures do not present a stimulus to the subject and ask if he perceives it; rather, these procedures present an exteroceptive stimulus and ask the subject to render a judgment concerning its relationship to behavior. To respond correctly, subjects must be able not only to discriminate their behavior, but to assess correctly its relationship to the feedback stimulus. There are data which indicate that under some circumstances subjects have difficulty correctly assessing the relationship of outcomes to their behavior, even when both behavior and outcome are highly discriminable. Jenkins and Ward (1965) reported that subjects' judgments of control in a simple two-response, two-outcome procedure tended to relate not to the actual contingency between behavior and outcome, but to the number of trials on which the desired outcome occurred ("success"). The problem posed by this result can be illustrated by reference to a contingency discrimination task in which multiple feedback presentations occur with equal probability on both contingent and non-contingent trials (Brener & Jones, 1974). The presence of feedback on both types of trial on a task in which subjects are given the opportunity to base decisions on perceived control of the feedback display may bias judgments toward a null outcome, even when some aspect of response state is in fact discriminated. Errors in judgment arising from this source may contribute to the observation that subjects who are successfully discriminating some feature of their behavior after training on a contingency discrimination task nevertheless respond incorrectly on approximately 25% of the trials presented to them (Brener & Jones, 1974).

The contribution of this judgmental process to performance on discrimination tasks is difficult to assess since so little is known about it. It is reasonable to assume that errors arising from this source are more prominent during the early stages of discrimination testing, where subjects are actively engaged in assessing the relationship of feedback to their behavior. There is also reason to assume that errors depend upon details of the discrimination task as well as upon properties of the response system that is to be discriminated. Errors may be more frequent on tasks that call for a judgment after multiple feedback presentations, where the relationship of feedback to behavior may be clouded by presentations that occur as a consequence of aspects of response state other than those which the subjects have discriminated. The likelihood of this happening would appear to be substantial in multi-determined physiological systems such as those that control cardiovascular and sudomotor responding (Obrist, 1975; Roberts & Young, 1971). The problem may be less severe for response-state as opposed to contingency discrimination procedures, where the subject's task is to denote which of two internal response states is identified by the feedback stimulus. The basis for this conjecture is that subjects tend to select (and can presumably discriminate the occurrence of) skeletal-motor responses that produce desired outcomes when a contingency between behavior and outcome is present, even though concurrent assessments of perceived control appear to be unaffected by contingency manipulation (Jenkins & Ward, 1965). Subjects tested by response-state discrimination methods may be less likely to define the task as one of assessing whether they can control the feedback display, since they are told and may subsequently confirm that feedback is conditional upon behavior on both types of test trial.

Some appreciation of the implication of these problems for assessment of the relationship between discrimination and control can be obtained by reference to the results of Figure 1. The explanation of these findings advanced earlier leads one to predict that subjects should be able to discriminate changes in heart rate prior to exteroceptive feedback training. However, the data presently available on the discrimination of changes in heart rate (Brener, Giacinto, & Baker, 1976) and the occurrence of discrete heart beats (Brener & Jones, 1974) in untrained subjects are unfavorable to this prediction. The failure of untrained subjects to discriminate these properties of cardiac function could nevertheless be a consequence of the circumstances under which the discrimination test was conducted. For example, detection of discrete heart beats may be easier following the performance of somatomotor responses which elevate the heart rate (as in Group I/HR and IF/HR in Figure 1), insofar as contractile properties of the heart are altered under these conditions. Detection of beats may be more difficult if such activities are discouraged, as was likely done in the Brener & Jones (1974) study. Performance of somatomotor responses may also facilitate discrimination of changes in heart rate insofar as these activities generate heart rate differences which are larger and more easily discriminated. Another problem is that untrained subjects may fail to perform correctly during the initial stages of a response-state or contingency discrimination test, not because afferentation deriving from the response is indiscriminable, but because they have had insufficient opportunity to correctly assess the relationship between interoceptive and exteroceptive stimulus events. Improvements in performance which occur subsequently over the course of discrimination or biofeedback training such as those described by Brener et al. (1976) may derive in part from improved accuracy at judging this relationship.

A discrimination theory applied to the results of Figure 1 also predicts that subjects should not be able to discriminate skin conductance activity prior to explicit biofeedback training. The available data on this question are more favorable (Lacroix & Mignault, 1976; Stern, 1972) but can be questioned on grounds similar to those discussed for heart rate. It is apparent that the predictions of discrimination theory with respect to the state of initial discriminability are not likely to fall on the basis of a few experimental tests.

Discrimination theory further specifies that performance under the instructional condition alone (Groups I/SC and I/HR, in Figure 1) depends upon the discriminability of interoception deriving from cardiac and sudomotor effector action. A direct test of this assertion is complicated by the fact that variations in electrodermal and heart-rate responding are likely to be associated with more discriminable activities that may serve as a basis for choice behavior during a discrimination test. The feasibility of resolving this question depends upon how much is known about correlates of the response as well as upon other properties of the response system. Extensive knowledge of the correlates of cardiac activity, and the discrete nature of the ventricular contraction, appear to make possible relatively firm conclusions about the basis of performance on some cardiac discrimination tasks. For example, Whitehead, Drescher, and Blackwell (1975) adapted a response-state discrimination procedure to the detection of discrete heart beats by requiring subjects to discriminate between trials on which a discrete visual stimulus was presented either 128 or 384 milliseconds following each heart beat. Subjects given knowledge of results after each trial were able to perform successfully on this task. Successful performance could not have been produced by a simple judgment as to whether the subjects could or could not influence the feedback display, because such attempts would have affected feedback frequency on both types of trial and could therefore not have provided a basis for distinguishing between them. It is also unlikely that afferentation deriving from deliberate somatomotor or respiratory maneuvers served as a basis for response choice, since it is unlikely that these maneuvers could have been performed with sufficient frequency or precision on any given trial to serve as an alternative referent for temporal judgments. Consequently one can conclude with some certainty that the referent for temporal judgments must have been the discrete ventricular contraction. Assessment of the basis for sudomotor discrimination, on the other hand, appears to be more difficult, owing to the slow and variable features of this response, and to greater difficulty in specifying and measuring its possible correlates.

The nature and extent of the above complications is such as to suggest that a discrimination analysis of the phenomena depicted in Figure 1 is not open to a convincing empirical test. The most serious obstacle appears to be that of assessing the discriminability of cardiac and sudomotor effector action prior to explicit feedback training. Untrained subjects may fail when tested initially on discrimination task, not because they are unable to discriminate afferentation arising from these effector processes, but because they have been provided with insufficient opportunity to assess the relationship between exteroceptive and interoceptive stimulus events. Extended discrimination testing does not circumvent this problem, because subjects may learn eventually to identify response-related sensations on the basis of the feedback contingency that is implicit in the discrimination procedure. Moreover, these sensations may arise from processes which are correlated with visceral responding, rather than from visceral activity itself. These considerations may explain why Diekhoff (1976) reported successful discrimination of skin resistance responses following application of an extended response-state discrimination procedure, even though subjects were not told whether they responded correctly or incorrectly following each discrimination trial. It is likely that subjects in Diekhoff's experiment learned to discriminate correlates of sudomotor effector action on the basis of the feedback contingency that was contained in the discrimination task. Such learning might have occurred if target responding were produced by response processes, such as deliberate respiratory or somatomotor maneuvers, that were themselves highly discriminable.

The problems discussed above appear to raise a more general problem for discrimination theories which propose that biofeedback training enhances visceral perception. At the moment it is difficult to see how, given our inability to control the stimulus whose detectability to be assessed, we can establish unambiguously whether or not biofeedback training alters detectability in the sense that the subject is made more aware of sensations produced by, or correlated with, the response. One reason for this view is that improvements in performance which occur as a result of biofeedback training may derive from a variety of processes other than enhanced detectability, such as the necessity to correctly associate exteroceptive and interoceptive stimulus events. A further problem that seems particularly applicable to the case of sudomotor discrimination is that the interoceptive events identified by feedback presentation before and after training may be different. This problem is so severe in this instance as to merit illustration by example. Lacroix and Mignault (1976) have reported that although subjects are unable to discriminate the occurrence of discrete skin-potential ("sweating") responses when tested on a response-state discrimination task prior to biofeedback training, their ability to discriminate following such training is substantial. These results indicate that subjects who comply successfully with an instruction to change sudomotor activity in the absence of feedback are also able to discriminate some aspect of response state, as a general statement of discrimination theory predicts. The versions of discrimination theory described earlier, however, make different statements about the sensory basis of this result. Theories which argue that biofeedback training enhances visceral perception would interpret the outcome to mean that experience with an explicit feedback contingency enhanced the detectability of afferentation related to the performance of discrete electrodermal responses. However, it is equally possible that the response states identified by feedback presentation before and after training were different. For example, discrete skin-potential responses which were identified by feedback presentation during the initial discrimination test may have been produced by an arousal-like process which is known to affect sudomotor function (Roberts & Young, 1971), whereas the responses identified by feedback during the post-discrimination test may have been produced by deliberate cognitive or somatomotor maneuvers which were acquired by the subjects over the course of biofeedback training. In the absence of some way of controlling or specifying the response state whose discriminability is to be assessed, the possibility of ascertaining whether biofeedback training alters the subject's awareness of sensations produced by or correlated with the response so as to produce novel sensory experiences seems very remote.

CONCLUSION

These considerations lead one to ask whether there is any profit to be gained by depicting learned control as a discrimination process. For the present, the attractiveness of this view derives not from its testability in any rigorous sense, but from its considerable organizing power and the attention it focuses on a likely consequence of biofeedback training that has received little systematic study in the available literature. It needs to be stressed that successful performance on properly conducted discrimination tasks has been reported, and that at least with respect to cardiovascular responses some conclusions about the source of afferentation that has been discriminated are possible (Brener et al., 1976; Whitehead et al., 1975). These reports indicate that subjects are able to discriminate some aspect of response state and suggest the feasibility of examining variables that determine performance on discrimination tasks. There are also sufficient data to indicate that performance on discrimination tasks is improved by biofeedback training (see Brener, this volume, for a review). Although the prospect of unravelling the mechanisms responsible for this effect appears limited at the present time, the attempt has hardly begun. It would seem reasonable in view of the substantial evidence for visceral perception to continue the study of these phenomena, even if for the moment our ability to draw conclusions about the basis for discrimination performance is in many instances less than we would like.

It is not possible to specify an optimum procedure for discrimination testing without regard to the purpose of the test and the properties of the visceral or CNS response that is to be discriminated. However, an adequate assessment of whether biofeedback training has rendered discriminable some aspect of response state must provide subjects with an opportunity to engage in those response strategies they are assumed to have identified on the basis of exteroceptive feedback. It would also seem desirable to avoid, where possible, complicating the discrimination task by presenting subjects with exteroceptive feedback that is unrelated to behavior, as is done in the contingency discrimination procedure. Response-state discrimination methods do not obviate the need to judge the relationship of feedback to behavior, but they do not appear to pose any more serious an obstacle to successful performance in this respect than does biofeedback training.

REFERENCES

Baron, J. An EEG correlate of autonomic discrimination. Psychonomic Science, 1966, 4, 255-256.

Black, A. H. Summary: The nature of operant and voluntary control. In P. A. Obrist, A. H. Black, J. Brener, & L. V. DiCara (Eds.), Cardiovascular psychophysiology: Current issues in response mechanisms, biofeedback, and methodology. Chicago: Aldine, 1974.

Black, A. H., Cott, A., & Pavloski, R. The operant learning theory approach to biofeedback training. In G. E. Schwartz & J. Beatty (Eds.), Biofeedback: Theory and research. San Francisco: Academic Press, in press.

Brener, J. A general model of voluntary control applied to the phenomena of learned cardiovascular change. In P. A. Obrist, A. H. Black, J. Brener, & L. V. DiCara (Eds.), Cardiovascular psychophysiology: Current issues in response mechanisms, biofeedback, and methodology. Chicago: Aldine, 1974.

Brener, J., Giacinto, J., & Baker, J. Visceral perception: Some studies of heart rate discrimination. Handout presented to the NATO Symposium on Biofeedback & Behavior, Munich, 27-30 July 1976.

Brener, J., & Jones, J. M. Interoceptive discrimination in intact humans: Detection of cardiac activity. Physiology & Behavior, 1974, 13, 763-767.

Brener, J., Kleinman, R. A., & Goesling, W. J. The effects of different exposures to augmented sensory feedback on the self control of heart rate. Psychophysiology, 1969, 5, 510-516.

Brown, B. B. Awareness of EEG-subjective activity relationships detected within a closed feedback system. Psychophysiology, 1971, 7, 451-464.

Diekhoff, G. M. Effects of feedback in a forced-choice GSR detection task. Psychophysiology, 1976, 13, 22-26.

Edelberg, R. The relationship between the galvanic skin response, vasoconstriction, and tactile sensitivity. Journal of Experimental Psychology, 1961, 62, 187-195.

Epstein, L. H., & Stein, D. B. Feedback-influenced heart rate discrimination. Journal of Abnormal Psychology, 1974, 83, 585-588.

Gatchel, R. J. Frequency of feedback and learned heart rate control. Journal of Experimental Psychology, 1974, 103, 274-283.

Gibson, E. J. Improvement in perceptual judgments as a function of controlled practice or training. Psychological Bulletin, 1953, 50, 401-431.

Jenkins, H. M., & Ward, W. C. Judgment of contingency between responses and outcomes. Psychological Monographs, 1965, 79, 1-17 (Whole No. 594).

Kamiya, J. Operant control of the EEG alpha rhythm and some of its reported effects on consciousness. In C. T. Tart (Ed.), Altered states of consciousness: A book of readings. New York: Wiley, 1969.

Kuno, Y. Human perspiration. Springfield, Illinois: Charles C. Thomas, 1956.

Lacroix, J. M., & Mignault, F. B. Effects of feedback training on the discrimination of skin potential responses. Submitted for presentation at the annual meetings of the Society for Psychophysiological Research, San Diego, California, October 1976.

Lacroix, J. M., & Roberts, L. E. Determinants of learned electrodermal and cardiac control: A comparative study. Psychophysiology, 1976, 13, 175. (Abstract)

Lang, P. J., & Twentyman, C. T. Learning to control heart rate: Binary vs. analogue feedback. Psychophysiology, 1974, 11, 616-629.

Levenson, R. W. Feedback effects and respiratory involvement in voluntary control of heart rate. Psychophysiology, 1976, 13, 108-114.

Obrist, P. A. The cardiovascular-behavioral interaction - As it appears today. Psychophysiology, 1976, 13, 95-107.

Roberts, L. E., & Young, R. Electrodermal responses are independent of movement during aversive conditioning in rats, but heart rate is not. Journal of Comparative and Physiological Psychology, 1971, 77, 495-512.

Staudenmayer, H., & Kinsman, R. A. Awareness during electromyographic biofeedback: Of signal or process? Biofeedback and Self-Regulation, 1976, 1, 191-199.

Stern, R. M. Detection of one's own spontaneous GSRs. Psychonomic Science, 1972, 29, 354-356.

Upton, A. R. M., & Longmire, D. The effects of feedback on focal epileptic discharges in man: A preliminary report. Le Journal Canadien des Sciences Neurologiques, 1975, 2, 153-167.

Whitehead, W. E., Drescher, V. M., & Blackwell, B. Lack of relationship between autonomic perception questionnaire scores and actual sensitivity for perceiving one's heart beat. Psychophysiology, 1976, 13, 177. (Abstract)

Wilcott, R. C. Effects of high environmental temperature on sweating and skin resistance. Journal of Comparative and Physiological Psychology, 1963, 56, 778-782.

NOTES

1. Black et al. (in press) have also questioned the assumption that the ability to discriminate afferentation produced by a response is necessary for control of that response. This assumption is challenged primarily on the basis of data which suggest that subjects can control occipital alpha after biofeedback training even though they are unable to identify brief instances of this response in a discrimination test. However, the procedure used by Black et al. (in press) to assess the discriminability of alpha can be questioned on several of the accounts raised later in this paper. The nature of these objections is such as to indicate that predictions of discrimination theory pertaining to the relationship between discrimination and control do not appear to be open to convincing empirical test.

2. Inspection of Group I/HR in Figure 1 shows that subjects evidenced substantial control of skin conductance when instructed to control heart rate. Thus it is clear that untrained subjects possessed the ability to alter electrodermal responding, but that they failed to utilize this skill when the behavioral goal was specified as a change in "palmar sweating." It may be that reference to sweating switched the subjects onto thermoregulatory strategies that were difficult to execute and may have had little effect on volar sweat glands, which appear to respond to thermal stimulation only when such stimulation is rather intense (Wilcott, 1963).

3. This explanation does not reduce the issue of whether feedback effects are obtained solely to the question of whether interoceptive referents are available in the absence of exteroceptive feedback. Other requirements have to be met if feedback effects are to be observed. As mentioned above, one of these requirements is that subjects must be given at least a limited opportunity to engage in activities that produce target responding. It should also be noted that other factors may prevent expression of feedback effects, even when exteroceptive feedback serves a prosthetic function. For example, response strategies may be suggested to the subject which are less than optimal and interfere with discrimination of response state (Lacroix & Roberts, 1976).

4. An important requirement of response-state and contingency discrim-

ination tasks when knowledge of results (reinforcement) is provided is that trial presentation must be independent of choice behavior and reinforcement history on previous trials. If this requirement is not met, the possibility exists that response choice may be a function not of the internal sensory state identified by feedback presentation, but of the subject's appreciation that one choice is more likely to be reinforced than another (that is, that one type of trial is more likely to occur than another). An example of the difficulty that may be encountered when this requirement is not met is discussed by Black et al. (in press). It should be noted further that attempts have been made to assess interoceptive discrimination without employing an exteroceptive stimulus to designate response state. For example, Epstein & Stein (1974) instructed subjects to press a button whenever they sensed that their heart rates exceeded an average rate established during a prior 10-minute adaptation period. Successful performance on such tasks when knowledge of results is given for correct choices does not provide unambiguous evidence for discrimination, because this procedure does not allow separation of reinforcement and discrimination effects. These procedures also appear less desirable in that subjects are required to define by reference to an arbitrary standard the interoceptive stimulus they are to discriminate, as well as to indicate when instances of the stimulus have occurred. This procedure appears more complex than contingency or response-state discrimination procedures, which dispense with the need to define the stimulus with respect to a referent and insure further that the visceral states which provide the occasion for choice behavior are constant over the course of discrimination testing.

The research reported herein was supported by Grants from the Ontario Mental Health Foundation (No. 345) and the National Research Council of Canada (A132), to L. E. Roberts. I thank Richard Marlin and John Lyons for their comments on some of the problems discussed in this paper.

INTER-EFFECTOR INFLUENCES IN OPERANT AUTONOMIC CONTROL

H.D. Kimmel and R.A. Burns
University of South Florida

Almost from the very beginning of research on operant reinforcement of autonomically mediated responses, the possibility has been considered that contingencies explicitly introduced in relation to a particular autonomic response might influence other autonomically mediated behaviors. For example, Shapiro, Crider, and Tursky (1964) examined skin potential levels and heart rates in conjunction with the administration of positive reinforcement contingent upon the frequency of skin potential responses. They concluded that their observed operant conditioning effect on skin potential response frequency was independent of changes in the other autonomic measures. Subsequently, Crider, Shapiro, and Tursky (1966) obtained quite similar results in a replication of their first study. In both of these studies, basal skin potential levels and heart rates actually declined during training in both experimental and control groups and skin potential levels tended to be slightly higher and heart rates slightly lower (the latter increasingly so) in the group reinforced for emitting spontaneous skin potential responses than in the control group. But these consistent differences were not statistically significant.

Similarly, Miller and Banuazizi (1968) reported that curarized rats reinforced with intracranial shock for either increases or decreases in heart rate or intestinal contractions showed appropriate operant conditioning effects in the reinforced response independent of changes in the other. Again, however, a consistently higher heart rate was found in animals reinforced for intestinal contractions than in those reinforced for intestinal relaxation. The statistical significance of this heart rate difference was not reported, probably because the effect did not change appreciably across conditioning trials. Likewise, Hamano and Miyake (1972) operantly conditioned human skin resistance responses with no apparent changes in heart rate, and Schwartz (1972) conditioned increased blood pressure levels and decreased heart rates conjointly and separately. In general, the conclusion of all of these authors has been that specific changes may be brought about in a particular autonomic effector by operant reinforcement without concomitant changes occurring in other ones.

In conflict with this general conclusion, other studies have reported inter-effector influences in operant autonomic conditioning. Schell and Grings (1971) reinforced skin resistance responses using a signaled avoidance paradigm and found significantly higher heart rates in their yoked controls than in the avoidance group, in addition to the explicitly hypothesized electrodermal differences. Gavalas (1967) presented positive reinforcement contingent upon emitted skin resistance responses during ten daily sessions and found higher heart rates in her yoked controls than in the reinforced group on eight of the ten days. The significance of this effect was not reported. In a study procedurally resembling the Miller and Banuazizi (1968) experiment on intestinal contractions and heart rate, Kimmel and Kimmel (1967) reinforced emitted skin resistance responses in one group of subjects and digital vasoconstrictions in another, in addition to measuring both responses and running noncontingent controls. They found that the concomitant reinforcement effect on one autonomic response significantly depended upon which of the two responses was explicitly reinforced. When the vasomotor response was reinforced, the frequency of both it and the skin resistance response were higher in the experimental group than in the controls. But when the skin resistance response was explicitly reinforced, its frequency was higher in the experimentals than in the controls, but the frequency of emitted vasoconstrictions was unchanged in the experimental group and increased in the controls. Kimmel and Kimmel attributed this complex outcome to the fact that the initial operant rate of the skin resistance response was almost twice that of the vasomotor response, resulting in adventitious intermittent reinforcement of the former when the latter was explicitly reinforced and reinforcement for omission of vasomotor responses when the skin resistance response was reinforced. Because of the relevance of the vasomotor data obtained by Kimmel and Kimmel to the results and arguments presented below, they are reproduced in Figure 1.

More recently, we have been examining inter-effector autonomic operant conditioning effects in monkeys. Our basic plan was to compare an instrumental conditioning paradigm with a classical one. The instrumental paradigm involved two different visual discriminative stimuli (tonic stimuli), a Sidman avoidance schedule being used in the presence of one of

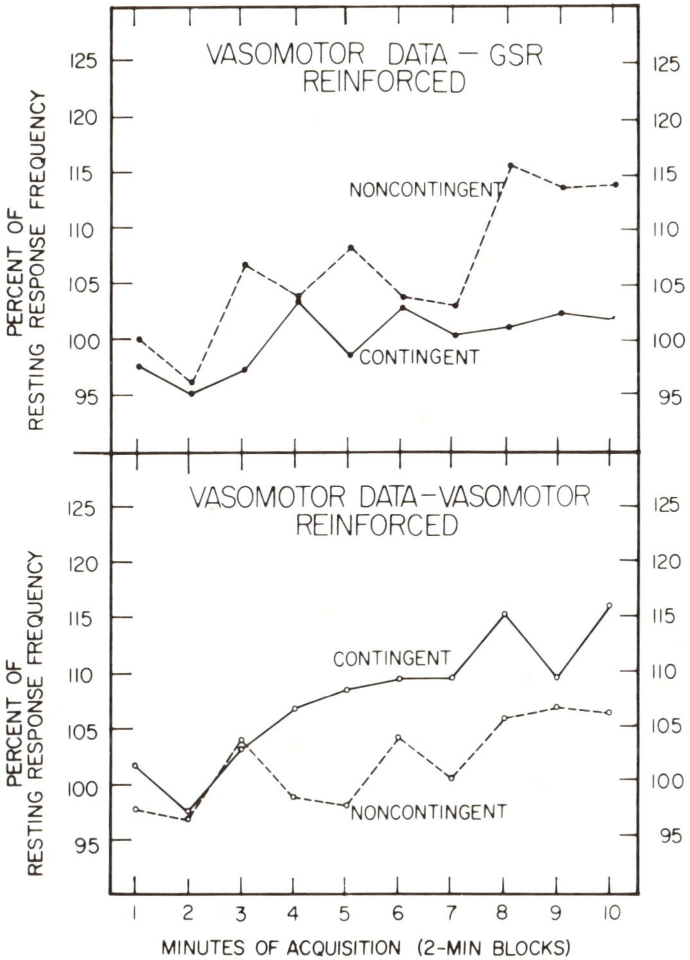

Figure 1. Frequency of digital vasoconstriction responses in subjects receiving reinforcement contingent upon the presence or absence of skin conductance responses (upper panel) and vasomotor responses (lower panel). From Kimmel and Kimmel, 1967.

these stimuli and a response contingent punishment schedule being used in the presence of the other. The classical conditioning paradigm analogously also contained two different tonic visual stimuli, with paired tone-shock trials being administered in the presence of one and unsignaled shock in the presence of the other. This unusual classical conditioning paradigm is a type of transswitching procedure (Asratyan, 1965), in which the visual discriminative stimuli are analogous to Asratyan's "switching agents."

METHOD

Subjects

Four adult male *Cebus albifrons* monkeys were assigned to the two experimental conditions, two in each condition. These animals were in matched pairs on the basis of initial unelicited skin conductance response measures.

Apparatus

The animal was restrained in a primate chair with a hole at the lower back of the chair permitting the tail to protrude for attachment of shock electrodes. The chair also contained an attachment so that the active electrodermal electrode made contact with the plantar surface of the foot. The electrodermal electrodes were of the zinc-zinc sulphate type, in teflon cups filled with saline paste. Two electrocardiographic electrodes were employed to measure heart rate. These were taped to shaved areas on the left and right sides of the animal's chest. The primate chair was placed inside of a sound-attenuated chamber with the animal facing a panel which presented visual stimuli. A speaker located behind the animal delivered continuous white noise at 80 db as well as delivering the phasic auditory conditioned stimulus to the subjects in the classical condition (the latter was a 1,000 Hz pure tone, 5.0 sec in duration with an intensity of 80 db).

Procedure

The instrumental condition involved alternating segments of S^D and S^Δ, consisting of red and green visual stimuli. Durations of these segments could range from 3.0 to 5.0 minutes, with a mean of 4.0 minutes. Sessions averaged 48 minutes in duration, not including an initial period for electrode polarization. Sixteen sessions were run, on alternating days.

During S^D a Sidman shock-shock schedule of 40 seconds was administered for the first six sessions. This was changed for the remaining sessions to shock-shock 20 seconds. The shock was 3.0 mamps in intensity and 0.1 sec in duration, administered to the animal's tail. A response-shock interval of 40 seconds began following each criterion electrodermal response (at least 2 microohms).

Responses within 5 secs following shock did not result in shock postponement. During S^{Δ} a response-contingent punishment schedule was run using the same criterion response.

The animals in the Classical condition received the same schedule of visual discriminative stimuli as was presented to the Instrumental animals. During S^{D} classical paired trials of a pure tone CS and shock (ISI of 4.9 seconds) were run. Inter-trial intervals ranged from 21 to 54 seconds with seven classical trials per S^{D} segment. During the seven S^{Δ} segments unpaired shocks were administered on the same random ITI schedule.

RESULTS

Frequency of Skin Conductance Response

The frequency of skin conductance responses in the presence of S^{D} and S^{Δ} in the instrumental and classical conditions, averaged over the sixteen sessions, is shown in Table 1. Two noticeable differences may be seen; classical animals tended to make more responses overall and there was a tendency for the instrumental animals to make more responses in the presence of S^{D} than in the presence of S^{Δ}. The difference between groups was not significant ($F(1,2) = 2.30$) but the interaction between groups and discriminative stimuli was highly significant ($F(1,2) = 72.06$).

Table 1

Frequency of SCR per Stimulus Segment Averaged Across Sixteen Daily Sessions

	Conditions		
Treatments	S^{D}	S^{Δ}	Total
Instrumental	8.21	5.23	6.72
Classical	12.12	13.14	12.63

Table 2

Average Skin Conductance Levels (micromhos) in S^D and S^Δ in Instrumental and Classical Groups

Treatments	Conditions S^D	S^Δ
Instrumental	37.90	38.60
Classical	48.49	48.51

Basal Skin Conductance

The basal skin conductance level was measured during the five second period prior to each shock in the Instrumental subjects and prior to each conditioned stimulus during S^D or unconditioned stimulus during S^Δ for the Classical subjects. Table 2 shows the average of the skin conductance measures in micromhos in the Instrumental and Classical animals for the two discriminative stimuli, across all sessions. The Classical animals had substantially higher skin conductance levels but showed no difference between discriminative stimuli. The Instrumental animals tended to have higher skin conductance levels during punishment (S^Δ) than during avoidance (S^D).

Neither the overall difference between the Instrumental and Classical groups ($F(1,2) = 2.63$), nor the interaction between Groups and Discriminative stimuli ($F(1,2) = 3.30$), were significant. A separate evaluation of the S^D - S^Δ difference within the Instrumental animals only, yielded an $F = 23.65$, but only a single df for error is available for this test.

Baseline Heartrate

Heart rate was measured during the five second interval prior to each phasic stimulus (CS or US) and averaged for each S^D and S^Δ segment.

Table 3 shows these measures for the Instrumental and Classical groups in the presence of S^D and S^Δ, averaged across all sessions. The

Table 3

Baseline Heart Rate (BPM) in Instrumental and Classical Groups During S^D and S^Δ

Treatments	Conditions S^D	S^Δ
Instrumental	221.5	227.5
Classical	204.4	203.0

fact that the Instrumental animals' heart rates tended to be higher is evident. In addition, the Instrumental animals had higher heart rates during the presence of S^Δ than during S^D, while the reverse was true for the Classical animals. Analysis of variance revealed that this interaction between Groups and Discriminative stimuli was significant ($F(1,2) = 31.18$), even with only 2 df for error.

DISCUSSION

In the Instrumental animals, with S^D signaling available shock-postponement and S^Δ signaling punishment, some 60% more responses occurred during S^D than during S^Δ. Since the overall number of shocks received during the presence of the two discriminative stimuli were approximately equal, this difference in response frequency must be taken as persuasive evidence of operantly conditioned stimulus control of the skin conductance response. The animals in the Instrumental condition selectively reduced and redistributed the number of skin conductance responses and substantially increased the efficiency with which they coped electrodermally with the discriminative paradigm. Unlike the findings of Greene and Sutor (1971) in a related study using human subjects, the monkeys' basic strategy was one of reducing responding systematically during punishment while holding response frequency steady during avoidance.

Of particular interest in the present context was the fact that heart rates also differed during S^D and S^Δ in the Instrumental animals but not in the Classical animals. In the case of the heart rate measure, the Instrumental animals' rates during S^{Δ} exceeded S^{D}. The importance of this result lies in the fact that the skin conductance response was what explicitly determined instrumental reinforcement, not heart rate. Nevertheless heart rate came under tonic stimulus control as a consequence of the differences between the electrodermal reinforcement contingencies associated with the discriminative stimuli.

The basis for this heart rate difference is not immediately apparent. Our initial assumption was that the Instrumental monkeys' adaptation to the experimental situation via electrodermal responding might have been achieved at the cost of increased arousal in terms of heart rate, especially during the punishment periods when an environmental demand for reduced electrodermal behavior existed and when the animals did in fact reduce responding to some 20% of their initial levels. But the heart rate effect may also have itself been adventitiously instrumentally conditioned rather than being merely compensatory. To examine this possibility more closely, we looked at the monkeys' heart rates during periods immediately following shifts from the avoidance to the punishment discriminative stimulus and vice versa, at times before any shocks occurred. Figure 2 shows these data averaged in blocks of four sessions.

As is shown in Figure 2, heart rates increased during the initial sessions and subsequently declined more rapidly immediately following transitions to avoidance than transitions to punishment. The avoidance-punishment difference was significant, $\underline{t} = 3.19$, but the interaction of this and blocks of sessions was not. The stimulus-controlled differentiation of heart rates seems to fit an associative hypothesis more parsimoniously than a non-associative, compensation explanation. We are inclined towards this view, analyzing its possible mechanism as follows.

Kimmel and Kimmel (1967) found that the frequency of digital vasoconstrictive responses increases when human subjects are given positive reinforcements at times when skin conductance responses are not occurring, but does not increase when reinforcements are given at times of nonoccurrence of vasoconstrictions. These results were depicted in the noncontingent curves in the upper and lower sections of Figure 1. Snyder and Noble (1966) have shown that brief episodes of cardiac deceleration accompany digital vasoconstrictions. Indeed, they instrumentally conditioned the frequency of occurrence of vasoconstrictions and simultaneously found an increase in the degree of these concomitant decelerations. To the extent that our monkeys may have emitted some vasoconstrictive responses in conjunction with skin conductance responses and others independent of skin conductance responses (some 16% of Kimmel and Kimmel's

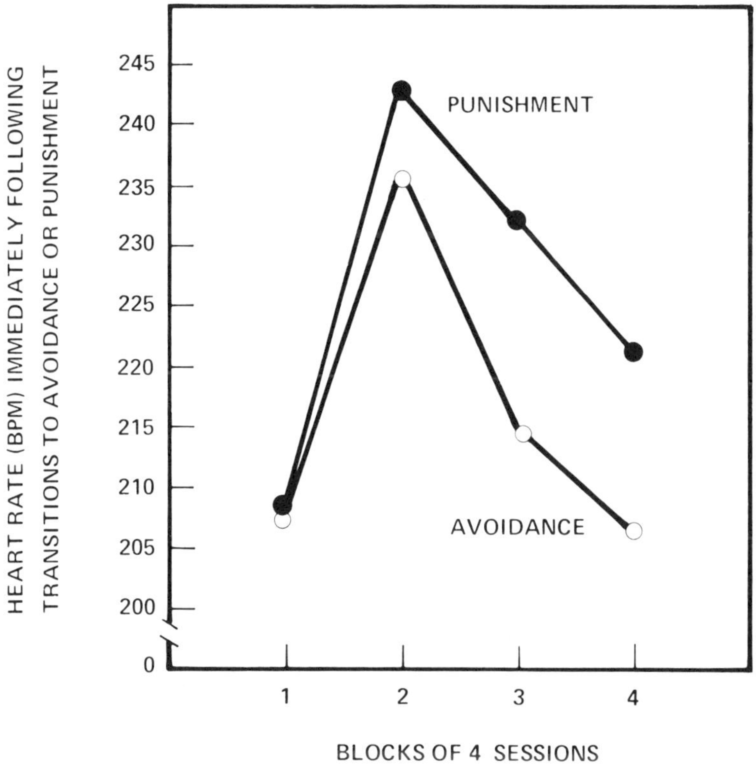

Figure 2. Heart rates in Instrumental monkeys following shifts to avoidance or punishment, averaged in blocks of four sessions.

humans' operant-level skin conductance responses were accompanied by vasoconstrictions and 30% of their vasoconstrictions were accompanied by skin conductance responses), the animals may have been receiving both adventitious intermittant avoidance and punishment training of the vasoconstriction response. Specifically, the initial increase in heart rate shown in Figure 2 may have resulted from an initial tendency for vasoconstrictive responses (i.e., cardiac decelerations) to be punished by shock during both avoidance and punishment periods, reducing their initial frequency of occurrence and consequently increasing heart rate. As the monkey learned to reduce the frequency of skin conductance responses during punishment, however, vasoconstrictions were less often punished. This would account for the slight reduction of heart rate following the second block of four sessions. During the avoidance periods, however, the shock-

shock interval was reduced from 40 to 20 seconds following the sixth session, but the number of shocks actually received remained essentially unchanged. The animals, as noted above, were actually avoiding more efficiently. Since some 30% of emitted vasoconstrictions initially may have been accompanied by skin conductance responses (based on Kimmel and Kimmel's data), the vasoconstriction response may have increasingly benefitted from intermittent avoidance reinforcement during the avoidance periods and more rapidly begun to increase in frequency. This would account for the more rapid and steeper decline in heart rate during the avoidance than in the punishment periods in the last two blocks of four sessions. The tortuousness of this logic to the contrary notwithstanding, we think it makes sufficient sense to justify its empirical evaluation in follow-up study of monkeys' skin conductance and heart rate behavior. In every published instance of inter-effector influence mentioned previously, in which cardiovascular changes were found to be associated with reinforcement of some other autonomic response, the nature or direction of these changes is predictable from the foregoing logic and data, although present space limitations preclude a detailed review of these cases.

In conclusion, there is reason to believe that the current belief that reinforcement-feedback contingent upon the occurrence or nonoccurrence of autonomically mediated responses influences only the explicitly determining response may be incorrect. Other autonomic responses may be concomitantly influenced to the extent that the reinforcing events adventitiously occur in significant temporal relation to their presence or absence. In particular, responses of the cardiovascular system, such as vasoconstrictions or brief episodes of cardiac acceleration or deceleration, themselves being quite susceptible of instrumental reinforcement, are likely to be modified in various degrees and fashions when other autonomic responses with which they have some partial direct or reciprocal correlation are used to determine the occurrence of the reinforcing events. That this may be the case should not be at all surprising, given the extent to which the autonomic nervous system functions as a complex, integrated regulator of the entire internal environment.

REFERENCES

Asratyan, E. A. Compensatory adaptation, reflex activity, and the brain. New York: Oxford, 1965.

Crider, A., Shapiro, D., & Tursky, B. Reinforcement of spontaneous electrodermal activity. Journal of Comparative and Physiological Psychology, 1966, 61, 20-27.

Gavalas, R. J. Operant reinforcement of an autonomic response: Two studies. Journal of the Experimental Analysis of Behavior, 1967, 10, 119-130.

Greene, W. A., & Sutor, L. T. Stimulus control of skin resistance responses on an escape-avoidance schedule. Journal of the Experimental Analysis of Behavior, 1971, 16, 269-274.

Hamano, K., & Miyake, S. Studies on modification of spontaneous autonomic activity: III. The relation of strength of reinforcer to instrumental modifiability of autonomic response. Japanese Psychological Research, 1972, 14, 38-42.

Kimmel, H. D., & Kimmel, E. Inter-effector influences in operant autonomic conditioning. Psychonomic Science, 1967, 9, 191-192.

Miller, N. E., & Banuazizi, A. Instrumental learning by curarized rats of a specific visceral response, intestinal or cardiac. Journal of Comparative and Physiological Psychology, 1968, 65, 1-7.

Schell, A. M., & Grings, W. W. Avoidance conditioning of the GSR: Nature of the response. Psychophysiology, 1971, 7, 402-407.

Schwartz, G. E. Voluntary control of human cardiovascular integration and differentiation through feedback and reward. Science, 1972, 175, 90-93.

Shapiro, D., Tursky, B., & Crider, A. Differentiation of an autonomic response through operant reinforcement. Psychonomic Science, 1964, 1, 147-148.

Snyder, C. W., & Noble, M. E. Operant conditioning of vasoconstriction. Paper presented at the meeting of the Psychonomic Society, St. Louis, 1966.

NOTE

This work was supported with a grant from the U.S. Army Medical R & D Command, No. DAMD 17-74-C-4121.

BIOFEEDBACK AND PHYSIOLOGICAL PATTERNING IN HUMAN EMOTION AND CONSCIOUSNESS

Gary E. Schwartz
Department of Psychology, Yale University
and
Department of Psychiatry, Yale University School of Medicine

INTRODUCTION TO PATTERN SELF-REGULATION

Although we do not usually think about it, we are continually self-regulating complex patterns of neurophysiological processes in our dynamic commerce with the external environment (Schwartz, 1975). Until very recently this fact was virtually ignored by scientists and laymen alike. A major reason for the failure to recognize and appreciate the self-regulation of patterns of brain processes is that the very brain processes involved in patterned neural self-regulation are normally unobservable and not available to direct conscious experience (Schwartz, in press, a). The development of biofeedback procedures for patterns of electrocortical activity serves the important function of bringing these unconscious neural processes, albeit indirectly, into human awareness. Furthermore, pattern biofeedback procedures make it possible for researchers to now manipulate patterns of brain processes differentially as a method for exploring their functional relationship to human experience and behavior.

To the extent that emotion and consciousness are emergent properties of neural patterning in the central nervous system (Schwartz, 1975; John, 1976), it becomes an intriguing paradox when we recognize that the brain is ultimately responsible for its own regulation (and that of the body) yet it has no conscious awareness that it is responsible, or even involved, in its self-regulation. Space precludes a more detailed discussion of neural patterning and the brain self-regulation paradox (see Schwartz, in press, a). However, the more general issue relating biofeedback, physiological patterning and emergent property to human emotion and consciousness is considered.

BIOFEEDBACK, PATTERNING AND EMERGENT PROPERTY

A thesis slowly emerging from biofeedback research is that patterns of physiological responses can be both self-generated and processed by the brain, producing unique cross-system interactions and perceptual gestalts that make up a significant component of human behavior and subjective experience (Schwartz, 1975). The concept of pattern here refers not simply to viewing, in isolation, combinations of processes, but rather goes beyond the individual components making up the pattern to recognize the novel, interactive or emergent property that patterns can acquire. Simply stated, the whole can have properties which are qualitatively and/or quantitatively different from the sum of its parts, and yet be dependent upon the organization of its parts for its unique properties. This phenomenon is seen at all levels of physics and chemistry, and extends through biology and neuropsychology (Weiss, 1969). The term synergism is also used to describe patterning and emergent property, as recently elucidated in the comprehensive volume by Fuller (1975).

The concept of emergent property or synergism needs to be considered in patterning. Although it is not a new concept, with few exceptions it is still ignored. In the area of consciousness, neuropsychologists concerned with this problem employ a similar idea when they speak of cell assemblies (Hebb, 1974), hyperneurons (John, 1976), holograms (Pribram, 1971), dynamic neural patterns (Sperry, 1969), or functional systems in the brain (Luria, 1973). In the area of emotion, the concept relating physiological patterning to emergent property has a long history, beginning with William James (1890) who described emotion as the brain's perception of patterns of visceral consequences of its action. More recent investigators such as Schachter and Singer (1962), have added biocognitive processes to the visceral activity as an integral part of this pattern. Modern comprehensive theorists like Tomkins (1962) and Izard (1971) stress the interaction of combinations of neurophysiological systems, including the processing of discrete patterns of postural and facial muscle activity, as the neural mechanisms underlying the emergent experience of emotion.

Evidence for patterning of central nervous system activity, and consequently peripheral nervous system activity, in human emotion and consciousness is evolving from two major research directions. The first is an extension of traditional psychophysiology, where differential patterns of electrocortical and peripheral physiological responses are monitored while subjects engage in complex cognitive/affective tasks. For example, recent data from our laboratory has documented that complex cognitive/affective tasks can be meaningfully dissected into their underlying neuropsychological subcomponents that have predictable effects on patterning of hemispheric activity (Schwartz, Davidson, & Maer, 1975). The data indicate that in right handed subjects, verbal versus spatial cognitive processes differentially involve the left and right hemisphere respectively. In addition, the right hemisphere seems to play a special role in the nonverbal components of emotion. Consequently, questions involving both verbal (left hemisphere) and emotional (right hemisphere) processes (e.g., "What is the primary difference in the meanings of the words 'anger' and 'hate'?") accordingly elicit evidence of dual hemispheric activation. Questions that involve both spatial (right hemisphere) and emotional (right hemisphere) processes (e.g., "Picture your father's face--what emotion first strikes you?") elicit evidence of accentuated right hemispheric involvement.

The second research direction is more recent in origin and involves the use of biofeedback. At the simplest level, it has been pointed out that the self-regulation of patterns of responses using pattern biofeedback procedures can have different emergent consequences from those observed when controlling individual functions alone (Schwartz, 1976). This basic observation provides the foundation for the hypothesis that by training subjects to voluntarily control patterns of visceral and motor responses, it is possible to assess central and peripheral linkages between physiological responses and their relationship to human behavior and consciousness (Schwartz, 1975). The development of this hypothesis is interesting in that it emerged somewhat unexpectedly in basic cardiovascular research concerned with the self-regulation of patterns of systolic blood pressure and heart rate. Details regarding the theory, development, measurement and interpretation of patterning in biofeedback are comprehensively discussed in a recent review (Schwartz, in press, b) and will only briefly be described here.

RELAXATION AND THE SELF-REGULATION OF PATTERNS OF SYSTOLIC BLOOD PRESSURE AND HEART RATE

In an experiment designed to determine the ease with which subjects could regulate the relationship between their systolic blood pressure and heart rate, a procedure was developed for administering binary (yes/no) feedback and reward for patterns of blood pressure (BP) and heart rate (HR): $BP^{up}HR^{up}$, $BP_{down}HR_{down}$, $BP^{up}HR_{down}$, $BP_{down}HR^{up}$ (Schwartz, 1972). In order to evaluate the specific effects of the binary feedback and reward itself, minimal instructions were given to subjects. They were not told what functions were to be controlled, nor were they told what direction(s) the functions were to change.

The results indicated that subjects rapidly learn to regulate both functions in the same direction ($BP^{up}HR^{up}$ or $BP_{down}HR_{down}$), and to a lesser degree, regulate the functions in the opposite direction (BP^{up}-HR_{down} or $BP_{down}HR^{up}$). These findings are contrasted with those obobtained in the earlier studies which also used minimal instructions but provided feedback and reward for BP itself (Shapiro, Tursky, Gershon, & Stern, 1969; Shapiro, Tursky, & Schwartz, 1970a) or HR itself (Shapiro, Tursky, & Schwartz, 1970b). With BP feedback (BP^{up} or BP_{down}), changes in BP were obtained independently of HR, while with HR feedback (HR^{up} or HR_{down}), changes in HR were obtained independently of BP.

In post-experimental interviews conducted with the subjects given feedback for BP or HR alone, no differences between the up and down conditions could be gleaned in terms of subjective report. However, when reports were obtained from subjects given BP-HR pattern feedback, the subjects trained to decrease both their BP and HR ($BP_{down}HR_{down}$) spontaneously reported feelings of relaxation, floating sensations and calmness, a subjective gestalt that could be predicted to be associated with a more integrated decrease in multi-physiological systems (Benson, 1975; Davidson & Schwartz, 1976) (see Table 1) (cited in Schwartz, 1976).

This accidental observation represents the first instance of a subjective report emerging with pattern biofeedback that did not spontaneously appear when the single responses comprising the pattern were independently regulated. It stimulated our recent research on the regulation of

Table 1

Mean values in response to the question:
"Rate from 1 (very little) to 5 (very much) how well relaxation/calm helped you to control your physiological responses."
(from Schwartz, 1976)

$BP^{up}HR^{up}$	$BP^{up}HR_{down}$	$BP_{down}HR^{up}$	$BP_{down}HR_{down}$ (a)
0.8	0.9	0.8	3.2

(a) $F(3,36) = 5.069$, $p < .01$

patterns of EEG and heart rate and subjective relaxation (Hassett & Schwartz, 1975), voluntary control of patterns of facial muscle activity and heart rate and the experience of anxiety (Schwartz, Davidson, Weinberger, & Lenson, in preparation), and the voluntary control of patterns of EEG symmetry and asymmetry and cognitive processes (Schwartz, Davidson, & Pugash, in press).

RELAXATION AND THE SELF-REGULATION OF PATTERNS OF OCCIPITAL ALPHA AND HEART RATE

A second procedure for training patterns of physiological responses is derived from a motor skills model (Schwartz, Young, & Vogler, in press) and involves coordination training (Hassett & Schwartz, 1975). Rather than quantifying patterns of physiological responses in real time and providing feedback for the presence or absence of a specific pattern, the coordination training procedure involves single system feedback for the individual responses making up the patterns, followed by multiple feedback for coordinating the combinations of responses.

Applying this approach to the regulation of patterns of occipital alpha (OA) and heart rate, Hassett and Schwartz (1975) conducted an experiment in which subjects were first given single system feedback training for OA control as well as HR control in one session. Then, in a second session, subjects were given practice periods with dual feedback for OA and HR simultaneously. Subjects were instructed to practice voluntary coordination of the two responses at their own pace, making them change separately or together, in the same or opposite direction. The results were quite striking, demonstrating that subjects could rapidly learn to generate, during test trials, all eight possible combinations of OA and HR: OA^{off} or OA_{on}; HR^{up} or HR_{down}; $OA^{off}HR^{up}$ or $OA_{on}HR_{down}$; or $OA^{off}HR_{down}$ or $OA_{on}HR^{up}$.

Analysis of post experimental subjective reports replicated and extended the Schwartz (1972) findings. Of the four self-regulated patterns of OA and HR, decreases in multi-system activity ($OA_{on}HR_{down}$) were more closely associated with subjective reports of relaxation. Interestingly, one female subject given eight sessions of coordination training reported spontaneously that she found the $OA_{on}HR_{down}$ pattern so relaxing that she began to practice it on her own outside of the laboratory.

These data highlight the general issue of pattern self-regulation and have important implications for theories comparing different self-regulation procedures. For example, a hypothesis that received popular notoriety was that since 1) during passive relaxation procedures such as transcendental meditation, increases in occipital alpha (OA_{on}) are often observed (Davidson & Schwartz, 1976), and 2) with the aid of biofeedback, subjects can learn to self-regulate increases in occipital alpha (Hardt & Kamiya, 1976), then 3) occipital alpha biofeedback can be used to produce a rapid, electronic meditator! The fallacy of this line of reasoning is that single system biofeedback, as described above, tends to result in specificity of learning, whereas biocognitive procedures such as transcendental meditation tend to involve the natural, albeit unconscious, self-regulation of complex patterns of responses (e.g., increases in alpha and theta frequencies over much of the cortex, which is expressed via the peripheral nervous system as decreases in heart rate, blood pressure, sweat gland activity, oxygen consumption, respiration, rate, etc.).

To the extent that the cognitive and behavioral concomitants of transcendental meditation and other complex self-regulation procedures reflect emergent properties of the unique patterns of the underlying neurophysiological systems, then the probability of replicating these patterns using simple biofeedback procedures would seem small. Questions that need to be raised are: 1) Is it possible, using biofeedback procedures, to fully replicate the psychophysiological pattern comprising meditation?; 2) What combination of responses and biofeedback procedures would be necessary to match the pattern of physiological changes that naturally occur during meditation?; 3) If it is possible, is it worth the effort?

My own response to these questions is divided according to the different needs of basic research versus clinical application (Schwartz, 1975, 1976). The pattern biofeedback approach provides a new research paradigm for investigating how different physiological systems combine to produce unique subjective gestalts and behavioral correlates; at this level, the approach promises to be fruitful. However, if the physiological patterns produced during meditation or other relaxation techniques are themselves of therapeutic value, then they should be induced and practiced using the non-electronic, easily portable and generalizable machinery of our own biocognitive systems.

ANXIETY AND THE SELF-REGULATION OF PATTERNS OF FACIAL MUSCLE ACTIVITY AND HEART RATE

Patterning theories of emotion (Tomkins, 1962; Izard, 1971) posit that the emergent experience of different emotions involves the differential patterning of skeletal and visceral responses by the brain. Within the skeletal system itself, patterning of facial muscle activity (by the brain) as expressed overtly in facial expression is considered to be a key factor. Recent research from our laboratory has demonstrated that when subjects are simply instructed to self-generate different classes of affective imagery (i.e., happy, sad and angry imagery; in Schwartz, Fair, Salt, Mandel, & Klerman, 1976), different patterns of facial muscle activity are generated which can be measured electromyographically. Interestingly, these subtle muscle patterns are typically not apparent in the overt face. Further, predictable differences in the underlying covert facial expressions are found between subjects differing in specific mood states such as in patients suffering from depression (Schwartz, Fair, Salt, Mandel, & Klerman, 1976, in press).

One extension of this research is to combine the self-regulation of facial activity with visceral activity as a means of assessing how patterns across these two major systems interact in the emergent experience of emotion. In a recent experiment (Schwartz, Davidson, Weinberger, & Lenson, in preparation), subjects were specifically instructed to increase and decrease their heart rate using biofeedback under 1) normal resting conditions, and 2) while simultaneously tensing the muscles in their forehead (FT) region.

Since previous research indicates that 1) unlike minimally instructed subjects, subjects deliberately instructed to increase their heart rate with biofeedback immediately draw on complex cognitive/affective strategies involving negative emotions such as anxiety (Bell & Schwartz, 1975), and 2) forehead muscle tension (loosely referring to tension in the frontalis, corrugator and related muscles) is observed in the overt frightened and anxious face (Ekman & Friesen, 1975), we predicted that self-regulation of the pattern of high heart rate and forehead tension ($HR^{up}FH^{up}$) would result in a more intense experience of anxiety than the regulation of either component alone (HR^{up} or FT^{up}).

Forty-two subjects were run in a 3 x 2 within-subject design with HR biofeedback (rest, HR_{down} and HR^{up}) crossed with forehead facial tension (rest and FH^{up}). The means for heart rate, integrated forehead muscle tension (EMG), and anxiety scores using Izard's differential emotions scale (Izard, 1972) administered after each trial, are shown in Table 2.

The results can be briefly summarized as follows: 1) Self-regulation of heart rate with biofeedback is not affected by the simultaneous tensing of the forehead region, though during HR resting conditions subjects show slightly elevated heart rate when tensing the forehead; 2) Subjects can readily tense their forehead while regulating their heart rate with biofeedback. Interestingly, however, forehead muscle tension covaries with heart

Table 2

Mean scores for Heart Rate, Forehead EMG, and Anxiety ratings during the regulation of Heart Rate with biofeedback (rest, HR_{down} and HR^{up}) and Forehead Facial Tension (rest and FT^{up}) (from Schwartz, Davidson, Weinberger, & Lenson, in preparation)

	Condition		
Condition	Rest	HR_{down}	HR^{up}
	Heart Rate (in bpm)		
Rest	66.8	67.4	74.6
FT^{up}	68.4	67.9	75.2
	Forehead EMG (in integrated units)		
Rest	17.1	18.0	28.1
FT^{up}	45.3	39.7	56.5
	Anxiety (from 1 to 14)		
Rest	4.47	5.24	8.84
FT^{up}	6.75	6.89	9.75

rate control during FT rest as well as FT^{up} conditions; and 3) Increased heart rate regulation itself (HR^{up} during FT rest) and forehead tension itself (FT^{up} during HR rest), are each accompanied by reported increases in the subjective experience of anxiety (relative to the basic resting condition). Finally, and most importantly, the highest rating of subjective anxiety occurs during $HR^{up} FT^{up}$ pattern regulation.

These data indicate that self-regulated facial forehead tension and self-regulated heart rate increases each contribute to subjective anxiety. When they are regulated as a pattern, moreover, they combine in an additive sense to contribute to the total emergent experience of anxiety. Using this particular pattern of facial muscle tensing and heart rate, the additive effect of FT and HR appears relatively specific to anxiety. On ratings of anger, for example, the subjective reports vary with heart rate control but they are minimally influenced by the tensing of the forehead region itself. Future research can more explicitly manipulate different patterns of facial muscle activity in combination with visceral activity. It might be predicted that generating the muscle pattern of an angry face, coupled with HR^{up}, could lead to a greater subjective experience of anger; generating the muscle pattern of a happy face, coupled with HR^{up}, could lead to a greater subjective experience of happiness.

The point at this stage of research is to illustrate how patterns of skeletal and visceral responses can interact and contribute to the emergent experience of unique emotions, or blends of emotions. This provides a possible rapprochement between "arousal" versus "pattern" theories of emotion, and helps to delineate new questions for basic as well as clinical psychophysiological research regarding the regulation and behavioral treatment of affective disorders.

COGNITIVE PROCESSES AND THE SELF-REGULATION OF PATTERNS OF EEG SYMMETRY AND ASYMMETRY

One of the most challenging frontiers in biofeedback research is to specify what patterns of brain processes underlie the self-regulation of visceral and skeletal effectors, and to determine how these patterns of brain processes ultimately generate the emergent experience of emotion and consciousness. Research on the former question has been recently reviewed elsewhere (Schwartz, in press, b). One example of research on the latter question involves the assessment and regulation of patterns of specific EEG changes and their relationship to subjective experience.

Schwartz, Davidson, and Pugash (in press) conducted an experiment addressing two questions: 1) is training for EEG parietal asymmetry using pattern biofeedback accompanied by predictable cognitive concomitants?; and 2) are the cognitive concomitants of training for simultaneous bilateral activation of the hemispheres a simple additive combination of the two asymmetry patterns, or do they represent a unique cognitive gestalt not readily predicted from the two asymmetry training conditions?

Bilateral parietal EEG was recorded from 20 right handed subjects and filtered for 8-13 Hz activity. Using a procedure adapted from the Schwartz (1972) blood pressure-heart rate pattern study, patterns of alpha (A) presence and absence across the left (L) and right (R) hemispheres were assessed 10 times per second and automatically counted. All subjects

Table 3

Mean self reported cognitive mode on a 1 - 7 scale for each of six thought categories during each biofeedback treatment, and difference scores for each of the three comparisons and significance levels (based upon 2-tailed t-tests for correlated means) (from Schwartz, Davidson, & Pugash, in press)

	Condition			Difference Score		
Thought Category	$LA^{off}RA_{on}$ (D1)	$LA_{on}RA^{off}$ (D2)	$LA^{off}RA^{off}$ (I)	D1-D2	D1-I	D2-I
Verbal	3.92	2.40	2.35	1.52*	1.57**	0.05
Visual	3.55	4.65	5.10	-1.10*	-1.55*	-0.45
Numerical	2.80	1.85	2.55	0.95	0.25	-0.70
Musical	2.85	2.25	2.05	0.60	0.80	0.20
Nothing	2.45	2.40	4.35	0.05	-1.90**	-1.95*
Emotional	4.00	4.00	2.60	0.00	1.40*	1.40+

** $p < .02$ * $p < .05$ + $p < .10$

received binary feedback for EEG symmetry training ($LA^{off}RA^{off}$--Integration) and EEG asymmetry training ($LA^{off}RA_{on}$ and $LA_{on}RA^{off}$--Differentiation).

Evidence for significant regulation in all three feedback conditions was obtained. As shown in Table 3, analyses of the post-feedback questionnaires revealed that the $LA^{off}RA_{on}$ pattern was associated with significantly more verbal cognitions, while the $LA_{on}RA^{off}$ pattern was associated with more visual cognitions.

Importantly, the cognitive findings from the symmetry training pattern ($LA^{off}RA^{off}$) suggest that the generation of this EEG pattern is not simply the sum of the two differentiation patterns; such a model would predict increases in both visual and verbal cognitions during EEG integration. It is important to recognize that the production of bilateral parietal activation may be accomplished in a myriad of ways, few of which naturally involve the simultaneous generation of verbal and visual thought. Rather, the activation of both hemispheres may typically involve the generation of complementary behavior and cognition. For example, a number of subjects in the experiment reported visualizing an image and holding the image in awareness. Interestingly, this strategy is similar to some meditation techniques which require the generation and maintenance of an image in consciousness. Banquet (1973) has reported that such a technique, at certain points during the meditation, is associated with bilateral activation in the EEG (i.e., increments in beta activity in both hemispheres).

These data highlight the use of pattern biofeedback procedures to explore the relationship between neurophysiological patterning and subjective experience. The challenge of recording and training more complex central nervous system EEG patterns as a means of assessing brain/consciousness relationships may reflect one of the most significant contributions to be made by future biofeedback research.

SUMMARY AND CONCLUSIONS

This chapter has developed the thesis that a fundamental theoretical question underlying emotion and consciousness concerns the emergent property of patterning of neurophysiological processes and their expression via the peripheral nervous system as patterns of skeletal and visceral activity. It is suggested that research on biofeedback and the regulation of combinations of responses extends the concept of emergent property by providing a new paradigm for systematically investigating physiological relationships in the intact human. Self-regulation as a general research strategy can be useful to the extent that it enables researchers to isolate component parts of neural/humoral systems and then examine how they combine to produce unique physiological and associated subjective states.

Research indicates that the regulation of patterns of responses can produce effects that are qualitatively and/or quantitatively different from the regulation of single components. Systematic comparison of the emergent properties of different self-regulated patterns of responses then becomes an important research direction. Although this principle has basic as well as clinical implications (Schwartz, 1974, 1975, 1976, in press, b), there are limitations to the use of pattern regulation procedures that need to be considered. For example, it is not inconceivable that the act of regulating a particular pattern of responses will have emergent consequences that are somewhat different from those found when a similar pattern is generated by other means. If future research should document this to be true, it will restrict the general applicability of the approach accordingly. On the other hand, such a finding could provide a further key to the unique characteristics of self-regulation processes themselves.

REFERENCES

Banquet, J. P. Spectral analysis of EEG in meditation. Electroencephalography and Clinical Neurophysiology, 1973, 35, 143-151.

Benson, H. The relaxation response. New York: William Morrow, 1975.

Davidson, R. J., & Schwartz, G. E. The psychobiology of relaxation and related states: A multiprocess theory. In D. I. Mostofsky (Ed.), Behavior modification and control of physiological activity. Englewood Cliffs, New Jersey: Prentice-Hall, 1976.

Ekman, P., & Friesen, W. V. Unmasking the face. Englewood Cliffs, New Jersey: Prentice-Hall, 1975.

Fuller, R. B. Synergetics. New York: Macmillan, 1975.

Hardt, J. V., & Kamiya, J. Conflicting results in EEG alpha feedback studies: Why amplitude integration should replace percent time. Biofeedback and Self-Regulation, 1976, 1, 63-76.

Hassett, J., & Schwartz, G. E. Relationships between heart rate and occipital alpha: A biofeedback approach. Psychophysiology, 1975, 12, 228. (Abstract)

Hebb, D. O. What psychology is about. American Psychologist, 1974, 29, 71-79.

Izard, C. The face of emotion. New York: Appleton-Century-Crofts, 1971.

Izard, C. Patterns of emotions. New York: Academic Press, 1972.

James, W. Principles of Psychology. New York: Holt, 1890.

John, E. R. A model of consciousness. In G. E. Schwartz & D. Shapiro (Eds.), Consciousness and self-regulation: Advances in research (Volume 1). New York: Plenum, 1976.

Luria, A. R. The working brain. New York: Basic Books, 1973.

Pribram, K. H. Languages of the brain. Englewood Cliffs, New Jersey: Prentice-Hall, 1971.

Schachter, S., & Singer, J. E. Cognitive, social and physiological determinants of emotional state. Psychological Review, 1962, 69, 379-399.

Schwartz, G. E. Voluntary control of human cardiovascular integration and differentiation through feedback and reward. Science, 1972, 175, 90-93.

Schwartz, G. E. Toward a theory of voluntary control of response pattern in the cardiovascular system. In P. A. Obrist, A. H. Black, J. Brener & L. V. DiCara (Eds.), Cardiovascular psychophysiology. Chicago: Aldine, 1974.

Schwartz, G. E. Biofeedback, self-regulation and the patterning of physiological processes. American Scientist, 1975, 63, 314-324.

Schwartz, G. E. Self-regulation of response patterning: Implications for psychophysiological research and therapy. Biofeedback and Self-Regulation, 1976, 1, 7-30.

Schwartz, G. E. Psychosomatic disorders and biofeedback: A psychobiological model of disregulation. In J. D. Maser & M. E. P. Seligman (Eds.), Psychopathology: Experimental models. San Francisco: Freeman, in press. (a)

Schwartz, G. E. Biofeedback and patterning of autonomic and central processes: CNS-cardiovascular interactions. In G. E. Schwartz & J. Beatty (Eds.), Biofeedback: Theory and research. New York: Academic Press, in press. (b)

Schwartz, G. E., Davidson, R. J., & Maer, F. Right hemisphere lateralization for emotion in the human brain: Interaction with cognition. Science, 1975, 190, 286-288.

Schwartz, G. E., Davidson, R. J., & Pugash, E. Voluntary control of patterns of EEG parietal asymmetry: Cognitive concomitants. Psychophysiology, in press.

Schwartz, G. E., Davidson, R. J., Weinberger, D. A., & Lenson, R. Voluntary control of patterns of facial muscle activity and heart rate: Effects on anxiety. In preparation.

Schwartz, G. E., Fair, P. L., Salt, P., Mandel, M. R., & Klerman, G. L. Facial muscle patterning to affective imagery in depressed and nondepressed subjects. Science, 1976, 192, 489-491.

Schwartz, G. E., Fair, P. L., Salt, P., Mandel, M. R., & Klerman, G. L. Facial expression and imagery in depression: An electromyographic study. Psychosomatic Medicine, in press.

Schwartz, G. E., Young, L. D., & Vogler, J. Heart rate regulation as skill learning: Strength-endurance versus cardiac reaction time. Psychophysiology, in press.

Shapiro, D., Tursky, B., Gershon, E., & Stern, M. Effects of feedback and reinforcement on the control of human systolic blood pressure. Science, 1969, 163, 588-589.

Shapiro, D., Tursky, B., & Schwartz, G. E. Control of blood pressure in man by operant conditioning. Circulation Research, 1970, 27 (Suppl. 1), 27-32. (a)

Shapiro, D., Tursky, B., & Schwartz, G. E. Differentiation of heart rate and blood pressure in man by operant conditioning. Psychosomatic Medicine, 1970, 32, 417-423. (b)

Sperry, R. W. A modified concept of consciousness. Psychological Review, 1969, 76, 532-536.

Tomkins, S. S. Affect, imagery, consciousness. (2 Vols.). New York: Springer, 1962.

Weiss, P. A. The living system: Determinism stratified. In A. Koestler & J. R. Smythies (Eds.), Beyond reductionism. Boston: Beacon Press, 1969.

NOTE

This research was supported in part by an award from the Stress Grants Program of the Roche Psychiatric Institute and by the Advanced Research Projects Agency of the Department of Defense and monitored by the Office of Naval Research under contract N00014-70-C-0350 to the San Diego State College Foundation. The chapter was completed while the author was on leave from Harvard University as a Visiting Associate Professor of Psychology at the Department of Psychiatry, University of California, San Francisco.

BIOFEEDBACK AND THE REGULATION OF COMPLEX PSYCHOLOGICAL PROCESSES

David Shapiro
Department of Psychiatry
University of California at Los Angeles

With the growth and diversity of research on the regulation of physiological responses by means of biofeedback and instrumental learning, investigators have become more and more attracted by the possibilities that these methods may provide for the analysis and modification of complex psychological processes. From early on in the development of the field, writers have speculated about the implications of biofeedback and other methods of self regulation and voluntary control, and a variety of reports have described case studies exemplifying these potentials. Examples of complex processes that have been discussed in this context are: states of consciousness, creativity and imagination, learning potential, attention and vigilance, problem solving capabilities, relaxation, coping with stress, and various perceptual and subjective reactions in pain, anxiety, fear, and other emotional states. Aside from the possible influence or control over such psychological processes, a biofeedback strategy of research may help elucidate and objectify so-called private events which have required sole dependence on introspective and verbal reports for their specification.

A great deal of attention has been paid to the effects of modifying various electrocortical activities, such as the EEG alpha rhythm, on verbal reports of associated mental activities and "feeling states" (Brown, 1970, 1971; Nowlis & Kamiya, 1970). This research has not been without controversy, however, and some investigators have emphasized the significance of cognitive and physiological processes, other than those specifically attributable to consequences of changes in the particular EEG rhythm, in bringing about particular alterations in subjective states (e.g.,

Beatty, 1972; Beatty & Kornfeld, 1972; Paskewitz, Lynch, Orne, & Costello, 1970; Walsh, 1974). In a thorough recent examination of relations between self-regulated occipital alpha rhythm, control strategies, and states of consciousness, Plotkin (1976a) concludes, "thus, if the alpha experience is more likely to occur with alpha feedback than without it, this is due to the special circumstances that make up the feedback situation and not due to alpha feedback per se." Without question, there are complex methodological problems involved in determining whether or not a particular physiological correlate of a subjective state is a necessary component of that state and in deciding whether or not biofeedback or other behavioral means of altering particular physiological activities are critical to the observed change in state (see Hardt & Kamiya, 1976; Plotkin, 1976b). Indeed, the central issue of all psychophysiological research is concerned with establishing necessary and sufficient interrelations of psychological, behavioral, and physiological processes.

Although there are clearly complicated theoretical issues involved in describing and characterizing internal states vaguely labelled as "letting go," "pleasant feeling," or "feeling detached and unfocused," certain empirical consequences of using EEG biofeedback to control a brain rhythm continue to be explored, regardless of the exact mechanism involved, on purely practical considerations. An important direction in this research is shown in a lawful relationship that has been demonstrated between operantly regulated cortical activity and a particular behavior. Using the theta rhythm (3-7 Hz) of the occipital-parietal EEG as an index of brain activity associated with arousal processes that determine monitoring efficiency under monotonous conditions, it was found that suppression of this EEG activity by operant methods enhanced efficiency in a radar monitoring task, whereas theta augmentation further degraded task performance (Beatty, Greenberg, Deibler, & O'Hanlon, 1974). Several features of this study can be singled out. First, a relatively straightforward relationship was assumed to exist between the target behavior, and the physiological function to be regulated by the individual. Second, the target behavior can be clearly defined and reliably quantified. It is very obvious from a research standpoint that a behavioral index of vigilance has advantages over measures of particular private events. In the case of states of consciousness, it is difficult to establish a single agreed-upon index or means of characterizing a state, although various indices are possible, e.g., alertness, clarity, intensity, extensity, etc.

It is natural for researchers particularly interested in such subjective phenomena to turn their attention to the EEG or to other measurable electrocortical processes in the assumption that what is happening in different brain structures may be critical to consciousness. However, it is also apparent that our present state of knowledge of EEG correlates of complex psychological processes is quite limited. The significance of a biofeedback strategy depends very much on knowledge of what specific physiological responses or patterns of response are related to what particular behavioral or psychological states and therefore worth exploring. On the other hand, a biofeedback strategy may be employed as a means of examining the possible significance of different physiological processes. This conclusion has been neatly summarized by Stoyva & Kamiya (1968): "The major point to be made here is that the use of operant techniques in combination with the physiological indicator (alpha) and the verbal report provides substantial construct validation for the hypothetical internal state by means of converging operations.... For example, it may be possible for Ss to discriminate and control other types of EEG waves in addition to the alpha rhythm; for instance, beta, delta, and theta waves, rhythms characteristic of alertness, rhythms claracteristic of drowsiness. If such a degree of discrimination and control proves possible, it could give psychologists a means of exploring and mapping a variety of conscious states, thus providing a powerful tool for the introspective method. It may also develop that, if S's ability to report about a limited number of private events can be sharpened in this way, then this new skill may transfer to other private events as well; so that S becomes more generally reliable--and sensitive--in the reporting of private events."

My interest in this general area of research was in the possibility of using biofeedback techniques to modify emotional reactions to particular stressful or aversive stimuli or to modify anticipatory emotional responses to such stimuli. The broad aim of the research to be described was clinical--to explore the therapeutic potential of biofeedback methods as a means of helping individuals adapt to stressful events or cope with specific anxieties and phobias. Typically in clinical biofeedback studies, the individual is given training in quiet "resting" laboratory conditions for the purpose of modifying ongoing physiological activities, such as blood pressure, heart rate, or skin temperature. The implicit basis for this approach is that a relatively permanent modification of "basal" physiological activity is desirable and that it can be accomplished with biofeedback training under relatively non-stimulating laboratory conditions. Little attention, however, has been given to abnormal physiological reactions that are under the control of specific eliciting stimuli or situations. In such instances, the relevance of typical laboratory biofeedback training of basal activity can be questioned in terms of its appropriateness for the relevant situations in everyday life that would appear to induce the abnormal reaction.

The work started with the general assumption that autonomic nervous system responses constituted an important source of information relevant to emotional states such as anxiety, fear, and so on. A series of studies was undertaken in collaboration with my associates to determine if biofeedback techniques could be useful in the control of such visceral components of emotional reactions and therefore in the behavioral regulation of such reactions. The assumption is a greatly oversimplified one, of course. The seat of emotion does not reside solely in activities of visceral organs; rather, emotional reactions are probably best viewed as complex patterns of verbal, skeletal-motor, visceral, and cognitive or other central nervous system events (Lang, 1969; Mathews, 1971). Nonetheless, that visceral components are often predominant in emotion is a fundamental proposition in many domains of psychological research, and the literature of psychophysiology is filled with studies documenting the association between particular visceral responses and emotional reactions such as fear, anxiety, and so on (see Lang, Rice, & Sternbach, 1972). This literature will not be reviewed here.

The methodology employed in this research followed from several studies reporting that discrete electrodermal responses to stimuli in humans could be relatively increased or decreased by biofeedback and operant conditioning methods (Shnidman, 1970; Shnidman & Shapiro, 1970). In these studies, a simple stimulus (visual or auditory) was presented for a few seconds, and the subject was reinforced either for the presence or the absence of a criterion electrodermal response. A similar methodology was employed by Kimmel, Pendergrass, & Kimmel (1967) with the aim of modifying orienting reactions of children and facilitating learning. In this case, the stimuli were more complex than simple tones or lights. They were geometric objects which subsequently were to be placed in their appropriate forms. The results suggested that operant conditioning of electrodermal responses, the physiological index of orienting, could transfer to performance on an intellectual task, although the results of the study were somewhat complicated.

In a variant of this same procedure, an attempt was made to see whether operant control of electrodermal responses to slides of snakes could be similarly accomplished (Shapiro, Schwartz, Nelson, Shnidman, & Silverman, 1972). The subjects were volunteers who reported fear of snakes. Again, the results were positive. In this case, electrodermal reactivity to complex fear-related stimuli could be relatively increased or decreased. Moreover, there was some suggestive evidence that reported fear of snakes could also be modified accordingly, as measured by comparisons of snake-fear questionnaire responses obtained before and after the training session.

In subsequent research, a number of basic changes were made in the research strategy. Rather than deal directly with phobic or anxiety subjects who are inevitably heterogeneous in regard to their "emotional" state, specific relatively easily controlled laboratory stressors were used that were assumed to have uniform aversive quality for normal volunteer subjects selected from a college-student population. Secondly, heart rate was chosen as the variable of interest because of its association with fear and anxiety (Lang, Rice, & Sternbach, 1972) and because of the finding that instrumental learning of heart rate altered emotional reactivity in rats (DiCara & Weiss, 1969). In this latter study, rats trained to decrease heart rate under curare in order to avoid electric shock showed good subsequent learning of a free-moving skeletal-motor response. When trained to increase heart rate, they showed poor subsequent avoidance learning. Moreover, there is a large literature indicating that heart rate is relatively easily controlled voluntarily by most subjects and that biofeedback may facilitate such control. Unlike electrodermal reactivity which tends to be discrete in character, heart rate changes continuously over time from heart beat to heart beat, so that visceral control could be demonstrated over longer intervals of stressful stimulation.

In a first study along these lines, subjects were given feedback and rewards for either increasing or decreasing their heart rate in 15 sec periods in which they were anticipating receiving aversive localized electrical shock stimuli (Sirota, Schwartz, & Shapiro, 1974). Both phasic heart rate changes during these anticipatory fear periods were altered as well as tonic heart rates over trials. Average effects (tonic and phasic) reached a maximum of about 10 bpm, comparing differences between heart rate increase and decrease groups. The phasic data are all the more interesting in not showing the typical biphasic or triphasic heart rate pattern often obtained in classical heart rate conditioning.

A second study replicated the heart rate results in all essential details (Sirota, Schwartz, & Shapiro, in press). It also replicated the basic finding that the heart rate training was associated with consistent variations in perception of intensity of the electrical stimuli. Heart rate increase was related to a relative augmentation in the perceived intensity of the stimuli, and heart rate decrease was related to a relative diminution of the perceived intensity. These effects were particularly relevant for those subjects who reported experiencing cardiac reactions to fear situations in everyday life, subjects who were designated as "Cardiac Aware." This research led to the conclusion that a combination of physiological and cognitive factors, i.e., both appropriate heart rate changes and a suitable cognitive set or belief about the psychological significance of the physiological change, are necessary for the learned control of a physiological response to transfer effectively to a related behavior.

The fact that heart rate changes appear to be associated with changes in perception of the noxious stimuli is consistent with various psychophysiological theories and data (James, 1890; Slaughter & Kahn, 1974; Morganstern, 1974; Obrist, Webb, Sutterer, & Howard, 1970; Wolpe, 1958; Lacey & Lacey, 1970). However, other cognitively-oriented research has suggested that simply the belief that a physiological response is changing in a certain way during the experience of stressful or emotional events may be sufficient to produce an increment or decrement in emotionality (Valins & Ray, 1967; Schachter & Singer, 1962). Sirota (1976) attempted to investigate the relative contribution of physiological factors (change in heart rate) and cognitive factors (belief that heart rate is changing) using basically the same biofeedback procedures. Different combinations of veridical and non-veridical feedback and instructions were employed, but the complex manner in which feedback and instructions interacted did not achieve a sufficient disentanglement of the cognitive and physiological factors. Nonetheless, the basic phenomenon was replicated, and the findings in general reaffirmed the importance of both cognitive and physiological factors in facilitating the transfer of learned heart rate change to perception of the intensity of an aversive stimulus.

The aim of the next study was to examine the effects of voluntary control of HR on reactions to another stressful stimulus--the Cold Pressor (CP) test. This study is presented in detail to give a clearer picture of procedures and findings. The work is in progress, and the findings should be considered preliminary, pending more comprehensive analysis. The CP test, which requires immersion of an extremity in ice water for a minute or more, is often used as a means of evaluating cardiovascular responses to stress. Reactions to the CP test are related to the physical properties of the cold stimulus, and the pain elicited by it, as well as "cognitive factors, learning, and expectancies" (Lovallo, 1975). In this study, the CP test was immersion of the hand in ice water for 30 sec; this period was chosen inasmuch as peak physiological and psychological effects are observed in this shorter period. In contrast with the previous studies on control of anticipatory heart rate reactions, in the present study subjects were asked to control their heart rate while the stressful stimulus was being experienced.

Four groups of nine subjects (volunteer males) were studied (see Table 1). For each subject, a session consisted of 34 cycles. All subjects were given two CP tests (cycles 3 and 34). Groups 1 (Increase) and 2 (Decrease) were given 25 voluntary heart rate control trials (cycles 4-

Table 1

Experimental Design

	Group			
	Increase	Decrease	Voluntary Control (Decrease)	Habituation
Cycle	1	2	3	4
1–2	Base	Base	Base	Base
3	Cold Pressor 1	Cold Pressor 1	Cold Pressor 1	Cold Pressor 1
4–28	Feedback	Feedback	Reading	Reading
29–33	Voluntary Control (no feedback)	Voluntary Control (no feedback)	Voluntary Control (no feedback)	Reading
34	Cold Pressor 2	Cold Pressor 2	Cold Pressor 2	Cold Pressor 2

Procedure and Analysis: Each cycle consists of 55 sec. In cycles 3 and 34, Sec 5–35 is signalled to subject for the cold pressor test. In cycles 4–28, Sec 5–35 is the feedback period in Groups 1 and 2. In cycles 29–33, Sec 5–35 is the voluntary control period for Groups 1, 2, and 3. In the analysis, Sec 0–5 is base period and Sec 35–55 is a post or recovery period. These periods are always unsignaled. Following each cycle, an additional blank period of 10 sec is used for data handling.

28) assisted by visual meter feedback (cardiotachometer) and monetary bonuses for criterion changes, increase heart rate in Group 1 and decrease in Group 2. Groups 3 (Voluntary Control--Decrease) and 4 (Habituation) read magazines during a comparable period of time (about 30 minutes), while the same measurements were taken during the 25 cycles. Then, Groups 1, 2, and 3 were given 5 voluntary heart rate control trials; Groups 1 and 2 were asked to do the same thing that they did during the feedback trials, and Group 3 subjects were simply asked to decrease their heart rate voluntarily. During this part of the experiment, Group 4 subjects continued to read magazines without interruption. Subjects were offered monetary bonuses at the conclusion of these trials as an incentive to concentrate on the task. Finally, all subjects were given a second CP test. For this second test, Groups 1, 2, and 3 were asked to change their heart rate as previously while their hand was immersed in the ice water. Group 4 subjects were given the second CP test with no special instructions, as a simple control for habituation.

The experiment was run by a digital computer (DEC PDP-11/GT-40 System). The R-wave in each heart cycle was detected with a software routine, and the period or time in milliseconds between successive R-waves in each trial cycle constituted the basic data. All intermediary calculations were made in terms of heart period, and the resulting mean values were subsequently transformed into rate for purposes of graphing and statistical analysis.

The data are shown in Table 2. In all analyses, the index of heart rate change was derived by subtracting the average heart rate in the base period (Sec 0-5) from the average heart rate in the critical period (Sec 5-35). Response to CP-1 varied from -6.8 bpm to 19.0 bpm; only five out of the 36 subjects showed a decrement in rate. The heart rate response to CP-1 was significantly higher in the Decrease feedback group than in the Voluntary Control group; all other group comparisons showed equivalent values. In the second CP test, the range of rate change was -4.2 bpm to 24.2 bpm; five values were negative. The feedback increase group showed a significantly larger mean change (16.6 bpm) than the other three groups, which did not differ from each other. In view of the unequal initial values, the primary analysis of difference between groups was made by comparing the change in CP-2 with CP-1, by subtracting the latter from the former. All feedback Increase subjects increased their heart rate (average increase of 11.5 bpm) from CP-1 to CP-2, and all but one feedback Decrease subject decreased their rate (average decrease of 3.4 bpm). In the Habituation group, all but one subject increased rate, and in the Voluntary Control group, four subjects increased and five subjects decreased their heart rate. As seen in Table 2, Increase and Habituation did not dif-

Table 2

Average Heart Rate Change (bpm)

	Group			
	Increase	Habituation	Vol. Control (Decrease)	Decrease
Trials	1	4	3	2
Cold Pressor 1	5.1	4.1	3.5	9.7
Cold Pressor 2	16.6	7.5	3.8	6.4
Cold Pressor 2 -Cold Pressor 1	11.5	3.4	0.3	-3.4
Feedback Trials	5.2	0.0	-0.2	-1.8
Voluntary Control Trials	2.7	0.2	-0.6	-4.1

Note: Index of heart rate change is obtained by subtracting average heart rate of base period (Sec 0-5) from signaled period (Sec 5-35), averaged over subjects, per trial or trials. Groups that are connected by a line are not significantly different in mean heart rate change. Note that only Groups 2 and 3 are significantly different for Cold Pressor 1.

fer from each other, and Voluntary Control and Decrease did not differ from each other in these comparisons.

Table 2 also gives the average data and statistical comparisons for the feedback and voluntary control trials. To summarize these data, the four experimental groups line up consistently. Group 1, given increase training with feedback, increased their rate during feedback trials more than Group 2, given decrease training. Both of these groups differ in the appropriate direction from Groups 3 and 4. During the voluntary control (no feedback) trials, Group 2 showed a significant heart rate decrease compared to the other three groups. Decrease heart rate feedback training appeared to facilitate voluntary control without feedback.

The data are more or less consistent with expectation. Subjects changed their heart rate in the appropriate direction during feedback and voluntary control trials. During the second as compared to the first CP test, appropriate responses were also shown. The increase feedback group showed an 11.5 bpm difference (increase) in heart rate compared to 3.4 bpm for the Habituation group, but this difference of 8.1 bpm was not significant. The decrease feedback group showed a relative slowing of 3.4 bpm in rate, a significant decrease as compared with the Habituation group but not as compared with the Voluntary Control (decrease) group. The latter procedure was not better than simple habituation. Finally, it should be noted that subjects who were given increase and decrease feedback training and who were also asked to change their heart rate voluntarily during the CP test changed their relative heart rate in the appropriate direction more than they did during simple non-demanding feedback trials, about twice as much.

Pain rating data are shown in Table 3. The four groups did not differ in their rating of the pain of the first CP test. In the second CP test, the ratings are consistent with the heart rate results. The two feedback groups differed from each other and from the two control groups in the appropriate direction. Table 3 gives the means and comparisons for the difference in CP-1 and CP-2 ratings and in the direct comparison of the two CP tests by subjects. In both scales, the means are in accord with expectation, although all the adjacent comparisons do not reach statistical significance. The two feedback groups are significantly different in all critical comparisons.

Finally, correlations were computed between Cardiac Awareness scores and two indices of the experimental effects--change in heart rate from CP-1 to CP-2, rating of CP-2. Cardiac Awareness is indexed by the degree to which subjects reported "loud pounding heart" and "increase in heart rate" in everyday fear or anxiety. In the feedback Increase group and in the Voluntary Control (decrease) group, the correlations were 0.57 and 0.63, respectively, between Cardiac Awareness and the CP-2 rating. All other correlations were close to zero. In addition, change in heart rate did not correlate appreciably with ratings or change in ratings of the painfulness of the CP tests.

The results may be summarized as follows:

1) Comparing the two feedback groups with the two controls during training trials, bidirectional changes in heart rate were observed. During 5 voluntary control trials, the group having prior feedback training for decreasing heart rate lowered their rate, as compared with the group

Table 3

Average Pain Ratings

	Group			
	Increase	Habituation	Vol. Control (Decrease)	Decrease
Cold Pressor Ratings	1	4	3	2
Cold Pressor 1 (1 = no pain, 10 = unbearably painful)	6.2	6.0	5.4	5.1
Cold Pressor 2 (1 = no pain, 10 = unbearably painful)	6.7	6.0	5.5	4.0
Cold Pressor 2 -Cold Pressor 1	0.5	0.0	0.1	-1.1
Comparison of Cold Pressor 2 with Cold Pressor 1 (1 = much less painful, 10 = much more painful)	6.7	6.0	5.5	4.0

Note: Groups that are connected by a line are not significantly different in mean pain rating.

not having the training. In fact, the decrease group seemed to improve when feedback was removed. The group having prior feedback training for increasing heart rate did not maintain their control as well during the voluntary control trials as they did during training trials.

2) Heart rate data for the CP test after training accord by and large with the feedback and control procedures. The effect is clearest in the increase feedback group; it showed an average increase in heart rate during the second CP test that was three times greater than during the first CP. In contrast, the decrease feedback group reduced their heart rate by about two-thirds. Although the feedback decrease group showed a greater relative decrease in heart rate during CP-2 as compared with the habituation control, the decrease was not significantly lower than the change observed

in the group given simple voluntary control instructions and no feedback. The increase in heart rate observed in the CP-2 compared to CP-1 for the feedback increase group was not significantly greater than the change observed in the habituation control, although the observed increase was much larger on the average. Differences in initial heart rate reaction to the first CP test complicate interpretation of these findings.

3) The subjective ratings suggest further that voluntary control procedures using biofeedback methods may be useful in the regulation of self-reports of pain related to the stress of ice water immersion. By and large, bidirectional pain reports were observed in the two feedback groups, compared to the two controls. The rating of CP-2 best exemplifies the self-report findings. For example, in regard to the two conditions designed to reduce pain ratings, in the feedback decrease group only one out of nine subjects rated the second CP with a value greater than 5; in the voluntary control decrease group, six out of nine subjects rated the second CP with a value greater than 5. The pain rating means for the four groups line up in the same order as the means for the various heart rate indices. This correspondence of heart rate and subjective report does not extend, however, to within-group correlations of the various indices of change.

4) Cardiac Awareness was more likely to be correlated with higher ratings of the second CP in the feedback increase and the voluntary control decrease group. A small positive correlation was also shown in the feedback decrease condition. In the habituation control, the correlation was close to zero. In this context, subjective reports of heart rate awareness would seem to be most related to greater pain and/or anxiety about the ice water immersion. In previous research, Cardiac Aware subjects were more likely to reduce their ratings of the intensity of electric shock when given heart rate decrease training during anticipatory reactions to the stimuli. This relationship does not appear to apply when heart rate control is actually attempted during the stressful stimulus itself or during this particular ice water stressor.

The report of this last study is based on short-cut and non-parametric statistical analyses of several indices of heart rate and pain rating change. It seems fair to conclude, however, that voluntary control procedures may be useful in understanding and possibly managing pain reactions and responses to stressful stimuli, more generally. We need further to distinguish pain and anxiety components in this kind of study, to examine indices of stress response other than simple verbal ratings, and to evaluate other concurrent physiological processes.

This paper summarizes research on the use of biofeedback and operant conditioning methods as a means of altering physiological responses assumed to be associated with complex psychological processes. The major purposes of the research are to determine whether physiological activity occurring in anticipation of or directly in response to rather strong eliciting stimuli such as electric shock or ice water can in part be modified and whether this results in an alteration of judgments of the intensity of the stimuli. The answer to both questions is positive. In some respects, learned control of visceral activity appears to be of a greater magnitude in situations placing a "demand" on subjects, that is, under conditions of stressful or aversive stimulation, than under mild non-stimulating, non-demanding conditions typically employed in biofeedback research studies. Perceptions of the intensity of the aversive stimuli appear to vary consistently with the degree of learned physiological control exhibited. The most promising results so far have been obtained using heart rate voluntary control training. This research supports the conclusion that direct feedback control of autonomic functions which are appropriate for given subjects in terms of their normal emotional responding may be useful as a means of controlling or modifying emotional states or reactivity.

From a clinical standpoint, biofeedback training for relevant physiological responses appears to offer a valuable behavioral strategy for changing anxiety, fear, or pain reactions. A recent paper by Gatchel and Proctor (1976) demonstrates this clinical potential in showing that learned heart rate control is an effective therapeutic technique for reducing anxiety in speech-anxious subjects. Further research will need to examine more closely the psychophysiological mechanisms involved and to compare the utility of the biofeedback method with other behavioral strategies such as relaxation and suggestion.

REFERENCES

Beatty, J. Similar effects of feedback signals and instructional information on EEG activity. Physiology and Behavior, 1972, 9, 151-154.

Beatty, J., Greenberg, A., Deibler, W. P., & O'Hanlon, J. F. Operant control of occipital theta rhythm affects performance in a radar monitoring task. Science, 1974, 183, 871-873.

Beatty, J., & Kornfeld, C. Relative independence of conditioned EEG changes from cardiac and respiratory activity. Physiology and Behavior, 1972, 9, 733-736.

Brown, B. Recognition of aspects of consciousness through association with EEG alpha activity represented by a light signal. Psychophysiology, 1970, 6, 442-452.

Brown, B. Awareness of EEG-subjective activity relationships detected within a closed feedback system. Psychophysiology, 1971, 7, 451-464.

DiCara, L. V., & Weiss, J. M. Effect of heart-rate learning under curare on subsequent noncurarized avoidance learning. Journal of Comparative and Physiological Psychology, 1969, 69, 368-374.

Gatchel, R. J., & Proctor, J. D. Effectiveness of voluntary heart rate control in reducing speech anxiety. Journal of Consulting and Clinical Psychology, 1976, 44, 381-389.

Hardt, J. V., & Kamiya, J. Some comments on Plotkin's self-regulation of electroencephalographic alpha. Journal of Experimental Psychology: General, 1976, 105, 100-108.

James, W. The principles of psychology. New York: Holt, Rinehart & Winston, 1890.

Kimmel, H. D., Pendergrass, V. E., & Kimmel, E. B. Modifying children's orienting reactions instrumentally. Conditional Reflex, 1967, 2, 227-235.

Lacey, J. K., & Lacey, B. C. Some autonomic-central nervous system interrelationships. In P. Black (Ed.), Physiological correlates of emotion. New York: Academic Press, 1970.

Lang, P. J. The mechanics of desensitization and the laboratory study of human fear. In C. M. Franks (Ed.), Behavior therapy: Appraisal and status. New York: McGraw-Hill, 1969.

Lang, P. J., Rice, D. C., & Sternbach, R. A. Psychophysiology of emotion. In N. Greenfield & R. Sternbach (Eds.), Handbook of psychophysiology. New York: Holt, Rinehart & Winston, 1972.

Lovallo, W. The cold pressor test and autonomic function: A review and integration. Psychophysiology, 1975, 12, 268-282.

Mathews, A. M. Psychophysiological approaches to the investigation of desensitization and related procedures. Psychological Bulletin, 1971, 76, 73-91.

Morganstern, K. Heart rate deceleration through the use of a reaction time task as a treatment for the reduction of analogue fear: Cardiac inhibition therapy. Unpublished doctoral dissertation, The Pennsylvania State University, 1974.

Nowlis, D. P., & Kamiya, J. The control of electroencephalographic alpha rhythms through auditory feedback and the associated mental activity. Psychophysiology, 1970, 6, 476-484.

Obrist, P. A., Webb, R., Sutterer, J., & Howard, J. The cardiac-somatic relationship: Some reformulations. Psychophysiology, 1970, 6, 569-587.

Paskewitz, D. A., Lynch, J. J., Orne, M. T., & Costello, J. The feedback control of alpha activity: Conditioning or disinhibition. Psychophysiology, 1970, 6, 637-638.

Plotkin, W. B. On the self-regulation of the occipital alpha rhythm: Control strategies, states of consciousness, and the role of physiological feedback. Journal of Experimental Psychology: General, 1976, 105, 66-99. (a)

Plotkin, W. B. Appraising the ephemeral "alpha phenomenon": A reply to Hardt and Kamiya. Journal of Experimental Psychology: General, 1976, 105, 109-121. (b)

Schachter, S., & Singer, J. Cognitive, social and physiological determinants of emotional state. Psychological Review, 1962, 69, 379-399.

Shapiro, D., Schwartz, G. E., Nelson, S., Shnidman, S., & Silverman, S. Operant control of fear-related electrodermal responses in snake-phobic subjects. Psychophysiology, 1972, 9, 271. (Abstract)

Shnidman, S. R. Instrumental conditioning of orienting responses using positive reinforcement. Journal of Experimental Psychology, 1970, 83, 491-494.

Shnidman, S. R., & Shapiro, D. S. Instrumental modification of elicited autonomic responses. Psychophysiology, 1970, 7, 395-401.

Sirota, A. D. Heart rate feedback and instructional effects on subjective reaction to aversive stimuli. Unpublished doctoral dissertation, The Pennsylvania State University, 1976.

Sirota, A. D., Schwartz, G. E., & Shapiro, D. Voluntary control of human heart rate: Effect on reaction to aversive stimulation. Journal of Abnormal Psychology, 1974, 83, 261-267.

Sirota, A. D., Schwartz, G. E., & Shapiro, D. Voluntary control of human heart rate: Effect on reaction to aversive stimulation. A replication and extension. Journal of Abnormal Psychology, in press.

Slaughter, J., & Hahn, W. Effects on avoidance performance of vagal stimulation during previous fear conditioning in rats. Journal of Comparative and Physiological Psychology, 1974, 86, 283-287.

Stoyva, J., & Kamiya, J. Electrophysiological studies of dreaming as the prototype of a new strategy in the study of consciousness. Psychological Review, 1968, 75, 192-205.

Valins, S., & Ray, A. A. Effects of cognitive desensitization on avoidance behavior. Journal of Personality and Social Psychology, 1967, 7, 345-350.

Walsh, D. H. Interactive effects of alpha feedback and instructional set on subjective state. Psychophysiology, 1974, 11, 428-435.

Wolpe, J. Psychotherapy by reciprocal inhibition. Stanford, California: University Press, 1958.

NOTE

The author's research is supported by National Institute of Mental Health Research Grant MH-26923 and Office of Naval Research Contract N00014-75-C-0150. The author is indebted to his associates who collaborated in several of the studies summarized in this paper: Gary E. Schwartz, Alan D. Sirota, Ronald Victor, and J. Alberto Mainardi. Portions of the paper were taken from a report presented at the Seventh Annual Meeting of the Biofeedback Research Society, February 27-March 3, 1976, Colorado Springs, Colorado (Victor, R., Shapiro, D., & Mainardi, J. A. Voluntary control of heart rate: Effects on heart rate and pain during the cold pressor test).

RESEARCH ON THE SPECIFICITY OF FEEDBACK TRAINING: IMPLICATIONS FOR THE USE OF BIOFEEDBACK IN THE TREATMENT OF ANXIETY AND FEAR

Peter J. Lang
Department of Psychology
University of Wisconsin at Madison

The purpose of this paper is to describe a series of experiments from our laboratory on visceral learning, and to present the implications of this work for the use of biofeedback in the treatment of anxiety. In this research we tested the hypothesis that feedback of information from a visceral organ would facilitate instructions to reduce that organ's activity level. The specific goal of our procedures was the slowing of heart rate. This response was chosen for evaluation because of the ease and reliability of heart rate measurement, and also, because increments in heart rate are associated with emotional arousal, whereas a slow pulse characterizes the relaxed state. Underlying our experiments was an assumption that the learned control of cardiac rate is a skills learning task. Thus, our strategy has been to examine such variables as instructions, information input, display characteristics, and incentives, to determine if these parameters would modify heart rate response acquisition in a manner similar to their effect on motor skills learning.

INFORMATION AND PERFORMANCE

Feedback procedures are based on the assumption that learned control over a bodily response is facilitated by information about activity in the relevant organ system. Thus, our initial experiments concentrated on this information variable. Lang and Twentyman (1974) studied two groups of subjects in a feedback task. Both groups were instructed to speed and slow heart rate over the course of a four session training period. The groups differed in the information characteristics of their feedback displays. One group received only binary information (an indication whether performance was good or poor), while the other group was provided with a continuous analogue display of heart activity. During the slowing training of the binary information group, interpulse intervals which exceeded in length the median pulse interval observed without feedback, resulted in the word GOOD appearing on an oscilloscope screen in front of the subject. Shorter intervals yielded no signal. Thus, subjects were informed on each pulse if their performance was better than or inferior to their previous standard. However, they could not monitor all changes in the organ system, nor did they have information concerning the degree to which a response exceeded or fell short of criterion. Subjects in the analogue group observed a continuous analogue representation of interpulse intervals. This was presented as successive lines on the oscilloscope screen, proportional to each interval between "R" waves of the EKG. The heart line intersected a target line (representing the subject's median non-feedback heart interval), providing the subject also with a continuous estimate of his relative performance.

The two conditions differed dramatically in the amount of information provided, and when instructed to increase heart rate, subjects in the analogue condition (high-information group) showed superior performance to that of binary subjects. However, this difference between conditions was not observed for heart rate slowing. While subjects were able to decrease heart rate on instruction relative to resting rates, this effect was not enhanced by the analogue display.

Working in our laboratory, Gatchel (1974) obtained similar findings. Separate groups of subjects were trained in heart rate speeding and slowing, utilizing displays which varied systematically in information content. One group was provided with a summary of performance only every 10 heart beats; a second group received a summary every 5 beats; a third group observed the continuous analogue heart interval display. When instructed to speed heart rate the analogue group showed the best performance, followed by the 5-beat group, and trailed by the 10-beat group. Thus, more frequent information resulted in better performance at the feedback task. However, this was again not true for slowing. While feedback subjects showed greater instructed slowing than controls, the amount of deceleration was unrelated to frequency of information.

INCENTIVES AND FEEDBACK

The above results prompted the conclusion that the mechanism of heart rate speeding and slowing are different, and that activating and tropotrophic cardiac changes are differentially responsive to experimental manipulation. A more recent study by Lang and Twentyman (1976) provided some additional support for this thesis. In this experiment the effects of monetary incentives were assessed. Subjects who received money for improved performance were compared with a group receiving no special rewards. During feedback trials, the incentive subjects were superior in performance to non-incentive subjects. This was particularly marked for heart rate speeding, and the incentive effect was clearly significant when only speeding sessions were analyzed. This difference was reduced for slowing, and did not achieve significance for slowing feedback alone. Furthermore, there was a suggestion that subjects performed better specifically in the absence of feedback. Thus, it was found that subjects' maximal slowing occurred in the incentive group, when they were under instructions to slow heart rate, but when they were no longer receiving feedback. At this point the incentive subjects did have heart rates significantly slower than the non-rewarded subjects.

The weight of data indicates that subjects can reduce heart rate on instructions, but manipulations of feedback variables do not appear to influence rate or degree of acquisition. These results have prompted us to change our experimental strategy, and to examine alternative procedures to feedback which might be expected to generate heart rate slowing. Two methods that we are now investigating involve the enlistment of muscle mediation and the modification of cognitive processes. The former approach is designed to produce visceral change through the modification of somatic muscle activity. The latter approach involves the reduction of visceral arousal through cognitive maneuvers such as meditation and related self-instructions.

MUSCLE MEDIATION

Obrist has been a vigorous advocate of the view that changes in heart rate are generally secondary to changes in muscular activity (Obrist, Webb, Sutterer, & Howard, 1970). He argues that cardiovascular and somatic responses are coupled neurophysiologically, and that neural events in the brain initiate tandem changes in the two systems. From this perspective, the most efficient way to reduce activity in the visceral system is to lower the general level of muscular tonus. This procedure is the same one advocated for many years by Jacobson (1938) and developed by Wolpe (1958) as a specific inhibitor of fear responses.

In a recent study Cuthbert (1976) tested the hypothesis that training in the reduction of muscle activity would produce a greater reduction in heart rate than direct pulse-interval feedback. Three groups of subjects were studied over four heart-rate slowing training sessions. The first group received analogue heart interval feedback, in the same manner as in our previous studies. The second group observed a similar display, but the oscilloscope pattern was controlled by muscle activity rather than the EKG. In this group the length of the horizontal lines were proportional to frontalis muscle potentials, with longer lines indicating a reduction in tonus. As for heart rate feedback, a vertical target line was provided so that the subject had a continuous display of his relative performance. The third group observed a display similar to that of the feedback groups, but it was generated by the computer and unrelated to the subjects' physiology. Group 3 subjects were instructed to track the display and press a hand-held microswitch whenever one of the horizontal lines terminated. All subjects were told that the purpose of this training was to facilitate heart rate reduction.

Training sessions involved five three-minute Feedback periods during which subjects observed their displays and five three-minute Transfer sessions, during which they saw no display, but were under instruction to continue heart rate reduction. At the end of each Transfer period subjects saw a "scoreboard," which indicated their heart rate during Transfer and the number of beats per minute reduction from rest.

Analysis of variance showed clearly that, during feedback trials, both the EMG and HR feedback groups reduced heart rate significantly more than did tracking subjects. Furthermore, there was no difference between Feedback groups in either degree of heart rate reduction or frontalis EMG change. Thus, the data argue that feedback procedures designed to produce a tropotrophic change yield essentially similar results, regardless of the target variable.

The results for transfer trials were even more surprising. There was no difference between the three groups in Transfer heart rate. When tracking subjects were relieved of the necessity of performing the tracking task, they slowed as much as did the feedback groups. Furthermore, there was a tendency for all groups to have slower heart rates during transfer than for feedback.

These latter results argue that the information processing demands of feedback procedures interfere with the individual's efforts to achieve a state of lowered arousal. Furthermore, the fact that tracking subjects could reduce heart rate to the level of the other groups during transfer, argues that feedback subjects did not acquire a special skill during feedback that they subsequently applied during transfer. There is indeed no evidence that precise feedback facilitates arousal reduction. Nevertheless, it must be pointed out that all subjects observed the "scoreboard" after transfer. Many subjects reported that this was valuable as information, as well as motivating, and helped them in the heart rate slowing task. Previous findings would support this assertion, and it presently seems reasonable to conclude that gross information about performance does help arousal reduction. However, the above experiment provides no support for the hypothesis that high density information about organ function facilitates a relaxation task.

COGNITIVE SET AND VISCERAL ACTIVATION

Benson has proposed that low levels of visceral activity and metabolic rate can be achieved through a simple meditation exercise, modeled after Transcendental Meditation (Benson, Rosner, Marzetta, & Klemchuk, 1974). The procedure involves no feedback of physiological responses. Subjects are simply instructed to relax their muscles and attend to their respiration. They are further told to say the word "one" silently as they expire, to not think about anything, to remain passive and relaxed, and to let all thoughts drift away. Benson and co-workers have reported marked reductions in oxygen consumption, and lowered visceral tonus among subjects practicing this method. He reports that these relaxation effects appear early, beginning within the first session, and that the method is useful in countering the effects of stress.

Cuthbert (1976) undertook a second experiment in our laboratory, designed to compare the efficacy in reducing heart rate of Benson's meditation procedure and pulse interval feedback. Subjects were trained over three sessions. During the first two sessions, feedback subjects were administered the same procedure as in previous experiments, including five feedback trials, and five transfer trials followed by the "scoreboard." Meditation subjects practiced the Benson procedure during both the feedback and transfer periods. They also saw their "scoreboard" at the end of transfer. During the final, third session all subjects were simply told to reduce heart rate over a continuous fifteen minute period, and neither feedback nor the "scoreboard" were administered to either group. The purpose of this last session was to provide a test of learning outside the original training context, and over a period of time more characteristic of the typical meditation session.

Analysis of the training sessions showed that significantly greater heart rate deceleration was obtained for meditation than feedback subjects, both during the period when feedback subjects observed the display and during the transfer periods. Meditation subjects also showed more stable respiratory patterns and more reduction in frontalis muscle tension than did the feedback group. During the third session, the group difference increased further. Feedback subjects showed little benefit of training, while the meditation group reduced heart rate progressively over the fifteen minute test period.

In addition to the heart rate data, the most dramatic difference between the two groups was in respiration. Meditation subjects showed little change over trials in either rate or depth of breathing. Heart rate subjects showed significantly greater variability. Brener (1974) has already speculated that heart rate feedback encourages respiratory maneuvers which are counter productive to relaxation. It is possible that this contributed to the poorer performance of heart rate feedback subjects.

We have recently undertaken a replication of the above experiment. The data are not as yet completely analyzed. However, it is already clear that the meditation group in this new experiment is less dramatically different from heart rate feedback subjects than in the Cuthbert study. Nevertheless, they did perform at least as well as feedback subjects. Thus, while we cannot be sure that meditation instructions are specially powerful, the conclusion that feedback does not significantly enhance instructed heart rate slowing received strong confirmation.

CONCLUSIONS

I believe that these data have important implications for the use of biofeedback in the clinical situation. Our results permit us to conclude the following: 1) Heart rate slowing is best effected when that response is part of a general reduction in activation. 2) Heart rate slowing is as readily produced by cognitive exercises as by intensive cardiac feedback. 3) Neither heart rate nor muscle potential feedback is uniquely effective in producing a lowered state of arousal, and these methods are equal in reducing muscle potentials and decelerating heart rate. 4) The evidence suggests that high-density feedback may interfere with cardiac rate slowing, prompting respiratory changes and cognitive activity which maintain arousal.

These conclusions argue against the general use of biofeedback as a routine treatment for anxiety. Methods such as instructed muscle relaxation and meditation exercises are much less expensive and are likely to be equally effective. It would certainly be of value for the therapist to monitor the effects of such relaxation instructions and perhaps periodically provide patients with a "scoreboard." However, the use of continuous heart rate or

EMG feedback is not warranted by the research results.

The above conclusions should not be taken to mean that biofeedback can find no place in the clinical enterprise. There is ample evidence that feedback methods can be used to produce very specific changes in organ systems, fractionating or reinforcing normal psychophysiological patterns (Lang, 1975; Schwartz, 1974). When a clinical problem is defined by a deviation in a specific system (e.g., high blood pressure or Reynaud's disease), then biofeedback may yet prove to be an appropriate treatment method. Furthermore, we have already noted that degree of visceral control under feedback conditions varies with such variables as age and disease state (Lang, Troyer, Twentyman, & Gatchel, 1975). It is quite possible that biofeedback may play an increasingly important role in the diagnosis of psychosomatic disorder. Finally, the feedback methodology is an important laboratory tool, which is uniquely capable of dissecting relationships between physiological and behavioral systems in the intact human being (Lindholm, 1975). Thus, I do not anticipate that the clinical exploration of biofeedback will be any less intensely pursued in the near future. Nevertheless, I think the available data justify the conclusion that high-density visceral feedback does not provide a uniquely powerful treatment for anxiety or other broad system stress responses.

REFERENCES

Benson, H., Rosner, B. A., Marzetta, B. R., & Klemchuk, H. P. Decreased blood pressure in borderline hypertensive subjects who practice meditation. Journal of Chronic Disease, 1974, 27, 163-169.

Brener, J. Factors influencing the specificity of voluntary cardiovascular control. In L. V. DiCara (Ed.), Limbic and autonomic nervous system research. New York: Plenum, 1974.

Cuthbert, B. N. Voluntary slowing of heart rate: A comparison of various techniques. Unpublished doctoral dissertation, University of Wisconsin, 1976.

Gatchel, R. J. Frequency of feedback and learned heart rate control. Journal of Experimental Psychology, 1974, 103, 274-283.

Jacobson, E. Progressive relaxation. Chicago: University Press, 1938.

Lang, P. J. Acquisition of heart rate control: Method, theory, and clinical implications. In D. C. Fowles (Ed.), Clinical applications of psychophysiology. New York: Columbia University Press, 1975.

Lang, P. J., & Twentyman, C. T. Learning to control heart rate: Effects of varying incentive and criterion of success on task performance. Psychophysiology, in press.

Lang, P. J., Troyer, W. G., Twentyman, C. T., & Gatchel, R. J. Differential effects of heart rate modification training on college students, older males, and patients with ischemic heart disease. Psychosomatic Medicine, 1975, 37, 429-446.

Lang, P. J., & Twentyman, C. T. Learning to control heart rate: Binary vs. analogue feedback. Psychophysiology, 1974, 11, 616-629.

Lindholm, J. M. Heart rate control and reaction time performance in human subjects. Unpublished doctoral dissertation, University of Wisconsin, 1975.

Obrist, P. A., Webb, R. A., Sutterer, J. R., & Howard, J. L. The cardiac-somatic relationship: Some reformulations. Psychophysiology, 1970, 6, 569-587.

Schwartz, G. E. Toward a theory of voluntary control of response patterns in the cardiovascular system. In P. A. Obrist, A. H. Black, J. Brener, & L. V. DiCara (Eds.), Cardiovascular psychophysiology. Chicago: Aldine, 1974.

Wolpe, J. Psychotherapy by reciprocal inhibition. Stanford: University Press, 1958.

BIOFEEDBACK, VERBAL INSTRUCTIONS AND THE MOTOR SKILLS ANALOGY

Derek Johnston
Oxford University

Biofeedback has been largely atheoretical in its orientation; there does, however, seem to be a sizeable body of opinion that regards learning to voluntarily control a visceral response as analogous to learning a conventional motor skill. This view has been most clearly proposed by Lang, e.g., "the acquisition of voluntary control over a viscus is a skill ... it requires an organised sequence of activities, movements and symbolic information such as those required to play darts or hit a tennis ball accurately." (Lang, 1975). Brener (1974), Engel (1972), and Schwartz (1974) take a similar position.

Although this view is appealing and offers potentially powerful insights into visceral control, it has not been extensively discussed or tested. This paper will describe two experiments that test aspects of the analogy and review the evidence on cardiovascular self control in the light of these experiments.

It is clear from the quote from Lang that the motor skill being analogised is one, such as darts, that demands very precise control. However in most feedback experiments such precision is not required, the subject simply being asked to vary some physiological function in a specified direction.[1] To many skills theorists this does not meet the definition of a skill. For example, Adams (1971), following Bartlett (1948), defines skill as requiring a graded response, one that has both direction and a specific magnitude. As most skills research is on adults it may well be appropriate to regard directional movements with no specific end point as not requiring skill. However, very early in training, for example in childhood, these responses presumably had to be learned and may have shown some of the characteristics of a skill at that time. If the visceral responses we study are truly novel, then it might be fruitful to regard them as requiring skill to control even directionally. In this case the motor skills literature allows one to make various predictions about the characteristics of such control. I shall concentrate on the four that seem most relevant to the current level of development of cardiovascular biofeedback research.

1) That knowledge of results (KR) is vital to learning (Thorndike, 1931).

2) That performance improves with training (Bilodeau, 1969).

3) That in general the more information provided by KR, the better is learning (Bilodeau & Bilodeau, 1958; Gill, 1975; Trowbridge & Cason, 1932).

4) That control changes and becomes more specific with training (Jones, 1962).

If, however, purely directional cardiovascular control is more accurately regarded as similar to a simple movement, such as pressing a dynamometer, then extrinsic KR would not have a vital function and purely verbal information, given prior to the task, would enable comparable control.

In both experiments to be described a comparison is made between verbal instructions suggesting possible methods of controlling the relevant cardiovascular function with those instructions plus feedback. If it is appropriate to consider such control as a skill then feedback should enable greater control than instructions alone and this control should, with training, increase in extent and/or become more specific, i.e., limited to the system being fed back.

The first experiment, fully described in Johnston (1976), was a single session study of heart rate control in which verbal instructions encouraging the limited use of skeletal mediators was compared with those instructions plus binary feedback. The heart rate results are shown in Figure 1. Feedback did not add to the effect of the instructions and control did not increase over the session. A measure of general movement showed that activity was closely related to the heart rate change and this relationship did not diminish over the session, i.e., there was no evidence of the response becoming more specific.

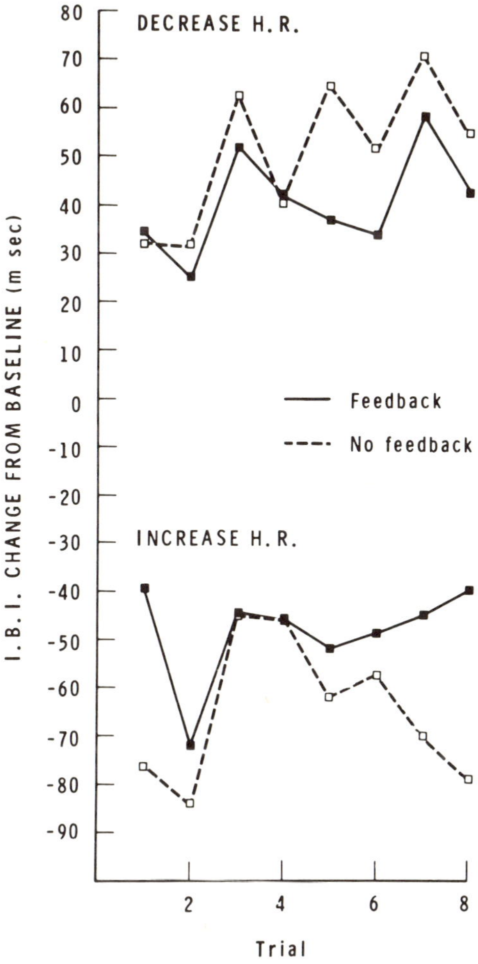

Figure 1. I. B. I. change from intertrial baseline.

These results are somewhat embarrassing for the skills analogy. However the amount of training provided was very limited and heart rate may be peculiarly susceptible to simple instructions. An analogous study was therefore carried out taking blood flow in the skin as the response system and using 8 training sessions. It was believed that this system would maximize feedback effects--firstly, because skin blood flow is less somatically linked than heart rate and secondly because promising reports of skin temperature control have recently appeared (Roberts, Kewman, & McDonald, 1973; Roberts, Schuler, Bacon, Zimmerman, & Patterson, 1975; Steptoe, Mathews, & Johnston, 1974). However the use of skin temperature as an index of blood flow is not entirely satisfactory. It is a very inadequate and sluggish measure (Greenfield, 1963) and pilot work has suggested that it is very susceptible to artifactual manipulation by the subject. Our measure of blood flow was the amplitude of the pulse detected by a photocell on the index finger of one hand (Cook, 1974). Subjects were requested to control the blood flow in one finger and the flow in this finger was used to drive an analogue feedback display. On each session they were required to both increase and decrease blood flow. Two groups of eight volunteers were trained. One group received both instructions explaining that relaxation would increase blood flow to the hand and tension reduce it and the visual feedback for all eight sessions. The other group received only the verbal instructions for the first four sessions and then the feedback for the remaining four. This allowed both a between and a within subject comparison of the feedback effect. The other measures taken were pulse amplitude from the contralateral (non-control) finger, pulse interval, respiration rate, and forearm electromyogram (EMG) for the control arm. Subjects' arms were placed in rests designed to minimize movement throughout the experiment. For the reasons advanced at this conference by my colleague Dr. Steptoe, all data were analyzed both from an initial and an intertrial baseline.

In Table 1, the means for the comparison of feedback and instructions are shown. Control was demonstrated but in no case was there a

Table 1

Pulse Amplitude in Control Finger, Mean Log. Proportion of Baseline

	Conditions		
	Instructions and Feedback Sessions 1-4	Instructions Sessions 1-4	Instructions Followed by Feedback Sessions 5-8
Initial Baseline			
Increase	-0.10	-0	-0.15
Decrease	-0.23	-0.15	-0.32
Intertrial Baseline			
Increase	0.01	0	0.02
Decrease	-0.13	-0.04	-0.10

significant difference between the feedback plus instructions with instructions alone, although the effect approached significance in one out of the four comparisons. Figure 2 shows the results for the control finger over the eight sessions. No improvement in control was shown, either within a session or over the eight sessions. This figure also shows that the response did not become localized in one finger as the non-control finger tracked the control finger throughout. Heart rate, respiration rate and EMG were all higher in the decrease condition, consistent with the tension/relaxation instructions, and this effect did not differ between groups or over sessions.

These results are consistently negative for a skills theory of visceral learning; KR was not vital and control did not improve or become more specific with training. These comparisons of explicit directive instructions and feedback appear to be unique in the cardiovascular literature, although Beatty (1972) reports similar results in training electroencephalographic activity, but other studies do bear on the skills analogy and there have been several experiments examining parameters that are important in motor learning. Lack of space will ensure a rather dogmatic description of this evidence.

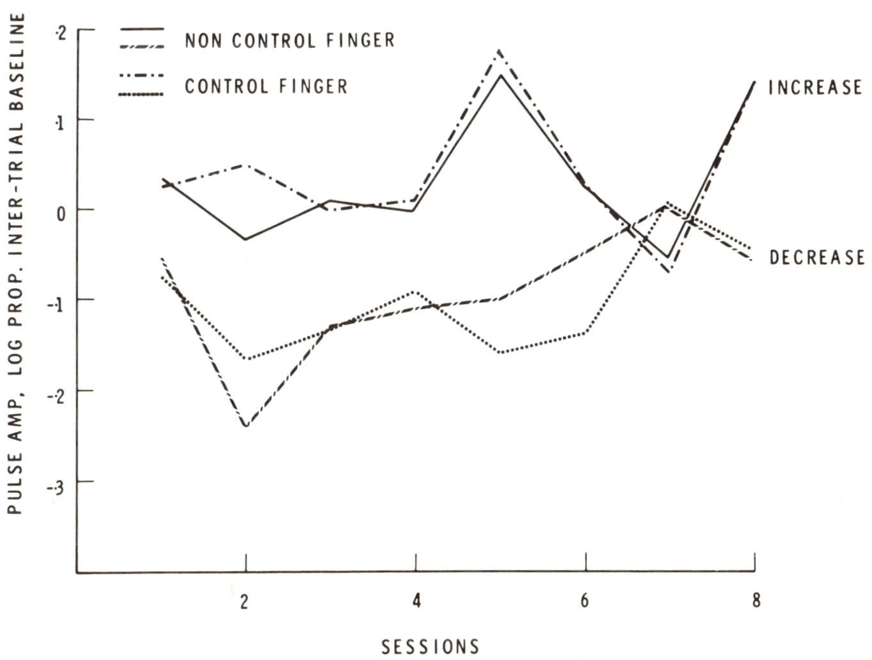

Figure 2. Pulse amplitude change from intertrial baseline.

IMPROVEMENT IN CONTROL WITH TRAINING

In heart rate studies the results are equivocal as to whether control improves over a session but it probably does from an initial but not from the more conservative intertrial baseline (Boucard & Courson, 1976; Blanchard, Scott, Young, & Edmunsen, 1974; Lang & Twentyman, 1974; Sirota, Shapiro, & Schwartz, 1975). Improvement over sessions has been reported by some (Brener, Kleinman, & Goesling, 1969; Gatchel, 1975; McCanne & Sandeman, 1975; Wells, 1973) but not others (Blanchard et al., 1974; Johnston, 1976; Stephens, Harris, & Brady, 1972; Young & Blanchard, 1974) and it is worth noting that Brener et al. (1969) demonstrated that such improvement can occur without feedback.

Experiments on blood pressure control have shown within session improvements in control (Brener & Kleinman, 1970; Steptoe & Johnston, 1976) and increase in control over sessions effects are reported by Steptoe (1976) over four sessions and Benson, Shapiro, Tursky, and Schwartz (1971) appear to have shown improvement over many sessions in hypertensives. Brener and Kleinman (1970) and Steptoe and Johnston (1976) found no improvement over two sessions, the latter, in fact, finding evidence of some deterioration in the second session.

As stated earlier, the published literature on vascular control provides the most impressive demonstration of the power of feedback. I am aware of three published and two unpublished major studies that are relevant to the acquisition issue (Roberts et al., 1973; Roberts et al., 1975; Taub & Emurian, 1976; Steptoe et al., 1974; Surwit, Shapiro, & Feld, 1976). The study by Taub suffers from idiosyncratic data reduction and reporting and cannot be evaluated while the Steptoe et al. study is of a preliminary nature. Surwit et al. produce results that, for blood flow, are very comparable to those of the present study with clear evidence of control but no evidence of acquisition over the five sessions of training. Roberts et al. (1975), however, in a study of the control of temperature in one hand relative to the other, obtained very profound within and between subject improvements over sixteen sessions of training. It is not clear from the report how this group controlled for the possible artifactual manipulation of the temperature probe and so a replication with more specific attention to this control is essential; but this study remains an important and impressive demonstration of the gradual acquisition of a highly specific response with the presumptive aid of feedback.

INCREASING SPECIFICITY WITH TRAINING

There is very little data on increasing specificity of a cardiovascular response with training. No heart rate studies provide convincing evidence one way or the other. Steptoe has carried out the most comprehensive examination of increasing specificity with blood pressure feedback (Steptoe, 1976; Steptoe & Johnston, 1976a, 1976b) but has not found convincing evidence of it. Roberts et al. (1975) claim that, in their study of the differential control of hand temperature, the response was initially a generalized one occurring on both hands and gradually becoming more specific and localized in one hand; unfortunately they provide no data to support this.

THE MORE INFORMATION PROVIDED BY KR THE BETTER IS LEARNING

I have concentrated on the very general characteristics of response acquisition which might be anticipated if controlling the viscera is a skill. Direct tests of parameters that might effect such learning are potentially much more powerful. A number of relevant studies on the importance of the information provided by the feedback have been carried out. The motor skills literature suggests very strongly that the more information provided by the KR the better is learning with the possible exception of very detailed information (Gill, 1975). It certainly appears to be the case that KR that provides magnitude information is better than simple binary, right/wrong information (Trowbridge & Cason, 1932) and that information after every response is better than less frequent information (Bilodeau & Bilodeau, 1958) and these are the variables that have been examined in heart rate control experiments. It is important to note that the motor skills data suggests that these variables affect the rate with which the response is acquired, more information leading to more rapid acquisition, rather than affecting asympotic performance.

Brener et al. (1969), Johnston (1976) and Young and Blanchard (1974) have varied the information presented by the feedback signal by varying respectively the percentage of trials in which information was given, the criterion level at which reinforcement was given and by giving either binary or analogue information. They all obtained negative or equivocal results.

Two studies by the Lang group have shown that informational variables can affect performance in a heart rate speeding task, Lang and Twentyman (1974) by comparing analogue and binary feedback and Gatchel (1975) by varying the frequency with which feedback was given. The support for a skills view found in these studies is, however, very limited since they both appear to show that the absolute level of performance achieved diminished with decreasing information, rather than, as would be predicted from the skills literature, rate of acquisition being affected. This suggests that information is not operating in the same way in the heart rate task as in a motor skill task and may be having its effect on performance rather than learning.

The experiments reported in this paper and examination of the literature on cardiovascular feedback provide little support for the notion that purely directional cardiovascular control is a skill. Feedback seems to add little to some forms of verbal instruction, performance does not reliably show acquisition effects, specificity does not improve with training, and learning does not improve as the information provided by feedback is increased. This suggests that such control is best conceptualized as similar to formally identical motor acts that are purely directional. It may well be that the motor skills analogy is appropriate for visceral control situations that are more similar to traditional motor skill tasks, i.e. ones involving a specific magnitude as well as a directional component, and if this is so then the analogy is as yet untested. A possible exception is when a truly novel response is required. Increasing the blood flow in one area of the body relative to another may be such a response and it may not be coincidental that such a task has produced the most impressive evidence of acquisition.

REFERENCES

Adams, J. A. A closed-loop theory of motor learning. Journal of Motor Behaviour, 1971, 3, 111-149.

Bartlett, F. C. The measurement of human skill. Occupational Psychology, 1948, 22, 31-38.

Beatty, J. Similar effects of feedback signals and instructional information on EEG activity. Physiology and Behavior, 1972, 9, 151-154.

Benson, H., Shapiro, D., Tursky, B., & Schwartz, G. E. Decreases in systolic blood pressure through operant conditioning techniques in patients with essential hypertension. Science, 1971, 173, 740-752.

Bilodeau, E. A. Principles of skill acquisition. London: Academic Press, 1969.

Bilodeau, E. A., & Bilodeau, I. M. D. Variable frequency of knowledge of results and the learning of a simple skill. Journal of Experimental Psychology, 1958, 55, 603-612.

Blanchard, E. B., Scott, R. W., Young, L. D., & Edmundsen, E. D. Effect of knowledge of response on the self control of heart rate. Psychophysiology, 1974, 11, 251-264.

Brener, J. A general model of voluntary control applied to the phenomena of learned cardiovascular change. In P. A. Obrist, A. H. Black, J. Brener, & L. V. DiCara (Eds.), Cardiovascular psychophysiology. Chicago: Aldine, 1974.

Brener, J., & Kleinman, R. A. Learned control of decreases in systolic blood pressure. Nature, 1970, 226, 1063-1064.

Brener, J., Kleinman, R. A., & Goesling, W. J. The effects of different responses to augmented sensory feedback on the control of heart rate. Psychophysiology, 1969, 5, 510-516.

Boucard, C., & Corson, J. A. Heart rate regulation with success and failure signals. Psychophysiology, 1976, 13, 69-74.

Cook, M. R. Psychophysiology of peripheral vascular changes. In P. A. Obrist, A. H. Black, J. Brener, & L. V. DiCara (Eds.), Cardiovascular psychophysiology. Chicago: Aldine, 1974.

Engel, B. T. Operant conditioning of cardiac function: A status report. Psychophysiology, 1972, 9, 161-177.

Gatchel, R. J. Frequency of feedback and learned heart rate control. Journal of Experimental Psychology, 1974, 103, 274-283.

Gill, D. L. Knowledge of results, precision and motor skill acquisition. Journal of Motor Behaviour, 1975, 7, 191-198.

Greenfield, A. D. M. The circulation through the skin. In W. F. Hamilton (Ed.), The handbook of physiology. Section 2: Circulation. (Vol. 2). Washington, D. C.: American Physiological Society, 1963.

Johnston, D. W. Criterion level and instructional effects in the self control of heart rate. Biological Psychology, 1976, 4, 1-17.

Jones, M. B. Practice as a process of simplification. Psychological Review, 1962, 69, 274-294.

Lang, P. J. Acquisition of heart rate control: Method, theory and clinical implications. In D. C. Fowles (Ed.), Clinical applications of psychophysiology. New York: Columbia University Press, 1975.

Lang, P. J., Sroufe, L. A., & Hastings, J. E. Effects of feedback and instructional set on the control of cardiac rate variability. Journal of Experimental Psychology, 1967, 75, 425-431.

McCanne, T. R., & Sandman, C. A. Determinants of human operant heart rate conditioning: A systematic investigation of several methodological issues. Journal of Comparative and Physiological Psychology, 1975, 88, 609-618.

Roberts, A. H., Kewman, D. G., & MacDonald, H. Voluntary control of skin temperature: Unilateral changes using hypnosis and feedback. Journal of Abnormal Psychology, 1973, 82, 163-168.

Roberts, A. H., Schuler, J., Bacon, J. G., Zimmerman, R. C., & Patterson, R. Individual differences and autonomic control: Absorption, hypnotic susceptibility and unilateral control of skin temperature. Journal of Abnormal Psychology, 1975, 84, 272-279.

Schwartz, G. E. Toward a theory of voluntary control of response patterns in the cardiovascular system. In P. A. Obrist, A. H. Black, J. Brener, & L. V. DiCara (Eds.), Cardiovascular psychophysiology. Chicago: Aldine, 1974.

Sirota, A. D., Schwartz, G. E., & Shapiro, D. Voluntary control of human heart rate: Effect on reaction to aversive stimulation. Journal of Abnormal Psychology, 1976, 83, 261-267.

Stephens, J. H., Harris, A. H., & Brady, J. U. Large magnitude heart rate changes in subjects instructed to change their heart rates and given exteroceptive feedback. Psychophysiology, 1972, 9, 283-285.

Steptoe, A. Blood pressure control: A comparison of feedback and instructions using pulse wave velocity measurements. Psychophysiology, in press.

Steptoe, A., & Johnston, D. W. The control of blood pressure: A comparison of instructions and pulse wave velocity feedback. European Journal of Behaviour Modification, 1976, in press. (a)

Steptoe, A., & Johnston, D. W. The control of blood pressure with pulse wave velocity feedback. Journal of Psychosomatic Research, 1976, in press. (b)

Steptoe, A., Mathews, A., & Johnston, D. The learned control of differential temperature in the human earlobes: Preliminary study. Biological Psychology, 1974, 1, 237-242.

Surwit, R. S., Shapiro, D., & Feld, J. L. Digital temperature autoregulation and associated cardiovascular changes. Psychophysiology, 1976, 13, 242-248.

Taub, E., & Emurian, C. S. Feedback aided self regulation of skin temperature with a single feedback locus: 1. Acquisition and reversal training. Biofeedback and Self-Regulation, 1976, in press.

Thorndike, E. Human learning. New York: The Century Company, 1931.

Trowbridge, M. H., & Cason, H. An experimental study of Thorndike's theory of learning. Journal of General Psychology, 1932, 7, 245-258.

Wells, D. J. Large magnitude voluntary heart rate changes. Psychophysiology, 1973, 10, 260-269.

Young, L. D., & Blanchard, E. B. Effects of auditory feedback of varying information content on the self control of heart rate. Journal of General Psychology, 1974, 91, 61-68.

NOTES

1. A possible exception to this point and therefore a feedback situation that meets Adams' definition of a skill may be those studies that required the subjects to reduce heart rate variance by keeping a cardiatachometer driven display within some prescribed region, e.g. Lang, Scroufe, & Hastings (1967).

This research was supported by a grant from the Medical Research Council. I would like to thank Michael Gelder and Andrew Steptoe for their comments on an earlier version of this paper.

PAVLOVIAN AND OPERANT-BIOFEEDBACK PROCEDURES COMBINED PRODUCE LARGE-MAGNITUDE CONDITIONAL HEART-RATE DECELERATIONS

John J. Furedy
University of Toronto

There are some autonomically mediated changes such as heart-rate acceleration which have been shown by research of the last decade to be eminently affectable by operant-biofeedback procedures (e.g., Lang, 1974). However, as recent reviews of this sizeable body of research have clearly shown (e.g., Blanchard & Young, 1973), cardiac deceleration is quite refractory to biofeedback conditioning techniques. Specifically, biofeedback techniques which apply reinforcement or information from the outset in the operant-informational framework seem to be relatively ineffective in producing learned decelerations of anything over the order of 1-3 beats per minute (bpm), once proper controls for such factors as relaxation are instituted, and adequate samples of subjects (permitting statistical evaluation of the data) are tested.

As suggested by my title, through the use of more traditional Pavlovian methodology, we have succeeded in producing much larger, learned decelerations than those obtained with biofeedback. The first section will briefly present our specific procedures and the data obtained by these means. However, consistent with Popper's (1960) dictum that there is no "logic" of scientific discovery, our findings appear to have raised more questions than they have answered. Accordingly, in the second section of this paper, I shall indicate a number of puzzles and problems for various theories of conditioning and learning raised by our evidence.

THE DATA

As detailed elsewhere (Furedy & Poulos, 1976, Exp. I), a negative (from head up to down) body tilt of 90^0 produces a highly reliable, nonhabituating, fast-recruiting (over 70% of the total deceleration occurring from one beat to the next), and large-magnitude (over 30 bpm) cardiac deceleration (unconditioned response, UR). Also, we have reported that pairing a conventional tone as conditional stimulus (CS) with the tilt unconditional stimulus (US) in a Pavlovian paradigm produces a decelerative conditional response (CR) of about 5 bpm, but that the gap (in terms of magnitude between the UR and CR) is puzzlingly large as well as providing a CR only slightly larger than that obtained with conventional biofeedback techniques (Furedy & Poulos, 1976, Exp. II and Conclusion section).

Recently, however, we have developed a form of the Pavlovian preparation which produces a phasic decelerative CR of over 10 bpm, as shown in the mean performance of the 12 Experimental Group subjects (normal college students) in the left panel of Figure 1. The US is the same tilt as used before, but both the CS and the general procedures are rather unorthodox. Specifically the CS is a tape-recorded order to "drop," which, by instructions leads the subject to do the following things: drop his head back onto a pillow on the tilt table, but not so quickly as to jerk or tighten his neck muscles; imagine that he is actually being tilted back on the table (i.e., the US); to help him imagine this tilting, roll his eyes back as if being tilted while keeping his eyes open at all times; and to relax during the whole process. Obviously, this sort of CS requires more active participation by the subject as well as more subject-experimenter interaction than in the more conventional preparations such as human eyelid conditioning with their "neutral," passive, non-instructed CSs such as conventionally presented tones or lights. Finally, the experimenter monitors heart rate and whenever he sees short-latency and single-beat accelerations occurring either immediately after the CS or the US, he eliminates these by reminding the subject to stay relaxed at all times in order to avoid such accelerations.

Now, all this clearly involves more than the Pavlovian temporal pairing of a neutral CS with a decelerative US, and the cardiac behavior confirms that this is so. Specifically, in the performance of the 12 Control subjects shown in the left panel of Figure 1, there is a deceleration of some 4 bpm to the imaginational head-drop CS where, during acquisition, that CS has followed the US by 17 sec on the 16 US-CS trials (backward conditioning control). Nevertheless, as that panel of Figure 1 also clearly shows, and as confirmed by statistical analyses ($p < .005$), the operation

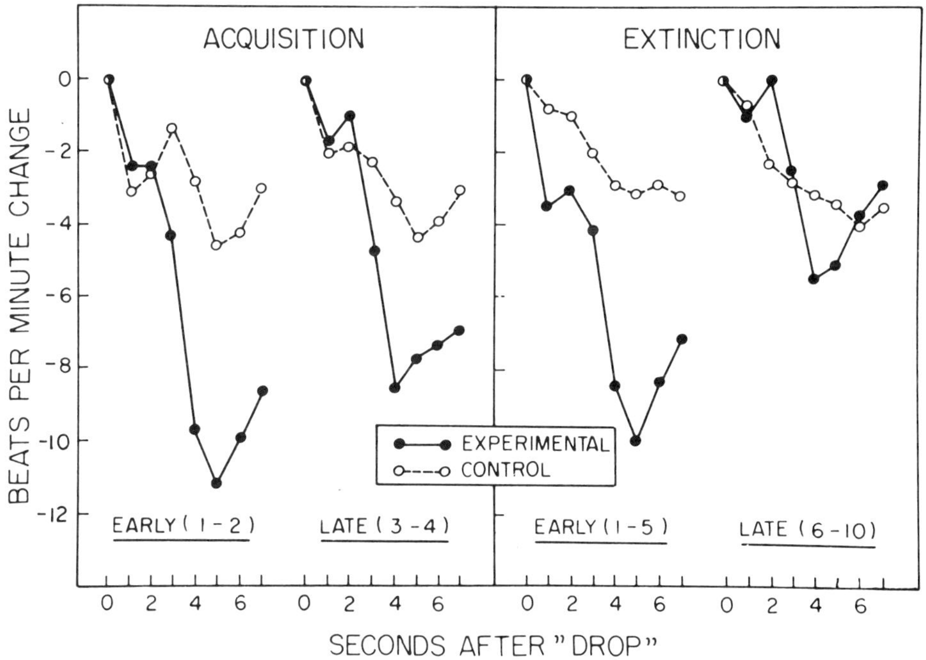

Figure 1. Mean heart-rate changes over seven seconds following initiation of the "drop" CS during acquisition and extinction of 12 Experimental and 12 Control subjects. (Acquisition data based on 4 CS-alone test trials interspersed among the 16 CS-US or US-CS tilt-paired training trials; Extinction data based on all ten CS-alone trials presented during Extinction.)

of pairing the CS with the US at a forward CS-US interval of .5 sec in the Experimental Group produced a much larger deceleration. Moreover, this CR resembled the UR, i.e., had a recruitment speed of the same order as the UR, i.e., approximately 70% of the deceleration occurring from one beat to the next. In addition, as shown in the right panel of Figure 1, the Pavlovian extinction procedure (i.e., presenting the CS in the absence of the US) produced, by the second block of 5 trials, decelerations of approximately the same magnitude in the Experimental and Control Groups. So, while the preparation is by no means simple, the results of this systematic experiment are clear. Imaginational Pavlovian conditioning of the form described produces large-magnitude, fast-recruitment decelerations for which the Pavlovian pairing operation is seen to be a necessary component, and which decline to control levels when Pavlovian extinction is introduced (Figure 1).

It now seemed that the magnitude and form of these Pavlovian based decelerations, which renders them readily distinguishable from the background of normal sinus arrhythmic variations (approximately 5 bpm) in cardiac rate (allowing record readers to discriminate between CS-elicited responding and such arrhythmic variations on over 80% of trials), would facilitate the application of operant or Skinnerian shaping methods. In this integration of the Pavlovian approach with operant-biofeedback techniques, the method was to first train subjects in Pavlovian acquisition trials (CS-tilt US pairings), and then present a period which involved both a Pavlovian extinction procedure (no tilts) and verbal graded reinforcement ("good," "very good," and "excellent") contingent on decelerative CR magnitude with the CS considered as a discriminative stimulus (S^D) in the presence of which the decelerative response was reinforced. Following the principles of operant shaping, the reinforcement criterion was shifted according to performance, with the experimenter aiming to maintain an 80% schedule of "good" or better during the (at least) 15 trials of this discrete-trial operant-shaping procedure. This, then, is a form of feedback which differs from conventional procedures only inasmuch as it is introduced following a Pavlovian training procedure.

The results of these preliminary studies suggest that the operant-feedback procedure indeed produces strong decelerative learning. Although carried out during what constitutes Pavlovian extinction a procedure which in itself causes the decelerative CR to return to control levels (see Figure 1, right panel), the institution of the operant shaping procedure not only prevented any decrease in CR magnitude, but it actually resulted in increases of over 40%. Decelerations of up to 40 bpm were obtained at the end of Pavlovian extinction by operant shaping in one young (12 years) subject.

More systematic evidence for the efficacy of operant shaping is also available from an experiment where Pavlovian and operant methods were simultaneously introduced by employing a longer (5 sec) CS-US interval. A separate experiment has shown that lengthening the CS-US interval produces significantly lower ($p < .05$) levels of decelerative CRs (about 7 bpm as compared to the levels shown in Figure 1), but the longer CS-US interval allows both measurement and contingent reinforcement of the CR on all paired CS-US trials, since there is no confounding by the UR until at least 7 sec following CS onset. In the simultaneous Pavlovian-operant arrangement, two groups of 5 subjects were run for 20 CS-US trials and given graded verbal reinforcement as described above. However, for the "finely-shaped" group, the reinforcement criterion was shifted up or down by 1 bpm according to performance on the immediately preceding trial; for the "crudely-shaped" group, the criterion was set on the basis of initial performance, although reinforcement was still contingent in the sense that only decelerations meeting the criterion were reinforced. Despite the small sample size involved, the finely-shaped group performed significantly, $p < .01$., better than the crudely-shaped group in the sense that the former group's decelerations increased in magnitude over trials, in contrast to the slight decrease in decelerations of the latter group.

THEORETICAL PROBLEMS

In this section of the paper, I would like to briefly draw your attention to results obtained with the tilt conditioning preparation which seem either not subsumed by or in direct contradiction to most major theories of classical and operant conditioning. One symptom of this state of affairs, especially as regards the Pavlovian phase of our research, is that the development of the effective conditioning preparation described above was preceded by a long, tortuous, and certainly not deductively-directed assay of a wide variety of procedures in over a dozen experiments. The results of these experiments, including that described in detail above, and some later studies, can be classified (albeit crudely) into the following levels of attained decelerative CR conditioning: "none" (no significant learned deceleration), "some" (4 or 5 bpm deceleration, as, e.g., in Experiment II of Furedy & Poulos, 1976), and "substantial" (about 10 bpm deceleration).

Thorndike's Belongingness Principle

This principle, described as one of Thorndike's "minor concessions to the gestalt psychologists" (Hilgard & Bower, 1966, p. 28), refers to the importance of the relationship between the CS and US (or, more precisely, the UR) in determining the strength of conditioning. Perhaps because of vagueness in specifying what constitutes a close relationship, and hence the inability to predict relative degrees of "belongingness," most other major theories of classical conditioning have little to say about this principle. Thus, for example, cognitive-contingency theories (cf., e.g., Dawson & Furedy, 1976; Rescorla, 1967), the newer Wagner-Rescorla model (cf., e.g., Wagner & Rescorla, 1972), the much older general stimulus substitution framework (cf., e.g., Furedy & Poulos, 1976; Jones, 1962), the strict S-R contiguity-reinforcement position (cf., e.g., Furedy & Schiffmann, 1974), and the instrumental preparatory-adaptive interpretation (e.g., Perkins, 1968) all pay scant attention to belongingness. Yet, since none of these latter theories seemed to be helpful to use in our specific dilemna of the tremendous gap between the 4-bpm CR and the 35-bpm UR, it was to Thorndike that we first turned. However, the results of these initial efforts suggested that perhaps the other theories were right to ignore the belongingness principle. Specifically, when we maximized belongingness, at least in terms of physical CS:US similarity by using a "short" (10^0) tilt combined with a tone as the compound CS, the levels of conditioning obtained were not above the "some" levels obtained with the tone-alone CS. Perhaps the head-drop component of the compound CS producing the "substantial" CR levels described above can be considered to increase the Thorndikian belongingness factor, although the definition of belongingness is so loose and vague that this sort of assertion cannot be made on non-circular grounds. In any case, as noted in the next section, even this form of belongingness was not, in itself, sufficient to produce a significant improvement in learned deceleration.

Cognitive Involvement

The notion that instructions to imagine the US when receiving the CS would facilitate conditioning is not only not derivable from such non-cognitive theories as the S-R contiguity-reinforcement position, but it is also treated as irrelevant by the currently popular cognitive-contingency account. This account does stress a cognitive factor, but that factor has to do with knowledge or awareness of the contingency or temporal relationship between the CS and US. That sort of contingency, of course, is patently obvious to the dullest of our subjects, so that arguments about the precise relationship between contingency awareness and amount of conditioning (cf., e.g., Dawson & Furedy, 1976) are beside the point here. The cognitive involvement which seems relevant is that of imagining the US, and an added dimension of complexity is introduced by our finding that, as in the case of belongingness, cognitive involvement per se was not sufficient to produce improvement: Experiments which combined the tone with efforts to imagine the tilt US at CS onset yielded no increase in decelerative CR levels. It was only when cognitive involvement was combined with the "more belonging" head-drop CS that the decelerative CR reached the "substantial" level. Yet, as indicated in the previous section, we also have evidence that the imagining-belongingness interaction is bidirectional, inasmuch as in a recent experiment which compared conditioning between head-drop CS groups who were and were not presented with the imagine-the-US instructions, the performance of the latter group was significantly, $p < .05$, inferior to that of the former group.

Stimulus Salience

Pavlov's initial formulations suggested that CS salience increased conditioning, and more recent formulations such as the Wagner-Rescorla (1972) model have also stressed the importance of increasing CS salience relative to the background. Pavlov himself, of course, restricted his dog's movements and strove to eliminate stimulation unrelated to the US and CS in order to increase stimulus salience. Following this principle, we initially blindfolded our subjects in order to make both the US (body tilt) and, more importantly, the CS (tone) "stand out" from the background. However, the stimulus salience principle does not just appear to be irrelevant for our outcomes, but it actually contradicts them. Blindfolded subjects showed no conditioning, whereas, as we have indicated (e.g., Furedy & Poulos, 1976) the increase of external, CS-irrelevant background stimulation by removing the blindfold increased decelerative conditioning to some 4 bpm.

Backward Conditioning and Contiguity-Reinforcement Theory

According to Jones' strict S-R contiguity-reinforcement position, which had received some direct (e.g., Furedy, 1969) and indirect (e.g., Furedy & Schiffmann, 1974) support from previous work with other autonomic Pavlovian conditioning preparations, some or even optimal early levels of conditioning should be attained if the CS were placed about 2 sec following US onset during training trials. As detailed elsewhere (Furedy & Poulos, 1976), this prediction follows from the relatively long onset latency of the decelerative UR (over 2 sec), and the assumption of the Jones position that what is important for optimal conditioning is not the CS-US but the CS-UR interval. We tested this prediction, but found to our chagrin that this backward US-CS arrangement with tone as CS not only failed to produce the 4-bpm level obtained previously (Furedy & Poulos, 1976, Experiment II), but actually yielded no evidence for any learned deceleration whatsoever.

Adding Affect to the US

After the first couple of tilt trials (which are rather startling to the subjects), most subjects report that the tilt US is neither pleasant nor unpleasant. Now, it is a fairly well documented empirical generalization that even if a US elicits entirely satisfactory URs, for example, in the case of light as the US and pupillary constriction as the UR (cf., e.g., Young, 1965), conditioning cannot be obtained, presumably because the US is affectively neutral. Confirmation of this affect interpretation comes from the fact that if a shock is used as the US, then conditioning is readily obtained (cf. also Bruner, 1969, for another response system). In addition, such theories of Pavlovian conditioning as the instrumental interpretation (Perkins, 1968) would also seem to require that the US have affect, because otherwise the "preparatory" CR is not adequately reinforced by its modification of an affectively neutral US. One theoretical problem presented by our results, especially in the case of the substantial form of the conditioning preparation is why we should have been so successful without having to add affect to our US. Moreover, when we did an experiment in which affect was added by presenting a shock concurrently with the tilt US, we found that the addition of at least this sort of negative affect, if anything, reduced conditioning.

Indeed, considering the relative neutrality of our tilt US, the fact that we have been able to obtain any decelerative conditioning at all would seem to be in direct contradiction to the instrumental interpretation of classical conditioning. In its various forms (cf., e.g., the preparatory-response theory of Perkins, 1968), this position has held an extensive and prolonged sway in the minds of many theorists. Essentially, the position is that what appears to be a classically conditioned CR is learned only because the CR is "instrumental" in modifying the US (e.g., Pavlov's dog learns to salivate to the bell because salivation makes the food taste better). In other forms of human autonomic classical conditioning such as that of the GSR with shock as the US, I have reported data to contradict this position--for example, in experiments wherein the relationship between anticipatory GSR CRs and the rated intensity of the immediately following shock was examined and found, contrary to the theory, not to be negative (e.g., Furedy, 1970). However, in the case of the present decelerative Pavlovian preparation, it would seem that no such additional data based on US ratings are necessary for the contradiction to become apparent between our results and the instrumental interpretation. It is hard even to speculate about the instrumental preparatory-adaptive mechanism through which the decelerative CR might be learned. In the classical Pavlovian case, there is at least a plausible connection between the (taste of the food) US and the (salivary) CR, although this is not, of course, to say that this is, in fact, the mechanism of learning. But what is the analogous "instrumental" connection between the (tilt) US and the (decelerative) CR in the present preparation? Clearly a stimulus substitution position accounts far more easily for our results which, from an instrumental interpretation, appear paradoxical.

The Distinction Between Operants and Respondents

Skinner's (1938) operant-respondent distinction in terms of the skeletal-autonomic distinction has, of course, been brought into serious question during the last decade. But I think it is fair to say that one aspect of his dichotomy which remains relatively uncriticized is the notion that, in general, contingent reinforcement will be more effective in the learning of emitted operants (e.g., bar pressing for food) than in the learning of elicited respondents (e.g., salivation learned to bell through pairing of bell with food). The strong version of this position, of course, is that elicited respondents are totally unaffected by contingent reinforcement, which can operate only on the learning of emitted operants. However, there is no need to hold to the strong version for one to see the paradox inherent in the present results when viewed in the context of previous operant-biofeedback based research on cardiac deceleration (e.g., Blanchard & Young, 1973). Briefly, it appears that whereas contingent reinforcement (or feedback) has been relatively ineffective in promoting the learning of spontaneous emitted "operant" decelerations (i.e., the traditional biofeedback paradigm), our results indicate that such reinforcement is effective in promoting the learning of nonspontaneous, CS-elicited "respondent" decelerations. Moreover, the latter class of deceleration responses seem highly sensitive to relatively fine differences in shaping procedures, as indicated by the significant difference alluded to at the end of the Data section between the group for which the respondent was "finely shaped" and that for which the respondent was "crudely shaped."

In summary, then, we appear to have succeeded in discovering how to teach the human heart to produce large-magnitude decelerations. The "logic" of this discovery, however, appears to have as unstable a foundation as do many of our current ideas concerning the nature of classical and operant conditioning.

IMPLICATIONS

The apparent gravity of the theoretical problems raised by our two-stage procedure should not obscure the procedure's potential for improving both our understanding and control of human cardiovascular function. In this section I shall try to sketch, in brief outline, the directions that future work may take.

First, on the understanding or basic-research side of the coin, there is the obvious point that the initial, Pavlovian, stage of the procedure, despite (or perhaps because of) its operational and theoretical complexity, offers a human Pavlovian heart-rate CR of greater magnitude and clarity than has been produced by procedures employing more conventional USs such as shocks. Hence we may now hope to explore the empirical laws of human Pavlovian heart-rate conditioning with greater power than has been possible with conventional Pavlovian procedures (cf. also Furedy & Poulos, 1976, pp. 94-95).

Similarly, the second operant-feedback part of the present procedure may allow a finer-grain elucidation of the principles of operant conditioning (and perhaps of complex motor-skills learning), as they apply to human heart-rate deceleration. The reason for this optimism is again that although the operational and empirical basis of our learned decelerations appear extremely complex, it is nevertheless clear that we now have a response of adequately large magnitude which should lend itself to easier experimental manipulation than has been possible with the smaller human decelerations produced by conventional biofeedback-alone-based procedures (cf., e.g., Blanchard & Young, 1973).

The second set of implications relates to the behavioral control of cardiovascular function. At least for cardiac deceleration, the raising of potential applications has been premature, since the behavioral control exerted by conventional biofeedback methods has been unimpressive (c.f., e.g., Blanchard & Young, 1973). The present two-stage Pavlovian-feedback method, however, makes it more sensible to consider applications, since at least in the laboratory the decelerative control achieved appears more adequate.

One point bearing emphasis, however, is that in contrast to most conventional biofeedback methods, the potential application of the present technique is to the control of phasic rather than tonic functions. Specifically, and as detailed elsewhere (Furedy & Poulos, 1976, pp. 92-94), the ultimate applied goal is that of modifying phasic maladaptive increases in cardiovascular output (which, for example, are part of the "fight-or-flight" reflex), rather than trying to teach someone to lower, for example, his tonic resting heart rate from 80 to 70 beats. It should be clear that this sort of phasic behavioral control is of at least as much potential clinical relevance as the tonic sort, since cardiac dysfunctions like paroxysmal atrial tachycardia (PAT) and angina pectoris episodes are phasic at least at the symptomatic level. On the other hand, the claim that the present behavioral control technique is in fact applicable to such dysfunctions requires a number of empirically testable, but as yet untested, assumptions, not the least important of which being the assumption that what has worked for normal subjects will also work for cardiac patients. Evidence for this sort of transfer involving the (deceleration-inducing) driving reflex to PAT patients has been reported by Wildenthal, Leshin, Atkins, & Skelton (1975). Encouraging also is the fact that the present Pavlovian-feedback form of behavioral control produces not only the heart rate decelerations reported here, but also parallel increases in the T-wave component of the electrocardiogram. It appears, therefore, that the imaginational form of conditioning used here induces both parasympathetic activation as well as sympathetic withdrawal at least in our normal population of subjects. If clinical tests indicate that these self-controlled ANS changes can be made readily available to patients through the imaginational-Pavlovian-feedback training method employed here, then, of course, the potential clinical implications sketched in here will have been actualized. My guess is that the extent of that actualization will depend on our ability to increase our understanding of the complex and inter-related roles of psychological mechanisms of (imaginational) learning and physiological mechanisms of cardiovascular function.

REFERENCES

Blanchard, E. B., & Young, L. D. Self-control and cardiac functioning: A promise as yet unfulfilled. Psychological Bulletin, 1973, 79, 145-163.

Bruner, A. Reinforcement strengths in classical conditioning of leg flexing, freezing and heart rate in cats. Conditioned Reflex, 1969, 4, 24-31.

Dawson, M. E., & Furedy, J. J. The role of awareness in human differential autonomic classical conditioning: The necessary-gate hypothesis. Psychophysiology, 1976, 13, 50-53.

Furedy, J. J. Test of the preparatory-adaptive-response interpretation of aversive classical autonomic conditioning. Journal of Experimental Psychology, 1970, 84, 301-307.

Furedy, J. J., & Poulos, C. X. Heart-rate decelerative Pavlovian conditioning with tilt as UCS: Towards behavioural control of cardiac dysfunction. Biological Psychology, 1976, in press.

Furedy, J. J., & Schiffmann, K. Interrelationships between human classical differential electrodermal conditioning, orienting reaction, responsivity, and awareness of stimulus contingencies. Psychophysiology, 1974, 11, 58-67.

Hilgard, E. R., & Bower, G. H. Theories of learning. New York: Appleton, 1966.

Jones, J. E. Contiguity and reinforcement in relation to CS-UCS intervals in classical aversive conditioning. Psychological Review, 1962, 69, 176-186.

Lang, P. J. Cardiovascular self-control: Determinants of performance and clinical implications. Paper presented in Symposium on "Biofeedback Conditioning," 3rd Congress of the International College of Psychosomatic Medicine, Rome, September 1975.

Perkins, C. C., Jr. An analysis of the concept of reinforcement. Psychological Review, 1968, 75, 155-172.

Popper, K. R. The logic of scientific discovery. London: Hutchinson & Co., 1960.

Rescorla, R. A. Pavlovian conditioning and its proper control procedures. Psychological Review, 1967, 74, 71-80.

Skinner, B. F. The behavior of organisms: An experimental analysis. New York: Appleton, 1938.

Wagner, A. R., & Rescorla, R. A. Inhibition in Pavlovian conditioning: Application of a theory. In R. A. Boakes & M. S. Halliday (Eds.), Inhibition and learning. New York: Academic Press, 1972.

Wildenthal, K., Leshin, S. J., Atkins, J. M., & Skelton, C. L. The diving reflex used to treat paroxysmal atrial tachycardia. Lancet, January 4, 1975, 12.14.

Young, F. A. Classical conditioning of autonomic functions. In W. F. Prokasy (Ed.), Classical conditioning: A symposium. New York: Appleton-Century-Crofts, 1965.

NOTE

This research was supported by Medical Research Council Grant MA-4889 of Canada. In the general area of investigation, I have been helped by the work of the following over the past four years: F. Carusi, S. Ginsberg, R. Heselgrave, F. Klajner, L. MacKay, C. Poulos, and K. Schiffmann. The formulation of the ideas expressed in the present paper has especially benefited from discussions with and comments from F. Klajner.

BLOOD PRESSURE CONTROL WITH PULSE WAVE VELOCITY FEEDBACK: METHODS OF ANALYSIS AND TRAINING

Andrew Steptoe
Department of Psychiatry, Oxford University
Warneford Hospital, Oxford

A number of reports concerning the voluntary control of blood pressure have appeared in recent years and many advances in the understanding of this phenomenon have been made (Shapiro, Schwartz, & Tursky, 1972; Schwartz, 1972; Brener, 1974). But a detailed examination of some aspects of this control is hampered by difficulties in monitoring blood pressure continuously and in producing a flexible feedback system. This paper describes experience with pulse wave velocity as a measure of blood pressure change and as a tool for investigating cardiovascular control.

The theoretical basis for the use of pulse wave velocity as an index of blood pressure change has been presented elsewhere (Gribbin, Steptoe, & Sleight, 1976). Pulse wave velocity, which is the rate of propagation of the pressure pulse through the arterial tree, is inversely related to arterial distensibility. This latter can be expressed as the change in volume of the vessel (ΔV) consequent on an alteration in pressure (ΔP). Since the relation between ΔP and ΔV is linear over the physiological range, changes in pulse wave velocity indicate arterial pressure fluctuations. Such a function has been demonstrated in both bench and clinical experiments (Gribbin et al., 1976).

As a feedback measure, pulse wave velocity offers distinct advantages over existing methods of continuous pressure monitoring. Since it does not require periodic or sustained limb occlusion, recordings can be carried out for extended intervals without discomfort. In the experiments to be described here, pulse wave velocity was estimated by detecting the

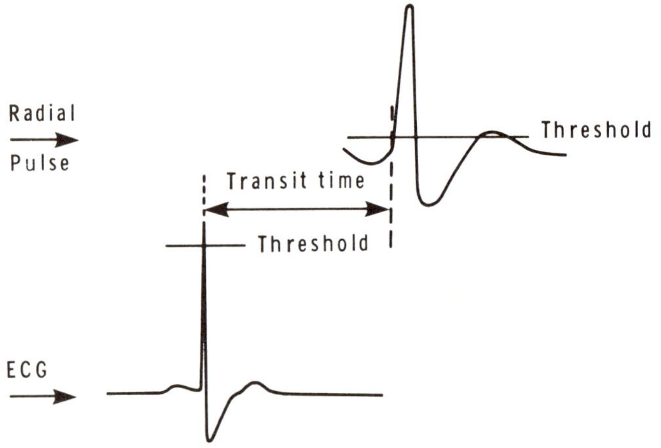

Figure 1. Triggering thresholds for the determination of Transit Time.

interval between the EKG and the radial pulse at the points on the waveforms shown in Figure 1. The resulting transit time is inversely related to mean arterial pressure (Steptoe, Smulyan, & Gribbin, 1976). Transit time may be monitored on every cardiac cycle so a beat to beat analogue display of pressure changes can be provided. It is therefore possible to give subjects a greater amount of information about their blood pressure than with binary feedback systems. The feedback displays that have been used are of the type outlined in Figure 2. The length of the horizontal line is determined on each cardiac cycle by the transit time, while the vertical and stars are part of a binary system for rewarding changes in pressure.

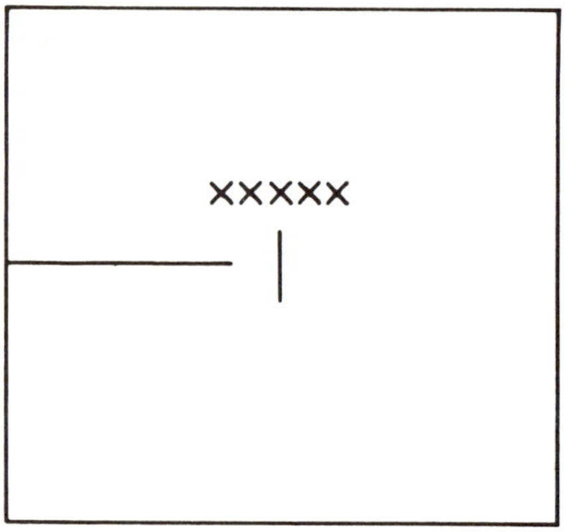

Figure 2. Transit time feedback display.

A major methodological issue in cardiovascular self control is the type of assessment to be employed. Blood pressure changes have commonly been measured from the initial baseline level, but such an analysis cannot distinguish modifications due to feedback and experimental contingencies from those consequent on adaptation or prolonged immobility in the laboratory. An alternative method of analysis, in which modifications are measured from a running baseline sampled throughout sessions, has been suggested (Schwartz, 1974). The two types of assessment may lead to rather different conclusions, as can be seen in the following data.

These results are taken from a study in which subjects were instructed to raise or lower blood pressure with the assistance of transit time feedback (Steptoe & Johnston, 1976a). The scores for the eight feedback trials expressed as changes from the initial level can be seen in Figure 3. Since transit time is inversely related to arterial pressure, an increase in transit time indicates a fall in pressure. It is evident that subjects attempting to lower blood pressure show a gradual lengthening of transit time over trials, while pressure is maintained near the initial

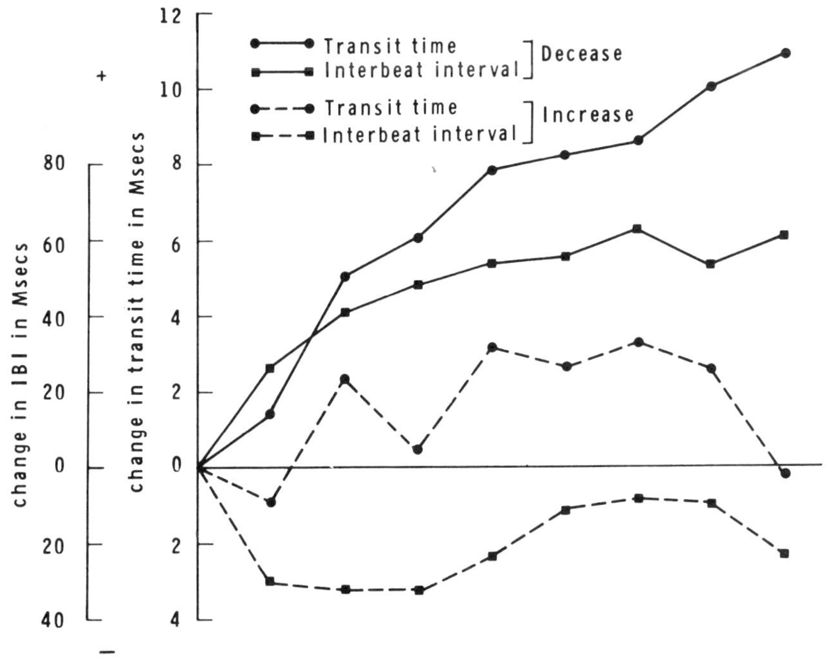

Figure 3. Transit time and Interbeat interval during trials, expressed as changes from the initial baseline.

level in the increase condition. This pattern of results is similar to that observed in experiments on systolic pressure control (Shapiro, Tursky, Gershon, & Stern, 1969; Fey & Lindholm, 1976). The modifications in transit time are associated with alterations in interbeat interval, as subjects lowering pressure tend to produce a reduction in heart rate.

However, assessment of cardiovascular activity during the rests separating each trial suggests that transit time and interbeat interval do not remain constant but gradually increase over the session. These data can be examined in Figure 4; the lengthening of transit time over the running baseline, indicating a fall in arterial pressure, shows that much of the apparent control in the decrease condition is due to tonic fluctuation. When modifications are analyzed from the running baseline, transit time changes are actually greater in the Increase condition.

The analysis from the initial baseline therefore favors the experimental condition which is compatible with the cardiovascular fluctuations that occur nonspecifically in the laboratory setting. In this experiment, reductions in cardiovascular arousal have thereby been inflated. However,

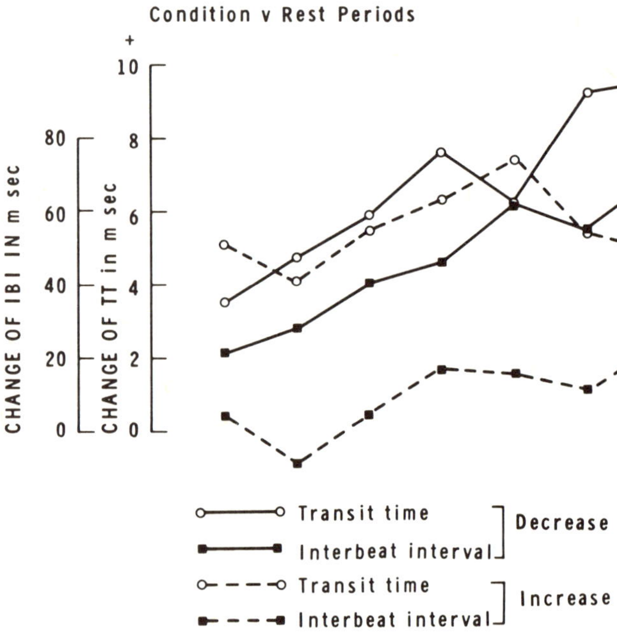

Figure 4. Transit time and interbeat interval during intertrial rests expressed as change from the initial baseline.

assessment from a running baseline punctuating trials is also contaminated by the fact that intertrial rests may not be immune to the influence of experimental contingencies. Thus in Figure 4, transit times in the increase and decrease conditions diverge late in training. Both types of analysis may be necessary for full understanding of the nature and source of modifications.

A second issue which has been examined using pulse wave velocity feedback is the influence of the instructions given to subjects attempting pressure control. In studies reported in the literature, subjects have been told either to control the "physiological responses" associated with the exteroceptive feedback, or to control blood pressure itself (Shapiro et al., 1972; Brener & Kleinman, 1970; Fey & Lindholm, 1975). In both cases, cardiovascular modifications may occur as a function of the instructions alone, perhaps through the initiation of greater and lesser degrees of physical activity, or through the production of sensory states which have been associated with high and low pressure in the past. Previous data suggest that even with non-directive instructions, normotensives and hypertensives can make significant modifications in pressure without the aid of exteroceptive feedback, although the evidence is not entirely consistent (Redmond, Gaylor, McDonald, & Shapiro, 1974; Brener, 1974; Steptoe & Johnston, 1976b). An instructional effect of this type will be modulated by the subjects' physiological sophistication, his general knowledge of cardiovascular function, and the incentives provided.

A detailed analysis of this problem was therefore undertaken in a study in which modifications with pulse wave velocity feedback were compared with those produced on instruction alone (Steptoe, 1976). The 20 subjects in an instruction group (Group 1) were told to increase or decrease blood pressure during trials, and they were given no knowledge of success or assistance with strategies. They were however told to attempt "psychological" control, and not to alter their physical activity or breathing pattern. It should also be noted that these subjects were informed that they would be paid according to their success at pressure control, although they did not of course discover their precise earnings until the end of the study.

A further 20 subjects attempted control with similar instructions but with the aid of pulse wave velocity feedback during trials (Group F). In addition to the analogue visual display and binary reward schedule (Figure 2), they also received limited auditory feedback. Ten subjects in each group were instructed to raise and ten to lower pressure; no subjects attempted both increases and decreases.

The four experimental sessions were divided into 4 minute trials separated by 2 minute rests, during which physiological monitoring was continued. The overall trial scores, assessed as change from the initial baseline, are shown in Figure 5. It is evident that both groups discriminate successfully between increase and decrease conditions by producing the appropriate transit time modifications. Furthermore, in both Group F and Group I there is a gradual divergence between increase and decrease conditions, and this is statistically significant. Thus even without exteroceptive feedback, subjects show a consistent pattern of pressure control, and indeed an improvement as "training" proceeds. The modifications in Group I are probably greater than those obscrved by Brener (1974) in instruction only conditions; the difference may be related to the strong incentives for pressure change in the present study. This finding emphasizes the importance of testing feedback against equivalently instructed no feedback conditions.

As far as the comparison of feedback and instructions is concerned,

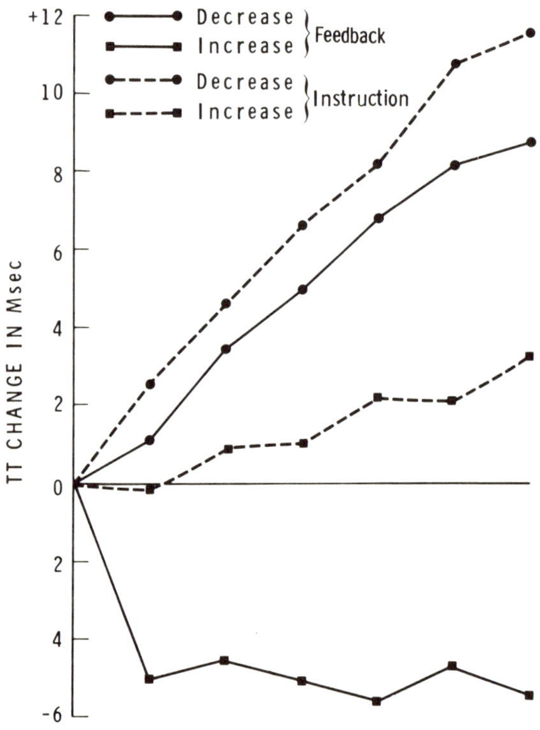

Figure 5. Transit time: Overall trial scores averaged over sessions expressed as change from initial baseline.

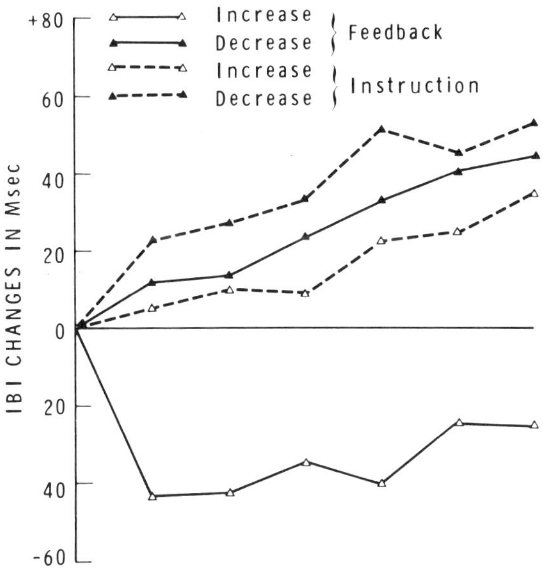

Figure 6. Mean change of Interbeat Interval from initial baseline: Overall feedback trial scores averaged over sessions.

a difference is apparent in the increase condition only. In this condition, Group I shows an attenuated reduction in pressure whereas an elevation above the initial level is seen in Group F. This difference attains borderline significance ($F(1,18) = 4.05$, $p < .06$). In contrast, similar and statistically indistinguishable lengthenings of transit time are found in the two decrease groups.

The interbeat interval data will briefly be described, since they reveal some interesting points. The means for the 6 feedback trials are shown in Figure 6; there are distinct differences from the transit time data, although the same pattern of results is observed. Both groups exhibit a separation between increase and decrease conditions, but this is seen from trial 1 onwards and does not enlarge over the session. Thus there is no progressive divergence between direction conditions equivalent to that found in transit time (Figure 5). The implication is that transit time is being modified to some extent independently of interbeat interval. But this limited specificity of control is not a feedback effect, since it is apparent in Group I as well as Group F. It must therefore be concluded that temporally independent responses in the variable associated with exteroceptive feedback cannot necessarily be considered indications of the functional significance of that feedback.

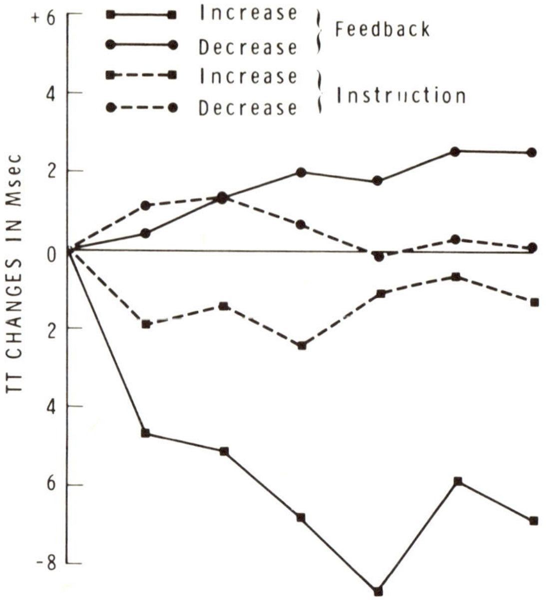

Figure 7. Transit time: Rest/Trial scores averaged over sessions.

The data that have been described thus far are overall trial scores assessed from the initial level. When changes from the running baseline are examined, a rather different pattern is observed. The transit time data averaged over all four sessions can be seen in Figure 7. As might be expected, the decreases are severely curtailed, since much of the lengthening of transit time in the overall trial scores is due to alterations over the running baseline. Modifications in Group F are now superior not only in increase but also in the decrease condition, and this is supported statistically ($F(1,36) = 7.71$, $p < .01$). It appears that while enhanced pressure elevation with feedback is a robust phenomenon, greater reductions are only manifest when assessment is made from the level actually present at the onset of each trial. Although subjects in Group I continue to discriminate between increase and decrease, the modifications are small and vary little over trials. When the mean changes in each session are examined (Figure 8), improved control over sessions is shown by Group F, particularly in the increase condition.

These results suggest that the distinction between pressure control with instructions and feedback is intimately related to the type of analysis undertaken. Greater reductions with feedback are apparent only from the running baseline, overall trial scores being similar in the two groups. The reason for this is that the levels of cardiovascular activity vary over

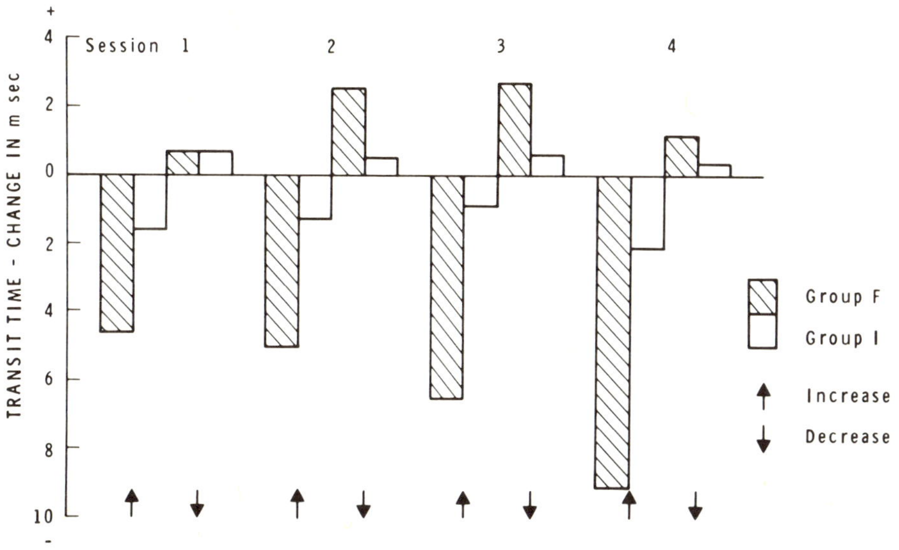

Figure 8. Transit time: Rest/Trial scores averaged over trials.

the running baseline, not only as a function of the length of time in the laboratory, but also according to experimental conditions. In Figure 9, the group curves for alterations in the running baseline are shown. Group I in the decrease condition exhibits a greater lengthening of transit time over rests than Group F, countering their reduced rest/trial scores.

This difference in pressure alterations over the running baseline raises the possibility that although the instructions and contingencies operating on the two groups are similar, there are other features of the experimental setting which are not equivalent. It should be noted that while feedback subjects were attending to a constantly varying visual display, those in Group I were sitting in a quiet laboratory with very little stimulation. The conditions under which feedback was provided had arousing qualities which countered the optimum milieu for pressure decreases. Group I thus produced a greater nonspecific reduction in cardiovascular activity, obscuring the comparison of feedback with instructions.

If this explanation is correct, it is probable that a more appropriate instructional condition is one in which subjects attempt pressure modifications in the presence of displays and stimulation equivalent to that received in feedback training. Hence the noncontingent influences on cardiovascular function should be equated across groups. Such a comparison was carried out in a further experiment with 20 subjects. Half the people

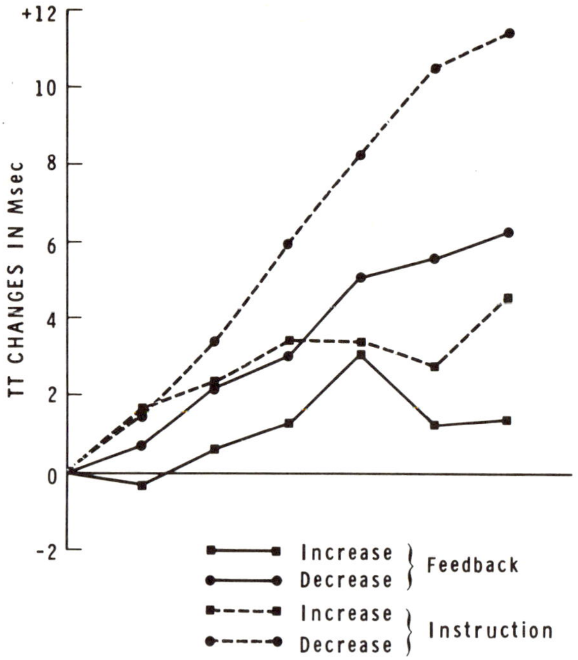

Figure 9. Transit time during intertrial rests; change scores from initial baseline.

were instructed to lower pressure with the aid of the feedback display used before. The other ten subjects (Group T) were instructed to lower pressure without any assistance, in the same way as Group I in the previous study. However they were simultaneously presented with a simulated display of the type outlined in Figure 2. It is important to point out that Group T did not believe that the display referenced arterial pressure, so that this was not a "pseudofeedback" comparison. The design also differed from the study by Brener and Kleinman (1970) in which the control group was told to remain vigilant to the display without attempting pressure modifications.

Figure 10 shows the overall trial effects averaged across the two experimental sessions. The greater lengthening of transit time in Group F, representing a larger fall in arterial pressure, is confirmed by the Group by Trial interaction ($F(5,90) = 2.58$, $p < .05$).

It can therefore be concluded that when pressure reductions in feedback and instruction groups are attempted under similar experimental

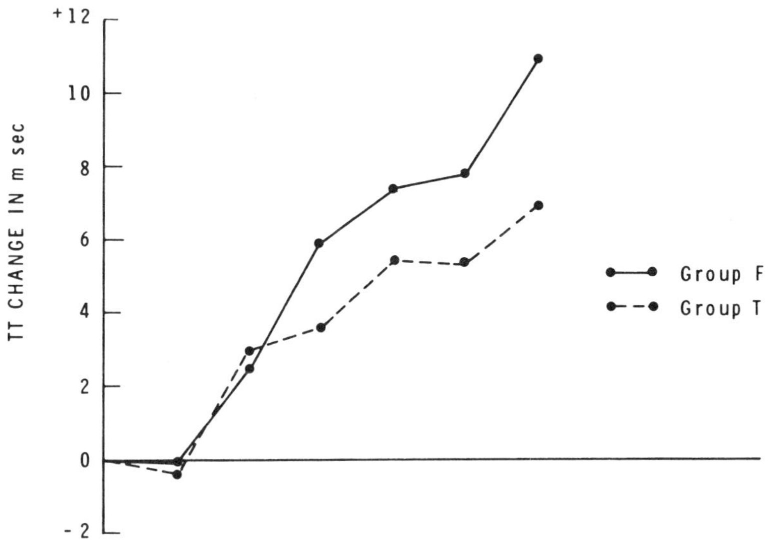

Figure 10. Transit time: Overall trial scores for Feedback and Instruction (T) groups averaged over sessions.

conditions, the modifications are greater in the former. But in a quiet, relaxing environment, substantial decreases occur regardless of the presence of exteroceptive feedback. So it is not surprising that when subjects are asked to lower pressure in an undistracting laboratory setting, feedback training has failed to produce notable effects over and above those shown by instructional and relaxation procedures. Yet this may not be because pressure feedback is ineffective, but because the training milieu is inappropriate. It can be argued that the superiority of feedback control in arousing surroundings should be exploited, by explicitly training subjects who are simultaneously occupied with other tasks. As pressure will thereby be elevated above resting levels, a wider scope for feedback effects will be available. Furthermore, such control is closer to that required in a clinical or applied program. An effective training procedure must lead to pressure control outside the laboratory in the subject's every day life, when preoccupation with other matters is inevitable. A step towards mimicking these conditions can be made by introducing distracting tasks, and this may also help to evaluate the relation of feedback control to other skills and other forms of learning.

REFERENCES

Brener, J., & Kleinman, R. A. Learned control of decreases in systolic pressure. Nature, 1970, 226, 1063-1064.

Brener, J. A general model of voluntary control applied to the phenomena of learned cardiovascular change. In P. A. Obrist, A. H. Black, J. Brener, & L. V. DiCara (Eds.), Cardiovascular psychophysiology. Chicago: Aldine Atherton, 1974.

Fey, S. G., & Lindholm, E. Systolic blood pressure and heart rate changes during three sessions involving biofeedback or no feedback. Psychophysiology, 1975, 12, 513-519.

Gribbin, B., Steptoe, A., & Sleight, P. Pulse wave velocity as a measure of blood pressure change. Psychophysiology, 1976, 13, 86-90.

Redmond, D. P., Gaylor, M. S., McDonald, R. H., & Shapiro, A. P. Verbal instructions and relaxation in hypertension. Psychosomatic Medicine, 1974, 36, 285-297.

Schwartz, G. E. Voluntary control of human cardiovascular integration and differentiation. Science, 1972, 175, 90-93.

Schwartz, G. E. Toward a theory of voluntary control of response patterns in the cardiovascular system. In P. A. Obrist, A. H. Black, J. Brener, & L. V. DiCara (Eds.), Cardiovascular psychophysiology. Chicago: Aldine Atherton, 1974.

Shapiro, D., Tursky, B., Gershon, E., & Stern, M. Effects of feedback and reinforcement on the control of human systolic blood pressure. Science, 1969, 163, 588-589.

Shapiro, D., Schwartz, G. E., & Tursky, B. Control of diastolic blood pressure in man by feedback and reinforcement. Psychophysiology, 1972, 9, 296-306.

Steptoe, A. Blood pressure control: A comparison of feedback and instructions using pulse wave velocity measurements. Psychophysiology, 1976, in press.

Steptoe, A., & Johnston, D. The control of blood pressure using pulse wave velocity feedback. Journal of Psychosomatic Research, 1976, in press. (a)

Steptoe, A., & Johnston, D. The control of blood pressure with instructions and pulse wave velocity feedback. European Journal of Behavioural Analysis and Modification, 1976, in press. (b)

Steptoe, A., Smulyan, H., & Gribbin, B. Pulse wave velocity and blood pressure change: Calibration and applications. Psychophysiology, 1976, in press.

NOTE

This work was supported by the Medical Research Council, UK.

CORONARY BIOFEEDBACK: A CHALLENGE TO BIOENGINEERING

Frederick A. Ernst and R. Karl Kordenat
Cox Heart Institute
Kettering, Ohio

Most animal studies of visceral and glandular learning have provided the foundations for interesting and often successful applications to various psychophysiologic disorders. Very often the focus of these treatment efforts has been on cardiovascular function with attention to such diverse clinical phenomena as cardiac arrhythmias and conduction problems (Engel, 1972), essential hypertension (Shapiro et al., 1970), and disorders involving problems of blood flow such as Raynaud's disease (Surwit, 1974) and migraine headache (Sargent et al., 1974).

Foundations

Most notable of the basic foundations for biofeedback was the work of Miller and his colleagues who were able to bring a wide variety of autonomically-mediated visceral and glandular responses under operant control (Miller, 1969). Several studies demonstrated operant manipulations of cardiovascular function including heart rate (Trowill, 1967; DiCara & Miller, 1968a), blood pressure (DiCara & Miller, 1968b), and regional blood flow (DiCara & Miller, 1967, 1968c; Carmona, Miller, & Demierre, 1974).

A remarkable degree of response specificity was demonstrated in the cardiovascular studies, particularly in the control of vasomotor activity and blood flow. Operant manipulation of differential vasomotor activity in ears, kidneys, and gastric wall of rats served to destroy cherished convictions amongst physiologists and psychologists that the autonomic nervous system is "vegetative" in character and therefore not capable of mediating these kinds of highly specific cardiovascular events. Although there has been some difficulty replicating this work (Miller & Dworkin, 1974) similar findings have since emerged from several laboratories which strongly confirm the basic tenets and which leave questions of future applicability clearly researchable (Engel & Gottleib, 1970; Fields, 1970; Hahn & Slaughter, 1971; Harris, Findley, & Brady, 1971).

Coronary Blood Flow & Heart Disease

In light of the encouraging findings relative to the control of regional blood flow, a most obvious yet hitherto totally unexplored area would appear to present itself with potential clinical ramifications of a most profound nature, namely, coronary circulation. The coronary arteries are richly innervated by both sympathetic and parasympathetic branches of the autonomic nervous system (Milnor, 1974) quantitatively unsurpassed by any other arterial system in the body (Ruch & Fulton, 1960). In fact, Gorlin (1974) points out that the coronary system is estimated to be capable of dilation "to a degree sufficient to increase coronary flow five times without changes in any other mechanical supply factor" (p. 110). Since the tonic state of the coronaries is a slight degree of constriction (Milnor, 1974) the potential for commensurate independent decreases in coronary blood flow would seem important from both a basic and a clinical standpoint.

Indeed myocardial infarction and angina pectoris are clearly disorders of insufficient blood flow. However, in spite of the fact that these types of ischemic heart disease cause more deaths than any other disease, virtually no systematic attention has been afforded this important problem of blood flow by biofeedback scientists.

Although atherosclerotic disease is the most frequent cause of inadequate coronary blood flow, a significant frequency of angina pectoris and myocardial infarction has been observed in the absence of any atherosclerotic obstruction (Roberts, 1972; Edwards, 1969; Hackel et al., 1969). A syndrome known to cardiologists as Printzmetal's variant angina pectoris is frequently observed in patients in whom angiography reveals little or no coronary obstruction while blood flow is partially or completely blocked by arterial spasm. Japanese scientists (Endo et al., 1976; Yasue et al., 1974) have recently documented the autonomic role in this disorder by inducing spasms and ischemia with associated ECG changes by injections of parasympathomimetic agents (methacholine and pilocarpine) in patients with the Printzmetal syndrome. This autonomic influence is therefore fully recognized if not completely understood.

Purpose

In an extensive research project on learned control of coronary blood flow in dogs, we are beginning to explore this relatively uncharted area. Thus far, our efforts have focused on "involuntary" coronary blood flow changes learned by association in the context of the Pavlovian (respondent) conditioning paradigm, and on "voluntary" bi-directional coronary blood flow changes learned by an aversive contingency (the operant escape-avoidance paradigm). Since the animal literature has proven so stimulating to the growth of clinically significant biofeedback applications conceivably a demonstration of learned control of coronary circulation might ultimately provide the basic foundations for the feasibility of modifying blood flow to ischemic pre-infarcted myocardial tissue in man. The present report describes the results of our efforts to date.

METHOD

Subjects

Twelve mongrel dogs ranging in weight from 10-25 kg were used in the study. Eight of these animals were available for uncomplicated coronary flow data analysis of respondent conditioning. Two of these animals were employed in the operant paradigm without previous exposure to the respondent procedures. The present report describes the results of typical respondent and operant conditioning of cardiovascular function with a primary focus on coronary blood flow as the specific target of operant control.

Apparatus

The primary apparatus was an Astrodata physiological monitor with a Honeywell 1508 Visicorder for light-sensitive paper recordings. Mean and pulsatile aortic and coronary blood flow were monitored through Statham electromagnetic flow probes. Heart rate ECG was measured through electrodes situated at contralateral limbs of the animal and central aortic blood pressure was monitored by a catheter positioned in the left femoral artery the tip of which was situated in the descending portion of the aortic arch. The catheter was connected to a Statham P-23-DB pressure transducer. A Harvard respirator was used during open chest surgery and during the conditioning procedures because of the paralysis induced by succinylcholine. Monophonic headphones were used for the presentation of the audio conditioned stimulus (CS) (1000 Hz tone) and a shock stimulator delivered a 8-m.a. A/C shock unconditioned stimulus (UCS) to the animal's left hindleg via two electrode plates (3 cm x 3 cm). Scheduling and programming of the CS, UCS, and the operant contingencies were controlled by an Aardvark Electronics Sandbox I event programmer.

Surgical Procedure

The procedure for implanting the flow probes has been described in previous work from this laboratory (Kezdi et al., 1969). Prior to the initiation of experimentation animals were allowed to fully recover from surgery (usually 4-7 days) during which rectal temperature, white blood count, and hematocrit were monitored.

Experimental Procedure

Each subject was run singly by being placed and secured in a surgery table immediately after which Anectine (succinylcholine chloride) (0.2 mg/kg/hr) was administered intravenously. Upon respiratory arrest the animal was respirated mechanically at a rate of 10 - 18 cycles per minute with an inspiration/expiration ratio of 1 : 1. The connector ends of the implanted flow probes were then connected via cables to Statham flow meters the output of which is directed to a Tektronex oscilloscope and Honeywell Visicorder via the Astrodata amplifying system. The audio headphones were then secured to the animal's head by adhesive tape. A small area of the dog's left hind leg was shaven and the two electrode plates were subsequently positioned at the shaven site to deliver the UCS through electrode paste. The blood pressure catheter and ECG electrodes were then situated and the animal was allowed to acclimate to the setting during which electrical calibrations for the various measures were adjusted. This was generally accomplished within 30 - 60 minutes. Prior to the initiation of the experiment, the animal's eyes were covered by a cloth towel and a white noise was begun through the headphones.

Respondent Conditioning Procedure

Following acclimation, the CS was presented alone for a 30-second period several times spaced by a 4-minute variable inter-trial interval. Physiological recordings were automatically taken during the CS presentation and during 30-second pre-CS and post-CS periods. This phase of the experiment was designed to assess the course of Pavlovian habituation.

The CS was then consistently paired with an overlapping 10-second UCS after which both were terminated simultaneously. Ten such acquisition trials were presented during which physiological readings were taken including pre-CS and post CS-UCS periods. Following acquisition, CS-only trials were begun initiating experimental extinction.

Periodic blood samples were drawn from the arterial catheter prior to and during the experiment for blood pH and gas analysis. Normal levels were maintained by controlled respiration.

Operant Conditioning Procedure

After several days recovery, two animals were returned to the table for operant procedures. In one, a second session was designed to shape operant decreases in coronary flow and a third to shape operant increases. The operant contingency was implemented by establishing a reference voltage for mean coronary flow change which programmed the termination of either the tone or the tone and shock. In this case the duration of the shock was not limited to the 10-second period utilized in the respondent procedure and could only be terminated if the criterion voltage change were achieved. Progressively greater changes were shaped by manipulating the reference voltage.

In fixed-criterion escape-avoidance training, shaping was not employed. A criterion increase in coronary flow was established and remained constant for all 55 trials. Reaching criterion in 20 sec or less terminated the tone and prevented the initiation of the shock (avoidance response). Reaching criterion in greater than 20 sec terminated the tone and shock (escape response).

RESULTS

Respondent Learning

Figure 1 is a recording from one animal illustrating a dramatic increase in mean coronary flow (C. F.) subsequent to the onset of shock (UCS). Tachycardia and an increase in central aortic pressure (B. P.) accompany the change in coronary flow while aortic flow (A. F.) remains essentially unchanged during the stimulus period. Figure 2 and 3 illustrate early and late acquisition of the respondent coronary flow CR to the tone (CS). Most animals tested thus far seem to acquire the CR quite rapidly

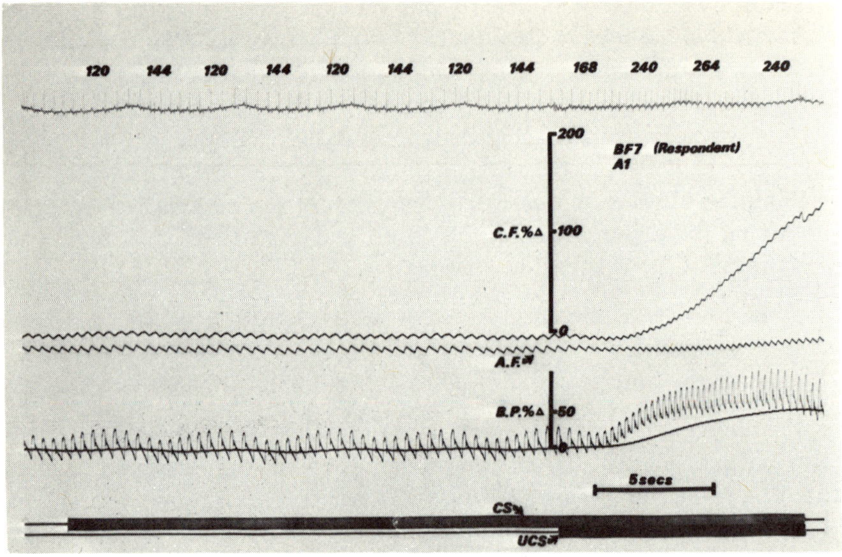

Figure 1. Respondent conditioning of coronary blood flow, acquisition trial #1.

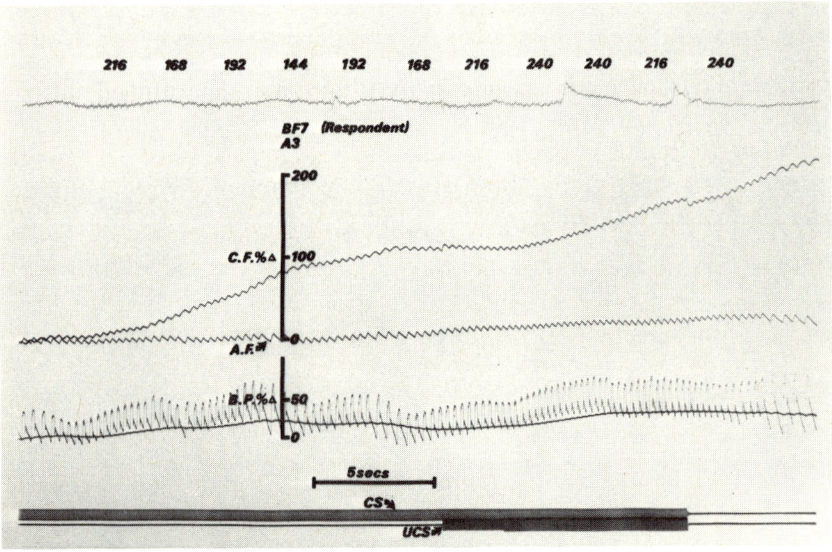

Figure 2. Respondent conditioning of coronary blood flow, acquisition trial #3.

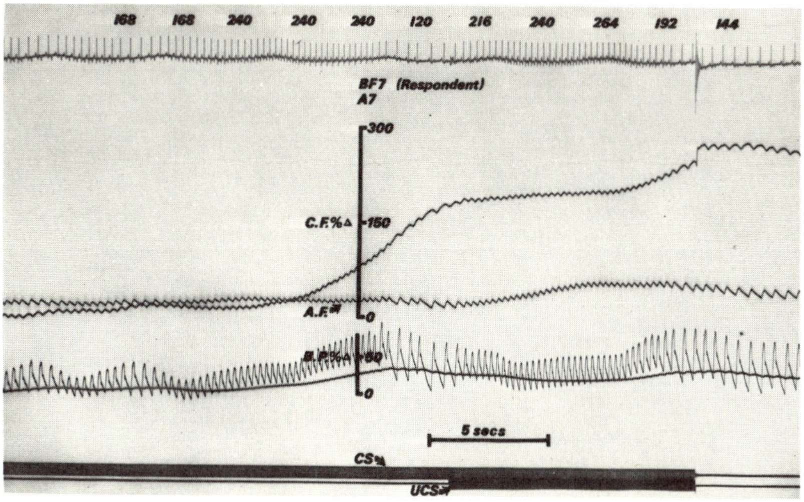

Figure 3. Respondent conditioning of coronary blood flow, acquisition trial #7.

but the difference in the magnitude of this response varies considerably between subjects. Pavlovian inhibition of delay can be observed for coronary flow, blood pressure, and heart rate after relatively few CS-UCS pairings as reflected in Figure 3. Conditioned and unconditioned increases in coronary blood flow have been replicated in all of eight animals. The accompanying cardiovascular changes for these same animals include conditioned and unconditioned increases in aortic flow and central aortic blood pressure with bi-phasic conditioned and unconditioned changes in heart rate, stoke volume, and peripheral resistance. Moreover, simultaneous changes in blood pressure and peripheral resistance are most closely correlated with coronary flow during respondent acquisition (Ernst, Kordenat, & Sandman, 1977).

Operant Learning

Figure 4 is the polygraph record of the first trial of operant decreases for an animal who had been subjected to respondent habituation, acquisition, and extinction three days previous. A slight respondent CR is reflected prior to the onset of the shock and a further unconditioned increase develops during the UCS. The animal is allowed to escape from the tone and shock when the mean coronary flow has decreased by only 7% from baseline values. This decrease is shaped gradually across trials until a

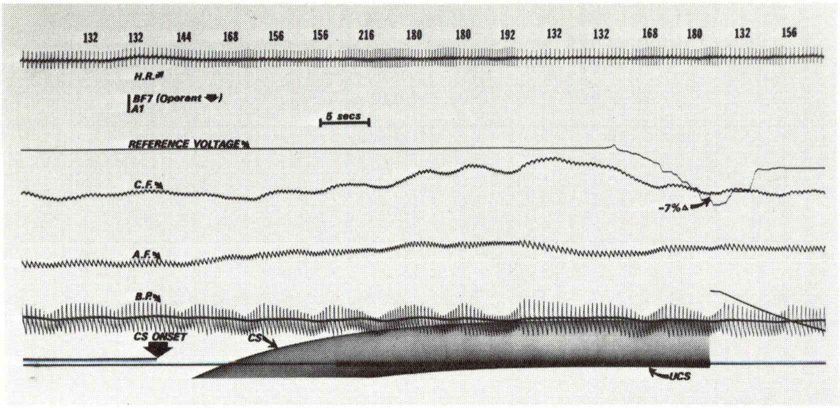

Figure 4. Operant conditioning of decreases in coronary blood flow, acquisition trial #1.

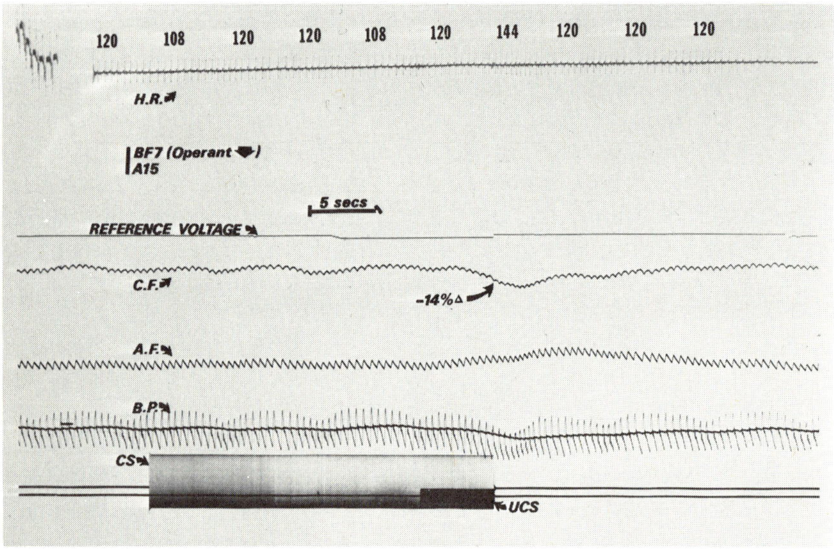

Figure 5. Operant conditioning of decreases in coronary blood flow, acquisition trial #15.

consistent 14% decrease is emitted within 15 trials. Figure 5 shows trial 15 in which the shaped decrease terminates tone and shock. In 60 subsequent trials no more than a 14% decrease is emitted on any given trial but an overall downward shift in baseline coronary flow of 20% is also noted across these remaining trials. (Operant decreases of comparable and greater magnitude have been replicated in three other animals to date.) Furthermore, the speed with which the target response is emitted increases significantly across trials ($F(4,56) = 32.17$, $p < .005$). Figure 6 illustrates the per-cent change in coronary flow shaped across fifths of conditioning. Corresponding changes in aortic flow, blood pressure, and heart rate are also shown. Most significant is the apparent early influence of aortic flow and pressure which dissipates almost entirely in late acquisition. The rather stable influence of heart rate on the target coronary response almost always amounts to one extrasystole at the time of the emitted decrease in coronary flow.

In a subsequent session three days later this same animal was shaped to emit operant increases in coronary flow. The first trial is illustrated in Figure 7. Of particular significance in this trial is the carry-over of emit-

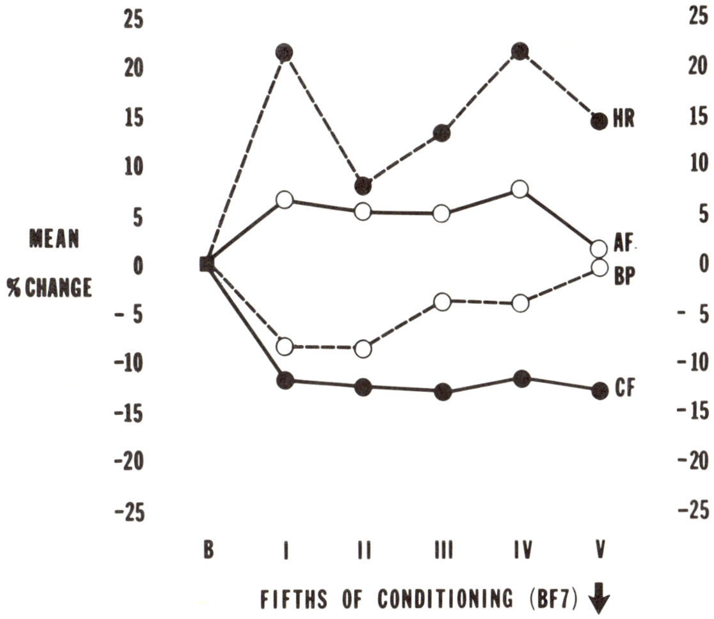

Figure 6. Mean per-cent changes in coronary blood flow, aortic blood flow, blood pressure, and heart rate over Vincentized trials of operant acquisition for decreases in coronary blood flow.

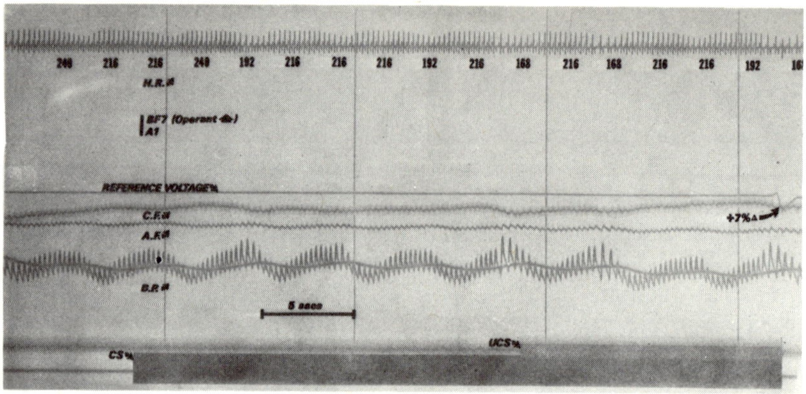

Figure 7. Operant conditioning of increases in coronary blood flow, acquisition trial #1.

ted decreases which were learned in the previous session. Two distinct decreases can be observed in the polygraph record which are punished by shock onset. Eventually a small increase is reinforced by tone and shock termination. Figure 8 (acquisition-trial #15) illustrates the effects of shaping further increases until a 20% increase is consistently achieved. As with the decreases in flow, the shaping is accomplished within 15 trials.

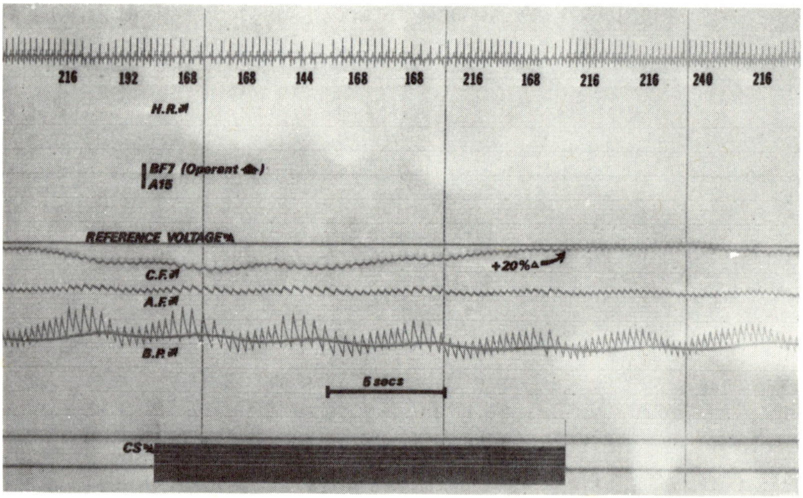

Figure 8. Operant conditioning of increases in coronary blood flow, acquisition trial #15.

Figure 9 presents the shaping of increases in coronary flow for this animal across fifths of conditioning and includes the corresponding changes in aortic flow, blood pressure, and heart rate. The degree of variability in the latter three measures can probably be attributed to the relatively small number of observations upon which the graph is based (25 trials).

In another animal who was also previously subjected to respondent habituation, acquisition, and extinction, a fixed-criterion operant procedure was attempted in which a criterion increase of nearly twice the baseline coronary flow was necessary for the animal to escape from or avoid shock. The subject in this procedure had to increase a baseline coronary flow of 116-146 cc/min to a mean of 225 cc/min. Figure 10 illustrates the course of avoidance acquisition for the criterion change. The mean latencies of the criterion changes for blocks of 5 trials are clearly decreasing across trials. In the first 15 trials the subject avoided only 33% of the shocks by emitting the criterion change within 20 seconds. In the last 15 trials 87% of the shocks were avoided.

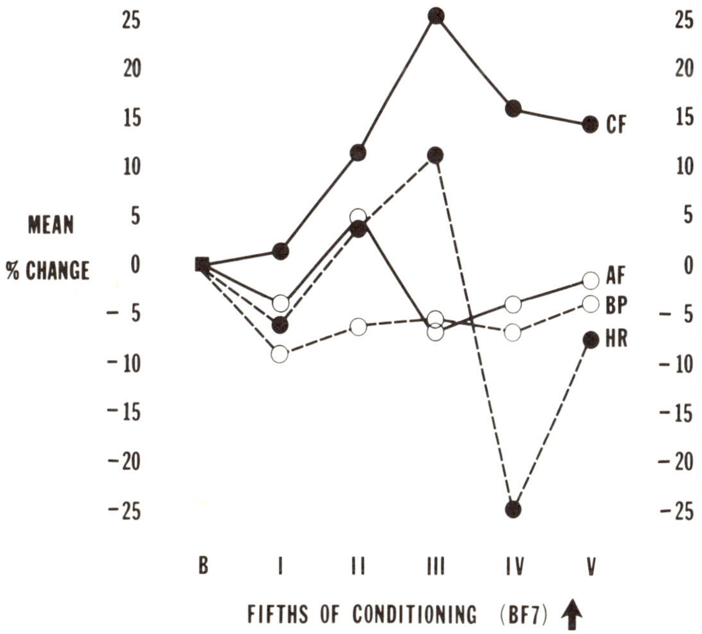

Figure 9. Mean per-cent changes in coronary blood flow, aortic blood flow, blood pressure, and heart rate over Vincentized trials of operant acquisition for increases in coronary blood flow.

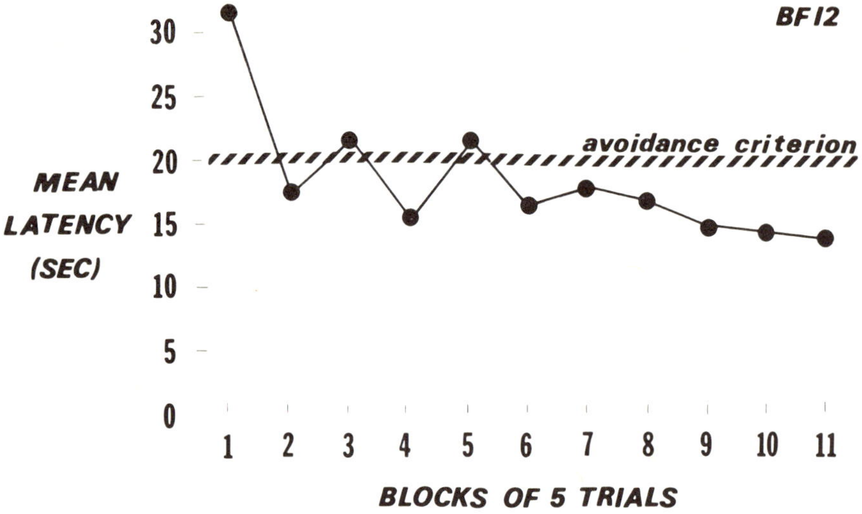

Figure 10. Mean latencies of criterion coronary blood flow increases reflecting learned avoidance across blocks of five trials.

DISCUSSION

These results are submitted as evidence that coronary blood flow can be modified by the kind of learning procedures which have provided the only substantive basis for biofeedback applications. The present study also provides confirmation of earlier work demonstrating operant control of visceral behaviors (e.g., Miller, 1969) and extends the range of applicability of operant procedures to an autonomically-mediated behavior of profound clinical significance.

If operant learning is accepted as an adequate model for "voluntary" behavior, these results suggest that organisms can achieve voluntary control of coronary blood flow. Therefore, modern biofeedback techniques might possibly be employed in the clinical modification of coronary flow in patients with coronary and ischemic heart disease. The Printzmetal syndrome would appear to be the most obvious first target of this effort because of the well-documented role of the autonomic nervous system in the etiology of the problem. The implication of the present results that coronary vasoconstriction can be learned when it is reinforced by the reduction of stress may also shed light on a potential etiologic component of the Printzmetal syndrome.

However, at present there are no adequate non-invasive methods of measuring human coronary blood flow continuously in a fashion which might allow for the arrangement of the discriminative signals so important to biofeedback techniques. While coronary angiography seems clearly inadequate for this purpose, advances in echocardiography offer some potential for the future.

This problem of measurement presents a challenge to bioengineering whose solution could provide biofeedback scientists with an exciting new area of research and biofeedback practitioners with a potential opportunity to alleviate the suffering caused by the most common of serious diseases.

REFERENCES

Carmona, A., Miller, N. E., & Demierre, T. Instrumental learning of gastric vascular tonicity responses. Psychosomatic Medicine, 1974, 36, 156-163.

DiCara, L. V., & Miller, N. E. Instrumental learning of urine formation by curarized rats. Psychonomic Bulletin, 1967, 1, 23-24.

DiCara, L. V., & Miller, N. E. Changes in heart rate learned by curarized rats as avoidance responses. Journal of Comparative and Physiological Psychology, 1968, 65, 8-12. (a)

DiCara, L. V., & Miller, N. E. Instrumental learning of peripheral vasomotor responses by the curarized rat. Comparative Behavior Biology, 1968, 1, 209-212. (b)

DiCara, L. V., & Miller, N. E. Instrumental learning of vasomotor responses by rats: Learning to respond differentially in the two ears. Science, 1968, 159, 148-158. (c)

Edwards, J. W. What is myocardial infarction? Circulation (Supplement IV), 1969, 39 & 40, 5-12.

Endo, M., Hirosawa, K., Kaneko, N., Hase, K., Inoue, Y., & Konno, S. Printzmetal's variant angina: Coronary arteriogram and left ventriculogram during angina attack induced by methocholine. The New England Journal of Medicine, 1976, 294, 252-255.

Engel, B. T., & Gottleib, S. H. Differential operant conditioning of heart rate in the restrained monkey. Journal of Comparative and Physiological Psychology, 1970, 73, 217-225.

Ernst, F. A., Kordenat, R. K., & Sandman, C. A. Respondent control of coronary blood flow. Manuscript in preparation for submittal, 1977.

Fields, C. Instrumental conditioning of the rat cardiac control system. Proceedings of the National Academy of Science, 1970, 65, 293-299.

Gorlin, R. Physiology of the coronary circulation. In W. Hurst et al. (Eds.), The heart. New York: McGraw-Hill, 1974.

Hackel, D. B., Estes, E. H., Walston, A., Koff, S., & Day, E. Some problems concerning coronary artery occlusion and acute myocardial infarction. Circulation (Supplement IV), 1969, 39 & 40, 31-37.

Hahn, W. W., & Slaughter, J. Heart rate responses of the curarized rat. Psychophysiology, 1971, 7, 429-435.

Harris, A. H., Findley, G. D., & Brady, J. B. Instrumental conditions of blood pressure in the baboon. Conditional Reflex, 1971, 6, 215-226.

Kezdi, P., Stanley, E. L., Marshall, W. J., & Kordenat, R. K. Aortic flow velocity and acceleration as an index of ventricular performance during myocardial infarction. The American Journal of the Medical Sciences, 1969, 257, 61-71.

Miller, N. E. Learning of visceral and glandular responses. Science, 1969, 163, 434-445.

Miller, N. E., & Dworkin, B. R. Visceral learning: Recent difficulties with curarized rats and significant problems for human research. In P. Obrist et al. (Eds.), Cardiovascular psychophysiology. Chicago: Aldine, 1974.

Milnor, W. R. Cardiovascular system. In V. B. Mountcastle (Ed.), Medical physiology. St. Louis: Mosby, 1974.

Roberts, W. C. Coronary arteries in fatal acute myocardial infarction. Circulation, 1972, 45, 215-230.

Ruch, T. C., & Fulton, J. R. Medical physiology and biophysics. Philadelphia: Saunders, 1960.

Sargent, J. D., Walters, E. D., & Green, E. E. Psychosomatic self-regulation of migraine headache. In L. Birk (Ed.), Biofeedback: Behavioral medicine. New York: Grune & Stratton, 1974.

Shapiro, D., Tursky, B., & Schwartz, G. E. Control of blood pressure in man by operant conditioning. Circulation Research (Supplement I), 1970, 26 & 27, I-27 to I-32.

Surwit, R. S. Biofeedback: A possible treatment for Raynaud's Disease. In L. Birk (Ed.), Biofeedback: Behavioral medicine. New York: Grune & Stratton, 1973.

Trowill, J. A. Instrumental conditioning of the heart rate in the curarized rat. Journal of Comparative and Physiological Psychology, 1967, 63, 7-11.

Yasue, H., Touyama, M., Shimamoto, M., Kato, H., Tanaka, S., & Akiyama, F. Role of autonomic nervous system in the pathogenesis of Printzmetal's variant angina. Circulation, 1974, 50, 534-539.

NOTE

The research reported here is part of a study which was submitted by the senior author in partial fulfillment of the Ph.D. degree in Clinical Psychology at The Ohio State University. The advice and guidance of Dr. Curt Sandman is gratefully acknowledged. The project has been supported by grants from the Miami Valley (Ohio) chapter of the American Heart Association.

BIOFEEDBACK CONTROL OF STOMACH ACID SECRETIONS AND GASTROINTESTINAL REACTIONS

Peter R. Welgan
Department of Psychiatry and Human Behavior
University of California, Irvine

In the past fifteen years the focus of biofeedback research with humans has been directed toward the modification of psychophysiological and medical disorders which could be conveniently monitored from the surface of the body. Research on such problems as headaches (Budzynski, Stoyva, & Adler, 1970), epilepsy (Sterman, MacDonald, & Stone, 1974), and stress related disorders (Benson, Rosen, Marzetta, & Klemchuk, 1974) has produced encouraging results with such recording methods.

However, because of the attention devoted to surface measurements, as well as the extreme difficulty encountered in monitoring deep visceral organ function in humans, the study of a wide range of disorders has been ignored. Research problems in this area are both ethical and technological. The invasive techniques required for the measurement of many organ functions involve risk to the subject. Catheterization or surgical implantation of physiological probes necessary for this type of monitoring tend to be restricted to life saving situations.

Further, the present level of development of biofeedback technology and instrumentation has created limits to deep visceral function research. The virtual lack of sophisticated non-invasive microprobes, designed for continuous monitoring of such systems as the gastrointestinal tract and blood chemistry changes, have restricted study of this field.

In animal research, where these limits are not as stringent, encouraging studies have been reported. Early work by Miller and Banuazizi (1968) has suggested that intestinal and cardiac function may be instrumentally modified. Miller (1969) and Ainslie and Engel (1974) add further support to the belief that with proper probes, learned changes in organ function could be achieved.

In 1969, this investigator began a series of studies to extend deep visceral biofeedback research to the human analog. These studies had two objectives: 1) to obtain a reliable measurement of glandular changes in the gastrointestinal tract, and 2) to attempt to produce experimental changes in stomach pH, as well as hydrochloric acid concentration and volume.

Basically, the methodology developed to obtain continuous feedback of stomach pH required the on-line pH measurement of acid secretions continuously aspirated from the stomach. To obtain these measurements, a nasogastric tube was placed under fluoroscopic control in the antrum of the stomach. Stomach contents were then aspirated under low vacuum and briefly collected in a special vessel. Changes in pH were measured with standard pH electrodes and displayed to the subject. The collection of stomach contents permitted additional in vitro analyses of acid concentration and volume changes.

The results of early studies (Welgan, 1974) with ten peptic ulcer patients using this biofeedback method indicated that acid concentration and volume declined while pH increased significantly from a baseline resting condition.

A second study with ten ulcer patients suggested that similar declines in acid concentration and volume were not entirely a result of physiological adjustments due to deactivation of the nervous system, since acid changes occurred only after pH feedback.

Based on these earlier findings, two additional studies were performed to determine the effect of pH feedback and placebo on short and long term training of these three gastric responses.

EXPERIMENT 1

Method

Subjects. Twenty-seven peptic ulcer subjects were selected for this study. The presence of peptic ulcer was confirmed by medical diagnosis. Subjects were randomly assigned to one of two groups. Nine subjects were placed in a True Feedback Group (TF) and eighteen subjects in a False Feedback Group (FF).

Apparatus. Stomach contents were aspirated under continuous vacuum (3 mm Hg) with a Gomco Thermotic Drainage Pump through a multilumen tube designed to prevent nasogastric tube plug-up by obstructions in the stomach (e.g. mucus, stomach wall enclosures). Acid changes in the gastric secretions were monitored on a Beckman pH meter and graphically recorded on a Grass recorder. Beckman electrodes were mounted in the nasogastric tube, 1 foot from the subject's face. Electrodes were inserted vertically in the wall of a 1 x 2 inch collection cylinder so that the electrode tips were continously immersed in approximately 0.3 ml of gastric secretions. Volumes exceeding this amount drained into another collection vessel. This procedure assured a reliable and continuous recording with a minimum of contamination of stomach samples from residual secretions.

Procedure

The study was conducted between 8:00 AM and 12:00 PM after the subject had fasted for 12 hours. A nasogastric tube was passed under fluoroscopic control so that its tip was positioned in the most dependent portion of the stomach. The subject was then placed in a semi-reclining position. During the experiment, the subject's saliva was continuously removed from his mouth with a vacuum ejector.

Experimental task. The experimental task consisted of a 15 minute basal period followed by three 15 minute training periods. Stomach content samples from each of these periods were kept for in vitro analysis of acid concentration and volume changes.

True Feedback Group. Following the 15 minute basal period, subjects were presented with a true display of pH of acid secretions and given a standard set of instructions to try to increase pH.

False Feedback Group. Control subjects were given the same set of standard instructions to increase pH while receiving false (reverse) feedback of pH during their attempt to increase pH. In this condition, perceived increases actually represented pH decreases.

Results

pH. The highest pH during the entire experimental period was averaged across subjects within each group. Changes in pH above 4.0 were not used since it was expected that these samples were contaminated with alkaline bile. Contaminated secretions were discarded.

Results in Table 1 showed that there were no significant differences in stomach pH between the True and False Feedback Groups ($t = 1.35$, $df = 25$, N.S.) during the first session.

Acid concentration. The smallest acid measure in milliequivalents of HCL (mEq) from the three 15 minute in vitro analyses for each subject was averaged for each group. In Table 1, it can be seen that acid concentration did not differ significantly between groups ($t = 1.46$, $df = 25$, N.S.).

Volume. The greatest volume (cc) was selected from the three in vitro analyses and averaged for each group. Table 1 indicates that the True Feedback Group significantly reduced its volume of secretions compared to the False Feedback Group ($t = 2.51$, $df = 26$, $p < 0.05$).

Table 1

Means and Standard Deviations of Highest pH and Volume and Lowest Acid Concentration Measures in a One Hour Training Session

		Stomach Responses		
Groups		pH	Acid Concentration (mEq)	Volume* (cc)
True	$\bar{X}$	2.66	.0202	10.1
Feedback	SD	1.67	.0169	8.1
	N	(n=9)	(n=10)	(n=10)
False	$\bar{X}$	1.83	.0368	20.7
Feedback	SD	0.74	.0393	13.4
	N	(n=18)	(n=17)	(n=18)

* $p < .05$

EXPERIMENT 2

A second study was conducted to determine if ten training sessions would have a greater effect on stomach acid changes than a single training session.

Method

Subjects. Eight peptic ulcer patients who have presently completed ten training sessions served as subjects in this study. All subjects met the same requirements as those of Experiment 1. Five subjects were randomly assigned to a True Feedback Group (TF) and three subjects were randomly assigned to a False Feedback Group (FF).

Procedure

The procedure in Experiment 1 was used in Experiment 2 except that the groups were trained for ten sessions. Usually sessions were scheduled twice a week for five weeks.

Results

pH. The subjects' highest pH in each training session was averaged for each group. Group sizes were too small to perform customary analysis of variance tests, however tests for linear trends of session means (Table 2) showed that the TF Group significantly increased pH over sessions compared to the FF Group. Preliminary tests indicated that pH in the TF Group was significantly higher ($p < 0.05$) than pH in the FF Group during six training sessions.

Acid concentration. The smallest acid concentration level (mEq) obtained from the three 15 minute experimental periods was averaged for each session. A linear trend test of session means (Table 3) revealed no significant differences ($t = 0.98$, $df = 6$, N.S.) between groups over sessions.

Volume. The greatest stomach secretion volume obtained (cc) among the three 15 minute experimental volumes, was averaged for each session. A linear trend test of mean volume changes over sessions showed no significant differences between groups ($t = 1.29$, $df = 6$, N.S.). However, average volume changes over ten sessions was significantly less in the

Table 2

Means and Standard Deviations of Highest pH Measures during Ten Sessions for True and False Feedback Groups

Groups		Treatments									
		1	2*	3*	4*	5*	6	7*	8*	9	10
True Feedback	$\bar{X}$	2.38	2.38	2.40	2.46	2.68	2.30	2.84	3.08	2.26	2.22
	SD	.91	.86	.82	.88	1.05	.90	1.03	1.14	.96	.68
False Feedback	$\bar{X}$	1.67	1.40	1.53	1.57	1.53	1.73	1.53	1.60	1.47	1.63
	SD	.25	.33	.05	.09	.05	.12	.19	.29	.31	.12

* $p < .05$

TF Group than in the FF Group ($t = 3.62$, $df = 6$, $p < 0.01$). Further tests showed that the TF Group produced significantly ($p < 0.05$) less acid volume in seven sessions and consistently less acid than the FF Group throughout all sessions.

Discussion

In general, the trend of the present results is consistent with earlier findings. Feedback of stomach pH seems to have an effect on stomach glandular secretions. Stomach pH tends to increase slowly and in very small increments. The volume of secretions discharged by the stomach glands, however, appears to be most sensitive to modification. Gastric secretions change both within and across extended training sessions. The unusually large volume differences observed between TF and FF Groups may be partially a result of the fact that the FF Group was actually being trained to decrease pH and perhaps indirectly increase secretion volume. The absence of any significant difference in acid concentration between groups is inconsistent with earlier findings, but may suggest that the TF Group, nevertheless, secreted less acid by volume, since secretion volume in this group was significantly lower than in the FF Group.

Research is presently under way which is designed to analyze the relationship between gastric motility, cortical, and muscular changes asso-

Table 3

Means and Standard Deviations of Lowest Acid Concentration (mEq) Measures during Ten Sessions for True and False Feedback Groups

Groups		Treatments									
		1	2	3	4	5	6	7	8	9	10
True	$\bar{X}$	.0161	.0213	.0148	.0121	.0465	.0128	.0122	.0096	.0173	.0156
Feedback	SD	.0171	.0185	.0174	.0179	.0743	.0108	.0167	.0094	.0191	.0155
False	$\bar{X}$	.0300	.0289	.0230	.0357	.0224	.0218	.0185	.0301	.0294	.0292
Feedback	SD	.0011	.0033	.0106	.0217	.0200	.0134	.0074	.0203	.0143	.0233

ciated with the observed changes in pH and volume. Systematic studies of these relationships are unavailable in the literature.

Even though the results of the current studies seem to be consistent with earlier research, imperfect measurement techniques continue to obscure findings. Occasional contamination of stomach contents from bile refluxing through the duodenum destroys the stomach sample for a period of time and measurement can only resume after the stomach and pH monitoring system are cleared of the alkaline solution. The expected loss of some fluid through the duodenum and occasional collapse of the stomach wall around the tip of the nasogastric tube present problems for accurate measurement of stomach glandular functions.

Solutions to many of these problems must await advances in the technology of continuous gastric function analyses.

SUMMARY

Two studies were performed to train increases in stomach pH and decreases in acid concentration and volume of glandular secretions using biofeedback of stomach pH. In Experiment 1, two groups of ulcer patients were presented with either True (TF) or False (FF) feedback of pH during a one hour training session. No significant changes occurred between groups in pH or acid concentration, however, glandular secretion volume significantly declined in the True Feedback Group. In Experiment 2, pH training was extended over ten sessions. Significant increases in pH and declines in se-

Table 4

Means and Standard Deviations of Highest Volume Measures (cc) during Ten Sessions for True and False Feedback Groups

Groups		Treatments									
		1	2**	3*	4*	5	6*	7	8**	9**	10*
True	$\overline{X}$	5.7	4.2	4.5	8.8	4.8	6.5	5.5	4.5	3.4	7.5
Feedback	SD	5.2	4.2	7.0	8.3	3.2	4.2	1.5	3.0	3.5	4.7
False	$\overline{X}$	21.7	21.6	19.6	22.0	22.0	29.7	23.3	28.3	23.0	28.0
Feedback	SD	13.1	6.2	7.3	7.5	12.8	16.7	14.3	7.6	4.3	10.2

* $p < .05$ ** $p < .01$

cretion volume were found in the True Feedback Group compared to the False Feedback Group. There were no differences in acid concentration between groups. The results are discussed in terms of the present level of biofeedback technology and problems involved in recording deep visceral organ functions.

REFERENCES

Ainslie, G. W., & Engel, B. T. Alteration of classically conditioned heart rate by operant reinforcement in monkeys. Journal of Comparative and Physiological Psychology, 1974, 87, 373-382.

Benson, H., Rosen, B., Marzella, R., & Klemchuk, H. M. Decreased blood pressure in pharmacologically treated hypertensive patients who regularly elicited the relaxation response. The Lancet, 1974, 289-291.

Budzynski, T. H., Stoyva, J. M., & Adler, C. S. Feedback-induced relaxation: Application to tension headache. Journal of Behavior Therapy and Experimental Psychiatry, 1970, 1, 205.

Miller, N. Learning of visceral and glandular responses. Science, 1968, 163, 434-445.

Miller, N., & Banuazizi, A. Instrumental learning by curarized rats of specific visceral response, intestinal or cardiac. Journal of Comparative and Physiological Psychology, 1968, 65, 1-7.

Sterman, M. B., MacDonald, L. R., & Stone, R. K. Biofeedback training of the sensorimotor electroencephalogram rhythm in man: Effects on epilepsy. Epilepsia, 1974, 15, 395-416.

Welgan, P. R. Learned control of gastric acid secretions in ulcer patients. Psychosomatic Medicine, 1974, 36, 411-419.

BIOFEEDBACK AS TREATMENT FOR CARDIOVASCULAR DISORDERS: A CRITICAL REVIEW

Bernard T. Engel
Gerontology Research Center
National Institute of Aging
Baltimore City Hospitals

Cardiovascular disorders are the most significant causes of human morbidity and mortality in western society. Annual deaths from cardiovascular diseases exceed all other causes combined. The range of cardiovascular disorders is great; and the number of disorders toward which biofeedback efforts have been directed is few. Furthermore, even with respect to specific problems where biofeedback has been tried, the conditions under which treatment has been tested are limited and the number of patients who have been studied is small. In addition, there is considerable variability in methodology among the various studies, and none of them was designed to permit one to make direct comparisons among methods.

CARDIAC DISEASE

Most of the studies of biofeedback in patients with cardiac disease either attempted to show that feedback had some effect on cardiac function, or attempted to elucidate a behavioral or physiological mechanism. Almost all of these studies focussed on heart rate training, and most of the patients studied had one or more cardiac arrhythmia. With few exceptions, none of the studies were designed to evaluate therapy, per se. However, some of these studies included either follow-up data or independent clinical evaluations so that it is possible to estimate their therapeutic potential.

Patients with Supra-ventricular Tachyarrhythmias

Sinus tachycardia. Patients with histories of sinus tachycardia have been studied in at least three laboratories (Engel & Bleecker, 1974, pp. 456-476; Scott, Blanchard, Edmundson, & Young, 1973; Vaitl, 1975, pp. 205-217). However, almost none of the patients had histories of any other cardiac disease, and most of the patients had significant psychiatric disorders. Sinus tachycardia in such patients is a benign cardiac disfunction which is secondary to the psychiatric disorder. The results from these studies are cardiologically interesting only in that they indicate that it is possible to produce large reductions in heart rate in such patients, and that these effects will persist outside of the laboratory.

Paroxysmal atrial tachycardia. Biofeedback studies of two patients with histories of paroxysmal atrial tachycardia (PAT) have been reported (Engel & Bleecker, 1974, pp. 456-476). Many patients with PAT are badly frightened by their arrhythmias; however, unless there are other indications of cardiac pathology, this arrhythmia has no cardiologically significant sequellae. One of the two patients reported above did have significant cardiac disease (congestive heart failure), and in his case there was evidence of clinically important changes: The patient's clinical status shifted from functional class III to class I after he learned to maintain a slower heart rate with a normal sinus rhythm. Objective changes included an increase in exercise tolerance, and a decrease in heart size (measured by roentgenograms). Changes first observed in the laboratory persisted during clinic visits over the next five months.

Atrial fibrillation. Patients with atrial fibrillation have been trained to increase and decrease their ventricular rates using operant conditioning techniques (Bleecker & Engel, 1973). The study was done primarily to determine the autonomic mechanisms of such behavior. One finding of potential clinical interest was reported for one patient who was able to produce an atrio-ventricular, junctional escape rhythm consistently while voluntarily slowing his ventricular rate. This result suggested that biofeedback might be useful in defining the degree of digitalization necessary to maintain such patients adequately. This observation has not been extended.

Patients with Ventricular Arrhythmias

Studies of patients with premature ventricular beats (PVC) have been reported by investigators from at least two laboratories (Engel & Bleecker, 1974; Weiss & Engel, 1973; Miller, 1975, p. 349; Pickering,

1975). In general the results indicate that some patients can learn to control this arrhythmia, and that the degree of control possible is clinically significant. A few patients were followed for periods of a year or more (Engel & Bleecker, 1974; Weiss & Engel, 1973), and these patients continued to maintain reduced levels of PVCs. One of the studies was particularly interesting because it involved a patient with a parasystolic ventricular rhythm (Pickering, 1975). Before training this patient's ectopic focus became manifest at a heart rate of 78 beats/min. After training she was able to speed her rate to about 106 beats/min before ectopic beats appeared. This shift in rate-related ectopic activity occurred not only during the conditioning sessions but also during bicycle exercise.

Patients with Conduction Defects

There have been two published reports of studies of patients with conduction defects (Bleecker & Engel, 1973; Weiss & Engel, 1975). In one paper it was reported that a patient with electrocardiographic evidence of intermittent Wolf-Parkinson-White disease was able to learn heart rate control, and independently to learn to control her cardiac conduction patterns. The patient's ability to control her conduction patterns transferred since she evinced reliable cardiac control in the clinic ten weeks after completion of her laboratory studies. The other published study of patients with conduction defects reported that patients with third degree heart block were unable to modify their ventricular rates.

Comment

The only studies of patients with cardiac disease which purported to evaluate the therapeutic value of biofeedback were those with patients with sinus tachycardia in the absence of any other cardiac disease. As noted above, these patients suffer from psychiatric disorders rather than from a cardiac disease. Thus, any evaluation of these studies should be made in terms of psychiatric criteria rather than in terms of cardiological criteria. With respect to the other studies reviewed above, the results seem clearly to show that clinically significant changes can be produced in patients with a variety of different cardiac arrhythmias. There is insufficient data to permit one to evaluate the therapeutic effectiveness of biofeedback either as a primary therapy or as an adjunctive therapy. However, the data seem to be strong enough to justify clinical trials of biofeedback. Such studies should include a variety of laboratory assessment procedures, and also should include a variety of outcome measures.

VASCULAR DISEASE

Most of the studies of biofeedback in vascular disease have been with patients with high blood pressure although there also have been a few studies of patients with Raynaud's disease or with migraine headache. Many of the studies of patients with vascular disorders have been reported at meetings but have not appeared in the scientific literature so that it is difficult to judge their quality. Furthermore, many of the patients were trained either to relax specific muscle groups, to raise hand temperature or to raise the electrical resistances of their skin even when there was no evidence that muscle tone, hand temperature or skin resistance was in any way disturbed in the patients. Often, even the published reports have been limited to a review of symptom change and no objective evidence of effect was reported.

High Blood Pressure

Because of space limitations I will comment only on studies of patients with high blood pressure. Furthermore, I will not consider any of the studies in which relaxation methods were used exclusively, or in which such methods were used in conjunction with biofeedback. The first kind of studies is excluded because the focus of this review is on biofeedback, and the second kind of studies is excluded because it is not possible to dissociate the effect of biofeedback from the effect of relaxation.

The first published study of the use of biofeedback to regulate blood pressure in patients was reported by Benson, Shapiro, Tursky, and Schwartz (1971). The investigators showed that some patients with high blood pressure could be trained to lower their pressures in the laboratory. This study did not include any pre-treatment or follow-up data, nor were any other parameters or clinical change reported. These findings were subsequently confirmed and extended in several ways in a comparable sample of patients, and by independent investigators (Kristt & Engel, 1975). This second study reported pre-conditioning baseline data and three-month follow-up results. The follow-up studies showed that the patients were able to retain their abilities to control their pressures during the follow-up period; and these studies also indicated that most of the patients sustained a significant reduction in blood pressure throughout the follow-up period. Laboratory studies also showed that the patients were able to learn to raise as well as to lower blood pressure, and that these changes in blood pressure occurred in the absence of any changes in heart rate, EEG alpha-wave activity or breathing rate. It also should be noted that neither group of investigators claimed that the effects they had observed were therapeutic.

Two other groups of investigators also have reported significant positive results in studies of blood pressure biofeedback. One group showed that hospitalized patients could learn to lower systolic and diastolic blood pressures relative to a baseline blood pressure taken before any training sessions were begun (Elder, Ruiz, Deabler, & Dillenkoffer, 1973). The findings are interesting because the effect of feedback alone appeared to be better than merely relaxing or trying to lower pressure without feedback. The significance of the results is very limited, however, because: 1) no pre-hospitalization baseline data were reported; 2) the role of concurrent therapy was not assessed; and 3) the laboratory data were reported as percentage change from a single pre-training baseline value so that it is not possible to determine whether the patients were lowering their pressures or merely habituating to their hospitalization. In a subsequent report from this group (Elder & Eustis, 1975), 22 outpatients, most of whom also were being treated pharmacologically, were seen weekly over about 8 weeks and then were studied after one month. The difference between the pretreatment baseline values and the follow-up values were small (8/3 mm Hg), but they were statistically significant. It also is difficult to evaluate these findings since the conditioning data are reported as percentage change from pre-treatment baseline values.

The last study to be reviewed here is especially interesting since it included not only blood pressure change data but also data from a paper and pencil test of brain function (Goldman, Kleinman, Snow, Bedus, & Korol, 1975). The results showed that as blood pressure fell performance on the test of cerebral function rose. However, the data are much too limited to warrant any speculation on their clinical significance. It should be noted that this is the only published study of biofeedback and blood pressure which attempted to assess clinical change in some parameter other than blood pressure.

Comment

The clinical potential of biofeedback in patients with high blood pressure is much less clear than in patients with cardiac arrhythmias. Before any attempt is made to implement clinical trials, additional data are needed. In particular, additional indices of clinical changes are needed (see Stone and DeLeo (1976) for an example of such a study using relaxation to lower blood pressure); and the relative effectiveness of relaxation methods and feedback methods should be compared.

A POINT OF VIEW

Behavioral research with patients with cardiovascular disorders is bringing together groups of scientists who have never worked together in the past. Furthermore, each of the groups has very different traditions; and each has very different ways of collecting and evaluating data. I believe that we are now at a stage where the scientists are just beginning to learn one another's language and one another's facts. I anticipate that we will soon be seeing a number of collaborative studies among these scientists. As these studies find their way into the scientific literature, the therapeutic role of biofeedback in patients with cardiovascular disorders will become clear.

REFERENCES

Benson, H., Shapiro, D., Tursky, B., & Schwartz, G. E. Decreased systolic blood pressure through operant conditioning techniques in patients with essential hypertension. Science, 1971, 173, 740-742.

Bleecker, E. R., & Engel, B. T. Learned control of cardiac rate and cardiac conduction in the Wolf-Parkinson-White symdrome. New England Journal of Medicine, 1973, 288, 560-562.

Bleecker, E. R., & Engel, B. T. Learned control of ventricular rate in patients with atrial fibrillation. Psychosomatic Medicine, 1973, 35, 161-175.

Elder, S. T., & Eustis, N. K. Instrumental blood pressure conditioning in out-patient hypertensives. Behavioral Research and Therapy, 1975, 13, 185-188.

Elder, S. T., Ruiz, Z. R., Deabler, H. L., & Dillenkoffer, R. L. Instrumental conditioning of diastolic blood pressure in essential hypertensive patients. Journal of Applied Behavior Analysis, 1973, 6, 377-382.

Engel, B. T., & Bleecker, E. R. Application of operant conditioning techniques to the control of the cardiac arrhythmias. In P. A. Obrist, A. H. Black, J. Brener & L. V. DiCara (Eds.), Cardiovascular psychophysiology. Chicago: Aldine, 1974.

Goldman, H., Kleinman, K. M., Snow, M. Y., Bedus, D. K., & Korol, B. Relationship between essential hypertension and cognitive functioning: Effects of biofeedback. Psychophysiology, 1975, 12, 569-573.

Kristt, D. A., & Engel, B. T. Learned control of blood pressure in patients with high blood pressure. Circulation, 1975, 51, 370-378.

Miller, N. E. Applications of learning and biofeedback to psychiatry and medicine. In A. M. Freedman, H. I. Kaplan & B. J. Sadock (Eds.), Comprehensive textbook of psychiatry, III. Baltimore: Williams and Wilkins Co., 1975.

Pickering, T., & Gorham, G. Learned heart-rate control by a patient with a ventricular parasystolic rhythm. Lancet, February 1975, 252-253.

Scott, R. W., Blanchard, E. B., Edmundson, E. D., & Young, L. D. A shaping procedure for heart-rate control in chronic tachycardia. Perceptual and Motor Skills, 1973, 37, 327-338.

Stone, R. A., & DeLeo, J. Psychotherapeutic control of hypertension. New England Journal of Medicine, 1976, 294, 80-84.

Vaitl, D. Biofeedback -- Einsatz in der Behandlung einer Patientin mit Sinustachykardie. In H. Legewie & L. Nusselt (Eds.), Biofeedback - Therapie. München, Berlin, Wien: Urban und Schwarzenberg, 1975.

Weiss, T., & Engel, B. T. Evaluation of an intra-cardiac limit of learned heart rate control. Psychophysiology, 1975, 3, 310-312.

Weiss, T., & Engel, B. T. Operant conditioning of heart rate in patients with premature ventricular contractions. Psychosomatic Medicine, 1971, 33, 301-321.

BIOFEEDBACK AND MEDITATION IN THE TREATMENT OF BORDERLINE HYPERTENSION

Richard S. Surwit
Harvard Medical School

and

David Shapiro
University of California
at Los Angeles

Because essential hypertension affects about 10 percent of the general population, behavioral manipulation of blood pressure has received much attention as a possible clinical tool (Shapiro & Surwit, 1976). Over the past six years, a number of different behavioral techniques have been clinically applied to the control of hypertension. The main purpose of this study was to compare the efficacy of three such methods in the treatment of essential hypertension.

No behavioral technique has received more recent interest as a treatment for hypertension than training patients to control their pressure through direct biofeedback of blood pressure (BP) change. Shapiro, Tursky, Gershon, and Stern (1969) developed a method to monitor and feedback changes in BP by holding cuff pressure constant and measuring the presence or absence of Korotkoff sounds. In this fashion, beat by beat blood pressure changes were fed back to normal subjects to produce small but reliable increases and decreases in either systolic or diastolic blood pressure (Shapiro et al., 1969; Shapiro, Tursky, & Schwartz, 1970). Schwartz (1972) found that larger reductions in blood pressure could be obtained when feedback was provided for decreases in both heart rate and blood pressure.

Direct blood pressure feedback has been used in a number of case studies with hypertensive patients. Benson, Shapiro, Tursky, and Schwartz (1971) were able to produce systolic changes up to 34 mmHg in a series of five patients. Goldman, Kleinman, Snow, Bidus, and Korol (1975) reported decreases of 4 mmHg systolic and 13 mmHg diastolic in a seven-patient sample. Kristt and Engel (1975) also reported success in lowering systolic pressure with a similar method. However, their procedure included training subjects with feedback both to increase and to decrease systolic pressure in order to establish voluntary control.

Another treatment technique based on biofeedback has been reported to be effective in treating essential hypertension. Moeller (1973) demonstrated that training patients to reduce frontalis electromyographic (EMG) activity through feedback led to systolic and diastolic pressure reductions of 13 percent in 36 essential hypertensive patients following 4 months of training.

Finally, meditation-relaxation has been used in a number of clinical studies to achieve reductions in blood pressure in patients suffering from essential hypertension. Without any electronic equipment to provide biofeedback, Benson, Rosner, Marzetta, and Klemchuk (1974a, b) demonstrated that patients instructed in a procedure based on transcendental meditation (Maharishi, 1966) achieved blood pressure reduction. This occurred in borderline hypertensives as well as those also taking antihypertensive medications. After 25 weeks of regular practice, meditating subjects not on medication showed average decreases of 8 mmHg systolic and 4 mmHg diastolic pressure. The group being treated pharmacologically displayed similar reductions in pressure over a 20-week trial. Stone and DeLeo (1976) recently used a similar type of meditation in comparison to a no-treatment control and found that meditation produced small (5-10 mmHg) but significant reductions in blood pressure which were accompanied by reductions in plasma dopamine-beta-hydroxylase activity and in furosemide stimulated venous activity.

Taken together, these results suggest a strong case for the utility of behavioral procedures in the treatment of hypertension. However, it is not clear which of these methods is more effective than others or whether effects are maintained over time. It is also difficult in these studies to separate the nonspecific placebo effect from active treatment variables. The present investigation attempted to answer these questions by comparing the separate effects of three behavioral procedures in patients with essential hypertension: BP - direct feedback for reduction in both blood pressure and heart rate (Schwartz, 1972); EMG - EMG feedback for reduction in frontalis and forearm muscle tension; RELAX - a form of meditation-relaxation training (Benson et al., 1974 a, b). It was assumed that placebo effects would not differ across groups in that all treatments were "active" and could be expected to produce some change.

METHOD

Subjects considered for the study were volunteers on or off antihypertensive or psychotropic medication with a history of at least one year of labile or sustained systolic and/or diastolic hypertension (average systolic BP $\geq$ 140, average diastolic BP $\geq$ 90), who were less than 60 years old, and who had no evident organic etiology for hypertension or major complications thereof, and no other serious illness.

Twenty-seven potential subjects whose histories met these criteria were then seen for a detailed medical examination. Subjects meeting the criteria of the study were assigned to one of three groups matched for age, sex, current use or non-use of relevant medication, type of blood pressure elevation (systolic and/or diastolic), and lability or stability of hypertension. Blood pressure was considered labile if the subject had a history of normal systolic and diastolic readings bracketed by elevated readings and unrelated to medication effects. The BP and EMG groups were initially assigned 9 members each, and the RELAX group, 8 members. However, 1 subject from the BP group dropped out of the study, and 1 subject from the EMG group was dropped because of persistent tachycardia, leaving 8 subjects in each group. The mean age and blood pressures for the BP, EMG and RELAX groups were: 46 years, 157/95; 48 years, 155/94; and 45 years, 156/92, respectively. Both the BP and EMG groups consisted of 6 men and 2 women while the RELAX group consisted of 7 men and 1 woman. Approximately half of the subjects in each group were labile and half were taking antihypertensive or psychotropic medication.

Subjects were scheduled to attend 10 sessions (twice weekly for 5 weeks) plus a follow-up eleventh session approximately 6 weeks after the tenth session. The first 2 1-hour sessions constituted a baseline period and the remaining 8 sessions (1 to 1-1/2 hours each) consisted of blood-pressure reduction training trials according to the method for the given group.

During baseline and training sessions, subjects sat in a semi-recumbent lounge chair in the training room and were connected to equipment to measure frontalis EMG, forearm EMG, EKG and respiration. In addition, blood pressure was measured and tracked by the constant cuff method as described by Shapiro et al. (1969) and Tursky, Shapiro, and Schwartz (1972). At the start of each session the subject was isolated in the training room and three initial blood pressure (auscultatory method) readings were remotely taken from the apparatus room. These readings were averaged to approximate the median systolic pressure, which was used as the initial constant cuff pressure setting.

For the BP group, BP and heart rate changes were fed back by using the pattern procedure described by Schwartz (1972). A simultaneous reduction in BP (absence of Korotkoff sound) and heart rate on a beat of the heart resulted in auditory (beep) and visual (cumulative digital meter) feedback. If 75% or more of the potential Korotkoff sounds were present during a one-minute trial, the constant cuff pressure was raised 2 mmHg on the next trial; conversely, if there were 25% or fewer Korotkoff sounds, the cuff pressure was decreased 2 mmHg on the next trial. A similar shaping procedure simultaneously was used for heart rate. BP and heart rate were tracked in the same way for the other groups, but no cardiovascular feedback was provided.

For each group, training sessions consisted of 20 one-minute trials with the blood pressure cuff inflated to the median systolic pressure, alternating with 10-second rests with the cuff deflated. Feedback, where used, was given only during the 20 one-minute trials.

The EMG group heard a change in click signal frequency and observed the deflection of an analog meter as average EMG activity varied. The forearm extensor and frontalis EMG readings were averaged, and the integrated output of this signal was used to drive a voltage controlled oscillator, which produced auditory clicks directly proportional to average muscular activity. The integrated average of the two EMG signals also drove the analog meter. The task of the EMG group was to lower EMG activity.

The RELAX group was asked to meditate following the relaxation method of Benson et al. (1974a, 1974b) during each training session. Briefly, these subjects were instructed to relax and then to recite the word "one" on each breath. They were told to remain passive and to bring their attention back to the word "one" if their thoughts drifted. At the end of each session, subjects in each group were shown a cumulative graph of their progress in lowering blood pressure.

After the first training session, each subject received home practice sheets and was instructed to practice lowering blood pressure as much as possible between sessions. They were asked to record the frequency of this practice, and the record sheets were collected at the following session for the remaining eight sessions.

RESULTS

Pre-Treatment Baseline Data

To determine if the three treatment groups differed in average blood pressure prior to the beginning of training, a two-way analysis of variance (ANOVA) was made of the three treatment groups and the five pre-treatment repeated measures of baseline BP: 1) average BP based on prior medical history; 2) average BP obtained in the physician's examination; 3) average BP at the beginning of baseline session 1; 4) average BP at the beginning of baseline session 2; 5) average BP at the beginning of training session 1. Results of the ANOVA showed that baseline differences between treatment groups were not significant for either systolic or diastolic pressure. However, it may be noted in Table 1 that

Table 1

Pre- and Post-Treatment Blood Pressure (mmHg)

Sessions	Groups BP n=8	EMG n=8	RELAX n=8	All Subjects n=24
Pre-Treatment				
Prior Medical History (average pre-study)	157/94	155/94	156/92	156/94
Physician's Exam.	158/104	166/105	170/100	165/103
Baseline Session 1 (initial value)	144/91	141/87	146/88	144/89
Baseline Session 2 (initial value)	139/88	140/86	146/88	142/87
Training Session 1 (initial value)	140/89	140/88	137/87	139/88
Post-Treatment				
Follow-up Session (initial value)	139/84	137/88	137/85	138/86

pressure varied considerably under the different conditions of observation. Pressures were highest for the physician's examination and previous medical history and lowest for the two baseline sessions and the initial training session. Differences among the five baseline measurements were significant for both systolic and diastolic values ($p < .001$).

Treatment Data

The primary treatment data consisted of systolic BP values obtained during eight sessions of treatment, 20 values per session, representing the median systolic pressures derived from the constant cuff method for each one-minute trial or period of observation. An ANOVA was carried out on these data, for the three treatment groups with repeated measures for eight sessions, 20 trials within each session. A significant main effect was obtained for trials ($p < .001$). On the average, pooling sessions and treatment groups, the initial value was 140.2 and the 20th value was 136.8 mmHg. No other main effects or interactions were statistically significant. The three groups did not differ from each other in the amount of systolic BP change observed either during any one session or over sessions.

Average first and last BP values for each session are shown in Table 2. As can be seen, reductions in pressure over the 20 trials were larger in baseline sessions than in training sessions. An ANOVA comparing baseline session 2 with training session 6 (the best training effect) supports this conclusion ($p < .01$). Secondly, note that the RELAX group showed an immediate drop in pressure at the very first trial of training session 1, while the other two groups showed a slight increase, as compared with baseline session 1. The findings may reflect a difference between the task or problem-solving orientation of the BP and EMG feedback procedures and the simple passive relaxation orientation of the RELAX procedure.

Follow-up Data

At the 6-week follow-up no significant differences were obtained between groups. Comparing the three groups, average systolic and diastolic values were quite comparable (Table 1), and the first and last trial values were also very similar (Table 2). Comparing these values to the medical history or to initial value obtained by the physician, the reductions in pressure for all subjects were 18/8 and 27/17 mmHg, respectively. However, comparing these same follow-up values to the values obtained at the beginning of the first training session (actual third pre-training contact with

Table 2

Systolic Blood Pressure (mmHg)
First and Last Trial Values

Sessions		BP n=8	EMG n=8	RELAX n=8	All Subjects n=24
		Groups			
BASELINE	1	141-136	142-134	142-142	142-138
	2	138-134	140-132	145-136	141-134
TRAINING	1	143-142	142-140	137-136	141-139
	2	140-139	141-137	138-134	140-137
	3	138-137	145-140	138-133	140-137
	4	137-137	138-137	140-138	138-137
	5	137-136	141-134	139-134	139-135
	6	134-128	141-140	138-132	138-133
	7	143-142	143-140	139-133	142-138
	8	143-139	146-143	139-133	143-138
FOLLOW-UP	1	139-135	136-130	137-134	138-133

the laboratory), the reductions were quite small--1 mmHg systolic and 2 mmHg diastolic.

Associated Changes During Treatment

An ANOVA comparable to the one carried out on systolic pressure was done on heart rate during training. No significant effects related to treatment group were found. As in the case of systolic blood pressure, a significant main effect for trials was observed ($p < .001$). On the average, there was a 3 bpm decrease in HR during sessions from trial 1 to trial 20. There were no significant effects over sessions.

DISCUSSION

The purpose of this study was to compare the effectiveness of three different behavioral methods of lowering blood pressure in patients with essential hypertension. It was expected on the basis of previous studies that the procedures would be effective to some degree. This was not the case. There is little evidence either during the course of the treatment sessions or in the six-week follow-up session of a significant reduction in pressure in any group. If one takes the initial pressure values immediately prior to the beginning of training as a baseline, the average reductions for all 24 patients at the time of the follow-up was 1 mmHg systolic and 2 mmHg diastolic. No one treatment procedure was obviously superior to any other. For each of the methods employed in this study, several earlier studies have been cited which reported average reductions in pressure ranging from 5 to 15% of pre-training baseline values. The failure to obtain even small reductions in the present study is therefore quite puzzling. Some speculations can be offered on the reasons for this failure and the apparent inconsistency between previous and present findings.

First, differences between this study and previous reports must be taken into account. Unlike previous investigations involving the use of direct blood pressure feedback, this study required that subjects lower their heart rates as well as their blood pressures. Because many subjects did not have high heart rates, this may have made the task exceedingly difficult. Also, previous studies involving behavioral treatment of hypertension through direct blood pressure biofeedback used patients with sustained hypertension whose pressures were usually higher than subjects studied here. Subjects in the Benson et al. study showed average pretraining systolic pressures of 165 mmHg, and Goldman et al.'s sample averaged 167 mmHg, whereas our subjects showed average pretraining pressures of 141 mmHg during the first three laboratory exposures prior to training. It is completely possible that the effectiveness of behavioral treatment follows the law of initial values (Wilder, 1950) and that only patients with exceedingly high pressures will show substantial benefit from behavioral intervention.

Another difference between this study and previous reports is that the present investigation gave all subjects a rather limited amount of training and attention. Only eight training sessions were used in the present study as compared to up to 34 sessions in the Benson et al. report, or 42 sessions in the Kristt and Engel study. It is of interest, however, that the one subject studied by Benson et al. who had both similar baseline pressures and number of training sessions showed a similar reduction in pressure as subjects in our study. Also, in the Goldman et al. study in which only nine treatment sessions were used, systolic reductions of only 4% were observed although diastolic changes were much larger.

Meditation-relaxation seemed as effective in lowering blood pressure within sessions as either biofeedback technique. Furthermore, decreases in blood pressure from meditation-relaxation were more consistent over sessions than changes achieved through biofeedback. Due to its inherent simplicity, it could be seen to have some advantage over other methods. However, the blood pressure reduction achieved in one of the baseline sessions during simple rest was larger than those produced in any of the subsequent treatment sessions. Therefore, it is not clear as to whether changes achieved through the withdrawal of stimulation and motivational demands are as therapeutically meaningful as changes achieved through more active coping.

Finally, rather large differences were observed between pressure levels obtained in the medical history and in our physician's examination as compared with the levels obtained in quiet laboratory conditions, particularly after a few baseline, non-task, recording sessions. These differences range up to 20 mmHg systolic and 15 mmHg diastolic. They attest to the potency of real-life variables (e.g., doctor's examination) versus the lack of potency of non-stimulating, laboratory conditions. Such variability has been noted repeatedly in the literature (Julius & Shork, 1971). Engel (personal communication) has suggested that the physician effect or habituation to the physician and medical situation may account in part for the placebo effect noted in hypertensive research (see Miller, 1974). It is obvious that we need to pay more attention to the sources of variability in blood pressure, particularly in patients with essential hypertension, as these sources may tell us more about the nature of the disorder and give us clues about the design of appropriate behavioral treatment procedures.

REFERENCES

Benson, H., Rosner, B. A., Marzetta, B. R., & Klemchuk, H. M. Decreased blood-pressure in pharmacologically treated hypertensive patients who regularly elicited the relaxation response. Lancet, 1974, 7852, 289-291. (a)

Benson, H., Rosner, B. A., Marzetta, B. R., & Klemchuk, H. M. Decreased blood pressure in borderline hypertensive subjects who practiced meditation. Journal of Chronic Disease, 1974, 27, 163-169. (b)

Benson, H., Shapiro, D., Tursky, B., & Schwartz, G. E. Decreased systolic blood pressure through operant conditioning techniques in patients with essential hypertension. Science, 1971, 173, 740-742.

Goldman, H., Kleinman, K. M., Snow, M. Y., Bidus, D. R., & Korol, B. Relationship between essential hypertension and cognitive functioning: Effects of biofeedback. Psychophysiology, 1975, 12, 569-573.

Julius, S., & Shork, M. Borderline hypertension: A critical review. Journal of Chronic Diseases, 1971, 23, 723.

Kristt, D. A., & Engel, B. T. Learned control of blood pressure patients with high blood pressure. Circulation, 1975, 51, 370-378.

Maharishi Mahesh Yogi. The science of being and art of living. London: International SMP Publications, 1966.

Miller, N. E. Preface. In N. E. Miller, T. X. Barber, L. V. DiCara, J. Kamiya, D. Shapiro, & J. Stoyva (Eds.), Biofeedback and self-control, 1973. Chicago: Aldine, 1974.

Moeller, T. A. Reduction of arterial blood pressure through relaxation training and correlates of personality in hypertensives. Unpublished doctoral dissertation, Nova University, Fort Lauderdale, Florida, 1973.

Schwartz, G. E. Voluntary control of human cardiovascular integration and differentiation through feedback and reward. Science, 1972, 175, 90-93.

Shapiro, D., & Surwit, R. S. Learned control of physiological function and disease. In H. Leitenberg (Ed.), Handbook of behavior modification and behavior therapy. New York: Prentice-Hall, 1976.

Shapiro, D., Tursky, B., Gershon, E., & Stern, M. Effects of feedback and reinforcement on the control of human systolic blood pressure. Science, 1969, 163, 588-589.

Shapiro, D., Tursky, B., & Schwartz, G. E. Control of blood pressure in man by operant conditioning. Circulation Research (Supplement 1), 1970, 26-27, 27-32.

Stone, R. A., & DeLeo, J. Psychotherapeutic control of hypertension. New England Journal of Medicine, 1976, 294, 80-84.

Tursky, B., Shapiro, D., & Schwartz, G. E. Automated constant cuff-pressure system to measure average systolic and diastolic blood pressure in man. IEEE Transactions on Biomedical Engineering, 1972, 19, 271-276.

Wilder, J. The law of initial values. Psychosomatic Medicine, 1950, 12, 392.

NOTE

This research was supported by National Institute of Mental Health Research Grants MH-26923 and MH-25104, Training Grant MH-06415, and Office of Naval Research Contract N00014-75-C-0150. Computing assistance was obtained from the Health Sciences Computing Facility, UCLA, supported by NIH Special Research Resources Grant RR-3.

BIOFEEDBACK AND DIFFERENTIAL CONDITIONING OF RESPONSE PATTERNS IN THE SKELETAL MOTOR SYSTEM

Eberhard E. Fetz
Departments of Physiology & Biophysics and Neurological Surgery and Regional Primate Research Center
University of Washington at Seattle

While biofeedback techniques are being extensively applied in operantly conditioning an impressive variety of central and autonomic nervous system responses, our ignorance of the neural mechanisms underlying operant learning remains virtually complete. Indeed, we still have the most elementary and speculative conception of how the nervous system initiates a simple voluntary motor response, no less how the occurrence of such a response can be modified by reinforcement. Our understanding of neural mechanisms underlying operant responding will probably advance soonest in the skeletal motor system, for several reasons. A basic understanding of the neural pathways converging onto spinal motoneurons has emerged from a century of anatomical and electrophysiological studies. More recently developed experimental techniques now make it possible to study activity of identified neurons in awake animals trained to perform relevant motor responses. In such experiments, biofeedback techniques could prove particularly useful in investigating functional relations between elements of the skeletal motor system. We will first review some relevant facts concerning the functional organization of the final elements in the skeletal motor system and then consider past and potential applications of biofeedback techniques to investigate this system.

FINAL ELEMENTS OF SKELETAL MOTOR SYSTEM

Figure 1 diagrams some of the basic elements of the peripheral skeletal motor system which are of present concern. The functional peripheral element is the motor unit, comprised of a single motoneuron and its asso-

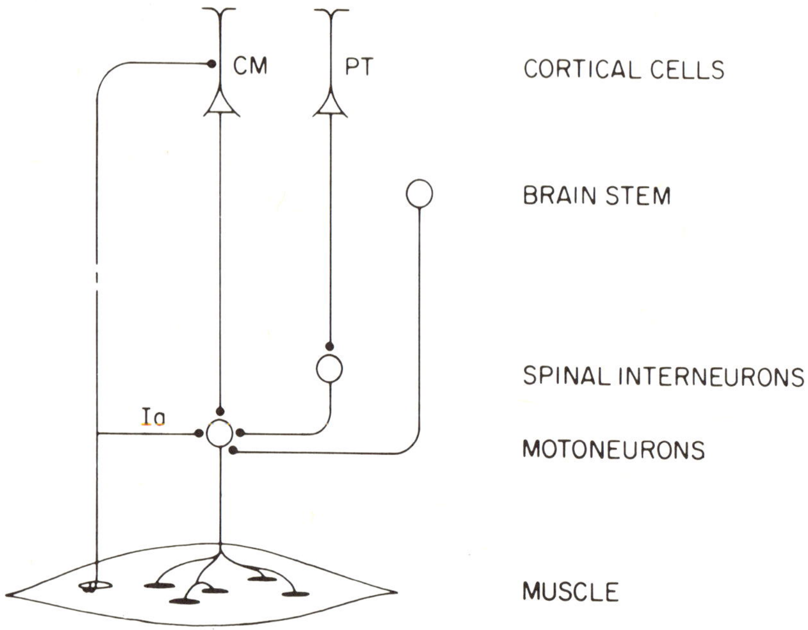

Figure 1. Schematic representation of the final elements of the skeletal motor system considered in text. A motoneuron and its associated muscle fibers comprise the motor unit. Motoneurons are influenced by corticospinal cells, both monosynaptically via corticomotoneuronal (CM) cells and polysynaptically via other pyramidal tract (PT) cells which synapse on spinal interneurons. Presence of sensory feedback loops and other descending motor systems are also indicated.

ciated muscle fibers, all of which are activated as a unit when the motoneuron fires. Skeletal limb muscles typically are comprised of several hundred such motor units. Activity of each unit produces a contractile twitch tension which summates with the twitch tension of other units to produce the net force output of the muscle. Depending on load, this force then produces a change in the muscle length and of the limb position. As net active tension increases, motor units appear to be recruited in a systematic sequence, in order of increasing motoneuron size (Henneman, Somjen, & Carpenter, 1965). In general the relation between electromyographic (EMG activity of a muscle and net tension is not linear, but under isometric conditions, ($\Delta P=0$), net tension is approximately proportional to rectified EMG activity.

The neural pathways converging onto the motoneuron arise from cells in diverse areas: spindle receptors of the same muscle, spinal interneurons, brain stem nuclei, and cerebral cortex. The relative functional importance of each of these systems remains of current experimental interest. A convenient candidate for study in behaving animals are the corticospinal or pyramidal tract (PT) cells, which arise primarily from motor cortex. In the primate some PT cells terminate directly on motoneurons (Kuypers, 1960). The excitatory potency of the corticomotoneuronal (CM) synapse has been demonstrated by stimulating cortex and recording intracellularly the evoked membrane potentials in individual motoneurons. Maximal stimulation, activating all of the cortical cells converging onto a motoneuron (called the motoneuron's "colony") typically produces a depolarization of 2-3 millivolts in forelimb motoneurons of the baboon, insufficient by itself to activate the motoneuron (Phillips & Porter, 1964; Preston & Whitlock, 1961). Less intense cortical stimuli recruit fewer CM cells and evoke smaller EPSPs. Minimal EPSPs are on the order of 100 microvolts (Porter & Hore, 1969), comparable to those produced by single Ia afferent fibers (Mendell & Henneman, 1971). Repetitive activation of the corticospinal cells is nevertheless quite effective in eliciting motor responses (Porter, 1970).

In addition to this basic corticomotoneuronal connection, one must remember the existence of the following important elements: proprioceptive feedback from muscle receptors to both motoneurons and supraspinal cells, other descending systems from brainstem (rubrospinal, reticulospinal, vestibulospinal) converging onto the motoneuron, and higher order cells converging on PT cells. These complexities defeat efforts to generate a simple neural model of motor control and certainly preclude any notion that motor cortex cells are the final controllers of motoneurons. Nevertheless, understanding the role of motor cortex cells in movements is an important first step, and a variety of experimental strategies have been applied to investigating the functional relations between motor cortex cells and motor units.

BASIC BIOFEEDBACK PARADIGM

Before considering applications of biofeedback techniques to investigating corticomotoneuronal relations, it is worth reviewing the basic variables found in most biofeedback studies, as diagrammed in Figure 2. Biofeedback experiments involve a reinforced response, R+, which is the activity on which reinforcement (S^R) is contingent. As the biofeedback literature attests, a large variety of CNS and ANS responses have served as reinforced responses. In addition to the reinforced response, there is also a set of responses which occur simultaneously, but which are not directly reinforced, namely, the correlated responses (RO). The subject is also exposed to several relevant stimuli which potentially affect the subsequent

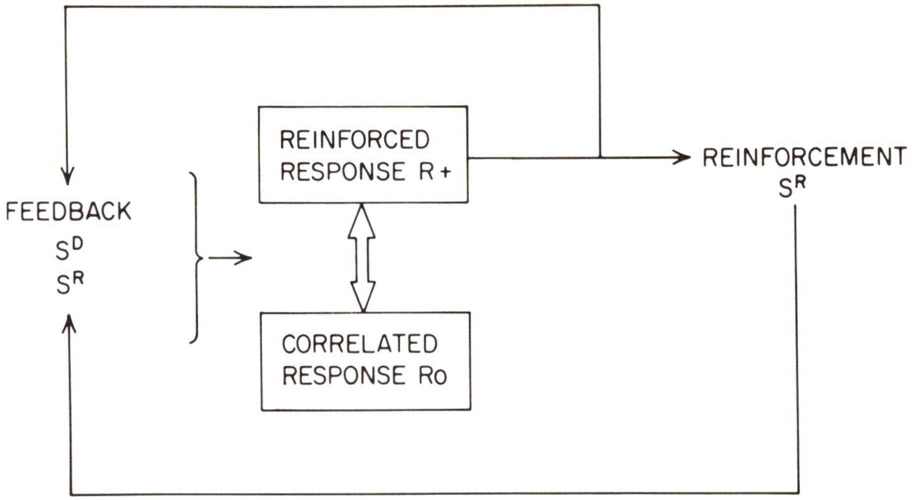

Figure 2. Schematic of basic variables in biofeedback experiments. Reinforcement (S^R) and exteroceptive feedback are contingent upon occurrence of the reinforced response (R+). Correlated responses (RO) which occur in association with R+ may have a variety of functional relations with R+ (see text). The discriminative stimuli (S^D), reinforcement, and feedback may affect subsequent responses directly, as well as through operant conditioning.

responses. The first is the reinforcing stimulus (S^R), e.g., food, intracranial stimulation, etc.; and the discriminative stimuli (S^D) which signal the availability of the reinforcer. Of course, the essential element in biofeedback experiments is the exteroceptive feedback concerning the value of the reinforced response. By having explicit auditory or visual feedback concerning otherwise unconscious responses, the subject can better learn to control these responses. The diagram suggests that these stimuli may potentially affect subsequent responses. These stimuli could have unconditioned effect on either the reinforced or the correlated response. For example, intracranial stimulation reinforcement has a general arousing effect on motor responses; visual feedback may desynchronize alpha waves etc. These effects need to be controlled by use of noncontingent reinforcement or, better yet, bidirectional conditioning of the reinforced response.

The relations between R+ and RO are often of considerable experimental interest. The reinforced response may be either causally or adventitiously related to the correlated response. Among the causally related RO are those which produce, or "mediate," R+; those which are produced by R+; and those which may be produced along with R+ by yet another RO. Any of these possibilities produce a correlation between RO and S^R which tends to sustain the occurrence of RO. Besides such causal relations, the simultaneous occurrence of RO may also be accidental; in this case, its occurrence could be superstitiously maintained. However, independent fluctuations between RO and S^R should tend to make RO eventually drop out, i.e., spontaneously dissociate from R+. The nature of the functional relations between R+ and RO can often be further tested by preventing the occurrence of RO (e.g., by paralyzing agents) or by differentially reinforcing the occurrence of R+ in the absence of RO (making RO now part of a more extensive reinforced response, $R+_2$).

INVESTIGATIONS OF SKELETAL MOTOR SYSTEM

Many experiments on the functional relations between the final elements in the skeletal motor system (Figure 1) may be understood in terms of the above concepts. A common experimental strategy is to reinforce particular movements (R+ = position or force trajectory) and observe correlated activity of motor units or motor cortex cells. For example, to investigate the relation of motor units to force, a useful motor response is a gradual increase in muscle tension. As net tension increases, new motor units are recruited into activity and the firing rate of active units increases slightly. Each motor unit has a specific level of net tension at which it is recruited; this means that each unit has a fixed recruitment order relative to other motor units of that muscle. This recruitment order appears to be the same, independent of which pathways are used to activate the motor units (Henneman, Somjen, & Carpenter, 1965). Moreover, motor units appear to be recruited in order of increasing size. This relationship --called the "size principle"--implies that any convergent pathway to a muscle affects all its motoneurons equally. If true, this principle represents an enormous simplification in the functional organization of motoneuron pools. Consistent with this hypothesis is the finding of Mendell and Henneman (1971) that single Ia afferent fibers send terminal connections to virtually all homonymous motoneurons. Whether this principle can be violated by trained voluntary effort remains an important experimental issue. The prediction that the recruitment of a given unit invariably occurs at a fixed level of net tension could be tested by attempting to dissociate motor unit activity and net tension. Another testable prediction is that two units of the same muscle with substantially different recruitment levels could not be activated without the lower threshold unit. Harrison and Mortensen (1962) and Basmajian (1973) reported that any of several motor units in hand muscles could be activated in isolation under conditions of free limb movements. Henneman, Shahani, & Young (1976) attempted to replicate these results, without success in 6 of 9 subjects; 3 subjects had sporadic, but unreliable, success in activating either of two units whose recruitment levels were close. Hannerz (1974) has shown that rapid phasic contractions may sometimes preferentially activate high threshold units, but confirms the difficulty of doing this under maintained levels of force. Further direct tests of the size principle using appropriate biofeedback would clearly be of considerable experimental interest.

The strategy of reinforcing specific movements has also proven useful for investigating correlated responses in motor cortex cells. In monkeys trained to move a handle through similar displacements but against different loads, Evarts first observed that activity of many precentral PT neurons covaried more strongly with the net force exerted or its derivative than with displacement (Evarts, 1967, 1968). Precentral cells related to jaw movements showed a less consistent relation to force, being strongly activated during the initial reaction-time bite, but sometimes being negligibly related to subsequent force components (Luschei, Garthwaite, & Armstrong, 1971). Humphrey, Schmidt, and Thompson (1970) found that both force and position parameters of a recurrent wrist movement could be predicted from the weighted average activity of a population of precentral cells, with an accuracy increasing with the number of cells included.

While these studies confirm that activity of precentral cells is correlated with movement, the details of the unit-muscle relationships remain unresolved. Interpretation of motor cortex cell responses typically proceeds in terms of the simplest view--namely that these cells are directly involved in activating specific muscles. Consistent with this view are those cells covarying closely with major agonists of the movement. Other cells, whose activity exhibits more complex or less intense covariation with the pretrained movement are often assumed to be directly related to other muscles, whose involvement is correspondingly less direct. While this model may be true for some precentral cells, it risks oversimplifying the relation of many motor cortex cells to movements.

The issue in question concerns the topographical relations between specific precentral cells and muscles. It is quite conceivable, for example, that a given motor cortex cell may be functionally related to activation of several different limb muscles. Moreover, it may be related in more subtle ways than simple covariation. To investigate such questions, biofeedback conditioning techniques have been used to train monkeys to contract specific arm muscles in isolation, and correlated activity of motor cortex cells was observed (Fetz & Finocchio, 1971, 1975). In these experiments, there was a set of {R+} consisting of isolated, isometric contractions of four representative arm muscles--a flexor and extensor of wrist and elbow--and the correlated response, RO, was the activity of specific motor cortex cells. Isolated muscle activity was differentially reinforced by using a voltage proportional to the weighted sum of activity in all muscles, the weights being positive for the muscle to be activated and negative for the muscles to be suppressed. Besides receiving fruit juice reinforcement when this voltage exceeded a threshold, the monkey had continuous visual feedback via an illuminated meter whose deflection was proportional to the voltage. After several weeks of training the monkey could be rapidly shaped to activate any of the four muscles in relative isolation. In these experiments, most motor cortex cells were found to become active with more than one of the four arm muscles. For example, a single precentral cell could be activated with either the wrist flexor or elbow flexor. Other PT cells were activated with both biceps and triceps, i.e., antagonists of the same joint. Still others were active in the same way with all four muscles, suggesting stronger relation to the occurrence of the response than its topography. These results suggest that many motor cortex cells have a higher order relation to muscles than the one-to-one relation of motoneurons. Figure 3 illustrates the activity of a PT cell which fired with both biceps (Figure 3C) and triceps (Figure 3D) under isometric conditions, but showed negligible modulation in relation to activation of the wrist flexor (Figure 3A) or extensor (Figure 3B).

Experiments in which R+ was a peripheral response (limb movement or muscle contraction) while RO was motor cortex cell activity have revealed that in a given cortical area many motor cortex cells may not be strongly related to the pretrained responses. Whether these cells are related to other responses or not related to any can be investigated by the reverse experimental strategy, namely, reinforcing activity of the cortical cell and observing the correlated motor response (Fetz, 1969; Fetz & Baker, 1973). Using this approach the movement or "motor field" associated with each isolated motor cortex cell can be characterized, much as the receptive field of individual sensory cortex cells can be characterized (Fetz, 1974). When R+ was an operant burst of motor cortex cell activity and RO was free limb movement, a variety of correlated motor responses were observed for different precentral cells. For some cells operant bursts were repeatedly associated with specific movements of a certain joint. For other cells operant bursts occurred with more generalized and variable movements; these movements sometimes became more specific and repeatable as reinforcement of cell activity continued, suggesting that many components of the response which dropped out may have been adventitiously correlated with the cell, whereas the components which remained may have had a stronger, possibly causal relationship with the cell. For other cells operant bursts continued to be associated with a variety of dif-

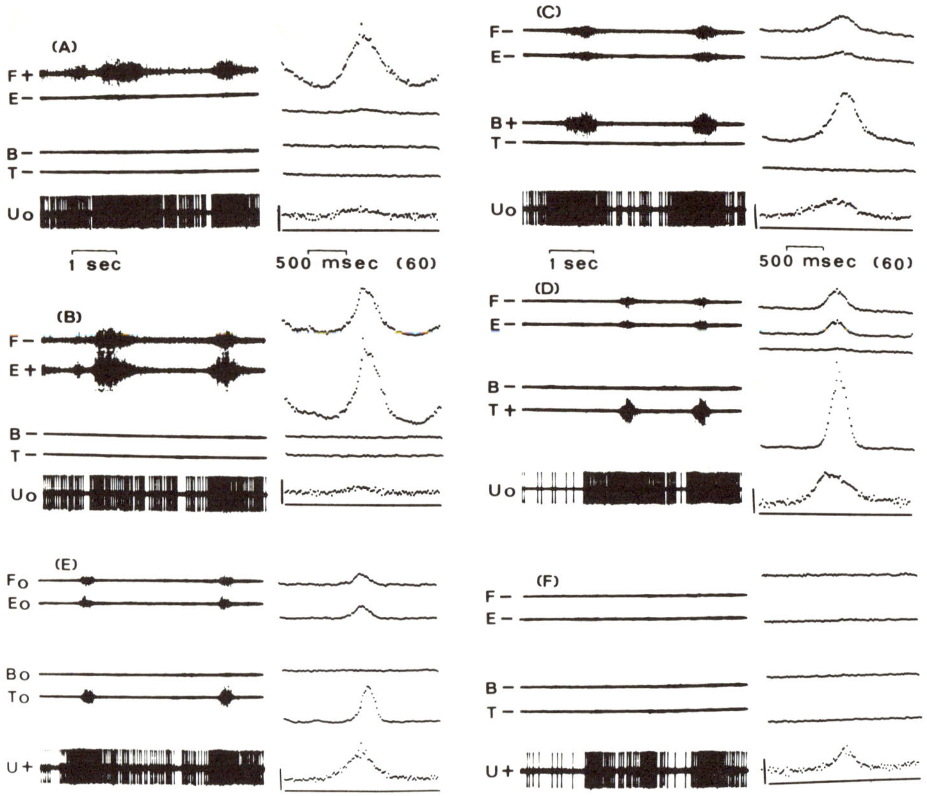

Figure 3. Activity of a precentral pyramidal tract cell and four representative arm muscles during isometric operantly conditioned response patterns. Examples of two successive responses shown at left; averages over 60 responses at right. EMG activity of flexor carpi radialis (F), extensor carpi radialis (E), biceps (B), and triceps (T), and responses of precentral unit (U) are labeled with a "+" or "−" to indicate that activity or suppression of that element was reinforced, and with a "0" to indicate that activity was not included in the reinforcement contingency. (A)-(D): reinforcement of isolated EMG activity in each arm muscle--(A) flexor carpi radialis, (B) extensor carpi radialis, (C) biceps, (D) triceps. (E): reinforced operant unit bursts with associated muscle activity. (F): reinforced unit bursts and muscle suppression. All EMG activity shown at same gain; vertical bars calibrate 50/sec unit firing rate. (From Fetz & Finocchio, 1975).

ferent movements and it was impossible to identify a common component. Finally, some cortical cells were repeatedly activated in operant bursts without any observable correlated motor response. In a given region of motor cortex, examples of each type of cell were found interspersed (Fetz & Finocchio, 1975).

While visual observation of motor responses provides qualitative information concerning the movements associated with operant bursts of a motor cortex cell, recording of EMG activity provides a more quantifiable measure of the extent and time course of correlated muscle activity. The patterns of EMG activity associated with operant bursts of a cell were found to be more repeatable under isometric conditions than under conditions of free limb movement. We have called the set of muscles which are coactivated with operant bursts of a precentral cell the cell's "motor field," as a behavioral analog of the receptive field of sensory cortex cells. For example, when bursts of activity of the cell in Figure 3 were reinforced, the motor field included triceps, flexor carpi radialis and extensor carpi radialis (Figure 3D). Clearly, the unit-muscle correlations seen when the cell was reinforced are not necessarily the same as those seen when muscle activity was reinforced. In Figure 3 the only correlation which consistently appeared under both conditions was the unit-triceps correlation. This correlation was also observed during active extension of the elbow (Fetz & Finocchio, 1975, Figure 6). In contrast, the correlation with wrist muscles appeared only when the unit was reinforced, but not when the wrist muscles were activated. This suggests that some muscles in the "motor field" may not always be consistently correlated under other behavioral conditions. However, the muscle which was most consistently correlated with the cell under different circumstances was usually the muscle which was most strongly activated with operant bursts (e.g. triceps in Figure 3). For the cell in Figure 3, the unit-biceps correlation was the least consistent under different behavioral conditions; unit and biceps activity were positively correlated when biceps was reinforced (3C), not correlated when the unit was reinforced (3E), and negatively correlated during active elbow movements, i.e., the unit was suppressed while the biceps was activated during elbow flexion. This suggests that unit-muscle correlations may depend strongly on the behavioral circumstances, and that they should be tested under a variety of conditions to determine which ones are the most consistent.

DISSOCIATION OF CORRELATIONS

As argued elsewhere (Fetz, 1974; Fetz & Finocchio, 1975), the "strongest" unit-muscle correlations are those which involve the most intense coactivation of cells and muscle and those which appear most consistently under different behavioral conditions. However, even the strongest unit-muscle correlations could be changed by operantly reinforcing their dissociation. Thus, for the PT cell in Figure 3, the unit-triceps correlation, which appeared during triceps activity, unit reinforcement, and active elbow extension, could be dissociated when the monkey was reinforced for activating the cell and suppressing all muscle activity (Figure 3E). Similar dissociation was achieved for all precentral cells tested in this study and appeared to be as easy to shape as isolated muscle activity. Thus, operant reinforcement of the dissociation revealed a degree of plasticity in these correlations which was not apparent when either units, muscles, or movements were the reinforced responses. In retrospect, this result might not be considered surprising since the effect of a single precentral cell, even those which have direct corticomotoneuronal connections, is subthreshold for firing the motoneuron and could in principle be easily overridden by the combined effects of other descending pathways. The fact that these cells and motor units can be so independently activated, however, does reveal an unexpected degree of flexibility in the system. In contrast to motor units, whose activity cannot be readily dissociated--if at all--from activity of homonymous motor units, motor cortex cells appear to have more flexible relations to muscle activity and force. Similarly, pairs of adjacent cortical cells which covaried strongly during both active and passive limb movements could be activated independently when the monkey was differentially reinforced for increasing activity of one cell and suppressing the other (Fetz & Baker, 1973). Clearly, operantly conditioning specific patterns of responses in these cells and muscles provides more extensive and detailed information concerning their functional relations than could be obtained by reinforcing movements alone.

CONNECTIONS REVEALED BY CROSS-CORRELATIONS

The fact that many motor cortex cells covary strongly and consistently with muscle activity raises the issue of their anatomical relationship. Some of these cells may have direct corticomotoneuronal connections; many more probably have indirect connections via spinal interneurons, brainstem neurons, or other corticospinal cells. Strong correlations--in the sense of consistent covariation--between motor cortex cell and muscle activity may suggest a functional relationship, but cannot establish the existence of a direct CM connection. Since many unconnected cells and muscles may be coactivated, such covariation is not sufficient to establish a connection. Moreover, since the effect of a direct CM connection is subthreshold for activating the motoneuron, consistent coactivation is not even a necessary consequence of a connection. An extensive search for an independent method of establishing connections led to the finding that cross-correlation procedures could be used to detect monosynaptic CM connections. A convenient approximation to a true cross-correlation is the spike-triggered average, which preferentially summates those post-synaptic events consistently correlated with the action potentials triggering the average. Mendell and Henneman (1971) first used this technique to establish that action potentials in single Ia afferent fibers were followed by monosynaptic EPSPs in virtually all homonymous motoneurons. We have found that triggering an average from action potentials of motor cortex cells and summing rectified EMG activity of covarying muscles may reveal the effects of direct CM connections (Fetz, Cheney, & German, 1976). For certain cells, the average EMG exhibits a transient post-spike facilitation (PSF) following the cortical spike at a latency consistent with known conduction times and having a time course resembling the shape of electrically evoked CM-EPSPs (Phillips & Porter, 1964; Preston & Whitlock, 1961). The simplest interpretation of this PSF is that it is mediated by a direct monosynaptic CM connection. Of 201 precentral cells strongly covarying with either flexion or extension of the wrist, 54 were followed by PSF in one or more muscles. The possibility that a single CM cell may facilitate motoneurons of more than one muscle via divergent terminal connections was tested by averaging EMG activity of 5 different synergistic muscles. Of 41 cells followed by PSF in at least one of the 5 muscles, 10 exhibited PSF in more than half of the muscles. Thus, the set of muscles followed by PSF for a given cell--called the cell's "muscle field"--may include at least several different synergists of a joint. Seventy-five percent of the cells had PSF in one or two of the 5 muscles, suggesting more restricted muscle fields.

CONCLUSION

In summary, we now have several fruitful strategies for investigating the functional organization of the final elements of the motor system. The observation of consistent covariation between cells and muscles during certain motor responses provides evidence of a functional relationship. Operantly conditioning specific response patterns in cells and muscles with biofeedback is a particularly powerful technique for testing the strength and stability of such covariations. More recently, the spike-triggered average, as a convenient approximation to a cross-correlation, has proven capable of detecting the existence and extent of anatomical connections. Clearly the most interesting work lies still ahead--namely to combine these techniques to test the covariation of cortical cells whose anatomical connections to motoneurons may be independently established.

REFERENCES

Basmajian, J. V. Muscles alive. Baltimore: Williams & Wilkins, 1973.

Chang, H. T., Ruch, T. C., & Ward, A. A., Jr. Topographical representation of muscles in motor cortex of monkeys. Journal of Neurophysiology, 1947, 10, 39-56.

Evarts, E. V. Representation of movements and muscles by pyramidal tract neurons of the precentral motor cortex. In M. D. Yahr & D. P. Purpura (Eds.), Neurophysiological basis of normal and abnormal motor control. Hewlett, New York: Raven Press, 1967.

Evarts, E. V. Relation of pyramidal tract activity to force exerted during voluntary movement. Journal of Neurophysiology, 1968, 31, 14-27.

Fetz, E. E. Operant conditioning of cortical unit activity. Science, 1969, 163, 955-957.

Fetz, E. E. Operant control of single unit activity and correlated motor responses. In M. Chase (Ed.), Operant control of brain activity. Los Angeles: UCLA Press, 1974.

Fetz, E. E., Cheney, P. D., & German, D. C. Corticomotoneuronal connections of precentral cells detected by post-spike averages of EMG activity in behaving monkeys. Brain Research, 1976, 114, 505-510.

Fetz, E. E., & Baker, M. A. Operantly conditioned patterns of precentral unit activity and correlated responses in adjacent cells and contralateral muscles. Journal of Neurophysiology, 1973, 36, 179-204.

Fetz, E. E., & Finnochio, D. V. Operant conditioning of specific patterns of neural and muscular activity. Science, 1971, 174, 431-435.

Fetz, E. E., & Finocchio, D. V. Correlations between activity of motor cortex cells and arm muscles during operantly conditioned response patterns. Experimental Brain Research, 1975, 23, 217-240.

Fetz, E. E., & Wyler, A. R. Operantly conditioned firing patterns of epileptic neurons in motor cortex of chronic monkey. Experimental Neurology, 1973, 40, 586-607.

Hanerz, J. Discharge properties of motor units in relation to recruitment order in voluntary contraction. Acta Physiol. Scand., 1974, 91, 374-384.

Harrison, V. F., & Mortensen, O. A. Identification and voluntary control of single motor unit activity in the tibialis anterior muscle. Anatomical Record, 1962, 144, 109-116.

Henneman, E., Shahani, B. T., & Young, R. R. The extent of voluntary control of human motor units. In M. Shahani (Ed.), The motor system: Neurophysiology and muscle mechanisms. New York: Elsevier, 73-78.

Henneman, E., Somjen, G., & Carpenter, D. O. Functional significance of cell size in spinal motoneurons. Journal of Neurophysiology, 1965, 28, 599-620.

Humphrey, D. R., Schmidt, D. M., & Thompson, W. D. Predicting measures of motor performance from multiple cortical spike trains. Science, 1970, 170, 758-762.

Kuypers, H. G. J. M. Central cortical connections to the motor and somatosensory cell groups. An experimental study in the rhesus monkey. Brain, 1960, 83, 161-184.

Luschei, E. S., Garthwaite, C. R., & Armstrong, M. E. Relationship of firing patterns of units in face area of monkey precentral cortex to conditioned jaw movements. Journal of Neurophysiology, 1971, 34, 552-561.

Mendell, L. M., & Henneman, E. Terminals of single Ia fibers: Location, density and distribution within a pool of 300 homonymous motoneurons. Journal of Neurophysiology, 1971, 34, 171-187.

Olds, J. Operant conditioning of single unit responses. Proceedings of the 23rd International Congress of Physiological Science, 1965, 372-380.

Phillips, C. G., & Porter, R. The pyramidal projection to motoneurons of some muscle groups of the baboon's forelimb. Progress in Brain Research, 1964, 12, 222-242.

Porter, R. Early facilitation at corticomotoneuronal synapses. Journal of Physiology, London, 1970, 207, 733-745.

Porter, R., & Hore, J. Time course of minimal corticomotoneuronal excitatory postsynaptic potentials in lumbar motoneurones of the monkey. Journal of Neurophysiology, 1969, 32, 443-451.

Preston, J. B., & Whitlock, D. G. Intracellular potentials recorded from motoneurons following precentral gyrus stimulation in primates. Journal of Neurophysiology, 1961, 24, 91-100.

BIOFEEDBACK IN THE TREATMENT OF NEUROMUSCULAR DISORDERS

Pola Engel-Sittenfeld
Nervenklinik der Universität München
Abteilung für Experimentelle und Klinische Psychologie

In this chapter the published papers and few yet unpublished abstracts on the treatment of neuromuscular disorders through biofeedback are reviewed. The term "neuromuscular disorders" as it is used here includes some areas that usually are not treated by physical rehabilitation methods, but render themselves apparently to biofeedback treatment, e.g. recto-sphincter responses (Kohlenberg, 1973; Engel, Nikoomanesh, & Schuster, 1974). Here as in the other cases described in the review, a muscular response that in healthy persons is voluntary, has lost this property due to disease and an attempt is made to reinstitute regular activity through operant conditioning procedures. Since the first major review on clinical applications of biofeedback (Blanchard & Young, 1974) the literature in this specific part of biofeedback research has vastly grown, including a large variety of approaches. Where some researchers seem to be mainly design oriented, others try to use biofeedback methods from a more clinical point of view. The earlier articles focus strongly on the technical side of biofeedback and describe in detail the application of this new method to a variety of disorders, resulting in rather anecdotal case reports (e.g., Marinacci & Horande, 1960). This broad range of intentions and resulting designs make it difficult for the reader to find out which disorders have been treated, the nature of the treatment, and the success of the outcome. The present review is therefore organized around the clinical symptom, and is mainly descriptive in nature. Final conclusions are only drawn in areas where the accumulated evidence is large enough to allow such a decision. In quite a few instances, judgements are left to the reader, who might or might not be willing to accept the evidence for his particular intentions.

HEMIPHLEGIA

The first report on the treatment of neuromuscular disorders with biofeedback (Marinacci & Horande, 1960) includes the treatment of hemiphlegia through EMG feedback. The authors succeeded in reeliciting neuromuscular potentials and developing twenty percent function in the previously nonfunctioning muscles of the left upper extremity of a patient within one hour.

This short training time is even lowered in a later report on 20 cases of hemiphlegia (Andrews, 1964). The patients, with a duration of illness between one and fourteen years, whose condition had become static following traditional physical therapy were treated with the help of visual EMG feedback. Seventeen of the twenty patients learned to generate motor unit activity in a previously nonfunctioning muscle within five minutes or less.

In a series of papers Brudny and collaborators (Brudny, Korein, Levidow, Grynbaum, Lieberman, & Friedman, 1974; Brudny, Korein, Grynbaum, Friedman, Weinstein, Sachs-Frankel, & Belandres, 1976) reported on 39 hemiparetic patients in whom the nonfunctional upper extremity was treated. The treatment goal in this case was to decrease volitionally spasms in spastic muscles and increase the strength of atrophied or paretic muscles rather than just demonstrate motor unit activity. All patients who were accepted into this study had failed to respond to traditional therapy after a long duration of disease. The treatment consisted typically of three to five weekly forty-minute sessions of visual plus auditory EMG feedback. After a training period of eight to twelve weeks, twenty-seven patients had achieved assistive capacity or actual prehension of the trained extremity. Twenty had retained significant functional gains after a three months to three years follow-up.

The authors also report on the retraining of the lower extremity in six patients, three of whom achieved previously absent ankle dorsiflection in a sitting or standing position, but showed only little carry over during actual ambulation.

In a well described procedure Johnson and Garton (1973) treated ten patients with foot dorsiflection paralysis, due to hemiphlegia of at least one year's duration. The treatment goal in this study consisted in gross foot dorsiflection and ambulation. After three thirty-minute training sessions in the laboratory, where patients received EMG feedback derived from needle-electrodes, training proceeded with a portable EMG feedback unit which the patients could take home and practice with twice daily for thirty minutes. Three of the patients developed a sufficiently functional and safe gait to eliminate the need of a short leg brace. In two patients no functional change was evident. The other five showed some functional improvement.

Amato, Hermsmeyer and Kleinman (1973) trained a patient with left hemiparesis with spastic overlay and spastic gait to inhibit spastic muscle activity in his gastronemicus muscle while simultaneously dorsiflexing his left ankle. After two months of training, the active range of motion of the left ankle had increased as well as the patient's gait, an improvement that apparently generalized to the nonfeedback condition. No follow-up data are reported.

Recently, Gavin and Stephen (1976) reported on the treatment of five hemiphlegic patients who received up to 107 training sessions. The authors defined treatment goals for every patient individually and found marked improvement in all of them. The training procedure consisted in relaxation training for spasms which started with forehead EMG feedback followed by feedback from involved musculature. Additionally, tapes with relaxation instructions for home training were used. Follow-up data are not available as some of the patients still underwent therapy at the time of the report.

In this as in all former reported studies, the only available control consists in the long duration of disturbance and patients' failure to respond to traditional therapy. In one recent study however, (Basmajian, Kukulla, Narayan, & Takebe, 1975), the authors used a parallel control group in the treatment of chronic footdrop in twenty hemiparetic stroke patients. While the ten experimental patients received twenty minutes of biofeedback training from the tibialis anterior muscle and twenty minutes of traditional physical therapy for forty minutes three times a week, the control patients received physical therapy only.

Results showed, that the combined physical therapy plus biofeedback group gained twice as much in strength of dorsiflection and range of motion. Three patients of this group improved enough to eliminate the need for their short leg braces.

In conclusion, there is no doubt that even after a longstanding disuse of muscles previously believed to be paralyzed, muscle activity can be reelicited if single motor unit firing can be detected in a relatively short time, even so it is reported to take longer for spastic subjects compared to normal controls (Harrison & Connolly, 1971) and in quadriplegic patients the control seems to be poorer (Simard & Ladd, 1971). The degree to which functional improvement can be achieved however, differs widely, in terms of treatment goals as well as in terms of necessary training time. Even if the psychological effect on a patient, who for the first time in years, learns that he can produce activity in one of his extremities, might be dramatic, it still might be a long way from this first movement to the functional use of such an extremity. It has been shown however, that biofeedback can enhance this process.

POLIOMYELITIS

Again, Marinacci and Horande (1964) pioneered in describing EMG feedback treatment of over twenty poliomyelitis patients--unfortunately again quite anecdotally. Apparently some degree of functional improvement was reached in the patients, who had been paralyzed from two to eight years. The treatment consisted in the increase of muscle volume through reactivation of single motor units.

Swaan, van Wieringer, and Fokkema studied the effect of EMG feedback and traditional physical therapy on the unwanted activity of the peroneus longus muscle in four hemiphlegic and three poliomyelitis patients. Patients received six sessions of combined physical therapy and EMG feedback. Results of the feedback trials provided lower EMG values and larger knee ankles than the physical therapy trials. The design however was obviously inappropriate to control for cumulative treatment effects and no clinical observations on the practical value of the treatment or follow-up data are reported.

Gavin and Stephen (1976) reported on the treatment of three polio patients, two of whom at that time still underwent therapy. One patient who had finished therapy reached his therapeutic goal, namely the development of muscle potential in his right calf and the extinction of inappropriate substitution of foot muscles in walking movements, within twenty-one training sessions. The other two patients showed marked improvement after twenty and sixty-six hours of training respectively. The patients had a long static condition before they started therapy.

The small number of polio patients treated so far with biofeedback allows no valuation of the method at the present time. As in the treatment of other symptoms, clinical value and treatment specific effects will have to be demonstrated.

CEREBRAL PALSY

Two groups of authors have reported on the treatment of cerebral palsy patients. Spearing and Poppen (1974) treated one specific disturbance, namely footdragging, in an athetoid cerebral palsy patient, using an ABA design and a loud horn as negative auditory feedback whenever the foot was dragged. Over the treatment, the patient reduced footdragging from about ninety percent of all steps to about two percent. During a three months treatment reversal, he went back to baseline conditions, indicating a need for booster sessions, if one considers the treatment reversal as follow-up. The result was treatment specific in another respect as well: The patient did not generalize the treatment effect to his untrained foot.

This is interesting in so far as the second group (Finley, Niman, Standley, & Ender, 1976; Finley, Niman, Standley, & Wansley, 1976) took a different approach in treating cerebral palsy patients with EMG feedback from the forehead in the attempt to alleviate muscle hypertonicity, one of the major habilitative problems in cerebral palsy. All participants in the study had a longstanding illness history and had shown to be refractory to conventional forms of therapy. The seven patients who took part in the first study received a baseline speech and motor evaluation prior to six weeks of auditory and visual EMG feedback relaxation training from the forehead. Accompanying a drop of almost fourteen microvolts (peak-to-peak) frontal EMG on the average, patients and their parents reported subtle improvements in various speech and motor functions, a finding that was confirmed by objective post-treatment evaluation, where all patients showed improvement in motor functions and only two, who had no speech at all to start with, did not improve in speech functions.

In the second study the authors treated four cerebral palsy children. This created a new problem, as the feedback signal itself was not reinforcing enough for this type of patient, and therefore a schedule was devised, where each subject received self-selected items as reinforcement for a certain amount of frontal relaxation that in turn was controlled by audiovisual EMG feedback from the forehead. An ABAB design was used. Over the first six-week treatment period all children showed substantial decreases in frontal EMG levels and concomitant speech functions; all but one had improved motor functioning. After the treatment reversal period, all children showed some deterioration of functioning, but regained and even improved their previously reached performance level again during the second four-week treatment period. As in the first study, a correspondence of low frontal EMG level and amount of improvement in speech and motor skills was seen.

These studies demonstrate two points: While the results indicate that EMG feedback might be helpful in the retraining and rehabilitation of cerebral palsy patients, booster sessions or probably constant home training seem to be important to keep up treatment effects. Secondly, in children and probably also in more disturbed adult patients, an additional reinforcer besides the feedback information might be necessary, thus bridging the gap between biofeedback and traditional operant conditioning techniques.

TORTICOLLIS

Torticollis is a disturbance of movement and postural control of the head and neck, often associated with neck muscle spasms and relatively refractory to a wide variety of treatments, including analytical psychotherapy, surgical intervention, and various types of medication. EMG feedback has been applied to this disturbance in a relatively large number of patients.

In the first published study (Cleeland, 1973) ten patients, three of whom had received prior medical treatment, were trained with a combination of electrical shock and EMG feedback whenever the muscle tension of their neck surpassed a certain threshold, that was lowered with progress. Number of training sessions varied from eight to twenty-three. Eight of the ten patients showed a substantial reduction of spasmodic activity; in six this improvement was stable for a mean follow-up period of nineteen months. Again we have a combination of traditional behavior therapy methods--shock as negative reinforcement--with biofeedback; the author reports that eight patients improved when shock was added to the EMG feedback. Another important observation is the tendency for younger patients with shorter symptom duration to improve most, a fact that should be considered in selecting patients for feedback training.

Brudny and collaborators have treated forty-eight patients with torticollis since their first report in 1974 (Brudny et al., 1974; 1976). Their approach to neuromuscular rehabilitation usually was twofold: to teach patients how to relax and inhibit spastic activity and simultaneously try to increase the force of atrophied muscles, a symptom combination that occurs frequently in torticollis, when one sternocleidomastoideus muscle is constantly tense while the opposite side of the neck is completely flaccid. Symptom duration in this patient group lasted from three months to thirty-five years. Most patients had undergone a variety of medical treatments, including crythalamectomy. Twenty-six of the forty-eight cases achieved meaningful or major improvement in activities of daily living and partially a decrease of medication. During the follow-up from three months to three years, seven of the patients had regressed, leaving a success rate of about 40 percent. One should consider however, that this promising result was achieved with patients sitting; results under conditions of standing, walking, or mental stress are not available at present. Of course these data will be decisive for the further valuation of the clinical usefulness of the biofeedback treatment of torticollis.

DISORDERS OF FACIAL MUSCULATURE

The treatment of blepharospasm, a disturbance that consists of spasms of the eye-lids and surrounding musculature which can result in eye closure and facial spasms, is reported in two abstracts. While Ballard (1972) used a combination of shock and feedback from eyeblink potentials, Stephenson (1976) in a recent report treated a patient with relaxation training plus EMG feedback from the forehead. In the first report a follow-up of nine months yielded an absence of troublesome spasms. In the second study, the decrease of spasm was accompanied by a substantial decrease of frontal EMG level and a slight increase of finger temperature. The patient was symptom free during a six months follow-up. Both studies had sufficiently long baseline periods where patients had failed to respond to traditional treatment approaches to exclude nonspecific treatment effects.

Marinacci and Horande (1960) report on the successful treatment of five cases of Bell's palsy, an inability to close the eye that results from face paralysis. Forty percent restorative functions were achieved with a shaping procedure for single motor unit control. After a duration of dysfunction up to 23 years, treatment duration took up to two years. No follow-up is reported.

In a very impressive report, Booker, Rubow, and Coleman (1969) described the training of a woman to use nerve axons for facial expressions which originally innervated the trapezius and sternocleidomastoideus muscles and were connected surgically to facial musculature after an automobile accident. The patient had previously received two attempts of conventional therapy over two years. The feedback training consisted in twelve sessions of EMG-feedback followed by home training with the help of visual feedback from a mirror--a procedure that previous to the EMG training had shown no effect. After using shoulder movement for some time to generate facial expression, the patient finally succeeded just to "think" of those movements in order to exhibit them. After four months follow-up a slight regression had occurred that could be eliminated by three booster sessions.

Netsell and Cleeland (1973) used acoustical EMG feedback from the elevator labii superioris to reduce lip hypertonicity in a 64-year old Parkinsonian patient. Five thirty-minute training sessions resulted in considerable progress toward removing the undesirable retraction as well as a correlated eye squint and wrinkling of the forehead and thus facilitated lip movement during speech.

Brudny (1976) treated four patients with facial spasms, two of whom learned to control their spasms sufficiently to return to work; also episodic recurrence was reported.

The present reports certainly demonstrate the usefulness of feedback methods in retraining peripheral nerve injuries. As most of the studies are presented in the form of single case reports, it is difficult however to draw conclusions for general applications. The disorders that have been treated certainly demand highly individualized clinical procedures. If such an approach is to represent scientific evidence, however, it should include long baseline and long follow-up observations, which are missing in all but one of the above studies.

TREATMENT OF INVOLUNTARY MOVEMENTS

Feedback in combination with Jacobsonian relaxation training was used in one case (MacPherson, 1967) to control choreiform movements with a good success that held up through a one-year follow-up period.

In seven distonic patients, five of whom previously to EMG feedback had undergone brain surgery, Brudny et al. (1974, 1976) achieved some success in reducing spasm activity and correcting head positions. However, three of the six improved patients regressed during the follow-up period.

Nusselt and Legewie (1975) trained two Parkinsonian patients with feedback from their hand tremor amplitude and found that patients succeeded to block tremor during feedback phases better than during no feedback control phases.

Again, the number of patients treated so far is too small to allow judgement. As it is the case with other symptoms, generalization from the laboratory situation to real seems to be problematic and should be considered part of the treatment schedule.

PERIPHERAL NERVE INJURY

Two authors (Brudny, 1976; Marinacci & Horande, 1960) report on the treatment of peripheral nerve injury with EMG feedback, apparently with varying results: While one patient achieved the use of a transferred wrist flexor tendon for wrist extinction within two thirty minute sessions, others needed up to 18 months to reach some benefit. Marinacci and Horande's report on a total of ten patients indicates that feedback facilitates recovery even after reconstructive surgery or atrophy of disuse, due to neuronitis, edema, infection or causalgia.

RECTOSPHINCTER RESPONSE

Studies from two independent research groups could demonstrate the usefulness of feedback training in controlling rectosphincter response. Kohlenberg (1973) treated a 13-year old boy who was considered for cholostomy by reinforcing increases in pressure exerted on a fluid filled balloon that was inserted into the boy's rectum. Visual feedback was provided through a water column connected to the balloon. Additional reinforcement consisted in money for an increase in pressure. Even so no clinical follow-up data are reported, it seems that during treatment anal sphincter pressure increased and the boy was not soiling for periods as long as eight hours. Surgery was apparently not performed.

In a very convincing study by Engel and collaborators (Engel, Nikoomanesh, & Schuster, 1974) six ambulatory patients with daily incontinence due to organic lesions, aged from six to fifty-four, were treated in a maximum of four training sessions. All patients were lacking the normal reflex contraction of the external sphincter in response to distension of the rectum, and the six year old child showed in addition no reflex relaxation of the internal sphincter, a response that in contrast to external sphincter reaction is under autonomic control. Patients tried to modify their reaction with the help of visual feedback from a polygraph according to instruction, a task that all of them learned quite readily, and were finally weaned from the feedback. After a follow-up period that ranged from six months to five years, four of the patients were completely continent, the two others markedly improved.

These last studies demonstrate one point very well, namely that a muscular response that most people master but in patients is lost due to organic lesions can be brought under voluntary control quite readily with the help of external feedback. Additionally, Engel and collaborators could demonstrate that the internal sphincter response, which presumably is involuntary as it is under autonomic control, can be trained by the same mechanisms. As the authors conclude correctly, this result is an indication for the possibility to apply feedback techniques to other gastrointestinal smooth muscles.

DISCUSSION

In conclusion, the results of biofeedback treatment of neuromuscular disorders seem promising--if one has realistic expectations. In most reported studies a longstanding disabling condition could be improved; in the case of rectosphincter responses some patients were completely symptom free after treatment. This outcome is certainly not disappointing considering the variety of symptoms treated, the multitude of underlying ethiological entities and the amount of previous treatment attempts.

As is to be expected from a new treatment approach there exists quite a number of problems: The highly individual procedure that is often necessary makes group studies and exact replications difficult. One strategy to overcome this problem is demonstrated in the study by Engel et al. (1975), securing long baseline and long follow-up periods.

A second difficulty lies in the generalization from successful laboratory performance to the real life situation: This should be recognized and treatment schedules should be devised that from the beginning include home practice, if possible also without external feedback devices, in order to make patients aware of internal cues and independent of the apparatus.

A last point that seems to be important for scientific documentation is the clear definition of a circumscribed treatment goal. It must be clear to the patient as well as to the reader, if as a result single motor unit firing or functional use of an extremity can be expected. This clarification will probably keep unrealistic expectations from this area of research, whose promising results call for further clinical evaluation.

REFERENCES

Andrews, J. M. Neuromuscular re-education of the hemiphlegic with the aid of the electromyography. Archives of Physical Medicine and Rehabilitation, 1964, 45, 530-532.

Amato, A., Hermsmeyer, C. A., & Kleinman, K. M. Use of electromyographic feedback to increase inhibitory control of spastic muscles. Physical Therapy, 1973, 53, 1063-1066.

Ballard, P., Doerr, H., & Varni, J. Arrest of a disabling eye disorder using biofeedback. Psychophysiology, 1972, 9, 271.

Basmajian, J. V., Kukulka, Narayan, & Takebe. Biofeedback treatment of foot drop after stroke compared with standard rehabilitation technique: Effects on voluntary control and strength. Archives of Physical Medicine and Rehabilitation, 1975, 56, 231-236.

Blanchard, E. B., & Young, L. D. Clinical applications of biofeedback training. Archives of General Psychiatry, 1974, 30, 573-589.

Booker, H. E., Rubow, R. T., & Coleman, P. J. Simplified feedback in neuromuscular retraining: An automated approach using electromyographic signals. Archives of Physical Medicine and Rehabilitation, 1969, 50, 621-625.

Brudny, J., Grynbaum, B. B., & Korein, J. Spasmodic torticollis: Treatment by feedback display of the EMG. Archives of Physical Medicine and Rehabilitation, 1974, 55, 403-408.

Brudny, J., Korein, J., Levidow, L., Grynbaum, B. B., Lieberman, A., & Friedman, L. W. Sensory feedback therapy as a modality of treatment in central nervous system disorders of voluntary movement. Neurology, 1974, 24, 925-932.

Brudny, J., Korein, J., Grynbaum, B. B., Friedman, L. W., Weinstein, S., Sachs-Frankel, G., & Belandres, P. V. EMG feedback therapy: Review of treatment of 114 patients. Archives of Physical Medicine and Rehabilitation, 1976, 57, 55-61.

Cleeland, C. S. Behavioral technics in the modification of spasmodic torticollis. Neurology, 1973, 23, 1241-1247.

Engel, B. T., Nikoomanesh, P., & Schuster, M. M. Operant conditioning of rectosphincteric responses in the treatment of fecal incontinence. The New England Journal of Medicine, 1974, 646-649.

Finley, W. W., Niman, C., Standley, J., & Ender, P. Frontal EMG biofeedback training of athetoid cerebral palsy patients: A report of six cases. Biofeedback & Self-regulation, 1976, in press.

Finley, W. W., Niman, C., Standley, J., & Wansley, R. A. Electrophysiologic behavior modification of frontal EMG in cerebral palsy children (Manuscript). Tulsa, Oklahoma: Research Psychology Department Children's Medical Center, 1976.

Gavin, J., & Stephen, K. Biofeedback muscle re-education: A review of ten clinical cases. 1976.

Harrison, A., & Connolly, K. The conscious control of fine levels of neuromuscular firing in spastic and normal subjects. Developmental Medicine and Child Neurology, 1971, 13, 762-771.

Jacobs, A., & Felton, G. S. Visual feedback of myoelectric output to facilitate muscle relaxation in normal persons and patients with neck injuries. Archives of Physical Medicine and Rehabilitation, 1969, 1, 34-39.

Johnson, H. E., & Garton, W. H. Muscle re-education in hemiphlegia by use of electromyographic device. Archives of Physical Medicine and Rehabilitation, 1973, 54, 320-325.

Kohlenberg, R. J. Operant conditioning of human anal sphincter pressure. Journal of Applied Behavior Analysis, 1973, 6, 201-208.

MacPherson, E. L. R. Control of involuntary movement. Behavior Research and Therapy, 1967, 5, 143-145.

Marinacci, A. A., & Horande, M. Electromyogram in neuromuscular re-education. Bulletin of the Los Angeles Neurological Society, 1960, 25, 57-71.

Netsell, R., & Cleeland, C. S. Modification of lip hypertonia in dysarthria using EMG feedback. Journal of Speech and Hearing Disorders, 1973, 38, 131-140.

Nusselt, L., & Legewie, H. Biofeedback und systematische Desensibilisierung bei Parkinson-Tremor: Eine Fallstudie. Zeitschrift für Klinische Psychologie, 1975, 4, 112-123.

Simard, T. G., & Ladd, H. W. Differential control of muscle segments by quadriplegic patients: An electromyographic procedural investigation. Archives of Physical Therapy, 1971, 447-454.

Spearing, D. L., & Poppen, R. Single case study: The use of feedback in the reduction of foot dragging in a cerebral palsied client. The Journal of Nervous and Mental Disease, 1974, 159, 148-151.

Stephenson, N. L. Successful treatment of blepharospasm with relaxation training and biofeedback. Paper presented at the 7th Annual Meeting of the Biofeedback Research Society, Colorado Springs, February 27 - March 2, 1976.

Swaan, D., van Wieringer, P. C. W., & Fokkema, S. D. Auditory electromyographic feedback therapy to inhibit undesired motor activity. Archives of Physical Medicine and Rehabilitation, 1974, 55, 251-254.

EMG FEEDBACK STRATEGIES IN REHABILITATION OF NEUROMUSCULAR DISORDERS

Gary DeBacher and John V. Basmajian
Department of Rehabilitation Medicine
Emory University

One of the most promising areas of application of electromyographic (EMG) biofeedback is in rehabilitation of neuromuscular disorders. In this context EMG biofeedback training falls into a category which rehabilitative specialists call neuromuscular education. Regardless of the condition being treated, neuromuscular education has three basic aims. Abnormal muscle activity (spasticity, athetoid movements, tremor, spasms, etc.) must be reduced. Useful strength and control must be restored in weak or paralyzed muscles and inappropriate movement patterns wherein muscles hinder one another or participate in primitive reflex patterns must be replaced by normal synergy.

EMG feedback training contributes to each of these aims. Small variations in abnormal muscle activity can be detected and used to shape reductions. Similarly, tiny vestiges of EMG activity in paralyzed muscles can be measured and shaped to functional levels. And EMG feedback from component muscles may allow a patient to control abnormal movement patterns.

Training inhibition of abnormal muscle activity in most cases is simply the training of muscular relaxation. We may distinguish between general relaxation of skeletal muscles throughout the body and learned relaxation of specific muscles, sometimes called differential relaxation. Since abnormal muscle activity in neuromuscular disorders is usually confined to specific muscles, training the subject to relax just those muscles is the more efficient approach, the one adopted by most clinical researchers thus far. However, isolated reports suggest that general relaxation training may be under-rated as a means of reducing abnormal muscle activity. Jacobsen (1936) provides a case report in which training in general progressive relaxation and in differential relaxation while using some limbs alleviated the spasticity and associated symptoms in a young girl with Little's disease. Jacobsen apparently did not use his EMG equipment to provide feedback to his patients, although he was providing some muscle feedback by careful observation and coaching. More recently, Finley and Niman (1975) used forehead EMG biofeedback to train general relaxation in four athetoid cerebral-palsied patients. Mild improvements occurred in various speech and motor functions measured after six weeks of training.

Thus a reduction in spasticity, athetoid movements, tremor, etc. may persist for a time after deep general relaxation. What is the mechanism? Since arousal or anxiety will usually increase abnormal muscle activity, a procedure which reduces arousal can reasonably be expected to reduce the excitatory effects of cortical activity on the spinal cord. Whether brief periods of deep relaxation have more direct effects on spinal reflex mechanisms, such as by reducing gamma efferent impulses to muscle spindles, has not been established. Denhoff and Robinault (1960, p. 287) in reviewing the opinions of physiotherapists regarding progressive relaxation and other relaxation techniques in treatment of the cerebral-palsied, note that such training is difficult and time-consuming and that many patients cannot be so trained. Ancillary use of EMG biofeedback might greatly simplify training and make it effective for more patients. They could then use deep relaxation several times a day to achieve a mild reduction of their symptoms.

Consider local relaxation, where a particular muscle must be trained to relax. The subject will usually also relax contiguous muscles in the course of training (DeBacher, 1972), in part because surface electrodes pick up some EMG from those muscles. This extraneous EMG can be eliminated by using intramuscular fine-wire electrodes (Basmajian, 1974) or substantially reduced by placing surface electrodes very close together and filtering out frequencies below about 90 Hz. And if the goal is to relax the target muscle while using the contiguous muscles, this should be incorporated in the training situation.

Jacobs and Fenton (1969) used EMG feedback to train local relaxation to break the pain-spasm-pain cycle in victims of neck injury. Such training has been used to treat one-sided overactivity in the sternocleidomastoid muscle in victims of spasmodic torticollis (Cleeland, 1973; Brudny et al., 1974). Instances where individual spastic muscles have been relaxed with EMG feedback training are reported by Brudny et al. (1974), and by Amato, Hermsmeyer, and Kleinman (1973), and we have seen similar results in our own clinic.

One of the most impressive applications of EMG biofeedback in rehabilitation is the training of useful strength in an initially paralyzed muscle. The procedure bears several resemblances to that used for training voluntary control of single motoneurons, discovered by Harrison and Mortensen (1962), and investigated by Basmajian and many others (Basmajian, 1974). One must have equipment capable of detecting the smallest quanta of muscle activity, single motor units, each of which is that subset of muscle fibers which contracts in response to a nerve impulse from a single motoneurone. The most effective form of feedback is the least derived, the amplified EMG voltage displayed on an oscilloscope and played over a loudspeaker so the subject can immediately perceive any response to his efforts. And in both instances the critical learning hinges on how the subject manipulates just a few motor units. But here there are marked differences. In single motor unit (SMU) training to selectively activate just one motor unit the subject must suppress all of its neighbors; the skill is substantially inhibitory. A patient struggling to reactivate a paralyzed muscle seems to be engaged in excitatory efforts: He searches ways to build the firing of two or three motor units into that of dozens. Whether single motor unit control will gain a place in rehabilitation is unclear. Ladd and Simard (1972) have investigated SMU control as a means for amputees, thalidomide victims, etc., to control artificial electric limbs. Gray (1971) trained SMU control in the paretic muscles of two subjects with local nerve damage. After a number of weekly sessions, electromyography and strength testing showed marked improvement. Harrison and Connolly (1971) trained four diplegic spastic subjects to discretely control very low amplitude spikes in spastic forearm muscles while inhibiting other EMG activity. Although the spikes may have represented more than one motor unit (due to limitations of their recording technique), the results are interesting in that the spastic subjects achieved about the same degree of control as normals. The authors do not mention any improvement in function from this procedure. Petajan and Jarcho (1975) have shown that Parkinson's disease patients cannot manage normal recruitment and control of single motor units. Production of minimal contractions was very difficult, and in patients with tremor any motor units activated tended to fire at the tremor frequency. But after L-Dopa drug therapy ability to generate minimal contractions and to isolate and control single motor units was regained in most patients.

These studies suggest that EMG biofeedback training of single motor units may have considerable potential as a measure of neuromuscular function, to analyze neuromuscular deficits, and possibly as a means of training more normal neuromuscular function. While achieving greater strength or reducing spasticity by training single motor unit control seems initially implausible, the combination of inhibitory and selective excitatory skills developed in such training may transfer to other motor behavior. Heretofore, the relationship of SMU control studies to the rest of EMG biofeedback research has been primarily inspirational: Other investigators were sufficiently impressed by SMU control to try EMG biofeedback in training other less subtle responses.

The initial success of Marinacci and Horande (1960) in restoring function in paralyzed muscles with EMG biofeedback actually predates the discovery of SMU control by Harrison and Mortensen in 1962. But there were few similar reports (Andrews, 1964; Marinacci, 1968; Booker, Rubow & Coleman, 1969) prior to the explosion of interest in biofeedback in the '70s. Then Johnson and Garton (1973) reported success in treating "foot-drop", or paresis of the ankle dorsiflexors, in a series of hemiplegic stroke victims; and Brudny et al. (1974) demonstrated that weak or paralyzed muscles in a variety of conditions could be strengthened with EMG feedback training.

In a study at Emory University (Basmajian, Kukulka, Narayan & Takeba, 1975), EMG feedback was combined with conventional physical therapy to treat chronic foot-drop in 20 hemiparetic stroke patients. Ten patients received 40 minutes of therapeutic exercise three times a week for five weeks. The other ten received 20 minutes of biofeedback training of the tibialis anterior muscle and 20 minutes of therapeutic exercise for the same schedule of sessions. Both groups improved, but the biofeedback group gained about twice as much in dorsiflexion strength and range of motion. Three of the biofeedback subjects improved enough in dorsiflexion to discard their short leg braces and walk with a normal heel-and-toe gait pattern. EMG feedback in this study was from a miniature battery-powered device now available commercially, the Emory/Basmajian Myotrainer. More recently this device has been used along with range of motion exercises to increase joint motion in patients recovering from lacerations of flexor tendons of the hand (Kukulka, Brown & Basmajian, 1975). Subsequently it was found that the use of finger electrogoniometers to provide motion feedback was more effective. In this case, finger motion is an unequivocal indication of correct muscle action while an EMG device using surface electrodes will also pick up wrist flexor activity, thus confusing training.

There are few published reports where EMG feedback has been used to inhibit an abnormal muscle synergy or to restore a normal synergy. Booker et al. (1969) treated a patient whose left facial nerve had been severed in an accident. The distal portion was reinnervated with a surgically transferred portion of the left spinal accessory nerve. Following reinnervation, the patient could produce contractions of the left facial muscles only by means of an exaggerated movement of the left shoulder. The goal was to break up this abnormal synergy and to train a normal symmetrical synergy of the left and right facial muscles. This was done in two stages by having the subject track target signals with an EMG feedback signal derived from the paralyzed facial muscles. To restore facial symmetry, a target signal was derived from the normal right facial muscles. Swaan et al. (1974) used auditory EMG feedback to teach hemiplegics and polio victims to suppress an undesirable synergistic contraction of the peroneus longus muscle during knee extension. Several clinics, including our own, have used EMG feedback to treat dyssynergic co-contraction of the extensors and flexors of the hands and fingers in spastic patients. One approach is to use separate EMG feedback devices for flexors and extensors. We have also used our computer to derive a single signal which represents the ratio times the difference of EMG activity in the flexors and extensors.

To illustrate an integrated approach to a cluster of neuromuscular problems, we will describe our own application of EMG biofeedback to the treatment of spasticity. It is based conceptually on a training task hierarchy and technologically on a PDP-8E computer which controls training and data acquisition. Before discussing these in more detail we must outline the nature of spasticity. If one asks a normal subject to relax, and proceeds to briskly flex and extend his arm or leg, no resistance is encountered. EMG investigation (Leavitt & Beasley, 1964) shows that adult normal subjects completely inhibit any stretch reflex response from this passive stretching. However in spastic subjects a reflex muscular contraction occurs, proportional to the velocity of stretch and subsiding rapidly when stretch ceases. This is spasticity in the strict sense. Other methods of stimulating the muscle spindles through stretching also produce an abnormal response in spastic muscles. Striking the muscle tendon with a reflex hammer causes an excessively large response with after-discharge and abnormal spread to distant muscles. If a muscle vibrator is applied to elicit the tonic vibration reflex or TVR (Hagbarth, 1973), the resulting contraction is larger in spastic muscles and develops more quickly. Unlike normals, spastic subjects generally cannot voluntarily inhibit the TVR. Some other abnormal phenomena such as clonus or spasms are directly related to the elevated response to stretch stimuli.

It is easy to see why this abnormal stretch reflex reactivity contributes to disordered movement and posture. But spasticity is invariably accompanied by other neuromuscular abnormalities which cannot be explained in terms of stretch reflex reactivity. Although spastic muscles can and do relax when the patient is comfortable and at rest (Hoefer & Putnam,

1940; Basmajian & Szatmari, 1964), stimuli such as distracting noises or conversation or the use of a normal contralateral limb may set off EMG activity. Some degree of paralysis is almost invariably present in spastic limbs: The same muscles which readily manifest spastic reflex activity may show little or no response to voluntary effort. Selective control of muscles and movements is replaced by primitive flexion or extension synergies. Reciprocal inhibition of flexors and extensors is often lost so that a muscle may be overpowered by its antagonist. Thus the clinical appearance of the spastic patient and his difficulties with activities of daily living are often less due to spasticity itself than to the related deficits in strength and control.

Spasticity may be seen following stroke, in cerebral palsy, in multiple sclerosis, in cases of physical trauma to the head or spine, etc. It is complex in etiology and not completely understood, but a major factor is interruption of inhibitory and selective influences of the brain on the spinal cord. An especially interesting population for treatment is adult hemiplegic stroke victims, where the side of the body controlled by the injured hemisphere is spastic and paretic and the opposite side is substantially normal. This has some advantages for training since a subject can first practice an unfamiliar feedback task with a normal limb to better understand what he is to do.

Obviously no single training task would suffice to test EMG biofeedback effectiveness for all facets of spasticity, or to train all the skills essential to meaningful improvement. Also, pilot studies have shown that overtly similar spastic hemiplegics can differ markedly when abnormal activity is analyzed electromyographically. These differences imply individual training needs which again require different training paradigms. Therefore we have organized a number of training tasks into a sequence of gradually increasing difficulty. Subjects first practice relaxing normal and then spastic muscles in the resting state where we can be fairly confident of their success. They are then reinforced for using feedback to maintain control of spasticity while being introduced to gradually more difficult task requirements. Since training of each subskill begins only after prerequisites have been mastered, the probability is increased that subjects will succeed at the more difficult tasks.

The training task hierarchy is grouped into three sequences. In the first, the spastic limb rests unused; the subject masters resting relaxation and then learns to maintain it during distracting noise, tactile stimuli, or concurrent use of a contralateral limb. Neurophysiologically speaking, muscle stretch stimuli are factored out while the subject learns to handle arousal or "overflow" stimuli. This corresponds to the minimun level of useful improvement biofeedback might provide, the ability to keep a spastic limb relaxed while resting or sitting engaged in deskwork, reading, conversation, etc.

In the second level of training the focus is on stretch stimuli. Learned control of resting relaxation is first established and then passive stretch of the spastic muscles is gradually introduced at increasing rates. The flexors and extensors of the elbow, the wrist, the knee, or the ankle are the focus of such training; the distal part of the limb is attached by a fitted plastic splint to the radial arm of a Cybex Isokinetic Dynamometer which is used to control the rate of limb motion.

Experience with pilot subjects indicates that while their limbs may be distinctly spastic on clinical observation, after they adapt to the Cybex and the experimental situation the spasticity may be absent except at very high velocities (over 100°/sec) which are not practical for training. Thus we are also trying other means of stimulating muscle spindles, using muscle vibrators or an automated reflex hammer. Spastic subjects cannot inhibit the tonic vibration reflex, at least not without EMG feedback. The vibration intensity can be varied to produce only as much TVR as the subject can manage. The vibration frequency must be kept to 100 Hz so that by filtering out all EMG frequencies below 130 Hz we can avoid the electromechanical artifact created by vibration of the electrodes.

We became intrigued with the idea of using a reflex hammer on reading in Jacobsen (1938) that some of his best subjects during deep relaxation would show no reflex response when the patellar tendon was struck. This suggested that subjects might even learn to manipulate stretch reflex responsitivity independently of other muscle activity. Normally, muscle tension elsewhere in the body has a marked influence on tendon reflexes, as in the clinical Jendrassik maneuver (Ott & Gassel, 1969). Therefore, initial training must be done with the subject thoroughly relaxed. The computer monitors EMG activity via an array of electrodes on the limbs and trunk and will fire the automated reflex hammer only when the subject is thoroughly relaxed. The hammer is then fired once per second and the subject sees a visual representation of the size of the reflex response on the feedback display screen. His task is to learn to decrease or increase the size of the response without resorting to the equivalent of Jendrassik maneuvers. Later he can be trained to inhibit the size of the tendon reflex while engaging in graded isometric contractions in certain muscles of the body. In these different ways we hope to see if subjects can learn to inhibit excessive stretch reflex responsivity while engaged in normal activity.

The third stage in the hierarchy is the most complex, since subjects are trained to develop in strength and phasic control of flexors and extensors, as well as the ability to inhibit abnormal co-contraction, one aspect of the dyssynergy occurring with spasticity. Again the limb is attached to the Cybex which is first set at zero velocity. Resting relaxation is re-established and on signal from the computer, the subject attempts an isometric extension. He receives visual feedback representing the extensor which is to be strengthened and the flexor which he must inhibit. After 20 seconds he is signaled to relax both muscle groups as quickly as possible, an important ability to develop in a spastic subject. When the muscles are relaxed below criterion, the subject is signaled to attempt isometric flexion while inhibiting the extensors. This is followed by the rapid relax task, and so on. Once the subject has learned to isometrically extend and flex while inhibiting co-contraction, isokinetic motion is added by having the computer release the Cybex arm during an isometric effort. By gradually combining such steps we may be able to train subjects to isokinetically flex and extend the limb without interruption.

Each subject sits with limbs comfortably supported, facing a screen on which the computer generates feedback displays, instructional signals, and reinforcement scores. EMG levels are represented by vertical bars. The display includes a criterion level which is programmatically revised in terms of the subject's recent performance. When the subject surpasses the criterion, a numerical score on the screen is incremented; this score is the basis for monetary incentive payments. EMG from up to four muscles and information on the position of the limb being trained is processed continuously and stored along with a record of stimulus and task conditions on disc memory for later analysis. Repeated baseline testing without feedback is the primary measure of progress. Training is highly individualized and no control groups are employed. However we can compare changes in trained and untrained spastic muscle groups within the same subject.

The overall purpose of the project is to develop and document the most effective strategies for treating spasticity. We anticipate that it will then be possible to transfer these strategies to the clinic where they can be carried out with simpler equipment on the many disabled patients who can profit from EMG feedback training.

REFERENCES

Amato, A., Hermsmeyer, C. A., & Kleinman, K. M. Use of electromyographic feedback to increase inhibitory control of spastic muscles. Physical Therapy, 1973, 53, 1063-1066.

Andrews, J. M. Neuromuscular re-education of the hemiplegic with the aid of the electromyograph. Archives of Physical Medicine and Rehabilitation, 1964, 45, 530-532.

Basmajian, J. V. Muscles alive: Their functions revealed by electromyography. (3rd ed.). Baltimore: Williams & Wilkins, 1974.

Basmajian, J. V., Kukulka, C. G., Narayan, M. G., & Takebe, K. Biofeedback treatment of foot-drop after stroke compared with standard rehabilitation technique: Effects on voluntary control and strength. Archives of Physical Medicine and Rehabilitation, 1975, 56, 231-236.

Basmajian, J. V., & Szatmari, A. The effect of largactil (chlorpromazine) on human spasticity and the electromyogram. A. M. A. Archives of Neurology, 1955, 73, 224-231.

Booker, H., Rubow, R., & Coleman, P. Simplified feedback in neuromuscular retraining: An automated approach using electromyographic signals. Archives of Physical Medicine and Rehabilitation, 1969, 50, 621-625.

Brudny, J., Korein, J., Levidow, L., Grynbaum, B., Lieberman, A., & Friedman, L. Sensory feedback therapy as a modality of treatment in central nervous system disorders of voluntary movement. Neurology, 1974, 24, 925-932.

Cleeland, C. S. Behavioral technics in the modification of spasmodic torticollis. Neurology, 1973, 23, 1241-1247.

DeBacher, G. A. Operant shaping of local muscular relaxation in normal children (Doctoral dissertation, University of Pennsylvania, 1972). Dissertation Abstracts International, 1973, 34, 3338-B.

Denhoff, E., & Robinault, I. P. Cerebral palsy and related disorders: A developmental approach to dysfunction. New York: McGraw-Hill, 1960.

Finley, W. W., & Niman, C. EMG biofeedback and cerebral palsy. Proceedings of the Biofeedback Research Society. Sixth Annual Meeting, 1975. Biofeedback Research Society, UCMC #C268. (Abstract)

Gray, E. R. Conscious control of motor units in a neuromuscular disorder. Electromyography, 1971, 11, 515-517.

Hagbarth, K.-E. The effect of muscle vibration in normal man and in patients with motor disorders. In J. E. Desmedt (Ed.), New developments in electromyography and clinical neurophysiology. (Vol. 3). Basel, Switzerland: S. Karger, 1973.

Harrison, A., & Connolly, K. The conscious control of fine levels of neuromuscular firing in spastic and normal subjects. Developmental Medicine and Child Neurology, 1971, 13, 762-771.

Harrison, V. F., & Mortensen, O. A. Identification and voluntary control of single motor unit activity in the tibialis anterior muscle. Anatomical Record, 1962, 144, 109-116.

Hoefer, P. F. A., & Putnam, T. J. Action potentials of muscles in "spastic" conditions. Archives of Neurology and Psychiatry, 1940, 43, 1-22.

Jacobs, A., & Fenton, G. S. Visual feedback of myo-electric output to train muscle relaxation in normal persons and patients with neck injuries. Archives of Physical Medicine, 1969, 50, 34-39.

Jacobson, E. Progressive relaxation. Chicago: University Press, 1938.

Johnson, H. E., & Garton, W. H. Muscle re-education in hemiplegia by use of electromyographic device. Archives of Physical Medicine and Rehabilitation, 1973, 54, 320-322.

Kukulka, C. G., Brown, D. M., & Basmajian, J. V. A preliminary report: Biofeedback training for early finger joint mobilization. American Journal of Occupational Therapy, 1975, 29, 469-470.

Ladd, H. W., & Simard, T. G. Bilaterally controlled neuromuscular activity in congenitally malformed children: An electromyographic study. Interclinic Information Bulletin, 1972, 11, 9-16.

Leavitt, L. A., & Beasley, W. C. Clinical application of quantitative methods in the study of spasticity. Clinical Pharmacology and Therapy, 1964, 5, 918-941.

Marinacci, A. Applied electromyography. Philadelphia: Lea & Febiger, 1968.

Marinacci, A., & Horande, M. Electromyogram in neuromuscular re-education. Bulletin of the Los Angeles Neurological Society, 1960, 25, 57-71.

Ott, K. H., & Gassel, M. Methods tendon jerk reinforcement: The role of muscle activity in reflex excitability. Journal of Neurology, Neurosurgery and Psychiatry, 1969, 32, 541-547.

Petajan, J., & Jarcho, L. Motor unit control in Parkinson's disease and the influence of levadopa. Neurology, 1975, 25, 866-869.

Swaan, D., Van Wieringen, P. C. W., & Fokkema, S. D. Auditory electromyographic feedback therapy to inhibit undesired motor activity. Archives of Physical Medicine and Rehabilitation, 1974, 55, 251-254.

NOTE

This work was supported in part by NINDS Grant #NS 12280 and by Rehabilitation Services Administration Grant #16-P-56808.

WHY SHOULD MUSCULAR RELAXATION BE CLINICALLY USEFUL? SOME DATA AND 2½ MODELS

Johann Stoyva
University of Colorado Medical Center

A growing body of evidence, much of it accumulated over the past several years, indicates that muscle relaxation is a powerful variable and one which can be clinically useful. Our own work with electromyographic (EMG) feedback was triggered by reports in the older literature concerning the effects of progressive relaxation (Jacobson, 1938) and autogenic training (Schultz & Luthe, 1959). With both these older techniques--essentially ways of training a "cultivated" low arousal condition--a number of successes with anxiety and stress-linked disorders have been reported. Similarly, in the behavior therapy technique of systematic desensitization, muscle relaxation has been utilized as a response incompatible with anxiety (Wolpe, 1973).

Application to Tension (Muscle Contraction) Headache

Briefly put, it seems that muscle relaxation may be viewed as an anti-stress response (see Stoyva & Budzynski, 1974). For example, in our own work with tension headache, a common stress-related disorder, we have found that feedback-induced relaxation is a useful treatment modality. Our pilot observations (Budzynski, Stoyva, & Adler, 1970) were later confirmed in a controlled study by Budzynski, Stoyva, Adler, and Mullaney (1973).

This finding has been replicated in a number of other independent investigations--Raskin, Johnson, and Rondestvedt (1973), Wickramasekera (1972), and others (see Table 1 for summary data). Recently, an extensive

Table 1

Frontal EMG Feedback in Tension Headache

Authors	No. of Patients	Symptom Duration & Baseline Length	Design & Controls
Budzynski, Stoyva, & Adler (1970)	5	2 to 40 years	No control group
Budzynski, Stoyva, Adler, & Mullaney (1973)	18	Severe headache mean of 7.7 years. Mean age was 36. 2 week baseline on EMG and headache measures	Controlled group outcome study: 1 treatment group, 1 no-treatment group, 1 placebo-suggestion control group receiving pseudofeedback
Raskin, Johnson, & Rondestvedt (1973)	10	All 10 patients had severe chronic anxiety, six also had insomnia and 4 of the 10 also had tension headaches. 8 weeks of baseline symptom recording	N=10, no control group
Wickramasekera (1972)	5	3 weeks baseline	Pseudo-EMG feedback followed by genuine EMG feedback

Table 1

Continued

Type and Duration of Training	EMG Response	Clinical Outcome	Follow-up
Frontal EMG feedback 2 to 3 half-hour sessions per week for 4 to 13 weeks. Twice a day home practice of relaxation	Mean decrease from 5.7 μV to 3.5 μV	All 5 patients showed decreased headache activity	3 month follow-up showed headache improvement was retained, especially if relaxation practiced
Frontal EMG feedback 2 half-hour sessions per week for 8 weeks. Twice a day home practice of relaxation for placebo-suggestion group and experimental group	Frontal EMG significantly lower in treatment group	Headaches significantly lower in treatment group ($p<.001$). Medication reduced or eliminated	Headache alleviation retained during 3-month follow-up. EMGs lower in treatment group
Frontal EMG feedback for 5 sessions/week. Trained to criterion of 2.5 μV over 2 to 12 week period & home practice	Levels decreased from ½ to 1/8 of starting values	4/4 improvement in tension headaches. 4/10 moderate or better improvement in anxiety symptoms	Not indicated
3 weeks of pseudo-EMG feedback, 12 weeks of real frontal EMG feedback. Two 30-minute sessions per week for 18 weeks	Decrease in group EMG data	Apparent decrease in headache intensity & frequency	Not indicated

Table 1

Continued

Authors	No. of Patients	Symptom Duration & Baseline Length	Design & Controls
Hutchings, Reinking, & Morgret (1976)	18	Mean age = 23 yrs. All had headaches $\geq$ 3 times/week (28 day baseline)	6 patients got frontal EMG feedback, 6 got modified Wolpe-Jacobson relaxation training, 6 got combined EMG feedback and Wolpe-Jacobson relaxation training
Reinking & Hutchings (1976) (follow-up to preceding study)	18	Same as Hutchings et al. above	Same

controlled study by Hutchings and Reinking (1976) has again documented the usefulness of EMG feedback in the treatment of tension headache. Moreover, EMG feedback proved significantly superior to progressive relaxation training in the reduction of headache activity. In a follow-up study, Reinking and Hutchings (1976) noted that continued practice of relaxation was significantly associated with maintenance of headache alleviation. They noted also that in the case of two patients whose headaches had returned, there again occurred a marked reduction in headache activity after they had relearned the relaxation response.

The use of feedback-assisted relaxation for tension headache is an example of a very direct biofeedback approach--the abnormal response is directly monitored and modified. There is also evidence that muscle re-

Table 1

Continued

Type and Duration of Training	EMG Response	Clinical Outcome	Follow-up
18 day training period. 10 half-hour relaxation training sessions for each patient	Significant decreases	Both EMG feedback groups superior to verbally instructed relaxation group (28 days)	7 patients seen at 12 month follow-up. 4 were symptom-free, 3 had regained headaches. Resting EMG levels of the latter were significantly higher. 2 of the 3 headache patients were again given EMG training. Both EMG levels and headache activity decreased sharply. Authors concluded that regular relaxation practice important in continued headache alleviation
Same	Same	Same	Same

laxation can be useful in a more indirect way for certain disorders thought to be stress-related. Exactly why muscular relaxation should be useful for such disorders is not at all obvious and much needs to be learned--particularly as to what the mechanism of action might be (more about this in the next section.

Chronic Anxiety

Recent evidence shows that EMG feedback training can be useful for chronic anxiety patients. Given the typically refractory nature of this affliction, these results are quite encouraging. Raskin et al. (1973) found frontal EMG feedback training in combination with daily practice of relaxation to be moderately useful for several patients suffering from severe chronic anxiety. The ten patients had been troubled by severe anxiety symptoms for at least three years. And previous therapeutic efforts by those same investigators--treatment with individual psychotherapy and medication--had not been successful. After considerable biofeedback training, patients proved able to achieve relaxation to a criterion point of 2.5μV or less on frontal EMG levels. One patient showed dramatic lessening of all his anxiety symptoms. Three other patients found relaxation to be useful in controlling previously intolerable situational anxiety.

In a controlled study, Townsend, House, and Addario (1975) compared chronically anxious patients given EMG feedback training to a matched control group treated with group psychotherapy. In the feedback group, there were significant decreases in EMG levels, mood disturbance, trait anxiety--and, to a lesser extent, state anxiety--that did not occur in the psychotherapy group.

An extensive controlled study has been reported by a Montreal group --Lavallee, Lamontagne, Pinard, Annable, and Tetreault (1975). Forty patients with chronic free-floating anxiety were randomly assigned to one of four groups in a 2 x 2 factorial design: EMG feedback and diazepam, EMG feedback and diazepam placebo, EMG feedback placebo and diazepam, and both placebos.

During treatment, the effects of EMG feedback plus diazepam were additive in reducing muscular tension. Although all active treatment groups reduced their anxiety after treatment, diazepam-treated subjects (with or without feedback) did less well than other subjects on anxiety measurements, adjuvant medication usage and home practice. The results indicated that EMG feedback treatment without diazepam had a more prolonged therapeutic effect for chronically anxious patients.

In this laboratory, we have worked with a number of chronically-anxious patients on a case-by-case basis over the past seven or eight years (Budzynski & Stoyva, 1975). Our observations are of interest since they indicate that patients are able to master the relaxation response if they persist in their biofeedback training. This step, however, is only a beginning. Once relaxation has been mastered, it is useful to add other interventions such as systematic desensitization, assertive training, modelling and role-playing. In other words, the patient must not only learn to relax, he must also learn to re-shape his coping responses.

Insomnia

Sleep-onset insomnia is another disorder for which some useful results have been reported with muscular relaxation--although it should be stressed that the findings have been less than uniformly positive (see Table 2). In the four experiments described in Table 2--all of which have utilized the arduous, but critical, step of all-night EEG monitoring--one yielded negative results. Although Hauri, Phelps, and Jordan (1976) reported their patients were sleeping better, this was not reflected by any improvement in sleep latencies as measured by the EEG criteria. Positive results, however, have been reported by Freedman and Papsdorf (1976), by Coursey, Frankel, and Gaarder (1976), and Borkovec (1976). The first two studies employed primarily frontal EMG feedback; Borkovec (1975) used a modified form of progressive relaxation.

Essential Hypertension

Several studies suggesting that muscle relaxation can be useful in the management of essential hypertension have been reported (see Table 3). Various types of relaxation training have been employed. For example, Jacobson (1970) reports that cases of moderate essential hypertension respond successfully to progressive relaxation--pressures decrease to within normal range. Klumbies and Eberhardt (see Luthe, 1969, Vol. II, pp. 70 to 72), using autogenic training with a group of young adult essential hypertensives, have reported decreases of 35 mm systolic and 18 mm diastolic over a 4-month period. A recent Canadian study (Smith, Black, Vanderwel-Johnston, & Cott, 1975), in which a variant of autogenic training was employed, reports pressure decrements of 15 mm systolic in their hypertensive group. Control patients, who received direct feedback of blood pressures per se, failed to show any significant decrement. Patel (1975) in several studies has noted favorable results using a combination of feedback-assisted relaxation and a Yogic relaxation exercise. Moeller (1973) using techniques of EMG feedback-assisted relaxation developed in this laboratory, has also reported significant decrements in pressure. Another recently-published study suggests that regular relaxation training, in addition to decreasing blood pressure, has hormonal consequences as well. Stone and DeLeo (1976) employed a simple (non-feedback) relaxation technique with 19 young male hypertensives. Treated patients showed significant reductions in blood pressure. They also showed significant reductions in plasma dopamine-beta-hydroxylase activity and in furosemide-stimulated renin activity. The authors suggest that a reduction of peripheral adrenergic activity contributes importantly to the reduced hypertension observed with the relaxation technique.[1]

Table 2

Summary of Studies Using Muscle Relaxation in Insomnia

Authors	No. of Patients	Symptom Duration & Baseline Length	Design & Controls
Hauri (1976)	10	Chronic insomnia for over 2 years, sleep latency over 30 mins. less than 90% of bed-time spent asleep	Each patient slept 3 nights in lab both before and after EMG training
Freedman & Papsdorf (1976)	18	Mean age = 23. Sleep latency ≥ 60 mins. at least 4 times/week, 6 months duration	6 patients got EMG feedback, 6 got brief progressive relaxation training, 6 did Williams "limbering" exercises
Coursey, Frankel, & Gaarder (1976)	22	Chronic insomnia, mean = 14 years. Sleep latency over 35 mins.	EMG feedback group and autogenic training group. Controls received five 45 minute sessions/ week for 6 weeks. Control group received electrosleep therapy
Borkovec (1975)	30	Moderate sleep-onset disturbance, college students. Non-use of drugs	10 got progressive relaxation, 10 were placebo patients, 10 no-treatment. Counter demand set present for first 3 weeks

Table 2

Continued

Type and Duration of Training	EMG Response	All Night EEG Data & Clinical Outcome	Follow-up
Frontal EMG feedback 2 to 3 times per week for a mean of 22 sessions	Decreased, amount not reported	Negative results. Patients claimed they slept better, but this not reflected in all-night EEG recordings	Not reported
Frontal EMG feedback for 6 half-hour sessions	Decreased	Both treatment groups showed decreased sleep latency (from 42 to 14 mins.)	Not reported
Two 45 min. sessions of EMG feedback per week + 15-20 mins. daily home practice with portable EMG device. Other group received modified, autogenic training for two 45-min. sessions/week + Home practice of AT, 6 weeks of training	Not reported	Sleep EEGs both before and after training. Half of relaxation patients improved on all 3 criteria. None of electrosleep controls improved to this degree	At 1 month successfully treated patients retained shorter sleep latencies & greater sleep efficiency (All night EEG data and daily sleep logs)
Brief training in progressive relaxation over 1 month period. Details not given	Not reported	2 pre-nights, 2 nights during training, 2 nights after training. Only progressive relaxation patients showed shorter time to sleep-onset (from 31 mins. to 11 mins.)	At 1 year follow-up gains retained by treatment group. Controls showed no improvement over baseline (verbal report)

Table 3

Summary of Relaxation Training with Essential Hypertension

Authors	No. of Patients	Symptom Duration & Baseline Length	Design & Controls
Klumbies & Eberhardt (1966), (in Luthe, 1969)	83	Details not given, but college student population. Pressure data based on mean of many measures for each patient. Precise base data not given	57 dropped out, 26 remained. No control group
Patel (1975)	34	Known hypertensives. Had been on anti-E.H. drugs for at least 6 mon. Diastolic pressure $\geq$ 110 on 2 separate days. Mean age = 59. BP baselines on 3 separate days	"Blind" measurement of BP. Random assignment to groups. In phase 1 Es got full training for 6 wks. In phase 2, former controls now got full relaxation training for 6 weeks.
Smith, Black, Vanderwel-Johnston, & Cott (1975)	16	Labile hypertensives, mean age = 41 (21-51). Symptom duration not given. 1 lab baseline session	4 groups of 4 patients each approximately matching for age, medication & starting baseline pressures
Stone & DeLeo (1976)	19	None previously treated. Mean arterial pressure 105 mm (mean of 14 measures over 10-14 days). Mean age of 28 years in both groups	14 experimentals, 5 controls. Base pressures similar in the 2 groups

Table 3

Continued

Type & Frequency of Training	Clinical Outcome	Follow-up
Learned autogenic standard exercises. Practiced 6 to 10 times/day, about 5 minutes each time	Mean drop of 35 mm systolic & 18 mm diastolic over 4 months. Biggest drop in first month	Not given, but patients seen for 5-15 months in study
Es got relaxation training 2/wk for 6 weeks + home practice 2/day. Initially, got talks on stress, E.H. & relaxation. Then got verbal relaxation training + GSR or EMG FB. Controls spent same lab time relaxing without instructions. No home practice for controls	In phase 1, Es decreased 26.1 mm systolic & 15.2 diastolic. Cs decreased 8.9 mm systolic & 4.2 mm diastolic. In phase 2, Cs decreased 28.1 mm systolic & 15.0 mm diastolic	Pressures in original treatment group remained low for at least 3 months. Pressures taken every 2 weeks
4 types of training: 1) autogenic-type relaxation, 2) autogenic-type relaxation & FB of systolic BP, 3) only FB of systolic BP, 4) control group had repeated BP measurements in each session. Each patient got one 75-minute session/wk for 9 weeks. Controls also told to alter BPs during training & pressures measured frequently during session	The 2 relaxation conditions showed significant decrease in BP (about 15 mm). BP feedback group did not decrease. 4/8 patients in relaxation groups decreased to normotensive range. 3/4 successful relaxation patients had combined relaxation and BP feedback	Successful patients remained in normotensive range for extensive follow-up
2ce/day, Es sat upright & counted breaths subvocally for 10-15 mins., period of 6 months. Controls seen 1/month for BP measurement	Reductions in BP, supine: 141.3 to 132.3, 90.3 to 82.2. Upright: 146.2 to 131.4, 95.3 to 85.2. ($p < .05$) + reductions in DbH & plasma - renin activity (only in treatment group)	None reported

Effects on Other Bodily Systems

The last three examples--chronic anxiety, sleep-onset insomnia and essential hypertension--indicate that muscle relaxation somehow acts to affect other bodily systems in a way which is opposed to the effects induced by stress (see also Stoyva & Budzynski, 1974). Several observations are consistent with such a view. For example, Connor (1974) found that when he gave subjects only a brief training in progressive relaxation, they showed smaller GSR and heart rate responses when exposed to a stressor than did the controls. In this laboratory, Budzynski (1969) noted that muscle relaxation produces a lessened ability to discriminate paired flashes of light--a sign of decreased cortical arousal (Venables & Wing, 1962). Similarly, muscle relaxation training is a useful prelude to the induction of EEG theta rhythms, a drowsy condition (Sittenfeld, Budzynski, & Stoyva, 1976). Indeed, subjects with high baseline muscle tension levels were only able to learn the subtle response of theta enhancement after training in muscle relaxation.

Gellhorn's Model

A specific model designed to account for the multiple effects of muscle relaxation has been proposed by the neurophysiologist Gellhorn who conducted extensive research on the relations between the striate muscle system and the autonomic nervous system (Gellhorn, 1967). A major impetus to Gellhorn's formulation of this model was his noting of similarities in the physiological consequences of progressive relaxation, autogenic training and certain forms of meditation.

In the model proposed by Gellhorn and Kiely (1972), they first cite the work of Hess concerning the distinction between ergotropic and trophotropic systems. The ergotropic syndrome consists of an increase in sympathetic discharges, in elevated skeletal muscle tone and in cortical excitation (EEG desynchronization). The trophotropic syndrome is associated with increased parasympathetic discharges, relaxation of skeletal muscles and lessened cortical EEG excitation (as in sleep).

Gellhorn and Kiely propose that the balance between ergotropic and trophotropic systems may be altered in two fundamentally different ways: 1) by direct stimulation of ergotropic or trophotropic "centers" in the hypothalamus or other cerebral areas; 2) by indirectly altering the activity of these two systems. This may be accomplished either by input from the cerebral cortex, or by changing afferent input impinging on the reticular formation and hypothalamus. Particularly effective in changing proprioceptive input are discharges from the muscle system. Gellhorn (1958) has shown, in animal preparations, that reduction of proprioception through curare-like drugs greatly reduces the ergotropic responsiveness of the hypothalamus and diminishes hypothalamic-cortical discharges. Also, the loss of muscle tone produced by these drugs results in behavioral sleep. In other words, there is a shift towards trophotropic activity.

Gellhorn and Kiely (1972) suggest it is this mechanism which accounts for many of the similarities among progressive relaxation, autogenic training, Wolpe's systematic desensitization procedure and certain techniques of meditation. In each, muscular relaxation results in reduced proprioceptive input to the hypothalamus, a diminution of hypothalamic-cortical discharges and in a dominance of the trophotropic system through reciprocal innervation.

An experiment by Hodes (1962) produced evidence very much in accord with the Gellhorn-Kiely model. When he injected Flaxedil (a curare-like drug) into the veins of cats they became sleepy, and their EEGs changed from the desynchronized pattern characteristic of an alert state to a synchronous pattern characteristic of a less alert state. But was this effect really due to muscular relaxation, or was it instead the result of a direct action of the drug on the central nervous system? It appears that the latter was not the case, because when Hodes injected the drug directly into the brain, through the carotid artery, then the earlier effect was not produced. This observation means that the Flaxedil did not block synaptic transmission in the brain. It is known, however, to block transmission at the myoneural junction (thus leading to paralysis). In interpreting the signs of sleep observed in his cats, Hodes suggested that the probable mechanism involved was a feedback system from muscle receptors to sites in the central nervous system.

To summarize this section: There is increasing evidence from various sources that muscle relaxation produces effects on other bodily systems. These effects, since they involve a shift from sympathetic to parasympathetic dominance, could reasonably be interpreted as being opposite in nature to effects attendant upon the defense-alarm reaction.

I think that the Gellhorn Model, or some modification of it, will turn out to be significant in our understanding of the physiological and clinical consequences of muscular relaxation. But I also think that muscle relaxation may be viewed within an even broader conceptual framework than that provided by the Gellhorn-Kiely formulation. The development of such a framework begins with the question: What do we think is going on in the various disorders we endeavor to treat with biofeedback training? The disorders we refer to are those which have variously been called stress-related, psychosomatic or functional in nature. And they appear somehow to be linked with the characteristic emotional responding of the individual.

A PSYCHOPHYSIOLOGICAL MODEL OF STRESS RESPONDING: ASSUMPTIONS

If we examine the literature on biofeedback clinical applications--in the stress area--one very notable deficiency we encounter is the general absence of any explicit rationale for such training. Why are we doing this? What reason is there to think that biofeedback training in any way impinges upon the causal mechanisms presumably involved in the disorder?

In the case of muscle relaxation, we see two end points--an initial muscle relaxation phase followed by some degree of clinical improvement. For example, anxiety may be diminished or blood pressure decreased. But what is going on between the two end points? What might be the connecting links between the biofeedback intervention and the presumed pathophysiology of the given disorder?

I think the examination of this question leads us into a cluster of assumptions which have generally not been made explicit. Further, I think that these assumptions lead to the development of a working model concerning the place of biofeedback and other self-regulatory techniques in the alleviation of certain stress disorders.

Learning of Maladaptive Learning Patterns

If we look at stress-linked disorders such as essential hypertension, anxiety problems, tension and migraine headache, we note that we are not born with these things. They begin gradually and seem to be tied in with life's experiences--with the habitual daily interaction between the individual and his environment. There is a slow evolution of pathology. What may begin as a normal reaction--increased blood pressure, peripheral vasoconstriction, HCL secretion, dilation of the extracranial arteries, bronchial constriction, contraction of the scalp muscles--eventually becomes pathological. An experimental psychologist would be likely to say that these are, no doubt, learned disorders--or conservatively put, there is a learning component present. But what kind of learning is going on? One point of view involves a straightforward operant conditioning model. For example, a child reports a headache. This is followed by a concerned parent saying, "Well, you don't have to take the arithmetic exam today." Through such reinforcement, the disorder develops.

Personally, I think this position is an oversimplified position--that a maladaptive response is directly reinforced. For one thing, this model ignores physiological mechanisms and the various ways in which these could become connected with environmental events. It also ignores the fact that, when the individual reacts to threat, multiple integrated physiological responses are brought into play--i.e., not just a single system is active, but many are active simultaneously. Finally, the model fails to account for how reinforcement might occur--that is, how can a physiological response be accurately reinforced when it is not visible to the reinforcing agent?

The model I would like to propose grows out of psychophysiological research and does, indeed, involve learning, but it also includes cognitive and physiological processes. Briefly put, it amounts to a cortical triggering of the individual's defense-alarm reaction. It grows out of two major sets of observations.

Instability in the System

If we look at individuals with stress-linked disorders, we see ample evidence that there exists an instability in the principally afflicted system. For example, sufferers from migraine headache, even in periods of remission, show pulsations of the superficial temporal artery larger than those seen in normals (Lance, 1973). These pulsations become more variable in the 3-4 days preceding an attack. The Australian neurologist, Lance (1973), using a thermovision camera, has observed that these patients characteristically show asymmetry of skin temperature between the left and right side of the head. Additionally, they show the well-known symptom of cold hands. Lance has characterized migraine headache as a "hereditary, paroxysmal vascular instability."

Such instability in the system can be reflected in various ways. It may be: 1) subject to unstable oscillations, 2) or given to maximal responding for long periods of time, or 3) show slowness of return to baseline after a perturbation (homeostatic deficiency--failure of negative feedback mechanisms).

Response Stereotypy

A major way in which this instability manifests itself is in response stereotypy. The afflicted system responds powerfully, especially when the individual is subjected to stress. I think a major contribution to psychophysiology research over the past quarter century has been that the individual, especially if he has a psychosomatic disorder, has a "preferred" response to stress. He is likely to be hyperreactive in the afflicted system.

What is the evidence for this? Let me cite a few studies that are fairly important. An early experiment was one by Malmo and Shagass (1949) in which they compared patients with cardiovascular symptoms--palpitations, hypertension, fainting--with another group of patients who had chiefly muscle-related symptoms; e.g., head and neck pains. These patients were exposed to a Wolff-Hardy thermal pain stimulus--a spot of heat focused on the forehead. There were considerable differences between the two groups. What it amounted to was this: When they were stressed, patients with cardiovascular complaints showed high heart rate variability, etc.--that is, cardiovascular type responses. On the other hand, patients with head and neck pains showed high neck muscle variability under stress. Another study by Moos and Engel (1962) examined essential hypertensives versus arthritics. The patients were subjected to five different stresses. There was considerable evidence of response stereotypy, i.e., a similar type maximal response to various stresses, at least in most of the patients. For example, in the essential hypertensives, 15 out of 20 showed strong specificity in their phasic blood pressure response under stress--there appeared to be a profile of reactivity for the individual.

In Cameron's (1944) work with anxiety cases it was noted that these patients fell into different types in terms of which physiological system was maximally responsive. For some it was the muscle system, for others it was the cardiovascular system, and for others it was the gastrointestinal system. There were also mixed types--both muscular and cardiovascular, for example.

Another observation concerns peptic ulcer patients. Over 20 years ago, the Chicago surgeon Dragstedt found that when ulcer patients were asleep their gastric HCl secretions were 3-20 times as great as those of normal subjects. In recent years, Kales and his group have also examined ulcer patients during sleep. EEG was also monitored, both in ulcer patients and in normal controls. During sleep HCl secretion rates in ulcer patients were at least twice those of the normal controls. Again, with asthmatics, it has been noted that a variety of stress situations will serve to trigger bronchial construction or obstruction. Finally, in our own studies of tension headache (Budzynski, Stoyva, Adler, & Mullaney, 1973), we found that even under resting conditions, tension headache patients had frontal EMG levels about twice those seen in normal patients of approximately the same age. And, with migraine patients, it has been noted by investigators such as Dalessio (1972) that the amplitude of pulsation in the extracranial temporal artery--even on days when they are not suffering from an attack--is about twice that of normals. Another intriguing observation by Dalessio was that migraine patients also showed marked variability in temporal pulse amplitude and that this variability began to increase 3-4 days prior to an actual attack.

The Second Step--Frequent Triggering

As indicated above, there is considerable evidence that response stereotypy is a central feature of patients suffering from psychosomatic and stress-linked disorders. But is this stereotyped reactivity sufficient by itself to lead to pathology in the system involved? Probably it is not. The psychophysiologist Sternbach (1966)--who formulated the present model some years ago--postulates that what is required is a frequent triggering of the preferred response. If the individual remains in a low stress environment and in a condition of little inner turmoil, the stereotyped response will not be elicited very often. However, if circumstances occur where there is a frequent triggering of this response, then trouble is likely to develop.

To take one example: Warfare, especially frontline combat, leads to frequent elicitation of the stress (defense-alarm) reaction. In World War II, Graham examined the blood pressure of young soldiers who had seen almost continuous combat for a 60 day period. In this group of healthy young men, 25% showed blood pressures of more than 140/90 mm--sufficient to classify them as hypertensives. Yet, once they were out of the combat zone for a few weeks, their pressures returned to normal levels.

A similar point of view has been advanced by Folkow (see Folkow and Neil, 1971), the Swedish cardiovascular physiologist. He proposes what is really a psychophysiological model of the genesis of essential hypertension. Initially, there is a cortical elicitation of the defense-alarm reaction. If prone individuals--blood pressure responders--are frequently stressed, longterm elevations in blood pressure are likely. Folkow states that the stressor episodes must be frequently elicited--and that the triggering stimuli are most probably the events, seemingly trivial, of everyday living.

The Third Step--Homeostatic Failure

But to move on to the next major postulate in the model: Is frequent elicitation of the individual's preferred response enough to bring about pathological changes? Probably not. There can be frequent episodes of increased blood pressure, muscle tension, increased gastric HCl secretion, etc. without pathological consequences provided that one critical condition is met--that the response readily returns to prestimulation or resting levels. But if the response is elicited frequently enough to prevent return to resting levels, this is where the trouble starts and is what may constitute a critical watershed in the development of stress-linked disorders. In other words, a failure of homeostatic control--in the sense of a slowness of return to baseline--gradually develops. We think this concept is likely to be a fruitful one for further investigation, and that it will mesh well with biofeedback thinking and applications.

Considerable evidence supports the idea that some failure of homeostasis is present in anxiety and stress-related disorders. One classic example is the study by Malmo, Shagass, and Davis (1950) concerning the startle response in patients with chronic anxiety. The startle response involved firing a pistol (a blank cartridge) and then studying the subject's reaction. Malmo, in examining the forearm EMG levels of both normals and chronically anxious patients, noted that the latency of the response was practically identical in both normals and anxiety neurotics, i.e., both reacted just as quickly and both showed the same curve of increasing muscle tension levels. But there was one fascinating difference. Normal subjects began decreasing tension levels in fairly short order. Those of the chronically anxious patients not only did not decrease, they continued rising--after those of the normals had begun going down. Malmo made similar observations of blood pressure during a mirror-drawing task, a mild stress situation. Pressure increases in normals levelled off shortly; those of the chronically anxious patients continued rising during the task.

Malmo interprets these results as indicating that chronically anxious patients suffer from a defect in homeostasis. We are very much in agreement. This apparent failure of homeostasis is physiologically (and perhaps experientially) a central feature of the disorder. A very good article documenting this point is by Lader (1969). He reviews an extensive body of literature indicating that patients with generalized anxiety are highly aroused physiologically and show great difficulty in returning to baseline levels after being stimulated. Similar evidence of such defective homeostasis has been noted in many of the stress-linked disorders.

Additional Components--Cortical Triggering and Social Reinforcement

Lest the reader should regard the above model as being excessively simple-minded, and that it ignores large bodies of data, two important additional components of it should be emphasized: 1) there is a cortical triggering of the individual's defense-alarm reaction--of which his preferred response is a part. Moreover, what is perceived as a threat is a highly idiosyncratic matter (cf. Lazarus, 1966). 2) the individual's response stereotypy is somehow reinforced; precisely how this occurs is not known. One possibility is that it is the overt behavior of the individual which is reinforced. For example, a youngster becomes anxious about something; this is followed by behavioral activation (and its attendant physiological arousal) in an effort to cope with the psychological stressor. His behavior is reinforced--and along with it his characteristic pattern of physiological arousal. Over the years, many reinforcements of this pattern occur. See Stoyva (1976) for additional discussion of these points.

Limitations of the Model

It may be objected that the proposed model does not really allow us to say "this is how stress disorders originate." I would have to agree with such a statement. Until we can experimentally produce a given disorder, we can only make tentative statements as to etiology. However, there is a large body of evidence that the mechanism postulated here--cortical triggering of the defense-alarm reaction--will at the very least act to exacerbate such maladaptive response stereotypy as is already present. Dozens of examples of this may be seen in the works of Harold Wolff (1968) who, in a great many studies, demonstrated that the technique of stress interviews would exacerbate the symptoms of psychosomatic patients.

Implications for Clinical and Experimental Work

Even though it is premature to say we know the origin of stress-related disorders in any precise way, the proposed model (Figure 1) does offer some specific suggestions for biofeedback work:

1) One biofeedback approach is to attack the physiological basis of a particular disorder in a direct fashion. Can the maladaptive (or painful) response stereotypy be modified? This is the way in which much clinically-oriented biofeedback work has proceeded (see Table 1 for examples).

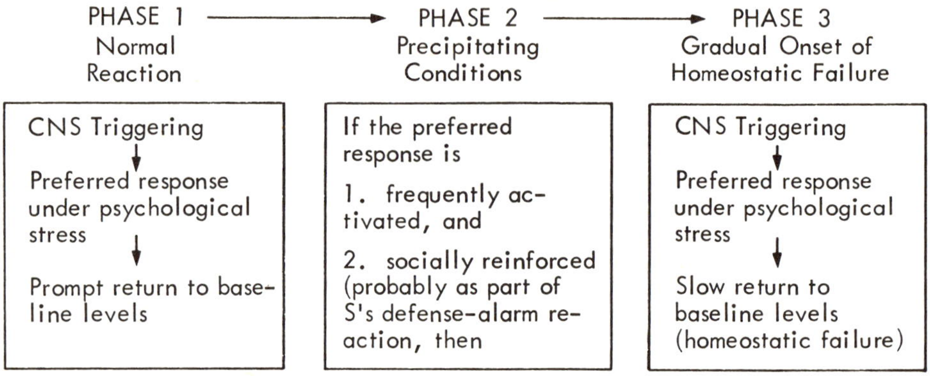

Figure 1. Stages in homeostatic-failure model of stress disorders.

2) The model suggests that we can attempt to modify more than one aspect of maladaptive responding. For example, in addition to measuring frontal EMG levels at rest, we should also measure them when the patient is exposed to stressful stimuli. Does the patient respond less powerfully than prior to training? Thus, after biofeedback training, do patients with disorders such as migraine headache, tension headache, chronic anxiety or essential hypertension show diminished reactivity?

3) In terms of the model, an important additional question is whether, after biofeedback training, various types of patients show improved homeostasis in the afflicted system; i.e., is there evidence of faster recovery to baseline levels after exposure to a stress episode? We predict that, in many disorders, pathology will be abated as recovery time improves.

4) Finally, the model suggests that a useful aspect of certain biofeedback procedures may be to "defuse the cortical trigger." A prominent feature of many types of biofeedback training is a shift to a non-striving mental condition--e.g., with frontal EMG, temperature, theta EEG or EDR feedback. And conceptual activity shifts from normal reality-oriented cognitions to a drifting condition in which directed thinking is absent. Actually, a major virtue of regularly practicing the various relaxation proce-

dures may mainly be that for a couple of times a day the individual shuts off his stress response. The effects of such a practice are likely to be reflected in many physiological systems.[2]

REFERENCES

Borkovec, T. D. Progressive relaxation treatment of sleep disturbance. Paper presented at the Second Annual Meeting of the American Association for the Advancement of Tension Control, Chicago, October 1975.

Budzynski, T. H. Feedback-induced muscle relaxation and activation level. Unpublished doctoral dissertation, University of Colorado, 1969.

Budzynski, T. H., & Stoyva, J. M. EMG-biofeedback bei unspezifischen und spezifischen Angstzustanden. In H. Legewie & L. Nusselt (Eds.), Biofeedback-Therapie: Lernmethoden in der Psychosomatik, Neurologie und Rehabilitation (Fortschritte der Klinischen Psychologie). Volume 6. Munchen-Berlin-Wien: Urban & Schwarzenberg, 1975.

Budzynski, T. H., Stoyva, J. M., & Adler, C. S. Feedback-induced muscle relaxation: Application to tension headache. Behavior Therapy and Experimental Psychiatry, 1970, 1, 205-211.

Budzynski, T. H., Stoyva, J. M., Adler, C. S., & Mullaney, D. J. EMG biofeedback and tension headache: A controlled outcome study. Psychosomatic Medicine, 1973, 35, 484-496.

Cameron, D. E. Observations on the patterns of anxiety. American Journal of Psychiatry, 1944, 101, 36.

Connor, W. H. Effects of brief relaxation training on autonomic response to anxiety-evoking stimuli. Psychophysiology, 1974, 11, 591-599.

Coursey, R., Frankel, B., & Gaarder, K. EMG biofeedback & autogenic training as relaxation techniques for chronic sleep-onset insomnia. Proceedings of the Biofeedback Research Society Seventh Annual Meeting, 1976, 8.

Dalessio, D. J. Wolff's headache and other head pain. New York: Oxford University Press, 1972.

Folkow, B., & Neil, E. Circulation. New York: Oxford University Press, 1971.

Freedman, R., & Papsdorf, J. D. Biofeedback and progressive relaxation treatment of sleep-onset insomnia: A controlled, all-night investigation. Biofeedback and Self-Regulation, in press.

Gellhorn, E. The influence of curare on hypothalamic excitability and the electroencephalogram. Electroencephalography and Clinical Neurophysiology, 1958, 10, 697-703.

Gellhorn, E. Principles of autonomic-somatic integrations: Physiological basis and psychological and clinical implications. Minneapolis: University of Minnesota Press, 1967.

Gellhorn, E., & Kiely, W. F. Mystical states of consciousness: Neurophysiological and clinical aspects. The Journal of Nervous and Mental Disease, 1972, 154, 399-405.

Hauri, P., Phelps, P. J., & Jordan, J. B. Bio-feedback as a treatment for insomnia. Proceedings of the Biofeedback Research Society Seventh Annual Meeting, 1976, 34.

Hodes, R. Electrocortical synchronization resulting from reduced proprioceptive drive caused by neuromuscular blocking agents. Electroencephalography and Clinical Neurophysiology, 1962, 14, 220-232.

Hutchings, D. F., & Reinking, R. H. Tension headaches: What form of therapy is most effective. Biofeedback & Self-Regulation, in press.

Jacobson, E. Progressive relaxation (2nd ed.). Chicago: University Press, 1938.

Jacobson, E. Modern treatment of tense patients. Springfield, Illinois: Charles C. Thomas, 1970.

Lader, M. H. Psychophysiological aspects of anxiety. In M. H. Lader (Ed.), Studies of anxiety. Ashford, Kent: Headley Brothers, 1969.

Lance, J. W. The mechanism and management of headache (2nd ed.). London: Butterworth, 1973.

Lavallee, Y., Lamontagne, Y., Pinard, G., Annable, L., & Tetreault, L. Effects of EMG feedback, diazepam and their interaction on chronic anxiety. Proceedings of the International College of Psychosomatic Medicine, Third Congress. Rome, 1975.

Lazarus, R. S. Psychological stress and the coping process. New York: McGraw-Hill, 1966.

Luthe, W. (Ed.) Autogenic therapy. Volumes I - VI. New York: Grune & Stratton, 1969.

Malmo, R. B., & Shagass, C. Physiologic studies of reaction to stress in anxiety and early schizophrenia. Psychosomatic Medicine, 1949, 11, 9-24.

Malmo, R. B., Shagass, C., & Davis, J. F. A method for the investigation of somatic response mechanisms in psychoneurosis. Science, 1950, 112, 325-328.

Moeller, T. A. Effects of EMG feedback and relaxation training in essential hypertensives. Unpublished doctoral dissertation, Nova University, 1973.

Moos, R. H., & Engel, B. T. Psychophysiological reactions in hypertensive and arthritic patients. Journal of Psychosomatic Research, 1962, 6, 227-241.

Patel, C. Randomised controlled trial of yoga and bio-feedback in management of hypertension. The Lancet, 1975, July 19, 93.

Raskin, M., Johnson, G., & Rondestvedt, J. W. Chronic anxiety treated by feedback-induced muscle relaxation. Archives of General Psychiatry, 1973, 28, 263-267.

Reeves, J. L. EMG-biofeedback reduction of tension headache: A cognitive skills training approach. Biofeedback and Self-Regulation, in press.

Reinking, R., & Hutchings, D. Follow-up and extension of "Tension Headaches--What Method is Most Effective?" Proceedings of the Biofeedback Research Society Seventh Annual Meeting, 1976, 60.

Schultz, J. H., & Luthe, W. Autogenic training: A psychophysiological approach in psychotherapy. New York: Grune & Stratton, 1959.

Sittenfeld, P., Budzynski, T. H., & Stoyva, J. M. Differential shaping of EEG theta rhythms. Biofeedback and Self-Regulation, 1976, 1, 31-46.

Smith, S. L., Black, A. H., Vanderwel-Johnson, C., & Cott, A. Successful behavioral treatment for hypertension: A study of methods and predictors. Paper presented at the Canadian Psychiatric Association Meetings, Calgary, Alberta, September 1975.

Sternbach, R. A. Principles of psychophysiology: An introductory text and readings. New York: Academic Press, 1966.

Stone, R. A., & DeLeo, J. Psychotherapeutic control of hypertension. The New England Journal of Medicine, 1976, 294(2), 80-84.

Stoyva, J. M. A psychophysiological model of stress disorders as a rationale for biofeedback training. In F. J. McGuigan (Ed.), Proceedings of the second meeting of the American Association for the Advancement of Tension Control. Blackburg, Virginia: University Publications, in press.

Stoyva, J. M., & Budzynski, T. H. Cultivated low arousal--an anti-stress response? In L. V. DiCara (Ed.), Recent advances in limbic and autonomic nervous systems research. New York: Plenum, 1974.

Townsend, R. E., House, J. F., & Addario, D. A comparison of biofeedback-mediated relaxation and group therapy in the treatment of chronic anxiety. American Journal of Psychiatry, 1975, 132, 598-601.

Venables, P. H., & Wing, J. K. Level of arousal and the subclassification of schizophrenia. Archives of General Psychiatry, 1962, 7, 114-119.

Wickramasekera, I. Electromyographic feedback training and tension headache: Preliminary observations. American Journal of Clinical Hypnosis, 1972, 15, 83-85.

Wolff, H. G. In S. Wolf (Ed.), Harold G. Wolff's 'Stress and disease.' (2nd ed.). Springfield, Illinois: Charles C. Thomas, 1968.

Wolpe, J. The practice of behavior therapy. New York: Pergamon Press, 1973.

NOTES

1. It should be noted that a recent carefully-executed experiment by Surwit and Shapiro (1976; see pp. 403-412 of this volume) failed to show significant decreases in blood pressure over a 5-week training period. This lack of training effect was true for each of the three groups employed: a group receiving blood pressure feedback through the constant cuff pressure method, an EMG feedback group and a relaxation group. The discrepancy between this study and the four studies described in Table 3 underscores the need for determining what the causal links might be between muscle relaxation and blood pressure. With this knowledge we should be able to decide which cases of essential hypertension could be helped by a systematic relaxation training and which could not. It should be emphasized that essential hypertension is a very broad diagnostic category. Thus, it seems unlikely that the same causal mechanisms are involved in every case or that relaxation training will be helpful in every case. Therefore, an eminently reasonable endeavor is to try to identify the subgroup of hypertensives who do respond favorably to relaxation training.

2. The observant reader may wonder what happened to "model $2\frac{1}{2}$" -- since in this paper only the Gellhorn-Kiely model and the homeostatic-failure model shown in Figure 1 are described. The reason for this omission is that at the present time "model number $2\frac{1}{2}$" is not sufficiently elaborated to warrant inclusion. Essentially, it is an attempt to grapple with the question of how extensive a "segment of physiological responding" needs to be altered in order for such an approach to be useful in changing a maladaptive stress response.

We are happy to acknowledge support from the National Institute of Mental Health Research Scientist Development Award K01-MH-43361; from National Institute of Mental Health Grants MH-25940 and MH-15596; and from the Advanced Research Projects Agency of the Department of Defense (contract monitored by the Office of Naval Research under contract N00014-70-C-0350 to the San Diego State University Foundation).

CLINICAL IMPLICATIONS OF BIOFEEDBACK

Heiner Legewie
Max-Planck-Institut für Psychiatrie
Munich

During the past several days we have had the opportunity of hearing about a large number of ways in which biofeedback methods can be used clinically. The clinician interested in applications found himself confronted with a wide range of views on the therapeutic usefulness of biofeedback. Thus Sterman and Stoyva reported mainly positive and clinically relevant results. Bernard Engel and Engel-Sittenfeld on the other hand were more cautious in their judgement of clinical relevance. Finally, Black, Surwit, Laverne Johnson and Lang came to rather negative conclusions. I got the feeling that these differing evaluations are due in part to differing areas of application but also in part to the temperament and attitude of the particular speaker.

After these introductory remarks I no longer want to conceal my own personal view. According to the theory of cognitive dissonance, my attitude should really be extremely positive because of the preparations for the Symposium. But in spite of my great efforts to bring all the conflicting information into consonance I have not been able to do away with my scepticism about the clinical use of biofeedback.

In my talk I certainly do not want to combine the excellent original contributions and summaries of the last few days into some sort of supersummary. Rather, I would like to present some reflections on the possible mechanisms involved in the therapeutic effects of biofeedback. As far as possible I shall elaborate on these reflections using examples from the talks given here at this Symposium, but I shall also mention a few other relevant studies. In conclusion I shall discuss some alternatives to biofeedback therapy and the need to integrate biofeedback into a more comprehensive behavior modification approach.

As a starting point I take the assumption that the general goal of therapy in biofeedback application is control of or compensation for disturbed psychophysiological functions. In the following discussion the various therapeutic approaches to attaining this general goal will be divided in three categories, according to the mechanisms mediating between biofeedback training and clinical symptom control:

1) In direct symptom control the function trained is an immediate correlate of the clinical symptom--the mechanisms can be described as a straightforward learning process.

2) In indirect symptom control the function trained usually is a correlate of a higher-level system which controls the symptom. When considering the mechanisms here a distinction must be made between two factors, the learning process to control the higher-level function and the relationship between this function and the symptom.

3) Certain applications of biofeedback have been found, in which a therapeutic effect is attained even though training results in only nonspecific or doubtful changes. Such apparently paradoxical results indicate that the therapeutic effect is not directly related to the biofeedback training per se but that indirect mechanisms of another kind are mediated by biofeedback.

DIRECT SYMPTOM CONTROL

The most convincing examples of direct symptom control in organic disturbances are seen in the treatment of neuromuscular disorders, which are discussed in detail in the papers of Engel-Sittenfeld and DeBacher and Basmajian. In their view these disorders cannot simply all be treated with one standard method, rather, each patient requires an individual assessment of his functional deficits depending on the kind of disorder, individually defined training goals and a corresponding therapeutic procedure.

A superb example of this kind of application is, in my opinion, the study by B. Engel et al. (1974) on the treatment of bowel incontinence using biofeedback of the rectosphincter response. Equally impressive is the project design of DeBacher and Basmajian in which a computer-controlled man-machine system with the aid of biofeedback is used for functional training in patients with spastic paralysis. A large-scale project recently started by Brudny and coworkers (personal communication) with 200 apoplectics, half of whom are going to be treated with conventional physical therapy and the other half with physical therapy plus biofeedback training, will in a few years permit a clear statement on the practical therapeutic relevance of biofeedback training for health care in neuromuscular rehabilitation.

Another area of application is that of organically determined cardiovascular disorders, which B. Engel discussed. According to Engel's cautious judgement the results so far are at least promising enough that clinically oriented studies seem justified.

The boundary between organic and psychosomatic functional disturbances is not fixed, and in some cases it cannot even be defined. Tension headaches, tics, stuttering, hypertension and migraine are examples of psychophysiological disorders for which a direct control of symptoms with biofeedback training has been attempted.

Stoyva has presented a detailed review including papers now in press on the treatment of tension headache with frontalis EMG feedback. In the area of psychosomatic disorders this use of biofeedback is one of those relatively well investigated so far. As to how the method works, however, it is not yet clear to what degree therapeutic success is due to a direct influence on the symptomatic functional disturbance (control of the assumed cause, i.e. spasms in the muscles of the head) or whether success is due to the therapeutic effects of general relaxation.

Stuttering is a psychophysiological disorder with direct EMG correlates. In our laboratory a severe stutterer with extreme tonic-clonic spasms of the muscles used in articulation underwent specific functional training (Legewie et al., 1975). Using biofeedback of the muscle groups affected during speech, the patient learned in increasingly difficult speaking situations to keep muscle innervation at a level low enough to permit smooth speech flow. Similar results in the treatment of stutterers have been reported by two other groups (Hanna et al., 1975; Lanyon et al., 1976).

Attempts at therapy of psychophysiological disorders through direct symptom control have also been made with the cardiovascular system. The results of Pickering and coworkers indicate the possibility of direct control of blood pressure in humans. However, the studies on hypertension reported by Black, B. Engel, Stoyva and Surwit and Shapiro seem to indicate a more general influence on the high blood pressure mediated by relaxation responses. Regarding vascular regulatory disorders such as Raynauld's disease or migraine, according to B. Engel's evaluation, in spite of quite a few publications there have hardly been results which can be taken seriously which indicate direct symptom control.

SYMPTOM CONTROL VIA HIGHER LEVEL SYSTEMS

One of the most fascinating and most original attempts to achieve therapeutic effects through the control of a complex subsystem of the central nervous system is the treatment of epilepsy via feedback of the sensorimotor rhythm (SMR) in the EEG, which Sterman described in detail. Earlier attempts at direct suppression of paroxysmal activity in the EEG had been rather unsuccessful. From careful animal experiments Sterman and his coworkers deduced SMR training would influence a thalamocortical system. This system is assumed to be involved in the suppression of motor excitability and thereby in counteracting the seizure process in epileptics. The first therapeutic case studies were extremely successful and were replicated by other groups. With amazing methodological elegance Sterman then went from these very promising results to a controlled therapeutic study with 40 patients, and he reported here on first results with three of these patients.

Laverne Johnson in his review touched on a few of the puzzles posed by SMR feedback therapy. That one and the same training procedure seems to have a specific anticonvulsive effect with quite different forms of epilepsy contradicts past experience in epilepsy research. Equally unexplainable is Sterman's finding that the SMR cannot be found in 30% of healthy subjects. Furthermore, the relationship between successful training and therapeutic effectiveness appears to be extremely complicated. Sterman reported on one patient in his new study who with SMR feedback showed a significant reduction in epileptiform EEG activity and clinical seizures but whose trained EEG frequency (12-15 Hz) showed no significant change during training. These contradictions belong to the "hard nuts" of biofeedback research which it is to be hoped will be cracked in the next few years!

With psychosomatic disorders biofeedback methods are used most frequently to induce a general state of relaxation. This therapeutic approach and the theory behind it were discussed in detail by Stoyva for such different kinds of disorder as tension headache, chronic anxiety, insomnia, and essential hypertension. Here we can only speak of the therapeutically effective control of a function if first, biofeedback relaxation can be shown to be more effective than competing methods of relaxation and if second, relaxation leads to symptom control outside the laboratory.

The mainly positive results for EMG relaxation training which Stoyva reports are at variance with the results of Black, Laverne Johnson, Lang, and Surwit and Shapiro, who could not determine any superiority of various feedback methods (EEG, heart rate, blood pressure, EMG) for the induction of relaxation as compared with methods using no equipment. A basic difficulty with any feedback-induced relaxation training was discussed by Lang: for physiological reasons the information processing of the feedback signal leads to an orienting response. All of the known proposals for resolving this dilemma in relaxation training, for example the introduction of a kind of "passive volition" (Green et al., 1970), involve the paradoxical requirement that the subject learn to disregard the feedback signal although it is being presented to him.

The fact that in spite of this the superiority of feedback methods could be demonstrated in some studies may be due in part to various indirect therapeutic mechanisms of biofeedback training. It is these mechanisms which I shall discuss next.

INDIRECT THERAPEUTIC MECHANISMS

Biofeedback as a Placebo

In his review on placebo effects in psychotherapy, A.K. Shapiro (1971, p. 458) has listed the following as criteria for especially effective placebos: "expensive, fashionable, elaborate, detailed, time-consuming and dangerous treatments." He also indicates the importance of the "intellectual and emotional investment...which may explain, in part, the reports of almost universal effectiveness accompanying the introduction of new therapies."

All of these criteria--with the exception of dangerousness--apply exceedingly well to biofeedback therapy, and frequently are given even more weight through the advertising of equipment manufacturers. For many researchers and clinicians there is also massive pressure to succeed, due to expensive equipment and research funds, which may contribute to therapeutic success in the sense of the Rosenthal effect (Rosenthal, 1966). As is well-known, strong placebo effects can even lead to long-lasting improvements in the most severe organic disorders (A.K. Shapiro, 1971). Thus in evaluating the numerous anecdotal case reports in the biofeedback literature it would be wise to first consider the empirically well-documented placebo effect.

Increasing Suggestibility

Suggestion is considered to be one of the essential components of the placebo effect. In procedures such as autogenic training and hypnosis however, autosuggestion and heterosuggestion are used intentionally in a more specific way. The fixation method of inducing hypnosis (Weizenhofer, 1957) provides a model which would also be appropriate for intentionally increasing suggestibility via biofeedback. The hypnotist has his subject fix his eyes on an object a short distance away and then observes the eyes. As soon as he sees that this strenuous fixation becomes less intense he gives the subject feedback about double images and other signs of fixation fatigue which occur. This "biofeedback," the accuracy of which the subject can check through his own perceptions, increases the subject's susceptibility to the following hypnotic suggestion.

Especially when biofeedback techniques are used for relaxation, e.g. in the treatment of tension headache, anxiety, hypertension or insomnia, but also when used for neuromuscular re-education similar mechanisms can be hypothesized: through successful biofeedback training a certain functional control is attained, which by itself is perhaps minimal and clinically irrelevant (e.g. in the case of heart rate deceleration), but which nevertheless can lead to an increased susceptibility to further suggestion relating to relaxation and therapy.

When increasing suggestibility using biofeedback, however, the question must be raised whether the same effects can be attained equally well using other methods, as for example is indicated by the results of Black and Surwit and Shapiro for reduction of blood pressure in hypertension and of Lang for reduction of heart rate.

Increasing Motivation

For a number of therapy techniques, including drug therapy, the importance of the motivation of patient and therapist for successful treatment has been stressed by numerous investigators (A. K. Shapiro, 1971). Based on this fact the use of methods aimed at intentionally increasing motivation has been recommended for psychotherapy (Goldstein, 1975). It is not possible, however, to clearly separate intentional increases in motivation from global placebo and suggestion effects.

The potential of biofeedback in increasing motivation in both patient and therapist became abundantly clear to me during a visit to a rehabilitation center at which a paraplegic had been under intensive treatment with

EMG-feedback for many months. Because of technical problems the feedback equipment when in use showed hardly anything other than noise and movement artifacts from cables and electrodes. Nevertheless the patient, who prior to the introduction of "biofeedback" therapy had had a "hopeless" baseline for more than two years, showed definite improvement, something which almost certainly would not have come about without the biofeedback equipment. The effects of intensive physical therapy and intensive training at home would not have been possible without the increase in motivation in both the patient and the rehabilitation team facilitated by biofeedback.

Probably even more effective than motivation increases via electrode artifacts are increases by showing that there are motor units in paralysed muscles which can be activated. That the importance of increasing motivation should not be underestimated is shown very impressively in the reports by Suzanne Owen (e.g. 1974), who had been a paraplegic for ten years, on her own treatment over a period of several years.

Patients repeatedly stress that one of the ways in which biofeedback increases motivation is through the visible and measurable experiences of success which the feedback provides. This is true as much for neuromuscular reeducation as for other applications like the induction of general relaxation. EMG-feedback or feedback of other relaxation responses can lead to increased motivation when used with these techniques and thus also to indirect therapy effects which are often falsely interpreted as direct effects of the training itself.

Cognitive Mechanisms

In his classic experiments on the two-factor theory of emotional states Schachter (1964) showed that the perception of a physiological arousal state is interpreted as a positive or a negative emotion, depending on the particular environmental stimuli. Conversely, Valins (1966) and Valins and Ray (1967) showed that by manipulating the perception of an arousal state via false heart rate feedback different interpretations of environmental stimuli may be induced. An overview on cognitive processes mediating the effects of false feedback can be found in a paper by Liebhart (in press).

Shapiro mentioned the possibility that even with correct heart rate feedback the cognitive interpretation of aversive stimuli may be influenced by knowledge of the heart rate. I would like to discuss the possible therapeutic use of these cognitive mechanisms of biofeedback on the basis of a study on heart rate feedback by Vaitl (1975). With chronic anxiety and numerous very frequent complaints relating to the autonomic nervous system (e.g. headache, neurotic heart disturbances, insomnia) an important role appears to be played by the cognitive misinterpretation of physiological arousal responses. According to a hypothesis suggested by P. Lang (1971), the perception of quite harmless arousal responses can act as an anxiety-producing stimulus if there is a suitable predisposition toward such an interpretation. The increase in anxiety then causes a further increase in the arousal response, and a vicious circle results leading to an anxiety attack.

Using this model Vaitl (1975) treated seven patients with paroxysmal sinus tachycardia and accompanying anxiety: By using heart rate feedback he tried to "break into" the vicious circle and stop the amplification of a harmless arousal response. In discussing the mechanism involved, Vaitl writes that "the patients felt they had been desensitized against fear of sudden and unexplainable heart acceleration. The fact that they were shown actually to be able to influence their heart rate affected the extent of their anticipatory anxiety. What happened with their heart was no longer a process over which they had absolutely no control and whose irregularities gave cause to phobic reactions."

This example shows how "irrelevant" functional control using biofeedback can lead to indirect therapeutic effects via cognitive processes.

In the application of biofeedback the indirect mechanisms discussed probably interact in a complex way with the direct effects of functional control. Research on the different components involved in effectiveness and the taking into account of these components should lead to better decisions in the future on when to use biofeedback training, how to conduct the training and how to evaluate the methods used.

BIOFEEDBACK AND BEHAVIOR MODIFICATION

The "Best Available Alternatives"

In a methodological article Miller & Dworkin (1977) advocate that the clinical value of biofeedback training be demonstrated through a comparison with the "best available alternatives." Now what are these alternatives? For organic disorders such as neurological, neuromuscular or cardiovascular diseases the usual therapeutic approach is the use of standard procedures of somatic medicine; biofeedback training if used at all is generally an additional form of intervention. On the other hand, for "psychosomatic disorders" in the broader sense biofeedback methods are in competition with other psychotherapeutic methods, and on these latter methods there is much less agreement about effectiveness (Bergin, 1971).

In comparative studies on the treatment of psychosomatic disorders such as have been reported on here by Black, Stoyva and Surwit and Shapiro, biofeedback training is for the most part compared with other methods of relaxation. Miller & Dworkin (1977) have pointed out one of the main reasons why biofeedback and relaxation methods must often fail with functional disorders: The disorders are usually maintained by massive reinforcement in the patient's everyday life, be it that the symptoms afford the patient additional attention or that they permit him to avoid aversive situations. This is certainly a truism for anyone who has experience with biofeedback techniques therapeutically and not solely in academic research projects, and it holds for both functional disorders and those which are primarily organic.

Nonetheless the conclusion is seldom drawn that it is of primary importance to analyze and modify the relationship between the symptoms and the environmental factors which maintain them and that, in contrast, a feedback signal presented twice a week for an hour or even every day can be of only secondary importance.

An alternative approach to the treatment of psychosomatic disorders has been developed by Fordyce et al. (1973) and Wooley et al. (1975). Here symptoms such as chronic pain are considered to be components of the illness behavior of patients who are playing a sick role because of environmental circumstances and lack of social skills.

I would like to illustrate this approach briefly with two examples although I am not aware of any comparative study in which biofeedback methods have been compared with such a behavior modification approach.

In a pain clinic Fordyce et al. (1973) treated 36 patients who had had chronic pain for many years and for whom after many unsuccessful treatment attempts no more medical treatment alternatives were available. Behavior analysis revealed the following typical components of pain behavior: the taking of analgesics, complaining, sighing, grimacing, physical passivity and frequent breaks during various activities. Individual therapy goals were determined for each patient to reduce his pain behaviors. Through consistent extinction of pain behavior and reinforcement of alternative behaviors, through training in social skills and through involvement of family members in treatment highly significant and clinically relevant improvement was achieved for all therapy goals, and this was maintained over a period of two years, as verified by a follow-up study.

Our own experience with patients treated on an outpatient basis point in the same direction. Fourteen patients who had prolonged psychosomatic symptoms following head injuries were treated with a behavioral training program geared to the illness behavior (Legewie-Pertzborn et al., in preparation). The subjects' complaints were, among others, chronic headache, functional cardiovascular symptoms, irritability, difficulties in concentrating and social problems. In eight two-hour group sessions, including role-playing, the patients learned first to see through the social mechanisms involved in their illness behavior and then to develop alternative social skills for attainment of attention and recognition. All of the patients showed marked improvement in their psychosomatic symptoms and in addition, improvement in other behavioral areas. Up to now I have not personally seen any similar success with a comparable amount of therapeutic effort using biofeedback methods.

Biofeedback as Part of a More Comprehensive Treatment Approach

In the heyday of biofeedback many of us believed we were on the right path to a new key paradigm for explaining and treating psychosomatic disorders (Miller, 1969). But in spite of the tremendous growth of the biofeedback movement these hopes have proved to be false. Shall we now completely give up the therapeutic application of biofeedback in favor of "better alternatives"? In concluding my talk I would like to suggest another approach: We should try to integrate biofeedback as one technique among many others into a more comprehensive treatment approach for psychosomatic disorders. The examples of treatment of illness behavior already mentioned seem to me to point in the right direction for developing such an approach. With other psychosomatic illnesses such as high blood pressure or coronary diseases, probably quite different interactions between life style and symptoms are of importance, but maybe a basically similar behavior modification approach for both treatment and prevention can be applied.

The basis of such an approach is a thorough behavioral analysis involving both psychophysiological and social aspects. The behavioral analysis leads to the definition of individual therapy goals and to the selection of the most suitable intervention techniques for attainment of these goals. Within the framework of such a therapy plan it would be possible to compare biofeedback methods with other forms of intervention (Legewie &

Nusselt, 1975). Compared with the way biofeedback is commonly used today this approach would require a major shift in emphasis. Biofeedback methods would then no longer be the center of focus; rather, they would take on the role of a technical tool which would have to prove itself in competition with other tools. It then becomes essential that on the one hand the biofeedback methods used require less effort than is now the case and on the other hand either the therapist must have thorough training in behavior modification or preferably the biofeedback methods must be used in multidisciplinary treatment centers.

In the last hundred years major steps forward in somatic medicine have repeatedly been cancelled out by a steady increase in illnesses and suffering which have resulted from the living conditions and life style we have created for ourselves. In order to meet the challenge of these problems in the future as was the case with the infectious diseases of the past, we need a new and comprehensive approach to the treatment and prevention of psychosomatic illness. Clearly biofeedback does not provide this approach--but perhaps it can play some modest part in it.

REFERENCES

Bergin, A. E. The evaluation of therapeutic outcomes. In A. E. Bergin & S. L. Garfield (Eds.), Handbook of psychotherapy and behavior change. New York: Wiley & Sons, 1971.

Engel, B. T., Nikoomanesh, P., & Schuster, M. M. Operant conditioning of rectosphincteric responses in the treatment of fecal incontinence. The New England Journal of Medicine, 1974, 646-649.

Fordyce, W. E., Fowler, R. S., Lehmann, J. F., Delateur, B. J., & Sand, P. L. Operant conditioning in the treatment of chronic pain. Archives of Physical Medicine and Rehabilitation, 1973, 54, 399-408.

Goldstein, A. P. Relationship-enhancement methods. In F. H. Kanfer & A. P. Goldstein (Eds.), Helping people change. New York: Pergamon Press, 1975.

Green, E. E., Green, A. M., & Walters, E. D. Self-regulation of internal states. In J. Rose (Ed.), Progress of cybernetics: Proceedings of the International Congress of Cybernetics, London 1969. London: Gordon & Breach, 1970.

Hanna, R., Wilfling, F., & McNeill, B. A biofeedback treatment for stuttering. Journal of Speech and Hearing Disorders, 1975, 40, 270-273.

Lang, P. J. The application of psychophysiological methods to the study of psychotherapy and behavior modification. In A. E. Bergin & S. L. Garfield (Eds.), Handbook of psychotherapy and behavior change. New York: Wiley & Sons, 1971.

Lanyon, R. I., Barrington, C. C., & Newman, A. C. Modification of stuttering through EMG biofeedback: A preliminary study. Behavior Therapy, 1976, 7, 96-103.

Legewie, H., Cleary, P., & Rackensperger, W. EMG-recording and biofeedback in the diagnosis and therapy of stuttering: A case study. European Journal of Behaviour Analysis and Modification, 1975, 1, 137-143.

Legewie, H., & Nusselt, L. Biofeedback-Therapie. Lernmethoden in der Psychosomatik, Neurologie und Rehabilitation. München: Urban & Schwarzenberg, 1975.

Legewie-Pertzborn, H., Legewie, H., Foid, J., & Brinkmann, R. Verhaltenstherapeutische Rehabilitation nach Schädelhirntrauma. In preparation.

Liebhart, E. H. Information search and attribution. Cognitive processes mediating the effects of false autonomic feedback. Psychological Bulletin, in press.

Miller, N. E., & Dworkin, B. R. Critical issues in therapeutic applications of biofeedback. In G. E. Schwartz & J. Beatty (Eds.), Biofeedback: Theory and research. San Francisco: Academic Press, 1977.

Owen, S. M. Biofeedback and muscle re-education - A personal experience. Paraplegia News, 1974.

Rosenthal, R. Experimenter effects in behavioral research. New York: Appleton-Century-Crofts, 1966.

Schachter, S. The interaction of cognitive and physiological determinants of emotional state. In L. Berkowitz (Ed.), Advances in experimental social psychology. New York: Academic Press, 1964.

Shapiro, A. K. Placebo effects in medicine, psychotherapy and psychoanalysis. In A. K. Bergin & S. L. Garfield (Eds.), Handbook of psychotherapy and behavior change. New York: Wiley & Sons, 1971.

Vaitl, D. Biofeedback-Einsatz in der Behandlung einer Patientin mit Sinustachykardie. In H. Legewie & L. Nusselt (Eds.), Biofeedback-Therapie. München: Urban & Schwarzenberg, 1975.

Valins, S. Cognitive effects of false heart-rate feedback. Journal of Personality and Social Psychology, 1966, 4, 400-408.

Valins, S., & Ray, A. A. Effects of cognitive desensitization on avoidance behavior. Journal of Personality and Social Psychology, 1967, 7, 345-350.

Weitzenhoffer, A. M. General techniques of hypnotism. New York: Grune & Stratton, 1957.

Wooley, S. C., Blackwell, B., Epps, B., & Harper, R. A learning theory treatment model for illness behavior. Psychosomatic Medicine, 1975, 37, 1.

CONTRIBUTIONS OF BIOFEEDBACK METHODS TO THE UNDERSTANDING OF VISCERAL AND CENTRAL NERVOUS SYSTEM FUNCTIONS

Jackson Beatty
Department of Psychology
University of California at Los Angeles

In this final chapter I would like to explore some of the scientific issues that have emerged from experimental investigations employing biofeedback procedures as they have emerged in this symposium. Some perspective may be gained by considering the types of experimental questions that have been posed here and the general issues to which they are addressed. It is my belief that the nature of these questions has changed somewhat in the past decade, and that the field of "biofeedback research" is now more diverse and complex than it was at its inception. This results from the fact that the field is unified only at the level of method or procedure and that these methods have been used by different investigators to pursue a variety of substantive questions.

THE OPERANT MODEL OF VISCERAL AND CNS PLASTICITY

The question that dominated biofeedback research in its earliest years and excited the interest of the scientific community concerned the rules of plastic change for visceral and central nervous system (CNS) functions. It was Miller's proposition that visceral and CNS events may be modified by contingent reinforcement in the same manner that the overt behavior of the skeletal musculature may be conditioned. One set of laws, the principles of instrumental conditioning, might hold for all mammalian response systems in which learning could be demonstrated. The initial experiments of Miller and his students, principally DiCara, were prepared as demonstrations of instrumental conditioning of visceral processes (Miller, 1969). In these experiments it was first necessary to show that all the properties of instrumentally conditioned skeletal responses appear also in visceral responses when the appropriate reinforcement contingencies are applied. This is the question of demonstration.

It was also necessary to show that such responses of the viscera were under the control of the autonomic nervous system, which regulates visceral function, and not mediated by learned responses of the skeletal musculature that might affect the viscera through any of several well-known somatic-visceral linkages. Thus the demonstration of instrumental learning in the viscera is deeply linked to the issue of response mediation.

The use of the curarized rat as an experimental preparation in which visceral learning could take place without direct skeletal muscle mediation seemed initially to be an elegant if difficult procedure for demonstrating that common laws of learning apply for both skeletal and visceral events (Miller, 1969). In the curarized animal, the activation of the striated musculature is blocked at the neuromuscular junction. However, the difficulties associated with this approach have become increasingly clear (Dworkin & Miller, 1977); unless extreme care is taken to stabilize major parameters of visceral functioning, demonstrations of instrumental conditioning of these processes may be difficult to evaluate. The instability of the curarized rodent preparation became apparent when a number of attempts to replicate the original work from Miller's laboratory were unsuccessful (Dworkin & Miller, 1977). These failures of replication cloud the validity of Miller's early conclusions. At this time, it would be prudent to regard the demonstrations of specific operant regulation of visceral function in the curarized preparation as insufficient to establish the principle that common laws apply to both skeletal and visceral learning.

The twin questions of demonstration and mediation form a focus for the experimental investigation of the rules governing the plasticity of visceral responses. In the present symposium, at least two presentations are concerned with both these issues.

In the paper presented by Dr. Pickering and his colleagues, Drs. Brucker, Dworkin, Frankel, Mathias and Miller, the logic of the curare experiment was applied to the study of visceral learning in man. In the first experiment, Pickering showed that poliomyelitis and muscular dystrophy patients who had virtually complete paralysis of the skeletal musculature could learn to increase or decrease diastolic blood pressure when provided with appropriate response-contingent reinforcement. As in the earlier experiments using the curarized rat, blood pressure changes were specific and not reflected in differential patterns of heart rate or respiratory activity. The demonstration that response-contingent reinforcement produces specific changes of blood pressure in patients deprived of most control of the skeletal musculature provides some plausible evidence for instrumental conditioning of visceral responses.

Pickering's second experiment is, to me, more intriguing and is reminiscent of some of Karl Lashley's work on the variety of mechanisms by which learned overt behaviors are executed (Lashley, 1950). Pickering was able to demonstrate discriminant control of blood pressure in a series of four patients with cervical transections of the spinal cord. Thus both the direct sympathetic mechanisms for the regulation of diastolic pressure and the indirect mechanism of regulation through striate muscle activation were excluded. Diastolic pressure control appeared to be mediated by the vagus, suggesting a plasticity of visceral function, not simply in the regulation of a particular cardiovascular parameter, but in the choice of the mechanism by which such control is accomplished.

Visceral learning and its mediation also are central issues in the presentation of Drs. Harris, Goldstein and Brady. Harris has presented data from a series of experiments examining the effects of long-term exposure to response contingent reinforcement of blood-pressure changes in the baboon. He reports that prolonged training may produce profound increases in diastolic pressure under schedules rewarding increases and punishing decreases. Under the reversed contingency, however, no changes in diastolic pressure relative to basal levels appear. Thus, increases are responsive to reinforcement but the effects of contingency are not symmetrical. Harris has approached the question of mediation by the ingeneous use of pharmacological agents that block specific sympathetic adrenergic transmitters in an attempt to clarify the mechanism by which reinforcement-contingent shifts in diastolic blood pressure are effected. The results indicate the participation of both adrenergic and non-adrenergic mechanisms in learned blood-pressure regulation in baboon.

The demonstration of instrumental conditioning of visceral events also appears in other papers in the symposium. Dr. Welgan's attempts to instrumentally condition stomach pH represents one of the few current programs investigating the plasticity of gastrointestinal functioning.

Thus several lines of evidence appear to support the proposition that visceral responses may be modified using the techniques of operant conditioning. Yet as compelling as these data may be, the last several years have brought confoundings of various sorts. Some stubborn data has appeared that is not easily reconciled with the idea that a simple and general set of rules governs the plasticity of bodily responses. For example, Dr. Garcia (Garcia & Koelling, 1966) has previously reported a series of experiments indicating that the behavioral effects of a reinforcer in instrumental conditioning are not as general as has previously been supposed (Skinner, 1938). This sort of specificity in the relation between response and reinforcer is more commonly associated with classical conditioning procedures than with instrumental paradigms (Hilgard & Marquis, 1940). In his paper with Rusinak at this symposium, Garcia raised the possibility that the mechanism by which visceral responses are instrumentally modified is different than the mechanism which operates for overt behavior of the skeletal musculature. The learning of visceral responses may be more like the learning of taste aversion, which Garcia and Rusinak term incentive modification through homeostatic utilization.

Further complications for the operant model of visceral plasticity are introduced by Dr. Furedy. Furedy has obtained large magnitude conditioned cardiac decelerations using a two stage procedure in which a modified classical conditioning procedure is first employed to elicit sizeable heart rate decelerations after which quite standard operant procedures are introduced during the Pavlovian extinction period to maintain or increase these decelerations. The theoretical problems posed in the interpretation of these experiments are substantial, as Dr. Furedy has so clearly indicated. The fact that none of the theories of instrumental conditioning currently available can account for such data suggests that the operant models of visceral plasticity are either in substantial error or at least incomplete in some serious ways.

ALTERNATIVE MODELS OF PLASTIC CHANGE

The question then arises as to whether any other type of model can account more completely for the phenomena of visceral and CNS plasticity. Four speakers have directly addressed this issue in this symposium. Dr. Lang has proposed that visceral learning might be conceptualized as a form of skill learning and reports data showing that in some cases this model seems to hold, whereas in other instances, it does not. Dr. Johnston, in his presentation, also addressed this issue and concluded that the motor skills analogy is not particularly appropriate for the analysis of cardiovascular conditioning. Taken together, it appears that the motor skills analogy may be less useful than the operant model as a theoretical mechanism for understanding the plastic properties of the viscera.

Another conceptual framework proposed in these meetings is that of cybernetic theory. In an intricate paper, Dr. Anliker has elegantly outlined cybernetic theory and indicated several ways in which the principles of cybernetic analysis might be useful for understanding data obtained using biofeedback methods. Unfortunately, rather little data is available that is appropriate for judging the applicability of cybernetic theory to the phenomenon of feedback-dependent visceral learning.

However within the framework of cybernetic theory, Dr. Mulholland investigated other aspects of feedback control of physiological functioning. Mulholland (1977) has used EEG-contingent visual stimulation as a unique method for investigating the alpha rhythms of the human brain. In his paper to this symposium, Mulholland has extended this method to provide a quantitative index of feedback control that is derived from systems theory. This provides a technique for assessing the degree to which electrocortical events recorded from various regions of the scalp are generated by processes that are functionally related to the visual system feedback loop.

Cybernetic or systems theory is most directly concerned with describing the ways in which some classes of complex systems are regulated. It does not address directly the question of plasticity or system adaptation. Although it is conceivable that the systems approach will identify relevant higher-order variables in the regulation of visceral or CNS systems that would make the plastic properties of these systems more understandable, the specific form that such a contribution might take is at the moment unclear.

And so we are left with many puzzles as answers to the question: What rules govern the learning of visceral and CNS responses? Contained within these puzzles is a deeper understanding of the nature of plastic change in the brain and viscera, yet the question is not resolved.

VISCERAL PERCEPTION

That visceral responses may be brought under some degree of control using instrumental conditioning procedures strongly suggests that the relevant portions of the central nervous system must have some information concerning the momentary state of visceral processes. Thus, the initial demonstration of operant regulation of the viscera served to reopen the investigation of visceral perception, a topic that was directly addressed by several participants in this symposium.

Dr. Brener, in his comprehensive review of the area of visceral perception, clearly indicated the difficult nature of the problem. Strong presumptive evidence from a variety of sources indicates that visceral afferents carry information about visceral functioning to the brain, probably at high as well as lower levels. Further, certain aspects of behavior suggest that such information is utilized in our daily functioning. The difficulty in objectively measuring visceral perception lies in the apparent impossibility of experimental control of the physical stimulus, a condition that has been critical to the development of an adequate psychophysics for the other sensory modalities. For this reason, the problem of visceral perception has been approached obliquely, in an attempt to define the properties of the interoceptive system by a series of converging procedures, each one of which by itself being inconclusive.

One method of sidestepping this difficulty is to treat visceral perception as a problem of multiple measurement of autonomic events in which the results of physical measurement methods are compared in various procedures to the judgment of the subject. Thus visceral perception is reduced to a discrimination problem for visceral events or states. The strength of this approach is that it permits the acquisition of some information concerning visceral perception. The weakness is that the procedure reveals little concerning the afferent channels utilized in making the discrimination. Thus it is impossible at this time to establish that visceral perception is mediated by visceral afferents, and not by other afferent systems about which much more is already known. Brener's own work in this area represents an important contribution to the solution of a critical but recalcitrant scientific problem.

A related set of issues was raised by Dr. Roberts in an analysis of the role of visceral perception in visceral learning. Roberts argues that the role of external feedback in human visceral learning may be in training the discrimination of interoceptive cues that enable the learner to later exercise control of a particular visceral function without concurrent feedback support. This suggests that feedback will be most useful in training control of visceral response systems for which appropriately labelled discriminations are not already established. Roberts uses discrimination theory to account for several of the problems that arise when comparing the effects of feedback and instruction in the regulation of visceral processes. It appears from the work of Roberts and others that a treatment of visceral perception is a necessary part of any fully adequate theory of visceral learning.

BIOFEEDBACK AND THE PATTERNING OF PHYSIOLOGICAL RESPONSES

A fourth question that has been addressed here concerns the interrelationships between various physiological systems and the ways in which biofeedback procedures may affect them. This is the issue of patterning of physiological responses which was considered in detail by Drs. Kimmel and Schwartz.

The question of response patterning was examined in the paper by Drs. Kimmel and Burns. In a complex experiment contrasting paired operant and Pavlovian procedures in which reinforcement was contingent upon skin conductance responses, systematic variations of heart rate were also observed. Kimmel interprets these results as the independent, adventitious conditioning of a cardiovascular response which is partially correlated with the response of interest, skin conductance. Thus Kimmel suggests independence of learned control in systems which are partially correlated at other levels.

Schwartz, in his presentation, made the provocative argument that the effects of training patterns of physiological responses may differ qualitatively from those obtained by training any of the component processes in isolation. In single-system training, specificity of control typically results, so that learned control of heart rate leaves blood pressure relatively unaffected. When complex patterns of physiological responses are learned, Schwartz argues that emergent properties of the physiological pattern may appear; for example, subjects trained to lower both blood pressure and heart rate report subjective relaxation, in contrast to subjects trained to lower either parameter alone. Schwartz reports similar results in an experiment investigating the regulation of blood pressure and forehead muscle tension on the experience of anxiety.

The issues Schwartz raises are exceptionally important, not only within the context of biofeedback research, but in physiology and physiological psychology more generally. With some significant exceptions, we know very little about momentary patterns of activity within the nervous system. In part, this stems from the technical difficulty of measuring concurrent processes and in part from the theoretical problems associated with interpreting such data. Regardless of the ultimate acceptance of such ideas as emergent behavioral phenomena, there can be little question that the study of spatial patterning of CNS and visceral activity provides a powerful approach to the understanding of brain function and behavior.

BRAIN FUNCTIONS

Just as operant procedures have proved to be useful tools in neurophysiology and psychopharmacology (Thompson & Schuster, 1968), the extension of these methods to the regulation of directly measured physiological processes can further our understanding of brain function. The use of biofeedback procedures in basic neurophysiological research is most elegantly represented by the work of Dr. Fetz and his colleagues in their investigations of the mechanisms of motor control. Fetz has used response-contingent reinforcement as a dissecting tool to test the integrity of correlational relationships observed between patterns of single unit activity and muscular activation. For example, the motor fields of single cortical cells may be defined by operantly regulating the activity of a cortical unit and observing the resulting patterns of electromyographic activation in the periphery. The plasticity of the pyramidal motor system may be demonstrated by reinforcing specified patterns of central and peripheral activity. That cortical bursts during electromyographic silence may be obtained under operant control suggests the involvement of more complex regulatory systems.

Similarly, the possible relation between the sensorimotor rhythm and suppression of epileptiform activity was suggested, as Dr. Sterman reported, by observations made of the effects of an epileptogenic agent upon seizure activity in cats previously trained to produce the sensorimotor rhythm. Although that finding was in part serendipitous, the logic of the discovery remains: Operant manipulation of brain events can lead to new knowledge of brain function.

BIOFEEDBACK AND BEHAVIOR

Finally, let us consider the question posed by the title of this symposium: Biofeedback and behavior. Can learning control of physiological processes have behavioral consequence? This, after all, is the question that for many of us is of greatest concern. For the clinician concerned with relaxation therapies, the treatment of behavioral disorders and similar matters, behavioral effects are the whole reason for including biofeedback procedures in a program of therapy. For psychologists concerned with applied problems of human performance, again the question of behavioral effects is paramount. For those interested in the relations between brain or visceral events and subjective experience, emotion or feeling states, the same question is posed: Does biofeedback affect behavior?

There are, of course, many instances in which the learned regulation of particular physiological processes do not have effect upon the behavior measured. Dr. Johnson reviewed data from a large number of experiments both published and unpublished in which the behavioral effects of biofeedback training appear to be minimal. Perhaps the enthusiasm generated by early publications in this literature was seriously misdirected. However, some compelling and apparently stable relations between brain and behavior have emerged in this meeting, and it is to those investigations that we now turn our attention.

For example, Dr. O'Hanlon has reported results from a series of experiments that he and I have performed in collaboration. We investigated the effects of learning control of a particular brain rhythm, theta frequency activity in the posterior cortex, that had previously been related to behavioral drowsiness. We found that when appropriate procedures were employed, bidirectional discriminant control of the proportion of theta activity in the electroencephalogram can be obtained quite reliably. Further augmentation procedures increased and suppression procedures decreased this measure of EEG activation about the levels recorded from a no-treatment control group. Since posterior theta frequency activity is an indicator of behavioral arousal, it was not surprising to find that regulating this theta index by operant procedures affected performance on an arousal-sensitive task, monotonous monitoring of a complex display for infrequently occurring signals. Under alerted conditions, feedback regulation of theta is, to the best of my knowledge, without behavioral effect. But under environmental conditions in which performance may depend upon arousal, an effect of learned regulation may be seen.

The other treatment of theta frequency activity in this symposium was presented by Dr. Birbaumer. Birbaumer's work, however, does not address the issues raised by the work O'Hanlon reported, as in Birbaumer's first experiment, posterior theta activity reflecting stage 1 sleep was specifically excluded, whereas this is precisely the phenomenon that O'Hanlon and I were trying to capture. Birbaumer's second experiment was concerned with frontal theta, which has no known relation to activation level or performance in vigilance tasks.

The problem of individual differences in brain-behavior relations was introduced by Drs. Orne and Wilson in their presentation. They stress the necessity of dealing with individual variation in future work on the physiological basis of behavior, an important question that is too frequently overlooked.

In this context, mention should also be made of Dr. Plotkin's intriguing experiments investigating the relations between regulation of alpha activity and subjective experience. Much of the early interest in the learned regulation of alpha activity stemmed from the presumed relation between alpha and meditative states. Plotkin was able to show, not only that the incidence of alpha activity is relatively unrelated to changes in subjective experience--that after all had been noted previously by other investigators, but that the control of the subjective experience was a function of social variables operating within the experimental situation. Alteration of subjective experience depends upon the set of expectations provided and the participant's perceived success or failure in producing the desired response pattern. One might also note that these findings do not necessarily contradict Schwartz's report that a subjective experience of relaxation may result when a complex of variables is regulated, but not when alpha alone is augmented.

Finally, the experiments reported by Shapiro are particularly interesting. Shapiro suggests that feedback regulation of autonomic functions that are involved in emotional responding in individual subjects may effectively modify emotional states or organismic reactions to environmental stressors. In these investigations, the behavioral effects of visceral regulation may be detected when the organism is challenged but not under baseline conditions.

From these data we are led to the conclusion that biofeedback procedures are most likely to produce behavioral consequences when they are used to regulate well-specified physiological processes for which brain/behavior relations are known to exist.

IN SUMMARY

In summary, then, where do we stand? I believe that the papers presented in this symposium reflect scientific advances in some areas of psychophysiological research using the methods we have come to characterize as "biofeedback procedures." Both the nature of this work and the climate surrounding it have changed, however, in the past ten years. The focused characteristics of the initial pioneering work have given way to more diversified objectives and experimental strategies. The promise that the primary barrier to the operant regulation of visceral and CNS function lay in the preconceptions of the scientific community appears to be largely unfulfilled. But what remains are a set of methods which are useful in particular research contexts. New problems have appeared and complexities of some of the original problems have increased. These issues are interesting in their own right.

We are left, I believe, with new tools, some new information and some new problems. One does not sense the approach of a major scientific discovery, but rather a productive period of normal science. (In predictions of this sort one can often be quite wrong. But the point is not one of seeing the future, rather it is to accurately assess the state of affairs at the moment.) The presentations that we have heard this week speak well for the healthy state of biofeedback research as an approach to a limited set of research problems. The next advances will come not from the demonstration that visceral and CNS events are conditionable, but rather from the substantive knowledge that has been gained in particular areas of inquiry by using conditioning procedures as a key to release other information about man, his physiology and his behavior.

REFERENCES

Dworkin, B. R., & Miller, N. Visceral learning in the curarized rat. In G. E. Schwartz & J. Beatty (Eds.), Biofeedback: Theory and research. San Francisco: Academic Press, 1977.

Garcia, J., & Koelling, R. A. Relation of cue to consequence in avoidance learning. Psychonomic Science, 1966, 4, 123-124.

Hilgard, E. R., & Marguis, D. G. Conditioning and learning. New York: Appleton-Century-Crofts, 1940.

Miller, N. Learning of visceral and glandular responses. Science, 1969, 163, 434-445.

Mulholland, T. B. Biofeedback as scientific method. In G. E. Schwartz & J. Beatty (Eds.), Biofeedback: Theory and research. San Francisco: Academic Press, 1977.

Thompson, T., & Schuster, C. R. Behavioral pharmacology. Engelwood Cliffs, New Jersey: Prentice-Hall, 1968.

NAME INDEX

SUBJECT INDEX